**RABBI SHLOMO CARLEBACH
LIFE, MISSION, AND LEGACY**

MODERN JEWISH LIVES • VOLUME 4

Rabbi Shlomo Carlebach

Life, Mission, and Legacy

**Dr. Natan Ophir
(Offenbacher)**

URIM PUBLICATIONS

Jerusalem • New York

Rabbi Shlomo Carlebach: Life, Mission, and Legacy
by Dr. Natan Ophir (Offenbacher)

Series: Modern Jewish Lives – Volume 4
Series Editor: Tzvi Mauer

Copyright © 2014 by Natan Ophir (Offenbacher)

Typeset by Ariel Walden

Printed in Israel. First Edition.

ISBN: 978-965-524-143-3

Urim Publications
P.O. Box 52287, Jerusalem 91521 Israel

www.UrimPublications.com

Portrait of Rabbi Shlomo Carlebach on front cover
Pastel drawing by Mike Horton

Library of Congress Cataloging-in-Publication Data

Ophir, Natan.
  Rabbi Shlomo Carlebach : life, mission, and legacy / Dr. Natan Ophir
(Offenbacher). — First edition.
     pages cm. — (Modern Jewish lives ; v. 4)
  Includes bibliographical references and index.
  ISBN 978-965-524-143-3 (hardcover : alk. paper) 1. Carlebach, Shlomo. 2.
Rabbis—United States—Biography. 3. Jewish musicians—United
States—Biography. I. Title.
  BM755.C2745O64 2014
  296.8'332092--dc23
  [B]
                            2013031262

Dedicated to my beloved parents,
my greatest fans
and most astute critics.
They decided that it was high time
that I publish this book.
With their loving persistence,
they made sure I did it.

Contents

Foreword

My father, Rabbi Shlomo Carlebach, feels incredibly present today. Though it has been eighteen years since he's passed away somehow he continues to inspire, uplift, and touch souls worldwide. His music speaks volumes and emits a physical presence that is intensely alive. It's beyond mere verbal definition. As the years pass, it seems that my father's spirit is inspiring us even more.

My father avoided the creation of tangible footprints in this world. He lived in abstract and spiritual realms. His gifts were not to be limited by words or intellectual concepts. He could not be captured in the physical realm. To organize him would be like catching snowflakes and expecting them to maintain their pristine presence while being sorted and stacked. His legacy was preserved because his fans and followers had the foresight to chase him around with tape recorders. My family and I remain grateful to all those who have documented his thoughts, music, and moments of Divine inspiration.

From the many excerpts I've read, I know that Dr. Natan Ophir has worked to clarify the diversified aspects of my father's rich career. He has recounted relevant events and unearthed a surprising wealth of factual evidence. Undeterred by the daunting task, Natan has worked to present a comprehensive portrayal that will now enable others to come forth and fill the many spaces in time. I appreciate his sincere connection to my father's legacy, and I know the world will benefit greatly from his devoted efforts at constructing this first book-length biography.

I pray when you, dear friends, read this book about my father, you will look beyond the stories and find a glimpse into his soul. More than anything else, it is clear we have so much to learn from him, so much to gain from his challenges and successes. As was his way, let us find the strength to truly and deeply emulate his love, generosity, and kindness. We must see every human being as a treasure filled with grace and dignity. In his honor, for the sake of our children and for the future of our world, let us seek new ways to hasten a utopian era of love, peace, and redemption.

With love, Neshama Carlebach

Preface

Despite the fact that Rabbi Shlomo Carlebach is considered a major figure in the history of twentieth century Jewry, no full length biography has been published that details the unfolding of his life and career. True, many articles and books were published with stories and anecdotes, but not a documented accounting with a historical timeline. My rather presumptuous goal was to compose what is called a "critical biography." As opposed to subjective and interpretive biographies, this genre entails meticulous research, detailed footnotes, and scholarly annotations in order to piece together dates, names, and places. The aim is to evaluate the life of the subject by setting forth minutiae that become meaningful through the prism of the historical backdrop and the colorfulness of the cultural settings.

One reason it is difficult to write a biography about Reb Shlomo is because he was continuously on the move, or as he jokingly phrased it, his home was in the airport. He accumulated more mileage than any other Jewish personality of the twentieth century and his life intersected in significant ways with thousands of people. This biography is therefore merely a first attempt at documenting his career, and those whose stories have been inadvertently omitted are invited to fill in the lacunae.

What happens when an author becomes so deeply immersed in writing a biography that he begins to dream about his subject? Well, this can be revelatory. One day Shlomo appeared in my dream and said:

> Natan, my friend, you never really know who the other person is. You are bound to misjudge me unless you can discover my inner secrets. But gevalt, one thing I ask. All my life I tried to discover the good in every person. I found holiness in the outcasts, treasures in the beggars, and righteousness in the rebels. My goal was to fix the world with empathy and to counter hatred with love. I proclaimed a faith in One God who directs each person towards Goodness. So I ask of you that when and if you discover mistakes

13

that I made, don't castigate me, just fix them. *Oy*, this world I left behind needs *mamash* such a fixing!

When I woke up, I realized that despite my intent to write an objective or critical biography, it was inevitable that I would be influenced ever subtly by Reb Shlomo's imperative requiring a continuous quest for goodness, empathy, and optimism. It is hoped that this bias does not impair the possibility for a balanced analysis of one of the most colorful and controversial Jewish figures of the twentieth century.

In sum, the purpose of my book is not only to document the life and career of Reb Shlomo via the prism of the cultural and sociological developments of his time, but also to provide a new framework to evaluate the unique form of heartfelt Judaism, joyous optimism, and soulful rejuvenation that he inspired.

Acknowledgements

The underlying assumption throughout this biography is that Shlomo's life and message needs to be explained through the prism of the people with whom he interacted. I thank the hundreds of people who shared their stories, photos, and archival treasures – their help is acknowledged individually in the footnotes and is referenced in the index (over 200 who were interviewed are marked with an asterisk).

I thank Neshama Carlebach for writing the beautiful foreword. A thanks to the authors of the testimonials, especially to Reb Zalman Schachter-Shalomi who was kind enough to Skype me several times. I acknowledge the many friends of Shlomo who taught me how incredibly far-reaching his impact was, and I apologize to the many others whose stories I have not yet documented.

My grateful appreciation to Mike Horton whose pastel drawing adorns the cover and whose artistic designs grace my websites. I thank Tzvi Mauer for adding this book as the fourth volume of his wonderful series Modern Jewish Lives. Tzvi suggested aeons ago that I publish a book and he guided me through the labyrinth of publishing. A special thanks to the expert and patient editor, Batsheva Pomerantz. Others who read through entire chapters and made extensive corrections include Shonna and Rabbi Yitz Husbands-Hankin, Sarah Kauffman, Jeffrey Levine, and Aaron Reichel.

Among those who encouraged the book, I would like to mention Yaakov Moshe from Raanana, who believes "that the Carlebach vision of Judaism and his unique *derekh*, music, and teachings are helping to bring this generation closer to Hashem and to fellow human beings."

A unique appreciation to my five adult children for forgiving me for being overly preoccupied with giving birth to this book at the expense of not spending more time with them and with my grandchildren.

My most important debt of gratitude is to my beloved parents, Prof. Elmer (Eliezer) and Dr. Esther Offenbacher, who persistently encouraged me to finish the book even if it might have some errors and oversights, reassuring me that I can always apologize in a second volume. It is with deep emotion that I dedicate this book to them.

Introduction

As I put the final touches on this book, the musical play, *Soul Doctor: The Journey of a Rockstar Rabbi*, is about to be featured on Broadway. One of the very few prominent Jewish-themed musicals since *Fiddler on the Roof* and *Yentl*, the play dramatically portrays the legacy of Rabbi Shlomo Carlebach:

> A modern-day troubadour, he ignited the spirit of millions around the world with his soul-stirring melodies, transformative storytelling, and boundless love. *Soul Doctor* takes us on an exhilarating musical odyssey through the challenges and triumphs of this cultural phenomenon: his childhood escape from Nazi Germany, becoming a rabbinical prodigy in America; his unlikely friendship with Nina Simone, discovering Gospel and Soul music; his meteoric rise as a "Rock Star-Rabbi" in the 1960s, performing with Bob Dylan, Jefferson Airplane, and the Grateful Dead; his struggle to reconcile his deep traditional roots with his desire to reach people of all backgrounds in the "free-love generation"; and his personal conflicts trying to keep his family together while traversing the globe as a "*Soul Doctor*," bringing joy and song to the lonely, the searching, and the broken hearted.[1]

Rabbi Shlomo Carlebach is "regarded as the foremost composer of contemporary Jewish songs."[2] He performed at approximately 4,000 concerts, and produced about twenty-seven albums. He also created a new genre of storytelling intertwined with song, and innovated experiential modes of applying Hasidic values to modern life challenges. He gave

---

1. This description is from http://shlomomusical.com/about.php/, where 15 reviews are listed, but most relate to the earlier pre-Broadway performances. See ShlomoMusical.com, http://www.shlomomusical.com/press.php (accessed Aug. 7, 2012).

2. Obituary of Shlomo Carlebach, *American Jewish Yearbook*, vol. 96, 1996, 550. For a discussion of this appellation, see below, Chapter 13.

rabbinic ordination or semi-ordination to about fifty students, inspired thousands of followers, and touched the lives of countless people around the globe. Sometimes, his influence was quite extraordinary and transformative.

Although there is a wealth of stories and hagiographic collections,[3] there is no systematic study of the life, writings and influence of Reb Shlomo. As Prof. Shaul Magid phrased it: "apart from a few short essays written mostly by acolytes, his influence, both musically and religiously, is largely unexplored terrain."[4]

Why is Shlomo so conspicuously absent from Jewish Studies scholarship?

The first reason is because Shlomo was teaching an inspirational "heartfelt" Judaism, and his followers responded in kind, recounting wondrous stories and describing altruistic deeds. They did not write critical biographies.

A second reason is that Reb Shlomo was not a systematic teacher and did not author scholarly treatises. Even when he taught from a specific book, such as *Lights of Return* by Rav Kook or *Mei HaShiloach* by the Izbica Rebbe, he would use the text as a springboard for inspirational messages and anecdotal tales.

A third reason is that trying to capture the import of his teachings is like trying to hold streams of light and water in your hands. His stories lose their pathos when translated onto the printed page, and his exhortations pale without the musical accompaniment and jocular interludes.

When I began writing this biography, I realized that the first step is to reconstruct factual details of what Reb Shlomo did, where he went, whom he influenced and who influenced him. Only after that, could I begin to properly analyze his songs, stories, and teachings. My purpose here is to provide the documentation and to outline the historical settings. For a follow-up volume, I have collected an analysis of his teachings using literary, theological, and cultural perspectives.

In this book, I try to answer the following four types of questions:

1.   BIOGRAPHY

Who was Reb Shlomo? What was his background and family history? What motivated him? What did he do, where did he go, with whom did

---

3. The term hagiography refers to a biography that idealizes or idolizes its subject, and is often found in writings about saintly figures and venerated persons.

4. Shaul Magid, "Rabbi Shlomo Carlebach and His Interpreters: A Review Essay of Two New Musical Releases," *Musica Judaica Online Reviews*, Sept. 6, 2010.

he interact? Who helped develop his career? How was he influenced by the Hasidic Rebbes of Chabad, Bobov, Modzitz, and Amshinov? Why was he criticized and even ostracized by parts of the Jewish community while others viewed him as an altruistic saint and hidden *tzaddik*?

2.   MUSICAL SUCCESS

What were the early musical influences on Shlomo? Who were his friends in New York in the 1950s and 1960s, and how was he influenced by them? What albums did he record and what was their intent? Who helped him produce his recordings? Where did he perform? How did he become a musical success story?

3.   HIPPIES, HOUSE OF LOVE AND PRAYER, AND CULTURAL BACKGROUND

What is the cultural and historical background for Reb Shlomo's work, especially as relating to the hippie generation? How did Shlomo relate to their aspirations for free love, self-actualization, and communal living? What happened in California in the summers of 1966 and 1967, and how did it shape his outreach career? How did Reb Shlomo interact with the gurus and Swamis in San Francisco? To what extent did the hippie counterculture serve as a catalyst for Shlomo's inventive interpretations of religious practice and as a natural setting for his innovative theological exegesis? What took place in the House of Love and Prayer? Why were there actually two houses? What was Shlomo's impact on the Aquarian Minyan of Berkeley and on the Jewish Renewal Movement?

4. CAREER, MESSAGE, AND MISSION

What was Reb Shlomo's mission as a Chabad emissary in the years 1949–1955? What was the trajectory of his career in comparison to his colleagues, and especially to his co-emissary, Reb Zalman Schachter-Shalomi? How did he begin to develop his international career? What did he do in Israel, where did he perform, and what did he create? What role did he play in the struggle to free and inspire Soviet Jewry? What was his post-Holocaust message when he visited Poland? How did Reb Shlomo transmit values of love, joy, and hope? Finally, how have scholars, followers, and admirers evaluated Reb Shlomo's life accomplishments and impact?

By providing detailed answers to these questions, my goal is to evaluate Shlomo's career via the prism of the cultural and sociological developments of his time, the Holocaust, the Six-Day War, the Soviet Jewry struggle, Americanization, assimilation, the hippie phenomenon, the rise of the New Age, and other events that were channeling the course of Jewish life. It is also an attempt at providing a micro-history of the Carlebach phenomenon by exploring the vantage points of dozens of individuals who were influenced by Shlomo.[5] But above all, this book attempts to provide a new framework to appreciate the unique form of heartfelt Judaism and soulful rejuvenation that was inspired by Reb Shlomo.

---

5. Micro-history is a genre of historical scholarship that has become popular amongst contemporary social historians. When writing micro-history, the author analyzes a specific individual or community, and attempts to reach understanding of wider issues at play. In the particular case of Reb Shlomo Carlebach, his life was a continuous interaction with thousands of people around the globe. Therefore, this biography draws extensively on the memories of these individuals and their specific stories.

Bibliographic Sources

In 1973, Shlomo's father, Rabbi Naphtali Carlebach, published *The Carlebach Tradition: The History of My Family*.[1] In doing so, he was continuing the tradition of his father, Rabbi Salomon Carlebach, who in 1898 published a definitive study on how the Carlebach family story was intertwined with the history of the Jews in Lübeck and Moisling.[2] More recently, in 1995, a documentary film on the Carlebach family was produced for German TV,[3] and a book was published on the Carlebach rabbinical family.[4]

The first interview with Reb Shlomo was published in August 1959 by Dr. Eric Offenbacher, the music columnist for *Jewish Life*.[5] More than a dozen radio and newspaper interviews in Israel were produced in

1. Rabbi Dr. Naphtali H. Carlebach, *The Carlebach Tradition: The History of My Family* (New York: The Joseph Carlebach Memorial Foundation, 1973). Selections were printed in *Hakrev Ushma* (*Connections*) (a bi-monthly published by the Carlebach Shul) beginning in 1985, vol. 1, issue 5.

2. Rabbi Dr. Salomon Carlebach, *Geschichte der Juden in Lübeck und Moisling* (Lübeck: 1898).

3. The film, entitled *Die Carlebachs: Eine Familiengeschichte*, was produced by Hanno Brühl and edited by Fritz Breuer for WDR (West Deutscher Rundfunk), 1995. It describes the Carlebach family tradition through live interviews with 6 descendants: Felix Carlebach in Manchester, Julius Carlebach in Heidelberg, Miriam Gillis Carlebach in Kefar Hanoar in Israel, Rabbi Shlomo Carlebach in Brooklyn (the latter two are children of Rabbi Joseph Carlebach), and journalist Emil Carlebach in Frankfurt. My thanks to Menachem Daum for showing me this film, a copy of which can be found in the Leo Baeck Institute in New York.

4. Sabine Niemann (ed.), *Die Carlebachs: Eine Rabbinerfamilie aus Deutschland* (Hamburg: 1995). The book was published by the Ephraim Carlebach Foundation of Leipzig.

5. Eric Offenbacher, "Interview with a Jewish Minstrel," *Jewish Life*, Aug. 1959, 53–57. My thanks to Eli Genauer, Eric's son-in-law, for sending me this article which provides important documentation for Shlomo's life in the 1950s. On a personal note, I might add that Eric, a first cousin of my father, was close to our family, and we would fondly refer to him as Uncle Eric.

Hebrew,[6] the first extensive one was written by Pinchas Peli on March 28, 1964.[7]

In 1980, Emuna Witt sat down with Shlomo to prepare an autobiography.[8] In 1982, Howard Jay Rubin interviewed Shlomo and wrote an article entitled "Fixing the World."[9] In March 1985, Dan Shacham interviewed Shlomo near the Carlebach Shul in Manhattan.[10] The first video-interview was recorded by Menachem Daum during Reb Shlomo's trip to Poland in January 1989.[11]

Shlomo answered personal questions on many radio shows, beginning with a series of appearances on Lex Hixon's *In the Spirit* in the 1970s (see below, Chapter 11), WRTI 90.1 FM in 1974,[12] KQED in San Francisco in 1975,[13] Zachary Goldman[14] and Zev Brenner[15] in 1992. Also on Zev Brenner's Talkline Show, there was a special Shlomo Carlebach Hour where Shlomo would come on Motzei Shabbat at midnight with his *chevra* to the Staten Island Radio Show to be interviewed by Yankel

---

6. These are summarized in the Hebrew version of my biography of Reb Shlomo.

7. B. Pinchas, "*Barkhi Nafshi et Hashem*," *Panim El Panim*, March 28, 1964. This is the pen name of Pinchas Hacohen Peli. The article is reproduced in Brand, *Reb Shlomele*, 54–55.

8. Emuna Witt, "Reb Shlomo 1980," *Kol Chevra*, vol. 13, 2007, 1–6. A very special thanks to Emuna for being so generous in providing me with a wealth of materials about Reb Shlomo.

9. Harold J. Rubin, "Fixing the World – An Interview with Schlomo [*sic*] Carlebach." *The Sun*, issue 84, Nov., 1982.

10. Dan Shacham, "Rabbi Shlomo Carlebach: 'The Enfant Terrible' of Orthodox Jewry in the United States," *Israel Shelanu*, March 8, 1985, 29 [Hebrew].

11. My thanks to Menachem Daum for showing me copies of these interviews.

12. This is the Temple University radio station in Philadelphia. The interviewer was 20-year old Kenny Ellis.

13. My thanks to Nechama Silver (Yasskin) for sending me her transcription of the 1975 San Francisco radio interview from KQED (88.5 FM).

14. Zachary (Zecharia) Goldman, "His Life, His Music, His Stories," 1992. Most of the video was posted on YouTube in 3 parts. The interview begins after almost 5 minutes of guitar playing of Reb Shlomo with Neil Seidel (at segment 4:50): YouTube .com, http://www.youtube.com/watch?v=qZ4egMpfsxo&annotation_id=annotation _27336&feature=iv; http://www.youtube.com/watch?v=8R3G9d2hE4E&feature=iv& annotation_id=annotation_976268; http://www.youtube.com/watch?v=cMZzuvLd GBY&feature=iv&annotation_id=annotation_793120.

15. Zev Brenner is the founder of Talkline Communications. The interview was recorded on Jan. 14, 1992 and aired the following Sunday on Network, a New York radio and television company that broadcasts nationally. See TalklineCommunications .com, http://www.talklinecommunications.com.

Greenberg.[16] Shlomo was hosted in 1994 in Miami on *Insights 613*[17] and in Israel by Muli Shapira on Galei Tzahal (see below, Chapter 8). In New York, a weekly Friday 1:00 PM radio show on WLIR with Zwe Padeh entitled *Listen to Shlomo's Hour* was billed as Monsey and Rockland County's Most Popular Show.

Various disciples, friends, and reporters interviewed Shlomo. These include: Gitta Schreiber (1989),[18] Micha Odenheimer (1990),[19] Alon Teeger (1992),[20] Michael Lerner,[21] Michael Paley,[22] and Rabbi Meir (Micky) Rosen[23] (the latter three in 1993). Among dozens of obituaries

---

16. My thanks to Eliezer Garner for this information (Dec. 24, 2012). For a description of Zev Brenner's 2-hour weekly radio interviews and mention of the weekly performance of Shlomo Carlebach, see J.J. Goldberg, "Radio Schmooze," *The Jerusalem Report*, Jan. 27, 1994, 34.

17. *Insights 613* produced by Larry Brass. The interviewer, Shmuel, videotaped Reb Shlomo shortly before his concert in Miami Beach in Feb. 1994 (the concert itself was posted in nine parts on YouTube – part I can be found at http://www.youtube.com/watch?v=8wsS1wL_qDg – see below for details of this important concert). The interview was posted on YouTube.com, Part I: http://www.youtube.com/watch?v=O7_zuWW82yY&feature=player_embedded#!; Part II: http://www.youtube.com/watch?v=E6JOU60G5Qk&feature=related; Part III: http://www.youtube.com/watch?v=wo6Zx2V6P9c&NR=1.

18. Gitta Schreiber, "Shlomo Carlebach: An Exclusive Interview," *Country Yossi Family Magazine* 2, 4, Nov., 1989: 30–34.

19. Micha Odenheimer, "On Orthodoxy: An Interview with Rabbi Shlomo Carlebach," *Gnosis* 16, Summer 1990, 46–49.

20. Alon Teeger's recordings of Shlomo in Johannesburg, South Africa, Sept. 1992, contain answers not addressed in any other interviews. My thanks to the Teegers for showing me the transcripts by Rena Teeger.

21. Michael Lerner, "Practical Wisdom from Shlomo Carlebach," *Tikkun Magazine*, Sept.–Oct. 1997, vol. 12, no. 5, 53–56. Lerner, who sometimes frequented the Carlebach Shul in Manhattan, interviewed Shlomo in 1993. See SeferChabibi.blogspot.com, http://seferchabibi.blogspot.com/2008/01/tikkun-magazine-interview-with-rabbi.html.

22. Michael Paley, "His Gift Will Last Long after Others Have Faded." The interview, recorded in the fall of 1993, was published in 1996 in *The New Standard*, a publication no longer existing. Paley died tragically in Dec. 2006. The editor of the *New Standard* was Jason Maoz, who then became an editor at *The Jewish Press*, and Maoz republished the article for Shlomo's 15th *yahrzeit* in *The Jewish Press*, Nov. 11, 2009. See JewishPressAds.com, http://www.jewishpressads.com/pageroute.do/41404.

Rabbi Michael Paley also wrote an article entitled "Shlomo Carlebach and the Synagogue of the Future." *Contact, The Journal of Jewish Life Network*, 7:1, Autumn 2004, 13–14. There he describes how he first met Shlomo at a Boston concert in the late 1960s.

23. For the first part of this interview, see DixieYid.blogspot.co.il, http://dixieyid.blogspot.co.il/2010/10/great-video-interview-with-shlomo.html. The entire interview can be found at http://www.box.net/shared/h9zpz4hxk2 (27:44 minutes) and https://www.box.com/s/4029hmg3tsfs3g8kdiw2 (29:49 minutes). My thanks to

published after his death, of particular interest are Robert L. Cohen in *The Jewish Advocate*,[24] Ari Goldman in *The New York Times*,[25] Michael Lerner in *Tikkun*,[26] and Elli Wohlgelernter in *The Jerusalem Post*.[27]

The first book to include a biographical chapter on Reb Shlomo was completed in October 1996 in time for the second *yahrzeit* of Reb Shlomo. It was written in Hebrew by Meshulam H. Brandwein, promptly translated into English, and published in 1997 with many revisions and additions.[28] In 1997, another two books about Shlomo were published. Yitta Halberstam Mandelbaum collected "inspiring stories" in *Holy Brother*.[29] She depicted the wondrous deeds and secret acts of kindness of a "Latter Day Saint," a "Hidden Righteous Man."[30] The third book is a collection of memories and selected teachings compiled by Zivi Ritchie.[31] These three books, designed to provide inspiring stories, teachings, and anecdotes, formed the basis for the reconstruction of Shlomo's biography even in critical and academic writings. Some biographical information can also be found in the recollections recorded by Shlomo's twin brother, Eli Chaim, and by Shlomo's wife, Neila Carlebach, as well as by

---

Reb Mimi Feigelson who was present at the event and identified it as mid-July, 1993 at Yakar in Jerusalem.

24. Robert L. Cohen, "Shlomo Carlebach: Sweet Singer of American Jewry," *The Jewish Advocate*, Dec. 16–22, 1994.

25. Ari L. Goldman, "Rabbi Shlomo Carlebach," *New York Times*, Oct. 22, 1994.

26. Michael Lerner, "Recent Losses: Jerry Rubin and Shlomo Carlebach," *Tikkun*, Jan. 1995, vol. 10, no. 1, 7.

27. Elli Wohlgelernter, "Simply Shlomo," *The Jerusalem Post Magazine*, April 20, 1995. The actual interview took place shortly before Shlomo's death. The article was reproduced in Brandwein, *Reb Shlomele*, 78–79.

28. Meshulam H. Brandwein, *Reb Shlomele: The Life and World of Shlomo Carlebach*, trans. Gabriel A. Sivan (Efrat, Israel: 1997). On the book cover his name is spelled Brandwine, but inside the book it is Brandwein, and in the Hebrew version it is Brand. Citations from the Hebrew will be noted here as "Brand, *Reb Shlomele*" and from the English translation as Brandwein, *Reb Shlomele*.

29. Yitta Halberstam Mandelbaum, *Holy Brother: Inspiring Stories and Enchanted Tales about Rabbi Shlomo Carlebach* (Lanham, Maryland: 1997).

30. Ibid., xxiv. Mandelbaum described how her father, Rabbi Laizer Halberstam, a hasid "in a long black coat and big broad-rimmed hat," took her to Carlebach's concerts at Town Hall and The Village Gate (ibid., xv).

31. Zivi Ritchie, *Shlomo Carlebach: A Friend to Our Generation*, The Rabbi Shlomo Carlebach Center, 1997. Zivi (Ziv) Ritchie, the son of Dr. Joshua and Liliane Ritchie (see below, Chapter 11), produced a series of popular booklets in English and Hebrew with Shlomo's teachings organized according to themes: Ecstasy for the Soul (part one and two), Get High (uplifting sayings), Soulmates, Friends Listen to This, On Bar Mitzva, Peace, The Blessing of Children, Shabbos is Bliss, Am Yisrael Chai – Israel Lives.

several disciples, such as Aryae Coopersmith and David Zeller.[32] Again the materials were typically anecdotal. The result is that it is not easy to critically assess Shlomo's life and career. Prof. Shaul Magid put it rather sharply when he wrote: "much of what we know about him is hopelessly hagiographic."[33]

To meet this challenge, I began to collate, document, and analyze the circumstances of his life and career using sources scattered in recordings, YouTube videos, entries in encyclopedias,[34] and historical surveys.[35] I found a plethora of material in journals such as *The Jerusalem Report* and *Moment*,[36] Israeli and American newspapers, and on blogs such as those of Jonathan Chipman, Baruch Melman, and Shaya Rothenberg.[37]

---

32. Rabbi Eli Chaim Carlebach, "My Brother: Shlomo as a Young Man." This description was written some time before 1990 (when Rabbi Eli Chaim died). It was posted on the Reb Shlomo email list, Jan. 17, 1998, and uploaded by WUJS, June 3, 2006 and was available for some time at wujs.org.il. Neila Carlebach, "Remembering Shlomo," *The Canadian Jewish News*, Nov. 9, 1995. Aryae Coopersmith, *Holy Beggars: A Journey from Haight Street to Jerusalem* (El Granada, California: 2011). David Zeller, *The Soul of the Story: Meetings with Remarkable People* (Woodstock, Vermont: 2006).

33. Shaul Magid on Rabbi Shlomo Carlebach, in "Jewish Spirituality in America – A Symposium," *Havruta: A Journal of Jewish Conversation*, vol. 2, no. 1, Spring 2009, 18–21.

34. See Zalman Alpert, "Carlebach, Shlomo (1925–1994)," in Jack R. Fischel, Susan M. Ortmann, Zalman Alpert, Donald Altschiller, Alan Amanik, *Encyclopedia of Jewish American Popular Culture* (Santa Barbara, CA: Greenwood Press, 2009); Yaakov Ariel, "Shlomo Carlebach," in Marc C. Carnes (ed.), *American National Biography: Supplement 2* (Oxford: 2005), 77–78; Judah M. Cohen, "Carlebach, Shlomo," *Encyclopaedia Judaica*, eds. Michael Berenbaum and Fred Skolnik, 2nd ed., vol. 4 (Detroit: Macmillan Reference USA, 2007), 481–482.

35. For example, Jonathan D. Sarna, *American Judaism: A History* (New Haven and London: 2004). On Carlebach, see 345–349.

36. Yael Levine surveyed 20 articles in *The Jerusalem Report* that mention Shlomo during the years 1994–2000. Yael Levine, "Rabbi Shlomo Carlebach," *The Jerusalem Report*, 2000. A shortened version of this article appeared in *Kol Chevra*, vol. 7, 2000, 135–138.

Robert L. Cohen, "Jewish Soul Man," *Moment*, Aug. 1997, 58–64, 83. The article is available on the web: RlcWordsAndMusic.net, http://www.rlcwordsandmusic.net/PDF/RLC_Reb-Shlomo-MOMENT.pdf.

37. Rabbi Jonathan Chipman, Thoughts on Shlomo (archives), "An Abrahamic Soul" (2001), posted Oct. 30, 2004, by R. Chipman on HitzeiYehonatan.blogspot.com, http://hitzeiyehonatan.blogspot.com/2004_10_01_archive.html; Rabbi Jonathan Chipman, *Lekh Lekha* (Supplement) – "On Shlomo Carlebach: Rebbe and Minstrel," posted Nov. 9, 2006 by R. Chipman on his blog HitzeiYehonatan.blogspot.com, http://hitzeiyehonatan.blogspot.com/2006_11_01_archive.html.

See http://seferchabibi.blogspot.com. Rabbi Baruch Binyamin Melman became a close disciple of Reb Shlomo in Manhattan from 1985–1994, and joined him "in

The first collection of Shlomo's stories was published by Susan Yael Mesinai in 1994 and included thirty tales.[38] In 2004, Tzlotana Barbara Midlo organized thirty-six stories in five categories.[39] The first posthumous editing of Shlomo's teachings was published by Michael Ruben in 1997.[40] Ruben had met Shlomo at a concert in a Montreal synagogue[41] in the 1960s and became Shlomo's manager in Canada for three decades. Ruben not only recorded Shlomo's teachings but also wrote musical notation when Shlomo phoned with new *niggunim*, thus collecting some 100 original tunes.[42] Hebrew versions of Shlomo's stories and teachings were collated and annotated by Moshe David HaCohen, Yeruham Dan Cohen, Yahad Witt, and Shmuel Zivan.[43] Witt also edited recordings of Carlebach classes given by Reb David Herzberg, one of Reb Shlomo's disciples.[44]

---

about 300 concerts on the violin and mandolin." Currently, he serves as Rabbi of Temple Israel of the Poconos, Stroudsburg, Pennsylvania. See www.TempleIsraelof thepoconos.org.

Shaya's blog, JewishMusicArchive.blogspot.com, archives many musicians. The section on Reb Shlomo, http://shlomocarlebacharchive.blogspot.com, includes links to dozens of video recordings, songs, stories, concerts and interviews.

38. Susan Yael Mesinai, *Shlomo's Stories: Selected Tales* (Northvale, New Jersey: 1994). It was published a month before Shlomo's death and sold 10,000 copies within three years. For the story of how Mesinai began writing the book in 1979, see below, Chapter 11.

39. Tzlotana Barbara Midlo, *Lamed Vav: A Collection of the Favorite Stories of Rabbi Shlomo Carlebach* (Lakewood, New Jersey: 2004).

40. Michael Ruben (ed.), *The Teachings of Rabbi Shlomo Carlebach* (Northvale, New Jersey: 1997).

41. The concert was at The Tifereth Beth David Jerusalem Synagogue, Cote St-Luc, Montreal, Canada, popularly known as the Baily Shul because it is on Baily Road. Shlomo called him on stage with his tambourine and Michael became a devoted fan.

42. Heather Solomon, "Michael Ruben Celebrates Life," *The Canadian Jewish News*, March 1, 2001. See also Michael Ruben, *The Celebrator (The Badchen) and His Friends (A Music Therapist's Diary)*, (Cote St. Luc, Quebec, Canada: 1999).

43. Moshe David Hacohen, *For My Brothers and Friends: Teachings and Stories* (Jerusalem: 2003, 2nd edition [Hebrew]). Yeruham Dan Cohen, *All Together in Holiness* (Mevaseret Zion: 2003 [Hebrew]). Yahad Witt (ed.), *Depths of the Heart* (1996), *Open the Gates of the Heart* (2010 [Hebrew]).

For the past several years, Rabbi Shmuel Zivan has been publishing Shlomo's stories and teachings. Three volumes appeared on the holidays entitled *Lev HaShamayim (Heart of Heaven)*: High Holidays and Sukkot 2004, Passover 2005, Hanukkah 2006, and two volumes containing a total of 112 stories in a collection entitled *Sippurei Neshama (Soul Stories)*, 2009, 2011 [Hebrew].

44. *Sparks of David: Rabbi David Herzberg zt"l teaches Orot Shlomo – commentary of Rabbi Shlomo Carlebach zt"l on Orot HaTeshuva of Rabbi Abraham Isaac HaKohen Kook zt"l*. The book was published privately in Israel without specification of date and place. Yahad Witt published a similar work in Hebrew, *Talks of Rabbi Shlomo Carlebach, Orot Shlomo* (2009), 260–391.

Some disciples have published Shlomo's teachings anonymously.[45]

In recent years, there have been attempts at collating this material. Many recordings of teachings, concerts, and weddings that circulate among Carlebach fans are only recently becoming accessible.[46] The Shlomo Carlebach Foundation launched an ambitious project of transcribing Shlomo's teachings, stories, and songs.[47] The first volume was published recently.[48] Documentary filmmaker Menachem Daum assembled video and audio recordings towards producing a film about Reb Shlomo. Daum discovered rare footage on the Carlebach Family Tradition in a German film that was excerpted in a 1974 CBS documentary *To Be a Jew*. Boaz Shachak, a graduate of the Israeli film school Maaleh, created and directed an hour-long documentary film entitled *You Never Know*, produced by Daniel Paran (Israel, 2008) and shown on Israeli Television Channel 2.[49]

In the academic world, there has been but scanty research on Carlebach. In 2003, Sarah Lerer Weidenfeld wrote an MA thesis in Hebrew at Bar Ilan University on "The Musical Tradition of R. Shlomo Carlebach: A Definitive Analysis of His Works and Musical Style." Weidenfeld expanded this into a Ph.D. dissertation in English which she completed

---

45. For example: *Am Yisrael Chai – Israel Is Living – Rabbi Shlomo Carlebach Teachings and Stories.* The anonymous author-compiler provides no clues as to his identity, nor any indication of dates or places of the teachings. He justifies his book as a fulfillment of his teacher's wishes: "In 1994, Rabbi Shlomo Carlebach said to me, write everything down that I've given you. I told him that with HaShem's help I would. This book is the fulfillment of that promise to my dear friend, Shlomo."

46. For example, just after completing this manuscript, I was given a collection of video and audio recordings of 130 gigabytes which include dozens of events, weddings, and concerts – most of which have yet to be publicized on YouTube.

47. The collection currently includes about 12,000 audio hours and 500 video hours which are gradually being converted to digital files and transcribed so that Shlomo's legacy will be accessible online in an organized and professional manner. See more in the announcement at the end of this book and in the website www.shlomocarlebachfoundation.org.

48. The first volume contains 84 brief expositions relating, often tangentially, to the first 6 portions of *Bereishit* (Genesis). Shlomo Katz (ed.), *The Torah Commentary of Rabbi Shlomo Carlebach, Genesis, Part I* (Jerusalem: The Shlomo Carlebach Legacy Trust and Urim Publications, 2012).

49. For a trailer see http://www.thejewishcinema.com/video/you-never-know-shlomo-carlebach. The entire film is available at the links: http://www.youtube.com/watch?v=7np6jL8dHUU and http://www.youtube.com/watch?v=7np6jL8dHUU&feature=youtube_gdata. Shachak interspersed interviews with Itzik Aeisenstadt, Mimi Feigelson, Aryae Coopersmith, Charlie Roth, Yehuda Leuchter, Nechama (and Shmuel) Silver, and Yahavyahu. Also filmed were Yitshak Fried, Sinai Tor, Avraham, Zusha Frumin, and Moshe David Hacohen. Shachak included brief clips from Reb Shlomo speaking to Mimi Feigelson at Yakar in Jerusalem.

in 2008. It is entitled "Rabbi Shlomo Carlebach's Musical Tradition in Its Cultural Context, 1950–2005." Recently, two BA theses were written at Yale and Princeton,[50] and a doctoral thesis has been undertaken at Haifa University.[51] But besides this, very little has been written from an academic perspective, and almost none of Shlomo's teachings have been analyzed using scholarly tools.

What follows is an attempt at reconstructing the story of Reb Shlomo. I interviewed more than 225 people and accessed some 200 websites, but this represents but a small fraction of those who have "Shlomo stories" to tell. Obviously, I have missed many others. But I do hope that now with the chronological framework presented here it will be easier to locate many more stories and situate them in context.

I conclude with a personal note. I first met Rabbi Shlomo Carlebach when I was 16 years old. It was on a Thursday afternoon, October 2, 1969, the sixth day of Hol HaMoed Sukkot. I was attending the SSSJ rally for Soviet Jewry at the Hammarskjold Plaza near the United Nations and Reb Shlomo was leading in spirited singing. Two days later, October 4, 1969, Shemini Atzeret, I walked to the Carlebach Shul to see for myself what he was all about. To my diary, I confided that the soulful and ecstatic dancing was a completely different type of prayer experience than anything I had ever seen in any synagogue. I returned again the next Shabbat.

Until moving to Israel in August 1974, I lived with my family on 81st St. and West End Ave., merely two blocks from the Carlebach Shul. Occasionally, I would pinch-hit as the Torah reader. In my diary, I took note of the extraordinary sight: long-haired hippies, dancing ecstatically while the older generation looked on. When Reb Shlomo came, the hippies crowded around, listening eagerly. I was an undergraduate at Yeshiva University, and one time the "Singing Rabbi" was invited to our campus. We would have been incredulous then had someone told us that Reb Shlomo was sparking a neo-Hasidic renaissance that would transform Jewish lives around the globe.

History has an ironic sense of humor. The last time I spoke to Reb Shlomo was on a Friday afternoon, August 21, 1992, in the settlement of Beit El. He was spending the summer in Israel, and had come to celebrate the Shabbat bar mitzvah of Amitai Cohen, the son of Mordechai Cohen,

---

50. Benjamin Chaidell, "A Countercultural Tradition: Shlomo Carlebach and His Holy Hippielach," Yale University, Senior Essay in the Department of Religious Studies, April 11, 2011. Daniel Berry, "The Performance Art of Reb Shlomo Carlebach." Undergraduate thesis, Princeton University, 2009.

51. Moshe David Hacohen is examining Reb Shlomo's teachings at the House of Love and Prayer during 1969–1974 in the context of the 1960s counterculture.

Dr. Natan Ophir with his grandson, Hod Shlomo Ophir, who is named after Reb Shlomo Carlebach. Photo taken on May 23, 2012.

Shlomo's grand-nephew.[52] I took my 9-year old son, Menachem, to greet Reb Shlomo. We found him rushing in the corridor of the Beit El guest house. He stopped and gave Menachem a blessing. A little more than a decade later, at age 21, Menachem organized a Carlebach band in our home town, Maaleh Adumim. Today, his band, Regaim, continues as one of many Carlebach bands in Israel. When Menachem and Ortal had their second child, they named him Hod Shlomo. I asked Menachem why and he replied, "Reb Shlomo is my Rebbe." "But," I persisted, "you met Shlomo only once." Menachem responded:

> I memorized his tunes, read all his stories, and joined the Maaleh Adumim Happy Minyan that Michael Brand set up in Mitzpeh Nevo.[53] Before each holiday, my wife and I study his teachings and are inspired to do good and help others. When encountering problems and in troubled times, I sing Carlebach tunes or think about his stories. Then I am comforted. My soul is resuscitated.

One day, Menachem asked me to help him research a college paper to analyze Shlomo's songs. I ended up writing a 350-page book in Hebrew

---

52. Mordechai Cohen's grandfather was Dr. Marcus Cohn, brother of Shlomo's mother, Paula (Pessia) Carlebach.

53. See The Brand Family, "Nachalat Yehuda," *Kol Chevra*, vol. 6, 1999, 9–10.

containing a biography of Shlomo and an analysis of his teachings.[54] My parents asked me how long would it take for me to prepare an English translation, and I confidently replied, three months. But it took two years as I kept on discovering endless numbers of people who had Shlomo stories.

After I finished writing the book, my father discovered a letter which revealed that more than 100 years ago, my grandfather, Emile Offenbacher, had befriended Moshe Carlebach, the son of Rabbi Shlomo Carlebach of Lübeck. My grandfather was a member of the Orach Chaim Synagogue on Manhattan's Upper East Side from 1904, and Moshe Carlebach joined in 1906.[55] As a sequel, my father added that sometime around 1947 Rabbi Naphtali Carlebach was invited to Orach Chaim to lead the all-night learning program of Shavuot. After the early morning *Shaharit* service, my father accompanied Rabbi Naphtali on the half hour walk back to his Manhattan residence. So it seems, that unknowingly, the seeds of this book were planted somehow in my grandfather's synagogue. Or as Shlomo was wont to exclaim: You Never Know.

---

54. To order this book in Hebrew, please write to Meorot.info@gmail.com.

55. Esther Halberstadt, "More on the Carlebach Tradition," *The Jewish Observer*, Nov. 1996, 45.

Part A

The Mission

First Influences

1.   LÜBECK AND THE CARLEBACH RABBINICAL LEGACY

Reb Shlomo was proud of his ancestral lineage. He was wont to recount that his genealogy could be traced back to Aaron the High Priest via his maternal grandfather, Rabbi Dr. Asher Michael (Arthur) Cohn (the Basler Rav). Rabbi Cohn had been ordained at the Hildesheimer Rabbinical Seminary in Berlin and served forty-one years as the Chief Rabbi of Basel, Switzerland (1885–1926). He is famous for having hosted Theodor Herzl and the First Zionist Congress in Basel in August 1897.[1] It is also noteworthy that the Basler Rav hosted Rabbi Avraham Yitzhak HaCohen Kook sometime around 1915 when Rav Kook was stranded in Switzerland because of World War I.[2] From then on, the two families, Cohn and Kook, maintained close ties.[3] One of Reb Shlomo's humorous anecdotes was that he was almost born to Rav Kook's son, because there was a serious marriage proposal for Tzvi Yehudah Kook and Pessia, the only daughter of the Basler Rav who was 19 years old at the time. In the end, Pessia married Naphtali Carlebach in 1917.

Shlomo was named after his paternal grandfather, Rabbi Dr. Shlomo

---

1. Hermann (Tzvi Ahron) Cohn, "The Basler Rav," in Marcus Cohn, *The Basler Rav: Rabbi Dr. Arthur Cohn: A Collection of His Writings* (Jerusalem: 2012).

2. Rav Kook was vacationing at the German spa resort in Bad Kissingen when Germany declared war against Russia on Aug. 1, 1914. Russian citizens were rounded up and interred, but at the intervention of his host, R. Dr. Isaac Bamberger, R. Kook was allowed to depart for neutral Switzerland. There he lived in St. Gallen for over a year with his wife (Raize-Rivka) and their son (Tzvi Yehudah). On January 27, 1916, R. Kook was invited to London to become the Rabbi of Congregation Machzike Hadath.

3. In particular, the Basler Rav's second son, Rabbi Dr. Marcus (Mordechai) Cohn, became very close to Rav Kook in the 1920s and they corresponded often. Their warm connection led eventually to a dedication of the library in Mercaz HaRav Kook by the son of Marcus Cohen who was named Arthur after his grandfather. See Cohn, "The Basler Rav," p. 10, fn. 18, and the photo on p. 41.

(Salomon) Carlebach (1845-1919), who had studied at the University of Würzburg, and began writing a doctorate at the University of Berlin.[4] There in Berlin in 1869, he became close to Rabbi Azriel Hildesheimer.[5] When Rabbi Alexander Sussmann Adler, rabbi of Mosling and Lübeck,[6] died on December 16, 1869, Rabbi Hildesheimer recommended 24-year old Shlomo to be his successor. Rabbi Shlomo's inauguration took place on July 4, 1870 (Shabbat *Parshat Balak*). On January 20, 1872 he married Esther, the eldest daughter of Rabbi Adler. They had eight sons and four daughters, all born in Lübeck where Rabbi Carlebach spent his entire fifty-year career as rabbi.[7]

Most of R. Salomon's children remained in Germany. Two were bankers.[8] Interestingly enough, his son Moshe (1881–1939) sailed to New York in 1906 as a *kashrut* supervisor on the Canard Line Ships.[9] In New York he found a position in a meat import company that enabled him to observe Shabbat (a rarity in those years). His father was against his remaining in the *treife medinah* (unkosher land) and he returned to Germany.[10]

Five of Rabbi Salomon's sons served as rabbis in leading German communities.[11] Two of his daughters married rabbis.[12] Shlomo the grandson,

---

4. Rabbi Salomon Carlebach was born to Joseph Hirsch Carlebach in Heidelsheim, Germany on Dec. 28, 1845. The theme of his doctorate was the development of German drama until the time of Lessing, with particular reference to the Hebraic or biblical sources. Later, he received his Ph.D. from the University of Tubingen.

5. Rabbi Azriel Hildesheimer came to Berlin in 1869 as the first rabbi of the newly founded Orthodox congregation, Adass Jisroel. Eliav, Mordechai, and David Derovan. "Hildesheimer, Azriel." *Encyclopaedia Judaica*. Ed. Michael Berenbaum and Fred Skolnik. 2nd ed. Vol. 9. Detroit: Macmillan Reference USA, 2007, 103–104.

6. Lübeck is the second largest city in Schleswig-Holstein, northern Germany, and Moisling is a district of Lübeck.

7. Rabbi Carlebach died on March 19, 1919. Carlebach, *Carlebach Tradition*, Chapter 5.

8. Alexander (1872–1925), named after R. Salomon's father-in-law, was a banker in Lübeck. Simson (Shimshon) worked in Frankfurt for Baron Wilhelm von Rothschild. Shimshon perished in 1941 in the Jungfernhof concentration camp near Riga, Latvia.

9. His brother-in-law, Rabbi Leopold Rosenak was the head of *kashrut* supervision at the Canard Line Ships.

10. Esther Halberstadt, "More on the Carlebach Tradition," *The Jewish Observer*, Nov. 1996, 45.

11. The five sons who became rabbis: Emanuel (1874–1927) in Köln, Ephraim (1879–1936) in Leipzig, Joseph Tzvi (1883–1942) in Altona and Hamburg, David (1885–1913) in Halberstadt, and Hartwig (Naphtali) (1889–1967) in Berlin and Baden. See Juedischegemeinde.at, www.juedischegemeinde.at/Persoenlichkeiten/RabbiCarlebach.asp. Compare Carlebach, *The Carlebach Tradition*, chaps. 6, 9. See also Naphtali Carlebach, *Joseph Carlebach and His Generation* (New York: 1959).

12. Sylly (1884–1968) married Rabbi Leopold Neuhaus of Frankfurt. Bella (1876–1960) married Rabbi Leopold Rosenak. Miriam Carlebach (1886–1962) married

was fond of noting the deterministic nature of his rabbinical calling by noting that his grandfather, his namesake, had five sons and two sons-in-law who were rabbis. Shlomo added: "My father was always pumping into me and my brother that 'you have to be good rabbis.'"[13]

In a *festschrift* published on July 16, 1910 in honor of Rabbi Dr. Shlomo Carlebach's fortieth year as rabbi of Lübeck, there were thirty-seven articles, and these included expositions from all five Carlebach rabbinical sons.[14] Rabbi Joseph Tzvi Carlebach was the most famous. After his father's death in February 1919, he took over as the rabbi of Lübeck until 1922. Later he served as Chief Rabbi of Altona (1927–1935), and of Hamburg (1936–1942). Despite the Nazi atrocities, he bravely refused to abandon his community.[15] He was murdered in the Jungfernhof concentration camp in Bikernieki Forest about three kilometers from Riga on March 26, 1942.[16]

Shlomo's family ancestry was very important to him as a link to the pre-Holocaust life and tradition. During his later years, Shlomo would stop off in Germany to visit the gravesites in Lübeck,[17] and then perform concerts in Lübeck and Hamburg.[18] In 1992, when asked to describe a particular memorable concert, Shlomo mentioned how he had appeared in front of 10,000 Protestants in Hanover.[19]

William Cohen and their son was the famous Israeli Supreme Court judge Haim Herman Cohn.

13. Lerner, "Practical Wisdom," *Tikkun*, 53.

14. Moshe Stern (ed.), *To Shlomo, Jubilee Volume, Collection of Expositions and Scholarly Articles in Wissenchaft and Jewish History from His Relatives and Friends* (Hebrew and German) (Berlin: 1910).

15. To hear Shlomo tell about the heroism of his uncle Rabbi Joseph Carlebach in Hamburg during the last years of the Holocaust, see the video posted by Joel Goldberg, go4joel, http://www.youtube.com/watch?v=Drj1LQGLyv8. Shlomo relates the story as personal testimony that he heard in Stockholm from a Holocaust survivor.

16. See the biography and photographic descriptions assembled by the Das Joseph Carlebach Institut (JCI) http://www.jci.co.il/?cmd=carlebach.3. See also Shnayer Z. Leiman, "Rabbi Joseph Carlebach, Wuerzburg and Jerusalem: A Conversation between Rabbi Seligmann Baer Bamberger and Rabbi Shmuel Salant," *Tradition* 28:2 1994, 58–63. Rabbi Shlomo Carlebach, *Ish Yehudi: The Life and the Legacy of a Torah Great, Rav Joseph Tzvi Carlebach* (New York: 2008). Ze'ev Wilhem Falk, "Carlebach, Joseph." *Encyclopaedia Judaica*, 2nd ed. (Detroit: 2007), vol. 4, 481.

17. Menachem Daum interview with Shlomo in Poland, Jan. 4, 1989, segment 66:05.

18. Interview of Menachem Daum with Rabbi Yehoshua Witt who as Shlomo's concert manager accompanied him on these trips.

19. Shlomo in an interview with Alon Teeger, Sept. 1992. Hanover is 150 km south of Hamburg while Lübeck is 67 km from Hamburg. A similar story of Shlomo was remembered by Liliane Ritchie. She mentions a "Meeting of the Ways" jamboree in Hamburg for 10,000 people in the 1970s and describes how the Germans apologized

Shlomo was deeply influenced by his father, Rabbi Naphtali (Hartwig) Carlebach. Born in Lübeck in 1889, Naphtali served as a teacher in the Jewish Gymnasium of Leipzig. Like many rabbis in Germany, he completed a Ph.D. Like his father, he wrote about German drama at the University of Tübingen. At age 21, when he was a doctoral student in Berlin, he gave a talk for Shabbat *Parshat Mishpatim*, February 5, 1910, at the Synagogue of the Berlin Rabbinical Seminary on the topic of "Justice – Also before God."[20]

In 1917, Naphtali married Pessia (Paula) (1896–1980), the daughter of Rabbi Asher Cohn.[21] Naphtali assumed a job as an educator in the Jewish Gymnasium in Leipzig. At age 28 he became rabbi of the Pestalozzistraße Synagogue, which soon became the most popular Orthodox synagogue in western Berlin.[22] Their daughter Shulamit was born in 1919.[23] Then, on 18th Tevet, January 14, 1925, Pessia gave birth to the twin boys, Shlomo and Eliyahu (Eli) Chaim.

2.   BADEN (1931–1938) AND TELSHE (1938–1939)

Shlomo was 6 years old when his father accepted the position of Chief Rabbi of Baden, Austria,[24] a resort town, a half an hour's drive from

---

for the Holocaust. Liliane Ritchie, *Masters and Miracles: Divine Interventions – Messages of Love, Healing and Heart Wisdom* (Jerusalem: 2010), 49–51.

20. This was then published in the Jubilee Volume for his father as Hartwig Carlebach, "Gerechtigkeit – Auch Gegen Gott," in Moshe Stern (ed.), *To Shlomo, Jubilee Volume, Collection of Expositions and Scholarly Articles in Wissenchaft and Jewish History from His Relatives and Friends* (Berlin: 1910 [Hebrew and German]), 282–287.

21. For photos of Pessia (Paula) with her brothers Heinrich (Chaim), Marcus (Mordechai), and Hermann (Tzvi Ahron) together with her parents Rebbetzin Betty (Bayla) and Rabbi Asher Cohn, see the photo section here, and Cohn, "The Basler Rav," 41.

22. The Pestalozzistraße Synagogue was built in 1911–1912 on the initiative of Betty Sophie Jacobsohn, a businesswoman who donated the property on which it stands. It functioned as a private synagogue for several years until it was taken over by the Community in 1919. See Esther Slevogt, *Die Synagoge Pestalozzistraße* (Berlin: 2012).

23. The German name of Shulamit Carlebach (1919–2003) is listed variously as Linerle, Zerlina and Cerline. She married Rabbi Simcha Zissel Halevi Levovitz (1908–2001), the son of the famed Rabbi Yeruchom Levovitz, and they lived in Borough Park, Brooklyn. They had 3 sons who are rabbis – Yeruchom, Yisroel, and Osher Michoel – and a daughter who married Rabbi Avrohom Moshe Faivelson.

24. Rabbi Prof. Wilhelm Reich, who served for close to 50 years as Chief Rabbi of Baden, had died on July 24, 1929. See www.juedischegemeinde.at/Persoenlichkeiten/RabbiReich.asp.

The wedding of Rabbi Naphtali and Pessia Carlebach, 1917

Vienna. The official inauguration took place on August 9, 1931.[25] From 1934–1938, the Carlebach family lived at Helenenstraße 6, next to a beautiful park (Doblhoffpark) and one kilometer from the Great Synagogue on Grabengasse 14. They would frequently host guests who were vacationing at the Baden Spas. Among the visitors to later impact Shlomo's life was R. Yosef Yitzchak Schneersohn, RaYaTZ (1880–1950), the sixth Chabad Rebbe. He had traveled from Warsaw to the Baden Spas to find relief from his multiple sclerosis. In 1936 (or 1937), R. Naphtali brought his twin boys to the Rebbe who blessed them saying:

> I bless you, that you will some day be *Chassidishe Yidden* (Hasidic Jews), and don't be German little boys. Sleep with your *tallit katan* and serve Hashem with joy.[26]

In Baden young Shlomo began appreciating music. He was enthused by the waltz tunes in the public courtyard behind his house where they

25. See www.juedischegemeinde.at/Persoenlichkeiten/RabbiCarlebach.asp. See also Thomas E. Schärf, *Jüdisches Leben in Baden: Von den Anfängen bis zur Gegenwart* (Vienna: 2005). This book, detailing the history of Jewish life in Baden, was published in honor of the rededication of the Baden Great Synagogue in September 2005.

26. Lerner, "Practical Wisdom," 53; Brandwein, *Reb Shlomele*, 23–24.

Carlebach-Cohn Family, Berlin 1924. Left corner, Rabbi Naphtali and wife Pessia (seated) with daughter Shulamit; center, Rabbi Dr. Arthur (Asher Michael) and Betty Cohn; behind them, Marcus and Rose Cohn with daughter Etti (standing); right corner, Rabbi Heinrich and Lotte Cohn with daughter Ina (seated).

Eli Chaim, Shulamit, and Shlomo, the three Carlebach children around 1927

would dance "night and day" to the tunes of Johann Strauss. He was so enchanted by the classical music that he decided he wanted to play violin:

> I had two dreams in my heart. I wanted to be the biggest *lamdan* (Torah scholar) in the world, and also the greatest musician. When I was eight or nine, my mother bought me a violin, and I was ready to play, but then at that time my rebbe says to me, 'Right now, *mamesh*, the Ribbono Shel Olam is testing you. Because both don't go. Or you're learning or you're playing violin. So I gave up violin.[27]

It was in Baden that young Shlomo experienced the Hasidic song, joy, and prayer that were to shape his career. At age 7, the twin Carlebach brothers "were very thrilled" when their father introduced them to the second Tschortkover (Chortkov) rebbe, Rabbi Yisroel Friedman, who was living in Vienna.[28] Next door to Rabbi Naphtali's synagogue was a *shtiebel* where Tschortkover and Bobover Hasidim prayed. The Carlebach twins preferred attending there rather than their father's own synagogue.[29] As Eli Chaim explained:

> Our biggest excitement in Baden was the Beis Midrash at the Chassidic *shtiebel*. . . . Shabbos and Yom Tov started to have a new meaning for us. From them we really learned the true meaning of Yiddishkeit and Chassidus, real *davening* and learning. Each year they imported new *nigunim* from Poland and each first Pesach night, *Hallel* was a new experience with new songs. My brother and I practiced endlessly these *nigunim* to get them right.[30]

By practicing, the boys not only became expert in musical prayer innovations in *Hallel*,[31] but they also imbibed the Hasidic transformative singing. Indeed, on Reb Shlomo's first record album, the Hasidic style prayer in Baden was acknowledged as being the source of inspiration,

---

27. Wohlgelernter, "Simply Shlomo."

28. Eli Chaim, *My Brother*. The Chortkov Rebbe died on December 1, 1933 and his funeral left a memorable impression on the twin Carlebach sons.

29. This was revealed by Shlomo when he answered Rabbi Micky Rosen's question in a public discussion at Yakar in Jerusalem (summer 1993) as to how he grew up in a German *yekke* home yet became a Hasidic singer. Shlomo even claimed that his father would have preferred the Chortkov *shtiebel* himself had he not been obligated to his own synagogue. For a video of the interview see DixieYid.blogspot.co.il, http://dixieyid.blogspot.co.il/2010/10/great-video-interview-with-shlomo.html.

30. Eli Chaim, *My Brother*.

31. For the full version of Shlomo's *Hallel* tunes which he developed into a standard liturgical form, see http://www.youtube.com/playlist?list=PLnuftEmfAbZzX7L5PJJuPca6oNj1Sa_YR&feature=view_all.

where Shlomo's "heart was first captured by the Chassidic warmth."[32] It seems that these melodies created an indelible impression enabling Shlomo to invent new tunes easily and spontaneously.

Young Shlomo also learned Hasidic songs from Moishe Heschel, the brother of Rabbi Abraham Yehoshua Heshel, the Kopitchinitzer (Kopyczynce) Rebbe. Moishe was a Breslov Hasid and a traveling merchant. He is said to have taught the Carlebach twins a tune for *Nishmas Kol Hai*.[33]

R. Naphtali employed private instructors for his boys. Eli Chaim described the first tutors: "Our teachers, the Lutvoks, were very serious, and concentrated on the books and literature of the Talmud." But, in 1936, a new tutor was hired, a Hasid fond of nature who took the two 11-year old boys on picnics and outings. Eli Chaim later recalled:

> Baden is a very beautiful city at the end of the Alps as they plunge into the lowlands. He showed us the beauty of G-d's creation – the world.[34]

One of the private tutors in the Carlebach house was from the Ponevezh Yeshiva and another was from the Telshe Yeshiva. Shlomo described how he would sneak out late at night to study with his tutor:

> According to good German education, children at a certain time must go to bed so that they can be alert the next day. But I had a deal with my teacher, who was a young man living on the third floor, that after I was supposed to be asleep I would sneak out of my room and study with him, studying day and night.[35]

Young Shlomo was an avid reader and read many secular books from his father's vast library including novels, European philosophers, and classical literature.[36] But what influenced Shlomo most was the religious

---

32. Quotation from the jacket cover of the 1959 album. The record was re-issued in 2002 with changes, e.g., the percussion instruments were made louder. See CdUniverse.com, http://www.cduniverse.com/productinfo.asp?pid=7399942.

33. See Arthur Green and Zalman Schachter-Shalomi, "A Dialogue on the Beginnings of Neo-Hasidism in America," *Spectrum: A Journal of Renewal Spirituality*, vol. 3:1, Winter–Spring, 2007, 10–18. Part of this dialogue was reprinted as "A Conversation: Rabbi Zalman Schachter-Shalomi and Rabbi Arthur Green," in *Kol Chevra*, vol. 13, 2007, 25–28.

34. Eli Chaim, *My Brother*.

35. Lerner, "Practical Wisdom," 53. Reb Shlomo told a similar story to Zachary Goldman, *His Life*, segment 6:55. YouTube.com, http://www.youtube.com/watch?v=qZ4egMpfsxo&feature=watch_response_rev; http://www.youtube.com/watch?v=qZ4egMpfsxo&annotation_id=annotation_27336&feature=iv.

36. Neila Carlebach, "Remembering Shlomo," *The Canadian Jewish News*,

fervor in his father's house. He later described how his father "gave over Yiddishkeit to me" by experiential religiosity:

> Every Friday night, my father took me and my brother by the hand, and he walked around all over the house singing *Shalom Aleichem* with us, but with so much sweetness.[37]

Later, Shlomo was to recall how his parents inspired him to reach out to the world: "My parents put so much fire for learning and loving the world, and absolutely really loving the world."[38] In explaining why he befriended non-Jews, Shlomo described his impression about his father's personal friendship with the Cardinal of Vienna.[39] But "the most important thing" that he learned from his parents was a sense of responsibility "to make the world better." They taught me that "I have no right to walk even one street without doing a favor, or smile at least at one person on that street." This became the driving force of his life. As a young man he was so motivated that when he got on the subway, he would feel: "I've got to do a favor to somebody, talk to somebody." He wouldn't leave the subway until he found someone whom he could help.[40]

Shlomo was also deeply impressed by his parents' altruism and "open house" policy:

> All the great rebbes who came to be cured to Berlin and Vienna would first contact my father or my mother. I grew up in an atmosphere of helping people day and night.[41]

Rabbi Naphtali Carlebach was friendly with Rabbi Yosef Shlomo Kahaneman (1886–1969), Rosh Yeshiva of the Ponevezh Yeshiva. The story is told that R. Kahaneman came to Berlin to fundraise for his yeshiva and stayed at the Carlebach home. When Shlomo's mother, Pessia, overheard that the yeshiva was on the verge of bankruptcy, she pawned

---

Nov. 9, 1995.

37. Recording transcribed in Katz, *Torah Commentary*, Part I, 193. Similarly, R. Naphtali described the Friday night scene in his father's home (R. Shlomo, the grandfather) as including walking around the house singing "*Shalom Aleichem*" – Naphtali Carlebach's family memoir, Chapter 7.

38. Interview by Menachem Daum at Shlomo's home in Manhattan on Nov. 8, 1989, segment 24:15. My thanks to Menachem for the video of this rare interview.

39. Daum interview, segment 23:25. Shlomo: "My father was very close to the Cardinal in Vienna, and I can never thank my father enough for this bridge."

40. Daum interview, Nov. 8, 1989, segment 23:50.

41. Zachary Goldman, *His Life*, first part of the interview with Reb Shlomo, segment 5:30-6:15 in http://www.youtube.com/watch?v=qZ4egMpfsxo&feature=watch _response_rev.

her jewelry and valuables, and gave the money to save the Ponevezh Yeshiva.[42]

In 1937, the Carlebach family traveled to Lithuania for a bar mitzvah celebration in the Kahaneman family and ended up staying there several months due to a series of accidents and illnesses, and young Shlomo spent time learning in the Ponevezh Yeshiva. His older sister, Shulamit, recounted later how this brief learning experience made an indelible impact on Shlomo in appreciating the value of the Talmudic studies and motivated him to become a scholar.[43]

Shlomo and his twin brother reached the age of bar mitzvah on the 18th of Tevet, 5698 (December 22, 1937), and celebrated on December 25, Shabbat *Shemot* at the Great Synagogue on Grabengasse 14 in Baden.[44] Anti-Semitic sentiments were beginning to be felt more acutely. Shlomo was later to describe his fears of playing in the park: "Children would threaten us and say 'we will kill you.'" Nazi Germany invaded Austria on March 11–13, 1938 and incorporated Austria into the German Reich. A wave of street violence against Jewish persons and property resulted throughout the Greater German Reich.[45] On March 13, 1,871 Jews were deported from Baden. It was dangerous to be a Jew. Rabbi Naphtali Carlebach managed to organize a clandestine early Shabbat morning service in his home.[46] The handwriting was on the wall. In July 1938, the Carlebach family managed to obtain a permit to travel to Lithuania.[47] They left just in the nick of time. Kristallnacht on November 9–10, 1938 was a devastating pogrom and marked the start of the Holocaust. At least 91 Jews were killed in the attacks, and a further 30,000 arrested

---

42. Mandelbaum, *Holy Brother*, 116–117, who quotes R. Itzik Aisenstadt who said he heard the story in 1980 from R. Avraham Kahaneman at the annual dinner of Ponevezh. A similar version is told by Brandwein, *Reb Shlomele*, 169–171.

43. Mandelbaum, *Holy Brother*, tells this story in the name of Shulamit Carlebach (Levovitz). There is confusion as to the date and place. Halberstam mentions the city of Telz. However, this would be a different district than Ponevezh. She also cites the year 1938. My guess is that two separate trips were conflated, and that the Carlebach family was in Telz in 1938 after fleeing Austria.

44. See Hermine Grossinger in *Kol Chevra*, vol. 10, 2004, 179 and in *Kol Chevra*, vol. 6, 1999, 23. In his travels to Europe, Shlomo visited Baden and the Synagogue "many times" – see Yehoshua Witt, "Baden, Austria: Reb Shlomo's Home Town," *Kol Chevra*, vol. 6, 1999, 22.

45. United States Holocaust Museum, 1938: Key Dates, Ushmm.org, http://www .ushmm.org/wlc/en/article.php?ModuleId=10007761.

46. For Reb Shlomo's dramatic story in Vienna in 1938 about the clandestine early Shabbat morning *minyan* in his father's home and the heroism of "Moshele Gut Shabbos," see http://www.youtube.com/watch?v=irJyKmFoPa4&NR=1&feature=end screen.

47. See Offenbacher, "Jewish Minstrel," 54.

and incarcerated in concentration camps. Jewish homes, hospitals, and schools were ransacked, as the attackers demolished buildings with sledgehammers. Over 1,000 synagogues were burned, 95 in Vienna alone.

On November 10 in Baden, the Jews were rounded up and marched through the streets towards the synagogue where they were forced to listen to anti-Semitic lectures and sing the Nazi anthem "*Horst Wessel*." Then they were loaded onto trucks and taken to Dachau. As soon as they were deported, the mob set fire to the synagogue and pillaged their stores and homes.[48] The violent atmosphere induced one-half of Austria's Jews to emigrate penniless within half a year. By May 17, 1939, nearly half of Austria's Jewish population had emigrated, leaving only approximately 121,000 Jews in Austria.[49]

Seemingly, the Carlebach family had escaped. Arriving in the Lithuanian town Telšiai, 13-year old Shlomo and his brother learned in the preparatory *mechina* program of the Telshe (Telz) Yeshiva.[50] But the Nazi invasion of Poland in September 1939 brought the war closer to Lithuania. The Lithuanian police began interrogating foreigners. Naphtali had fallen through a malfunctioning hidden trap door in the rented house and was bedridden, yet somehow he managed to visit the Consul of Denmark and procure a visa to travel to Denmark.[51] There the Carlebach family succeeded in obtaining a visa to England where they boarded "the last trans-Atlantic ship bound for New York." Reportedly, the captain informed them: "Now you don't know what a miracle it is that you are on my ship, but one day you will know."[52] This narrow escape from the terrors of the Holocaust left a profound impression on Shlomo that was later to shape his life career.

---

48. YadVashem.org, www1.yadvashem.org/yv/en/exhibitions/kristallnacht/baden.asp. See there for photos of the humiliating march through the streets of Baden, the forced anti-Semitic sermons in the Synagogue followed by the deportation to Dachau and the burning of the Synagogue.

49. YadVashem.org, www1.yadvashem.org/yv/en/righteous/stories/historical_background/vienna.asp.

50. Witt, "Reb Shlomo," 2; Zivan, *Soul Stories*, vol. 2, 208.

51. Liliane Ritchie relates Shlomo's story how the consul liked Naphtali's answer to his challenge about King David's adulterous relationship with Batsheva and thus granted him a visa. Ritchie, *Masters and Miracles*, 46–48. See also Liliane Ritchie, "The Wandering Messenger," *Kol Chevra*, vol. 13, 2007, 44–45.

52. Reb Shlomo as told to Zachary Goldman, *His Life*, second part of the interview, segment 1:10–1:35 in http://www.youtube.com/watch?v=8R3G9d2hE4E&NR=1.

3.   BROOKLYN (1939–1945)

The Carlebach family settled in Williamsburg, Brooklyn at the end of 1939. During the Holocaust years, R. Naphtali served as rabbi of the Young Israel of Crown Heights on Eastern Parkway, a large, mainstream Orthodox synagogue, until he was succeeded by Rabbi Zvi Dov (Harold) Kanotopsky.[53] R. Naphtali suffered from a heart condition, and his wife Rebbetzin Pessia maintained the household, earning money as a book-binder.[54]

Shlomo spent his teenage years studying in the *haredi* yeshiva, Mesivta Torah Vodaas, in the Kensington neighborhood of Brooklyn. There he was influenced by Rabbi Shlomo Hyman (1892–1945) who had come from Vilna in 1935 to teach at the yeshiva. One day in 1942, Rabbi Aharon Kotler, visited Torah Vodaas. With the encouragement of R. Shraga Faivel Mendelovitz, principal of Torah Vodaas, R. Kotler began planning a *kollel* program. He chose the small resort town of Lakewood, New Jersey, outside the bustle of New York, as an ideal place for intensive full-time Torah learning. A building was found on 617 6th St. The program began in April 1943, shortly after Pesach, with fourteen students, some of whom had known R. Kotler from his days teaching in Kletzk in Poland. Shlomo and his brother Eliyahu Chaim, aged 18, joined this first group. Shlomo learned for six years with avid enthusiasm. In later years, Reb Shlomo recalled:

> When I was in yeshiva, I was learning so much, that not only did I not buy a newspaper; I didn't even look at the headlines! I didn't want anything in my head but the Torah.[55]

Chazkel (Charlie) Roth visited Lakewood and saw the Carlebach brothers studying: "Then, it was Reb Eli Chaim who joked around and always

---

53. My thanks to Shulamith Z. Berger, Curator of Special Collections, Yeshiva University for providing information from the YU Archives about the Young Israel of Eastern Parkway in the 1940s, and for referring me to R. Naphtali Carlebach's obituary in the *American Jewish Yearbook*, vol. 69 (New York: 1968), 605. There it states that he was Rabbi of Young Israel of Eastern Parkway until moving in 1945 to become the Rabbi of Kehilath Jacob. AjcArchives.org, http://www.ajcarchives.org/AJC_DATA/Files/1968_15_DirectoriesLists.pdf.

54. Brandwein, *Reb Shlomele*, 24; Shalomi, "A Conversation," 26.

55. This is what Reb Shlomo says in a Synagogue performance in the early 1990s. See video posted in Feb. 2008 by Emeto7 entitled *Rabbi Shlomo in Concert Part 7a*, http://www.youtube.com/watch?v=prN7W4eWUYo&feature=player_embedded#at=316. Similarly, he is quoted by his interviewer (Lerner, "Practical Wisdom," 53) as exclaiming that while studying at Lakewood, he "didn't want to have anything to do with the world."

sang *niggunim*, while Reb Shlomo was quiet and studious."[56] Shlomo was considered "one of the most promising young Talmudists in the country and pronounced an *illui*, a Torah genius, by R. Aharon Kotler."[57] It is reported that a particularly brilliant classmate, Willie Low (Ze'ev Lev),[58] was said to have remarked that there were only two students in Lakewood at the time who understood R. Aharon Kotler's class – himself and Shlomo.[59]

R. Kotler (1891–1962) was born in Sislovich, Poland and had been head of the yeshiva in Kletzk, Poland until the Holocaust. He escaped via Kobe, Japan, arriving in New York in April of 1941. With his founding of the Lakewood Yeshiva, he became a prominent figure in the American *haredi* world. R. Kotler was chairman of both the Grand Rabbinical Council of Agudas Israel and the Rabbinical Council of Torah Umesorah.[60] He pioneered the idea of a *kollel*, as a full-time learning program,[61] and Lakewood became a main source of *haredi* leadership.

Shlomo's disciples often stated that not only was he an outstanding student and protégé of R. Kotler, but that his mentor viewed him as his potential successor.[62] The story is told that the Lakewood Yeshiva students had a hard time following Rabbi Kotler's discourses and understanding

---

56. Chazkel Roth, "Vintage Reb Zalman Schachter-Shalomi," *Kol Chevra*, vol. 15, 2009, 190–191.

57. Zalman Schachter-Shalomi, "The Master of Virtuous Reality: Reb Shlomo Carlebach," in *Wrapped in a Holy Flame: Teachings and Tales of the Hasidic Masters* (San Francisco: 2003), 290. Cf. Mandelbaum, *Holy Brother*, 51–52, 73–74.

58. Prof. Lev (1922–2004), Israel Prize recipient in physics. He studied physics at Columbia University in New York from 1946 until 1950, and occasionally would visit Lakewood to hear the lectures of Rabbi Aharon Kotler.

59. Chipman, "Rebbe and Minstrel."

60. Mordechai Hacohen, "Kotler, Aaron," *Encyclopaedia Judaica*, 2nd ed., vol. 12 (Detroit: 2007), 323.

61. On the isolationist ideology of Rabbi Kotler preventing students from any activity except learning Torah full-time, see Yoel Finkelman, *Religion and Public Life in 20th Century American Jewish Thought*, Ph.D. dissertation, the Hebrew University of Jerusalem, August 2002, Chapter III, "Rabbi Aharon Kotler: Influence through Withdrawal," 101–169.

62. See, for example, Mandelbaum, *Holy Brother*, 73–74. She quotes Rabbi Kotler as having told Rabbi Feinstein that Shlomo Carlebach was "a rare, brilliant, and extraordinary young man learning in his Yeshiva . . . this student absorbs Torah learning in a unique way that he has never witnessed before, and that in all his years as Rosh Yeshiva he has never encountered such a mind." In a personal communication (Dec. 17, 2012), Yitta Mandelbaum clarified that the source for this is Joey Greenblatt who heard the story from his father Rabbi Ephraim Greenblatt who had heard it from his teacher, Rabbi Moshe Feinstein, in the late 1940s.

his Talmudic references. Shlomo would summarize and review the class for them. According to one report:

> Once a week the top class in the Mir Yeshiva would come from Brooklyn to listen to the discourse of Rabbi Aharon Kotler. It was not easy to follow the sources and reasoning, but after the class was over, there was one person who would explain and review the class for everyone else. This was Reb Shlomo.[63]

However, in a recent biography of R. Kotler, there is not a single mention of Shlomo.[64] The obvious reason is that Shlomo was considered a renegade for having defected to Chabad, played guitar, and hugged women. Nonetheless, the learning under R. Kotler established a chain of tradition for Shlomo which enhanced his reputation as a standard bearer of Orthodoxy even when he was ostracized because of his maverick style.

4.   MANHATTAN (1946–1951)

In 1945, the Carlebach family moved to Manhattan as R. Naphtali assumed leadership of Congregation Kehilath Jacob on 305 West 79th St. replacing Rabbi Jacob Meyer Segolovich.[65] Originally from Danzig, R. Segolovich had founded the synagogue in 1941.[66] After he passed away in 1944,[67] R. Naphtali purchased the rights to the synagogue, including the lease on the building,[68] and the Carlebach family lived on the second floor of the synagogue.

Shlomo's father suffered a heart attack in 1948. Shlomo stopped learning full-time in the Lakewood Yeshiva to spend more time at home in Manhattan.[69] He also began to frequent the Hasidic courts more often, especially Chabad, Modzitz, and Bobov. Sometime around 1950, when his father wasn't feeling well, Shlomo filled in to teach his weely Torah

---

63. Leiser Morawiecki told me (Jan. 8, 2013) that in 1972 he was told this story by a rabbi who was part of the Mir class that attended Rabbi Kotler's class.

64. Rabbi Yitzchok Dershowitz, *The Legacy of Maran Rav Aharon Kotler: A Vivid Portrait of the Teachings* (Lakewood, New Jersey: 2004).

65. The name is sometimes spelled Sagelowicz or Sagallovich.

66. Sagelowicz is listed as a founder of the Synagogue on the Certificate of Incorporation of Congregation Kehilath Jacob, Inc. (as a Religious Corporation under the laws of the State of New York). The Certificate was signed on December 26, 1941. I thank Daniel Goldschmidt, a current board member of Kehilath Jacob, for sending me this information.

67. Paley, "His Gift."

68. Daniel Goldschmidt wrote to me that "*Shuls* were bought and sold like stores and Naftali and his family took over the lease when they bought the congregation."

69. Witt, "Reb Shlomo," 3.

Shlomo spent his teenage years studying in Mesivta Torah Vodaas in the Kensington neighborhood of Brooklyn. Shlomo (front row) is in the center of a class picture, about 1943.

portion class. The students enjoyed it so much that they requested that he continue giving the class. Soon Shlomo set up a learning group called TSGG (or TASGIG), an acronym for **T**aste **A**nd **S**ee **G**od **I**s **G**ood, based on the verse in Psalms 34:9.[70] He explained this verse using a teaching of R. Nachman of Breslov to say that "you cannot begin to talk to people about God unless you have first given them a taste of how God is Good."[71] TSGG operated for a number of years as a co-ed program, the first such Hasidic outreach program in America. Chaim Waxman, who participated in this group when he was 15 years old, described how TSGG included "small groups of maybe ten to fifteen teenagers and young adults" who joined together "for singing and inspiration."[72]

Marilyn Schwadron (Hittner) was one of the participants in TSGG. One day in 1951 or 1952, Shlomo took his class to 770 Eastern Parkway for a *yechidus* with the Rebbe. Marilyn began corresponding with the Rebbe.[73] When the question arose of finding suitable employment that

---

70. Green and Schachter, "A Dialogue," 13. Cf. Cohen, R.L. "Jewish Soul," 61 where he uses the acronym TASGIG as does Mandelbaum, *Holy Brother*, xxix. However, Chaim Waxman, who participated in the program, told me the acronym used was TSGG.

71. This explanation was reported by Reb Zalman Schachter-Shalomi, March 19, 1994 at the Hillel of Berkeley gathering.

72. Personal correspondence, June 28, 2011, from Prof. Chaim Waxman.

73. My thanks to Eliezer Evan Schwadron, son of Marilyn Schwadron, for this information, Nov. 15, 2012.

Shlomo and his twin brother Eli Chaim, with their father Naphtali.
(Inset) Shlomo was learning at the Lakewood Yeshiva when he took a vacation
at Camp Torah Vodaas in the Catskill Mountains. Maybe summer, 1946.
Courtesy of Sheina Carlebach Berkowitz (Eli Chaim's Daughter)

would not hurt her Shabbat observance, the Rebbe advised her to have
Shlomo contact Rabbi Chaskel Besser. This was the beginning of a unique
friendship between the two men which, forty years later, led to Shlomo's
pioneering concert tour of Poland in January 1989 (see below).[74]

In 1950, Shlomo and his father attended a Hebrew language *ulpan*
taught by Prof. Isaac Barzilay. The class was held at the Jewish Theological
Seminary (JTS),[75] just four subway stops from their Manhattan residence.
Shlomo would practice playing the piano at JTS (only later in 1956 did he
take up the guitar). At JTS Shlomo made some lifelong friends with future
rabbis who later opened the doors to his performing at non-Orthodox
congregations. Jack Riemer was a student at JTS when he first met
Shlomo in the early 1950s. Riemer, who became one of the best-known
and most-quoted writers in the rabbinate, invited Shlomo to perform
several concerts over the years:

---

74. My thanks to Yisroel Besser for this information, Oct.–Nov. 2012.

75. Personal communication Aug. 5, 2012 from Rabbi Hayyim Halpern who also
participated in this class.

Eli Chaim and Shlomo, rowing summer vacation Catskill Mountains, probably summer 1948.

I arranged several visits for Shlomo at the synagogues where I served as rabbi in Boston, Massachusetts – at Temple Sinai of Swampscott and Marblehead (1957–1961), and Temple Beth Hillel in Mattapan (1961–1964); then in Dayton, Ohio at Congregation Beth Abraham (1964–1978), and finally in La Jolla, California at Congregation Beth El (1978–1986). Each time that Shlomo came he had a wonderful impact.[76]

When Shlomo would play the piano at JTS, people would stop to listen. It was an unusual sight to see a Chabad fellow playing Hasidic melodies at JTS. Sara Schafler-Kelman was one of those impressed. She invited Shlomo to a pre-Shabbat program at the Hillel Center on Convent Avenue. Shlomo was afraid that his English was not fluent and that his accent was Yiddish, but Sara answered that he could sing Hasidic tunes and need not speak much. She prepared a poster entitled

---

76. Personal interview with Rabbi Jack Riemer, Dec. 11, 2012.

Reb Shlomo, standing to the right of the table, half hidden, at a Bar Mitzvah celebration. Photo taken around 1948.

Courtesy of Rebbetzin Hadassa Carlebach

Rabbi Shlomo Carlebach (center) with a group that he brought to 770 Eastern Parkway, around 1950. This is a photo of the TSGG learning group that Reb Shlomo organized in his father's synagogue. Marilyn Schwadron (Hittner) is the second woman to the left of Shlomo. She has short black hair and is standing behind the two ladies in the front row.

Courtesy of Reb Zalman Schachter-Shalomi

Rabbi Naphtali Carlebach at Congregation Ohab Zedak (Belle Harbor, New York) at a testimonial banquet to honor Max Haas, January 8, 1966.
Courtesy of Linda Haas-Shapira

The Place of Music in the Hassidic Tradition. This was Shlomo's first invited performance for college students.[77]

Nine years later, in 1959, Sara attended a concert by Shlomo on Motzei Shabbat.[78] When she walked in with her husband, Rabbi Shmuel Schafler, and three of their children, Shlomo immediately recognized her:

> As soon as I entered the auditorium Reb Shlomo spotted me. He jumped off the stage, ran to meet and embrace me. I couldn't believe that so many years later he still remembered me. He said, Sara Edell – Do you know that *you were the first person who invited me to perform before an audience*? You were my very first sponsor. You gave me a title for my life's work.[79]

---

77. Personal interview with Sara Schafler-Kelman (née Edell), July 13, 2011. Born in Toronto on May 29, 1928, Sara had graduated the University of Toronto and had come to study for a teacher's degree at JTS. Sara was working as the assistant to Rabbi Arthur Zuckerman, director of the B'nai B'rith Hillel Foundation of City College and had been assigned the task of organizing Friday afternoon pre-Shabbat programs.

78. The concert took place at the Madison Jewish Center, a Conservative synagogue in Brooklyn around the corner from the Schafler home.

79. Personal interviews with Sara Schafler-Kelman, July–Aug. 2011. See also

Wedding performed February 25, 1950 by Rabbi Naphtali Carlebach for Max and Sonja Haas at Ratner's Restaurant, a famous kosher dairy restaurant on the Lower East Side of New York City.   Courtesy of Linda Haas-Shapira

During his early years in New York, Shlomo had been learning and conversing mostly in Yiddish. He began learning English in a special Columbia University program in 1951.[80] His teacher happened to be a vice president of the League for Arab Refugees, but Shlomo credits her not only in instructing him in "phonetic rudiments" of English, but also

Natan Ophir, "How Sara (Edell) Schafler-Kelman Arranged Reb Shlomo's First Piano Performance for College Students (Manhattan, 1950)," *Kol Chevra*, vol. 18, 2012, 109–110.

80. Apparently this was a course offered by The American Language Center through The School of General Studies. My thanks to Jocelyn Wilk, Public Services Archivist at Columbia University, for the information.

for encouraging him towards a singing career by pointing out that he had a "fine ear for sounds."[81] Becoming fluent in English at the age of 26, Shlomo developed an idiosyncratic grammar that became his hallmark. His mixture of Yiddish words such as *"mamash," "gevalt," "heilige,"* and *"nebech"* provided his listeners, some of whom were quite assimilated, with a nostalgic reminder of a Hasidic Eastern European life and culture that had been lost in the Holocaust. These expressions eventually became part and parcel of the modern Carlebach followers' mode of speech and a linguistic part of what one might call a neo-Hasidic identity.

5.   HASIDIC INFLUENCES (BOBOV, MODZITZ, AND CHABAD)

Shlomo learned from Bobov to tell stories, from Modzitz to sing tunes, and Chabad sent him on his life mission. All three rebbes had escaped the Holocaust. Their lifework in New York was a miraculous rejuvenation of Hasidic life.

⁂

The Bobover Rebbe *shtiebel* was very near the Carlebach residence in Manhattan. The Carlebach brothers enjoyed listening to the Bobover Rebbe's stories and tales.[82] He was known to have a "warm, outgoing personality, a welcoming smile, a rare gift for storytelling and an inexhaustible fund of Hasidic tales that attracted people to his table or festive meals."[83] Shlomo described these tales as a powerful way of healing broken hearts and generating love and understanding. Later he adapted and retold some of these stories. Shlomo once explained how impressed he was by the way the Bobover Rebbe told a story: "It was not only a nice story, it had a medicinal effect for both your head and heart." The Bobover identified emotionally with his stories and would arouse his audience to tears.[84]

The Bobover Rebbe, R. Shlomo Halberstam (1905–2000), was the son of R. Ben Zion Halberstam (1874–1941) of Bobov (Bobowa), Galicia in

---

81. Offenbacher, "Jewish Minstrel," 54.

82. My father, Prof. Elmer Offenbacher, recalls first meeting Shlomo Carlebach on the steps of the Bobover *shtiebel* in Manhattan sometime around 1947.

83. David Landau, *Piety and Power: The World of Jewish Fundamentalism* (New York: 1993).

84. Reb Shlomo often began a story about how he loved to tell about the Sanzer Rebbe by noting that he had heard it many times from the Bobov Rebbe, and each time the Rebbe would cry anew. Zivan, *Soul Stories*, vol. 2, 7. Cf. Midlo, *Lamed Vav*, 19, n. 1.

Southern Poland. He was one of the very few Hasidic rebbes to survive the Holocaust:

> In July 1941, Nazis overran Lvov in the Soviet Union, to which the Halberstam clan had fled from Galicia two years earlier. The SS clubbed to death his father, the Rebbe, his mother, Chaya, and most of his siblings. Somehow Shlomo escaped with his son, Naftali – but his wife and all his other children died in the camps . . . He shaved off his beard, and masqueraded as a Polish officer and even as a nun, to save Jews from the Nazis. He allegedly smuggled hundreds to freedom in false-bottomed coal trucks.[85]

In 1946, the Bobover Rebbe arrived in New York via Italy and England, and settled in Manhattan. Barely 300 Bobover Hasidim had survived. At the time, there were so few Orthodox Jews in his Manhattan neighborhood that his son was sent out into the streets to look for a *minyan*.[86] Shlomo Carlebach visited the Bobover Rebbe on the first Sukkot that the Rebbe celebrated in America (October 1946). Shlomo was very impressed by the Bobover storytelling at the ceremonious rejoicing of Simchat Beit Hashoeva despite the fact there were "only twenty people present."[87]

The Rebbe later moved to Bedford-Stuyvesant in Brooklyn, developed kindergartens, schools, synagogues, and Talmud academies as his father had done in Eastern Europe. He aided displaced persons to come to America, arranging for them job training in watch repair and the diamond industry. He encouraged his followers to enter the business world. When the crime rate rose in the beginning of the 1960s, he relocated to Borough Park.[88] An estimated 12,000 Bobover Jews live today in Borough Park,[89] and at the time of the death of the Bobover Rebbe in 2000, there were an estimated 120,000 members internationally.[90]

Eli Chaim and Shlomo both maintained a very close relationship with the Bobover.[91] Shortly before his wedding in 1972, Shlomo traveled

---

85. Lawrence Joffe, "Obituary: Rabbi Shlomo Halberstam: After escaping from the Nazis he revived an entire Jewish sect," *The Guardian*, London, Sept. 2, 2000.

86. "Rebbe Who Rebuilt Bobover Group from Ashes of Shoah Dies at Age 92," *Jewish Telegraphic Agency*, Aug. 3, 2000.

87. Zivan, *Heart of the Heavens*, 289–290 [Hebrew].

88. Jerome R. Mintz, *Hasidic People: A Place in the New World* (London: 1992), 11.

89. Jacques Gutwirth, *La Renaissance du Hassidisme: De 1945 à Nos Jours, Paris*, 2004 (translated into English by Sophie Leighton, *The Rebirth of Hasidism: 1945 to the Present Day* [London: 2005]).

90. Joffe, "Obituary."

91. Personal communication of Hadassa Carlebach (Nov. 2, 2012): "The Bobover Rebbe considered and treated Eli Chaim as a relative since up my genealogical tree

with several followers to the Rebbe to receive his blessings (see below, Chapter 11).

❋

Modzitz was a crucial Hasidic musical influence on the young Shlomo in the 1940s.[92] A famous Modzitz saying is that "the Heavenly palace of music *is* identical to the palace of *teshuva* (penitence)."[93] The second Modzitzer Rebbe, Shaul Yedidya Elazar Taub (1886–1947), fled Poland, traveled via Vilna, Lithuania, and Russia to Japan, and then arrived in San Francisco. In 1940, he settled in Williamsburg and began to rebuild. The Rebbe was a prolific musical composer, creating more than 700 compositions.[94] Particularly noteworthy, are his wordless melodies and songs of devotion and *devekus*.

Ben Zion Shenker, the "musical secretary" of Modzitz, was a close friend of Shlomo in Williamsburg.[95] Brooklyn-born Shenker was just a few months younger than Shlomo, and their families lived near each other in Williamsburg in the early 1940s. The Carlebach twins would walk with Ben Zion to the Rebbe's *tisch* in the neighborhood's Poylishe Shtibel.[96] They studied together in Torah Vodaas and during the summer vacations went with their classmates to Camp Mesivta in Ferndale, New York.[97]

An intriguing anecdote is told about Shlomo from one summer in the early 1940s. Shlomo's bunk was nicknamed "the bunk of the future

---

I share a grandmother with him. At every event, he used to sit Eli Chaim at the table near him."

92. While introducing the tune for "*Yah Ribon Olam*," in the recording *Shabbos in Shamayim*, Reb Shlomo credits the Modzitz Rebbe with giving the inspiration to compose tunes. He describes how as a teenager, he and his brother Eli Chaim, went to the Friday night *tisch* of the Modzitzer. On Modzitz tunes, see Sarah Friedland Ben-Arza, "The Tune in Modzitz Hasidut" [Hebrew], Piyut.org.il, http://www.piyut.org.il/cgi-bin/print_mode.pl?what=article&Id=761.

93. Reb Shaul Taub, *Imrei Shaul*, 309, quoting his father Reb Yisrael Taub.

94. Velvel Pasternak, "Hasidic Music and Modzitz: A Short Overview," *Journal of Synagogue Music*, vol. XVIII, no. 2, Dec. 1988, 9–15.

95. Ben Zion Shenker was born on May 12, 1925. See Sam Weiss, "Ben Zion Shenker," in *Nine Luminaries of Jewish Liturgical Song*, 2003, KlezmerShack.com, http://www.klezmershack.com/articles/weiss_s/luminaries/#shenker.

96. Modzitz.co.il, http://www.modzitz.co.il.

97. Camp Mesivta, the first yeshivish summer camp in America, had been founded by Rabbi Shraga Feivel Mendlowitz of Torah Vodaas in 1937. My thanks to Aaron Reichel for this information.

Roshei Yeshiva,"[98] and the counselor was O. Asher Reichel.[99] In later years, Shlomo, with a "twinkle in his eye," would tell various members of the Reichel family that had his counselor "given him a *klep* or a *frask*" (Yiddish for a smack), he "would have straightened out." The implication is that had he been disciplined more when young, he would have followed a more conventional rabbinic path and not have become the iconoclastic, independent, and creative world-influencing person that he turned out to be![100]

Important Torah personalities vacationed near the camp. One of them was the Modzitzer Rebbe. Shlomo and his friends, Ben Zion Shenker and Moshe Wolfson, spent long summer hours with him.[101] Shlomo recalled his impressions:

> We sat down on a rock beneath one of the trees and the Rebbe said, "Shloymele, I'd like to teach you the world of melody." Each *niggun* began very softly, then grew louder until it throbbed with a steady beat like all his Modzitz melodies.[102]

Ben Zion Shenker set an important precedent in 1950 as he began the first recordings of Hasidic non-cantorial music. In 1956, he formed the Neginah record label in order to produce the first commercial recordings of authentic Hasidic *niggunim*.[103] Shenker wrote over 400 original *niggunim*, many of which have been adopted throughout the Jewish world.[104] Tunes that Reb Shaul sang for prayers, such as the *Hallel*,

---

98. The bunk included several budding young Torah scholars such as Shraga Moshe Kalmanowitz who became the Rosh Yeshiva of the Mir Yeshiva.

99. Rabbi O. Asher Reichel (1921–2012) had been valedictorian at the Torah Vodaas elementary school and then again at Yeshiva College (class of 1942). He received ordination at the YU rabbinical school (RIETS) in 1944.

100. Aaron Reichel, personal communication, Oct. 25–26, 2012. Aaron reports that this comment was repeated several times by Shlomo to Rabbi Reichel and to his children.

101. Brand, *Reb Shlomele*, 24–25.

102. Brand, *Reb Shlomele*, 63–64.

103. Weiss, "Ben Zion Shenker." Cf. Sam Weiss, "Carlebach, Neo-Hasidic Music, and Current Liturgical Practice," *Journal of Synagogue Music*, vol. 34, Fall 2009. For an updated version of this article see KlezmerShack.com, http://www.klezmershack.com/articles/weiss_s/carlebach/weiss_s.carlebach.html#fn3. Cf. Mark Kligman, "Contemporary Jewish Music in America," in David Singer and Lawrence Grossman (eds.), *American Jewish Year Book*, New York: 2001, vol. 101, 88–140.

104. These include tunes such as *Eishet Hayil, Mizmor L'David, Hamavdil* and *LaYehudim*. See Weiss, "Shenker" and compare Modzitz.org, http://modzitz.org/music.htm.

influenced Shlomo and sometimes are recognizable in the "consistent, steady beat reminiscent of the march-like Modzitz melodies."[105]

⁜

The formative Hasidic influence on Reb Shlomo was Chabad. The RaYaTZ, R. Yosef Yitzchak Schneersohn, the sixth Rebbe of Chabad was one of the very few Hasidic rebbes to escape the Holocaust.[106] He was evacuated from Warsaw after the Nazi invasion in September 1939,[107] and arrived in New York on the S.S. *Drottningholm* on March 19, 1940.[108] Thousands came to greet his arrival, amongst them R. Naphtali Carlebach and his twin sons.[109]

The Rebbe settled in Crown Heights, Brooklyn, and set up headquarters at 770 Eastern Parkway. He began building day schools and yeshivas, and sending out emissaries to spread religiosity.

Shlomo was attracted to Chabad and studied *Tanya* even when he was learning at Lakewood.[110] After his twin brother Eli Chaim left Lakewood to study at the Chabad Yeshiva of the RaYaTZ, Shlomo went to consult the Rebbe. Shlomo recalled:

> I told him that I loved learning, but he told me that I should stop thinking just about what I personally loved to do, and focus more

---

105. Kligman, "Contemporary Jewish Music," 102. See HeichalHanegina.blogspot.com, http://heichalhanegina.blogspot.com/2006_04_01_archive.html that the tunes of Reb Shlomo for *Lecha Ezbach* (Psalms 116:17–19) and *Ani Maamin* were influenced by the Modzitz *Hamol al Maasecha*.

106. In Russia, the Rebbe had waged a desperate battle against the Bolshevik anti-religious decrees. He was interned in the Spalerno prison in Leningrad in 1927 and accused of counter-revolutionary activities. Then he was banished to Kostroma in the Urals, and later allowed to leave for Riga in Latvia. In 1934 he came to Warsaw, Poland.

107. For the story of how U.S. officials and Nazi soldiers enabled the Rebbe's evacuation, see Bryan Mark Rigg, *Rescued from the Reich: How One of Hitler's Soldiers Saved the Lubavitcher Rebbe* (Yale University: 2004).

108. For a picture of the RaYaTZ upon his arrival in New York in 1940, see Pekko. Naropa.Edu, http://pekko.naropa.edu/archon/?p=collections/findingaid&id=143&q=&rootcontentid=4400#id4400.

109. This was told by Reb Shlomo in Oct. 1994 to the reporter for the Chabad weekly *Kefar Chabad*. It was printed in an obituary article by the *haredi* newspaper *Yom HaShishi*, Oct. 28, 1994 (reproduced in Brandwein, *Reb Shlomele*, 212–213).

110. Brandwein, *Reb Shlomele*, 45, and in a slightly different version in Brand, *Reb Shlomele*, 35–36 as told by Rabbi Abraham Hayyim Flusberg to cantor Yair Subar. Flusberg states that he was a roommate of Shlomo in Lakewood.

on what the world needed. So I started doing that: talking to people about Judaism.[111]

From the sixth Rebbe, Shlomo absorbed a post-Holocaust urgency. Zalman tells how Shlomo explained his decision to leave Lakewood in order to study at the Lubavitcher Yeshiva:

> The Jewish world has just been destroyed in the Holocaust . . . The shepherds of our people are gone and there is no one to guide us . . . Lakewood grooms scholars, but Lubavitch grooms outreach workers . . . Hopefully, here at Lubavitch, I'll learn how to expand the souls of thousands . . . I left Lakewood because of the Six Million.[112]

On March 16, 1949, on Shushan Purim, Eli Chaim Carlebach married Hadassa, the daughter of Rabbi Schneur Zalman Schneerson,[113] a first cousin of Reb Levi Yitzchak, the father of the seventh Chabad Rebbe, R. Menachem Mendel Schneerson. The couple had five daughters.[114]

Rosh Hashana, September 24–25, 1949, was a turning point in Shlomo's life. He joined the RaYaTZ for the prayers and was awed how the Rebbe "was *davening* for the whole world," saving lives on the Day of Judgment: "You could see that this was a Jew who cared about the whole world."[115] Shlomo was overwhelmed by the emotional outpouring – the Rebbe's fervent crying during the reading about the sacrifice of Isaac was as if he were there sacrificing his own son:

---

111. Lerner, "Practical Wisdom," 53.

112. Mandelbaum, *Holy Brother*, 52.

113. Hadassa was born on Feb. 23, 1928 in Nevel, in the Ukraine. Her parents, Rabbi Zalman and Saranee Schneerson, fled Soviet rule and went to Palestine in 1935. From there, they moved to France where they spent the war years and in 1947 immigrated to America. For the heroic story of Rabbi Schneerson's establishment of children's homes and the only functioning wartime yeshiva in Marseilles, see the photos in the United States Holocaust Memorial Museum collection from Hadassa Carlebach, www.USHMM.org. For a studio portrait of Hadassa at a young age, see http://digitalassets.ushmm.org/photoarchives/detail.aspx?id=1170868. For a 3-minute clip of Hadassa speaking about her cousin, Chaya Mushka (Moussia) Schneerson (1901–1988), the wife of the Lubavitcher Rebbe, see http://www.youtube.com/watch?feature=endscreen&v=rV1fFoeM_Vc&NR=1.

114. Shterna Citron, now in Los Angeles, Calif.; Sheina Berkowitz, originally in Huntington Beach, Calif., now in Ramat Beit Shemesh, Israel; and three daughters in Brooklyn, New York: Billie (Yocheved Baila) Dayan, Fradie Laufer, and Esty (Esther Leba Leah) Kugel.

115. Herzberg, *Sparks of David*, 99–101.

I had the privilege to *mamash* see the way the Rebbe was crying on the second day of Rosh Hashana when they were reading *Akeidas Yitzchak, gevalt.* Just got a little taste, a little taste of how Avraham Avinu must have been crying. God should bless you and me, we should have a taste how beautiful the world is, how precious the world is to God.[116]

Shlomo was attracted to this deep empathy coming as it was right after the Holocaust. It was this fervent prayer style and emotional-spiritual ecstasy that made a deep impression on both Reb Shlomo and his lifelong friend, Reb Zalman Schachter-Shalomi,[117] inspiring them to become the Rebbe's first emissaries to the college campuses.

---

116. My thanks to Shlomo Katz for sending me this recording of Shlomo speaking in Jerusalem in Nov. 1989.

117. See "A Dialogue on the Baal Shem Tov with Rabbi Zalman Schachter-Shalomi and Maggid Yitzhak Buxbaum, moderated by Matisyahu Brown," *Spectrum: A Journal of Renewal Spirituality*, vol. 3, no. 1, Winter–Spring, 2007, 64–86.

CHAPTER 2

Launching an Outreach Career

1. HASIDUT IN AMERICA

To appreciate the task of Reb Shlomo as a Hasidic emissary and his role in the neo-Hasidic renewal, it should be noted that in the first half of the twentieth century, Hasidut was not a successful popular movement in America. True, thousands of Hasidim had immigrated to the United States after 1917. They had come as a result of anti-Jewish pogroms in the Ukraine, the ravages of World War I, and the repression of Judaism in the USSR. These immigrants founded hundreds or maybe thousands of congregations. However, the authoritative rabbinic leadership was mostly of Lithuanian origin. There were some Hasidic rabbis, but often these were merely *einiklekh*, i.e., basing their claim to rebbe status mostly upon their ancestry.[1] Sociologist Solomon Poll describes the Hasidic rebbes who were active at the time as *shtickel rebbes*, i.e., "somewhat of a Rebbe."[2] Hasidism had not earned its new reputation in America. As a movement, Hasidism was still suffering from the harsh criticism and accusations that they reflected what was wrong, outdated and backward in Eastern European Judaism.[3]

About forty-seven Hasidic rabbis immigrated to North America during the years 1893–1934. Of these, thirty-six established themselves in

---

1. See Ira Robinson, *Translating a Tradition: Studies in American Jewish History* (Brighton MA: 2008), Sect. II, Orthodox Judaism in North America, "The First Hasidic Rabbis in North America," 190–205; "Anshe Sfard: The Creation of the First Hasidic Congregations in North America," 206–222.

2. Solomon Poll, *The Hasidic Community of Williamsburg: A Study in the Sociology of Religion* (New Brunswick, New Jersey: 2006 [new edition]), 286, 115–125.

3. Robinson, *Translating a Tradition*, 208.

New York.[4] However, the vast majority of Hasidim who immigrated to the United States were not successful "in transmitting their style of religious life to the next generation."[5]

After the Holocaust, many more Hasidic leaders arrived as refugees in America. These included Rebbes from Belz, Bobov, Chernobyl, Lisk, Munkatch, Novominsk, Satmar, Skver, Stolin, Talin, Trisk, and Zanz.[6] By 1945, New York had become "full of Rebbes" especially in Brooklyn.[7]

The Hasidic communities they reconstructed were determinedly insular, and did not reach out to attract new adherents. The exception was the seventh Chabad Rebbe, R. Menachem Mendel, who initiated a revolutionary outreach approach. He was unique amongst the Hasidic leaders in that he had acquired secular knowledge, having studied philosophy, math, and physics at the University of Berlin, and civil engineering in Paris. It was easier for him to understand American culture and direct his emissaries accordingly, and to counter assimilation at a time when religious life in America was dramatically declining. The new generation of American "baby boomers," born after World War II,[8] was deserting religious life in both the Christian and Jewish communities.

Jewish baby boomers were disproportionately represented in the counterculture of the Hippie Movement as well as the Civil Rights Movement, anti-Vietnam War protests, and student rebellions.[9] But there was an added burden for the Jewish youth of the 1960s. They were the post-Holocaust generation. Many had relatives who perished in the Holocaust.[10] The tragedy was still alive. There was a lingering mixture of melancholy and anger. For some, God had deserted His people and so they left God.

By 1971, less than half of the Jewish population was affiliated with a synagogue.[11] Orthodox Judaism was being "written off as a vestige of the

---

4. Ibid., 215, n. 49. Robinson cites the list that appears in Tzvi Rabinowicz's *Encyclopedia of Hasidism*, to indicate that most of Hasidic rabbis were in New York – 12 in Manhattan, 10 in Brooklyn, and 4 in the Bronx. Others were in Chicago (5), Philadelphia (4), Boston (3), Detroit (2), St. Louis (2), and one each in Montreal, Toronto, Cleveland, Pittsburgh, and Milwaukee.

5. Robinson, *Translating a Tradition*, 207.

6. Chaim I. Waxman, "From Institutional Decay to Primary Day: American Orthodox Jewry Since World War II," *American Jewish History*, vol. 91, no. 3–4, Sept.–Dec. 2003, 405–422.

7. Robinson, *Translating a Tradition*, 215.

8. After World War II, the birth rate in America more than doubled, from 1.5 million a year in 1940 to 4 million a year in the 1950s.

9. See Chaim I. Waxman, *Jewish Baby Boomers* (Albany, New York: 2001), Chapter 1.

10. Waxman, *Jewish Baby Boomers*, 4–5.

11. Jack Wertheimer, "The Turbulent Sixties," in Jonathan Sarna, *The American*

immigrant past," with a mere 11 percent of American Jews identifying themselves as Orthodox.[12] Unlike the days of Eastern Europe, marrying a non-Jew was not seen as a crime worth sitting in mourning, but rather as a natural entrée into successful American life, and often justified as a rejection of antiquated parental values.

Into this deteriorating state of religious Judaism, Reb Shlomo appeared with a revivalist Hasidic message of song, joy, love, and dance. It was to these youth that Shlomo appealed with his soulful singing and stories that sentimentally and romantically reconstructed the pre-war Hasidic life. Shlomo's message was to vividly portray the brokeness with its antidote of hope, the six million crying along with the future Redemptive rejoicing. His singing-stories dramatized the heroism in Eastern European Hasidic communities and created an empathy with this lost heritage.[13]

The innovation of Reb Shlomo and Reb Zalman was to present a piece of the Hasidic heritage that would appeal to twentieth century American Jewish sensitivities. Similar to Martin Buber and Elie Wiesel, they recast the Hasidic stories by adding inspirational meanings palatable to the modern ear. Like Rabbi Abraham Heschel, they presented teachings drawn from Hasidut that spoke to existentialist needs and spiritual thirsting of a generation of Jewish baby boomers. It is not coincidental that the two "spiritual advisors" listed for the House of Love and Prayer were Heschel and Wiesel (see below).

The major novelty of his guitar playing was that Reb Shlomo adapted American folk singing methods to Hasidic music. Already in 1961, the music critic of *The New York Times* astutely observed that "Carlebach is trying to revive in an American context the tradition of the Hasidim in which music was used as a medium to gain spiritual release . . . to keep the vanishing tradition of Hasidic song alive."[14]

By way of comparison, if in 1945, after World War II, there were only some 20,000 Hasidim in the world, today there are between 350,000 and 400,000.[15] At least a part of this phenomenal exponential growth

---

Jewish Experience, 2nd edition (New York and London: 1986), 330–347.

12. Ibid., 346.

13. Cf. Yaakov Ariel, "Crisis and Renewal: From Crushed Hasidism to Neo-Hasidic Revival and Outreach," in Armin Lange, K.F. Diethard Romheld and Mattias Weigold (eds.), *Judaism and Crisis: Crisis as a Catalyst in Jewish Cultural History* (2011), 317–335. See also Yaakov Ariel, "Paradigm Shift: New Religious Movements and Quests for Meaning and Community in Contemporary Israel," *Nova Religio*, May 2010, vol. 13, no. 4, 4–22.

14. Robert Shelton, "Rabbi Carlebach Sings Spirituals," *New York Times*, Oct. 24, 1961.

15. Gutwirth, *La Renaissance*, 8.

is due to the *baal teshuva* movement and the outreach efforts such as those of Lubavitch. It is with this background that we can understand the revolutionary import of the first two Chabad outreach emissaries, Reb Shlomo and Reb Zalman.

2.   MISSION DEFINED (DECEMBER 10, 1949)

December 10, 1949 was a day that shaped the future of Shlomo's career. He came to the *farbrengen* of 19 Kislev,[16] the annual commemoration of the freeing from prison in 1798 of the founder of Chabad, Rabbi Shneor Zalman of Lyady. Traditionally, this is marked by a memorable singing of the "Rav's *Niggun*" (*Dem Rebben's Niggun*), a wordless tune attributed to the founder of Chabad. The four parts of the melody correspond to the four steps for elevating the soul to the highest spiritual regions.

The Rebbe was in poor health and only a few Hasidim were invited in at a time. Zalman recalls: "Along comes Beryl Chazkin, who was one of the *gabbaim* of the Rebbe, and he says, 'Shloimeh and Zalman, come in. The Rebbe has asked for you.'" When Zalman and Shlomo entered, the Rebbe told them: "It is worthwhile for you to start visiting the colleges" ("*Kedai az ir zolt onhoybn fohren in di colleges*").[17] At the time, Reb Zalman was serving as a congregational Rabbi in the Boston area, and he decided to begin by visiting the nearby colleges. He recorded "a couple of hours of Chabad *niggunim*," translated some of the Rebbe's teachings into English, and "fixed up" a dozen old pairs of *tefillin* from his synagogues. He then picked up Shlomo who had come to Providence by train, and they drove to Brandeis University.[18]

---

16. A *farbrengen* in Yiddish and German literally means "spending time together." In Chabad, it refers to a joyous gathering for song (in particular, inspirational wordless melodies), drinking a toast (*l'chaim*) and sharing Hasidic wisdom and inspirational stories. When the Rebbe spoke, this was often a time for an important public exhortation.

17. This is the quote told to me by Reb Zalman, July 13, 2011. See Rabbi Zalman M. Schachter-Shalomi and Joel Segel, *Davening: A Guide to Meaningful Jewish Prayer* (Woodstock, Vermont: 2012), 47–48. See also Shalomi, "Conversations," 14. A less dramatic version of this event can be found in an interview conducted by M. Herbert Danzger with Reb Zalman in the late 1970s. Zalman recalled the circumstances of the idea to visit college campuses: "The Rebbe was talking about people in universities. I said to Shlomo who was standing next to me, 'Next week is Hanukkah. Let's take the car and go to Boston . . . Let's see what we can do." See Herbert M. Danzger, *Returning to Tradition: The Contemporary Revival of Orthodox Judaism* (New Haven, Connecticut: 1989), 60–61.

18. This was the first year of Brandeis. Founded as the first secular academic Jewish institution of higher learning, the first class had merely 107 students.

The two Chabadniks arrived at a swinging dance at "The Castle," a Brandeis café. Zalman set up a tape recorder and led the singing. Shlomo told Hasidic stories. Later, at 3:00 AM, Zalman offered free *tefillin* to anyone who could put them on three times. He gave out all the thirteen pairs that he had brought. This predated the *tefillin* campaigns of Chabad.[19]

Next they visited Boston University where they discovered a Hillel director named Shabbatai doing "outreach work," and "even getting paid for it." It was then that Zalman realized that he should become a Hillel director. They completed visiting the Boston area colleges by going to Brown University where they found a sympathetic Hillel director.[20]

The fifth and sixth Chabad Rebbes had sent out *shluchim*, emissaries for specific tasks in keeping contact and helping their Hasidim living in the periphery. The sixth Rebbe had sent *shluchim* to save his Hasidim in the early days of the Holocaust. He directed his senior yeshiva students to provide voluntary religious education to Jewish students in New York's public school system. A few were sent outside of New York as for example R. David Moshe Lieberman who went in 1949 to serve as a rabbi and educator in Chicago.[21] But Zalman and Shlomo were the first outreach messengers to "lost souls" outside of the committed Hasidic camp, i.e., they were the first "*kiruv* workers." Underlying this activity was a Messianic urgency and a missionary zeal rarely seen before in Orthodox circles.[22] They set up a pioneering effort of outreach that Chabad would first begin to initiate on college campuses only twenty years later.[23]

---

19. My reconstruction is based on Green and Schachter, "A Dialogue," 14–17, as well as a Skype interview with Reb Zalman, Aug. 7, 2011, and Reb Zalman's recollections recorded on March 19, 1994 at Hillel of Berkeley. Cf. Samuel C. Heilman and Menachem M. Friedman. *The Rebbe: The Life and Afterlife of Menachem Mendel Schneerson* (Princeton: 2010), 168–169.

Beginning in 1967, Lubavitch became known for the *tefillin* campaigns in public areas from airports to street corners. See Heilman and Friedman, *The Rebbe*, 184.

20. Green and Schachter, "A Dialogue," 17–18. Danzger, *Returning to Tradition*, 61.

21. Aryeh Solomon, *The Educational Teachings of Rabbi Menachem M. Schneerson* (Northvale, New Jersey: 2000, 7).

22. My thanks to Aaron Reichel for pointing out that Rabbi Herbert S. Goldstein (1890–1970) was a unique exception of an American rabbi in the early 20th century who actively engaged in outreach work. He utilized methods "similar to those used by successful evangelists in an attempt to win back Jewish souls." His revivalist rallies earned him the title as "The Jewish Billy Sunday," i.e., the Billy Graham of his day. See Aaron I. Reichel, *The Maverick Rabbi: Rabbi Herbert S. Goldstein and the Institutional Synagogue – "A New Organizational Form,"* 2nd ed. (Norfolk, Virginia: 1986), 98–101.

23. The first Chabad house on a college campus was opened by Rabbi Boruch Shlomo Cunin in March 1969 at UCLA (University of California Los Angeles). Cunin

3. CO-EMISSARY REB ZALMAN

The outreach career of Reb Shlomo was intertwined with that of his co-emissary, Reb Zalman. Together they were instrumental in inspiring an avant-garde cultural phenomenon of the 1960s–70s and the ensuing Jewish Renewal Movement.[24]

Zalman Schachter was born on August 17, 1924 in Zholkiew, Poland.[25] In 1925, the Schachters moved to Vienna, Austria. His father, "a Belzer Hasid with liberal tendencies," had him educated in both a traditional yeshiva and a socialist Zionist high school.[26] When Zalman was about 12 years old he came by trolley to Baden to ask R. Naphtali Carlebach about the *kashrut* of a chicken liver.[27] That was when he first met the twin Carlebach brothers and they played ping-pong together.[28]

When the Nazis took over Austria, the Schachter family fled to Antwerp, Belgium. There, at age 15, Zalman discovered Chabad Hasidut, first in an Agudah Youth Group, and then in a diamond cutting shop where Chabad Hasidim would "learn Talmud while they sang Hasidic melodies." After the bombing of Antwerp, the Schachter family traveled with other refugees by coal train to an internment camp in Vichy France. After he was freed, Zalman gained admittance to the Chabad yeshiva in Marseilles. It was there, that he met the future seventh Rebbe of Chabad.[29] Upon receiving a visa, the Schachter family traveled to the United States via Algeria, Morocco, and the West Indies. After arriving in New York City in 1941, the 17-year old Zalman enrolled in the Chabad Tomchei Temimim yeshiva.

---

in 1972 also established a Chabad House at the University of California in Berkeley. Today there are Chabad houses around the world on about 130 college campuses.

24. For a survey of the origins, influences, ideology, and impact of the Jewish Renewal Movement see Shaul Magid, "Jewish Renewal Movement" in *The Encyclopedia of Religion*, 2nd ed. (Farmington Hills, Missouri: 2005), 7, cols. 4868–4874.

25. In the mid-1970s, he added the name Shalomi "to take the edge off Schachter" which in Yiddish means "butcher." Indeed, he came from a family of Hasidic butchers – his grandfather slaughtered meat for the Belzer rebbe. See Rodger Kamenetz, *Stalking Elijah: Adventures with Today's Jewish Mystical Masters* (New York: 1997), 18.

26. I have drawn much of this reconstructed biography from Reb Zalman's website RZlp.org, http://www.rzlp.org.

27. Zalman gives his age as "10 or 11" (Schachter, *Wrapped in a Holy Flame*, 290). However, elsewhere he states 12 (Green and Schachter, "A Dialogue," 26).

28. Unpublished interview with Reb Zalman recorded by Menachem Daum, June 1, 1995, segment 20:40. See also Schachter-Shalomi, Davening, 46.

29. Zalman Schachter, "How to Become a Modern Hasid," *Jewish Heritage*, 2, 1960, 33–40, Rzlp.org, http://www.rzlp.org/index.cfm?objectid=4C43B014-D614-E19E-2D D972305671977B.

Already then, during the Holocaust years, the sixth Rebbe was issuing fervent messages of how the rejuvenating of Chabad was the key to hastening the arrival of Moshiach. Zalman recalled:

> In 1943, I experienced a surge of imminent messianic expectation when the late Lubavitcher Rebbe, Rabbi Yossef Yitzchak Schneersohn issued his apocalyptic broadsides.[30]

One day in Brooklyn, Zalman met Shlomo and suggested that he join him at Tomchei Temimim, but Shlomo preferred to stay with R. Kotler in Lakewood. Reb Zalman describes R. Kotler as "one of those amazing *geonim*, prodigies of Talmud," and reports Shlomo as having responded: "If I go, there won't be anyone to take over where Reb Aaron left off."[31]

Reb Zalman taught Hasidut in New Haven, Connecticut from 1945–1947.[32] In 1947, he received ordination from the Central Lubavitch Yeshiva, and from two mentors, Rabbis Eli Simpson and Israel Jacobson. In 1948, he began teaching at the Achei T'mimim Yeshiva in Rochester, New York. From 1949–1952, Rabbi Zalman served as congregational rabbi and principal at Agudat Achim in Fall River, Bristol County, Massachusetts, and at Ahavath Achim, a synagogue 12 miles away in New Bedford. In the early 1950s, Zalman was busy with his congregation, raising a family, and studying at Boston University, so he fulfilled the Rebbe's mission mostly in the Boston area. Fall River is located 16 miles southeast of Providence, Rhode Island, and 46 miles south of Boston. This is the reason that Zalman and Shlomo began their outreach careers in campuses in the Boston area. Zalman explains: "Every once in a while, Shlomo would come by train to Providence, and I would pick him up, and the two of us would go and visit various places."[33]

As a committed Chabad Hasid, Zalman maintained a regular correspondence with the Rebbe, reporting on his activities.[34] In 1955, Zalman began studying for his M.A. at Boston University in the Psychology of Religion with a specialization in pastoral counseling. After attaining his M.A. degree, Zalman embarked on an academic career in Winnipeg,

---

30. HavurahShiraHadash.org, http://www.havurahshirhadash.org/rebzalmanart icle3.html.

31. Shalomi, "Virtuous Reality," 290.

32. Green and Schachter, "A Dialogue," 15. Reb Zalman described himself as being involved in founding the first Lubavitch Yeshiva in New Haven.

33. Personal interview with Reb Zalman recorded by phone on July 13, 2011.

34. He was in continuous contact with Rabbi Chaim Mordechai Aizik Hodakov (1902–1993), "the chief of staff" of the Lubavitcher Rebbe, who had the responsibility of speaking in the Rebbe's name and giving answers and guidance to the Rebbe's Hasidim.

Canada, and taught in the Department of Religion, University of Manitoba, eventually becoming an assistant professor (1956–1969). Simultaneously, he directed the B'nai B'rith Hillel at the university (1956–1967). One of the programs Zalman organized was a weeklong retreat for students at Winnipeg. He invited Reb Shlomo to help lead the program.[35]

In 1963, Zalman began doctoral work at Hebrew Union College, and soon was appointed to head the Department of Judaic Studies at the University of Manitoba. In the summer of 1966, Reb Zalman participated in a symposium where thirty-eight prominent rabbis responded to five key questions. Zalman was the *only Hasidic representative* amongst the respondents.[36] He emphasized that all the assertions he made about Torah and *mizvot* were "in consonance with the normative standards of Orthodoxy – only being modified by Hasidism." He declared a full faith commitment to "all the *oughts* that my master, the Lubavitcher Rebbe, my repository of the faith, prescribes for me."[37] However, he opened up a Pandora's Box by describing his revelatory experiences of LSD:

> . . . when I can undergo the deepest cosmic experience via some minuscule quantity of organic alkaloids or LSD, then the whole validity of my ontological assertions is in doubt . . . After seeing what really happens at the point where all is One and G-d immanent surprises G-d transcendent and They merge in cosmic laughter, I can also see Judaism in a new and amazing light.[38]

This praise of "the sacramental potential of lysergic acid" led to Zalman's departure from Chabad.[39]

In 1968, Zalman completed a Ph.D. at Hebrew Union College in Cincinnati on the system of spiritual counseling in Chabad Hasidism,[40] and he then spent the academic year of 1968–1969 at Brandeis University where he studied ancient Semitic languages and taught a course in the

---

35. Carol Rose, "Memories that Continue to Hold Magic," *Kol Chevra*, vol. 7, 2000, 57–59. Rose describes how Shlomo took her to Zalman to stay in his house in Winnipeg for the week of the retreat.

36. Zalman M. Schachter, *The Condition of Jewish Belief: A Symposium Compiled by the Editors of Commentary Magazine* (New York: 1966), 207–216 (originally appeared in *Commentary Magazine*, vol. 42, no. 2, Aug. 1966, no. 2).

37. Ibid., 208–209.

38. Ibid., 213–214.

39. Kamenetz, *Stalking Elijah*, 19. Cf. Micha Odenheimer, "Wise guy, wise man," *Haaretz*, Oct. 2, 2005, http://www.haaretz.com/news/wise-guy-wise-man-1.171162. See also Raphael Ahren, "Reb Schneerson Skips the Acid Test," Nov. 26, 2007, NewVoices.org, http://www.newvoices.org/community?id=0004.

40. Later he was to sum up his discoveries in his book *Spiritual Intimacy: A Study of Counseling in Hasidism* (Northvale, New Jersey: 1991).

psychology of religion. This course was a stimulating factor in the publication of *The Jewish Catalogue*,[41] a countercultural guide to Jewish practice.

In the early 1970s, Zalman taught at the House of Love and Prayer, Esalen, the Lama Foundation, and SAT (Seekers of Truth). He led a month-long seminar entitled "Kabbalah" at the Hillel House of Berkeley climaxing on Sunday, June 16, 1974 with a *farbrengen* together with Reb Shlomo (see below, Chapter 5).

In the fall of 1975, Zalman left Winnipeg and began his career as a Professor of Religion at Temple University in Philadelphia. For Jews alienated from the existing forms of denominational Judaism, Reb Zalman was effectively creating "Jewish Renewal" as a neo-Hasidic alternative emphasizing devotion in prayer ("davenology"), mystical Hasidut, "psycho-spiritual breakthroughs," and a "paradigm shift."[42]

In 1987, Zalman retired from Temple University as Professor Emeritus. In 1995, he accepted the World Wisdom Chair at Naropa University in Boulder, Colorado, officially retiring from that post in 2004. Today, he lives in Boulder with his wife Eve, and is considered the major inspiration of the Jewish Renewal Movement.

By 1996, twenty-six Jewish Renewal communities had sprouted in fifteen states with seven more in Canada, England, Switzerland, and Brazil.[43] The story is still continuing as Reb Zalman inspires his disciples as "the first post-modern Hassidic Rebbe."[44]

In light of all this, it is not surprising that when "Neo-Hasidism" is defined in the recently published *Oxford Dictionary of the Jewish Religion*, it is Reb Zalman and Reb Shlomo who are identified as "the two persons most responsible for the development of a neo-Hasidic approach to Judaism in North America."[45]

4.   RIGHT HAND OF THE SEVENTH REBBE (1950–1955)

On Shabbat, January 28, 1950, the sixth Rebbe, the RaYaTZ, died. Shortly thereafter, even before he was elected to fill his father-in-law's position,

41. Richard Siegel, Michael and Sharon Strassfeld, *The Jewish Catalog: A Do-It-Yourself Kit* (Philadelphia: 1973). See "Soul Man: Interview by Alice Chasan," HavurahShirHadash.org, http://www.havurahshirhadash.org/rebzalmanarticle18.html.

42. Ellen Singer (ed.), *Paradigm Shift: From the Jewish Renewal Teachings of Reb Zalman Schachter-Shalomi* (Northvale, New Jersey: 1993), xx.

43. Kamenetz, *Stalking Elijah*, 21.

44. Aleph.org, https://www.aleph.org/betmidrash/rebzcontributions.pdf.

45. Arthur Green, "Neo-Hasidism," in Adele Berlin and Maxine Grossman (eds.), *The Oxford Dictionary of the Jewish Religion*, 2nd ed. (Oxford: 2011), 532.

R. Menachem Mendel sent Shlomo "to travel secretly" to the American yeshivas and teach Hasidut.[46] The seventh Rebbe was keen on paving Hasidic inroads into the classical yeshiva world, and Shlomo, who had spent six years in Lakewood, was suited for the task. The Rebbe gave Shlomo $200 to travel to Chicago. Shlomo arrived in the Skokie Yeshiva,[47] and presented himself as a businessman interested in studying. Late at night, he organized Hasidut learning. Shlomo repeated this in yeshivas in Cleveland[48] and Detroit.[49] Later, he told an interviewer that in this way he brought "hundreds of kids to Lubavitch" during the early 1950s.[50]

Reb Zalman explained why Shlomo was chosen by the Rebbe for this task of infiltrating the yeshivas and teaching Hasidut:

> After all, how can you begin these things? By first talking *divrei Torah*, explaining a difficult Rambam or interpreting a *Tosefot*, and only then adding a bit of *hasidut*. Shlomo, who had been study-ing with R. Aharon Kotler, had a much better way of doing this than I.[51]

R. Menachem Mendel gave his inaugural speech as the seventh Chabad Rebbe on January 17, 1951 (the first *yahrzeit* of the sixth Rebbe). He pro-claimed: "We are now very near the approaching footsteps of Messiah, indeed, we are at the conclusion of this period, and our spiritual task is to complete the process of drawing down the Shekhinah."[52]

Both the sixth and seventh Rebbes viewed the Holocaust as the last stage of the pangs of Redemption, the apocalyptic fulfillment of the

---

46. This is the report given in the *haredi* weekly newspaper *Yom HaShishi*, Oct. 28, 1994, based on a recorded interview with Reb Shlomo. The date is given as "the day after the sixth Rebbe died." This article is reproduced on pp. 212–213 in the Hebrew version of M. Brandwein's book on Reb Shlomele.

47. The "Skokie Yeshiva," i.e., the Hebrew Theological College, was founded in 1922 to train Orthodox rabbis to meet the needs of the American Jewish community by receiving a BA degree before ordination.

48. I assume that this is the Telshe Yeshiva which had opened in 1941.

49. I surmise that his visit to Detroit may have been connected to Rabbi A. A. Freedman and Rabbi Sholom Goldstein who had come from New York to Detroit in 1944 and 1946 respectively. They came at the urging of Rabbi Shraga Feivel Mendelowitz from Mesivta Torah VoDaas to lead Yeshiva Beth Yehuda. Later, in 1960, Reb Shlomo returned to Detroit to perform in concert for the students at Yeshiva Beth Yehuda (see below).

50. Danzger, *Returning to Tradition*, 59. When Danzger interviewed Shlomo some-time in the late 1970s, Shlomo explained that during the three years of 1951–1954, he was sent by the Rebbe to the *yeshivot* in New York, Chicago, Detroit, and Cleveland to talk to the students and teach them "Lubavitch Torah."

51. Personal interview with Reb Zalman, July 13, 2011.

52. Heilman and Friedman, *The Rebbe*, 4.

trials and tribulations (*Gog* and *Magog*) heralding the appearance of the Messiah. RaYaTZ asserted that this generation was the last in exile and would be the first of redemption, a message that his successor intensified.[53]

Shlomo described his relationship with the Rebbe as being very close.[54] He was honored with the role of *"hozer,"* to repeat the Rebbe's talks.[55] Shlomo later told an interviewer:

> From 1951 to 1955 I was, *mamash* [really], the Rebbe's right-hand man. Today, Lubavitcher sends out messengers all over the world, but then it wasn't yet organized . . . Zalman and I were the first messengers of the Lubavitcher Rebbe. Zalman and I were his representatives, teaching his message to the world.[56]

Shlomo would invite religious youth to study Hasidut with him in local synagogues such as Ezrath Israel in the Bedford Stuyvesant neighborhood.[57] Dov Gilor recalls how Shlomo organized the gatherings:

> In the early 1950s, Shlomo used to ask people in Boro Park to allow him to come to their basements and ask them to invite their young friends. He would come on Motzei Shabbat or Sunday evenings and tell inspirational stories and Hasidic teachings. For us as teenagers it was a great opportunity to socialize, and we learned to appreciate Hasidic tales.[58]

Sometime around 1951, the Rebbe sent Shlomo to Boston where he was hosted by the Krinsky family.[59] Their son, Pinchas Shmuel Krinsky, was 23 years old at the time. He had returned to Boston after studying at the central Chabad-Lubavitch yeshiva in Crown Heights, Brooklyn.

---

53. Ibid., 12.

54. For a rare photo of Shlomo in close consultation with the Rebbe, dated to 24 Tevet 5712 (= Jan. 22, 1952), see in the Lubavitch Archives facebook collection – http://www.facebook.com/photo.php?fbid=585112684848901&set=a.402691849757 653.112979.402581576435347&type=1&theater.

55. Although, Chabad mostly "disowned" Shlomo after he left the movement, this position of *"hozer"* for Shlomo seems accurate as it is mentioned in the Chabad Internet encyclopedia, Chabad.co.il, http://Chabad.co.il/Chabadpedia.

56. Lerner, "Practical Wisdom," 53.

57. My thanks to Rikki (Gordon) Lewin for this information. Her father, Rabbi Moshe (Morris) Gordon, was Rabbi of Shaare Tefilah in Bedford-Stuyvesant from the mid-1930s until the early 1950s. On the Ezrath Israel Synagogue, see Ellen Levitt, *The Lost Synagogues of Brooklyn*, 2009, 120.

58. Personal interview with Dov Gilor, June 23, 2012.

59. A son of the Krinsky family, Chaim Yehuda (Yudel), was later to become one of the most influential rabbis in Chabad and in American Judaism overall.

Don Wallace, who was 16 years old at the time, describes how Pinchas would visit his Bnei Akiva group on Shabbat and "try to bring us closer to Yiddishkeit and Lubavitch." That Shabbat when Shlomo visited the Krinskys, Pinchas arranged for the Bnei Akiva group to visit Friday night to sing with Shlomo and experience Hasidut.[60]

Shlomo felt that the Lubavitcher Rebbe "*mamash* gave me a new soul." His mission was to save lost Jews: "Every Yid I saw, I wanted to grab and say, *Gevalt!* Don't you know there is a Rebbe in the world?" He decided that whenever he would travel on the subway, he would look for a Jew to whom he could teach some Torah. One day, Erev Shavuot, May 29, 1952,[61] at 4:00 AM, after having had *yechidus*, a private audience with the Rebbe, Shlomo was on the subway. He found a boy of about 20 years old who was beaming with joy, and discovered that the fellow was planning to marry a non-Jew in a church that Shabbat. Shlomo convinced him to reverse his direction and brought him to the Rebbe at 4:30 AM. The Rebbe spoke to him until 7:30 AM:

> You know what the Rebbe was doing? Washing out his *neshama*. This wasn't just a little dust. The Rebbe had to do plastic surgery on his *neshama*. Cut very deep. The Rebbe opens the door and this boy's eyes are red with tears. The Rebbe says, take him to the *mikveh* and then to put on *tefillin* with him. I don't have to tell you the rest of the story. He was Shavuos in Lubavitch.[62]

During his years as a Chabad emissary in the early 1950s, Shlomo spent some time learning in Yeshivas Rabbi Chaim Berlin, a Lithuanian-style *haredi* yeshiva in Brooklyn where his first cousin, also named Shlomo Carlebach, was one of the Rosh Yeshiva's closest disciples.[63] This yeshiva

---

60. Personal correspondences from Don Wallace, June 28 – July 1, 2012.

61. My calculation of the date is based on Shlomo's mention of the second day of Shavuot as Shabbat which could only be in 1952 and would mean that his Wednesday visit to the Rebbe was May 28, 1952.

62. This is excerpted from a 15-minute eulogy that Reb Shlomo gave in July 1994 at Lincoln Square Synagogue in Manhattan for the *shloshim* of the Rebbe. The talk was posted on YouTube http://www.youtube.com/watch?v=E9_d1eVkw SE&feature=youtube. It was transcribed by Dovid Staloff and printed in *Chabad Lights*, Winter 1994/5, and re-edited for *Kol Chevra*, vol. 8, 2001, 137–138. See also HeichalHanegina.blogspot.com, http://heichalhanegina.blogspot.com/2007/06/lubavitcher-rebbe-ramash-ztvkl-personal.html. It was copied in Brandwein, *Reb Shlomele*, 219–225 and is quoted in Eugene and Annette Labovitz, *A Sacred Trust, Stories of Jewish Heritage and History*, Los Angeles, 1994.

63. Shlomo's cousin, Shlomo Carlebach (Salomon Peter Carlebach), was also named after their common grandfather. From 1966–1978, he served as the *mashgi-ach ruchani* of Yeshivas Chaim Berlin. He wrote a biography of his father entitled,

had a more flexible program than Lakewood, and students could learn part-time and take college courses. A rare first-hand testimony is offered by a fellow student, Rabbi Meyer Leifer:

> I was 18 years old when I first met Shlomo at Yeshivas Chaim Berlin. Shlomo had come from six years in Lakewood to study at Chaim Berlin. In both Yeshivas, he was considered an important *lamdan* and *talmid chacham*, one of the most respected students.[64]

Even after Shlomo left the Lakewood Yeshiva, he would return every so often to visit. Rabbi Leifer recalls how Shlomo would visit Lakewood occasionally on Motzei Shabbat, "and five or six of us would gather together with him, learn Torah, and sing Hasidic songs."[65]

In early December 1953, the Lubavitcher Rebbe called Shlomo in and told him emphatically that he won't talk to him again until he arranges to receive rabbinic ordination.[66] Shlomo went to R. Hutner who tested Shlomo on a discussion in Tractate *Hullin* about the topic of *ta'am k'ikar*, "a lingering taste is considered like the essence," and then celebrated with him his *semicha*.[67] In retrospect, this *semicha* was a deciding factor in Shlomo's career. His Orthodox rabbinical ordination became the key factor for his authoritative influence.

Reb Shlomo set out to influence college students. Interestingly enough, on June 20, 1954, he attended a day-long conference in Philadelphia on

---

Ish Yehudi: The Life and Legacy of a Torah Great, Joseph Tzvi Carlebach (New York: Shearith Joseph Publications, 2008).

64. A special thanks to Rabbi Leifer for taking the time to visit me and share his personal experiences, Dec. 17 and 24, 2012. A thanks also to his daughter Nicole for arranging the interview.

65. Rabbi Leifer was a close personal friend of Reb Shlomo and hosted him many times in his synagogue Congregation Emunath Israel (see below, Chapters 11–12). Born on Feb. 12, 1932, he studied in Yeshivas Chaim Berlin from 1948–1951 and in Lakewood from 1951–1954. Then from 1954–1957, he undertook a dual program, studying for his BA at Brooklyn College at night and in Yeshivas Chaim Berlin during the day.

66. The Rebbe's policy was to encourage his disciples to receive ordination in order to enhance their educational roles. See M. Avrum Ehrlich, *The Messiah of Brooklyn: Understanding Lubavitch Hasidism Past and Present* (Jersey City, New Jersey: 2004), 168.

67. Reb Shlomo can be heard in a 7-minute recording made in Nov. 28, 1982 describing how he received *semicha* from R. Hutner. My thanks to Yitzhak Dorfman for sending me this recording in Oct. 2009. It was uploaded by go4joel on May 31, 2011 – see YouTube, http://www.youtube.com/watch?v=lovFyKUCaC4; http://vimeo.com/21078987. Shlomo told a similar story to Alon Teeger in an interview in Sept. 1992, and there on p. 32, he gives the date of the Rebbe's request as Hanukkah (= Dec. 1953) which would mean that the *semicha* was given at the beginning of 1954.

Halacha, Science, and Philosophical Problems organized by AOJS, the Association of Orthodox Jewish Scientists.[68] Shlomo was the ninetieth registrant to sign in, and the only one to sign in as "Rabbi."[69] Previously, the Rebbe had initiated a meeting with the founders of AOJS.[70] It seems that Shlomo's visit was connected to his role as the Rebbe's emissary to college campuses.

Sometime in the early 1950s, a student from Columbia University heard that Shlomo was teaching Hasidut, and invited him to meet with students at Columbia. Shlomo was excited. He felt that "the gates were opening" and he went to consult the Rebbe.[71] Would it be right to teach a co-ed group at Columbia? It seems that although the Rebbe was far from enthusiastic, Shlomo persisted and began teaching Hasidut on the Columbia campus. Soon, he created a framework called "Hasidic Academics."[72]

Shlomo spent the Labor Day weekend, September 3–4, 1954 in Atlantic City, the resort destination in New Jersey frequented by many religious Jews. He spoke to people, inviting them to Hasidut classes in New York. On Motzei Shabbat, he walked into The Breakers, a rambling 450-room kosher hotel just off the boardwalk. One of the youth there asked if he was a rabbi and soon brought his friends. They spoke and sang together through the night. At 4:30 AM Shlomo brought out his *tefillin*, and the boys put them on, one after the other. Years later, Shlomo exclaimed: "It was one of the holiest nights in my life."[73]

---

68. One of the sessions was entitled A Chassidic approach to Torah and Science, and another one, Epistemological Considerations in Science and Religion. The conference took place at the Bnei Israel Synagogue in Logan.

69. My thanks to my father, Prof. Elmer Offenbacher, who showed me the signature of Reb Shlomo at this conference. It is also mentioned in p. 14, n. 36 in his article, Elmer L. Offenbacher, "The Association of Orthodox Jewish Scientists (AOJS): The First Two Decades (1947–1967)," *BADAD*, 15, Sept. 2004, 5–36.

70. Ibid. The Rebbe met on December 25, 1951 with two founders of AOJS, Elmer Offenbacher and Walter Feder. Their two-hour meeting revolved around philosophic and halachic questions arising from scientific developments, and how these should be communicated to college-aged students. They even considered a joint publication for college students.

71. Witt, "Reb Shlomo," 3.

72. Pinchas Hacohen Peli, "*Barkhi Nafshi et Hashem*," *Panim el Panim*, March 28, 1964. Peli told the story of a woman he interviewed from an assimilated New York family, who had become religious through Reb Shlomo's Brooklyn College outreach in the early 1950s.

73. Danzger, *Returning to Tradition*, 60. Danzger's interview with Shlomo took place sometime around the end of the 1970s.

5.   FROM CHABAD TO INDEPENDENT OUTREACH

Zalman and Shlomo were inspired by their Chabad experiences to use Hasidic music as an outreach tool.[74] During the 1950s, Zalman and Shlomo created their innovative outreach while operating within the Orthodox halachic structure. Thus, for example, in May 1955, Shlomo found a way to help a Jewish woman who had been impregnated by a non-Jewish boyfriend who deserted her. She did not want to have an abortion and shared her dilemma with Shlomo telling him that a Jewish boyfriend whom initially she had rejected still wanted to marry her. The problem was that if a woman is pregnant from someone who is not her husband, the *Halacha* requires waiting twenty-four months before marriage is allowed. The couple signed a contract commiting them to give up the baby for adoption. Shlomo met with Rabbi Moshe Feinstein, the leading halachic authority in the *haredi* world and explained the urgency. The next day, May 8, 1955, Rabbi Feinstein wrote a detailed responsa permitting the marriage.[75] Shlomo then hastened to organize the wedding.[76] This story illustrates three basic ingredients in Shlomo's nascent outreach career – a genuine concern to solve people's problems, a grasp of halachic nuances,[77] and an ability to proceed quickly with a practical solution.

Despite his initial enthusiasm, Shlomo was becoming frustrated. He tried a job in a small synagogue in Harlem, New York. He taught in various *yeshivot*, but had problems keeping discipline.[78] He felt inadequate in his *"kiruv"* mission. In 1955 he complained to the Rebbe that 90% of his audience would leave when he asked men and women to sit separately,

---

74. In a recent book, Reb Zalman describes how the sixth Rebbe, Yosef Yitzchak, assigned Shmuel Zalmanov with the task of preserving Chabad *niggunim*. This resulted in a two-volume collection entitled *Sefer HaNiggunim* containing 347 Chabad melodies ranging from short, catchy tunes to yearning and *devekus*. See Schachter-Shalomi, Davening, 44-46.

75. Rabbi Moshe Feinstein, *Iggerot Moshe, Even HaEzer* (New York: 1961), 32, 69–75. The responsa was addressed to "my friend, the honorable Rabbi Shlomo Carlebach *Shelita* [May he live to long and good life]," and is an indication that in May 1955 Shlomo was still on good standing in the *haredi* community.

76. The story is told with literary embellishments in two contradictory versions – Brandwein, *Reb Shlomele*, 225–227, and Zivan, *Soul Stories*, vol. 2, 151–152. Zivan adds a postscript that Shlomo met this woman many years later in Jerusalem at the Kotel and she thanked him for having enabled her to have a family with eight children!

77. In phrasing the halachic question, Shlomo explained how the couple had received a large sum of money committing them to having the baby taken for adoption, thus alleviating one of the main halachic concerns.

78. Offenbacher, "Jewish Minstrel," 54.

At 770 Eastern Parkway, Brooklyn, the headquarters of the Lubavitcher movement, around 1951. Reb Shlomo Carlebach wears a slanted gray hat, second from left. The Rebbe is speaking into the microphone.

and when he added that women couldn't sing, only one person remained: "So instead of spending two hours with people who wanted to know something about Yiddishkeit, I wasted my time on one idiot . . . I can't do outreach this way."[79]

The Rebbe did not provide Shlomo with a permit to allow women to sing with men. According to Shlomo, the Rebbe told him: "I cannot tell you to do it your way. But I can't tell you not to do it your way. So if you want to do it on your own, God be with you." Shlomo often would recount sadly: I was homeless. I was not with Lubavitch, I was not in Lakewood. The years 1955–1959 were very difficult because "I was really nowhere in the world."[80]

Reb Shlomo attended courses at Columbia University in subjects such as geology,[81] philosophy, and abnormal psychology.[82] The jacket cover of Shlomo's first album in 1959 says that Shlomo "attended Columbia

---

79. This is Shlomo's reconstruction of the exchange in his interview to Lerner, "Practical Wisdom," 54. Cf. Brandwein, *Reb Shlomele*, 26–27 and Brand, *Reb Shlomele*, 21. A similar version is recorded in Witt, "Reb Shlomo," 3.

80. Brenner, *Talkline*, segment 5:00; Lerner, "Practical Wisdom," 54.

81. Reb Zalman relates a story how in a geology class at Columbia, Shlomo challenged the Professor telling him that the world was created 5,700 years earlier – Skype interview with Reb Zalman, Aug. 7, 2011.

82. Offenbacher, "Jewish Minstrel," 54.

University and the new school of Social Research, and is now working towards his Doctorate in Philosophy."[83] The jacket covers of two albums in 1960 and 1963 go further, stating that Shlomo was "a graduate of Columbia University." However, it seems that Shlomo did not actually complete an academic degree.[84] One interesting story that is told, is that one day, as Shlomo walked from Columbia University through nearby Harlem, he was enchanted by the devotional singing of the "black brothers and sisters – they blew the roof off with that singing. They were talking to the Lord." Soon indeed, Shlomo was to discover that his enthusiasm and talents lay in the realm of spiritual music and not academics.

---

83. CdUniverse.com, http://www.cduniverse.com/productinfo.asp?pid=7399942.

84. Robert Hornsby, Director of Media Relations at Columbia University, wrote to me (Nov. 9, 2010): "We have no information on this individual in our records. There may have been some informal study for which there are no records, but he was not awarded a Columbia degree." Similarly, in response to my persistent questioning, Jocelyn K. Wilk, Public Services Archivist at Columbia, informed me on July 19, 2011, that there was no record of an enrollment for the name Shlomo Carlebach at Columbia University.

CHAPTER 3

Singing Rabbi Becomes Famous

1.   GUITAR-PLAYING RABBI, 1956–1958

In 1955, Shlomo was an advisor for the Yiddish play, *The Dybbuk*, which was playing in Greenwich Village.[1] He instructed the cast about Hasidic dances and Jewish weddings. Shlomo was so impressed by the guitar player who was using just two musical chords that he decided to learn guitar:

> From this point to buying an instrument was but a logical step. The Society for the Classic Guitar furnished a teacher, Miss Anita Scheer, who may be credited with noting down Shlomo's songs for the first time. She immediately recognized the inherent talent of the young composer, and her encouragement and advice guided him up to his public appearances.[2]

Shlomo would phone Anita Scheer when he invented new tunes and she would transcribe the notes. Thus his first songs such as *"Luley Torascho"* (Psalms 119:92) and *"Esa Einai"* (Psalms 121:1) were preserved. Anita influenced Shlomo in the direction of folk music and the flamenco style, and encouraged him to perform on stage.[3] Interestingly enough, Shlomo later was to incorporate the flamenco style into his *Kabbalat Shabbat* in the first few bars of *"Moshe v'Aharon"* (the concluding cantorial part of

---

1. *The Dybbuk* by Shlomo Ansky reflects the life of Jews living in the Polish-Russian countryside before World War I.

2. Offenbacher, "Jewish Minstrel," 55.

3. Anita Scheer (1935–1996) was a student of Carlos Montoya (1903–1993), a founder of the flamenco style of music and dance. Anita developed a career in folk music and appeared on stage with singers such as Bob Dylan and Pete Seeger and may have been instrumental in introducing Shlomo to them. She wrote the book

the fifth Psalm). It seems that Shlomo associated the flamenco with an old musical tradition connecting to the Levite music in the Temple:

> When I was learning how to play the guitar, my guitar teacher told me there was an old tradition that some Flamenco tunes went all the way back to the Temple. She said there were some old music manuscripts of flamenco with the signature Reuven Halevi.[4]

Before mastering the guitar, Shlomo would play the piano. In 1956–1957, he served a short stint as a "weekend" rabbi in Dorothy, Atlantic County, New Jersey.[5] Many of the congregants were Holocaust survivors, "simple Jews with broken hearts, and their children didn't come to the Synagogue. I didn't have much to do, so I began playing the piano and singing. At least that way, I was able to establish some sort of a rapport."[6]

Dorothy is about twenty miles west of Atlantic City. There Shlomo met and befriended Nina Simone who sang and played piano at the Midtown Bar and Grill on Pacific Avenue in Atlantic City.[7] The two encouraged each other to develop their singing careers at a crucial point in their development.[8] Nina introduced Shlomo to Harlem Gospel music. She produced her first album, *Little Girl Blue*, in 1958. It was a smash hit and she went on to record more than forty albums. An album of Simone which appeared in 1962 contained the song "Sinner Man," an American spiritual telling the sinner not to run from God. Shlomo adopted this song for his own performances early in his career.

One day in the late 1950s, Shlomo asked his friend Rabbi Meyer Leifer, to drive with him to Coney Island to hear Nina Simone play. When Meyer asked him why he maintained this unique friendship, Shlomo answered that he felt it vital to sympathize with the plight of the people who are discriminated against because of the color of their skin.[9] Later in his life, when asked to specify his greatest concerts, Shlomo related how he was "very good friends with Nina Simone," and once in Chicago, she had

---

Flamenco Guitar Method for Beginners, see TheFlamencoSociety.org, www.thefla mencosociety.org/id19.html; http://www.finefretted.com/html/desde_el_escritorio _sept__5__1.html.

4. This is the quote as remembered by Rabbi Moshe Stepansky (personal communication, Aug. 26, 2012). He was *gabbai* of the Carlebach Shul from 1987–2002, and today lives in Safed.

5. Offenbacher, "Jewish Minstrel," 54.

6. Adapted from Witt, "Reb Shlomo 1980," 4; Witt, *Open Gates of the Heart*, 220.

7. Nina Simone was the stage name of Eunice Kathleen Waymon, singer, songwriter, pianist, arranger, and civil rights activist associated with jazz music (1933–2003).

8. This meeting is dramatized in the Broadway musical "Soul Doctor."

9. Rabbi Meyer Leifer, personal interviews, Oct. 29, 2012, Dec. 17, 2012.

him join her on stage and "the whole night club got up and danced like crazy."[10]

Shlomo began frequenting Greenwich Village, the Bohemian center in lower Manhattan where writers, poets, artists, and students, later known as the "Beats," were creating a counterculture.[11] There he played alongside Richie Havens at Cafe Noir,[12] and befriended musicians such as Babatunde Olatunji,[13] Bob Dylan,[14] Peter Yarrow,[15] and Phil Ochs. The latter three were born to Jewish parents. Dylan, born in 1941 as Robert Allen Zimmerman, had a major influence on American popular music and is widely regarded as the preeminent poet-lyricist and songwriter of the last half of the twentieth century.[16] Peter Yarrow,[17] born in Manhattan in 1938, came to Greenwich Village in 1959 and in the 1960s became famous as part of the folk music trio, Peter, Paul and Mary.[18] Phil Ochs (1940–1976) arrived in New York in 1962 and became an integral part of the Greenwich Village folk music scene. There he had an incredible outburst of creativity and wrote hundreds of original songs. Ochs utilized the power of his lyrics to promote the anti-war protests and the

---

10. Interview of Alon Teeger in Sept. 1992, p. 18.

11. Beat culture included experimentation with drugs, sex, Eastern religions, and idealization of exuberant means of expression and being. The Beats had a pervasive influence on rock and roll, and popular music including the Beatles and Bob Dylan.

12. See below, Chapter 11 on Shlomo's appearance after Richie Havens in July 1984, his concert with Richie Havens in 1993, and also how Havens became famous at the Woodstock Festival.

13. Babatunde Olatunji (1927–2003), born in Nigeria, was a virtuoso of West African percussion. His first album, entitled *Drums of Passion* was released in 1959 by Columbia Records, and became an unprecedented, worldwide hit, selling over five million copies. See Babatunde Olatunji, *The Beat of My Drum: An Autobiography* (Philadelphia, 2005).

14. In a recording preserved in the Weisz collection, Shlomo tells his chevra in the HLP on Feb. 10, 1973 about his friendship with Bob Dylan.

15. On Shlomo's friendship with Peter Yarrow see Jeff Diamant, "Music helps Orthodox Jews make a spiritual link to God; Carlebach tunes have wide appeal," *Times - Picayune*, New Orleans, Aug. 5, 2006.

16. Robert Shelton notes that Rabbi Shlomo Carlebach tried to influence Dylan "to consider his obligations as a Jew," and that in 1974 Dylan showed "the *mezuzah* he wears" to a friend. See Robert Shelton, *No Direction Home: The Life And Music Of Bob Dylan* (New York: 1986), 413.

17. His parents' name was Yaroshevitz before they emigrated from the Ukraine to Rhode Island.

18. The trio Peter, Paul and Mary was mentored by Milt Okun who in the same years was advancing the musical career of Shlomo by arranging his early records (see below).

counterculture revolution.[19] These musicians influenced Shlomo's new career as a Jewish folk singer.[20]

Particularly significant was the impact of Pete Seeger, the iconic figure in the American folk song revival. Seeger achieved fame as the singing minstrel of the Civil Rights Movement of the 1960s.[21] Shlomo observed how Seeger connected to his audience, had people singing along and was a master at storytelling. Although Shlomo rarely ever sang English songs, he did sing three of Seeger's theme songs: "Don't You Weep Over Me," "Kumbaya,"[22] and "We Shall Overcome." The third song advocated a utopian vision of love and understanding.[23] Moreover, when Shlomo appeared in Israel in 1965, he prefaced his rendition of "We Shall Overcome" by telling his audience that he had just come from performing in San Francisco with Pete Seeger. He announced in Hebrew that Seeger is "truly one of the great people in the world, not only as a singer – he is simply a great person." Then Shlomo rendered his version of Seeger's song.[24]

Soon Reb Shlomo began taking his guitar to the Catskills, New York,

---

19. Marc Eliot, *Death of A Rebel: Starring Phil Ochs and a Small Circle of Friends* (New York: 1979); Michael Schumacher, *There But for Fortune: The Life of Phil Ochs* (New York: 1996).

20. Brandwein, *Reb Shlomele*, 29, writes that Reb Shlomo "appeared on the stage alongside Bob Dylan and Joan Baez." Many writers have repeated this statement of Brandwein and mistakenly connected this to a folk festival in San Francisco in the summer of 1963. Dylan and Baez, who were the popular stars of American folk music at the time, did appear together many times including May 17–18, 1963 at the Monterey folk festival in California, but it does not seem that Shlomo was there, and I have not yet found the evidence to document any Carlebach appearance with this duo in 1963 or at any other time.

21. Allan M. Winkler, *To Everything There Is a Season: Pete Seeger and the Power of Song* (New York: 2009).

22. To hear Reb Shlomo's version of "Kumbaya," see YouTube.com, http://www .youtube.com/watch?v=1ikatUUduPs&feature=em-subs_digest. Cf. Pete Seeger's version in 1963 in Melbourne, Australia at http://www.youtube.com/watch?v=3H -MeS6LhhU&feature=related. Seeger describes the "mysterious" origins of this song. He adds that the song needs some harmony and thus encourages the audience join in. The original song was an Afro-American spiritual prayerful tune in the 1920s entitled "Come By Yah." Later it was sung as "Come By Here." See Gary Stern, "Kumbaya, My Lord: Why We Sing It; Why We Hate It," *Journal News, New York's Lower Hudson Valley*, June 27, 2009, Lohud.com, www.lohud.com/article/20090627/ COLUMNIST/906270343/%5C-Kumbaya--My-Lord-%5C--Why-we-sing-it--why -we-hate-it. Cf. Samuel G. Freedman, "A Long Road From 'Come by Here' to 'Kumbaya,'" *New York Times*, Nov. 19, 2010, NYTimes.com, http://www.nytimes.com/ 2010/11/20/us/20religion.html?_r=3&scp=1&sq=Winslow%20Gordon&st=cse.

23. Originally a gospel musical composition by Reverend Charles Albert Tindley in 1901, it had become a key anthem of the Civil Rights Movement.

24. BooMp3.com, http://boomp3.com/mp3/28ghlko2pjg-we-shall-overcome.

and appearing in bungalow colonies such as Riverhaven[25] and hotels such as the Pioneer Country Club in the Catskills. In the summer of 1956, Irwin Borvick was working as a waiter in the Pine View Hotel in the Catskill Mountains when he heard that Shlomo was singing at the nearby Pioneer Hotel. Borvick went to the Pioneer and invited Shlomo to play at the Yeshiva University student Hanukkah party (December 1956). Borvick recalls:

> The concert was a huge success and hundreds of students stayed until after midnight. In the middle of the show, Shlomo announced "I have two new songs that I have just composed," and he began to play *"Esa Einai"* and *"Hashmienei et Kolech."*[26]

Meanwhile in Brooklyn, Shlomo took his guitar and began influencing yeshiva youth. Rabbi Dr. Tzvi Hersh Weinreb was a yeshiva boy in Borough Park, age 16, when he was invited in 1956 to a youth group led by Shlomo in a basement in Crown Heights:

> My yeshiva Rebbe forbade us from going, but we went anyway. Shlomo was the only person to whom my friends and I could bring our sophomoric, but agonizing questions of faith. He looked at us with no judgment or criticism, only concern. "Brothers, you're singing the wrong song. Sing a song with me." Then he took his guitar and began playing his song *"Ruach."* We sang for a long time. Our doubts became irrelevant. And then he shared his vision, "If we can find that song of faith together, we can change our whole generation."[27]

This is a striking example of the emotional-spiritual influence of Reb Shlomo on a generation of youthful seekers from religious backgrounds.[28] When Shlomo began singing and telling stories in the late 1950s, it was a time that the melancholy of the Holocaust still permeated American

---

25. Personal interview with Stuart Wax, July 13, 2011.

26. Personal interviews with Irwin Borvick in 2011.

27. Menashe Bleiweiss, "The Grateful Yid and the Grateful Dead: How Reb Shlomo Carlebach and Jerry Garcia Serenaded the Jewish Soul," *Jewish Spectator*, Winter, 1995–1996, MenasheBleiweiss.com, http://menashebleiweiss.com/articles/Grateful%20Yid%20and%20Grateful%20Dead.pdf. For a similar story, see Brandwein, *Reb Shlomele*, 65–68.

28. R. Weinreb went on to receive his rabbinic ordination from the Rabbi Jacob Joseph Yeshiva in New York and his Ph.D. from the University of Maryland. From 1989, he served as the spiritual leader of Congregation Shomrei Emunah in Baltimore and as Executive Vice President of the Orthodox Union from 2002. See OU.Org, http://www.ou.org/torah/author/Rabbi_Dr_Tzvi_Hersh_Weinreb.

Jewry. Moshe Waldoks was one of the young boys who heard Shlomo at the time. He reflected recently:

> Reb Shlomo Carlebach was important because he gave us permission to sing after the Shoah. I was a 10-year old boy when he came to my yeshiva in Brooklyn, the Yeshiva of Eastern Parkway, in the late 1950s. The Shoah was still very raw and it was Shlomo who taught us to sing in renewed joyous Hasidic melody.[29]

Perhaps it is a relevant observation that some twenty years later Moshe Waldoks co-edited a book on Jewish humor.[30] Indeed, Shlomo inspired people by creating a new joyous setting. But, many of his songs were also prayers of salvation in times of trouble and anticipation of Divine Intervention.

On August 5, 1957, Reb Shlomo led a special Tisha BeAv program at the home of the Brandwein family, which lived near the Carlebach family synagogue on the West Side. Hadassa Goldberg, who at the time was a senior in Central (Yeshiva University High School for girls) in Brooklyn together with the Brandwein daughter, recalls that after reading *Eicha*, everyone sat on the floor with lit candles: "Reb Shlomo played his guitar and told inspiring stories of yearning for Jerusalem by many Chassidic rabbis." Goldberg also heard Shlomo "many times in the SZO (Student Zionist Organization) of Hunter College in 1958–1959."[31]

Rikki (Gordon) Lewin was a sophomore at Hunter College when she met Shlomo at the Pioneer Country Club in the summer of 1957. Rikki was fascinated by Shlomo's singing on the lawn:

> As a journalism major, I was always alert to an interesting story. Shlomo was magical. His audience was entranced. He had adults who could barely carry a tune singing spiritedly.[32]

---

29. Personal communication from Rabbi Moshe Waldoks, Oct. 27, 2009. Waldoks was born on July 17, 1949 to Holocaust refugee parents. All of his father's family had been annihilated in the Ukraine and most of his mother's family were murdered at Auschwitz.

30. William Novak and Moshe Waldoks, *The Big Book of Jewish Humor* (New York: 1981). Moshe completed his doctorate in Eastern European Jewish Intellectual History at Brandeis in 1984 and received ordination as a post-denominational rabbi in 1996. Reb Moshe founded NishmatHayyim (see www.nishmathayyim.org) and currently is the rabbi at Temple Beth Zion in Brookline Massachusetts.

31. Personal communication from Hadassa Goldberg June 28, 2012. Hadassa went on aliyah with her husband Moshe in 1963.

32. Rikki Lewin, personal interviews, June 2012. See Natan Ophir, "The Origins of Reb Shlomo's First LP Record: The Account of Rikki (Gordon) Lewin," *Kol Chevra*, vol. 18, 2012, 107–108.

When Rikki returned home to Brooklyn, she contacted three recording companies. One of them asked to hear a sample of Shlomo's music. Thus, in the fall of 1957, Rikki arranged the first serious recording of Reb Shlomo singing. The taping session took place at his parents' home in Manhattan. An outgrowth of this meeting was the creation of an informal group whose purpose was to promote Shlomo:

> This resulted in performances at the Village Gate and other similar clubs. Murry Gerstel helped organize the business related issues.[33]

In December 1957, Rikki organized a party in her home. She played piano while Shlomo played guitar and then he joined her in a duet at the piano.[34] With the aid and prodding of friends like Rikki, a company called Zimra Records was formed and soon Reb Shlomo produced the two LP records that launched his professional career.

2.   LAUNCHING A MUSICAL CAREER, 1958–1959

Rabbi Gerald Friedman was a 17-year old studying in Mesivta Torah Vodaas when he discovered Reb Shlomo in the spring of 1958. Together with a few other Brooklyn Yeshiva teenagers, he followed Reb Shlomo into Greenwich Village and was enthralled by his music and message:

> We were hanging out at Shabsi's Pizza on Utica Ave. in Crown Heights. A few of us at Torah Vodaas and Chaim Berlin were straying from the *derech*, the straight and narrow path, and looking for something, who knows what. We found it in Shlomo and followed him around, especially when we started studying at Brooklyn College in the evenings. We often made our way into Greenwich Village after 11 PM. He was quite a presence, along with the jazz greats, folk singers, comics, and other attractions we lusted after. Imagine our excitement in discovering "one of ours" who was there "making it happen" – in the Village Gate, no less. I was one of Reb Shlomo's earliest groupies. He introduced me to a new kind of soulfulness.[35]

For the next thirty-six years. Gerald Friedman became a devoted follower of Reb Shlomo, davening and studying with him in New York,

---

33. Rikki Lewin, personal correspondence, June 8, 2012.

34. A Japanese journalism exchange student, who was a classmate of Rikki's, helped devise the theme for the party to center around Japanese food and ideas. Then she wrote it up in a Japanese newspaper with a couple of pictures, the first story about Reb Shlomo in Japanese.

35. Interview with Rabbi Gerald Friedman, Jan. 30, 2013.

New Jersey, and Israel. In 1977, Rabbi Friedman became the Hillel Director at the University of Florida, working on campus for twenty-two years. Often he would invite Shlomo to the campus: "Shlomo loved to come and meet his holy Hippelach, find new students, and go bike riding in that laid back setting."[36]

In mid-1958, Reb Shlomo was the star performer at a Young Israel convention keeping hundreds of people "awake all night singing along with him in virtually a trance-like ecstasy." This according to the laudatory report in *The Young Israel Viewpoint* where they also exclaimed:

> His magnetic spell attracts people of all types and ages, and the radiant look on their faces leaves no doubt as to whether they are enjoying themselves. Our many pleasant experiences, observing Shlomo Carlebach in action, leave us with a strong desire to enjoy more of his performances.[37]

But, just as Shlomo was discovering his uncanny skills of inspiring youth to become observant, he was still struggling to earn a living. A breakthrough came in the fall of 1958. A friend of Reb Shlomo from their days together in New York, R. Yecheskel Hartman heard that Reb Shlomo was struggling in New York, and invited him to work with the youth and teach in the St. Louis day school, the Epstein Hebrew Academy. Rabbi Hartman served both as the Midwest Regional Director of the OU (Union of Orthodox Jewish Congregations of America), and as rabbi of Congregation Tpheris Israel in University City, a suburb of St. Louis, Missouri.[38] He thus was able to provide Shlomo with an invaluable opportunity of working with youth. In what was his only long-lasting job, Shlomo served as youth director at Congregation Tpheris Israel from October 1958 to June 1959.[39]

Irene Goldschmidt (later Adina Mescheloff) was in the sixth grade at

---

36. Interview with Rabbi Gerald Friedman, Feb. 5, 2013.

37. "Chasidic Guitar," *Young Israel Viewpoint* 48, Sept.–Oct. 1958, 10–11. The report is cited in the first record back side in the section "comments from listeners." See also Sarna, *American Judaism*, 346, and Regina Stein, *The Boundaries of Gender: the Role of Gender Issues in Forming American Jewish Denominational Identity, 1913–1963*, Ph.D. dissertation, Jewish Theological Seminary, 1998, 59.

38. Rabbi Yecheskel (Charles) Hartman was the spiritual leader of Tpheris Israel from 1949 until 1967 when he moved to Israel. See Walter Ehrlich, *Zion in the Valley, Volume II: The Jewish Community of St. Louis* (Columbia, Missouri: 2002), 43. On Congregation Tpheris Israel and its various locations, see Flickr.com, http://www.flickr.com/photos/mohistory/3380606066, HistoryHappenedHere.org, http://www.historyhappenedhere.org/details.php?id=24 (temporarily offline in Sept. 2012).

39. Sue Ann Wood, "The Singing Rabbi," *St. Louis Post*, Jan. 10, 1993.

Rikki Lewin (Gordon) and Rabbi Carlebach at a concert in The Village Gate, Greenwich Village, New York City, 1957 or 1958   Courtesy of Rikki Lewin

the Epstein Hebrew Academy. She remembers how Shlomo taught her class Talmud:

> Seven girls from fifth and sixth grade were in the *limudei kodesh* class with Rav Carlebach (that is how we called him then). We learned Gemara Tractate *Berachot*. Most of what I recall from the class was his singing with us *"Borchi Nafshi," "Esa Einai,"* and similar *niggunim*. We did a lot of singing and listening to stories that year. His concerts had a packed audience in our *shul*, and we sang until the late hours of the night. We were inspired and uplifted by his presence and his never-ending stories.[40]

Later, when Shlomo's first record appeared in June 1959, the rave reviews printed on the jacket cover were from his fans in St. Louis (see below). Rabbi Yecheskel Hartman's salutation on the cover emphasized the spiritual power of Shlomo's songs:

> An exciting musical adventure in the realm of the spirit. An inexhaustible treasure of melodies which communicate man's need to believe and give expression to his transcendental hopes, aspirations, anxieties, and yearnings for salvation.

---

40. Adina Mescheloff, personal correspondence June 28–July 1, 2012.

Elsie Ellis and her husband Bob were members of R. Hartman's synagogue and they became very friendly with Shlomo. Elsie recalls:

> Rabbi Hartman recognized Shlomo's great potential. He hosted
> him in his large home and was his mentor. But R. Hartman was
> very busy and when Shlomo needed something he would phone
> my husband Bob and they would drive around. Shlomo had all
> kinds of unusual outreach interests. For example, he asked to visit
> the Black churches (they were then called Negroes or Blacks and
> not Afro-Americans). He introduced himself and sang his Hebrew
> songs. They loved him and he in return appreciated their gospel
> music. One day he brought about twenty Blacks to our synagogue
> to participate in his concert. Soon they were dancing in the aisles.
> We were enchanted by their excitement and sense of rhythm.[41]

Elsie also describes how Shlomo would receive a great deal of fan mail
from St. Louis teenagers, and she took upon herself the responsibility to
respond in writing for him. Elsie had also initiated a program bringing
together the sisterhood of her Orthodox Synagogue of Tpheris Israel
together with the women from the large Reform Temple in St. Louis,
and she had Shlomo come to sing and teach: "They were all enchanted
with Shlomo because they had never met an Orthodox rabbi like that."[42]

At the end of 1958, Rabbi Shlomo Carlebach was invited by the Yeshiva
University Community Service Division, Youth Bureau, to lead several
workshops in Jewish Music at the Teenage Torah Leadership Seminar at
the Lake House Hotel, Woodridge, New York. The weeklong program
was filled with interesting speakers and leading rabbis.[43] On Sunday,
December 28, 1958, at 5:00 PM, Shlomo, together with a YU student,
Hyam (Chaim) Wasserman, led a workshop about "Jewish liturgical and
festival music." Then on Monday, December 29, at 11:00 AM, Shlomo led
a workshop on "Israel Songs," and at 5:00 PM again on Jewish liturgical
music.[44]

Sometime around February 1959, Shlomo was invited to an Orthodox

---

41. Elsie Ellis, telephone interview, July 1, 2012.

42. Ibid.

43. The program was geared for high school and college youth who had little
religious background and included rabbis such as Haskell Lookstein of Kehilath
Jeshurun in New York; Moses Tendler, at the time assistant dean of Yeshiva College;
Morris Besdin, chairman of the Jewish Studies Program at YU, and David Hartman,
from the Jewish Studies Program at YU.

44. My thanks to Shulamith Z. Berger, Curator of Special Collections, Yeshiva
University, for sending me the entire program of the Torah Leadership Seminar (Jan.
14, 2013).

synagogue to give "one of his first concerts in New York." After the concert, at a private *Melaveh Malkah* he began composing a new song on the piano. But no one present knew how to write music and in those days, there weren't portable tape recorders. So at 1:00 AM, 16-year old Itzik Aisenstadt[45] went to wake up Kalman Kinnory,[46] the recording engineer at Vanguard Records, who set up a big and bulky recorder and preserved Shlomo's new melody, later known as "*Ye'erav Na*."[47]

In the beginning of 1959, Shlomo was invited by the high school senior class at the Talmudical Academy (TA) of Baltimore to perform a concert.[48] The event took place in the hall of the Shaarei Tzedek Synagogue,[49] and was such a success that Shlomo was invited many times thereafter to Baltimore. A brief video, recently posted on the Internet, provides a rare glimpse into how 35-year old Shlomo was able to inspire the youth into musical joy and dancing.[50] He is accompanied on the flute by Dr. Gershon Kranzler,[51] principal of TA, who knew Shlomo from their days together at

---

45. Itzik Aisenstadt, was Shlomo's lifelong friend and *chavruta* learning partner. A prominent Modzitzer Hasid, Itzik was expert at remembering Shlomo's tunes and "was known by Carlebachers as the Treasurer of the Niggunim." He died on Dec. 4, 2011 at age 67. For several tributes to Itzik and descriptions of his relationship to Shlomo see *Kol Chevra*, 18, 2012, 124–131.

46. Kalman Kinnory was born Feb. 10, 1923 and died March 4, 2009.

47. Interview of Itzik Aisenstadt with Eliezer and Michele Garner on the radio station WSIA, Staten Island. The interview was transcribed by the Garners and published as "Reb Itzik's Commentary on Shlomo's Melodies," *Kol Chevra*, 18, 2012, 134–135.

48. Eugene Fischer, a member of the TA high school senior class of 1959, relates that this event was in January or February of 1959 and was sponsored by his class to earn revenue to produce the class yearbook.

49. Rabbi Louis B. Friedlander (in Hebrew, Rabbi Elazar Bainish Friedlander), the grandfather of TA senior Jason Rosenblatt, was the rabbi of Shaarei Tzedek in Baltimore and he agreed to host the concert in the synagogue's hall. At the time, "those in authority did not know how to accommodate a public venue for Shlomo's performances and were reluctant to provide a venue for his style of *kiruv*" (Eugene Fischer, personal correspondence, Jan. 9, 2013).

50. A 3:29-minute video without sound was posted by Kesher, Jan. 1, 2013, www .box.com/s/xs18050jlf4f5wgjr9jo. This is the earliest video portrayal of Shlomo's concerts. In the opening picture are Trude Kranzler on right and Greta Schlossberg on the left and the photo was taken at the Kranzler home where Shlomo led an all-night program. At segment 1:41 onwards are TA students. The first row is Label Deutsch, Eugene Fischer, and Sam Koenigsberg and in the back row are Alan Katznelson, Jason Rosenblatt, and Henry Lazarus. In the dancing around Shlomo are Jason, Phil Kaliphon, Raqui Sugarman, Alan Baron, and others. The video was taken by Irv Klavan, a TA student at the time. My thanks to Eugene Fischer and Eli Schlossberg for the information (Jan. 6–10, 2013).

51. At segment 2:29–2:41, Gershon Kranzler can been seen playing the flute next

Mesivta Torah Vodaas, and hosted him after the concert for an all-night kumsitz in his home.[52] Kranzler was later to invite Shlomo some fifteen times to sing and inspire the students in TA Baltimore.[53] Kranzler, himself a composer of Jewish folk music, played piano and violin and encouraged the music tradition at TA,[54] even bringing a choirmaster from New York, Seymour Silbermintz.[55]

Eli W. Schlossberg was 9 years old when Reb Shlomo came to Baltimore. He described Reb Shlomo as "our Pied Piper" and pictured the impact that Shlomo made:

> He was awesome; we were in absolute awe as he jumped up and down strumming his guitar. We were simply transfixed, and for me, it opened up a new world of music. That night, Shlomo conducted a kumsitz at the Kranzler home on Devonshire Drive. It was an all-nighter.[56]

Reminiscing about the long-lasting effects of Reb Shlomo, Eli Schlossberg wrote:

> To this day I am in awe of that musical wizard and capturer of hearts. Shlomo made everyone feel special. One can say whatever about him, but the fact is that he turned many, many Jews on to Yiddishkeit. And it was he alone who restarted musical *simcha* after the Holocaust. *Klal Yisrael* had stopped singing, and now Shlomo was teaching our youth how to sing once again. . . .

---

to Reb Shlomo.

52. For biographical write-ups on Dr. Kranzler, see T.H. Weinreb, "Dr. Gershon Kranzler: Tiferet Personified," *Jewish Action*, Winter 5761/2000, OU.org, http://www .ou.org/publications/ja/5761winter/KRANZLER.PDF; Obituary, *The Baltimore Sun*, March 7, 2000, BaltimoreSun.com, http://articles.baltimoresun.com/2000-03-07/ news/0003070440_1_talmudical-academy-sociology-glyndon.

53. Personal communications from Eli Scholssberg, June 2011, Jan. 2013.

54. Eugene Fischer relates that music was encouraged at TA. Already in 1947, when he was in first grade, he sang in the cantata of 70–80 voices under the leadership of William Krumin who came from Washington D.C.

55. Eli W. Schlossberg, "TA the Way It Was," *Where What When: Baltimore's Jewish Family Magazine*, Feb. 2011, WhereWhatWhen.com, http://www.wherewhatwhen .com/read_articles.asp?id=855. See also Eli W. Schlossberg, "The Awesome Power of Music," *Where What When: Baltimore's Jewish Family Magazine*, Sept. 1, 2011, WhereWhatWhen.com, http://www.wherewhatwhen.com/archive/2011/09/the-awe some-power-of-music.

56. Eli W. Schlossberg, "The Sixties and Seventies: Turbulent Yet Wonderful Years – The Way We Were," March 2009, *Where What When: Baltimore's Jewish Family Magazine*, WhereWhatWhen.com, http://www.wherewhatwhen.com/read_articles .asp?id=549.

> Wherever Shlomo was, he brought friendship, *chesed*, unbeliev-
> able kindness, and tremendous *simcha* . . . He singlehandedly
> revolutionized *niggunim, nusach,* and *zemiros* . . . His impact on
> me in Jewish music made me dedicate the Carlebach Music Room
> in my home in his memory.[57]

Although Shlomo's music was valued for his rejuvenation of joy after the
Holocaust, many in the religious *haredi* world were perturbed by the
fact that he sang to mixed audiences of men and women. The question
arose whether it was permissible to even sing his tunes. On May 30, 1959,
Rabbi Moshe Feinstein wrote a responsa to Rabbi Shmuel Dishon allowing Carlebach tunes to be played at weddings (*Even HaEzer*, 1, 96). Rabbi
Feinstein does not mention Shlomo's name explicitly, but refers to him as
a Torah scholar who has gone off the path, and explains that he is not an
apikorus (a heretic) nor a *mumar lete'avon* (a transgressor for pleasure);
his transgression is merely "*kalut rosh* and *peritzut*" (light-headedness
and licentiousness) in that he performs before mixed audiences.

Shlomo was, however, invited to non-*haredi* places. In 1959, Shlomo
Carlebach gave a musical performance accompanied by pianist Shirly
Braverman at the Thomas Jefferson High School, in East New York, a
residential neighborhood located in eastern Brooklyn.[58]

Shlomo spent a good part of the summer of 1959 in the Catskills in
South Fallsburg, New York. Aaron Katchen was there that summer as a
17–year old waiter in the Laurel Park Hotel, a favorite haven for Orthodox
Jews. He remembers Shlomo walking through the dining room with his
guitar playing "*Esa Einai*" and "*Borchi Nafshi*."[59] Shlomo also entertained
on the lawn of Gartenberg and Schechter's Pioneer Hotel in the Catskills.
This popular glatt-kosher resort was the place for young religious singles
to vacation in the summer. Shlomo would sit on the lawn strumming his
guitar and people would gather for an impromptu concert.[60]

In a rare video filmed at the Pioneer Hotel in the summer of 1959, one
can see Reb Shlomo performing.[61] The cultural director at the Pioneer

---

57. Ibid.

58. My thanks to Dov Shurin for this information. Shurin was 9 years old, when
his father R. Yisroel Shurin, rabbi of the Mogen Abraham Congregation in East New
York, brought him to this concert.

59. Personal interview with Aaron Katchen, Feb. 14, 2013.

60. My thanks to Rikki Lewin for describing these events.

61. This video was filmed by Gertrude Ross. Together with her husband,
Morris, she frequented the Pioneer Hotel in the summer. The video was uploaded
by Gertrude's grandson, Azi Graber, on April 13, 2011, http://www.youtube.
com/watch?v=SuoLbRW4GKU. My thanks to Azi Graber for this information

Country Club, Dr. Morris Mandel, can be seen at segment 0:53–1:03.[62] Also seen in the audience is Goldie Stern, a freshman in college, who was working as a counselor in the Pioneer Hotel summer day camp.[63] Goldie and her classmates Lila Silver and Barbara Cohen became avid Carlebach fans. After the summer, they invited Shlomo to come regularly on Motzei Shabbat to lead a sing-along kumsitz in a circle on the floor in the finished basement of Goldie's home on 2816 Ave. I in Brooklyn.[64] Shlomo would share the new songs that he had composed:

> Shlomo would come with his right-hand man, a fun loving, tall guy with a French beret named Murry Gerstel.[65] We would sit for hours and sing Shlomo's original compositions such as *"Esa Einai"* and *"Hanshoma Loch."* Each song could take some twenty minutes.[66]

On August 29, 1959, Shlomo was invited again to the Torah Leadership Seminar organized by the Yeshiva University's Youth Bureau, Community Service Division.[67] Shlomo was supposed to arrive right after Shabbat to lead the *Melaveh Malkah* program. Chaim Wasserman, a YU student who served as an advisor at the Seminar, describes how several hundred teens anxiously awaited Shlomo who finally showed up after midnight, but soon, with his guitar, "whipped the crowd in a frenzy."[68] Later, to an interviewer in 1961, Shlomo described this as the most powerful concert performance of his to date – "the singing and dancing was four hours straight."[69]

(April 14, 2013). The video was copied by Joel Goldberg and posted on http://www.youtube.com/watch?v=FUqUuyGGUag&NR=1.

62. Morris Mandel published several books together with Leo Gartenberg, the co-owner of the Pioneer Hotel. Both men were Torah scholars and longtime columnists for *The Jewish Press*.

63. Goldie appears at segment 0:16–0:19.

64. Mel Isaacs, "A Teacher Can Influence Eternity," *Kol Chevra*, vol. 18, 2012, 194–195. My thanks to Goldie Isaacs for clarifying this story.

65. Brooklyn-born Murry Gerstel was living in Williamsburg at the time. He died on June 15, 2012.

66. Personal interview with Goldie Isaacs, Dec. 20, 2012.

67. The program took place from Aug. 26 – Sept. 7 at Camp Monroe, Monroe, New York.

68. R. Chaim Wasserman, "The First and Last Time We Met," *Kol Chevra*, vol. 13, 2007, 64–65. See Rabbi Moshe Pesach Geller, "I Remember," *Kol Chevra*, vol. 7, 2000, 102–106. In a personal interview, Rabbi Moshe Pesach Geller reminisced how his father, Victor B, Geller, the head of the YU Youth Bureau, brought him as a 7-year old youngster to this concert and as a result he became a lifelong devoted follower of Reb Shlomo (personal interview Jan. 14, 2013).

69. Yaakov Edelstein, "The Dancing Rabbi, R. Shlomo Carlebach," *HaTzofeh*, Aug.

On Hol HaMoed Sukkot in mid-October of 1959, Shlomo performed at the Yeshivah of Flatbush High School in Brooklyn. Avi Zablocki, at the time in ninth grade, recalls how Shlomo "really rocked and we were totally taken by him . . . mesmerized." Avi began "carrying Shlomo's guitar on the subway and accompanying him to various concerts." He and his friends from Bnei Akiva of Brighton Beach "became Shlomo's boys": "We would join him at concerts and dance up a storm, bringing in the audience with us."[70]

Sometimes friends from his yeshiva days invited Shlomo to perform. In 1959, Rabbi Yisroel Singer who had been Shlomo's *havruta* learning partner in Brooklyn invited him to the Hillel Hebrew Academy of Kehilat Beth Jacob in Beverly Hills, California. Yocheved Ehrman was in sixth grade at the time. She recalls Shlomo playing the piano and enchanting the children for two hours until their teacher sternly rebuked them for missing class.[71]

In 1959, Shlomo led a concert at the newly opened Kadimah day school in Buffalo, New York. At the time, Tova Snyder was 7 years old. She reports that her Hebrew teacher, Rabbi Hartman, spent a whole week teaching Shlomo's tunes to her class in preparation for the concert:

> I had tingles all week and sang your songs with my whole heart at the top of my lungs . . . This was my first experience with joy, love, and that intense, sweet prayer/song that comes from the heart and soul . . . I remember feeling deeply moved by the experience, carried away to a place I did not know existed. This was probably my first spiritual experience.[72]

At the end of December 1959, Reb Shlomo led a concert for Hanukkah sponsored by the Yeshiva University Yolanda Benson Society.[73] It took place at the George Washington High School near YU.[74]

Shlomo traveled extensively, gradually establishing "a home base" in

---

18, 1961.

70. Rabbi Avi Zablocki, "Memories," *Kol Chevra*, vol. 17, 2011, 118. See also Avi Zablocki, "My Very First Concert with Shlomo," *Kol Chevra*, vol. 18, 2012, 68–69.

71. Yocheved Ehrman, personal interviews, Aug. 2012.

72. Tova Snyder, "Blessings and Love," *Kol Chevra*, vol. 10, 2004, 118–119.

73. Yolanda Benson died at age 19 on Oct. 9, 1959 in a tragic traffic accident. Yolanda was an only child and had survived the Holocaust by hiding with Christian neighbors in Poland. Her parents found her after the war and gradually brought her back to Judaism. She was one of 28 participants in the first Yeshiva Youth Seminar, later renamed Torah Leadership Seminar. The Yolanda Benson Honor Society was established in her memory. See *YU Review*, Winter 2005, 15, www.scribd.com/doc/46285648/YESHIVA-UNIVERSITY-REVIEW-Winter-2005.

74. This was told to me by Rabbi Moshe Pesach Geller who was 7 years old at the

major cities such as Boston, Los Angeles, and Chicago where he would
return several times a year to sing and teach. In Chicago, Arnold and
Claire Gassel, and Arnold's sisters, Gertrude and Rita, hosted Shlomo
many times. The Gassels' three teenagers became fans of Shlomo and
together with their Bnei Akiva friends would join Shlomo for his formal
and informal concerts in Chicago.[75] Larry and Evelyn Yellin were living in
Aurora near Chicago when they heard exciting reports about the "Singing
Rabbi." They went to hear Shlomo in concert in Chicago and then invited
him to Aurora and Shlomo gave a concert program at Temple B'nai Israel:

> Shlomo was basically unknown at the time and we were appre-
> hensive how he would be appreciated so we invited the Bnei Akiva
> *chevra* from Chicago and indeed the youth were so enthusiastic
> that even the congregation old-timers were up and dancing. After
> the concert, we adjourned to our home where Shlomo, accom-
> panied by the Bnei Akiva youth on piano, guitar, and drum, gave
> forth with soul touching melodies and meaningful Torah messages
> till 2:00 AM. It was a night to remember.[76]

The crucial turning point in Shlomo's career came when fans such as Rikki
Lewin (see above) helped set up Zimra (Zimrani) Records to produce his
first two albums.[77] The songs selected were those that "the audiences had
asked to hear again and again."[78] Kalman Kinnory, a Holocaust survivor,
was the sound engineer. New York artist Jules Halfant (1909–2001) designed the attractive record covers.[79]

The key person to promote Shlomo was Milton Okun. Born in
Brooklyn on December 23, 1923, Okun was a child lover of opera, and a

---

time, but his father, Victor Geller, brought the whole family to the concert (personal
interview, Jan. 14, 2013).

75. Interview with Arnold Gassel, Sept. 22, 2012.

76. Personal communications from Larry and Evelyn Yellin in Sept. 2012.

77. The working address of Zimra Records is listed on his first two albums as 200
West 57th St., New York City. This is an elegant 16-story office building located in
midtown Manhattan directly across from Carnegie Hall. As late as 1969, Shlomo's
business card listed this as his New York address. My thanks to Kenny Ellis for sending me a copy of this card.

78. Edelstein, "The Dancing Rabbi." He also quotes Shlomo as stating that the
record company was supported "by three wealthy Jews interested in supporting the
spread of my music."

79. Halfant, who was known for his unique religiously influenced paintings, was
the art director for Vanguard Records from 1953 until the mid 1980s. Shlomo, on
his fifth record, thanks Jules Halfant "whose friendship and untiring efforts have
accompanied me since I began singing."

talented pianist and singer.[80] Okun, who later set up his own company, Cherry Lane Music, became an outstanding record producer[81] whose secret of success was his knack for discovering and mentoring musical artists such as John Denver,[82] Laura Nyro, and Placido Domingo. He transformed three unknown singers – Peter Yarrow, Paul Stookey, and Mary Travers – into the most successful group act of the 1960s folk boom. Okun also published the catalogue of songs of Elvis Presley. And he discovered Rabbi Carlebach.

In the late 1950s, Okun was "arranging and producing" for Vanguard Records when an employee there told him about the Singing Rabbi. Okun met Shlomo and the momentous decision was made to produce an album. Okun had been working full-time for Harry Belafonte as arranger and producer as well as the leader of his band. So Okun used members of Belafonte's band "as backup for Shlomo." The group of six musicians included four African-Americans from "the Baptist choir from the church down the street" where Reb Shlomo "used to visit all the time."[83] Okun described how Shlomo's mother, Rebbetzin Pessia, would come "to all the sessions," bringing "food and treats," and giving out "yarmulkes to wear," but he complained that he had difficulty in recording:

> He prayed while he sang. It's called *davening*. He would rock back and forth. . . . He couldn't stop himself. And I just couldn't get it right. We tried everything, even had someone holding the mic and moving it back and forth with him.[84]

Okun conducted the choir and orchestra for the first two albums of Shlomo, *Songs of My Soul* and *Sing My Heart*. The professionalism he added proved to be the crucial element in the success of this new genre of Hasidic music. The record jacket of the second album acknowledges Okun's contribution:

---

80. Okun began his career in the late 1940s as a music teacher in a junior high school in New York City, and in the early 1950s was hired as a pianist by Harry Belafonte.

81. See Milton Okun, *Along the Cherry Lane: My Life in Music* (Beverly Hills, California: 2011). My thanks to Howie Kahn for explaining about Milt Okun. See KnickerBockerVillage.Blogspot.com, http://knickerbockervillage.blogspot.com/search/label/milton%20okun. Okun garnered 75 gold and platinum Records and 16 Grammy nominations.

82. See at 13:00 in the autobiographical recording by Milt Okun (Nov. 2005). http://www.artistshousemusic.org/videos/milt+okun+full+interview. It is mostly a half hour tribute to John Denver whose music Okun arranged and produced.

83. Neshama Carlebach, personal correspondence, April 30, 2012.

84. *Along the Cherry Lane*, 103.

In his imaginative and vibrant arrangement of these original *niggunim*, Milton Okun has added a new dimension and a new intensity to the world of Chassidic melody.

Similarly, music connoisseur, Eric Offenbacher, began a laudatory review of Shlomo's first album by remarking how Okun had transformed Shlomo's music:

It is quite astonishing for those who know Carlebach's *niggunim* in their "naked" version how much "dressing up" a professional musician, experienced in the business of arrangements, can accomplish through coloration and promotion of detail by means of various solo instruments.[85]

Okun helped Shlomo produce his early albums.[86] He arranged the music and conducted the chorus and orchestra for the fifth album, *Wake up World*, in 1965, and Shlomo wrote a dedication to Milt Okun, "whose soul-stirring arrangements have brought my songs to the hearts of thousands." The cover picture of Reb Shlomo on this album was taken by Bernard Cole who had also prepared the album covers for the 1962 record of Peter, Paul and Mary, whose musical director was also Milt Okun.

3.   FIRST TWO LP HITS, 1959–1960

Reb Shlomo's first record, *Hanshomo Loch*, or in English, *Songs of My Soul*, appeared in June 1959. It was a culmination of several years of singing and teaching with Jewish youth especially in the greater New York area and in St. Louis. The record was sold for $4.98. Reportedly, 5,000 copies were sold in the first week.[87] For many a fan, Reb Shlomo would add a personal inscription.[88]

The album included themes of yearning and hope, songs for salvation, rebuilding of Jerusalem, and rejoicing. The rationale was defined on the jacket cover:

---

85. Offenbacher, "Jewish Minstrel," 56.

86. Okun, *Along the Cherry Lane*, 104: "We went on to make five more albums. He financed the sessions and sold the records himself."

87. Mandelbaum, *Holy Brother*, xxxi. Mandelbaum (personal communication) told me that her source for this report was Itzik Aisenstadt, Shlomo's longtime friend.

88. For example, he gave his record as a present to Rikki (Gordon) Lewin and wrote a dedication on the cover: "To my dear Rikki. One of my true friends I met with my guitar. One I would never like to miss. One I'll remember for long. Fondly, Shlomo." My thanks to Rikki for sending me a copy of this inscription.

For many years now, Shlomo, as he has become known, has put Jewish youth at the center of his heart. With them he shares the joy of countless *niggunim* (melodies) – many of them his own – and the delight of words of Torah as well as a multitude of inspiring stories. From this enthusiastic and yet simple brotherhood of youth, has sprung the need for this record.

On the record it is proclaimed that Rabbi Shlomo Carlebach has started "an electrifying movement among the young people in the American Jewish communities":

His songs are an unusual expression of feelings reflecting varying as well as blended moods of Jewish religious life. The deep but yet beautifully simple joy of the Chassidic mystic moods in combination with the overwhelming love for the study of the Torah as lived in the world of the *yeshivot*, permeate all of his music.[89]

Several people from the St. Louis area were quoted on the jacket cover with rave reviews. One of them was Daryle Makovsky, at the time a senior in the University City High School. The first time she had met Shlomo was on September 6, 1958 at the Motzei Shabbat *Selichot* service at Rabbi Hartman's synagogue:

Shlomo came on stage, and began singing and playing his guitar. Most of the Orthodox teens were there and we were mesmerized. His music was so spiritual, and we all began the *Selichot* with an uplifted feeling. After one of his trips to New York many of us went to greet him at the airport and he flattered us with an impromptu concert where we all sang with him. I guess we were his first groupies. He in turn referred to us as his boys and girls.[90]

Two months later, Reb Shlomo asked Daryle to compose a few lines to add to the jacket cover of his new record. Daryle wrote the following laudatory appreciation:

The atmosphere he creates by his music, scintillating personality, and intensity of religious feeling is indescribable. I was extremely elevated and somehow felt close to God. He has a rare gift of instilling faith in those who have none and strengthening it in others.

---

89. The original text from the 1959 album is reproduced at CDUniverse.com, http://www.cduniverse.com/productinfo.asp?pid=7399942.

90. Daryle Makovsky Spero, interview July 6 and July 8, 2012.

Similarly, Rabbi Gerald Jacobs, from the Young Israel of St. Louis is quoted in praise of the captivating melodies that appeal to both the religionist and the skeptic:

> The ineffable has found articulation in the soul stirring *niggunim* of Shlomo Carlebach. Having composed the music, he proceeds to a rendition of artistry and emotion. The cold blooded skeptic and the convinced religionist will find his soul keeping time with the captivating melodies.

When Eric Offenbacher interviewed Shlomo upon the appearance of his first record album, he sought to understand "the magic" that within just two years, from 1957 to 1959, had catapulted Shlomo "to musical fame and passionate adoration among America's Jewish youth." He asked Shlomo to define his uniqueness and Shlomo replied: "Some call me a balladeer, some call me a revivalist – maybe I'm both." Offenbacher labeled him the "Jewish Minstrel," and compared Shlomo to "the wandering minstrel of old" and to the troubadours:

> Like the troubadours of the Middle Ages, a stringed instrument to accompany him, he sings of love, a different kind of love to be sure, but an equally intense one, springing from the stirrings of a Jewish soul and the pouring out of a Jewish heart.[91]

The second album, entitled *Sing My Heart*, בָּרְכִי נַפְשִׁי appeared in 1960 with twelve original compositions of Reb Shlomo. Jules Halfant again designed the cover and Kalman Kinnory was the sound engineer. On the back cover was a photo of Reb Shlomo at Town Hall taken by David Gahr, the pre-eminent photographer of American folk musicians of the 1960s.[92] The songs were arranged by Milt Okun who again directed the choir.[93] This continued the success of the first album with folk-like melodies in a straightforward, easy-to-sing stepwise design.

4.   MUSICAL CAREER TAKES OFF IN THE EARLY 1960S

With the popular reception of his first two LP records, Rabbi Carlebach's professional career began to prosper. Newspapers took note of his unique style of involving the audience. On the jacket cover of his second

---

91. Offenbacher, "Jewish Minstrel," 53.

92. Bruce Weber, "David Gahr, Photographer of Musicians, Dies at 85," *New York Times*, May 29, 2008, NYTimes.com, http://www.nytimes.com/2008/05/29/arts/music/29gahr.html.

93. The record was republished in 2004 by Sojourn Records, http://www.sojourn records.com/prod/artist/shlomo_carlebach.

LP record (1960) there is a quote from *The National Jewish Post and Opinion*: "The ability to provoke passionate participation is the clue to and the keynote of his success." Similarly, *The London Jewish Chronicle* emphasized Carlebach's genuineness, fervor, and Hasidic fire:

> Carlebach pours out his deep-rooted faith, his wholehearted affirmation of belief, in soul-summoning melodies of his own composition. In interchanging intermingling moods he captures the gladness, the sadness, the warmth and the wonder, the frenzy, the fire of Chassidic life – as he himself has experienced it.

The esteemed *New York Times* music critic, Robert Shelton, wrote a favorable review:

> A great deal of enchanting melody with a distinctive Chassidic joy and lilt. Enthusiastic and affectionate response from the audience. He has the people with him and he can ask for no more.[94]

On Purim, March 13, 1960, Shlomo was hosted by Nechemia Polen at his home in Gary, Indiana.[95] Around that time in West Lafayette, Indiana, Rabbi Gerald (Gedaliah) Engel, the Hillel director at Purdue University hosted Shlomo at the Hillel Foundation's dining room. The college newspaper publicized a photo with the title of "The *Swinging* Rabbi" and a student who had met Shlomo at a 1959 summer religious youth conclave wrote in the Hillel bulletin, "Man, he's cool." Curious students were soon dancing in "a jam-session, Hassidic style." The party continued in Rabbi Engel's house where Shlomo played piano and spoke "reaching out gently for their Jewish souls." R. Engel concluded:

> Shlomo, who travels the length and breadth of the country to awaken youth, believes he can help young people hear the voice of their Maker through the medium of song.[96]

---

94. Robert Shelton (1926–1995), whose birth name was Shapiro, was the son of Russian Jewish immigrants. As a staffer for *The New York Times* during the years 1958–1968, he chronicled the 1960s folk music boom. His reviews when positive helped launch musical careers such as that of Bob Dylan. See Jon Parles, "Robert Shelton, 69, Music Critic Who Chronicled 60s Folk Boom," *New York Times*, Dec. 15, 1995.

95. A photo labeled "Purim 1960" shows Reb Shlomo in a Yeshivishe black jacket and hat at the Polen home in Gary, Indiana together with the three Polen children, Cheryl, Ranan, and Lauri. It appears in the *L'Koved Reb Shlomo Remembrance Journal* produced by The Carlebach Shul, Nov. 1995.

96. Gerald Engel, "The Singing Rabbi," *Congress Bi-Weekly*, July 25, 1960, 9–11.

Shlomo also became popular in some religious Day Schools. Here is one recollection from Prospect Park in Brooklyn:

> In the 1960s, Prospect Park Day School embarked upon ambitious and extensive outreach efforts to the nonreligious Brooklyn Jewish community. One of the ways the principal attempted to open our hearts and kindle our spirits was by introducing us to the music and stories of Rabbi Shlomo Carlebach. Shlomo Carlebach was in fact a ubiquitous and major presence at Prospect Park Day School; he constantly performed at school assemblies, *chagigas* (parties), and other events. He made a real impression upon us, and helped infuse our lives with religious fervor.[97]

Sometimes Reb Shlomo developed a close friendship with a local resident who then would host him on a regular basis. This is exemplified with Rabbi Eugene Labovitz who in 1948–1949 had studied with Shlomo in the Lakewood Yeshiva. In the winter of 1960, when Reb Shlomo was invited to the Miami Hebrew Academy, Eugene and his wife Annette attended the concert. That was the beginning of a unique friendship. The Labovitz home in Miami Beach became a teaching center for Reb Shlomo whenever he would visit Florida.[98] Eugene and Annette would often travel to San Francisco to be with Shlomo at the HLP when he was there for Shabbat. Yisroel Finman, a regular at the second HLP, explained the importance of these visits:

> The Labovitzes were a tremendous *chizuk* to the House of Love and Prayer. Back in the sixties and seventies almost nobody in any area of mainstream Judaism wanted anything to do with Shlomo or his crazy hippies. Gene and Annette were regulars when Shlomo came for his periodic visits.[99]

Shlomo was creating a revolutionary experience for high school age students. In December 1960, Shlomo led the singing and dancing at a Yeshiva University Seminar for 250 high school students in Ellenville, Ulster County, at the eastern base of the Catskill Mountains, 90 miles northwest of New York City. Steve Weinberg wrote about his memories:

---

97. Mandelbaum, *Holy Brother*, 108–109.

98. Eugene Labovitz was Rabbi at Congregation Ner Tamid in Miami Beach, Florida from 1958. He passed away recently on May 23, 2012. My thanks to Dr. Annette Labovitz for this information. For a recording of Shlomo at the Labovitz home singing *Niggun Neshama* in the early 1970s, see http://www.youtube.com/watch?v=5RwPph8WOas&feature=plcp.

99. Posting by Yisroel Finman on June 16, 2012 in the Shlomo Carlebach Google groups.

> Was this the guy who'd played for the Scranton Hebrew Day School earlier that winter and drove everyone wild?? The one they called the Jewish Elvis Presley!!?? . . . . Reb Shlomo kept telling me that my song and my dance was one with God. . . . We sang and we danced, *"Borchi Nafshi"* . . . I felt I was approaching some kind of ecstasy. The same *niggun* sung hypnotically over and over and over again . . . The dance spun round with all the energy we could muster, each dancer being energized at each turn with a fiery glance from Reb Shlomo's indescribable eyes and a broad smile from Reb Shlomo's gleeful, nodding face. It was as if he were pushing us round and round on a playground wheel with all the energy of his faith in God.[100]

Reb Shlomo also traveled outside of New York. In 1960, he came to Beth Yehuda, a religious Day School in Detroit, Michigan.[101] Two of his former classmates from Mesivta Torah Vodaas, Rabbi A.A. Freedman and Rabbi Sholom Goldstein,[102] were directing Beth Yehuda first as vice principals, and later as principals of the boys' and girls' schools respectively. Shlomo played his guitar and sang at the Mogen Avrom boys' building in the Beth Yehuda school. Rabbi Harry Maryles, who was in the eighth grade at the time, recalls his experience:

> I will never forget it. There he was on the *duchan* platform where the priestly blessing is given, singing the new songs on his first album. Neither he, nor I, nor anyone else in the room knew it at the time as he was yet still quite unknown, but he was about to change the face of Jewish music forever.[103]

The religious youth movements also invited Reb Shlomo. Around 1960, Shlomo led a *kumzitz* of the Zionist youth group Mizrachi Hatzair, in Kew Gardens, Queens, New York. The program was organized by Stanley Fisher (presently from Great Neck, New York).[104]

---

100. Steve Weinberg, communication in *What's Next?* (magazine edited and published by Rebecca Diamond Mallinger and Lev Mallinger [Bec N Lev] in Ojai, California), Winter/Spring 1995, 18.

101. DetroitYeshiva.org, http://www.detroityeshiva.org/Page.asp?ID=eed9ec58bb d7c9a0fbbd123e.

102. They had been sent by Rabbi Shrage Feivel Mendlowitz from Torah VoDaas to Detroit in 1944 and 1946 respectively. See Sidney M. Bokosky, *Harmony and Dissonance: Voices of Jewish Identity in Detroit, 1914–1967* (Detroit: 1991), 402.

103. My thanks to Rabbi Maryles for providing me information beyond what he wrote in his blog, HaEmtza.Blogspot.co.il, http://haemtza.blogspot.co.il/2006/06/ rabbi-shlomo-carlebach_11.html.

104. Fay Bluime, "He Brought Me Home," *Kol Chevra*, vol. 7, 2000, 66–68.

In 1960, Shlomo was invited to the national convention of NCSY (National Conference of Synagogue Youth) at the Monsey Park Hotel in Monsey, New York. Sixteen-year old Ilene Freedman from Charleston, West Virginia "felt such love and warmth at that convention . . . sitting on the floor, listening to Shlomo Carlebach, and participating in the NCSY Shabbat activities, made me want to be Shomer Shabbat."[105] Fourteen-year old Elchonon Oberstein came from Montgomery, Alabama, a place where "Yiddishkeit was not a popular commodity and Orthodoxy was considered passé." Oberstein described how he was so inspired by Reb Shlomo that he decided to attend Yeshiva University High School in New York.

> I was uplifted, inspired, and invigorated by his *davening* and his singing over the weekend. The sincerity, the passion, and the spirituality were new and enticing. . . . It was this experience that spurred me to go to yeshiva.[106]

Reb Shlomo was also invited to sing in private homes. At the end of December 1960, 27-year old Michael Kaufman hired Shlomo for $100 to be the guest performer at a *Hanukat Habayit* house dedication in Far Rockaway, New York. After the concert, Shlomo stayed until the wee hours of the morning reminiscing about Torah Vodaas (where Michael had also attended), Chasidic music, and what to do about the Jewish youth. Reflecting back today, Michael recalls that Shlomo's ideas "were already percolating" but he had not yet designed his grand vision.[107]

In the fall of 1961, Shlomo was invited to a Manhattan apartment to help launch the Yavneh student organization at City College. About thirty or forty college students sat on the living room floor of the home of 19-year old Tzilia Meyers (later Sacharow) while Reb Shlomo led the singing with his guitar.[108]

Shlomo reached a milestone in his career on October 22, 1961 when he appeared in the prestigious Town Hall at 123 West 43rd St. in Manhattan.

---

105. "Hundreds Register for First National North American NCSY Alumni Reunion," Jan. 17, 2006, OU.org, http://www.ou.org/general_article/hundreds_reg ister_for_first_national_north_american_ncsy_alumni_reunion.

106. Rabbi Elchonon Oberstein, "Early Days in Montgomery," *Where What When: Baltimore's Jewish Family Magazine*, March 2008, http://www.wherewhatwhen .com/read_articles.asp?id=435. Cf. Rabbi Leonard Oberstein, "My First Encounter with Orthodoxy – Shlomo Carlebach and NCSY," circa 1960, http://www.beyondbt .com, *Beyond Teshuva*, Aug. 12, 2009.

107. Michael Kaufman, personal interview, Sept. 21, 2011.

108. Personal interview with Tzilia Sacharow on June 2, 2012. Tzilia, who was born on October 6, 1942, was later involved in the first Ruach Retreat in July 1982 (see below, Chapter 11).

Again, *New York Times* music critic, Robert Shelton, wrote a favorable review. He described how Shlomo is reviving Hasidic music in an American context and classified him as a "singer of spirituals" who uses the flamenco style:

> The merits of Mr. Carlebach's performance were in his warm, communicable manner rather than in his musical acumen. His light baritone voice is not a big one and it fell into strain and hoarseness. When he tried a few falsetto flights it broke. His guitar playing is competent, but seems to owe more to flamenco than anything directly connected with his biblical and prayer texts. But Mr. Carlebach is trying to revive in an American context the tradition of the Hasidim in which music was used as a medium to gain spiritual release. . . . He may be unorthodox in his orthodoxy, but he was helping to keep the vanishing tradition of Hasidic song alive.[109]

The Town Hall performance provided Shlomo with an opportunity to prove to his parents that his decision to sing was correct. Shlomo's father had expressed his deep disappointment with Shlomo's favoring musical outreach over a standard rabbinical vocation. But then when Shlomo paused in Town Hall to publicly thank his father for coming to hear him, there was a new appreciation for Shlomo and his maverick career.[110] A similar first-hand testimony is offered by Goldie Isaacs:

> The Orthodox world had been pressuring Shlomo's parents to dissuade their son from his musical career. It was therefore a special moment at Town Hall when Shlomo stopped in front of a packed audience in the middle of his singing to acknowledge his father. The audience was electrified at what was an impressive sight of reconciliation between father and son.[111]

Reb Shlomo's popularity began to spread. *The Galveston Daily News* reported in December 1961 that Rabbi Carlebach "has appeared in synagogues in nearly every major city in the United States and Canada." The paper announced that Carlebach would be singing in Galveston, Texas on December 21, 1961 in the "first of the season's cultural programs sponsored by the Galveston Jewish Welfare Association." Interestingly

---

109. Robert Shelton, "Rabbi Carlebach Sings Spirituals," *New York Times*, Oct. 24, 1961.

110. Rabbi Meyer Leifer, personal interview, Dec. 17, 2012. Rabbi Leifer had heard directly from Shlomo's father about his initial disappointment.

111. Goldie Isaacs, interview, Dec. 20, 2012.

enough, the paper noted that Carlebach's repertoire included "a wide variety of songs ranging from Negro spirituals to the popular song *When Irish Eyes Are Smiling*."[112]

On Sunday, April 1, 1962, Shlomo appeared at the Yolanda Benson Memorial Concert at the Congregation B'nai Jeshurun auditorium in Manhattan.[113] Cantor Sherwood Goffin opened for Shlomo at this concert, and the two singers became good friends, sharing the stage together many times over the years.[114]

Sometimes, Reb Shlomo's appearances were a surprise. In the summer of 1962, Rabbi Meyer Fenster was running a B'nai B'rith summer program for 150 campers when Reb Shlomo showed up at the gate "to play for the kids here." After some hesitation about inviting a "hippie" with a guitar, R. Fenster arranged a performance, and the "program was electrifying," "a huge success – far beyond any expectation."[115]

Reb Shlomo was becoming known as a popular folk singer. Shlomo was later to exclaim to his interviewer that in 1962 he had performed in front of 30,000 people in Madison Square Garden.[116] But more often, he was invited by local Jewish communities. Thus for example, on October 31, 1962, *The Bridgeport Post* in Connecticut announced: "B'nai B'rith to Hear Folk Singer Tonight. Rabbi Shlomo Carlebach, chasidic folk singer, will inaugurate the 1962–63 season of the Jewish musical and cultural program."[117]

In the fall of 1962, Yisrael Winkelman (Medad)[118] was a 15-year old student at Yeshivas Chofetz Chaim Queens, a major Orthodox yeshiva located in Kew Gardens Hills, New York, when he first met Shlomo at a performance in the Forest Hills Jewish Center in Queens, New York. The Carlebach music was a big hit at Yisrael's high school. Among Yisrael's classmates were David Nulman, Baruch Chait, and Label Scharfman. They went on to become part of The Rabbis' Sons, a music group influenced by Reb Shlomo[119] which began producing albums in 1967, thus

---

112. *Galveston Daily News*, Dec. 17, 1961, 17. This popular and optimistic song ends with the line "Let us smile each chance we get."

113. The program was organized by Dr. Abraham Stern, director of the Yeshiva University Youth Bureau's YUSCY (Yeshiva University Synagogue Council Youth).

114. My thanks to Sherwood Goffin for this information. See below, Chapter 9, for their participation together at the rallies for Soviet Jewry.

115. Myron Fenster, *Up From the Straits: A Memoir*, 2011, 141–143.

116. Interview with Alon Teeger, Sept. 1992, p. 19.

117. NewsPaperArchive.com, http://newspaperarchive.com.

118. While in the Betar Youth movement in 1965, Yisrael Winkelman used the name Medad, and after going on aliyah in 1970, he officially Hebraized his name to Medad in 1973. Medad and his family moved to Shiloh in 1981.

119. The final album of The Rabbis' Sons was released in 1974 under the name

popularizing the new Hasidic music.[120] Yisrael explains why he and his friends were so impressed by Shlomo:

> Reb Shlomo's appearances were a natural development that strengthened our new identity. He fit in with the zeitgeist and permitted us an expression of soul that was not only "in" but also so completely Jewish. His kippah, beard, and Hebrew, together with his use of Chassidic and Kabbalistic terminology, were a statement of cultural and ethnic pride which was an amazing combination for us, whether at SSSJ demonstrations or on subway cars late at night when we sang Carlebach tunes and Israeli songs.[121]

On Sunday, December 22, 1962, Reb Shlomo gave a concert in The Garden Jewish Center, a synagogue in Flushing, New York. Ten songs were from the liturgy and two were folksongs ("Kumbaya" in English and "*Gevaldishe Bruder*" in Yiddish). This was his first recording to be bootlegged.[122] It was made into a record entitled *Rabbi Shlomo Carlebach Sings* and distributed a few years later by a company named Galton, who also added two songs from Shlomo's "single" released by Shlomo in 1966 entitled "*Chai*" and "*Ein KeEloheinu.*" This is an important "single" – the song "*Chai*" is better known as "*Am Yisrael Chai.*" On the "single," Shlomo is accompanied by an orchestra and choir arranged and conducted by Bob De Cormier.

Shlomo did not lodge a legal complaint about the bootlegging. Instead, he reportedly joked that only great singers such as the Beatles and Bob Dylan have their recordings pirated.[123] In the background, one can hear the spontaneous accompaniment that was Shlomo's hallmark. The congregation claps enthusiastically even after the music stops.

In mid-December 1963, Reb Shlomo played at a Hanukkah party

Baruch Chait and Old Friends. It included two tunes written by Shlomo – "*Od yishoma*" and "*Hasheveynu.*"

120. See below, Chapter 11 that Baruch Chait founded the record company Emes which in 1975 produced the album *Shlomo Carlebach and The Children of Jewish Song Sing Ani Maamin* with the participation of the Dave Nulman Orchestra.

121. Personal communication from Yisrael Medad, March 16, 2013.

122. The recording was later reproduced in 2002 by Neshama Carlebach and David Morgan with Sojourn Records, SojournRecords.com, http://www.sojournrecords.com/prod/artist/shlomo_carlebach.

123. My thanks to Howie Kahn for pointing this out. A bootleg is a recording of a performance not released officially by the artist. Sometimes, this is encouraged, as for example, The Grateful Dead encourages fans to bootleg, thus stimulating a dedicated following. In the case of Shlomo, he simply did not pay much attention to financial details, besides which his magnanimous nature allowed others to profit from his songs.

arranged by Howard Rothman[124] in the Brooklyn Army Terminal. Non-Jewish high ranking officers were sitting in the front row and in a short time they were also clapping along with Shlomo.[125] Similarly, in 1964, Rabbi Dov Peretz Elkins, chaplain at Ft. Gordon, Georgia, invited Shlomo to do a gig for some 250 Jewish GIs from New York City:

> He came and rocked their world. These were 18-year olds who hadn't been in a *shul* since age 13, and were turned on in a glorious and unforgettable way. That was my formal introduction to Shlomo . . . For 30 years since, I was flattered to be called by him, "the holy Rabbi Elkins." Even though I knew every one of his other holy rabbi friends were bestowed with the same title, it meant no less to me to have this priceless gift from my beloved holy friend.[126]

By 1964, Reb Shlomo had developed a substantial following around the world. Pinchas Peli, who interviewed him in March 1964, noted that Shlomo had a significant following of youthful Hasidim and was successfully creating a new and innovative form of Hasidut. Peli noted however that Shlomo's critics had labeled him as "The Jewish Elvis Presley" or "The Haredi Rock and Roll King," and some even threatened him with excommunication.[127]

By the early 1960s, although it was clear that Shlomo had a unique musical career, there was a major organizational problem. Shlomo was quick to help anyone in need and ready to perform wherever asked. This diffused his time and energy. One of Shlomo's early fans was Michael H. Steinhardt.[128] At age 19, he was "stirred and enthralled by the joy of Rabbi Carlebach's singing."[129] In 1963–1964, Michael set up a company called

---

124. Howard Rothman, Professor Emeritus at the University of Florida, writes a column called "The Music Maven" for the Jewish Council of North Central Florida's newspaper, *The Chronicle*. At the time, he was 25 years old and serving as a chaplain's assistant at Fort Hamilton, Brooklyn. He had first heard Shlomo in the late 1950s at the Pioneer Hotel and in Greenwich Village.

125. Howard Rothman, "A Different Carlebach," *The Chronicle*, Sept. 2007, 10, JCNCF.org, www.jcncf.org/ChronicleSept07.pdf.

126. Rabbi Dov Peretz Elkins, communication in *What's Next*, Winter/Spring 1995, 24.

127. [339] See the article by Pinchas Hacohen Peli (under the pen name B. Pinhas) in the Israeli weekly magazine *Panim El Panim*, March 28, 1964.

128. Steinhardt, born in 1940, was a financial whizboy, having graduated the Wharton School of the University of Pennsylvania at the age of 19. He eventually established a highly successful hedge fund company, Steinhardt Partners L.P. See Michael H. Steinhardt, *No Bull: My Life In and Out of the Markets* (New York: 2001).

129. Michael H. Steinhardt, "Universal Pleasures of Jewish Joy," *Contact: The Journal of Jewish Life Network*, Winter 2001, 304.

The Shabbos Express to help Shlomo channel his talents in a professional business-like manner and handle the financial aspects of booking events. However, Shlomo's new managers were unable to dictate new habits.[130] Shlomo continued to travel around the globe in magnanimous style but in disregard of conventional time and business.

5.   EUROPE IN THE EARLY 1960S

In 1959 on his first trip to Israel, Shlomo stopped off in Switzerland and visted his uncle's family living in Montreux. Mordechai Cohen was a child then, but he remembers how his father phoned the head of the nearby yeshiva, Etz Chayyim, and many young men soon filled their living room singing with Reb Shlomo late into the night.[131]

By 1960, Shlomo was receiving invitations throughout Europe. He traveled to Copenhagen, Denmark in August 1960, and to Antwerp, Belgium in September 1960.[132] Regine Sauerman and Lea Ressler were two of the participants in the performance in Antwerp.[133] They began spreading the word about the "singing Rabbi from America" and suggested to Jacques Bronstein in Paris that he invite Reb Shlomo. Bronstein was living at Toit Familial, the Jewish student house on 9 rue Guy Patin. He hosted Shlomo there in February, 1961, and along with ninety students, most of whom had come to Paris in the waves of immigration from Algeria, Morocco, and Tunisia. About 80 percent were not religious. A year later, Bronstein and his friends organized Reb Shlomo's first public concert in Paris, at the Bobino Music Hall in front of about 2,000 people.[134]

In July 1961, Shlomo was back in England. In London, he was invited to Yesodey Hatorah Secondary School for Girls in Stamford Hill. In Gateshead, he performed for religious *haredi* audiences connected with the Gateshead Yeshiva.[135] Shlomo also visited Manchester. Meir Persoff, at the time 19 years old, joined Shlomo on the train ride from Manchester to London, and interviewed him for *The London Jewish Chronicle*. Persoff described how teenagers at Stoke Newington Town Hall, an east London music venue, had joined Shlomo dancing "in an ecstasy of emotion." He noted that Shlomo's best audiences "are invariably teenagers, dissatisfied

---

130. Personal interview with Michael Steinhardt, Aug. 30, 2012.

131. Orna Cohen, "Holy Cousin, An Interview with Rabbi Mordechai Cohen," *Kol Chevra*, vol. 7, 2000, 75–76.

132. Regine Sauerman-Franco, personal correspondence, June 19, 2011.

133. Lea Ressler, personal correspondence, Oct. 5, 2012.

134. For a series of photos from this event and more explanations, see Natan Ophir, "The Story Behind the Photos," *Kol Chevra*, vol. 17, 2011, 211.

135. My thanks to Mordechai Beck for this information, Feb. 15, 2013.

with life, and striving to fill a vast vacuum. They are looking 'for something real.'" Persoff depicted Shlomo's impact on the teenagers with "hours of music, sometimes joyous, sometimes haunting."[136]

Gabriel A. Sivan was in his late 20s when he helped organize Shlomo's concert in the summer of 1961 in the Redbridge district of Essex, northeast of London. He quickly became an avid fan of the Carlebach music. Later he recalled how he enthusiastically sang Shlomo's tunes of hope and faith such as "*Yisrael Betach beHashem*," and they inspired him when he served as an Israeli soldier during the Yom Kippur War.[137]

In August 1961, when Shlomo visited Israel, he told newspaper reporter Yaakov Edelstein about his successful performances throughout Europe – in Belgium, Holland, England, and France (Paris, Strasbourg, and Marseilles).[138]

In 1964, Reb Shlomo was again invited by Bronstein and friends to perform in Paris at the annual benefit concert organized to fund the Toit Familial programming. The major supporter was French banker, Baron Alain de Rothschild, at the time age 54. Reb Shlomo tells the story of how "this concert raised $100,000 to support the kosher kitchen that offered daily meals for students who had come from Algeria and Morocco who *mamash* had nothing to eat." At the concert, R. Shlomo introduced a joyful optimistic song that he had invented on the plane coming over from New York. On the flight, "in the middle of the night I woke up and this melody just hit me." I put it on tape. The song's message was to go out in joy and come in with peace (Isaiah 55:12).

Shlomo describes how Baron Rothschild was sitting in the first row, and Shlomo asked him to bring some joy to all by joining him on stage and dancing. When Rothschild jumped on stage, the audience enthusiastically danced so much that they went out on the street. Shlomo reports how the police stopped traffic: "I would say that about 2,000 people were dancing right in the square, in the streets. One of the great nights in my life."[139]

Mordechai Beck was in art school in London in the early 1960s when

---

136. Meir Persoff, "Bible with a Beat," *The London Jewish Chronicle*, July 7, 1961. The article is reproduced in Brandwein, *Reb Shlomele*, 231.

137. In 1997, Sivan translated M. Brandwein's book on Reb Shlomo into English. See Gabriel A. Sivan, "Translator's Forward," in Brandwein, *Reb Shlomele*, 17–18.

138. Edelstein, "The Dancing Rabbi."

139. This recording of Reb Shlomo's explanation has been played often on Reb Shlomo Carlebach Radio, http://tunein.com/tuner/?stationId=95906& and on toker.fm. The story is corroborated by Dr. Jacques Bronstein who added that Baron Rothschild was the president of numerous institutions and a very generous benefactor – personal correspondence, July 3, 2011.

Reb Shlomo in Paris, February 1961   Courtesy of Dr. Jacques Bronstein

he first became enchanted with Reb Shlomo's music. Upon reading Gabriel Sivan's enthusiastic description in *The London Jewish Chronicle* about Reb Shlomo's 1960 album, *Sing My Heart,* he set out to purchase the record, eventually finding it in a London store. In the summer of 1964, Beck went to hear Shlomo sing in the Ilford United Synagogue in London and then followed him to a coffee-bar called "The Hole in the Wall":

> Shlomo steered his way down to that basement of this coffee-bar and through the waiting crowd like he was parting the Red Sea. There was something radiant about him that only increased as he began to strum his guitar and sing. By the end of the evening, everyone in the room (and it was jam-packed) was totally entranced. Reb Shlomo was such an antidote to all the Jewish experiences I had undergone in my years of searching. He was warm and friendly, easy and accessible. It was so different from the hard-edged Orthodox Jews of that time, and worlds away from the stiff upper lipped Anglo-Jews that frequented the so-called Orthodox synagogues.[140]

In sum, in the early 1960s, Reb Shlomo was becoming known in major Jewish communities around the world. His reputation spread as an enthusiastic rabbi who could awaken joy and hope.

---

140. Mordechai Beck, personal interview, Feb. 14, 2013.

6.   NEXT FOUR LP RECORDS, 1963–1967

Reb Shlomo's third LP, *At the Village Gate*, was released in March 1963 by Vanguard, a company founded in 1950 by Seymour and Maynard Solomon.[141] This was the *first time* that a religious Jewish artist had his album released by a major American record company and the International Music-Record Newsweekly, *Billboard*, took note of this unusual achievement.[142] Jules Halfant, the designer for Vanguard, played a significant role in designing the public image of Shlomo's early musical career.

This record was based on a live performance at The Village Gate, a nightclub in the heart of Greenwich Village where prominent jazz artists and comedians were hosted. The Gate was founded by Art D'Lugoff in 1958, who, although having grown up in a religious family in Brooklyn, was a self proclaimed "left wing atheist."[143] Nonetheless, he took a liking to Shlomo and provided him the venue to promote a joyous Judaism in The Village. In the year 1963 alone, D'Lugoff is said to have hosted Shlomo half a dozen times.[144]

Shlomo's performances were radically different from the standard jazz and comedy prevalent in the Village. No one else there sang Hebrew songs, and certainly not from the Jewish liturgy. The song *"Pitchu Li,"* translated as "Open the Gates of Righteousness" (Psalms 118:9), was chosen as the title. Shlomo, the former Chabad emissary, adapts to The Village Gate by rephrasing its message in universalistic religious-moralistic terms. He

---

141. VanguardRecords.com, http://www.vanguardrecords.com; http://www.van guardrecords.com/about.html; http://www.jazzdiscography.com/Labels/vanguard .htm; http://www.facebook.com/VanguardRecords?sk=info.

142. *Billboard* announced in Sept. 22, 1962, 50, that Vanguard had contracted Rabbi Shlomo Carlebach "who has received much attention for his performances of Hassidic and Hebrew repertory." Then on March 16, 1963, 32, *Billboard* noted: "Something different in the way of a folk album, this could readily capture public imagination." In particular, *Billboard* was impressed by the "artist's dynamic performances which get the audience stirred into active singing, clapping or humming with him."

143. He was born as Arthur Joshua Dlugoff in Harlem on Aug. 2, 1924 and he died Nov. 4, 2009. His father, Raphael, had been a yeshiva student in Slonim, Russia before immigrating to Brooklyn where he ran a vacuum cleaner and sewing-machine repair shop. Arthur's mother, Rachel Mandelbaum, was from Palestine and a relative of Rabbi Kook, first Chief Rabbi of Palestine. Art received a religious education in the Flatbush Yeshivah elementary school. For an hour-long interview with Art D'Lugoff by Harold Hudson Channer on Feb. 16, 1998, see WN.com, http://wn.com/The_Village_Gate.

144. Mandelbaum, *Holy Brother*, xxxii.

redesigns a parable of entry to Heavenly Gates that was well-known in the American-Christian ethic:

> While on the way to my concert at the Village Gate, I composed the melody *Pischu li Shaarei Zedek*, Open the Gates of Righteousness (Psalms 118:9). It occurred to me that at one time or another all of us have stood at the Heavenly Gates pleading for admission. When they did not open instantly many of us turned away in anger or despair, not realizing that we must be prepared to knock for a lifetime. This, my third record, is an invitation to young people who know that life without Him is empty. Let us with song and prayer and hearts of fire storm the Gates of Righteousness together. Meet you at the Gates.

Reb Shlomo's fourth record, *In the Palace of the King, Mikdash Melekh*, was also released by Vanguard Records. The cover photo was again taken by David Gahr. This record, released in 1965, is unique in the discography of Reb Shlomo because of the collaboration of Benedict Silberman, one of the most famous Jewish conductors at the time. Silberman was born in Latvia and became an eminent orchestral leader in pre-war Germany. He hid in Holland during World War II, and after the war became known as an outstanding orchestral director in Holland. Silberman arranged the best-selling Capitol album *Jewish Music (Melodies Beloved the World Over)*.

Reb Shlomo traveled especially to Europe to perform together with Silberman's choir and orchestra.[145] On the record cover, Reb Shlomo wrote a dedication to Silberman:

> Thank you for putting so much heart into my songs. Everyone who will hear this beautiful music will love you as much as I do.[146]

In the "liner notes" for this record, Sophia Adler framed Reb Shlomo's message in the historical setting of Hasidism, neo-Hasidism, Existentialism, and the Holocaust. Adler began by describing the sadness, perplexity, and yearning created in the aftermath of the atomic bomb, "the final mushroom":

> The malaise we all sense. We stand in a searing territory. The contemporary arts sing us the dirge and interpret for us our

---

145. For a sampling of the tunes on this record, see CDUniverse.com, http://www.cduniverse.com/productinfo.asp?pid=1420947.

146. This is the quote from the original jacket cover of the record *In the Palace of the King* as produced by Vanguard Records. The Israeli Hed Arzi production added "He died in 1964." However, that is a mistake, as Silberman died in 1971.

self-destructive soul sickness. In the shadow of the final mushroom we stand atrophying and baffled. Yet we all have a terrible
need for a path towards life and love within our civilization.

Adler then surveyed the visionary revival and musical expressiveness
created by the Baal Shem Tov in founding Hasidism:

> One of those radiant few, who have illumined man's hope, Israel
> Baal Shem Tov, founder of Hassidism, some two hundred years
> ago, burst upon the decaying European ghetto with a fiery voice
> of affirmation – a renewed vision of the dynamic soul of man. In
> the tradition of the Biblical poet David (a skillful player on the
> harp who danced before the Lord with all his might), Israel Baal
> Shem Tov re-awakened Jewish expressiveness in music and dance.
> Like the Negro tunes, Hassidic songs emerged from the deepest
> currents of longing within the soul of a despised minority. Built
> of subtly related but simple elements, sometimes almost an entire
> song around one note or a few words circularly repeated and re-
> examined till invested with a hypnotic intensity. Often a melody
> sung without real words, just tender and intimate little syllables
> that lifted its participants to a mystic fervor.

Adler emphasized the importance for modern Western culture of the ex-
istentialistic Hasidic revival of Martin Buber's stories and Marc Chagall's
paintings:

> Western culture is sensing the impact of the rich Hassidic heri-
> tage. Its shafts of insight are imbedded in the tales and anecdotes
> told by the Hassidim, and we witness their circulation among the
> seekers and thinkers of our time, in translations brought to the
> Western World by the philosopher Martin Buber. In painting,
> Marc Chagall transmuted into fervent colour and soaring me-
> lodic line the essence of his Hassidic forbears for the edification
> of Western culture.

All this builds up to Adler's placing the music of Shlomo in the tradition
of the Baal Shem Tov, as a folk singer speaking from the fibers of his own
being, offering a Hasidic spark of Divine fire "to melt estrangement and
soul weariness":

> Now a vibrant new Jewish personality has emerged to express
> the Hassidic heritage in the context of our times. Rabbi Shlomo
> Carlebach directly descended through a noteworthy rabbinic
> line of scholars seeks to make manifest the original message of

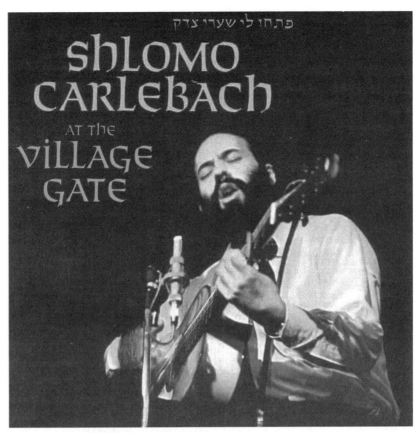

Album cover, At the Village Gate

Hassidism. Shlomo is an Orthodox rabbi, a man of God – but he is also a folk singer in the truest sense of the word. A bard who utters from the fibers of his own being, music and words that speak with the world around him. Shlomo is a link in our time to the heroic figure of the Baal Shem Tov. In his presence one may experience that glow of warmth and courage, the Hassidic spark of divine fire that melt estrangement and soul weariness.

Finally, Adler concluded by highlighting Shlomo's message for "today's youth" who are searching for meaning:

Young people gravitate toward Shlomo. Today's youth, pondering the irrevocable realities of the Brave New World it shortly must inherit, is listening for messages of meaning. In a climate of search and longing, music becomes exploration.

Album cover, Wake Up World

Essentially, Adler has summed up the neo-Hasidic innovation of Reb Shlomo and its attraction for the younger generation.

The fifth album, *Wake up World*, in 1965 was produced again by Shlomo's own record company, Zimrani Records. Similar to the previous records, the design was by Jules Halfant and the photo by David Gahr. As in the first two records, Milton Okun conducted the orchestra and arranged the music.[147] On the introductory jacket cover, Rachel Anne Rabinowicz wrote poetically about the inspirational power of this soul music:

> These are *neshama niggunim* of twilight and yearning, passion-fraught prayers that set the soul vibrating softly, rejoicings that rise in curling crescendo to the skies, and chords that kindle candles in the dark.

Reb Shlomo wrote a moving dedication on the jacket cover:

> This, my fifth record, is dedicated to all those asleep desperately trying to wake up – to all those crying in their sleep with no one to dry their tears. To those who woke up only to find a dark disappointing world, with no one to give them a little light. To those who found only a sleeping religion, searching frantically for a living G-d – a living Torah. To all those lost on the way – to those who are so far, and yet so unbelievably near. To you.

In 1967, Reb Shlomo participated in a very unusual album where he sang compositions that were not his own but those of a rabbinical colleague. This was Rabbi Eliyahu Hartman, the brother of Rabbi Yecheskel Hartman who had been Shlomo's host and mentor at Congregation Tpheris Israel in 1958/9. Eliyahu actually had a similar background to Shlomo in that he

---

147. The record was reproduced in digital format by Sojourn Records co-founder Mark Ambrosino, after having been unavailable for many years, ShlomoCarlebachMusic.com, http://shlomocarlebachmusic.com/?cat=1.

created musical compositions for biblical verses without having any formal musical training. While he was studying at Mesivtah Chaim Berlin in Brooklyn, he composed "some thirty songs, with lyrics taken from the Bible." In August 1960, Eliyahu received his ordination at Chaim Berlin and joined his brother for three years as associate rabbi of Tpheris Israel in St. Louis.

Rabbi Eliyahu Hartman's vision of producing some of his original compositions as a record came to fruition in 1967 when he produced his album *Rebuild Thy House* בְּנֵה בֵיתְךָ. It had a cover picture of the Western Wall with inserted photos of Reb Shlomo and cantor Sholom Katz[148] who were invited to each sing five of Hartman's compositions.[149] The lyrics that Shlomo sang all reflected the post Six-Day War hope and enthusiasm: "*B'nai Vescho*, Rebuild Thy House" (from the *Musaf* festival liturgy); "*Tiveeanu*" from the *Musaf* of the High Holidays is translated as "Bring us unto the mountain of Thy Holiness and cause us to rejoice in Thy House of Worship"; a Yiddish song "*Zul Shoin Zein*,"[150] translated here as "May the redemption come soon," and two verses from Psalms, "*Gal Einai*, Open my eyes so that I may see wondrous things from Thy law" (Psalms 119:18),[151] and "*Hodu LaShem*" translated as "Give thanks unto the Lord for His Kindness endures forever" (Psalms 118:1).

The total of six records produced from 1959 until 1967 were instrumental in spreading the musical reputation of Reb Shlomo. The next stage of his career underwent a dramatic change resulting from his direct encounters with hippies in San Francisco.

---

148. Born in Romania, Sholom Katz studied music in Vienna and came to the United States as a Holocaust survivor.

149. For all this information, see the record jacket cover.

150. This song can be heard at www.youtube.com/user/RabiShlomo#p/u/34/KA NUp17wiRg.

151. For this song, see www.youtube.com/watch?v=vonst11IrlM&feature=share.

CHAPTER 4

Holy Hippies Discovered

1. BERKELEY FESTIVAL, JULY 4TH WEEKEND, 1966

Shlomo's unique musical outreach career in San Francisco can be said to have begun in December 1965 when Ian Grand brought Shlomo to a Hanukkah concert.[1] It was there that young college students such as Aryae Coopersmith discovered the "Singing Rabbi."[2] But, the watershed event in Reb Shlomo's career was on the July 4th weekend of 1966 at the 9th Annual Berkeley Folk Music Festival. His Greenwich Village friends, Pete Seeger and Bob Dylan, encouraged him to perform.[3] Rabbi Shlomo Carlebach was the *only performer* to publicly and proudly identify as Jewish.[4] Here he was facing youth who had rebelled not only against the establishment, but also against Judaism. With sardonic wit, Shlomo described his experience: "I walk around with a *yarmulke* and *tzizit*, and I could see who is a Jew – those who kept away from me."[5]

On Thursday, June 30, at the festival's beginning, every performer was given an opportunity to present one song as a free promo. When Reb Shlomo got on stage he announced:

---

1. At the time, Ian was the head of the Experimental College in San Francisco. He had known Shlomo from 1958–1959 in St. Louis when as a 15-year old, Ian would visit Shlomo in his apartment and listen to Shlomo compose new tunes. See Coopersmith, *Holy Beggars*, 306–308.

2. Ibid., 21–24.

3. Ari L. Goldman in his *New York Times* obituary on Carlebach, Oct. 22, 1994.

4. The bands included Jefferson Airplane, Greenbriar Boys, and Los Halcones de Salitrillo. The singers were Pete Seeger, Robert Pete Williams, Alice Stuart Thomas, Sam Hinton, Charley Marshall, Phil Ochs, and John Fahey. For the detailed program see http://berkeleyfolk.blogspot.co.il/2011/08/berkeley-folk-festival-1966.html.

5. http://www.youtube.com/watch?v=X_9w7eWC-0s.

Folks, this is my first time in Berkeley. I don't know if you believe in God, but for five minutes, I'm begging you, believe in God with me.[6]

Shlomo started singing *"Am Yisrael Chai – Od Avinu Chai,"* which he had composed the year before for the Soviet Jewry rally (see Chapter 9). The simple Hebrew words resonated in their vibrancy and exuberance. Soon the youth were dancing. Eighteen-year old Michael Carter was passing by and with his six-string banjo joined the guitar players, "the four of us playing together as if we had rehearsed for days":

> I saw we were all watching Shlomo's fingers for the chord changes, so this was a new song for us all. There were perhaps fifty people surrounding us . . . Over what seemed like an hour, we were joined by more and more people singing, dancing, nearly blocking the plaza . . . Essentially, I became a part of the group that followed Shlomo wherever possible.[7]

Reb Shlomo recalled with his characteristic irony: "The moment the Jewish kids saw that the non-Jewish kids were dancing, suddenly I was *kosher l'Pesach*."

Twenty-year old David Zeller was taking a summer course at Berkeley when he met Shlomo at the Festival. Shlomo invited him for breakfast at the Durant along with another eighty hippies and then took them along to his concert at the Berkeley Hillel House. When they arrived, there were no seats left, so Shlomo informed the audience that the hippies were his accompaniment on stage. The singing, dancing, and learning with Shlomo at the Festival reshaped the entire direction of Zeller's life,[8] and he became a leading disciple eventually receiving rabbinic ordination from Shlomo.

Friday morning, Shlomo went searching for Shabbat meal hospitality and was directed to Rabbi Saul Berman, rabbi of Congregation Beth Israel in Berkeley. He innocently requested: "Just in case I find a couple of lonely Jews who also want to taste Shabbos, would it be OK if I bring them with me?" R. Berman agreed. Then, at 10:00 AM, Friday morning, Shlomo led a workshop and extended an open invitation to join a Shabbat meal. As a result, "400 people showed up." R. Berman later recalled: "we pooled

---

6. http://www.youtube.com/watch?v=X_9w7eWC-0s.
7. Michael Carter, "Memories of Reb Shlomo," *Kol Chevra*, vol. 16, 2010, 101.
8. Zeller, *The Soul of the Story*, 12–16.

all our Shabbat food and chopped it into teeny little pieces." There wasn't much food but there "was lots of *ruach* and love."[9]

Shlomo's recollection was typically hyperbolic. He told one interviewer that 1,000 kids showed up.[10] To another interviewer, Shlomo described how over 2,000 kids came.[11] He also described the anguished president of the local synagogue who bitterly complained about the Friday night hippie occupation.[12]

On Sunday, July 3, 1966, at 8:00 PM, Shlomo appeared on stage in between Jefferson Airplane, Alice Stuart Thomas, and The Gypsies.[13] Then on July 4 at 10:00 AM, Shlomo led a workshop entitled Jewish Folk Music. This was followed by the Festival's main event, the Jubilee Concert, where Shlomo appeared alongside the Festival's stars such as Pete Seeger, Phil Ochs and many others. R. Shlomo reflected afterwards upon his revelatory discovery. His music, teachings and stories could reach thousands of young spiritual seekers immersed in the 1960s culture of "sex, drugs, and rock and roll" and connect them with their true and genuine soul searching:

> In 1966, the greatest thing happened to me. I was invited to the Berkeley Folk Festival. There I saw all these thousands of young people who the world condemned as being dope addicts and I realized that they were yearning for something holy, and their souls were so pure, awesome![14]

For Reb Shlomo, this was a major breakthrough in a revolutionary type of outreach – appealing to a hippie generation, many who were alienated from their Jewish heritage.

---

9. Rabbi Berman as quoted by Mandelbaum, *Holy Brother*, 3–4.

10. Paley, "His Gift."

11. Brenner, *Talkline*, segment 8:30.

12. Lerner, "Practical Wisdom," 54. Similarly, Shlomo tells Shmuel, his interviewer in Miami Beach in Feb. 1994 that the Synagogue Rabbi had complained that the hippies came barefoot. See *Insights 613*, Part II, segment 1:25–1:45. See http://www.youtube.com/watch?v=E6JOU6oG5Qk&NR=1.

13. The concert took place in the Pauley Ballroom, the second floor of the Student Union of the University of California, Berkeley. See BerkeleyFolk.blogspot.com, http://berkeleyfolk.blogspot.com/2010_02_01_archive.html.

14. Lerner, "Practical Wisdom," 54, and the Miami interview of *Insights 613*.

2.   LOVE, PSYCHEDELICS, AND HIPPIES IN SAN FRANCISCO,
       1967

San Francisco of 1966 was the American Mecca of the emerging counterculture for seekers of spirituality. You could hear a different spiritual
teacher every night of the week. Thousands of young Jews were attracted
to Meher Baba, Krishna Consciousness, and Sufi Sam. Others found their
way to Suzuki Roshi from the San Francisco Zen Center or to Christian
evangelical groups such as the Children of God and Jews for Jesus. Into
this "Supermarket of Spirituality" entered Reb Shlomo and Reb Zalman,
blazing a trail of neo-Hasidic renewal. They became the Rebbes of the
Hippie Movement.

Reb Shlomo's career as "Rabbi of the hippies" is best understood
against the backdrop of the "turbulent '60s" when the first wave of baby
boomers were reaching college age, bringing with them a social tumult
that shook up American society. Many were angry and disillusioned.
They were being drafted into the Vietnam War, so they led anti-draft
protests. They fought for justice, civil rights, and women's equality.

The number of youth who lived a counterculture lifestyle was estimated at its peak as reaching 300,000. They were predominantly white
upper-middle class educated youths aged 17 to 25. Hippies created their
own social groups, played and listened to psychedelic rock, and embraced
the sexual revolution. They used marijuana, LSD, psilocybin, peyote,
and other psychotropic substances, and explored alternative states of
consciousness.

The San Francisco Bay Area was the center of the psychedelic cyclone.
By June 1966, an estimated 15,000 hippies had moved into Haight-
Ashbury. Many arrived without jobs, had little money, slept on sidewalks
and panhandled for food or sold marijuana.[15]

Saturday, January 14, 1967, was the date set by an astrologer to celebrate the dawning of a New Age, the Age of Aquarius. About 25,000 or
30,000 hippies joined the Human Be-In, a festival of poetry and music at
the Polo Grounds in Golden Gate Park in San Francisco.[16] This so-called
Gathering of the Tribes accentuated the fact that "the hippie phenomenon was real."[17]

Shlomo was gradually beginning to understand and interact with the

---

15. John C. McWilliams, *The 1960s Cultural Revolution* (Westport, Connecticut:
2000), 69.

16. Terry H. Anderson, *The Movement and the Sixties: Protest in America from
Greensboro to Wounded Knee* (New York: 1996), 172. Anderson cites the number
30,000. McWilliams, *The 1960s*, 72 gives the number as 25,000.

17. Todd Gitlin, *The Sixties: Years of Hope, Days of Rage* (New York: 1993), 215.

hippies in San Francisco. One place where he was invited was the *I-Thou Coffeehouse* on Haight Street, owned and managed by Laura Ulewicz. At this coffeehouse, Laura organized poetry readings, art exhibits and folk concerts. It was in February 1967 that George Gorner and Pamela Klein heard Shlomo at the I-Thou Coffeehouse. Subsequently, they began joining Shlomo for Shabbat when he was in San Francisco. Two years later, they asked Shlomo to perform their marriage.[18] The personal story of George Gorner illustrates a fascinating aspect of what it meant for Shlomo to encounter these students. George Gorner was born in 1943:

> I never had any interest in Judaism until I met Shlomo. My dad was a Holocaust survivor. His whole family was slaughtered at Babi Yar in the Ukrainian capital Kiev along with another 33,000 Jews. He became an avowed atheist. He was a violinist. For him Jewishness was something to hide so as to avoid discrimination and persecution. There was nothing Jewish in our house.[19]

George studied for his graduate degree in literature (poetry) at San Francisco State University. He lived a mile away from the first HLP which he attended regularly, and was deeply influenced by Reb Shlomo. At Shlomo's request, George wrote the lyrics *Lord Get Me High* which became one of Shlomo's classics (see Chapter 6).

On April 24–25, 1967, Reb Shlomo led the Pesach Seder in Northern California. Aryae Coopersmith and Eliezer (Sonny) Garner drove up from San Francisco. Eliezer describes this unusual Seder:

> Everyone was sitting on the floor around a table with no legs and Shlomo was in the middle of the group, sitting on the floor . . . That night there was a full eclipse of the moon, which gave the evening an even more surrealistic mood.[20]

By the seemingly incongruous juxtaposition of an Orthodox rabbi leading a Pesach Seder while sitting on the floor in the middle of a group of youthful hippie seekers, Shlomo was not only creating a sense of genuine acceptance; he was also transmitting a message that Jewish lore and ritual need not contradict the hippie quest.

The 1967 Summer of Love was a defining moment of the Hippie Movement.[21] It was an attempt to embrace a new lifestyle with communal

---

18. Coopersmith, *Holy* Beggars, 206–207, and phone conversation with George Gorner, Nov. 30, 2012. For the wedding details, see below, Chapter 5.

19. George Gorner, personal interview, Nov. 30, 2012.

20. See Eliezer Garner, "Close Encounters of the Best Kind," *Kol Chevra*, vol. 7, 2000, 50–51.

21. Peter Braunstein and Michael William Doyle (eds.), *Imagine Nation: The*

Poster for the 9th Berkeley Folk Music Festival, Fourth of July, 1966

living and free sharing of resources. Haight-Ashbury soon became the capital of the hippie revolution with estimates as high as 50,000–100,000 hippies.[22] About ten or twenty thousand of these hippies were of Jewish origin. This is the background for the most colorful part of Reb Shlomo's career, the House of Love and Prayer.

Not coincidentally, LOVE became a major focus of Reb Shlomo as he taught an altruistic form of love – *hesed* and caring. This is emphasized in the vision Shlomo outlined in the summer of 1967:

> Here's the whole thing, simple as it is. The House of Love and Prayer is a place where, when you walk in, someone loves you, and when you walk out, someone misses you.[23]

American Counterculture of the 1960s and '70s (New York: 2002), 7.

22. PBS.org, http://www.pbs.org/wgbh/amex/love/filmmore/pt.html.

23. Coopersmith, *Holy Beggars*, 68. Aryae Coopersmith says this in a recording on segment 37:20 in the documentary film, *You Never Know* by Boaz Shachak.

3.   PLANNING THE HOUSE OF LOVE AND PRAYER (1967–1968)

The first base for Reb Shlomo in the San Francisco area was a one-bedroom house of Alex and Miriam Scott in the town of Forest Knolls in Marin County. It was here on an open hillside, surrounded by fields, overlooking a redwood forest, where Shlomo led his Shabbat programming and began to crystallize a core group of *chevra*. Together they traveled to Shlomo's concerts on the West Coast. In July 1967, they went to Mexico City where Shlomo was hosted by the Jewish community. Alex and Aryae Coopersmith accompanyied him on stage.[24]

In August 1967, Shlomo arrived again in Haight-Ashbury. He walked up and down Haight Street, greeting thousands of hippies, hugging each one, giving out his business card, and inviting all for Shabbat at the home of Alex and Miriam Scott.[25] Soon the Scott one-bedroom home became rather small to accommodate all those invited. Ian Grand had a store-front center in San Francisco where he did his bioenergetic practice and workshops, and there he hosted several events for Reb Shlomo.[26] But it was obvious that a new solution was needed. Shlomo told his *chevra* that it was time to set up a place to welcome all the "holy beggars":

> It would be a place for all the holy beggars of the world, for all the young people who are hungry for a world of love and peace, who are hungry for a true friend, who are hungry for the Great Shabbos.[27]

Reb Shlomo's term "holy beggars" is a felicitous expression. Seemingly, a beggar is impoverished and begs for sustenance.[28] But the "holy beggar" is wandering the streets of the world, "begging not to take, but to give."[29] He is hungry, not for bread nor for water, "but to hear the Words of God" (Amos 8:11). He is begging "to turn over the whole world" and is offering a utopian gift of hope and redemption.[30] In Shlomo's kabbalistic-Hasidic

---

24. Coopersmith, *Holy Beggars*, 58–63.

25. Miller, "An Interview with Aryae Coopersmith," 62. Coopersmith tells a similar story in the recording of Boaz Shachak's movie, segment 36:00–37:00.

26. Aryae Coopersmith, personal communication, Nov. 25, 2012.

27. Coopersmith, *Holy Beggars*, 67.

28. Shlomo's innovative creation of the term "holy beggars" may have been influenced by the Hasidic dramatizations of the image of the beggar as a disguise behind which hides a righteous saint or a miraculous miracle worker.

29. Coopersmith, *Holy Beggars*, xviii. Compare Halberstam Mandelbaum, *Holy Brother*, 75: "A Holy Beggar is someone who is begging you to allow him to give."

30. The literary image of the beggar as bringing about ultimate redemption can be found in the story of *The Seven Beggars & Other Kabbalistic Tales of Rebbe Nachman of Breslov*, transl. by Aryeh Kaplan (Woodstock, Vermont: 2005). For explanations,

vision, these are the "holy hippies" who despite the external disguise are on a truly momentous spiritual quest.

Shlomo's newfound mission was to reach out to "holy beggars" who are "hungry like no generation before" because they are thirsting to "bring the great day of love and peace":

> We can't just stand by and abandon them to every newly minted guru and drug dealer on the planet. . . . We have to reach out to them.[31]

The attractiveness of this idea is that it unveiled a cosmic purpose in the hippie quest. It was interlaced with Shlomo's *midrashic* interpretation that even non-Jews, "hungry for God's presence," found their way to Mount Sinai, to join in receiving "the deepest secrets of the world."[32] The power of the idea was that it afforded the hippies, many of whom felt alienated by mainstream Jewish society, to link up to a legitimate spiritual pursuit that was defined as a core feature of Jewish belief, a longing to be God's partners in bringing about a better world. Aryae Coopersmith sums up the practical implications of Shlomo's vision:

> The Haight-Ashbury in the early days was an exciting, expansive center of creative energy, music, art, poetry, social experimentation, and spiritual exploration together with the sex, drugs, and rock and roll. Thousands of young Jewish spiritual seekers like me were being drawn to spiritual teachers from non-Jewish mystical traditions who showed up in San Francisco. These teachers were connecting with us in a much more vital way than our rabbis and synagogues had, and we were learning great things from them. Shlomo was there to "save" a whole generation of Jewish spiritual seekers from losing the opportunity to connect our lives with the great spiritual story and spiritual treasure of our own people.[33]

※

The House of Love and Prayer began in a three-story building that was rented on April 7, a few days before Pesach.[34] The House opened in May

see Adin Steinsaltz, *Beggars and Prayers: Adin Steinsaltz Retells the Tales of Rabbi Nachman of Bratslav* (New York: 1985). For a more recent translation, see Zalman Schachter-Shalomi, *Tale of the Seven Beggars: Rabbi Nahman of Bratzlav, Retold from the Yiddish by Rabbi Zalman Schachter-Shalomi* (Boulder, Colorado: 2012).

31. Coopersmith, *Holy Beggars*, 63.
32. Ibid., 66–68.
33. Personal communication from Aryae Coopersmith, Nov. 25, 2012.
34. For a description of how the $350 rental was pledged in March 1968 by John

1968. Aryae and his wife Ruthie, together with Alex and Miriam stayed on the second floor and organized the activities. The attic was decorated with Alex Scott's artistic stained glass on the sunny porch overlooking Golden Gate Park.[35] The first resident in the attic was Eliezer (Sonny) Garner. He was one of the few *chevra* able to pay rent because he was working at the time.[36]

The location was in the Richmond District about a mile from Haight-Ashbury, "the vibrant epicenter of the hippie movement.[37] The two most popular psychedelic rock bands, Jefferson Airplane and The Grateful Dead, played in the streets with psychedelic dances and open-air park events. The band community leaders provided free food, lodging, and health care to all. But drugs were rampant and each week, some twenty-five undercover narcotics agents would arrest an average of twenty hippies, usually for possessing marijuana.[38]

For many hippies, "religion" was a combination of a hippie life style with psychedelic music. This is illustrated by the response of The Grateful Dead drummer Mickey Hart about his Jewishness. The interviewer noted that his bar mitzvah picture was displayed in the Grateful Dead Family Album, but Hart responded: "I don't think it affected it one way or the other. My religion is rhythm. That's my God."[39]

The HLP both imitated and challenged this mode of living. By offering a Jewish version of communal life and music, the *chevra* were saying we can do this too, but we tune into the Jewish *neshama*.

Seaman, a Presbyterian seminary student in San Rafael who became a devoted follower of Reb Shlomo, see David Yisroel Miller, "How It All Began, An Interview with Aryae Coopersmith," *Kol Chevra*, vol. 7, 2000, 60–65. A similar story can be found in Coopersmith, *Holy Beggars*, Chapter 10, except that pseudonyms are used. Cf. Mandelbaum, *Holy Brother*, 6–7. See below for how Dr. Joshua Ritchie paid the first month's rent of $400.

35. Rachel Trugman, "Modzhitz Flash Mob," *Kol Chevra*, vol. 17, 2011, 31. For the artistic work of Alex Scott (later Elyah Succot) see below, Chapter 10.

36. Personal interview Dec. 20, 2012.

37. Vincent Tompkins (ed.), "Hippies," *American Decades*, 7, 1960–1969, Detroit, 2001.

38. *Time Magazine*, July 7, 1967.

39. USAToday.com, http://www.usatoday.com/community/chat_03/2003-06-13 -hart.htm. Born in Brooklyn, New York as Michael Steven Hartman on September 11, 1943, his mother Leah, also a drummer, raised him with only a little bit of Jewish identity. In his autobiography MickeyHart.net, http://mickeyhart.net/bio, Hart does not mention his Jewish ancestry.

CHAPTER 5

The House of Love and Prayer

1. FIRST HOUSE, ARGUELLO BLVD. (1968–1970)

The House of Love and Prayer is the most colorful part of Reb Shlomo's career.[1] The first House on 347 Arguello Boulevard existed for only two years. In June 1968, an official organizational structure was set up. Alex Scott was listed as "chairman," Aryae Coopersmith "president," and Donna Anderson "vice president." Two older couples who provided some stability to the group of youthful hippies were Moshe (Melvin) and Nadine Fohrman, and Marvin (Moshe Yitzchak) and Bernice Kussoy.[2]

Rabbi Abraham J. Heschel and Elie Wiesel were listed as "spiritual advisors" of the HLP. Reb Zalman had first met with Heschel in 1956 and Wiesel in 1960.[3] Notably, there was no name from the Orthodox establishment. This corroborates Reb Shlomo's lament that he had "turned to the Torah Giants in America" and beseeched them to help save the hippie youth, but they simply mocked him.[4] In April 1969, Shlomo published a

---

1. For a study on the HLP, see Yaakov Ariel, "Hasidism in the Age of Aquarius: The House of Love and Prayer in San Francisco, 1967–1977," *Religion and American Culture*, Summer 2003, vol. 13, no. 2, 139–165. Cf. Yaakov Ariel, "Can Adam and Eve Reconcile? Gender and Sexuality in a New Jewish Religious Movement," *Nova Religio*, May 2006, vol. 9, no. 4, 53–78.

2. Personal interview with Moshe Kussoy. See Aryae Coopersmith, "House of Love and Prayer – Mechitzah," *Kol Chevra*, vol. 6, Nov. 1999, 39–40. Cf. Coopersmith, *Holy Beggars*, 156–163.

3. See Rzlp.org, http://www.rzlp.org/index.cfm?objectid=E3C58300-D612-00A6 -A6FFA333C19F3C71. See items 45–46 in the photo collection of Pekko.Naropa.Edu, http://pekko.naropa.edu/archon/?p=collections/findingaid&id=143&q=&rootconte ntid=4407#id4407.

4. Shacham, "Enfant Terrible." Shlomo is quoted as saying: "I told them that now is a unique moment to capture the Jewish youth who are thirsty for true living Words, sweet can come from bitter, but they laughed at me. One of them said to me, go home

letter to the editor of the monthly *haredi* magazine *Beis Yaakov* asking if they would agree to publicize his version of what is happening in the Hippie rebellion in the U.S., but his request went unanswered.[5]

The HLP served as a free hostel for many hippies. Only a few paid rent.[6] People "moved into the basement, the attic, any nook and cranny of this large rambling house that was not already occupied by someone else."[7] For some, the HLP was an alternative to the communes of Haight-Ashbury, a crash pad with free room and board. Thousands came for classes, meals, Shabbat prayers and holiday events. The mailing lists indicate that in a short time some 2,500 people had visited.[8] The "regulars" stayed longer, some living in the commune for several years and others living nearby.[9]

An eyewitness account from the summer of 1968 is provided by Rabbi Marc Howard Wilson, who at the time was 19 years old:

> After we bid the Sabbath farewell, fifty or so of us crowded into the living room of the House, sitting on the floor, singing, clapping, swaying, holding on to each other shoulder-to-shoulder, embracing Shlomo's songs and stories. I recall most being surrounded by a feeling of all-wellness, wrapped in peace, welling up with love. Vietnam, draft cards, and political intrigue would have to wait. If only we could envelop the world in such a joyous, healing sensation. For me, it was a coming of age, truly a Summer of Love.[10]

Marc Wilson was one of the more textually knowledgeable youth at the HLP as he was studying at the Hebrew Theological College, Bet Midrash LaTorah in Skokie, Illinois, a suburb of Chicago. He helped lead the HLP learning programs in the summer of 1968:

> Shlomo would ask me to share *divrei Torah* and teach texts while he was on the road. At the HLP, they ordained me "Assistant

and eat cholent. Another Rabbi, who is now active in the *baal teshuva* movement, called me then a clown."

5. See *Beis Yaakov*, issues no. 118–119 (Nisan 5729), 16. Shlomo's letter was a response to Moshe Praeger's article criticizing the Hippie phenomenon.

6. See Garner, "Close Encounters." Nechama Garner, "Grandpa-Shlomo," *Kol Chevra*, vol. 13, 2007, 221–223.

7. Coopersmith, *Holy Beggars*, 165. Others who moved into the HLP in 1968–1969 included Joe Gutman, George Gorner, and Joseph Holman. See their entries on the blog/website http://holybeggars.ning.com/profiles/members.

8. Ariel, *Hasidism*, 162, n. 36; Ariel, *Adam and Eve*, n. 12.

9. See Aryae Coopersmith's website HolyBeggars.Ning.com, http://holybeggars .ning.com/profiles/members where more than 40 people filled out profiles indicating when they had been at HLP.

10. Personal communication with Rabbi Marc Howard Wilson, March 14, 2013.

Resident Messianic Prophet In Training." They gave me this rather humorous title so that they could name me the "director" of their "Chicago branch" for purposes of tax-exempt status, giving the address of my dorm room as "headquarters."[11]

The HLP was a focal point for celebrations and communal events. The House was just six blocks north of Golden Gate Park. Major events were held in the Park. Weddings were an opportunity for communality and a sense of continuity to an ancient tradition. Shlomo would tell the young couple that the Matriarchs and Patriarchs were under the wedding canopy, and even the souls of their future children.[12]

At the HLP, hippie originality was synthesized with the traditional Jewish demand for modest dress:

> Members of the House started a whole new Jewish style of dress . . . They adopted more colorful South Asian and Middle Eastern garments and experimented with "biblical garments" . . . Men, too, were innovative in that realm, wearing, for example, colorful vests and head covers. Such garments helped women and men adapt to observant Jewish norms while retaining hippie styles and tastes, and maintaining a sense of individuality and freedom.[13]

As many HLP activists left for Israel, a leadership crisis developed. David Deen (later Dovid Din) came in the summer of 1969.[14] Lynn Reichman remembers how David instituted regular learning sessions and a more formalized regimen such as a weekday morning *minyan*: "He walked around the House ringing a bell to wake everyone for *Shacharit*."[15]

In August 1969, Leo Skir, a freelance writer, spent eighteen days collecting impressions of the HLP in order to write a story for the magazine *Midstream*.[16] He then phoned to corroborate his information, but was told that the House leader, David Deen had moved to a commune on

---

11. Personal communication, March 14, 2013. See also Marc Wilson, "Holy Days Pass, Bittersweet Tears Linger," in marcmusing.blogspot.co.il, posted on Oct. 12, 2012. Compare Marc Wilson, "Tears Bitter and Sweet," Dec. 4, 2012, GreenvilleJournal. com, http://www.greenvillejournal.com/opinions/in-my-own-words/1782-tears -bitter-and-sweet.html.

12. Joshua Wiseman in an interview with David Herzberg broadcast on Israeli public radio on Sept. 12, 1995. Quoted by Ariel, "Adam and Eve," 65.

13. Ariel, "Adam and Eve" 58; Ariel, "Hasidism" 145–146.

14. See Coopersmith, *Holy Beggars*, 231–235 on various memories of how Dovid Din was invited and why he left the House.

15. Personal interview with Lynn Reichman, Jan. 16, 2013.

16. Leo Skir, "Shlomo Carlebach and the House of Love and Prayer," *Midstream: A Quarterly Jewish Review*, Feb. 1970.

Sutter St., and that the House was being reorganized. Indeed, the House was in a state of flux. About fifteen people had left for Israel, and another fifteen were planning to go soon.[17] So Skir decided to speak directly to Reb Shlomo. Shlomo promptly invited him to travel with him to San Francisco. On December 9, 1969, the two left LaGuardia Airport and arrived at the House at 8:15 PM where Shlomo led a Hanukkah program until 2:00 AM.[18]

Skir learned from Shlomo that the monthly budget needed to run the House was $750, of which $300 comes from the Jewish Federation "because we give free meals."[19] When Skir's report was published in the February 1970 edition of *Midstream*, it was critical of the sanitary conditions and physical neglect.[20] Aryae Coopersmith responded in a letter to *Midstream*. He described the remarkable success of the House in hosting between 100–200 people each Friday night, and influencing "thousands of young people":

> I have seen dozens of unhappy and desperate young people, who were ready to give up on a world that had no place for them, get their first real taste of the joy of Shabbos, their first overwhelming experience of what it is to be with people who love you, people who really care. I have seen young people who hardly knew they were Jewish who are now studying Hebrew and putting on *tephillin* every day.[21]

Rabbi Carlebach also responded with a letter to the editor.[22] He complained that "the old generation is deaf," they don't realize the needs of the American youth who are now "ready for the great Shabbos." He contrasted the typical synagogue which is "empty" of holiness, love, and soul-stirring prayer, as opposed to the HLP which is bringing "heaven down to earth." Reb Shlomo concluded with a plea: "Let's rebuild the Holy Temple again, here, everywhere, on every street, in the hearts of our young people who are waiting, ready, and who know, as nobody before ever knew, how much God is waiting for them." Reb Shlomo also lamented the situation in Israel where religious leaders "come with their

---

17. Aryae Coopersmith, "Communications," *Midstream*, vol. 16, no. 5, May 1970, 67–68.

18. Skir, "Carlebach", 27–29.

19. Ibid., 42.

20. Ibid., 39–40.

21. Coopersmith, *Midstream*, 68.

22. Shlomo Carlebach, "The Heart of Tomorrow," *Midstream*, vol. 16, no. 5, May 1970, 66–67.

middle-class, half-hypocritical religion which nobody wants to buy," and fail to appreciate the spiritual yearnings of the youth:

> The young people in Israel are waiting for a message from God who loves them as much as they love Him, but they are given a message of a God who only tells them what to do and when to do it – no soul, no love . . . They are ready for the Holy Temple. Their hearts are crying day and night while their souls are ready to die a thousand times for the Holy Land.[23]

Skir responded by explaining that he found it "difficult to talk of Love and Angels" when there was so much neglect of "physical things as having meals-on-time and clean floors." Skir criticized the lack of residential leadership:

> There is no resident head providing direction, giving form to the days so that there is a time for praying, time for study, and time for cleaning and preparation of meals.[24]

By 1970, it was becoming clear that the situation in the HLP was problematic. The men's dormitory was a dark and damp basement and the women slept in the slanted-roofed attic.[25] Yisroel Finman, who moved into the HLP in April 1970, described the sleeping conditions:

> The boiler room was the men's dormitory. What a nightmare! . . . One big old boiler over there, and bunk beds made out of wood . . . if there wasn't bunk bed space, you're on the stone floor in a sleeping bag.[26]

In retrospect, Shlomo's paradigm of unlimited love for all and his unique ability to see goodness everywhere, allowed the entry of all kinds of people. Many came simply to enjoy the free lodging and food. Some were genuine seekers who embraced Yiddishkeit. Others participated without committing themselves. But there were also those who camped out, and a few were problematic:

> They took full advantage of the free food and a place to crash, lived out in the basement, and created a little underworld, were into drugs and didn't connect to the HLP aims or activities – they took, but never gave.[27]

---

23. Ibid., 67.
24. Leo Skir, "Communications," *Midstream*, vol. 16, no. 5, May 1970, 68–69.
25. Trugman, "Modzhitz Flash."
26. Coopersmith, *Holy Beggars*, 237.
27. Personal communication from Ne'eman Rosen, Aug. 3, 2011.

Taking stock after two years of operation, the activists of the House met for "several heated meetings." They realized that a new start was necessary to continue outreach without the problematic "basement residents." There were the older couples, the Fohrmans and Kussoys, who worked and helped out financially. Louise, Chana, Adina, and Elana cooked for large numbers of people. An imbalance had been created between the "givers" and the "takers." An additional problem arose when a majority voted in favor of allowing smoking and music on Shabbat for those who so desired.[28] This was a red line for Reb Shlomo. The sense of community was disintegrating, and the House closed at the beginning of 1971.[29] Aryae suggested to Shlomo to set up a new type of House, more of a yeshiva, and ensure that Shlomo would be actively present at least four months a year.

> On a conference call with Shlomo in New York, we come up with a new plan: a House of Love and Prayer Yeshivah. This time we'll be more grounded. We'll buy a house, hire teachers, recruit students from all over the U.S., charge tuition, and build a community.[30]

For the next few months, the HLP did not have a central location and the *hevra* would meet at the homes of the older patrons – the Fohrmans, Kussoys, and Natalie Zarchin.[31] Meanwhile, in February, 1971, in the local *San Francisco Jewish Bulletin*, Shlomo was quoted as promising:

> To build a yeshiva here where Jews from all over the world can come to study and pray, presents a need for a full-time spiritual guide . . . I would very much like to stay here and give concerts only on weekends, if financially possible. My theory is that six million Jews who died in the Holocaust have come back as today's young people. Let's not lose them again.[32]

This "theory" of soul transmigration was mentioned above as being part of the inspirational directive that Shlomo received from the sixth Rebbe. As a kabbalistic idea, it is invoked here to give importance and urgency to the mission at hand – the saving of Jewish souls.

---

28. Ariel, "Hasidism," 154.

29. Coopersmith, "From House to Aquarian Minyan," in Victor Gross, Reuven Goldfarb, Yehudit Goldfarb, Nadya Gross and Miriam Stampfer (eds.), *Ancient Roots, Radical Practices, and Contemporary Visions – The Aquarian Minyan 25th Anniversary Festschrift* (Berkeley, California: 1999), 32.

30. Coopersmith, "From House to Aquarian Minyan," 32.

31. Personal communication from Ne'eman Rosen, Aug. 1, 2011.

32. *San Francisco Jewish Bulletin*, Feb. 1971, quoted in Coopersmith, *Holy Beggars*, 247.

2. SECOND HOUSE, 9TH AVE. (1971–1978)

The April 1971 brochure for the new HLP described a course of study to include basic Hebrew, Humash, Mishnah, Gemara, and Hasidut. The teaching was described as reaching three levels of experience – mind, heart, and soul:

> The fact reaches only as far as the mind.
> The story reaches as far as the heart.
> And the melody reaches all the way to the soul.
> *In this yeshiva you pass only when you learn the melody.*

A justification was presented for its co-ed nature, which at the time was quite revolutionary for the Orthodox yeshiva world:

> What a man can learn is only half the story.
> What a woman can learn is the other half.
> In Hebrew there is no such thing as a word with one letter.
> Every word must have at least two letters.[33]

The realtor, Henry Klein, located a three-story house at 1456 9th Ave. between Judah and Kirkham Sts. Two benefactors from New York, Michael Steinhardt and Stanley Stern, agreed to pay the monthly mortgage,[34] and additional funding came from Moses Feuerstein of Brookline, Massachusetts.[35] The bank mortgage was signed by Melvin Fohrman and Marvin Kussoy.[36]

Aryae, Yankala, Ne'eman, and Pesach painted the building, added carpets, and broke down the wall on the main floor with crowbars and hammers, so it could be a prayer area.[37] Aryae found redwood planks, which they put up vertically, to resemble the *Mishkan*, the Tabernacle.[38] All was finished just in time for the High Holiday services of September 19, 1971.[39] A large *sukkah* was built in the spacious backyard. Shlomo arrived during Hol HaMoed Sukkot, at the beginning of October 1971.[40]

The second House solved the problems of the uncontrolled camping out that had proved ruinous to the first House. For the first year, only

---

33. Coopersmith, *Holy Beggars*, 248.

34. Michael Steinhardt, personal interview, Aug. 30, 2012.

35. Coopersmith, *Holy Beggars*, 249.

36. Personal communication from Marvin Kussoy.

37. Interview with Yankala Shamas, Sept. 15, 2011. See also HolyBeggars.ning.com, http://holybeggars.ning.com/profile/SarahAriellaKauffman?xg_source=activity.

38. Ne'eman, email correspondence, Aug. 5, 2011.

39. Coopersmith, *Holy Beggars*, 248–250.

40. Coopersmith, *Holy Beggars*, 251.

Pesach and Ne'eman lived there. They were responsible for the daily functioning and greeting everyone.[41] The first floor served as the synagogue and library where everything took place – Shabbos meals, Shlomo teach-ins, and daily classes. The second floor was originally classrooms, but after about a year, Yankala and Shoshana Shemesh (Shamas) moved in and stayed until February 1973.[42] Then Nechama Yasskin (Silver) moved into their room[43] and Sarah Dickerson (Kauffman) joined her in June.[44]

New officers for the second HLP were elected on April 25, 1972.[45] Pesach Weitz became president and Steven Maimes, vice president. Steven helped organize teach-ins with Reb Shlomo, Reb Zalman, and Reb Gedaliah Fleer. Zalman led a Shabbat program from May 27–29, 1972.[46] Shlomo led a summer learning session from June 15 to July 4, 1972.[47] During 1972, Shlomo visited several times and is reported to have taught *Halacha* in the morning and Hasidut (R. Nachman of Breslov) at night.[48] Many classes were recorded.[49] He also taught Talmud. Coopersmith recalled:

> Learning Talmud with Shlomo is very different from learning Hasidic stories or mystical teachings with him. This is left brain stuff . . . dialectic logic . . . so we can understand the details of how God wants us to act.[50]

Aryae suggested transcribing Shlomo's teachings into print form.[51] The result was the appearance in February 1972 of the first issue of *Holy Beggars' Gazette* in a simple format of mimeographed pages edited by Elana Rappaport. After Steve Maimes joined as assistant editor and then as managing editor, the journal expanded to include literary

---

41. Ne'eman, email correspondence, Aug. 5, 2011. Ne'eman moved out after he was married in October 1972, and Pesach continued to take care of the House until March 1975. Pesach met his future wife when she "walked in through the front door." They were married during Hanukkah, in Dec. 1974.

42. They left for New York in Feb. 1973, eventually arriving in Israel shortly before the Yom Kippur War, Yankala Shamas, personal interview, Sept. 15, 2011.

43. Nechama Yasskin (Silver), personal interview, Oct. 6, 2012.

44. Sarah Kauffman correspondence. See below on her profile.

45. Coopersmith, *Holy Beggars*, 262.

46. Ibid., 263.

47. *Holy Beggars' Gazette*, vol. 1, no. 2, Iyar 5732.

48. Ne'eman, email correspondence, Aug. 7, 2011.

49. The Ami Weisz collection of 44 teachings of Shlomo includes recordings by Ne'eman Rosen at the second HLP over the course of 3 years, 1972–1974. For 1972, these include classes from Jan. 3 and Dec. 7.

50. Coopersmith, *Holy Beggars*, 251–252.

51. Ibid., 252–253.

Reb Shlomo and Aryae Coopersmith at the first House of Love and Prayer, 1968

compositions from HLP regulars and teachers. It was subtitled in August 1973 as "A Journal of Chassidic Judaism." A total of twelve issues were published.[52] The last issue appeared in 1977 with twenty-one selections, six from Shlomo including his stories "Wheel of Fortune," "Don't Give Up," and "A Meeting on the Road." Another thirteen contributors added their poems, stories, and literary creations. These last issues illustrate

---

52. Kalman Serkez took all the articles in the Gazette and turned them into a book – Kalman Serkez (ed.), *Holy Beggars Banquet – Traditional Jewish Tales and Teachings of the Late, Great Reb Shlomo Carlebach and Others, in the Spirit of the 1960s, the 1970s, and the New Age* (Northvale, New Jersey: 1998). The problem is that Serkez edited the materials into 126 sections, made extensive editorial revisions but did not indicate what was said by Reb Shlomo. The result is a conflation of contributions by other authors.

how Carlebach Hasidism was beginning to evolve to include a wide variety of ideas prepared by Shlomo's students, friends, and colleagues.

An innovation of the *kiruv* work at the second HLP was a dramatization of the Torah reading. Chava Cooper (Fried) described the pathos and communal participation in the Shabbat readings:

> David Herzberg used to read the Torah on Shabbos. . . . He would stop in between each *aliyah* and turn around, and explain the story with enthusiasm, wide eyes, and arms flying in the air. We could *hear* and *experience* it: "Yoseph's brothers have come before Yoseph . . . . Yoseph pretends not to know Hebrew. . . . then Yoseph cries. . . . I'm Yoseph your brother! *Od Avinu Chai*!? Is our father still alive!?" You would break down crying at this awesome reunion! It was drama happening now![53]

The HLP *chevra* would travel long distances to join Shlomo's concerts and Shabbat programs. Thus, for example, Chava Cooper, Sarah Kauffman, Baruch (Barry) Ring together with Pesach, and a friend of his all piled into Neil Rader's van and drove to Spokane, Washington, for a Shabbat program at a Conservative Synagogue, Temple Beth Shalom. Shlomo's concert took place on Motzei Shabbat, November 25, 1972.

#

When Shlomo would come to the HLP, hundreds of people would join him, especially for Shabbat. Here is the description by Nechama Yasskin (Silver):

> It was the job of those of us who lived there to prepare the food. I made the *challot*. Others made rice, vegetables, salad, and techina. Cakes appeared from somewhere. Reb Shlomo always paid the bill or got donations from friends. The *davening* with Reb Shlomo was "the highest of the high." People's lives were changed from the experience of being with Reb Shlomo. When he left, many helpless souls would come around looking for their holy friend. We were often overtaken by addicts, psychotics, "messianic visionaries," etc. It wasn't easy, but that was what it was all about. Being a friend to those in need.[54]

The HLP had become established as a far-out revolutionary phenomenon. A budding sociologist named Matthew Maibaum visited the HLP

---

53. Chava Cooper (Fried), personal communication, Aug. 25, 2011.
54. Nechama Yasskin (Silver), personal interview, Oct. 6, 2012.

in 1973 to conduct a "field study" and explain the remarkable way that Hasidism was being brought to American Jewish youth.[55]

Despite his good intentions, Shlomo actually taught at the HLP only sporadically. For example, his classes were recorded during 1973 on January 29, February 10, March 6, and June 26–July 7. In 1974, his recorded classes included March 6–13 and June 14–20.[56] But other teachers came to fill the HLP with exciting teach-ins. These included Rabbi Shaul and Tzivia Chill, Rabbi Gedaliah Fleer, who taught Hasidut of Rebbe Nachman of Breslov,[57] and Eliyahu Klein who was living in the neighborhood.[58] Mickey Moshe Shur was studying in Berkeley and he organized an interfaith conference which Reb Shlomo attended. Local rabbis in San Francisco also came to teach at the HLP. In 1974–1975, these included Rabbis Mordechai Cohen, Heshy Dachs, David Gottlieb, and Yehuda Mandelcorn.[59] The HLP had evolved into a bustling *baal teshuva* enterprise.

By 1975, the House was beginning to wind down. To a large extent, this reflected what was happening in San Francisco as hippie culture was on the wane. Unlike the utopian beginnings in 1966–1967, when peace, love, and communes were seen as harbingers of a visionary new society, the unsanitary conditions and drug abuse disfigured a deteriorating Haight-Ashbury. A vibrant neighborhood deteriorated into a decaying low-rent area "infested with vice and crime." Instead of gentle, peace-loving hippies, the area was taken over by questionable characters.[60]

Sometimes there was not even a *minyan* for Shabbat, and people walked to Rabbi Shalom Stern's Magain David Sephardim Congregation in the Richmond District of San Francisco.[61] The HLP encountered financial difficulties. Fundraising letters before the holidays of Pesach and

---

55. Matthew Maibaum, "Some appeals of Hasidism to American Jewish Youth: A Field Study," 1973. Cf. Matthew Maibaum, *The New Student and Youth Movements, 1965–1972: A Perspective View on Some Social and Political Developments in American Jews as a Religio-National Group*, Ph.D. Thesis, Claremont Graduate School, 1980.

56. These are recorded teachings with specific dates in the Ami Weisz collection.

57. Rabbi Fleer was born in New York in 1940, had studied at the Novardok Yeshiva in Brooklyn, Mirer Yeshiva, and Torah Vodaas. He received rabbinic ordination at Yeshivat Chasidei Breslov in Jerusalem in 1960. Gedaliah Fleer, *Rabbi Nachman's Fire: An Introduction to Breslover Chassidus* (New York: 1972). See Shalom Freedman, *In the Service of God – Conversations with Teachers of Torah in Jerusalem* (Northvale, New Jersey: 1995), 170.

58. My thanks to Nechama Yasskin (Silver) for providing these details.

59. Skype interview with Sarah Kauffman, Sept. 11, 2011.

60. McWilliams, *The 1960s Cultural Revolution*, 77.

61. Sarah Kauffman, personal communication, Aug. 13, 2011.

Rosh Hashana which used to bring about $5,000 each time, now brought much less.[62]

The House gradually began closing and the residents moved out.[63] Henry Klein, a HLP supporter, who as a realtor had helped in the original purchase, ensured that it was sold. Marvin Kussoy remembers that the proceeds of about $5,000 were sent to Shlomo.[64] Menachem Kallus recalls that in mid-July 1978, he had "the honor" of being the "last Shlomo-person" to sleep on the floor of the HLP, and the next day the new owners received the key from Reb David Herzberg.[65]

The closure reflects a more general phenomenon of how the "counter-cultural revolution" was fading away in the 1970s. The psychedelic 1960s with their optimistic expectations of enlightenment and peace gave way to a sober realization of the dangers of drugs and a return to the non-utopian style of living.

3.   EXPERIENCES OF HLP PARTICIPANTS

It is difficult to capsulate in words the unique spirit at the HLP. The following eight stories provide a glimpse into how lives changed as a result of the HLP experience. There were those who became very religious while others merely integrated a new spirituality into their lives. Some converted to Judaism.

⁂

Estelle Frankel had been "turned off to conventional Judaism":

> The deep spiritual longings I felt were not being addressed by organized religion, and the vision and music of universal love that filled the streets of San Francisco in the late sixties were far more compelling to me than the ethnocentrism and chauvinism I encountered at home and in the synagogue.[66]

---

62. Personal conversation with Alifa Saadya.

63. David and Alifa Herzberg moved out of the HLP in 1976 and were replaced by Rivka Yaffee and Chaya Mugg (personal communication from Alifa). Chava Cooper, personal conversation Sept. 1, 2011: "We moved out of the House on Feb. 16, 1977 when my fourth child was born."

64. Marvin Kussoy, personal conversation, Aug. 25, 2011.

65. Herzberg, *Sparks of David*, vii.

66. Estelle Frankel, *Sacred Therapy: Jewish Spiritual Teachings on Emotional Healing and Inner Wholeness* (Boston, 2003), Preface, ix–x.

In 1969, after graduating San Carlos High School in California, Estelle was on her way with friends to Canada when she was invited for Shabbat to the HLP. Her first encounter with Reb Shlomo "changed the course of my life and made it possible for me to find a spiritual home in Judaism."[67]

> I had the good fortune of meeting Rabbi Shlomo Carlebach and a group of hippies who were exploring the boundaries of religious ecstasy through song, dance, prayer, and meditation at the House of Love and Prayer in San Francisco. I have always considered this meeting auspicious, as it profoundly influenced the course of my life at a rather vulnerable point in my youth.[68]

Sixteen-year old Estelle was moved by the Shabbat experience of "people ecstatically singing and dancing, with light and love radiating from their faces."[69] After a few months at the HLP, Estelle decided to go study in Jerusalem:

> In many ways I owe my life to Reb Shlomo's love and his profound understanding of Judaism, for the peak spiritual experiences I had at the House of Love and Prayer opened up the possibility that my spiritual longings could find expression in Jewish form.[70]

#

Debbie Levine (Shapiro) was a teenager at the HLP in 1968–1970. She grew up in an atheistic family in San Francisco and joined Habonim, the secular Zionist youth movement. Debbie was 14 when Alex Scott spoke to the Habonim youth on Hanukkah, and invited everyone to visit the HLP. Debbie began going to the HLP and traveling to Shlomo's concerts. Debbie describes how she was moved by Shlomo's song of Shabbat:

> The audience swayed and passionately hummed along in harmony. As I, too, was carried away with the melody, it suddenly dawned

---

67. Estelle Frankel, "Broken Hearts and Shattered Vessels," *Kol Chevra*, vol. 13, 2007, 191.

68. Frankel, *Sacred Therapy*, ix.

69. Ibid., x.

70. Ibid., x. Estelle studied in Jerusalem from 1970–1978, attending Machon Gold Teachers College and the Michlalah College for Jewish Studies, and then teaching at several yeshivas, including Neve Yerushalayim and Shapell (Bruria). Today she works as a spiritual psychotherapist and teaches Jewish mysticism in Berkeley, California. See Facebook.com, http://facebook.com/estelle.frankel; SacredTherapy.com, http://www.sacredtherapy.com.

on me that the key to our continuity, to our national identity, lay in "singing the song of Shabbos."[71]

Debbie began observing Shabbat and falling out of step with her secular setting: "I was probably the only girl in my secular high school who had never tried drugs." Then she attended another Carlebach concert:

> Reb Shlomo stood on stage and began recounting the terrible tragedies that befell our nation – the Inquisition, the Crusades, the pogroms, the Holocaust. "One little nation, one little tiny nation," he intoned. "One little nation, among all the great nations that try to destroy her. And yet, we are still here, while the other nations have disappeared! What's the secret of our survival? *Am Yisrael Chai*, the Jewish nation is alive because *Od Avinu Chai*, our Father, God, is still alive. I was electrified. Here was a solution that in its utter simplicity had never occurred to me.

In May 1968, Debbie began frequenting the HLP every Shabbat and holiday: "I considered it my second home."[72] Her parents were perplexed and angered. Reb Shlomo and Aryae drove with Debbie to her parents' home to try and convince them to allow her to keep kosher:

> . . . it was a big tear scene. After the initial yelling and screaming, my parents went to the back room to speak with Reb Shlomo. After that, my parents allowed me to make a makeshift kosher kitchen in the basement.[73]

Debbie together with many HLP *chevra* would attend a Gemara class given by Rabbi Pinhas Lipner in San Francisco.[74] He suggested to Debbie that for her senior year in high school she enroll in the Beis Yaakov girls' religious high school in Denver, Colorado. But this was a small school with only thirty-five girls and Rabbi Meyer Schwab, the principal, was afraid to accept "the hippie girl" lest she have a detrimental effect on the religious girls. So R. Lipner asked Shlomo to speak to the principal. Shlomo pleaded and admonished R. Schwab: "Please take her to your

---

71. The story told here is based on an interview with Debbie Shapiro, Aug. 25, 2011. See also Coopersmith, *Holy Beggars*, 354–357.

72. http://holybeggars.ning.com/profile/221126?xg_source=profiles_memberList.

73. Interview with Debbie Shapiro, Aug. 25, 2011.

74. Rabbi Lipner had established the Lisa Kampner Hebrew Academy of San Francisco in 1969. This was the only traditional Jewish day school high school in San Francisco. See TheJewishRevolution.com, http://thejewishrevolution.com/history .html; HebrewAcademy.com, http://www.hebrewacademy.com/judaicstaff.html.

Entrance to the first HLP

school. And if you don't take her, her blood's gonna be on your head."[75]

Today, Debbie is a writer/teacher living in Jerusalem and working on her "fourth *minyan* of grandchildren." Recently, she reflected on what Reb Shlomo had done for her: "It was such a tremendous, tremendous mitzvah. He really wanted his Hasidim to join the real world – to make an impact with their creativity from within."

⁂

---

75. Coopersmith, *Holy Beggars*, 355–356.

Reb Shlomo with his followers in the first HLP

Reb Shlomo holds Asher Bottero at the second HLP, 1972. Asher's mother, Libby Rivka Bottero, had converted to Judaism in Seattle in 1968 and then came to the HLP with her baby son. Asher Yaffee was one of the very few children at the HLP.

Courtesy of Libby Bottero

In the 1970s.
My thanks to Moshe Kussoy for graciously supplying these
and many other pictures.

Yisroel (Ivan) Finman was born in Newark, New Jersey in 1951. He attended Weequahic High School, a public high school in Newark which was 70 percent black and 20 percent Jewish. The Hebrew teacher at the school was a member of Rabbi Eli Chaim Carlebach's congregation and had arranged for federal funds, "earmarked for cultural enrichment for inner city kids," to bring Shlomo to Weequahic High School. Ivan, a freshman in high school, met Shlomo and "was mesmerized":

Because of Shlomo's appearance at a predominantly black inner city high school, I wound up learning Torah instead of heading off to an ashram in India. I didn't need to find God in the Himalayas. God existed even in the inner city, even without acid. Were it not for Shlomo, my five children would not be immersed in the beauty of Yiddishkeit. They would probably have Sanskrit names.[76]

In high school, Ivan was involved in "radical leftist politics," but it was his psychedelic experiences that opened up "the doors of perception," and Ivan became involved in Far Eastern religions. He became a "long haired, bead wearing, pot smoking, meditating, chanting, yogi hippie." Then one day, a "tripping buddy" told him about those "crazy Jews living in a commune called the House of Love and Prayer."[77] In April 1970, Ivan moved into the HLP, staying there until its temporary closing in November 1970. He then spent a year and a half in Denver learning with Rabbi Shloimie Twerski before returning to San Francisco and rejoining the HLP community as one of its leading activists. Yisroel wrote in 2000:

Because of Shlomo, a visionary, iconoclastic disciple of the Holy Baal Shem Tov, today I am the spiritual leader of Rosedale Jewish Center.[78]

Yisroel also served as a congregational rabbi in Key West, Florida. Currently, he lives in Boca Raton, Florida, and defines himself as a "heavy Shlomo person, tempered by influence of close relationships with Rabbi Shloime Twerski and with the Bobover Rebbe."[79]

❉

Emma Chava Finman, at the time Stephanie, came to the second HLP where she met and married Ivan Yisroel Finman. Today she lives in Flatbush, Brooklyn, and identifies herself as a Carlebachian Modern Orthodox Liberal with five adult children. Chava describes her experience in the early 1970s:

---

76. Rabbi Yisroel Finman, "Shlomo, My Bubie and the Soul of Judaism," *Kol Chevra*, vol. 7, 2000, 72–74.

77. Ibid., 73.

78. Ibid., "Shlomo, My Bubie," 74.

79. Yisroel Finman, personal communication, Aug. 25, 2011. See also Coopersmith, Holy Beggars, 234–235; HolyBeggars.ning.com, http://holybeggars.ning.com/profile/YisroelFinman.

Shlomo's coming to town brought all the *chevra* from far and wide;
the HLP was packed and the energy was so high. This was the first
time I experienced a "holy" man treating us, as if we were the ones
connected to Hashem, truth, and Torah.[80]

\#

Barry (Reuven) Barkan was active in the HLP, and served as one of
Shlomo's regular drivers to the airport. Barkan grew up in Williamsburg,
Brooklyn, New York in an "assimilated" family. After graduating
Goddard College in 1966, he embarked on "an identity quest," searching
for "the spiritual lineage of the Baal Shem Tov," but couldn't find it in
the "Chassidic enclaves" in New York and Boston. One day in 1972, in
Eureka Springs, Arkansas, he encountered "a van-load of holy hippies
from the House of Love and Prayer." It was then that he met Joe Cooper,
Ivan Finman, and David Herzberg who invited him to visit the HLP.[81] A
year later, Barry was living in San Francisco and decided to visit the HLP
for Shabbat. It left an indelible impression:

> I encountered a visceral connection to the core of Jewish spiri-
> tuality that I never knew existed. By the time Shabbos was over
> I had found my tribal root . . . Shlomo walked into the House of
> Love and Prayer and embodied love. He made a genuine connec-
> tion with each person he touched. His *davennen*, his melodies,
> his singing, his stories, his dancing seemed to alter reality and
> transported me outside of time and space. The Baal Shem Tov,
> Reb Nachman, the Ishbitzer Rebbe, all became real and contem-
> poraneous characters.[82]

\#

Linda Elyad, born on June 2, 1949, grew up in Chicago in an all-Jewish
neighborhood. Her family background in "Jewish Reform religion"
disappointed her by "its lack of spirituality." Linda struggled with the
questions of "Why be Jewish?" and "Who needs it?" When she was 18,

---

80. HolyBeggars.ning.com, http://holybeggars.ning.com/profile/chavafinman?xg_
source=activity.

81. Ben Habeebe (a.k.a. Barry Barkan), "You Are Building It, and They Are Coming:
The Aquarian Minyan and the Field of Rebbetude," in Gross, Goldfarb, Goldfarb,
Gross and Stampfer (eds.), *Ancient Roots*, Radical Practices, and Contemporary
Visions, 73–80. Barry Barkan, "Honoring David and Neila," *Kol Chevra*, vol. 17, 2011,
111–112.

82. Barkan, "You Are Building It," 76.

she connected to Sri Nerode, "an 80-year old authentic East Indian Brahmin," who taught her yoga and meditation:

> Sri Nerode guided me about how to be a spiritual seeker . . . He strengthened me and blessed me for my journey through what turned out to be a huge, booming spiritual marketplace.[83]

In 1970, 21-year old Linda was living with her husband Jerome Freedman, and their toddler, Micah, in "comfortable, successful Westchester County, New York." But they felt that something was all wrong:

> We knew we had to make a new world for ourselves. We had to change spiritually and socially. . . . We saw ourselves as spiritual seekers, whose quest was to create a new, better, higher, social order.

The couple traveled through America on a "spiritual trip searching for a perfect commune to join." They met Reb Zalman in the summer of 1971 at a spiritual community called the Lama Foundation, 20 miles north of Taos, New Mexico. He suggested visiting the House of Love and Prayer:

> We found a tiny, crowded room with open-heartedness, kindness, joy, a gateway to a mind-expanding, deeply fulfilling experience of being in universal love. And it had an authentic Jewish flavor! Reb Shlomo Carlebach was the radiant source of that bursting, energetic flow. He made us sing and dance and be happy! Reb Shlomo showed us the "highest of the high" and the "deepest of the deep."[84]

Recently, Linda described how she was influenced by Reb Shlomo:

> The reason Reb Shlomo Carlebach is my Rebbe has to do with his spiritual qualities of *chesed*. It's important to understand that Shlomo Carlebach is Rebbe to many non-Orthodox Jews for reasons of transmission of spiritual qualities.[85]

---

83. This and the subsequent quotes from Linda Elyad are based on several Skype interviews and email correspondences in the months of Sept., Oct. and Nov., 2011. See also Linda Elyad, "How the Minyan Has Affected Me and My Efforts to Create a Jewish Renewal in Israel," March 14, 1999, in Gross, Goldfarb, Goldfarb, Gross and Stampfer, *Ancient Roots*, 55–62.

84. Personal communications with Linda Elyad, 2011. Eventually, Linda and Jerome divorced as Jerome went on Hindu and Buddhist spiritual paths while Linda followed Reb Shlomo and Reb Zalman. Linda later married Bill Finn from Phoenix, Arizona. She was instrumental in helping organize events for Reb Shlomo, "the most successful" was in Phoenix for about 800 people.

85. Personal communications, Fall 2011.

Another unusual facet of the HLP was the active participation of non-Jews and converts. Here are two examples.

⁜

Jean (Chaya) M. Knowlton grew up as a Catholic in Jackson, Michigan. As a college student, she began exploring higher states of consciousness and was influenced by *Be Here Now*, the "counterculture bible" for thousands of seekers of enlightenment, written by Richard Alpert (Ram Dass). In 1972, at age 21, Jean found her first taste of Jewish spirituality at the HLP and joined the community for a couple of years. She rented an apartment on 9th Ave., just up the street from the HLP, and "sometimes the overflow from the House would stay in our apartment."[86] Jean studied with Reb Shlomo, Reb Zalman, and Rabbi Stern, and converted to Judaism under their guidance.

⁜

Sarah Ariella (Dickerson) Kauffman was born in Niagara Falls, New York, September 27, 1942. She converted at the age of 22 with a Conservative rabbi in Buffalo, New York, and assumed the name Sarah. In January 1972, she moved to California where she attended Santa Rosa Junior College. One day, she spotted a poster advertising Shlomo's concert at Sonoma State (about 15 miles away). She attended the concert in March 1972 and it "changed my life." Sarah began attending the House on Rosh Hashana in 1972, and moved to live there in June 1973. Sarah described her role at the HLP:

> With all the people moving in and out, and those who came just for Shabbat or to stay a week or so, there was constant stimulation and excitement. I'd like to think I made a difference in some of their lives, particularly those young ones who asked for advice or homeless and disenfranchised people who just needed a warm meal and a hug.[87]

To sum up, the divergent variety of profiles illustrate a wide range of experiences at the HLP. But certain themes do recur. One is the communal-emotional impact that attracted many people. This feature is a

---

86. Personal communication, July 26, 2011.

87. Personal communications from Sarah Kauffman. She married her husband Raphael Kauffman on September 7, 1980 in Golden Gate Park.

prominent part of the Carlebach legacy and accounts for the widespread success of modern-day Carlebach *minyanim*.

4.   SIX HLP MARRIAGES

Reb Shlomo often emphasized the importance of marriage. Marital ceremonies were major musical happenings. The following six weddings illustrate this aspect of Shlomo's outreach and offer a glimpse into the life-changing events of the people whom he influenced from the HLP.

❀

On April 1, 1968, Ahouva (Phyllis) Steinhaus and Natan (Norman, Nossen) Schafer were married in Winnipeg. Reb Zalman performed the ceremony and Reb Shlomo led the *Sheva Brachot*. Previously, in June 1967, 20-year old Phyllis had dropped out of UCLA and was living in a Haight-Ashbury commune. She discovered the Shabbat celebrations of Alex and Miriam Scott in Forest Knolls and there she met Norman who had come from studying with Reb Zalman in Winnipeg.[88] They had celebrated their engagement in February 1968 on Shabbat with some fifty people in the greenhouse apartment of a friend on Nob Hill in San Francisco. There Shlomo introduced his song, "The Whole World is Waiting to Sing a Song of Shabbos."[89] In May 1969, they joined the first couples from the HLP to go on aliyah, to go to Israel.[90]

❀

On March 24, 1969, Reb Shlomo performed the marriage of Pamela (Pam) Klein to George Gorner[91] in Golden Gate Park near the HLP. *Life Magazine* was doing a feature story on weddings and they sent a camera crew to take pictures of the outdoor event. This was the first time that a major national media had picked up on Reb Shlomo's innovative San Francisco activities. The two full color photos provided a glimpse into a

---

88. Coopersmith, *Holy Beggars*, 49–50.

89. To hear Shlomo singing this song see the posting by Joel Goldberg, go4joel, http://www.youtube.com/watch?v=tsMg1uKHFiU.

90. Ahouva Steinaus, Skype interview, Sept. 11, 2011. For more on Natan Schafer, see below, Chapter 11 on both his Rabbinic ordination and second marriage.

91. See above, Chapter 4 on how George and Pam came to know Reb Shlomo in 1967. For the song that George wrote with Shlomo, "Lord Get Me High," see below, Chapter 6.

new wedding style that Reb Shlomo had designed.[92] The ceremony began at 4:00 PM in the park, and a couple of hundred strangers joined the HLP core group to create a musical happening. By nightfall, the park police asked the celebrants to move on, and the newlyweds were transferred by truck, complete with their *huppah*, to continue celebrating at the HLP.[93]

George was somewhat of a media celebrity because of his role in leading anti-war protest songs.[94] Years later, Shlomo recalled how George "was arrested for singing an obscene song and it turned out to be my '*Esa Einai*.' When he got married, because he was so famous, *Life Magazine* came to film the wedding."[95] In actuality, Gorner did not know Hebrew. He had simply adapted the tune for his lyrics condemning police brutality against peace demonstrators.

#

On March 5, 1972, Neil and Patricia Seidel were married by Reb Shlomo in Latigo Canyon in the hills above Malibu, in northwestern Los Angeles. Neil had grown up in a non-religious home and practiced Far Eastern Hindu meditation. He knew very little about Judaism.[96] It was his fiancée, Patricia Ann White, who suggested having a Jewish ceremony. Neil agreed on condition that "the Rabbi be a Jewish Holy man." Rabbi Joe Schonwald recommended Shlomo Carlebach, and in November 1971, Neil visited the HLP:

> When I entered the room, Shlomo was teaching and strumming. I joined in guitar, and a unique musical and spiritual relationship was born.[97]

Reb Shlomo performed the *huppah* in a 400-acre pastoral setting with dancing and singing that lasted for two hours. As there was no table at the outdoor ceremony, Shlomo used his guitar box for signing the *ketubbah*, the marriage contract. At the time, Neil was the lead guitarist with a

---

92. "The Free-form Wedding Game," *Life Magazine* 67, no. 13, Sept. 26, 1969, 95–96. Available on line at Google Books.

93. For a description of the wedding see Coopersmith, *Holy Beggars*, 205–209.

94. San Francisco State was a hotbed of campus protests during 1966–1968. Gorner explained recently: I was facing a lot of charges and had warrants out because I would take the microphone and sing protest songs during the demonstrations. In the end, I pled guilty to disturbing the peace. (Gorner, personal discussion, Nov. 30, 2012).

95. Reb Shlomo to his interviewer on Jan. 14, 1992 – Brenner, *Talkline*, segment 25:00.

96. Neil was born on Oct. 7, 1946 in New York. He graduated Fairfax High School in 1964 and California State University in LA in 1968.

97. Email exchanges with Neil in June 2012.

Reb Shlomo had the sign displayed prominently next to his chair in the second HLP, announcing the farbrengen on June 16, 1974 at the Hillel Foundation in Berkeley. The drawing shows two Hasidim dancing under the titles Reb Shlomo Carlebach and Reb Zalman Schachter, followed by a quote from Psalms 100:2. This was a landmark event as it marked the beginning of the Aquarian Minyan Berkeley.   Photo by Steven Maimes

HOUSE OF LOVE AND PRAYER

1456 Ninth Avenue ● San Francisco, California 94122 ● Phone (415) 731-9507

The second House of Love and Prayer, and backyard, 1974. Behind Shlomo are Yisroel (Ivan) Finnman, Joe Cooper and Avraham Sutton.

Photo by Steven Maimes

music band named Shanti. Over the years, while he developed his career as a professional musician in Los Angeles, he became close with Shlomo, performing dozens of concerts with him in California and traveling with him outside the state about ten times. The hundreds of hours performing and learning with Shlomo revolutionized his life:

> We eventually became *shomer Shabbos* as a result of Reb Shlomo. To say that the musical and spiritual relationship with Shlomo changed me would be an understatement.

⁂

On October 25, 1972, Reb Shlomo performed the marriage of Ne'eman and Malka Rosen at the Hillel House of Berkeley. On the wedding invitations Shlomo wrote that "the whole world is invited." The invites were distributed all over Haight-Ashbury and it became a special Carlebach happening with many people who didn't even know the couple.[98]

Ne'eman was a key figure in the refurbishing of the second HLP. He had first come to the HLP on Shabbat, July 10, 1970 during a "Ten-Day Teach-In":

> I had never heard of Shlomo, had never experienced Shabbos, and walked in reluctantly. I had been hitchhiking, searching for my purpose in life. After hearing Shlomo teach, tell stories, and sing, and experiencing the genuine warmth and friendliness of the people around me, I said to myself, "This is what I was looking for."[99]

Shlomo gave him the Hebrew name Ne'eman. He lived with Pesach Weitz on the third floor of the HLP and they were responsible for the functioning of the second HLP.

Malka was born as Jane Gorman on April 29, 1950 and grew up in a secular home. At age 16, she graduated from Christopher Columbus High School in the Bronx and attended City College of New York. At 19, she left school and moved to Kibbutz Ganigar in the Galilee. Then she found the HLP community in Kiryat Yovel and was deeply touched by their love and warm acceptance. She met Shlomo when he arrived to perform the wedding of Chanan and Channah Leah at the Kotel, the Western Wall:

> Meeting Shlomo transformed my life and launched my spiritual journey. He showed me a meaning and depth in Judaism that, to this day, I have yet to find in the existing religious world.[100]

---

98. Mandelbaum, *Holy Brother*, 9.

99. Ne'eman Rosen, personal communication, Aug., 2011.

100. The story told here is based on several discussions with Malka Gorman from Sept. 29 to Oct. 6, 2011.

*Photo taken by LIFE Magazine of the wedding of Pamela Klein (on right, hold-
ing bouquet) and George Gorner (head barely visible, next to Pamela), March
24, 1969. Natan Schafer is holding the bamboo poles for the huppah. Behind
Shlomo is Aryae Coopersmith in brown suede sport jacket. On the right, Alex
Scott is playing the guitar. Jon Hammond is playing accordion just behind
Reb Shlomo.*

Shlomo gave her the Hebrew name of Malka based on one of his Hasidic
parables/stories.[101] Malka was one of the first four students in 1970
at Neve Yerushalayim, the women's religious seminary established by
Rabbi Dovid Refson in Jerusalem. She then tried Sh'or Yoshuv women's
seminary in Far Rockaway, and from there went to the HLP where she
met Ne'eman. After giving birth to twin sons, the couple went to New
York, intending to join the HLP *chevra* in Israel. Instead they stayed in
Far Rockaway where Ne'eman studied in the *kollel* of the Sh'or Yoshuv
Yeshiva.[102]

---

101. Malkele was so poor that when Reb Elimelech of Lizensk visited her home, she
had nothing to offer. Broken-hearted, she boiled a pot of water, her tears falling into it
as she pleaded to God to add taste to the water. When Reb Elimelech tasted the soup
his soul was revived, the lesson being that with Malkele's soup you can bring people
back to life. The story was published in *The Holy Beggar Gazzette*, Spring–Summer,
1976 edition (see above). A rendition of this story is transcribed in Midlo, *Lamed Vav*,
181–183. See below in the context of Soviet Jewry.

102. The couple divorced in 1979, and eventually Malka left the Orthodox world.
Currently, she is a clinical psychologist in private practice in San Francisco.

\#

On April 11, 1973, Reb Shlomo performed the marriage of Donna Anderson, his business manager at the HLP,[103] to Steven L. Maimes. Reb Shlomo announced ceremoniously on a popular radio program called *The Meeting of the Way* that everyone was invited to the wedding.[104] The wedding thus became the first major event at the HLP where spiritual seekers from all the different paths came together for a purely Shlomo happening.[105] Steven studied philosophy and religion at San Francisco State University. When the second HLP opened, Steve moved nearby and attended regularly (1972–1975). There he met Donna. Steve not only organized educational events such as teach-ins (see above), but he also was co-editor of *The Holy Beggars' Gazette*, and ran a Judaic Book Service specializing in Hasidut and Kabbalah.[106]

\#

On August 31, 1975, Alifa Saadya and David Herzberg were married in the Shakespeare Garden of Golden Gate Park. Their marriage was performed by Rabbi Shalom Stern, the rabbi at the nearby Magain David Sephardim Congregation. The engagement *tenaim* was celebrated at the HLP on Motzei Shabbat, May 10, 1975 with Reb Zalman and Reb Shlomo officiating. Alifa was born in Indianapolis, Indiana, on January 16, 1948 as Phyllis Ann Smith.[107] At age 21, she began studying in nursing school in San Francisco. She heard about the HLP, and in August 1970 began visiting regularly on Shabbat. Under the guidance of Shlomo she converted to Judaism on June 20, 1974.[108] Three days later, on Shabbat, she asked Shlomo to give her a Hebrew name:

> On Shabbat at the HLP everyone was giving blessings. Shlomo was inspired and gave me the unique name of Alifa Pelait, אליפה

---

103. Donna was 14 years old when she first met Shlomo in April 1963 in New York. See Coopersmith, *Holy Beggars*, 299.

104. Donna Maimes, personal communication, Sept. 12, 2011.

105. Personal communication from Steve Maimes, Sept. 2, 2011.

106. Currently, Steve is a freelance writer and principal of SALAM Research in Rochester, New Hampshire. See Blogger.com, http://www.blogger.com/profile/1780 6391364675752537; SalamResearch.com, http://www.salamresearch.com/.

107. Her family had a Christian, Protestant, background. In her high school years, she lived in Mooresville, Indiana, a town founded by Quakers. Phyllis and her brothers attended the Mooresville Friends Meetings.

108. In the special set of 44 recordings of teachings from the HLP, collated by Alon Teeger, this is recording #24.

פלאית, literally, the wonderous Alifa. The name is a play on the letter *aleph*. Later, I learned that the *aleph*, being silent with no vowel sound of its own, is the moment before Creation, the letter before *beit* that begins the story of Creation.[109]

At the end of 1974, Alifa moved into the House, replacing Nechama Yasskin as the roommate of Sarah Dickerson (Kauffman). The two women did the cooking and organized much of the daily programming. After their marriage, David and Alifa lived at the House. Their daughter Shira was born in December 1975, and they left the HLP a few months later.[110]

David Herzberg was born in 1951 and grew up in a Modern Orthodox family in Jersey City, New Jersey. He studied at the Yeshiva of Hudson County for twelve years and was involved in the Zionist Bnei Akiva youth movement. David went to Israel in 1969 and served for a year as a volunteer in the army. Upon returning to America, he began a spiritual journey, eventually settling in at the HLP for a couple of years:[111]

> When I was freaking out in my young hippie days I ended up in San Francisco, and I stayed at the House of Love and Prayer . . . There was a wonderful library there that was filled with almost every book you could ask for in the world of *Chasidut*, which Shlomo himself put together.[112]

David spent many nights delving into these books at the HLP. In the last few years of the HLP, he served as "the *gabbai*, *shamash*, and spiritual leader,"[113] functioning in effect, as "Rabbi of the HLP" when Reb Shlomo was not there.[114] In 1980, he went on aliyah settling in Moshav Me'or Modi'im, and after his divorce in 1982, moved to Jerusalem where he taught *hasidut*. He remarried twice and died at a young age on July 23, 2002.

---

109. Personal interviews with Alifa Saadya in Oct. 2011.

110. The couple had two daughters, Shira and Razi. In February 1980, they went on aliyah to join their friends at Moshav Me'or Modi'im. They divorced in May 1982 and Alifa assumed the last name Saadya. Today, Alifa lives in Me'or Modi'im and works at the Hebrew University Vidal Sassoon Center for the Study of Antisemitism.

111. Shalom Freedman, "David Herzberg," *In the Service of God – Conversations with Teachers of Torah in Jerusalem* (Northvale, New Jersey: 1995), 215–228.

112. Ibid., 217.

113. Moshe Rothkopf, "Reb David," in *Sparks of David*, xiii.

114. Menachem Kallus, "Preface," in *Sparks of David*, vii.

5.   SPIRITUAL DIRECTIONS AFTER HLP

Most of those who passed through the HLP were in their twenties. As they matured, married, and found jobs, they reentered mainstream society usually taking with them their newfound spirituality. Basically, there were three types of spiritual directions after the HLP:

a.   an Orthodox religious path, sometimes *haredi*;
b.   aliyah to Israel, often accompanied by a Carlebachian type religiosity;
c.   innovative spiritual paths.

#

a. The first result was a natural outcome of Reb Shlomo's agenda to promote religiosity. He encouraged his students to find serious Torah learning venues. Some went to the Sh'or Yoshuv Yeshiva founded by Rabbi Shlomo Freifeld in 1967 in Far Rockaway, New York.[115] Others traveled to Jerusalem to the Diaspora Yeshiva founded by Rabbi Mordechai Goldstein after the Six-Day War.[116] This was the first yeshiva in Israel designed specifically to meet the needs of English-speaking spiritual seekers from the Diaspora.[117] In the summer of 1968, Rabbi Goldstein came to the HLP in San Francisco to recruit students.[118]

In the 1970s, additional *yeshivot* for *baalei teshuva* were founded in Jerusalem: The Shema Yisrael Yeshiva in 1970 (which changed its name to Ohr Samayach in 1972),[119] and Aish HaTorah in the Old City in 1974.[120] Neve Yerushalayim, the first women's seminary, was started in 1970 by Rabbi Dovid Refson.[121] Gradually, this grew into the phenomenon of *baal*

---

115. See ShorYoshuv.org, http://www.shoryoshuv.org/RabbiFriefeld.aspx. In 2003, the yeshiva moved to its current location in Lawrence, New York.

116. See below, Chapter 10, for the story of Rabbi Joe Schonwald and the first 8 students at Rabbi Goldstein's Yeshiva.

117. Thus, for example, when Eliezer (Sonny) Garner, one of the first residents of the HLP told Shlomo in 1969 that he wanted to become more religious, Shlomo sent him to the Diaspora Yeshiva, and he stayed there for six months. Personal interview, Dec. 20, 2012.

118. Coopersmith, *Holy Beggars*, 174.

119. It was founded by Rabbis Nota Schiller, Mendel Weinbach, Yaakov Rosenberg, and Noah Weinberg. See Danzig, *Origins of Return*, 67–68.

120. For a 4-minute film on the life of Rabbi Noah Weinberg (1930–2009), founder of Aish Hatorah, see http://www.aish.com/v/insp/82246137.html.

121. Nevey.org, http://www.nevey.org/nevehistory.php. See above how Malka Gorman was encouraged by Reb Shlomo to attend Neve Yerushalayim. She was one of the first four students at Neve.

teshuva yeshivas.[122] Shlomo encouraged many to attend these yeshivas, sometimes even arranging airfare and/or tuition.

Thus, the post-HLP path led to observant religiosity. This is exemplified in the stories of leading HLP activists such as Ne'eman and Pesach (described above), who after leaving the HLP began studying in Sh'or Yoshuv and eventually integrated into the American *haredi* world.

⁂

b. The aliyah directive was a natural outcome of the enthusiasm following the Six-Day War. In Reb Shlomo's theological view, the hippie revolutionary Summer of Love and the June liberation of Jerusalem were both part of a Messianic global transformation that began in 1967. In his mind, they were mutually dependent. He sang about the "Great Day of Shabbos," when the whole world will return to Jerusalem, and find universal peace, love, and true friendship with God. The first two couples of the HLP, Alex (Elyah) and Miriam Scott (Succot), and Natan and Ahouva Schafer left for Jerusalem in April–May 1969. Reb Shlomo dedicated to them his song, on his 1972 album, "Rebuild Jerusalem": "May the angels walk with you to guard you on your way" (Psalms 91:11). Eventually, about twenty people who were at the HLP moved to Moshav Me'or Modi'im and played an important role in developing this pioneering endeavor (see Chapter 8).[123]

Sometimes, the individual path went through multiple changes. One illustration of the complexity can suffice here. Jonathan Daniel had first met Shlomo in Berkeley in 1968[124] and soon became a regular at the HLP, participating in its programs until it closed. He studied for a year in Jerusalem from the summer of 1973, first briefly at the Diaspora Yeshiva and then at Ohr Somayach. Then he went to Portland, Oregon and became a chiropractor. Jonathan returned to Israel in 1980, living on Moshav Me'or Modi'im until 1982. His marriage took place at the Moshav

---

122. On the circumstances for the emergence of *baalei teshuva* see Danzger, *Returning to Tradition*, chapters 3–4.

123. These include Meira Burkey, Shoshana and Eliahu Galor, Alifa and David Herzberg, Moshe and Bernice Kussoy, Chaya and Avraham Leader, Mordechai and Morasha Levy, Liliane and Dr. Joshua Ritchie, Yankala and Shoshana Shemesh, Dina and Ben Zion Solomon, Rachel Trugman and Nechama Yasskin (Silver).

124. See below, Chapter 7. Born June 16, 1947, Jonathan studied at the University of California, Berkeley from 1966 to 1969. He first attended Shlomo's concert on May 26, 1968 at the Berkeley Community Theater. For an advertisement of this program see under "Today" in the *Oakland Tribune*, May 26, 1968 – http://newspaperarchive.com/oakland-tribune/1968-05-26/page-164, first column, second entry.

in 1985 (see below, Chapter 8). However, eventually he found his niche
in life in the U.S. as an alternative medicine practitioner and as a serious
spiritual seeker who studied Kabbalah and Hasidut with leading rabbinic
authorities.[125]

※

c. The third route is evidenced by those who adapted various aspects of
the spirituality that they found at the HLP. Some sought new versions of
the HLP ideal, created "Carlebach *minyanim*" and exported Carlebach
nusach to congregations around the world.

Many who passed through the HLP had an experience that they
found difficult to integrate when they went back into mainstream Jewish
life. The Shabbat high seemed to have lost its luster. Compared to the
camaraderie of the HLP, the typical synagogue seemed like a disjointed
collection of individuals following a predetermined liturgy, and prayer
services seemed dry and uninspiring. Having had a taste of "Love and
Prayer," they didn't always fit easily within the existing institutions. Some
of them created new spiritual paths.

This direction is exemplified in the Aquarian Minyan of Berkeley
(AMB).[126] The idea germinated during a month-long seminar led by Reb
Zalman which began Friday evening, May 17, 1974, at the Hillel House
of Berkeley.[127] The seminar climaxed with a *farbrengen* featuring Reb
Shlomo on June 16, 1974. Shortly after, seminar participants formulated a
vision of "a New Age Judaism" which eventually became to be considered
a progenitor of the Jewish Renewal Movement (see below). Although
they never acquired a building of their own, AMB established a spiritual
community whose purpose was "to revitalize prayer, liturgy, rituals and
teachings," with "innovative participatory services."[128] The AMB activists
created new modes of spiritual, kabbalistic, meditative, and ecumenical

---

125. Personal interview, March 28, 2013. Today, Jonathan is a chiropractor, Chinese
Medicine practitioner and homeopath in New York and Connecticut. My thanks to
Jonathan for sharing his story which I have condensed here.

126. I will use the shorthand AMB although the preferred term is The Minyan,
See AquarianMinyan.org, http://www.aquarianminyan.org/index.cfm?pageid=4&
siteid=1.

127. My thanks to Reuven and Yehudit Goldfarb, who generously provided me with
a wealth of information on the AMB.

128. AquarianMinyan.org, http://www.aquarianminyan.org/index.cfm?pageid=4
&siteid=1.

Second HLP 1973. Front row, Jonathan Daniel and Barry Ring. Above Jonathan is Chayah Leider. Near her is Mordechai Levy. Towards center is Sally Duensing (blonde) facing her boyfriend Ian Grand (with glasses and hand on beard).

experiences,[129] and this became a pioneering model of neo-Hasidic Renewal.[130]

Reb Zalman recalled:

> Shlomo and I divided the scene. Some from the HLP would come over to Berkeley and vice versa, for it was a trip of about three-quarters of an hour drive over the bridge. The two congregations were viewed as complementary and not inimical.[131]

Barry (Reuven) Barkan, an HLP activist who helped found the AMB, explained how AMB was created under the inspiration of Reb Zalman and Reb Shlomo, "two awesome, profound and prophetic teachers":

> Reb Zalman and Reb Shlomo were the sacred living bridges that enabled the tradition to take root in this West Coast community that was more oriented towards Woodstock, India, and Selma than Jerusalem, Sfat, and Bratzlov.[132]

---

129. For a description of these innovations, in particular what she calls "vernacular Kabbalah," see Chava Weissler, "Performing Kabbalah in the Jewish Renewal Movement," in Boaz Huss (ed.), *Kabbalah and Contemporary Spiritual Revival* (Beersheba: 2011), 39–95.

130. Yaakov Ariel, "From Neo-Hasidism to Outreach Yeshivot: The Origins of the Movements of Renewal and Return to Tradition," in Boaz Huss (ed.), *Kabbalah and Contemporary Spiritual Revival* (Beersheba: 2011), 17–37.

131. Reb Zalman Schachter-Shalomi, Skype interview, Aug. 2011.

132. Barkan, "You Are Building It," 74.

Barkan refers to them as the "two Zaydes of Jewish Renewal," but perhaps it would be more accurate to say that Zalman was the "father" of Jewish Renewal, and Shlomo was the "uncle," thus contrasting Reb Zalman's humorous note that he was the uncle of the HLP and Shlomo was the father.[133]

As the HLP began to wind down its activities in 1975–1976, the AMB became an attractive center for Reb Shlomo's followers in the Berkeley–San Francisco area. Aryeh Trupin joined AMB in 1974, was close to Reb Shlomo, and played with him in concerts for twenty years in both New York and the Bay Area. For him, Reb Shlomo was teaching the "melody" of a God who "is alive and living":

> Being with and playing music with Rabbi Shlomo Carlebach z"l really opened my heart to the immanent and transcendent God that is alive and living. Shlomo always said that knowing the words but not knowing the melody was like being in exile. Whenever I played with Shlomo, I had the experience of the exile being over.[134]

After the HLP closed, it was the AMB who would be instrumental in helping organize the visits of Reb Shlomo to California two or three times a year.

---

133. For a more precise definition of Shlomo's role in the development of the Jewish Renewal Movement see Magid, "Jewish Renewal," 4869 and 4872–4873.

134. *Nitzotzot*, vol. 25, no. 4, Summer 1999, 9.

Part B

The Impact

Getting High at the HLP

1.   LORD GET ME HIGH AND RETURN AGAIN

The hippie culture of the 1960s reveled in "getting high." "Tripping" was pandemic, with a wondrous reverence for marijuana.[1] Timothy Leary, icon of the 1960s counterculture, and a leading proponent of the therapeutic and spiritual benefits of LSD,[2] founded the League for Spiritual Discovery in September 1966 "to change and elevate the consciousness of every American."[3] Leary pronounced the phrase that became the slogan of the hippie generation: "Turn on, Tune in, and Drop out."[4]

Shlomo described Leary as "one of my best friends"[5] and that he came "a lot of times" to the HLP. Shlomo noted with humor that it was "a great honor" to hear that on Leary's LSD trips he would listen to Carlebach records.[6]

---

1. Stephen Gaskin, *Monday Night Class* (Santa Rosa, Calif.: Book Farm, 1970), new introduction to the revised edition, 2005.

2. Leary completed a doctorate in psychology in 1950 at the University of California, Berkeley. He began teaching at Harvard University in 1959 and during 1960–1962 conducted the Harvard Psilocybin Project with Prof. Richard Alpert (later Ram Dass) to find better ways to treat alcoholism and reform convicted criminals.

3. Jay Stevens, *Storming Heaven: LSD and the American Dream* (New York: 1987), xv; McWilliams, *The 1960s Cultural Revolution*, 17–18.

4. Timothy Leary in a press conference in New York on September 19, 1966. The archival recording was reproduced in the *American Experience* documentary on the Summer of Love, PBS.org, http://www.pbs.org/wgbh/amex/love/filmmore/pt.html.

5. In Leary's autobiography he refers to "the Rock and Roll Rabbi," supposedly a reference to Shlomo Carlebach. Timothy Leary, *Flashbacks, An Autobiography: A Personal and Cultural History of an Era* (Los Angeles: 1990 [first published May 25, 1983]).

6. Shlomo to his interviewer Shmuel in *Insights 613*, Part II: http://www.youtube .com/watch?v=E6JOU60G5Qk&feature=related, segment 3:00–3:40. Another

Shlomo even told a story of how he had once experimented with LSD in a uniquely Jewish way by having "his *chevra* turn on a tape recorder and ask him every ten minutes if he believes in God." Shlomo noted laughingly: "Indeed, they recorded me as responding in the affirmative, and I still have this recording." However, Shlomo observed proudly that the Shabbat experience at the HLP was "more powerful" than LSD, and that "even Timothy Leary agreed when he visited the HLP for Shabbat."[7] In later interviews, Shlomo remembered Leary as saying: "I may be into LSD, but it's only out of emergency. But, I see you Jews have the answer. Shabbos is the best drug in the world."[8] This remarkable declaration was corroborated by Rabbi Baruch Melman who personally questioned Leary about his relationship with Rabbi Carlebach:

> Leary's answer stunned me. He said succinctly, without skipping a beat, "If I had ever had a chance to listen to Shlomo's music before I ever took drugs, I would have never needed to take them in the first place, that's how powerful his music was!'" This counterculture icon admitted to me that his entire career mission of selling mind-altering psychedelic experience was duplicated and transcended by the powerful feelings of transcendental universal oneness aroused within him by the music of Reb Shlomo![9]

No wonder that a sign posted on the entrance door to the first HLP had proclaimed – "We get high on Shabbos."[10] Similarly, "Lord Get Me High," Shlomo's first original song in English, implied an alternative to the psychedelic high:

---

version is that when Leary informed Shlomo that he liked to listen to Shlomo's music while on acid trips, Shlomo responded that learning Talmud was superior. Shefa Siegel, "Shlomo Carlebach – Rabbi of Love or Undercover Agent of Orthodox Judaism?" *Haaretz*, Sept. 4, 2011, HaAretz.com, http://www.haaretz.com/culture/books/shlomo-carlebach-rabbi-of-love-or-undercover-agent-of-orthodox-judaism-1.382475.

7. This is a translation into English of the quote attributed to Shlomo by his interviewer (Nili) in *Maariv*, Sept. 9, 1970 (the Hebrew article is photocopied in Brand, *Reb Shlomele*, 160). Cf. Shacham, "Enfant Terrible," 29. See also Wohlgelernter, "Simply Shlomo," where he quotes Shlomo as saying that he never advocated drug use, but that he had tried drugs during the 1960s in order to better appreciate what was happening to the hippies.

8. See Paley, "His Gift." and Shlomo's interview in 1994 on *Insights 613*, Part II: http://www.youtube.com/watch?v=E6JOU60G5Qk&feature=related, segment 2:30–3:50.

9. Rabbi Baruch Melman, personal correspondence on Oct. 26, 2012. Melman spoke to Leary at a Whole Earth Conference in New York City in 1989.

10. Ritchie, *Masters and Miracles*, 35.

Lord get me high, get me high, get me high.
Lord get me high, get me higher. (2×)
Higher and higher, higher and higher . . .

This song was based on a tune that Shlomo sang to the words of *"Yasis Alayich Elohaiyich"*[11] when he performed the wedding of George Gorner, an avid song composer (see above, Chapter 5). Shlomo turned to the groom and asked that he prepare lyrics in English.[12] A week or so later Gorner succeeded.[13] Recently, George reconstructed more of the history of this song:

> We left a concert at Sonoma State University near Santa Rosa. Pam, my new bride, was driving my old Corvair that had had a fire, so there was no backseat, just a lot of cushions. The sun was coming up in an unbelievable sunrise. Out the window was some garish hotel with flamingos. Shlomo and I were huddled half asleep on the cushions. Shlomo looked up and said, "George, the Lord is quite an artist." That is when we began singing our new uplifting song "Lord Get Me High," and we continued all the way back to his motel in San Francisco.[14]

A precedent for this song is "Higher and Higher," recorded two years earlier (July 6, 1967) by the Afro-American singer, Jackie Wilson.[15]

---

11. This Carlebach song eventually became one of the most famous Jewish wedding tunes. The words are from the *"Lecha Dodi" piyut* of the Friday night prayer service, based on the verse in Isa. 62:5 about the rejoicing of God over Israel like a groom over a bride.

12. Shlomo tells this to Shumi Berkowitz in a video filmed in the summer of 1994 in Shumi's Ramat Gan apartment, http://www.youtube.com/watch?v=qL-gpu3htHo. See also http://www.youtube.com/watch?v=8eRSoMCH1Ho&feature=relmfu, segment. 4:40. For a picture of this event, see Brandwein, *Reb Shlomele*, 249.

13. Lynn Reichman added that the original first version of the English lyrics was composed after a wedding that Shlomo performed on Mt. Tamalpais in Marin County shortly before Pesach, March 1969. Lynn was walking down the mountain with the HLP group: "I was very happy at the House, but only 16 years old and living away from home for the first time. George noticed how lonely I felt and began humming the tune that Shlomo had sang at his wedding, spontaneously adding English words of comfort: 'God will make you high' (3×) . . . 'You are not alone' (3×) . . . 'God is always with you' (3×). When we arrived at the bottom of the mountain, and drove to the post-wedding party in Mill Valley, George rushed excitedly to Shlomo and exclaimed: 'I have some English lyrics for your song.'" Personal conversations with Lynn Reichman, Jan. 16, 2013. See also Lynn Reichman, "A Story about a Niggun," *Kol Chevra*, vol. 17, 2011, 26.

14. George Gorner, personal conversations and correspondence, Nov. 30, 2012.

15. For the many versions of this popular song, see En.Wikipedia.org, http://

Wilson's song begins: "We praise your name Lord. We lift you higher, higher, higher."[16] Shlomo transformed the theme and added a utopian Messianic continuation:

> Lord let me pray, just one prayer . . .
>> Lord let me say, let me say, let me say just one word
> Lord let me sing, let me sing just one song . . .
>> Lord let me live till the Great Morning comes.
> When the whole world will sing just one song.

Recently, George revealed that in the original lyrics there was a concluding line: "So high, that I really love my brother, so high that I know there's no Other." Shlomo would sing this, but eventually these lines fell out of use and were forgotten.[17]

Shlomo's second original song in English was composed in the summer of 1974 and is titled "Return Again."[18] The lyrics were again written with a Hippie disciple, Ronnie (Rafael Simcha) Kahn. They implore a rebirth as a "return to what you are . . . to the land of your soul."[19]

> Return to what you are, return to who you are,
>> Return to where you are. Born and reborn again (2×).
> Return again, return again, return to the land of your soul.
>> <Relive the joys of your fathers before you
>>> who died with the song of their Lord on their lips, They sing,>[20]
> Return Again, Return Again, Return to the land of your soul . . .

---

en.wikipedia.org/wiki/%28Your_Love_Keeps_Lifting_Me%29_Higher_and_Higher.

16. The lyrics are: Lord you are worthy of all our praise. Choir: higher, higher. I'll keep on lifting, lifting You high. Choir: higher, higher. "Higher and Higher" is also the name of Wilson's bestselling album of which 4 million copies were eventually sold.

17. George Gorner, Phone conversation Nov. 30, 2012.

18. Shlomo composed the original tune on a Thursday evening shortly after arriving in the Catskill Mountains to lead a Shabbaton in the summer of 1974. See Ben Zion Solomon, *Shlomo Shabbos*, 15.

19. The original version that Ronnie Kahn wrote was "return to the home of your soul," but Shlomo changed it to the "land of your soul." This according to a personal communication from Robert Cohen who was present in the summer of 1974 when the song was first composed. The expression "land of your soul" is a unique phrase coined by Reb Shlomo.

20. This additional line, seemingly hinting at the Holocaust generation, was added later by Reb Shlomo. It changes the import of the song to a much more Jewish message as opposed to the more universal theme of a self return to one's soul. For the complete song by Reb Shlomo, see http://www.youtube.com/watch?v=WgCMi9Mn VgY&feature=related.

This was expanded upon in a teaching printed in 1977, where Shlomo explained how "the greatest blessing is to be connected to your roots, to the roots of your own soul."[21]

It is with such innovations that Shlomo was able to effectively speak "Hippie language" and offer an attractive alternative to their value system of psychedelic spirituality.

2.   NEO-HASIDIC HIPPIE VALUES

How does an Orthodox Hasidic Rabbi relate to the hippie value system of psychedelics, rebellion, peace, and sexuality? R. Shlomo applied the Kabbalistic-Hasidic notion that a spiritual spark of goodness, love, and joy can be discovered underlying the seemingly "alien" quest. Thus, he was able to speak the hippie language, partake of their joys and sorrows, and gain their trust and love. His self-proclaimed mission was to bring a little Jewish holiness, a little Yiddishkeit to these "holy hippelach."

On the one hand, Shlomo imparted traditional Jewish messages, directing all who were ready to listen to marry Jewish, keep kosher, and observe Shabbat. He suggested Hebrew names, even inventing some original ones.[22] He encouraged visiting Israel and even settling there. But what distinguished his approach from the typical Jewish outreach was the way he tuned in and really appreciated the song and soul of a hippy generation. Speaking in Berkeley in 1967, Shlomo described the hippies as a new generation of young people who hear the Divine melody but "don't know the words." He exclaimed that this is the melody that was lost with the destruction of the Holy Temple.[23]

Shlomo's thesis was that the world would be fixed when the older generation listens to the hippies' melody and simultaneously "these inspired young people" learn some of the traditional words. It is only with this combination that the redemptive "new song to God" (Psalms 96:1) will be sung:

> The saddest thing today, friends, is that we have an older genera-
> tion that knows all the words. They know every word, and they
> guard every word, and they teach every word. But, they don't
> know the melody! . . . Today, a whole new generation of young

---

21. Shlomo Carlebach, "The Ingredients of Peace," in Elana Rappaport and Steven L. Maimes (eds.), *The Holy Beggars' Gazette*, Oakland, California, 1977, 3–4.

22. For example, to Barbara Midlo, Shlomo gave the name Tzlotana, which in Aramaic means "our prayer." For the name change of Phyllis Ann Smith to Alifa see above, Chapter 5, section 4.

23. Zeller, *The Soul of the Story*, 28.

people seems to be so far away from Judaism. But are they? They're moving to a different beat. They hear a heavenly melody. They're dancing a new dance. But, they don't know the words!

If we could just get the guardians of the tradition to listen to the new melody, and if we could just get these inspired young people to learn some of the words, then, like it says in Psalms, we could "sing a new song to God." We could really fix the whole world.[24]

Shlomo used an idiosyncratic term of "holy beggars." The hippies, who are penniless, hungry, and "tripping," are on a holy quest to receive God's Revelation. They may not be aware of their true inner spiritual motivation, but really they are *begging* to know and love God. In a talk in 1968, Reb Shlomo proclaimed that there are three levels to receiving the message from God:

Every day, every second, God is sending us messages. The only thing is, the messages come on different levels. One level is the fact: the fact can only reach as far as the mind. Then there's the story: the story reaches past the mind to the heart. But the deepest of all is the melody: the melody reaches all the way to the soul.[25]

One might say that the programming at the HLP was intended to provide all three components: Torah for the mind, stories for the heart, and melodious spirit for the soul.

Hippies preached altruism, joy, sincerity, and emphasized "love of nature, passion for music, and desire for reflection."[26] Shlomo reinterpreted the hippie lifestyle and values. Hippies emphasized "personal freedom" and their rallying call was "Don't trust anyone over 30." Shlomo readily accepted the hippie demand for freedom from hierarchical statuses. Despite his official rabbinical role, he preferred to be addressed informally by his first name, routinely eschewing formal titles. He advocated a laissez-faire approach of not telling people what to do or how to act. He resonated easily with freedom from scheduling – he lived in his own dimensions of timelessness. The hippies expressed freedom in flamboyant clothing and unkempt hair. R. Shlomo wore his hair long, and pinned up his beard with bobby pins.[27] In hippie-land he changed his attire, took off the suit, hat, and jacket, and appeared with a vest, suspenders, a Magen David

---

24. Ibid., 27–28.

25. Coopersmith, *Holy Beggars*, Preface, xvii.

26. Jentri Anders, *Beyond Counterculture: The Community of Mateel* (Pullman, Washington: 1990).

27. The practice of not cutting one's beard, common in Chabad, is based on a kabbalistic idea.

pendant, and an unusual velvet *kippah* with embroidery, usually silver Yemenite filigree. Shlomo wore a bead necklace in San Francisco but not in New York because "my mother doesn't like hippies." The necklace had "four-color beads for the four races (black, white, yellow, red) arranged seven-alike beads then another seven-alike."[28]

Hippie life embraced empathy, brotherhood, and communal living. These ideals were meant to replace capitalism, materialism, and the career-driven "rat race." Reb Shlomo brought Jewish equivalents that were meant to parallel and even compete with the teachings of his friends and colleagues such as Stephen Gaskin, Yogi Bhajan, Swami Satchidananda, and Pir Vilayat Khan (see below). The House of Love and Prayer exuded love and joy. The welcoming atmosphere was influenced by Shlomo's ideals of empathy, appreciation, and recognition of the goodness of each person. Shlomo had a talent to bring out the inner beauty of each person with a non-judgmental all-embracing love towards all. This expressed itself in his signature greetings of "Holy Brother/Sister" and "My Best Friend." The implications are stated by his wife Neila at their *Sheva Brachot* in December 1972:

> Shlomo says to everyone, "Ah! There's my top friend! There's my best friend!" When I first met Shlomo he told me I was top girl, and I was his best friend, and I got a little confused, because every single time he saw somebody *mamash*, that person was a top friend, a best friend. . . . When he looks into every single face here and he says, "you're my best friend, you're my top friend," there's nobody else in the world except you. You are his best friend, his top friend.[29]

For optimistic Shlomo each individual was "the best."[30]

3.   FRIENDLINESS AND COMMUNAL LIFE

This effervescent friendliness was at the core of the existence of House of Love and Prayer. It fit in as part of a neo-Hasidic ethic that nourished a warm communal life style. Reb Shlomo added a Jewish dimension to the hippie ideal of "free love" and brotherhood by explaining the halachic dimensions of interpersonal relations. In his teachings at the HLP in 1975 on *Sefer HaChinukh*, on mitzvah #238, "Don't Hate Your Brother in Your Heart," Reb Shlomo commented: "Probably 95 percent of the people hate

---

28. Skir, "Carlebach," 28.
29. *Holy Beggars' Gazette*, vol. 2, no. 1, April 1973.
30. For more on this, see below, Chapter 13.

each other because they misjudge each other." How can one eliminate this "hate?" Reb Shlomo quoted a book called *Yad HaKetana*, as saying:[31]

> What do you do if you hate people for no reason, and you can't get out of it? The only way out is loving people for no reason. Just love, because love is a very holy fire that will drag out all the darkness of hatred.[32]

Shlomo cited *Yad HaKetana* as noting that "free love," *ahavat hinam*, can rectify "free hate," *sinat hinam*, the unwarranted hate of the type that led to the destruction of the Second Temple.[33]

Shlomo's creation of the House of Love and Prayer should be understood in context of the commune phenomenon that began burgeoning after the 1967 Summer of Love. Thousands of communes were created in a period that has been dubbed "the greatest wave of communal living in American history."[34] From a sociological perspective, the HLP was similar to the urban communes that were set up then in Haight-Ashbury. But significantly, it was the only attempt at establishing a Jewish one. With but a rare exception, there were almost no other Jewish communes in twentieth century America.[35]

The significance of the HLP should also be contextualized as a Jewish alternative to the "Jesus Coffeehouses" which functioned as a 24/7 ministry outreach to troubled youth, runaways, alcoholics, and prostitutes. In August 1967, four hippie couples rented a storefront a block away from the intersection of Haight and Ashbury Streets[36] and turned it into

---

31. This book, *Yad HaKetana*, was printed anonymously, but has been identified as having been composed by Dov Barish Gottlieb, who died on Aug. 27, 1796.

32. Pesach Weitz and Ne'eman Rosen, "Shlomo's Teachings on Mitzvah 239, 'Rebuke a Fellow Jew Who Isn't Acting Correctly,'" *Holy Beggars' Gazette*, Winter–Spring, 1975, 45–46.

33. This idea was developed by Rav Kook in *Shemonah Kevatzim*, vol. 8, sect. 47, 414 (=*Orot HaKodesh*, vol. 3, 324). Rav Kook explains how the ability to discern the Goodness in each person creates a spontaneous and natural love for the other person and obscures the evil aspects.

34. Timothy Miller, *The 60s Communes: Hippies and Beyond* (Syracuse, New York: 1999), 67–69.

35. See Robert Sutton, *Modern American Communes: A Dictionary* (Westport, Connecticut: 2005), 12. The one Jewish commune listed is Arpin. This was a Jewish farm colony established in 1904 at Arpin, Wisconsin, 150 miles northwest of Milwaukee by the Jewish community for refugees from pogroms in Romania. It declined over the years. In 1940 there were only two families remaining and by 1958 everyone had departed.

36. Ted Wise, "the first hippie convert of the Jesus People," and his wife Elizabeth, together with another 3 couples, ran the storefront ministry linking the hippies to

a Jesus coffeehouse, christening it "The Living Room."[37] The commune was supervised by a group of Baptist pastors.[38] They promoted the Gospel through street evangelism, food sharing, and offering thousands of hippies a place to crash.[39] Many Jewish hippies in San Francisco were attracted, and reportedly, hundreds converted to Christianity.[40] The Evangelical Movement spread around the country. By September 1973, Moishe Rosen was able to found the Jews for Jesus organization with a home office on Haight Street. Messianic Jews began proclaiming that Jesus or Y'shua was the Messiah. Thousands of Jewish street Christians became aggressive witnesses to convert their Jewish brethren.[41]

Through all this religious and spiritual turmoil, the HLP was a Jewish oasis, the only Jewish commune in the Haight. Reb Shlomo's philosophy of life was that Jews needed to be offered genuine love, camaraderie, and empathy and then they would return home.[42] He encouraged his followers to develop communal living. In doing so, he was influenced not only by the Haight-Ashbury communes, but also by models of social interdependence of the Israeli kibbutzim that he had visited. His vision could also have been nurtured by the ideals of the communal support in the Hasidic courts in Brooklyn which he had frequented. As Reuven Goldfarb, an HLP regular, phrased it:

> Shlomo was into creating community – he regarded us all as *chevra*. He demonstrated unconditional love and modeled for us "mutual caring." He didn't judge people. He expressed concern. To this day, the *chevra* feel connected.[43]

---

evangelical churches throughout the U.S. See Paul R. Dienstberger, *The American Republic: A Nation of Christians*.

37. Stephen J. Nichols, *Jesus Made in America: A Cultural History from the Puritans to the Passion of the Christ* (Downers Grove, Illinois: 2008), 124–125.

38. Baptist pastor John MacDonald, from Mill Valley, California, assembled a group of colleagues and raised funds to lease the building. See Larry Eskridge, *God's Forever Family: The Jesus People Movement in America, 1966–1977* (Stirling, Scotland: University of Stirling, 2005), 93–95.

39. Randall Herbert Balmer, "Ted Wise," *Encyclopedia of Evangelicalism* (Louisville, Kentucky: 2002), 634. It is estimated that about 20,000 Hippies visited the Living Room during the two years that it operated – Eskridge, *God's Forever Family*, 93–94.

40. Paul R. Dienstberger, *The American Republic*, Chapter 10 "The Non Establishment Awakening", http://www.prdienstberger.com/nation/atbofcon.htm.

41. Dienstberger, *The American Republic*.

42. See below, Chapter 7, on Shlomo's address on Nov. 21, 1972 at Yeshiva University on love and empathy as the answer to the challenge of Jews for Jesus.

43. Personal interview, Aug. 2011.

A key feature of communal life was festive meals. The HLP residents would visit the farmers' market, especially on Fridays. Elana Schachter (Rappaport):

> When I was living at the House, I remember going down to the farmers market on Friday, and collecting produce from the people there that they didn't think would make it through the weekend. I remember one time there was a dumpster and they put this humongous squash in the dumpster . . . It was a hundred pound squash! It was damaged on one end, so we cut that off and used the rest. And bringing home cases of, I don't know, and Meira would turn it all into Shabbos food.[44]

The HLP residents developed an art of how to collect leftover foods, similar to the practice of the Diggers, a commune that set the tone in Haight-Ashbury in the 1960s.[45] The Diggers salvaged food from restaurant and supermarket overflow, prepared it in their communal kitchen, and brought it, twice a day, to the Panhandle extension of Golden Gate Park. They referred to this as "garbage yoga," gathering "society's leftovers" and distributing them as free food. The Diggers staged free concerts, provided free shelter, and ran free stores in which "customers" could take and leave items at will.

A major innovation of Reb Shlomo and Reb Zalman was to reshape the Hasidic concept of a *farbrengen*. An event was not called a concert, party or happening, but it was labeled a *farbrengen*, implying a congenial Hasidic camaraderie with inspirational songs, joyous dancing, and meaningful stories. The Carlebach *farbrengen* differed from what Shlomo had observed in Chabad in significant ways such as mixed-gendered dancing and an entrance fee, but by co-opting a Yiddish term, Shlomo transmitted a subtle but powerful message of Jewish continuity and uniqueness.

Similarly, Shabbat and holidays were communal events, a time to taste tranquility and experience "paradise" through singing, learning, and feasting that was essentially a Shlomo adaptation of the Hasidic *tish*. Thus an attractive social-spiritual experience could be offered to compete with the non-Jewish attractions.

---

44. HolyBeggars.ning.com, http://holybeggars.ning.com/profile/Tzfatree.

45. Named for 17th century utopian English farmers who raised food for the poor, the Diggers renounced capitalism, declaring that "money lust is a sickness." – McWilliams, *The 1960s Cultural Revolution*, 69.

4.   PURIFICATION, HEALING, AND PARADISE ON SHABBAT

Shabbat and holidays were the most attractive part of the HLP happening. HLP offered a community of spirituality and meaning, a Judaism with feasting, dancing, and learning. For spiritual seekers, including many non-Jews, this was a winning combination – celebrating religious tradition in a non-judgmental way so unlike what most had known from childhood.

Reb Shlomo would visit every two months or so, and then hundreds would join. He presented Shabbat as the opportune time to taste the sweetness of "paradise." Time stopped. The community exited the bustling rat race and discovered a high without drugs. It was created through singing, swaying, storytelling, Torah study, and camaraderie.

Aryae Coopersmith picturesquely depicted the emotional high of the first Friday nights at the HLP (May 1968):

> . . . we're transported to another dimension. *The joy is so intense
> that the only thing I can do is to sing, or shout, or dance for hours,
> or hug everyone, or just close my eyes and cry* . . . Hundreds of
> people show up every week to be with us for Shabbos. About 50
> will typically sleep on the floor of the prayer room and dining
> room. Services last until after midnight and we sometimes don't
> get to sleep until dawn.[46]

Reb Shlomo sought to discover the longing for a "real Shabbos," and he was critical of the way that most religious people observed Shabbat:

> Sometimes, I have the privilege of being with Jews who don't keep
> Shabbos, but, *gevalt*, are they longing for Shabbos. They are not
> longing for the type of Shabbos that most *frum* people have —
> some chicken soup, some noodles, the *Jewish Press*. They are really
> longing for the *Yom shekulo Shabbos*, for the true Shabbos, the real
> Shabbos, which is so much deeper.[47]

Reb Shlomo proudly told an interviewer how the HLP "was so mobbed on Friday night that people had to come through the window" and the prayers lasted "for 5 or 10 hours" with *seudah shlishit* continuing to the wee hours of the morning.[48]

Reb Shlomo emphasized the interplay of the ancient tradition to

---

46. Aryae Coopersmith, "From House," 30–34.

47. Rabbi Shlomo Carlebach in *Hakrev Ushma* (*Connections*), vol. 1, issue 4 Aug./ Sept. 1985.

48. Brenner, *Talkline*, segment 15:55.

the new innovations. He explained that just as the wine of Kiddush is best when it's old, so too this Shabbat is connected to antiquity, to the Shabbatot of the past. But it also needs to be new, just as the challah is best when it's freshly baked.[49]

Reb Shlomo recommended preparing for Shabbat with "purification" in the *mikveh*:

> Back in San Francisco I struck a deal with people who wanted to come to me for Shabbos that they had to go to the *mikveh* first. It was unbelievable – from noon to three it was men, and from three to six it was women. Then they started keeping the mitzvah of becoming clean before Shabbos.[50]

Although it is usually only religious married women who go monthly to the *mikveh*, in several Hasidic circles such as Belz and Breslov, *mikveh* is a regular part of religious life for males. But, for the youthful hippies this practice could relate to purification from sin in a new way. For those who may have had guilt feelings for having left their families, rebelled against tradition, and severed their ties with religion, *mikveh* was an innocent way of saying, yes, we can be pure, innocent and righteous.

Reb Shlomo used a Hasidic/Kabbalistic idea to highlight the importance of creating personal purity to receive the Shabbat:

> On Shabbos, new energy is coming down from Heaven, but the energy refuses to be received in dirty vessels, so for one second before Shabbos, purity and holiness also descend into the world.[51]

Reb Shlomo explained the significance of ritual immersion not only as a means towards purification and sanctity but also as a way to create closeness and become "surrounded by God's Heavenly Love." In a teaching at the Cougar Hot Springs near Eugene, Oregon on April 13, 1992,[52] Shlomo suggested a sequence of five meditative type focuses for dipping in the *mikveh*:

> The first time you go down to immerse yourself is to *cleanse* yourself. The second time is to *purify* yourself. The third time is to *sanctify* yourself. The fourth time is . . . the level of *Oneness*, the

49. Cf. Cohen, "Jewish Soul Man," 64.

50. Paley, "His Gift."

51. Rabbi Shlomo Carlebach, "The Soul of *Shabbos*," *Kol Chevra*, vol. 8, 2001, 10–11. Compare a slightly different version as transcribed in Rabbi Shlomo Carlebach "The Soul of *Shabbos*," *Kol Chevra*, vol. 6, 1999, 120.

52. Libby Bottero and Jesse Rappaport transcribed Reb Shlomo's talk on *mikveh* in *Kol Chevra*, vol. 10, 2004, 39–42. For more on this, see below in the section on Jewish Renewal in Oregon.

Divine Name *Yod-Heh-Vav-Heh*. However, the High Priest on Yom Kippur immersed five times: four times for the Holy Name, and the fifth is beyond everything, the deepest depths of Oneness.[53]

The first four dips signify the four letters of the Tetragrammaton. The stage beyond this is immersion on the highest level of the High Priest on the Day of Atonement. This sums up an ethical-spiritual paradigm aimed at discovering and reliving the "depths" of God's Oneness.

1. Cleansing sin
2. Purification
3. Sanctity
4. Oneness with the Divine
5. Beyond All, to the Deepest Depths.

Where did Reb Shlomo find this idea? The precedent for five types of intentions during five sequential immersions is found in Kabbalistic and Hasidic instructions. The meditative idea of focusing intentions on permutations of the Divine Name is found in the writings of sixteenth century Safed kabbalists. Detailed instructions in the name of the Ari serve as a guide in the pre-Shabbat immersion in the *mikveh*. The purpose is to transform thoughts into Love and Mercy.[54] The idea of meditations during ritual immersion as a means towards receiving Divine Illumination was then developed by the Baal Shem Tov.[55] Reb Shlomo in his teachings about the *mikveh* expands upon the meditative intentions popularized by R. Nachman of Breslov and thus offers an easy to appreciate version of a complex Kabbalistic meditative practice. This kind of idea, integrating *kavvanot* into the *mikveh* ritual, has been encouraged in the Jewish Renewal Movement.[56]

---

53. Ibid., 42, and see HavurahShirHadash.org, http://www.havurahshirhadash.org/shlomoarticle16.html

This experiential *mikveh* excursion is described below.

54. See Aryeh Kaplan, *Meditation and Kabbalah* (York Beach, Maine: 1982), Chapter 6, Sect. 3, *Kavanot*, 214–217. His source is *Shaar HaKavanot*, vol. 2, 25 and *Pri Etz Chaim, Inyan Shabbat*, 4.

55. See ibid., Sect. 3, 276–277 where the intentions of the Baal Shem Tov's immersion are summed up with different permutations of the Divine Name for each dip. Cf. Jonathan Garb, *Shamanic Trance in Modern Kabbalah* (Chicago: 2011), 126 that the Besht "ascribed all of his mystical levels and illumination (*he'ara*) to his frequent purifications, which were accompanied by a famous *kavvanah* that he developed." See p. 221, n. 42, that the Besht's *kavvanah* received numerous commentaries.

56. Carol Rose, "Introduction to *Kavvanot* for the Mikveh," in Shohama Harris Wiener and Jonathan Omer-Man (eds.), *Worlds of Jewish Prayer: A Festschrift in Honor of Rabbi Zalman M. Schachter-Shalomi* (London: 1993), 226–230. Carol Rose is a founding member of P'nai Or and a student of both Reb Zalman and Reb Shlomo.

Shabbat is a prime example of Reb Shlomo's neo-Hasidic renewal of tradition. In Hasidic life Shabbat is "the epicenter,"[57] the time when all gather to experience the spiritual dimensions of life. Shlomo reworded the Hasidic ideas using a language that was meant to speak to the hippie generation. He spoke about Shabbat as a healing "vitamin" to bring new energy to the soul, to fix brokenness and to relieve pain:

> Shabbos is the highest energy center in the world . . . Shabbos is the day when your soul is at the most, most high.[58]
>
> Shabbos is the strongest vitamin you can imagine, because it doesn't just nourish the body. It *mamash* heals the soul. On Shabbos, new energy flows down to us from Heaven in the absolutely purest way.[59]
>
> Shabbos showers upon us the deepest fixing in the world, and we can taste the completeness, the bliss, and the peace of the World to Come.[60]
>
> Shabbos invites all those who need new energy, all those who have been broken by the world of the six days, who need the world of Shabbos to make their brokenness whole again. Shabbos invites all those who have so far only felt the pain of life and are crying for the joy, the bliss, the unbelievable heavenliness of being alive in a world created by God.[61]
>
> Shabbos is back in Paradise. Paradise is a place where everything is good, everything is holy, everything is beautiful. Paradise is a place where suddenly it's clear to me that I can fix all my mistakes . . . Shabbos is the deepest healing in the world. . . . It gives you new brains, new eyes, new ears – what a *gevalt*, Shabbos.[62]
>
> There are three levels of serving God. There is a level of a servant, the level of a child, and there is the level of a friend. God has very few servants; God has very, very few children; and God has nearly no friends. But Shabbos morning, Shabbos morning, suddenly we look deep down into our hearts we know we are God's friends and we see we are *God's friends*.[63]

---

57. See for example, Garb, *Shamanic Trance*, 132.

58. SimpleToreMember.com, http://www.simpletoremember.com/articles/a/carle bach-*Shabbos*/.

59. Midlo, *Lamed Vav*, "The Last Few Minutes Before *Shabbos*," 209.

60. Ibid., "The Bliss of *Shabbos*," 232.

61. SimpleToreMember.com http://www.simpletoremember.com/articles/a/carle bach-*Shabbos*/.

62. Rabbi Shlomo Carlebach, "The Soul of *Shabbos*," *Kol Chevra*, vol. 8, 2001, 10–11.

63. Record Album, Rabbi Shlomo Carlebach Singing the Prayers of *Shabbos* Morning, vol. 2. Reb Shlomo also expresses this message in a concert in Nov. 1972

In encountering and engaging the "holy hippies," R. Shlomo effectively created a new "set and setting" to "get high" and to become "God's friends." It was through enhancing the ritual observances that he was able to respond to basic needs of healing from brokenness and to renew joy in living.

In retrospect, Reb Shlomo initiated a concept that soon became so popular that it received a new name – a "Shabbaton." The term entered modern parlance as a colloquial expression for a Shabbat experience replete with singing, spirited praying, communal meals and Torah study. But in actuality, this is a Neo-Hasidic innovation of Reb Shlomo. He redesigned the Hasidic Shabbat, expanded it to be gender inclusive, and pioneered ways of "getting high" on Shabbat. Today, the idea of a "Shabbaton" is taken for granted, but in the late 1960s the idea of transforming an Orthodox type celebration of Shabbat into a social-spiritual-emotional happening that is open to all was a rather avant-garde concept.

in Brookline, MA. See segment 39:00 at Archive.org, http://archive.org/details/NewEnglandJewishMusicForumAChasidicEveningFeaturingRebShlomo.

CHAPTER 7

Outreach and Wide-Reach

1. REB SHLOMO'S EXPANDING CAREER (1966–1969)

With five LPs to his credit, Shlomo's growing fame brought him invitations to a variety of venues. Thus, he appeared on March 13, 1966 at a major Conservative synagogue, West Suburban Temple Har Zion, in a suburb of Chicago, Illinois.[1] Two months later, Shlomo took part in the International Guitar Festival at Lake Geneva, Wisconsin which was held from June 10–12, 1966.[2] Afterwards, at a special press conference, Shlomo joined together in a common cause with Father J.L. de Lima, a Catholic priest who also performed at this Festival, to explain and justify the use of the guitar in religion.[3]

One secret of Shlomo's charisma was his ability to remember names. Often it was an individualized endearing form of the Hebrew name. In June 1966, Nechama Yasskin (Silver) met Reb Shlomo in Philadelphia at a concert sponsored by the Hillel House at Temple University:

> The concert went from 9:00 PM to 1:00 AM. It was contagious – pretty soon the whole audience was jumping on the pews of the hall and singing together. I was transported by the enthusiasm and the feeling of "high" that pervaded the room. Shlomo's voice penetrated the heart, his songs filled you with joy, and I was enthralled with the warmth that he showed everyone. Somehow, I got up the courage to go up to him and I said, "Hello, Rabbi Carlebach." He said, "No, call me Shlomo. And what's your name?" I told him my English name that I used since I was born, "Nanette." He said, "No, what's your Hebrew name?" I had to think fast, as I hadn't really

---

1. *Oak Park Oak Leaves*, March 10, 1966, 79.

2. *Billboard*, The International Music-Record Newsweekly, June 18, 1966, 34. For an announcement of the dates, see *The Milwaukee Sentinel*, April 9, 1966, 6.

3. *Billboard*, July 2, 1966, 55.

ever used it. "Well, I was named after my great-aunt who died in the Holocaust, Nechama." "Ah!" he said and then we parted. I met him again a few months later in Philadelphia at a Jewish coffee shop called Hamakom and was amazed when he waved and called out "Nechamala" – I was shocked to realize that he had remembered my name out of all the hundreds of people that he had met at the concert several months earlier.[4]

Nechama became one of Shlomo's devoted followers, living in both the HLP in San Francisco and then in Me'or Modi'im in Israel (see below).

In particular, Shlomo was interested in meeting college students. On Motzei Shabbat, October 29, 1966, Shlomo gave a concert in Berkeley.[5] Then in November 1966, he performed at the campus of CIT (Case Institute of Technology) in Cleveland, Ohio.[6] Sue Tourkin was in her first semester at the nearby Western Reserve University (WRU) and recalled her reaction:

> I was stunned by Shlomo's music and presentation. I understood most of the songs in Hebrew, but I was very ambivalent about his followers jumping wildly up and down on stage, and all of this sensation was in the auditorium of the Engineering School of CIT, Case Institute of Technology. I mean, this was a place for physics or for math lectures or boring scientists or mad scientists, but not for wild Chassidic hippie singers and dancers.[7]

Thanks to his best-selling LPs, Shlomo's career transcended denominational lines. On December 4, 1966, Reb Shlomo performed at the Peninsula Temple Beth El, a Reform congregation in the San Francisco Peninsula, San Mateo, California. The *San Mateo Times* reported about Shlomo Carlebach's popularity, performing "in practically every state and every city from Toronto to Texas," giving "standing room only concerts at New York's Town Hall," and completing "six European odysseys packing concert halls in London, Paris, Jerusalem, Rotterdam, and Rome."[8]

Similarly, the Hebrew Union College, California School, announced Shlomo's Hanukkah performance, Motzei Shabbat, December 10, 1966, at the Leo Baeck Temple in Los Angeles, lauding his "five best-selling

---

4. Nechama Yasskin (Silver), personal interview, Oct. 9, 2012.

5. *Oakland Tribune*, Oct. 23, 1966, 8.

6. Reb Shlomo returned to Cleveland in January 1967 and performed at the Hillel of Western Reserve. See below in the story of Hanna Tiferet Siegel. Later, in 1967, CIT united with Western Reserve to become Case Western Reserve University.

7. Sue Tourkin-Komet, "An Inter-Faith Date," *Kol Chevra*, vol. 7, 2000, 164–166.

8. *San Mateo Times*, Nov. 26, 1966, 7.

LPs circling the globe" and describing Shlomo as having "performed in practically every state and every city from Toronto to Texas," and having "crowded concert halls in London, Paris, Jerusalem, Buenos Aires, and Sydney." The publicity blurb stated that Shlomo had given several "Standing Room Only" concerts in New York's Town Hall.[9] Reading these accolades, one might conclude that Reb Shlomo in 1966 had reached the epitome of his career success.

In 1966, Pablo (Paltíel) Goldstein was a talented 16-year old musician when Reb Shlomo came to perform in Buenos Aires at the Opera Theatre at Corrientes Avenue. This was a turning point in Pablo's life. It was known that he could play Israeli music on his flute. Maestro Eduardo Schejtman invited Pablo as part of Shlomo's backup band. Pablo was deeply impressed by Reb Shlomo and soon became a leading force in the spread of Carlebach music in Argentina:

> My contact with this great man during the rehearsal and show was unforgettable. It changed my life forever. Reb Shlomo taught me the real meaning of Hasidut and through him I could justify my approach to Judaism through music. I promised to myself that EVERY child in Buenos Aires would know his music, so I gave lessons to other music teachers. I went on to dedicate many years of my professional work to play, arrange, and teach the wonderful music composed by Rabbi Carlebach. My goal was that every child in town should be able to sing and feel these extraordinary melodies with truly Jewish lyrics.[10]

Pablo Goldstein is but one example of how the Carlebachian music was spreading in the mid 1960s to Jewish communities around the world.

Among the many concerts performed in 1967: Motzei Shabbat, February 18, 1967, Reb Shlomo performed in Winnipeg, Manitoba;[11] on

---

9. Hebrew Union College announcement, "A Hanukkah Evening with Shlomo Carlebach," Dec. 10, 1966 – "Shlomo Carlebach," Nearprint Biography, American Jewish Archives (AJA), Cincinnati, Ohio. Since the seating capacity in Town Hall was 1,500 people, this means that the performances were quite a success. My gratitude to Kevin Proffitt, Senior Archivist for Research and Collections at AJA, and to Michelle Wirth (intern at the AJA,) for sending me a scan of the files on Rabbi Shlomo Carlebach.

10. Personal interview with Pablo Goldstein, Feb. 24, 2013. A special thanks to Oro Zahava Jalfon for telling me about Pablo and his prominent role in spreading Carlebachian music in Argentina. Pablo Goldstein completed his degree in music therapy in Buenos Aires. He founded "AVEMUS," the Venezuelan Music Therapy Association, and was its first president. In 2000, Goldstein was honored with Venezuela's National Music Prize.

11. *Winnipeg Free Press*, Feb. 17, 1967, 25.

February 28, 1967, the Hillel Foundation at Ohio University hosted Reb Shlomo;[12] on April 17, 1967, Shlomo was featured at a special cultural program at The Village Gate Theater for the benefit of America's Black Jews.[13]

The Six-Day War broke out on June 5, 1967. There was a news blackout from Israel, but the news from Arab sources was that the Israeli Air Force had been destroyed, the oil reserves in Haifa were on fire, and Arab forces were on the outskirts of Tel Aviv.

On June 6, 1967, WINS, the New York all-news radio station, reported that a few Jews were gathering at Dag Hammarskjöld Plaza as Israeli Foreign Minister Abba Eban was slated to arrive from Tel Aviv to address the UN. Two students in the Yeshiva University *semicha* and graduate studies program, Jonathan Helfand and Moshe Bernstein, heard the news on WINS and went to 47th St. where they found about thirty people demonstrating. Helfand recalls what happened next:

> Our numbers were growing and we didn't know what to do. Someone phoned Shlomo Carlebach and he arrived with his guitar. Moishe and I borrowed a police megaphone, jumped on top of a car, and introduced Shlomo. He began leading "*Am Yisrael Chai*" and within a short time we were loudly singing. This was an incredible event. Without amplifiers and no organization, we held a major rally in midday with several thousand people in spirited singing led by Shlomo. He never asked for a penny. It was clear to him that this was the mitzvah of the hour.[14]

Michael Steinhardt who was at this rally describes the mood:

> After several speeches, Shlomo Carlebach got up on the truck and said that in this time of danger it is difficult to speak. We can only pray for our soldiers who are dying and wounded to save Israel this very moment. He led the crowd by chanting a mournful *El Maleh Rahamim*, and then broke down in tears. I'll never forget his crying on that June night. After the rally was over, I went to him and asked what can I do for you. He said, I want to go to Israel.

---

12. *The Athens Messenger*, Feb. 23, 1967, 3. At the time, Jacob Mirviss was the Hillel director at Ohio University.

13. "Cultural Program Performed in New York for Benefit of Black Jews," *Jewish Telegraphic Agency*, April 18, 1967: "Taking part in the program were Theodore Bikel, Herschel Bernardi, the famed folk singer Shlomo Carlebach and Marian Seldes . . . Negro cantors Otto Brown and David Koton, Negro singers of Yiddish and Hebrew songs Raphael Palmer and Connie Thompson."

14. My thanks to Prof. Jonathan Helfand for this story told to me Aug. 23, 2012.

> So I paid for his ticket. Somehow, he managed to get on the next
> flight and soon was at the Kotel and visiting the wounded in the
> hospitals and sanatoria.[15]

Shlomo returned from Israel to New York on September 18, 1967 –
enough time in advance to be at his father's *shul* for the High Holidays –
the last time he would spend the holidays with his father. The synagogue
had been struggling and on some Shabbatot there wasn't even a *minyan*.
Ari Goldman, whose family moved into the neighborhood recalls that in
the early 1960s when he was 13 and his brother Shalom was 15, they were
asked by R. Naphtali to come Shabbat morning:

> He offered us a dollar, but my brother said, "You cannot take
> money for going to *shul*." So we began to go to help this Rabbi,
> and he also needed help with the services so we read the Torah.
> We felt we wanted to give to this rabbi, and also he was the father
> of this great Shlomo Carlebach.[16]

On December 23, 1967, Rabbi Naphtali Carlebach died.[17] Shlomo was in
the middle of a concert in San Diego, California when he was told that
his father had died. When it was suggested that he cancel the rest of the
concert, Shlomo is reported to have exclaimed:

> Many of these holy brothers and sisters have traveled very far
> to hear me. For some of them, it's their first taste of Yiddishkeit,
> maybe the only encounter they'll ever have with Torah. Their *ne-
> shomos* are thirsting for a word that will change their lives; their
> need to sing joyously is greater than my need to cry. I will cry
> later.[18]

Upon returning to his hotel room, he began sobbing and "didn't stop the
entire night." Toward dawn, he was humming a new melody for the verse
from Isaiah 25:8, *Umocho Hashem*, "God will erase the tears."[19] He trav-

---

15. Personal interview with Michael Steinhardt, Aug. 30, 2012. See also Steinhardt, *No Bull*, 90.

16. Videotaped interview of Ari Goldman by Menachem Daum, March 2007.

17. *The American Jewish Yearbook*, 1968, 605, in the obituary section cites the day of death as Dec. 23, 1967. This was Motzei Shabbat, the eve of 22 Kislev. See AJCA rchives.org, http://www.ajcarchives.org/AJC_DATA/Files/1968_15_DirectoriesLists. pdf. My thanks to Shulamith Z. Berger for sending me this reference. See also "Rabbi Carlebach, Former Leader of Congregation in Austria, Dies in New York, Aged 78," *Jewish Telegraphic Agency*, Dec. 26, 1967.

18. Mandelbaum, *Holy Brother*, 44.

19. Ibid., 45. Rabbi Meyer Leifer remembers that when Shlomo returned from Jerusalem, he shared the story of how he composed this song at the Kotel. Rabbi

eled to Jerusalem with the coffin to bury his father in Har HaMenuhot.[20]

In 1968, Shlomo took over his father's synagogue, Kehilath Jacob, on West 79th St. in Manhattan.[21] But because he was often away traveling, his twin brother, R. Eliyahu Chaim, who was rabbi of the Hillside Jewish Center in New Jersey, would come to lead the Kehilath Jacob congregation on selected Shabbatot and Festivals.

Even though Shlomo was in the first year of *aveilut* mourning for his father, he continued to perform. When he sang at Beth Tikvah – New Milford Jewish Center, New Jersey, Rabbi Halpern explained that Shlomo was permitted to perform despite the year of mourning because this is his occupational calling.[22] On March 21, 1968, Shlomo performed at a Conservative congregation, Temple Sinai in Long Beach, California[23] and came again for another concert on January 27, 1969.[24]

On April 28, 1968, Reb Shlomo officiated at the wedding of Michael and Judith Steinhardt near Scranton, Pennsylvania.[25]

In the photo section, one can see two rare mementos from Shlomo's life in 1967–1968. These photos, courtesy of Karen Blake (née Weizer), a very close friend and confidant of Shlomo at the time, provide a glimpse into his New York social life. They show him in Central Park, Manhattan in November 1967 and on a boat ride around Manhattan in June 1968.

On July 7, 1968, Reb Shlomo came to Berkeley to participate in the 11th Annual Folk Music Festival at the Hearst Greek Theater. *The Oakland Tribune* reporter was so impressed by Shlomo's songs of love and brotherhood that it was humorously recommended to have him solve the

---

Leifer: "To this day, we often hum this tune as a most meaningful consolation in times of trouble" (personal interview, Dec. 17, 2012). See also http://ningmp3.com/on ply.php?q=dTViVHhaYl9GVjA=&tl=Reb%20Shlomo%20Carlebach%20Tears%20I %20Heard%20the for a recording where Reb Shlomo explains that he was at the Kotel after his father's death and composed this song because the stones "were made out of our ancestors' tears." Rabbi Uzi Schwietze in his eulogy for Reb Shlomo recalled how Shlomo explained his composition of *Umocho* at the Kotel as a consolation for all people in mourning. See Brandwein, *Reb Shlomele*, 303.

20. See Brand, *Reb Shlomele*, 24 for a photo of the story in the *Haaretz* newspaper about Shlomo's "arriving last night" in Israel with his father's coffin. Brand dates the article to Feb. 12, 1968 which would mean that Shlomo arrived Feb. 11.

21. Http://www.carlebachshul.org.

22. Personal interview with Rabbi Hayyim Halpern, Aug. 5, 2012. Rabbi Hayyim (Harold) Halpern had become friendly with Shlomo when they studied Hebrew together at JTS in 1950 (see above).

23. *Press-Telegram*, March 21, 1968, 40.

24. *Press-Telegram*, Jan. 22, 1969, 62.

25. Personal interview with Michael Steinhardt, Aug. 30, 2012.

My thanks to Shlomo's close friend, Karen Blake (née Weizer) for sending me these rare photos of Shlomo in Manhattan (November 1967), and of his entertaining on a boat ride around Manhattan (June 1968).

In Central Park, Manhattan, November 1967

Shlomo in June 1968 Photo courtesy of Karen Blake

negotiating problems at the 1968 Paris Peace Conference and end the war in Vietnam:

> The rejoicing Rabbi Shlomo Carlebach lit a firecracker under the audience right at the start with his irresistible songs of love and brotherhood. With Shlomo Carlebach on our side who needs diplomats. Cut him loose with his Old Testament songs at the Paris Peace Conference and you'd get a treaty signed by the participants the same day over a luncheon of bagels and lox.[26]

One of the most memorable episodes in the life and legacy of Reb Shlomo took place toward the end of October 1968. Shlomo was invited by Allen Secher, rabbi of Congregation Ahavat Shalom in Northridge, North Los Angeles, for Shabbat in a program co-sponsored with students at California State University of Northridge. Rabbi Secher recalls:

> I had been innovating musical services and using multimedia techniques to inspire my congregation. We thought that to have an Orthodox rabbi lead us in singing Kabbalat Shabbat would be a startling revelation for my congregants. But little did we envision how dramatic it would be.[27]

Shlomo phoned from New York to tell his *chevra* at the HLP that he would be arriving on Friday in Los Angeles. A dozen *chevra* piled into two vehicles, Aryae Coopersmith's Volkswagen Beetle, and a Volkswagen van driven by Alex Scott (later Elyah Succot):

> It was a VW van, the type typically used by hippies in those days, and it looked it. With some blankets and cushions at the back of the van, it could comfortably hold ten or more people. We nicknamed it the Shabbos Express because we would all pile in to go to the *mikveh* before Shabbos. Or, when we traveled throughout California to be with Shlomo for Shabbos, that was our main vehicle.[28]

The *chevra* drove some seven hours from San Francisco and picked up Shlomo at the airport. The trip to Northridge would normally take only half an hour, but a truck jackknifed on the freeway and traffic was blocked up for miles.[29] It was already 5:00 PM. The sun was setting and Shabbat

---

26. *The Oakland Tribune*, July 6, 1968, 5, 31.

27. Personal interview with Rabbi Allen Secher on Nov. 21, 2012. The congregation had yet to acquire its own building and services were held on 9659 Balboa St. in Northridge, Los Angeles.

28. My thanks to Aryae Coopersmith for this explanation, Nov. 21, 2012.

29. Personal communication from Fred Schwartz, Nov. 30, 2012. Schwartz, a

was beginning. Shlomo announced that it was necessary to park, leave all their stuff in the cars and walk the rest of the way.

Meanwhile some 300 congregants waited anxiously. Someone heard that a truck had overturned and the Synagogue secretary was dispatched to find Shlomo, only to discover to her astonishment that Shlomo was prohibited from riding in a car on Shabbat. She tells the *chevra* that the Synagogue is a long distance away.[30] Shlomo with his natural charm asks to have her congregants invite all their friends and prepare a great celebration for when he arrives. Meanwhile, it began raining. Aryae reconstructs what happened next:

> It was after midnight and we had been walking for a few hours. Suddenly a car pulls up. It was Ron McCoy, host of the *Night Owl*, a live call-in show on LA radio station KFI. He had been alerted that the Singing Rabbi and his followers were walking in the rain. He asks Shlomo to explain the meaning of Shabbat. Soon thousands hear his radio broadcast of Shlomo's soliloquy about the joys of Shabbat. Some listeners drive out to see this unusual event. The rain turns into a torrential storm, yet even more visitors join to accompany the courageous Shabbat observers. Eventually there were about 200 people walking to honor the Shabbat devotion of the Carlebach group, all energetically singing Shabbat songs.[31]

The group stretched out the length of a block and became a "veritable parade for Shabbat." The weary voyagers arrived at 2:20 AM[32] and were greeted by a capacity crowd of some 400 or 500 people in the social hall.[33] There was a standing ovation, dry clothing and a kosher Friday night vegetarian meal. Then Shlomo led an ecstatic Friday night singing

---

member of the Ahavat Shalom Congregation, was present at this event.

30. Estimates of the actual distance range from 17 miles (Allen Secher), 20 miles (Eliezer Garner and Shlomo Carlebach) and 27 miles (Aryae Coopersmith).

31. I have reconstructed the story based partially on the account by Aryae Coopersmith, *Holy Beggars*, 96–106 and by Yitta Halberstam Mandelbaum, *Holy Brother*, 10–14. My thanks to Aryae and to Rabbi Allen Secher for their additions and corrections.

32. This calculation of 2:20 AM is from Shlomo's reconstruction of the event as told to Yankel Greenberg in a Staten Island radio interview in 1986 or 1987. My thanks to Eliezer Garner who shared the transcript of Shlomo's interview as transcribed by Miriam Rubinoff.

33. According to Fred Schwartz, the Carlebach entourage did not walk all the way to the planned destination in Northridge. Instead, a Jewish community center in Sherman Oaks was specially opened for them and the Ahavat Shalom congregants came there to join in the Shabbat program. Personal communications, Nov. 30–Dec. 4, 2012.

and dancing. Before walking back to the motel, Shlomo announced that Shabbat services would be held the next morning at 10:00 A M.[34]

This Shabbat walk in the rain was recorded in Carlebach lore and legend as an exemplary devotion to Shabbat. One of the participants was later quoted as stating:

> I will never forget that Shabbos walk with Shlomo Carlebach. Everyone who did that walk was transformed. We were a bunch of kids who didn't know anything about Shabbos until we took that walk, and this is how he taught us. After witnessing Shlomo Carlebach keeping Shabbos with such passion, devotion, and fervor . . . how could you not keep Shabbos after that?[35]

On Thanksgiving Weekend, November 28–30, 1968, Reb Shlomo was invited to perform at the Orthodox Union Annual Convention in Washington D.C. at the Shoreham Hotel. Jonathan Cohen, at the time, was a sophomore at Yeshiva University and keyboard player and lead singer with a band called The Chosen, one of the very first Jewish music bands. Jonathan recalls that they began playing at 2:00 A M after Shlomo had finished a two-hour concert.[36]

Towards the end of 1968, Shlomo was hosted by Rabbi Bernard M. Stein of Temple Israel of South Merrick in Long Island on the occasion of their new building at 2655 Clubhouse Road. Serena Stein recalls:

> Rabbi Carlebach had everyone singing and dancing in *shul*. When he finished his concert, he came with us to our home and continued playing and we all kept singing. The evening is still in my memory even though 43 years have passed. Shlomo Carlebach was one in a million.[37]

On Sunday, September 7, 1969, Shlomo performed the marriage of Diane Wolkstein and Benjamin (Benny) Zucker in a garden in Englewood, New Jersey – a ceremony which lasted three hours. Diane was one of

---

34. This is based on the description of Rabbi Allen Secher, Nov. 20–21, 2012.

35. Halberstam Mandelbaum, *Holy Brother*, 14. This citation is a paraphrase of what Eliezer (Sonny) Garner told Yitta Mandelbaum. Rabbi Garner told me that this incredible experience was "the major turning point in my life." For a CD recording of Garner's reconstruction of this story see Rabbi Eliezer Garner, *Tomorrow Will Be Shabbos* (CD), #15, "The Walking Shabbos" (4:03), Orpnimi: 2011, www.allmusic .com/album/tomorrow-will-be-shabbos-mw0001565901. Garner's original version was printed in the 1987 issue of *Hakrev Ushma* (*Connections*), p. 5.

36. My thanks to Prof. Jonathan Cohen for providing this information.

37. My thanks to Serena Stein for the pictures and information.

Rabbi Bernard Stein of Temple Israel, South Merrick with Reb Shlomo who performed in honor of the Temple's new building, 1968.

Courtesy of the Stein family

those deeply influenced by Shlomo to develop a professional career as an inspired storyteller:[38]

> Shlomo was my rabbi from 1968 until he died in 1994. I still consider him to be my rabbi as I have found no one to replace him in the way that he combined joyous singing, heart storytelling, and Torah learning. He had a profound effect on my life as well as on my career as a storyteller and writer. At Shabbat meals at the Carlebach Shul, Shlomo often invited me to tell stories. I arranged two major concerts at the American Museum of Natural History in which we both told stories.[39] When our daughter Rachel was born on December 27, 1971, I wanted a special name that would just be hers so we consulted Shlomo. He offered us Kashtiah (God is my rainbow) or Cholamiah (God is my dream). As dreams are very important to me, I chose Cholamiah. To this day, my daughter who is a poet, has dreams as intricate as novels. After Shlomo's passing, because I missed his transmission of Judaism so much, I went to Jerusalem to study Hebrew at the Hebrew University and spent eight years researching and writing *Treasures of the Heart: Holiday Stories that Reveal the Soul of Judaism.* I dedicated this book to Shlomo and his wisdom permeates the commentaries.[40]

In 1969, Shlomo's outreach to college campuses took all kinds of shapes and forms depending on the invitations. Rivka Zablocki, a freshman at Queens College, attended Shlomo's performance there one afternoon during Hol HaMoed. She recalls that his performance was limited to one hour as the room was needed the next hour for a class.[41] When he came again to the campus, Rivka brought along her younger sister Emuna. Years later, after she was married and moved to Jerusalem, Emuna hosted many Shlomo events in her home. After his death, she began producing *Kol Chevra*, the annual journal which plays a major role in creating a worldwide Carlebach community.

On Wednesday, Hol HaMoed Sukkot, October 1, 1969, Shlomo

---

38. See www.dianewolkstein.com. On another storyteller inspired and actually ordained by Shlomo as a *maggid* see below, Chapter 11, about Reb Yitzhak Buxbaum.

39. See below, Chapter 11 for the performance on March 6, 1989, and Chapter 12 on the one on Sept. 13, 1994.

40. Diane's book was published by Random House-Schocken, New York, September 2003. I last spoke by phone with Diane Wolkstein on Jan. 20, 2013. Sadly, she died on Jan. 31, 2013 following emergency heart surgery while on a trip to Taiwan working on her most recent project, the Chinese epic story of *Monkey King: Journey to the West.* May this excerpt be a small tribute to her memory.

41. Rivka Zablocki, "Little Did I Dream," *Kol Chevra*, vol. 7, 2000, 82.

traveled the 50 miles from the HLP to a concert in Santa Rosa. Gedalia Druin invited him to Santa Rosa Junior College to speak to his philosophy class.[42] Shlomo took his *lulav* and went outside on the grass with the students saying: "Stand very close around me as we shake the *lulav* because the *lulav* shakes the world."[43] Then he sang a Bobov tune for shaking *lulav* and created a very moving experience. Not too long after, at 21:56 and 23:19 (Pacific Time Zone), the city of Santa Rosa was severely shaken by two earthquakes of magnitude 5.6 and 5.7, respectively. The quakes were distinctly felt throughout the entire San Francisco Bay Area. Rachel Trugman who was there with Shlomo and later experienced this frightening earthquake, remarks today: "Now that is really called shaking up the world."[44]

On December 10, 1969, Shlomo returned with the HLP *chevra* to Gedalia Druin's morning class on the sixth day of Hanukkah at Santa Rosa Jr. College. Then he told stories related to Hanukkah in the weekly Wednesday gathering to an overflow auditorium of about 150 people.[45]

2.   HOLY MAN JAM AND MEETING OF THE WAYS (1969–1972)

Reb Shlomo's most innovative outreach was at hippie events and spiritual gatherings such as the Holy Man Jam and Meeting of the Ways. The Holy Man Jam Festival on October 3–9, 1969 took place at the Family Dog on the Great Highway, and featured rock bands, Hare Krishna chants, Middle Eastern music, and Transcendental Meditation. Reb Shlomo was unique as an Orthodox rabbi on a program with psychedelic gurus Timothy Leary and Alan Watts, and spiritual teachers Stephen Gaskin, Pir Vilayat Khan, and Swami Satchidananda.[46]

Shlomo developed special connections to these teachers and gurus. Sometimes it was Shlomo's students who facilitated the connections. Thus, for example, Jonathan Daniel was a regular visitor at the HLP programs from 1968 until 1973. He explains how he was instrumental in

---

42. Gedalia had done graduate work at the University of Oklahoma in philosophy and written about "the spiritual and ethical development of mankind." He and his wife Zahava met Shlomo in San Francisco in 1968 and moved to Israel in 1970. See Chapter 8 about their settlement in Migdal.

43. Personal communication with Rabbi Gedalia Druin, Oct. 4, 2012.

44. I thank Rachel Trugman for telling me the story of her experience of the earthquake (Sept. 13, 2012).

45. Skir, "Carlebach", 35–37.

46. HareKsna.com, http://www.harekrsna.com/sun/editorials/09-06/editorials 652.htm. Although Shlomo's name is not listed on the publicity advertisement here, it is mentioned on this site as one of the performers/presenters.

bringing Steve Gaskin and Shlomo together: "I attended Gaskin's famous Monday Night Classes and Sunday Morning Services. Gradually more and more HLP regulars joined. Soon the two teachers met and became close friends."[47]

Reb Shlomo participated in a Holy Man Jam Festival in July 1970 at the University of Colorado in Boulder.[48] Ne'eman described how eighteen members of the HLP drove to the Holy Man Jam on July 20, 1970:

> When the gurus did their things, there seemed to be no visible effect. But when Shlomo performed, hundreds of kids began dancing and singing in huge circles, exuding joy, warmth, and friendship all around.[49]

Natalie Zarchin recalls driving a van full of eight HLP chevra to Boulder, picking up Shlomo from the Denver airport and bringing him to the event.[50] After Shlomo led the ecstatic singing and dancing, Stephen Gaskin went on stage and said that "all the gurus tried to teach us how to get to that magical place but *Shlomo just took us there.*"[51] This compliment is revealing. Stephen Gaskin, the counterculture icon of San Francisco, was leading the popular weekly *Monday Night Class* where Californian hippies shared the meanings of their psychedelic experiences.[52] It was a place for self exploration and HLP regulars also attended.[53] Sometime in the mid-1970s Shlomo came to play at Gaskin's commune in Tennessee

---

47. Personal interview with Jonathan Daniel, March 28, 2013.

48. Reb Shlomo appeared alongside Alan Watts, Yogi Bhajan, Stephen Gaskin, Sri Gurudev, Swami Satchidananda, Chogyam Trungpa, and Zen Buddhist Bill Quan-roshi. For descriptions of this event, see DavidAndLilatResemer.com, http://www.davidandlilatresemer.com/?/david/lila; SikhiWiki.org, http://www.sikhiwiki.org/index.php/Siri_Singh_Sahib_Harbhajan_Singh_Khalsa_Yogi; Iyiny.org, http://www.iyiny.org/about/the_history_of_integral_yoga/.

49. Based on an interview with Ne'eman, Aug. 17, 2011.

50. HolyBeggars.ning.com, http://holybeggars.ning.com/profile/natomi?xg_source=profiles_featuredList.

51. Comment by Natalie Zarchin, March 26, 2007 at HolyBeggars.ning.com, http://holybeggars.ning.com/profiles/blog/show?id=563044%3ABlogPost%3A244&commentId=563044%3AComment%3A801.

52. Gaskin was born Feb. 16, 1935. In 1967, with the help of Ian Grand, head of the Experimental College in San Francisco, he organized a major weekly event in San Francisco State's Gallery Lounge. The number of participants swelled to as many as 1,000–1,500 people, and the location was moved, eventually settling in at Chet Helms's "Family Dog," a ballroom on the Great Highway, near the Pacific Ocean. See Gaskin, *Monday Night Class.* Compare StephenGaskin.com, http://www.stephengaskin.com/mnc.html.

53. Personal interview with Reuven Goldfarb, Aug. 19, 2011. See also Coopersmith, *Holy Beggars*, 302.

*Shlomo participated at
A Yoga of Joy event in
San Francisco,
June 27, 1971.*

and Gaskin remarked: "Before Reb Shlomo came to The Farm, 28% of the 1,800 people living here were Jewish. After he left, we were all 28% Jewish."[54]

On Sunday evening, June 27, 1971, Shlomo participated as a speaker-performer at A Yoga of Joy event in San Francisco. The program took place in The Family Dog on the Great Highway, but now under its new name, Friends and Relations Hall. The poster listed Shlomo Carlebach first, followed by Yogi Bhajan and Allen Ginsberg.

In 1971–1972, HLP activists joined with representatives of spiritual organizations in the San Francisco Bay Area to create an ecumenical council which they called the Meeting of the Ways. The purpose was to plan joint events, teachings, and concerts.[55] They even organized a weekly radio show hosted by Will Nofski.[56] As part of the preparations for a major gathering, there was discussion at Yogi Bhajan's center between Reb Shlomo, Pir Vilayat Khan, and Satchidanada. Donna Maimes reminisces:

> It was magic to listen to them talk to each other, rather than to their disciples. They talked casually and respectfully, mostly by telling stories. But in the end what was really clear is that they were all telling the same story. It was just an amazing time.[57]

---

54. This comment is quoted by Avraham Sand on his facebook site, Jan. 17, 2012. Bob Goldstein added that he was present at the time, and remembers Shlomo singing for a few hours on a Monday night in 1974 or 1975. Stephen Gaskin wrote to me (Sept. 2012) and verified this description adding that he was friends with Shlomo and that Shlomo approved of the "ruffles and flourishes" welcoming (Oct. 2, 2012).

55. It included representatives from the organizations of Satchidananda, Yogi Bhajan, Sufi Sam, Pir Vilayat Inayat Khan and others such as the Hare Krishna and Shugendo Buddhists groups.

56. Interviews Sept. 2011 with Steve Maimes and Donna Maimes.

57. Coopersmith, *Holy Beggars*, 256.

The ecumenical program in February 1972 with Buddhists, Sufis, Hindus, and Christians took place at the Nob Hill Masonic Center of San Francisco. Reb Shlomo began by singing "the Great Day is coming, and God is sending us holy teachers," implying his colleagues in the front row.[58] But, Shlomo asked rhetorically, how can ordinary people help? He then taught about the special joy of the drawing of the water in coming to the Temple on Sukkot, bringing "pure water from the deepest well in Jerusalem." The joy was expressed by water which is a gift from Heaven and unlike the other offerings at the Temple during the other holidays, is not dependent on personal wealth. Every person, from the greatest landowner to the humblest little beggar, pours their water over the holy stones. The *Levi'im* (Levites), the holy musicians, played and sang as the people danced in joy. Shlomo proclaimed: "If we want to lift the whole world up to Heaven, we can only get there by dancing on our feet."[59]

The Masonic Auditorium has a large round stage that juts out into the audience and is surrounded by 3,165 seats arranged in concentric semi-circles. Shlomo's hippies joined on the large round stage, and began jumping up and down as Shlomo sang, "Let's lift the whole world up to Heaven." Soon, 3,000 people were dancing in the aisles. Toward the conclusion, Shlomo asked everyone to draw close, "to bring the Great Day of Love and Peace." He invited the teachers in the front row to stand close to him on stage. Circles of people held each other in a trance-like dance of ecstasy.[60] Shlomo stopped and looked at the teachers:

> Some of you said that while we may be on different paths, the paths are all going to the same place. I respectfully disagree. If I may be so bold to say so, in my humble opinion, we are all on the same path. For now, while we are walking, just for a little longer, we are *just wearing different shoes*.[61]

To understand the significance of Shlomo's outreach to the world of gurus and Swamis it might be noted that although Jews constitute merely 2% or 3% of the American population, in the early 1970s they were disproportionately found in cults and movements influenced by Far East religions with estimates ranging from 25%–30%.[62] The secret of Shlomo's

---

58. Aryae Coopersmith speaks on video describing this and reading from p. 257 of his book, *The Holy Beggars*, HolyBeggars.com, http://www.holybeggars.com/videos.html.

59. Coopersmith, *Holy Beggars*, 257–258.

60. Adapted from Coopersmith, *Holy Beggars*, Chapter 27, 254–259.

61. Coopersmith, *Holy Beggars*, 261.

62. See Steven Shaw and George E. Johnson, "Jews on an Eastern Religious Quest

The ecumenical program at the Nob Hill Masonic Center of San Francisco, February 1972

success in reaching out to these movements was that he was perceived as offering a Jewish mode of experience without deprecating their path.[63]

3.   OUTREACH, INREACH, AND WIDE-REACH (1970–1973)

The international aspect of Reb Shlomo's career is illustrated in his performance in France in 1970 produced for La Television Française by Rabbi Josy Eisenberg, a French television producer. Shlomo can be seen and heard playing tunes from his early records: *Borchi Nafshi, Lemaan Achai, Esa Einai, Hanshomo Loch, Umocho Hashem,* and *Ein KeEloheinu.* This is one of the best quality recordings on YouTube from Shlomo's early years.[64]

One of Shlomo's pithy phrases was that we need inreach and not

and the Jewish Response," *Analysis* 41, Institute for Jewish Policy Planning & Research of the Synagogue Council of America, Nov. 1, 1973.

63. Compare below on Shlomo's visits to the Moonies and to the Transcendental Meditation Movement's Maharishi International University campus.

64. Five videos were posted on YouTube on March 4, 2013 by Kanal von israel-chanel: http://www.youtube.com/watch?v=ZTlP1ycke-U; http://www.youtube.com/watch?v=Lma21mlCHKQ&list=UUIzcA1h6A22_Gxu1Nzq3i9A&index=2; http://

outreach. He also humorously coined the term wide-reach.[65] But in reality, Shlomo's wide-reach was mostly a product of an impromptu inspiration. For example, in 1970, Shlomo was visiting Yeshiva University (YU) in Manhattan when he encountered a penniless couple who were despondent that they couldn't get married. Shlomo gathered a few YU fellows and performed the ceremony. Eli Schlossberg, who happened to be visiting YU for the weekend, described what happened:

> I was walking down a dorm hall, and I thought I was seeing an apparition, as coming toward me, bouncing down the hall, was Shlomo, just Shlomo. He greeted me with a hug, and said, "Holy brother, did you bring your guitar?" . . . Shlomo brought the young couple to the building and on the spot we made a wedding. Shlomo was careful to make sure all was halachically correct. The *seudah* was some cookies and cake.[66]

This is one of many stories illustrating the remarkable way Shlomo would use his rabbinical training to help people solve life's challenges. Schlossberg concludes:

> This wedding was just another mystery of his meaningful life. Whatever he did, he did with love and he was a person who spent his life creating joy for others.[67]

The demands on Reb Shlomo's time increased exponentially in the early 1970s. He was obligated to Kehilath Jacob, had promised his *chevra* in San Francisco to spend time with them "a few months each year" and was sought after for many an event. Thus for example, he led the singing on May 10, 1970, at the Israel Birthday "Be-In" in Central Park's Sheep Meadow in Manhattan celebrating Israel's 22nd Independence Day.[68]

---

www.youtube.com/watch?v=E1hdSSmQeyE; http://www.youtube.com/watch?v= hdDwZYoiOGM&list=UUIzcA1h6A22_Gxu1Nzq3i9A; http://www.youtube.com/ watch?v=_LDlidVcx4M.

Shlomo also performed in France a decade later, in 1980, and again a recording was produced by Josy Eisenberg (see below).

65. Shlomo in a talk at Lincoln Square Synagogue in Manhattan a month after the death of the Lubavitcher Rebbe: "Many great leaders talk about outreach, inreach, wide-reach. Outreach always rubs me the wrong way. Outreach means you are outside reaching out. The Rebbe was not outreach, the Rebbe was in-reach, *mamash* reaching into the depths of the *neshama*." http://www.youtube.com/ watch?v=E9_d1eVkwSE&feature=youtube.

66. Personal communication from Eli Schlossberg, June 12, 2011.

67. Eli Schlossberg, June 11–12, 2011.

68. "Gov. Rockefeller Proclaims May 11 Israel Independence Day in New York State," *Jewish Telegraphic Agency*, May 4, 1970. See also "Hippie Rabbi Leads New

That same week in May, Shlomo traveled to Romania, where he was received at the Great Synagogue in Bucharest by Rabbi Dr. David Moshe Rosen (1912–1994), the Chief Rabbi of Romanian Jewry. *Maariv* newspaper reported on May 17, 1970, that Rabbi Shlomo Carlebach, "the dancing Rabbi," spent a week in Romania, inspired the Jewish community in Bucharest, and composed a new tune for *"Oseh Shalom."*[69]

On Sunday evening, October 18, 1970, Shlomo was featured as the "Singing Rabbi" at New York City's Cultural Gala which took place during the Sukkot festival.[70]

Sometimes a Shlomo concert in a distant Jewish community could revolutionize the life of a young child. In the summer of 1971, Reb Shlomo visited Copenhagen, Denmark and performed at the Caroline Jewish Day School, the only Jewish school in Copenhagen. Chava Harris (at the time Eva Vainer) was in the third grade. She was enchanted and began listening regularly to Shlomo's records. Gradually, she became religious. At age 17, she made aliyah. Chava considers Shlomo as "the main person to bring me back to Yiddishkeit."[71]

Other people met Shlomo during their university days and then became attached to his teachings. In November 1971, Miriam Rubinoff met Shlomo at a concert in Northeastern University in Boston and then "attended every concert, teaching, and gathering he gave in the Boston area" until moving to New York in 1975 "to be closer to his shul."[72]

On the weekend of December 24–25, 1971, Reb Shlomo led a Shabbat program at the USY (United Synagogue Youth) Convention at the Sheraton Hotel in Washington D.C.[73]

In the early 1970s, Shlomo felt a driving need to reach out with love and care to all, answering whatever requests came his way. Despite his

---

York Fun," *The London Jewish Chronicle*, May 15, 1970 – article photographed in Brandwein, *Reb Shlomele*, 90.

69. Avraham Rotem, "With the Inspiration of a Visit to Romania," *Maariv*, May 17, 1970 [Hebrew]. The article is reproduced in Brand, *Reb Shlomele*, 143.

70. "City's Cultural Gala Features Singing, Dancing, Acting This Weekend." *Jewish Telegraphic Agency*, Oct. 16, 1970, http://archive.jta.org.

71. Chava Harris, personal interview, Sept. 19, 2011.

72. Posted July 16, 2012, http://holybeggars.ning.com/profile/MiriamRubinoff. Miriam's original name was Melissa Hopkins and she adopted the name Miriam upon her commitment to Orthodox Judaism. Born in Boston, Massachusetts, she attended Tahanto Regional High School, Boylston, Massachusetts and graduated from Massachusetts College of Art in 1975.

73. Bruce Ginsberg, who was 16 years old at the time, remembers how on motzei Shabbat, a phone line was hooked up so that Soviet Jews could listen to the concert (Bruce (Hashir) Ginsberg, personal communication, Nov. 28-30, 2012). A year before, Shlomo had clandestinely visited Moscow – see Chapter 9.

overloaded schedule, he sometimes committed himself to ongoing teaching. For example, from 1970–1972, Rabbi Joseph Polak, Hillel director at Boston University, arranged for Shlomo "to fly on Eastern Airlines every Wednesday for almost two years to teach Hasidut to students at Hillel."[74] Prior to that, R. Polak as Hillel director at Ohio University in Athens, Ohio had brought Shlomo to the campus once a semester and organized Shlomo's performances and teaching in nearby campuses such as Oberlin, Antioch and Ohio State.[75]

Reb Shlomo's reaching out to assimilated youth and redirecting their lives could occur at any time. On March 16, 1972, Reb Shlomo gave a concert in the Wilshire Boulevard Temple, a reform congregation in the Los Angeles area. Zusha Frumin was in his senior year at UCLA and his friend, Jonathan White, told him that he "had to meet this hippie rabbi coming to town." After the concert they went to the home of Liliane and Dr. Joshua Ritchie for a Rosh Hodesh Nisan party. Four years later, Zusha came to Israel and connected to Shlomo's *chevra*. He eventually settled in the Moshav and received rabbinic ordination from Reb Shlomo.[76]

In September 1972, during the presidential election campaign of Richard Nixon versus George McGovern, Shlomo was asked to sing at a political rally in Los Angeles in a heavily populated Jewish district. Yisroel Travis, who was 13 years old at the time, remembers this event as taking place at the corner of Fairfax and Beverly Boulevard opposite the CBS television studio:

> I was deeply affected by tunes such as *"Lemaan Ahai"* and *"Ufros Aleinu"* and I became a devoted lifelong follower of Reb Shlomo. Just like some people were fans of the Beatles or the Grateful Dead, so *lehavdil*, I was a hasid of Reb Shlomo, and for almost two decades, followed him all over, whenever I could hear him.[77]

Shlomo showed a new form of heart-warming Judaism that could change a person's life direction. This is what happened to 21-year old Yehudah

---

74. Rabbi Polak was born in 1942 in the Netherlands, survived the Holocaust and moved with his mother to Montreal, Canada. There in 1962, he met Shlomo at a concert at Concordia University and soon began accompanying him both in teaching Hasidism and guitar.

75. Personal interview with Rabbi Joseph Polak, Aug. 17, 2012. My thanks to Pinhas (Paul) Mandel who was a student at the time at Boston University for telling me about the outreach activities organized by Rabbi Polak.

76. Zusha Frumin, "Jerusalem!", *Kol Chevra*, vol. 16, 2010, 45–48. Personal communication with Zusha, Aug. 8, 2011.

77. Personal interview with Yisroel Shlomo Zalman Travis, April 8, 2013. See below, discography, about his collection of unknown Carlebach songs.

(Jerry) Katz on October 21, 1972 in Miami, Florida where Shlomo was leading a two-week teaching in Hasidut on the writings of Reb Nachman of Breslov. Yehudah had grown up in a traditional Jewish home and even attended Yeshiva University, but had left religious observance and found in The Grateful Dead band a "community and kindred spirit, a new form of spirituality." Upon encountering Reb Shlomo, Yehudah discovered a new way of understanding Judaism filled with joy and centered on the individual experience: "The Torah became alive with Reb Shlomo." Yehudah became close to Reb Shlomo for the next twenty-two years, performed with him often, and even served for a while as his musical director.[78]

By the early 1970s, Reb Shlomo had crystallized a unique style combining three types of presentation: singing-whistling-guitar playing, musical storytelling, and ethical-theological exhortations spliced with personal anecdotes. This is exemplified in a 60-minute appearance on November 14, 1972 at Congregation Kehillath Israel in Brookline, Massachusetts as part of the New England Jewish Music Forum concert of Hasidic music. Shlomo's message, based on Hasidic stories and personal vignettes, aimed at inspiring his audience to deepen their religious fervor, identify with the Hasidic *niggun*, become "friends with God," and pray for the day when the whole world will again hear the Divine Voice.[79]

On November 21, 1972, Shlomo spoke to an overflow crowd of Yeshiva University students at Furst Hall in the Manhattan campus at a symposium dealing with the challenge posed by Jews for Jesus. The program was organized by Aaron Reichel, president of the Yavneh chapter at Yeshiva University, to deal with the Jesus Movement which had become a high profile evangelical campaign.[80] At a rock and roll concert entitled Jesus Joy

---

78. Personal interview with Yehudah Katz on Aug. 31, 2011. See below, Chapter 9, on Yehudah's Los Angeles band, Promised Land, which accompanied Shlomo on the 10-day concert tour in Russia. Also see below, Chapter 12, on Shlomo and the wedding of Yehudah and Michelle in 1989 and his blessing to them in Los Angeles in 1993 before they went on aliyah.

79. Reb Shlomo is recorded from segment 35:00 to 101:00. See Archive.org, http://archive.org/details/NewEnglandJewishMusicForumAChasidicEveningFeatu ringRebShlomo. The recording is available in the collection of Archive.org, http:// archive.org/details/opensource_audio. For details of this concert, see the blog of Joshua Hammerman. Josh is the son of cantor Michal Hammerman who invited Reb Shlomo. See JoshuaHammerman.blogspot.com, http://joshuahammerman.blogspot. com/2011/11/shlomo-carlebach-zl-vintage-concert.html, Nov. 11, 2011.

80. A major event called Explo '72 took place in Dallas, Texas from June 12 to June 17, 1972. With a budget of almost $3 million, the goal was to train 100,000 high school and college students to become personal evangelists. The program climaxed with an all-day Christian music festival dubbed "The Christian Woodstock" with an

at Madison Square Garden on August 30, 1972, Moishe Rosen, founder of "Jews for Jesus," had exhorted Jews to follow him in converting.[81]

Reichel invited a panel of rabbis: Shlomo Carlebach, Melech Shachter, Charles Sheer, and Walter Wurzburger. A critical "right wing" view was presented by Rabbi Schachter, halachic legal specialist and professor at Yeshiva University. He characterized those who join the Jews for Jesus Movement as "lunatics who were not satisfied with one heavenly father but needed a son and a ghost also." He asserted that these converts are "*m'shumadim*," who suffer from "a mental sickness or self-hatred." The other rabbis on the panel argued for a softer approach. But it was Reb Shlomo who directed his criticism at the Jewish establishment for not responding to the non-religious Jews who are "knocking at our doors." Shlomo asserted with great pathos: "We should be *crying* when our brothers are dying . . . We are the ones that are sick, not them . . . We are the ones that are in bad shape . . . We have to become real Jews again." The thrust of his argument was that the Christian missionaries were succeeding because they offered a genuine love and empathetic concern: "If only our brethren would know that there is a Jew who cares and is waiting for them, then they will return home."[82]

As the Jews for Jesus Movement became more active on American campuses, Reb Shlomo decided to take action and train student activists how to respond more effectively. David Stahl remembers how he and some fifty other religious college students from the New York area came to a full-day seminar in 1973 at the Carlebach Shul:

> We were flabbergasted. In the packet of material, we each found a New Testament. Shlomo explained that these missionaries are familiar with the Jewish biblical sources and we have to become acquainted with theirs.[83] Shlomo spent the day preparing us to

---

estimated attendance of 180,000. For a summary of the news coverage, see http://www.webcitation.org/query?url=http://www.geocities.com/demonobsession666/explo72.html&date=2009-10-25+19:26:33.

81. The name of the movement at the time was Messianic Judaism, but after the slogan of "Jews for Jesus" was posted on flyers at San Francisco State University, the campus newspaper mistook the slogan for a movement, and the national media adopted it. See Paul Baker, *Contemporary Christian Music: Where It Came From, What It Is, Where It's Going* (Westchester, Illinois: 1985), 55, http://www.ccel.us/CCM.toc.html.

82. See Shlomo Charlop, "Symposium on Jews for Jesus is Held Here: Distinguished Panelists Address Capacity Crowd," *Hamevaser*, Yeshiva University Student Newspaper, Dec. 12, 1972, 1, 3. My thanks to Aaron Reichel for sending me this article and providing background information (Oct. 19–26, 2012).

83. For example, Shlomo pointed to erroneous Christian hermeneutics of the word

November 21, 1972, Yeshiva University, at the Furst Hall in the Manhattan campus at a symposium dealing with the challenge posed by Jews for Jesus. From left to right: Rabbi Melech Shachter, Rabbi Walter Wurzburger, Rabbi Shlomo Carlebach, Rabbi Charles Sheer, and Aaron Reichel. The program was organized by Aaron Reichel, president of the Yavneh chapter at Yeshiva University. Photo courtesy of Aaron Reichel

understand the Christian missionaries and counter their claims against Judaism.[84]

Shlomo would sometimes develop a specific theme message in a concert. Two of his live concerts in 1973 around the time of the Yom Kippur War focused on his unique wording of a vision of redemptive peace. Later, a record entitled *Songs of Peace* was produced posthumously based on these two concerts, one on Holocaust Memorial Day, April 29, 1973 in Hillside, New Jersey, and a second one in Toronto recorded by Shlomo's brother-in-law, Srul Glick.[85]

"almah" and he cited the Gospel reference to James as an older brother of Jesus to prove that the notion of a virgin birth was mistaken.

84. David Stahl, personal interview, Nov. 18, 2012.

85. The recording was transferred and produced afresh by Sojourn Records in

Back to Yeshiva University. It was the last week of December 1973. I was in my senior year at YU. Reb Shlomo was invited to our Hanukkah celebration in the basement of Furst Hall where we held *Cafe Yeshiva*. One of my classmates reported: "It was a wild *leibedik* night with lots of dancing. People were really turned on and excited for the next few days."[86] A picture of this memorable event was published in my YU yearbook graduating class.[87]

4.   YOGI BHAJAN, SUFI SAM, AND SWAMI SATCHIDANANDA

In 1973, a 90-minute documentary entitled *Sunseed* was filmed with interviews of ten New Age leaders including friends of Shlomo such as Yogi Bhajan, Pir Vilayat Khan, and Swami Satchidananda, as well as two former Jews, Sufi Sam and Baba Ram Dass (Dr. Richard Alpert). But the only practicing Jew among the ten was Shlomo Carlebach.[88] He was able to gain acceptance in these circles not only because of his non-judgmental way of appreciating others but also because of his outgoing personality where he radiated empathy and humor.

Reb Shlomo's participation at events such as the Holy Man Jam and Meeting of the Ways paved the way to personal friendships. The mutual respect with people like Pir Vilayat Khan and Swami Mahadevananda enabled Shlomo to enter the ashrams where he discovered many a wandering Jewish seeker. To appreciate this innovation, we compare Yogi Bhajan, Sufi Sam, and Satchidanada, three of the influential personalities with whom Shlomo interacted.

#

2009, SojournRecords.com, http://www.sojournrecords.com/prod/artist/shlomo _carlebach. For a review of this record see Magid, "Rabbi Shlomo Carlebach and His Interpreters."

86. My thanks to Yehuda L. Frischman for this recollection (personal correspondence Aug. 23, 2012).

87. My thanks to my YU classmates Sidney Slivko and Chaim Brickman for sending me a scan of this photo.

88. The film was directed by Fredrick Cohn and began showing on a daily basis at the Whitney Museum of American Art in Nov. 1973. The other personalities interviewed included Sri Brim Dass, Lama Anagarika Govinda, Swami Muktananda, and Maharaji Virsa Singh. See Nora Sayre, "Sunseed (1973) Film: Mysticism in U.S.," *The New York Times*, Nov. 3, 1973. For a listing of the ten participants, see Shii.org, http:// shii.org/knows/Sunseed. Compare the descriptions at Fandango.com, http://www .fandango.com/sunseed_v155560/plotsummary.

Classmates of the author, crowding around Reb Shlomo (left corner), clapping, singing and dancing at a Hanukkah party, December 1973 at Furst Hall. Pictured from the Yeshiva University class of 1974 are Norman Blumenthal, Mitchell Flaum, Marvin Stern, and Benjamin Yasgur.

Yogi Bhajan or Siri Singh Sahib (1929–2004) was born into a Sikh family in India. After immigrating to Canada, he arrived in Los Angeles in 1969 and began teaching a mix of Kundalini yoga, Tantrism and Sikhism (a blend of reformed Hinduism and Islam). Soon he established the 3HO Foundation (Healthy, Happy, Holy Organization), and by 1972, had created over one hundred 3HO yoga ashrams in the U.S., Canada, Europe, and Israel. In 1977, *TIME Magazine* featured an article about Bhajan:

> Nine years ago, he was an anonymous yoga teacher who owned little but a suitcase full of beads. Today he earns over $100,000 a year in lecture fees as Yogi Bhajan, the "Supreme Religious and Administrative Authority of the Sikh Religion in the Western Hemisphere." Thousands of American disciples in his Healthy-Happy-Holy Organization (3HO) revere the robust, bearded Bhajan as the holiest man of this era. With equal fervor, opponents denounce him as a charlatan and a heretic.[89]

---

89. James Wilde, "Religion: Yogi Bhajan's Synthetic Sikhism," *TIME Magazine,* Sept. 5, 1977, Time.com, http://www.time.com/time/magazine/article/0,9171,915413,00.html.

The *TIME* correspondent reported:

> Ashram members rise at 3:30 a.m. to practice yoga and meditate,
> sometimes while staring at a picture of Bhajan. . . . Full-fledged
> initiates follow Bhajan's every dictum on diet, medical nostrums,
> child rearing, even orders to marry total strangers . . . For most
> of the converts, the discipline of Bhajanism seems to have filled
> a deep spiritual vacuum. Many are in their mid-20s and come
> from upper-middle-class homes. . . . The adherents are flushed
> with the rosy beauty of new faith. "We got involved in Sikhism
> so we could re-establish a direction in our lives based on real
> principles," a young Jewish woman at a Los Angeles ashram told
> *TIME* Correspondent James Wilde.

Bhajan had indeed tapped into a deep spiritual vacuum. He attracted
thousands of youth in their mid-20s, offering them a spiritual alternative lifestyle. Many were disillusioned Jews. Rabbi Sammy Intrator recalls
how Reb Shlomo once visited Yogi Bhajan in New Mexico for an evening
of prayer and study with a thousand of his followers. After the program,
Reb Shlomo greeted each of the Yogi's followers and persisted in asking for their prior family names (after Indian names were cited), only to
discover Katz, Stein, Friedman, and one young man who admitted in an
unaccented Yiddish, *"Ich bin an Sanzar eyenickel"* (I am a grandson of
the *Sanzer Rebbe*).[90]

Yogi Bhajan viewed Shlomo as a friendly colleague and not antagonis-
tic competitor, and when Bhajan's 3HO Foundation organized the World
Symposium for Humanity in Vancouver in 1976, Reb Shlomo was invited
as the Jewish representative (see below, Chapter 10).

#

Sufi Sam, or Ahmed Murad Chisti (1896–1971), founded the Sufi Islamia
Ruhaniat Society and the Mentorgarden.[91] His students addressed him as
"Murshid," an Arabic term meaning "Exalted Teacher."[92] But in actuality,

---

90. Rabbi Shumel Intrator, "Sharing Memories," *Kol Chevra*, vol. 3, no. 1, Nov. 1996,
7–8.

91. See the website of Sufi Ruhaniat International, Ruhaniat.org, http://www
.ruhaniat.org/index.php?option=com_content&view=article&id=150&Itemid=143.

92. Mansur Johnson (formerly Otis B. Johnson, a college professor of English who
joined the hippies going to California in the 1960s) wrote a biography: *Murshid, A
Personal Memoir of Life With American Sufi Samuel L. Lewis*, Peaceworks, 2006.
There he defines Murshid as "the first Western-born Sufi teacher, Zen master, and
practitioner of Indian cosmic metaphysics." See below, Chapter 8 for the Peace

he was born Jewish as Samuel Leonard Lewis. His mother, Harriett (Rosenthal), was the daughter of Lenore Rothschild of the international banking family and his father, Jacob, was vice president of the Levi Strauss jeans manufacturing company. It was in 1967, while recovering from a heart attack, that Sam Lewis heard the voice of God saying, "I make you spiritual leader of the hippies." The remainder of his life he traveled around California teaching "Dances of Universal Peace" based on sacred phrases from religions he encountered. In 1968, he joined forces with Pir Vilayat Khan, the eldest son of his first teacher, and together they created "a great flowering of the Sufi work in the United States."[93]

In a personal letter dated November 12, 1969, Sufi Sam described how he met Shlomo and found "love and tenderness and Brotherhood on both sides."[94] Later, in July 1970, Sufi Sam embellished the description of his encounter with Shlomo: "We took one look at each other and there was a love-embrace."[95] Sufi Sam once visited the HLP and discovered "a number of my disciples there, both Jewish and non-Jewish."[96]

In a personal letter, December 15, 1969, Sufi Sam admitted having "plagiarized" his Dance of Universal Peace from Reb Shlomo with the justification that this is what I "feel the world needs."[97] Similarly, in a letter to a friend in Washington, dated September 27, 1969, Sufi Sam wrote:

> Some of my own disciples went off to join Rabbi Schlomo in this city who gives the Chassidic version of the same type of dances.[98]

Thus, it seems that the following anecdotal exchange between Sufi Sam and Shlomo is indeed an authentic reflection of the cultural-spiritual exchange:

> Sufi Sam: I have to tell you, I stole something from you.
> Shlomo: What?

Festival at Moshav Me'or Modi'im which was organized by disciples influenced by Sufi Sam.

93. Ibid.

94. Nov. 12, 1969, MurshidSam.org, http://murshidsam.org/Diaries1.html.

95. Coopersmith, *Holy Beggars*, 167 based on Murshid Samuel Lewis, "Sufi Vision and Initiation: Meetings with Remarkable Beings," diary entry, July 28, 1970.

96. Sufi Sam's letter is addressed to a person named Peter who was in "The Temple of Understanding" in Washington D.C. See http://murshidsam.org/Diaries1.html.

97. Letter to his friend Ram in San Francisco, MurshidSam.org, http://murshidsam.org/Documents/Diaries/1969.pdf.

98. Letter to Congressman Phillip Burton in Washington D.C., MurshidSam.org, http://murshidsam.org/Documents/Diaries/1969.pdf.

Sufi: The idea of using dance to bring all these people together in love and peace in our age.

Shlomo: Well, I stole it from the Baal Shem Tov.[99]

In December 1970, Sufi Sam fell down the stairs of his San Francisco home and suffered a brain concussion. He died shortly after, on January 15, 1971.[100]

#

Swami Satchidananda[101] was an anonymous Hindu when he was hosted in New York by the psychedelic artist Peter Max in 1966. His fame began on August 15, 1969, when he gave the opening invocation to close to a half-million people at the Woodstock Music Festival. He led a chant of a Sanskrit mantra, *"Hari Om,"* intended to remove suffering.

Woodstock was the epoch-making event of the Hippie era. It took place on the 600-acre dairy farm of a Jewish couple, Max and Mimi (Miriam) Yasgur, in the rural town of Bethel in Sullivan County, 43 miles southwest of the village of Woodstock, New York. The Yasgur farm turned into a countercultural mini-nation where "minds were open, drugs were used, and love was free." Of the estimated 400,000 to 500,000 participants, most were white upper-middle class, ages 17–23. A disproportionate number was Jewish.

Reb Shlomo asked plaintively why it was Satchidananda who addressed Woodstock and not the Lubavitcher Rebbe – it would have been a *gevalt* – it would have changed a whole generation.[102] Shlomo is expressing his conviction that a charismatic Jewish personality could have dramatically influenced the hippie movement and offered a Jewish mantra/chant instead of the Sanskrit one.

Reb Shlomo met with Satchidananda many times. Yehonatan Chipman was one of "a dozen of the *chevra*" who accompanied Reb Shlomo in mid-July 1971 to visit the Integral Yoga Institute of Swami Satchidananda in San Francisco. Shlomo played *"Hashiveinu HaShem Eilecha VeNashuva"* (God, return us to You and we shall return), and soon everyone was singing and dancing. He talked about Shabbat and they listened "with real

---

99. Coopersmith, *Holy Beggars*, 167.

100. Ruhaniat.org, http://www.ruhaniat.org/index.php?option=com_content&view=article&id=150&Itemid=143.

101. The title Swami means the "Knower who is a Master of Himself." The words, "sat, chid, ananda," mean Truth, Knowledge, and Bliss. Satchidananda founded "Integral Yoga" and "Satchidananda Ashrams International."

102. Lerner, "Practical Wisdom," 54.

interest and receptivity." Later on, Shlomo told his *chevra* that "many, if not most of the yogilakh and swamilakh were Jewish."[103]

In 1973, Shlomo was one of the seven speakers invited to give a presentation at Swami Satchidananda's ten-day yoga silent retreat in Monticello in Sullivan County, New York.[104]

In 1981, Zalman and Shlomo went to Yogaville, the ashram of Swami Satchidananda in Pomfret, Connecticut.[105] Shlomo played guitar and told stories, and soon the ashram people gravitated to him. The Swami strolled toward Shlomo and took him aside:

> "Shlomo," he asked a little petulantly, "Are you trying to take my people away from me?" "No, Swami," Shlomo responded politely but firmly, "I'm just trying to invite them to come back home."[106]

In this hippie generation, there were thousands of Jewish seekers who were enchanted by the *Om* chanting gurus. Wendy Shapiro was a devotee of Satchidananda. Later she became influenced by Shlomo, changed her name to Hannah-Sara, and married Rabbi David Zeller. She recalls that Shlomo admired Satchidananda saying that he was unique amongst the gurus – "he was *mamash* a *tzaddik*."[107]

✳

Shlomo's empathetic approach towards the spiritual imports from the Far East was radical for an Orthodox rabbi. His theological premise

---

103. Yehonatan Chipman, "Memories of Shlomo," *Kol Chevra*, vol. 14, 2008, 137–140.

104. The seven speakers represented the three traditions, Hindu, Jewish, and Christian. Afterwards, Satchidananda wrote: "Each of the speakers pointed the way to mutual acceptance and to an underlying unity." Swami Satchidananda, *Living Yoga: The Value of Yoga in Today's Life*, New York, 1977. In his book, Satchidananda included photos and biographical information of the invited speakers. See Judith Guttman, "He and His Art Make Heart," book review of Swami Satchidananda's *Beyond Words and Living Yoga*, in *Yoga Journal*, 21, July 1978, 61, 64. See also http://www.iyiny.org/about/the_history_of_integral_yoga.

105. The pictures of Reb Zalman at the Satchidananda Ashram are preserved in the University of Colorado Zalman Schachter Collection and labeled "81," presumably 1981. See items 67–68, 102, 116, Pekko.Naropa.edu, http://pekko.naropa.edu/archon/?p=collections/findingaid&id=143&q=&rootcontentid=4523#id4523.

106. This is the version told by Mandelbaum, *Holy Brother*, 72–73. Neila Carlebach, "Remembering Shlomo," in *The Canadian Jewish News*, Nov. 16, 1995, has a slightly different version. When asked by the Swami whether he was trying to steal his followers, Shlomo replied: "I was just borrowing some of mine back."

107. Personal communication from Hannah-Sara Zeller. See also Zeller, *The Soul of the Story*, 226.

was that after the Holocaust, it was necessary for God to send teachers from the Far East with teachings of love and devotion. He found a
basis for this provocative idea in the teachings of R. Mordechai Yosef
of Izbica's *Mei HaShiloach* where it is explained that the reason a *kohen*
(a priest) is not allowed to defile himself unto the dead (Leviticus 21:1)
is because he may become angry at God and conclude that the world
functions without Divine Love and Providence. The *kohen* needs to be in
a state of joy and see Divine Goodness, whereas death creates anger and
sadness.[108] Shlomo applied this idea to the post-Holocaust generation
saying that the anger at God contaminated the teachings. Therefore, God
sent teachers from India, Japan, and Tibet to renew a joyful spiritual
love for God. His message was recorded in 1974 or 1975 for a gathering
organized by Pir Vilayat Khan at the Paulie Ballroom in Berkeley where,
of the eleven spiritual teachers participating, ten had come from Jewish
backgrounds. Panelists spoke afterward of how it was "a pity" that there
had not been anyone to teach them this Jewish spirituality when they
were searching in the late 1950s and 1960s.[109]

This type of theological position is radical in that it gives legitimacy to
learning spirituality from the Far East. But it also explains how Shlomo
developed mutual trust with leading figures in the New Age spirituality
of the decade from 1966–1976.

---

108. *Mei HaShiloach, Parshat Emor.* For Reb Zalman's reconstruction of Reb
Shlomo's source as the Ishbitzer Rebbe on Lev. 21, see Rodger Kamenetz, *The Jew in
the Lotus: A Poet's Rediscovery of Jewish Identity in Buddhist India* (San Francisco:
1994), 157.

109. It was Reb Zalman who recorded and interpreted Shlomo's message. See
Schachter, *Wrapped in a Holy Flame,* 294–295 and the interview on April 25, 2001
with Reb Zalman in Harold Kasimow, John P. Keenan, Linda Klepinger Keenan
(eds.), *Beside Still Waters: Jews, Christians, and the Way of the Buddha* (Sommervile,
MA: 2003), 85–98.

CHAPTER 8

Israel

1. ISRAEL DISCOVERS THE DANCING RABBI (1959–1966)

Reb Shlomo's special connection to Israel began in August 1959 when he used the money earned from his first record to buy a plane ticket to Israel. He arrived and started singing: "I didn't think anyone would pay attention to me, so I was just sitting on street corners singing and slowly, slowly . . . And my first concert in Jerusalem that summer, thousands of people attended, it was *gevalt*."[1]

Shlomo visited Kibbutz Yavneh and Kibbutz Tirat Tzvi to where his relatives from his mother's side had come on aliyah. In Tirat Tzvi, he was hosted by Ephraim Adler, and his concert was well received. At Yavneh, he was hosted by Esther Adler whose husband Alexander had died a couple of years before. There the *yekke* kibbutz members had a hard time appreciating the Rabbi who was jumping up and down with a guitar.[2]

Israel began to discover the "Dancing Rabbi." Israel Radio scheduled a broadcast for 7:30 PM on Motzei Shabbat, March 5, 1960, entitled *The Story of Shlomo Carlebach, the Dancing Rabbi from America*.[3]

Shlomo returned to Israel towards the end of the summer of 1960. He was invited to perform at the famous Edison Theater on 14 Yeshayahu St. in Jerusalem.[4] Shlomo also entertained at the engagement party of Hannah Wallach just a block away from Edison.[5] The groom, Yonatan Shenhav,

1. Lerner, "Practical Wisdom," 54.

2. Two photos taken in 1959 at Kibbutz Tirat Zvi by Ephraim Yair (Adler) can be seen in *Kol Chevra*, vol. 8, 2001, 92.

3. *Davar* newspaper, March 4, 1960, 6. In an interview 30 years later, Shlomo credited his first manager in Israel, Moshe Heshin, with having invented the term "Dancing Rabbi." See http://video.yahadoot.com/5521.

4. A picture of this performance can be found in Brandwein, *Reb Shlomele*, 74.

5. Shlomo had known Hannah's mother, Penina Paula Wallach (Prenzlau), from the

vividly recalls how their guests, a dozen young adults, were impressed when Shlomo introduced his tune *"Esa Einai."* A year later, on August 7, 1961, the couple was married at Kibbutz Shaalvim and Shlomo arrived to lead the singing.[6]

Shlomo spent an entire month in Israel during August 1961, performing fifteen times all over the country.[7] Thus for example, he appeared in the cultural hall of the municipality of Petach Tikvah on August 29, 1961.[8] *Maariv* newspaper reporter Avraham Rotem described how the 31-year old "Dancing Rabbi" is appearing "three times a day before packed halls and exciting thousands of people."[9]

The American press picked up the story of how Carlebach created a commotion in Israel. They described a concert in Haifa where fans continued singing with Shlomo in the streets, creating such a hubbub that a man rushed out of his house in his pajamas and grabbed Shlomo's guitar. He ripped the strings and exclaimed: "My wife made me do it." Reb Shlomo had to protect him from a lynching. The press also described how "ticket holders got into such a hassle" trying to enter Heichal Shlomo in Jerusalem, that even Shlomo couldn't get in until the "police helped him fight his way to the stage with the buttons ripped from his shirt and the police in similar dishabille."[10]

A year later, on August 16, 1962, Shlomo again visited Israel, staying for a month, and it was mostly the young religious youth who received him.[11] Eliezer Jeselsohn was one of the religious youth who came to hear Reb Shlomo sing in the early 1960s. Eliezer was serving in the army in the Nahal and then as a Bnei Akiva *"communar"* activity coordinator in Beersheba. He recalls how songs like *"Esa Einai"* were readily learned

---

time that the Prenzlau family lived in Lübeck where Shlomo's grandfather and then his uncle were the rabbis for decades (see above).

6. My thanks to Shlomo Wallach, Hannah Wallach, and Yonatan Shenhav for the interviews on Aug. 26–30, 2012.

7. Edelstein, "The Dancing Rabbi."

8. The advertisement is reproduced in Brand, *Reb Shlomele*, 87.

9. Avraham Rotem, "The Dancing Rabbi is Exciting Thousands," *Maariv*, Sept. 4, 1961.

10. American newspapers around the country, from Pennsylvania to Ohio, picked up on this story when they wrote about Shlomo's performance in New York's Town Hall on Oct. 22, 1961. The story can be found in: *Simpson's Leader-Times*, Oct. 19, 1961, 6 (Kittanning, Pennsylvania); *The Cuero Record*, Oct. 20, 1961, 4; *The Bedford Gazette*, Oct. 23, 1961, 4 (Bedford, Pennsylvania); *The Evening Independent*, Oct. 23, 1961, 1 (Massillon, Ohio). See Brandwein, *Reb Shlomele*, 245–248 for variations on this story as told by Itzik Aisenstadt and cantor David Ullmann.

11. This was reported in the *Davar* newspaper on Aug. 17, 1962, 14.

Reb Shlomo Carlebach at the Kings Hotel, Jerusalem, 1959. From left to right: Yaakov Lerner, Reb Shlomo, Chaim Adler, Yaakov Tzuker, and Yosef Miletzky. Photo courtesy of Yaakov Lerner

Shlomo performing at the wedding of Hannah Wallach and Yonatan Shenhav on August 7, 1961 at Kibbutz Shaalvim. He is shaking the groom's hand. My thanks to Shlomo Wallach and his sister Hannah for providing these rare vintage photos.

at Reb Shlomo's concert in Tel Aviv at the Beit Zionei America cultural center in 1960, and at the Hias House in Beersheba in 1962.[12]

Religious educators began inviting Reb Shlomo. R. Yaakov Yosef Goldwicht, head of the Kerem B'Yavneh Hesder Yeshiva (where Torah studies are combined with service in the Israel Defense Forces), invited Shlomo to sing with his guitar with the yeshiva boys.[13] Rabbi Yosef Ba-Gad, founder of the Nehalim Yeshiva invited Shlomo to his yeshiva high school, and the students were so inspired that he would regularly invite Shlomo. He also arranged for Shlomo to appear at Tel Aviv's Mann auditorium. Years later, at Shlomo's funeral, R. Ba-Gad eulogized Shlomo: "There are no words to describe the spirit of holiness and faith which his songs and dances infused in hundreds of our pupils."[14]

The story is told that on March 10, 1963, Shlomo gave a Purim standing-room only concert at the Mugrabi Theater in Tel Aviv and was paid $3,000. The next day, in Jerusalem, he spent all his earnings to load a truck full of Purim *mishloach manot* – groceries, pastries, and wines – and distribute them individually to close to 100 needy families.[15]

On December 1, 1964, Reb Shlomo arrived for his eighth visit to Israel. Tehila Ofer of the *Haaretz* newspaper questioned him as to what he would do if he were the Chief Rabbi of Tel Aviv-Yafo. Shlomo answered, I would prowl Dizengoff St. and try to understand the youth. He is depicted as strumming a flamenco guitar and stirring his audience to spirited singing.[16]

In the spring of 1967, when Reb Shlomo visited Jerusalem, Gershon Winkler was a studious 18-year old in the ultra-Orthodox Bais Yoseph Novardok Yeshiva and reports that Shlomo's concert was "tabooed by *yeshivot* all over Jerusalem." Although the Rosh Yeshiva, Rabbi Eleizer Bentzion Bruk, was against his going to the concert of the "controversial singing rebbe," Gershon went and discovered a whole new approach to Torah learning:

---

12. Personal interviews with Eliezer Jeselsohn March 9–10, 2013. The HIAS House is the Hebrew Immigrant Aid Society hostel and most of the participants who came to the concert in Beersheba were new immigrants.

13. Brandwein, *Reb Shlomele*, 46 – picture of R. Shlomo in 1964 at Kerem B'Yavneh with the Rosh Yeshiva.

14. "Memorial Tribute by Rabbi Yosef Ba-Gad, Founder of the Nehalim Bnei Akiva Yeshivah," in Brandwein, *Reb Shlomele*, 297–298.

15. Mandelbaum, *Holy Brother*, 131–133. Mandelbaum told me that she heard this story from Itzik Aisenstadt who was Shlomo's manager in Israel at the time and accompanied him on this Purim venture in Jerusalem (personal communication, Dec. 17, 2012).

16. Tehila Ofer, "Prayer Accompanied by Guitar," *Haaretz*, Dec. 1, 1964 [Hebrew], printed in Brand, *R. Shlomele*, 64–65.

> I was swept by Shlomo's songs and tales and teachings . . . I
> returned that night to the dorm with my head spinning from
> Shlomo's teachings and stories, from this whole other way of
> understanding Torah that was rooted in the heart rather than the
> intellect.[17]

It seems that the seeds of rebellion were planted at this concert. Gershon,
the son and grandson of Orthodox rabbis, received his ordination at this
yeshiva, but soon set out on his own path, became active in the Jewish
Renewal Movement and developed what he called "Flexidox Judaism."[18]

2.   I HEARD THE WALL SINGING (1967–1968)

The Six-Day War was profoundly moving for Reb Shlomo. He traveled to
Israel in June 1967 and found his way to the Kotel for Shabbat. There he
created a tune for "*Yibaneh Hamikdash*"[19] and sang his famous song "*Am
Yisrael Chai*" in reverse, starting it with an ecstatic note of "*Od Avinu
Chai*."[20] Shlomo performed for the Israel Defense Forces in army bases
across the country. In Netanya at Beit HaHayal, he told the wounded
soldiers, "you are my *Rebbes*, and I am your *hasid*," and asked each one
individually to bless him that he should attain their meritorious level
of selfless devotion to others.[21] Shlomo's musical messages reflected a
Messianic fervor of relying upon Divine Providence. He later recapitu-
lated his excitement and utopian message of peace:

> After the Six-Day War, I was one of the first people to walk into
> the Old City and I walked up to every Arab and kissed them, our
> cousins. I went to the top people in Israel, and I said, If we want
> to live in peace with the Arabs, we need an army to make peace
> . . . Give me 5,000 free tickets to bring holy hippies from Los
> Angeles and San Francisco and we will go to every Arab house in
> the country and bring them flowers and tell them that we want to
> be brothers with them. We will bring musicians and we will play

---

17. Gershon Winkler, "Shlomo" in *Pumbedissa: An Open Forum for Uninhibited Discussion of Judaic Issues*, printed in *What's Next*, Winter/Spring 1995, 18.

18. Gershon Winkler, *The Way of the Boundary Crosser: An Introduction to Jewish Flexidoxy* (Oxford: 1998).

19. Ben Zion Solomon, *Shlomo Shabbos*, 30: "This *niggun* I made up the first Shabbos night by the Holy Wall in June 1967." See also Brandwein, *Reb Shlomele*, 273, where he dates a picture of Shlomo on his way to the Kotel in 1967.

20. Jacob Birnbaum, personal communication, March 10, 2013.

21. Brandwein, *Reb Shlomele*, 155, story reported by Rabbi Sar-El Davidovich.

at every Arab wedding and we want them to bring their bands to play at our weddings. We have to live together.[22]

Ten years later, in 1977, when it was announced that Anwar Sadat, was to visit Jerusalem, Shlomo sent a message to his friend Prime Minister Menachem Begin with a unique suggestion:

> How wonderful it would be for 5,000 young Israeli men and women to dance backward in front of Sadat's car all the way from the airport to the Knesset. And when Begin would visit Egypt, 5,000 young Egyptian men and women should dance in front of Begin's car from the Pyramids to his hotel. Afterwards, when I saw Begin, I asked him about it. Sadly enough, he said he never got the message, but that it was a great idea.[23]

At the end of August 1968, Shlomo arrived in Israel. The reporter in the *Davar* newspaper wrote that Shlomo would perform at the Bar Aton student club at Hebrew University, the Ohel Shem hall in Tel Aviv, in Haifa, and in kibbutzim.[24]

A major event was held on August 31, 1968 at Heichal Shlomo in Jerusalem and produced as a record entitled *I Heard the Wall Singing.* The album cover portrayed Reb Shlomo at the Kotel with an inspirational vision of yearning and noted that tickets "were sold out weeks in advance" and "thousands of Carlebach fans had to be turned away." On the record jacket cover was written:

> Those present at the concert that evening saw Shlomo Carlebach at his best. He sang many new compositions which were enhanced by his great joy and emotion of being in Israel once again.

The concert was recorded by the Brooklyn-based The Greater Recording Company and produced in stereo retaining the sounds of the participating audience. Immediately after his performance, Shlomo went to the Kotel and soon a large crowd gathered to join in prayer-singing. While reciting *Kaddish* he composed a new composition for *"VeYatzmach,"* emphasizing the Messianic message. This was also included in the two long-playing records produced.[25]

---

22. Abbreviated from Lerner, "Practical Wisdom," 56; cf. *Kol Chevra*, vol. 14, 2008, 34. A similar quote can be found in Zivi Ritchie, *A Friend to Our Generation,* 75.

23. This is the quote from Shlomo as remembered by Rabbi Moshe Stepansky (personal discussions, Nov. 10, 2010, Aug. 26, 2012).

24. Enriqo Macias, *Davar* newspaper, Sept. 2, 1968 [Hebrew].

25. The first record included six songs: *"Oseh Shalom," "V'sechezenoh," "Ana Hashem," "Korosicho," "Zochraynu," "Vehu Yashmiainu."* The second record included

Reb Shlomo with Israeli soldiers, 1967
Photo courtesy of Menachem Daum

With Israel's return to Jerusalem and the Temple Mount, Shlomo like many Jews, felt that the gates of heaven were opening. He invented new commentaries on the workings of Divine Providential Intervention. He applied his song "*Od Yeshoma*" (Jeremiah 33:10) as referring to the fulfill-ment of the Messianic vision of a rejuvenated Jerusalem. Inspired by the jubilation following the liberation of Jerusalem, he reiterated that the souls of the six million who perished in the Holocaust were coming alive again in Israel. He predicted that soon the three million Soviet Jews would join them in rebuilding Jerusalem. Shlomo used metaphoric imagery, mythical prototypes, and musical effects to create a dramatic rendition heralding the return to Jerusalem. Here is a song-tale performed as a commentary/exposition utilizing a famous verse from Psalms 114:4 that is well-known from the *Hallel* service. Shlomo's guitar accompaniment and vivid delivery introduce the tune into an emotionally charged setting. The fast beat lifts up the singing of the valleys and the dancing hills as describing the Messianic vision. In his sing-song, Shlomo opens with two exegetical questions on this verse:

---

the songs "*Venomar Lefonov*," "*Veyatzmach*," "*Umocho Hashem*," "*Benei Beitcha*," "*Mikimi*," "*Am Yisrael Chai*," and "*HaNeshomo Loch*."

Have you seen, have you seen the hills of Yerusholayim dancing?
Have you heard, have you heard their cry when they dance?

He answers with a song concretizing how the "people of the valley" will be reunited in dance with the "people of the hill," all together now on the Holy Hill of Jerusalem. Israel and the world will all sing together:

הֶהָרִים רָקְדוּ כְאֵילִים גְּבָעוֹת כִּבְנֵי צֹאן, מִלִּפְנֵי אָדוֹן חוּלִי אָרֶץ מִלִּפְנֵי אֱ־לוֹהַּ יַעֲקֹב.

Shlomo offers a synopsis of joyous singing of redemption:

Long time ago, long time ago, we all lived on the hills of Yerusholayim. But then we went into exile. We went into the valley. One valley was Inquisition. One valley was called Auschwitz. And the last valley was called Siberia.

So how can the hill dance as long as the valley is still in exile?

On the great day, on the great day, when from all the four corners of the world, from all the valleys, we will come back to Yerusholayim. The people from the valley will tell the people of the hill, "when you were crying, your tears rolled through the valley, and your tears are so high." And the people of the hill will tell the people of the valley, "your prayers go to the hill, and your prayers are so deep, your prayers are so deep." And the valley and the hill get together, the six million and the three million will dance together, Israel and the world will sing together. God and the angels, real God, guarding us, Yerusholayim and the whole world will dance together, on that Holy Hill.[26]

Essentially, Shlomo had created a theological Messianic reinterpretation using the poetic imagery of the Psalms to predict the utopian reunification. This song was published in Shlomo's record album produced in the fall of 1972 and entitled *Uvnai Yerusholayim,* "Rebuild Jerusalem."[27] The band that accompanied Shlomo was the Clei Zemer Orchestra directed by Noach Dear and John Neuman.[28] In the opening dedication, Shlomo wrote an ode to Jerusalem:

---

26. http://www.youtube.com/watch?v=BnBoG1q_Gdk&feature=related.

27. This album, released by Menorah Records in 1972, was originally intended to have two parts, but only one was published and thus it included only seven songs. The music was arranged by Mutty Parnes, the recording engineer was Pat Jaques, and the cover design was by Marcia Hartman.

28. This band appeared shortly thereafter at Shlomo's wedding in Dec. 1972. The Clei Zemer Orchestra existed for only a short time. It included Sid Statler (drums), Pete Sokolow (keyboards), Mickey Lane (bass guitar), Danny Rubinstein

Dedicated to Jerusalem, the city of G-d, the heart of the world, the soul of Israel. To Jerusalem, which is built with the fire of Auschwitz and the snow of Siberia, with every tear, with every prayer, with every song, with every dance. The city where man was first created and ultimately all of mankind will become human again. The city where man first prayed and where on the great day the whole world will pray together. The city where the river of tears began and where on the great day, the tears will begin to dance. To the city where G-d is nearer, the whole world closest, the city of peace – to Jerusalem.

Another one of the seven songs on this record was one of the most popular tunes that Shlomo composed, a musical interpretation of Psalms 137:5, *Im Eshkochaych* entitled "Jerusalem Is Not Forgotten." Shlomo added a commentary:

I would forget my right hand (my own soul) before I forget you Jerusalem. Even greater than all the joys of the world is the joy of knowing Jerusalem. Memory is the purest expression of the soul. One can be forced to know but not forced to remember. We only remember what touches our soul. We Jews cannot forget Jerusalem because we cannot live without it.

Then he added a moving sing-story explanation:

There is no pain in the world which can make us forget Yerusholayim. There is no joy in the world which can make us forget Yerusholayim. For two thousand years whenever we prayed, and we prayed all the time. We directed our thoughts, our feet, our minds to Yerusholayim. If you would have stopped a little Yiddilah on his way to the gas chambers and you would ask him what are you thinking about? He would answer, I am thinking of Yerusholayim, I'm on my way to Yerusholayim. If you'll stop a little Yiddilah on his way to Siberia, what are you thinking about? He will answer I'm thinking of Yerusholayim, I'm on my way, I'm on my way to Yerusholayim.[29]

(woodwinds), and Mutty Parnes (electric guitar). My thanks to Howie Kahn for this information.

29. To hear Shlomo singing the song and the musical explanation: http://www.youtube.com/watch?v=Xxivi4XqaFs. One of the best recordings of Reb Shlomo in this song, can be heard at http://ningmp3.com/onply.php?q=ZEdKU1JLQVRESXM=&tl=Shlomo%20Carlebach%20Imeshkochay%20Yerushalayim.

Reb Shlomo dramatized a nostalgic commentary on the importance of Jerusalem. For many Jews, the return to Jerusalem fulfilled ancient prayers, but for Shlomo, the stones of the Wall could be heard singing.

Reb Shlomo also composed a most remarkable song to mark the return of Israel to Jerusalem as a reworking of an Evangelist gospel song. The gospel theme is "My Lord is coming back" with an obvious Christological significance, whereas Reb Shlomo's refrain is:

> My Lord is coming back to the City of David.
>   My Lord is coming back for His Own.
> Oh, praise the Lord.

The triumphant irony of the song is revealed by comparing it to the gospel lyrics. Here Reb Shlomo has invented a moving rendition of a Jewish Messianic revival with lyrics such as:

> My Lord has come back after two thousand years of crying and suffering.
>   Yes, my Lord has come back.
> Yes, my Lord, He's seen me cry.
>   Yes, my Lord, He heard me pray.
> My Lord, He knows my heart, He heard my soul.
>   My friends, yes my brothers, yes my sisters.
> It was yesterday.
>   It was only yesterday.
> But today, but today, I have seen it with my own eyes.
>   Oh yes, Lord, I have seen it.[30]

3.   CARLEBACH AND THE HASIDIC SONG FESTIVAL

Shlomo's visits to Israel after the Six-Day War were marked by a growing enthusiasm for Hasidic folk music. One of the signs of the times was the popularity of the play *"Ish Hasid Haya"* ("Once There Was a Hasid"), produced by Dan Almagor, which opened in Tel Aviv on October 1968. It offered a secular interpretation to Eastern European Hasidic music and stories, and became a surprising hit being performed more than 600 times in Israel. The success inspired enthusiasts to solicit songs to be presented in an annual Hasidic Song festival. However, the only things

---

30. My thanks to Tzvi Moshe Cooper for sharing the original recording of this song by Reb Shlomo. It is prefaced with his explanation in Hebrew that God has returned to Mt. Zion after 2,000 years of our prayers.

"Hasidic" about most of these songs were that the lyrics were from the liturgy or from biblical sources.[31]

Nachum Beitle teamed up with Micki Peled of Solan Theater to produce the Festival. Menashe Levran, director of the Israeli Army Rabbinate's band, became the Hasidic Festival's choir and orchestra director. Shlomo was involved from the beginning. He later told an interviewer: "Together with my promoter, Nachum Beitle, I initiated the Hasidic Song Festival."[32] Indeed, in almost every one of the first ten festivals there was an entry of a song written by Shlomo. His tunes for *"VeHaer Eynenu"* and *"Od Yeshoma"* placed second in the years 1969 and 1972 respectively. *"Uvau Haovdim"* won first place in 1974.

The First Hasidic Song Festival was held on October 5, 1969, Motzei Simchat Torah at the Mann Culture Center in Tel Aviv. Shlomo's song, *"VeHaer Eynenu"* performed by Ha'Shlosharim (The Three'ngers),[33] won second place. Following up on this newfound popularity, Menashe Levran and Shlomo produced an album in 1970 entitled *VeHaer Eynenu* with the Israeli record company, Hed Arzi.[34] Levran conducted the choir and orchestra, and arranged the music for ten songs of Shlomo.

In the Second Hasidic Festival in 1970, the song *"Yevarechecha"* composed by David Vinkrants (sung by Ilana Rubina) took first place. David with his accordion was one of the frequent accompanists of Reb Shlomo.[35] The Tzemed Reim Duo of 22-year old singers, Israel Gottesdiener and Binyamin (Benny) Rosenbaum, sang R. Shlomo's tune for *"Shema Yisrael"* arranged by Arieh Levanon. On Motzei Shabbat, August 29, 1970, Tzemed Reim joined forces with Reb Shlomo in an evening of Hasidic music on Mt. Carmel, Haifa.[36]

In the Third Hasidic Festival in September 1971, Shlomo's tune for *"Hemdat Yamim"* from the *Amidah* in the Shabbat prayers was performed by the threesome Shovavey Zion.[37] This song was then incorporated into Shlomo's next record, which was produced in the fall of 1972.

---

31. Marsha Bryan Edelman, *Discovering Jewish Music* (Philadelphia: 2003). The excerpt "Reinventing Hasidic Music: Shlomo Carlebach" is available at MyJewishLearning.com, http://www.myjewishlearning.com/culture/Music/TOSyn agogueMusic/Hasidic_Carlebach.htm.

32. Shacham, "Enfant Terrible."

33. The three singers were Shalom Hanoch, Benny Amdurski, and Chanan Yovel.

34. For a recording of Shlomo singing *"VeHaer Eynenu"* with Levran's choir, see http://savethemusic.com/bin/archives.cgi?q=songs&search=performer&id=Shlomo +Carlibach.

35. For a photo of David Vinkrants accompanying Reb Shlomo, see Brand, *Reb Shlomele*, 216.

36. Brandwein, *Reb Shlomele*, 76 – Hebrew advertisement for the performance.

37. The three singers were Coby Recht, Chanan Yovel, and Kobi Oshrat. The latter

In the Fourth Festival in 1972, the Tzemed Reim Duo received second prize with Shlomo's tune for "*Od Yeshoma*."[38] In the Fifth Festival in 1973, Lew Pilschik sang Shlomo's "*Adir Hu*."[39] In the Sixth Festival in 1974, Shlomo's song "*Uvau Haovdim*" (Isaiah 27:13) was performed by Chocolate, Menta and Mastiq, and they won first prize. This song was then featured in Shlomo's concert recorded live in 1976 in the Mann Auditorium (*Heichal Hatarbut*) in Tel Aviv[40] and produced as a record.[41]

In the Ninth Festival in 1977, Jimmy Lloyd, an Afro-American singer living in Israel, sang Shlomo's tune for "*Ki VeSimcha*" (Isaiah 55:12) and Uzi Fuchs sang Shlomo's "*Meloch Al Kol Haolam*." In the Tenth Festival in 1978, The Brothers and Sisters[42] sang Shlomo's "*Omdot Hayu Raglenu Bishear'rayich Yerusahalyim*" (Psalms 122:2). This song was actually first sung by Reb Shlomo in June 1969 for the *Sheva Brachot* of Ayesha Joy Burkey at the HLP.[43]

The Diaspora Yeshiva Band (DYB),[44] a band strongly influenced by Reb Shlomo, was the audience favorite in 1977–1978, winning first place in both the Ninth Festival and Tenth Festivals with "*Hu Yiftach Libenu*" and "*Malchutcha*" respectively.[45] Then in 1980, they took second place with "*Pitchu Li Shaare Tzedek*."[46] With their beards, vests, and *tzitzit*, they

---

arranged the music. See Elyaqim Mosheh's Media Collection – http://elyaqimmedia. pbworks.com, Chasidic Song Festival.

38. For a record of this festival see www.ortav.com/sunshop/index.php?l=product _detail&p=355. On YouTube there is a 3-minute clip of several Tzemed Reim renditions of Carlebach songs including Od Yeshoma. In addition there is a recording of Reb Shlomo as he appeared on their pre-Shabbat program, *Shalom Lavo Shabbat*. Benny asks Shlomo, "Are you a rabbi or a singer?" He answers: "I am a Jew who is looking for God, for Israel, waiting for Mashiach, for the day that is entirely Shabbat, who is happy to see the joys of creation . . ." See http://www.youtube.com/watch?v= ojriwdEOdbY&feature=related.

39. *Adir Hu* received 11th place. For the 1973 Chassidic Song Festival record, see http://www.ortav.com/sunshop/index.php?l=product_detail&p=353.

40. http://www.youtube.com/watch?v=eHRYjQZ-VZM&feature=em-subs_digest-newavtr-vrecs. In this 9-minute clip, Reb Shlomo adds *chazzanut* and sings "*Harahaman*" and explains: The Merciful One should send us Eliyahu the prophet."

41. The record was produced by Nogah Productions of Nachum Beitle, T. Herskhovitz, and Sh. Gefen, and again distributed by Hed Arzi. The record contained eight songs including two versions of "*Od Yeshoma*."

42. See Bros-and-Sis.com, http://www.bros-and-sis.com/biography.shtml.

43. Ben Zion Solomon, *Shlomo Shabbos*, 33.

44. For a description and history of the DYB, see Ruby Harris, "The Band that Changed Jewish Music," *Jewish Magazine*, June 2007, http://www.jewishmag.com/ 114mag/band/band.htm.

45. For the record of the 1977 Hasidic Song Festival see http://www.ortav.com/ sunshop/index.php?l=product_list&c=66.

46. Ruby Harris told me that "*Hu Yiftach*" and "*Pitchu Li*" were composed by

looked like real Hasidim, yet their music was Jewish Rock. Two of the founding members of DYB were Shlomo's disciples, Ben Zion Solomon and Moshe Shur. Ruby Harris, who joined the DYB in 1976, notes that this was "the first Jewish Rock Band":

> Whatever Shlomo is to modern Jewish folk music, we were to Jewish Rock music. Shlomo loved us for that and always seemed very at home with us backing him up and performing together. Besides our original songs in DYB, we used to play many Shlomo songs, and when you "rock" them up, they seem to be custom made for rock n' roll.[47]

With events like the Hasidic Song Festival, the term "Hasidic music" acquired a new connotation as a genre of popular, easy to sing lyrics from traditional sources. The catchy tunes were adapted in synagogues around the world as easy to learn melodies that facilitated congregational singing. The songs were adopted in youth movements, summer camps, and religious celebrations. In sum, the Carlebachian musical style was beginning to evolve gradually into a neo-Hasidic cultural trend that was going beyond standard religious identities.

4.   JERUSALEM AND MIGDAL (1969–1973)

Shlomo's visit to Jerusalem in the summer of 1969 had some interesting events. On July 24, 1969, the evening of the Tisha BeAv fast, Shlomo and his *chevra* were on their way to the Kotel. The word spread that he would be leading *Eicha* and *Kinnot* with his guitar. Some *haredim* at the Kotel objected and blocked his way. A small riot ensued and police came. Shlomo announced: "*Chevra*, this is not the way," and the group retreated to the road under the Porat Yosef Yeshiva where Reb Shlomo shared his inspirational messages and Hasidic stories.[48] The next day or

---

Rabbi Yossil Rosenzweig, and "*Malchutcha*" by Reuven Sirotkin.

47. Personal communication, Nov. 13, 2012. Ruby adds: "Yossil Rosenzweig together with Avraham Rosenblum, our lead singer, penned what could be called the 'anthem of the Baal Teshuva Movement' with their song '*Tzadik Katamar Yifrach*', perhaps the first big hit in Jewish Rock history. Shlomo was the musician/singer/composer that made it all possible and paved the road."

48. Elli-Moshe Kline, "Saved from Drowning," *Kol Chevra*, 17, 2011, 106–107. Elli-Moshe (at the time Michael) was in Israel for his junior year abroad and went to the Kotel. Michael's father, Rabbi Oscar Kline, had studied with Shlomo in Torah Vodaas and Michael's first memory of Shlomo was from 1955 when Shlomo visited his home in Newark, New Jersey.

so, the Amshinover Rebbe brokered a peace and accompanied Shlomo to the Kotel.[49]

On Sunday, August 17, 1969, Shlomo performed at the prestigious Gymnasia Rehavia high school in Jerusalem. He implored the audience to join in singing, and noting that there was a group from the USY Israel Pilgrimage,[50] he admonished them: "Those who are here in Israel for the first time . . . you should be jumping and singing forty-eight hours a day!"[51]

Soon Shlomo's disciples began establishing a base in Jerusalem. Alex and Miriam Scott, who had hosted Shlomo's Shabbat programs in Forest Knolls near San Francisco (see above), came on aliyah in April 1969, first renting a small one-bedroom apartment in Jerusalem. Natan and Ahouva joined them in May 1969.[52] In the fall, they found a large Scandinavian all-wood house on 18 Shmaryahu Levine St. in Kiryat Yovel, overlooking the hills and trees of the Jerusalem Forest where they opened the House of Love and Prayer in Jerusalem.[53] Alex Hebraized his name to Elyah (Eliyahu) Succot.[54]

Shlomo was very proud of his first delegation of new *olim* (immigrants) to Jerusalem. On the jacket of a record album "dedicated to Jerusalem," Shlomo praised "our first group from the House of Love and Prayer in San Francisco," i.e., Alex and Miriam Scott, Natan and Ahouva Schafer, and dedicated to them his song "May the angels walk with you to guard you on your way" (Psalms 91:11).[55]

Elyah Succot invited many students to spend Shabbat at the House. Ruth (Freeman) Fogelman began coming at the end of October 1969.[56]

---

49. My thanks to Rabbi Moshe Waldoks for this information (Sept. 11, 2012). At the time he was a 20-year old student at the Hebrew University of Jerusalem.

50. The USY (United Synagogue Youth of the Conservative Movement) annual pilgrimage brought youth to Israel for the summer.

51. One of those present who was deeply impressed was 16-year old Kenny Ellis who was on a USY summer tour. He later was instrumental in inviting Shlomo to a radio interview in Philadelphia and to an ongoing series of Saturday evening concerts in Manhattan (see below, Chapter 11). My thanks to Kenny for sharing this event and the accompanying photo.

52. Coopersmith, *Holy Beggars*, 209–210.

53. Personal communication from Ahouva Steinhaus, Sept. 9, 2011.

54. Born in New Jersey during World War II, Alex Scott majored in art at Rutgers University and attended the San Francisco Art Institute of California. Influenced by Reb Shlomo, Alex became religious and today divides his time between learning in a *kollel* and painting as a professional artist. See SoferOfTzfat.com, http://www.soferoftzfat.com/Elyah%20Succot.htm.

55. The record, entitled *Uvnai Yerusholayim*, was released in the fall of 1972.

56. Ruth Fogelman, "Moments," *Kol Chevra*, vol. 15, 2009, 89.

The Diaspora Yeshiva Band

The Diaspora Yeshiva Band in 1980: Ruby Harris, Gedaliah Goldstein, Avraham Rosenblum, Ben Zion Solomon, Simcha Abrahamson, and Ted Glazer.

Born in London, England, she had arrived in Israel as a teenager, worked on a kibbutz for a year, and was about to start her studies in English Literature at Hebrew University. Ruth described her ecstatic Shabbat experience:

> This Shabbat was like no other I had previously experienced. We all sat on the floor with our brown rice, tehina, and Israeli salad on white paper-ware. We fed each other pieces of challah and it was an amazing spiritual sharing. We sang Shlomo's melodies such as "*Mizmor Shir*" and "Lord Get Me High." Yes, we actually got higher and higher as we sang. I felt as if I had left my seated position on the floor and was floating somewhere in upper space. Every so often, one of our hosts would tell a Shlomo story or saying.[57]

Ruth went regularly for Shabbat: "When I came home after Shabbat, people wondered what I was so high on because I was so high from

---

57. Personal interview with Ruth Fogelman. See also Ruth Fogelman, "Waking Up in Jerusalem," *Kol Chevra*, vol. 3, Nov. 1996, 21–22.

On August 17, 1969, Shlomo performed at the Gymnasia Rehavia high school
in Jerusalem.   Photo by Debby Appel

Shabbat." She met Reb Shlomo when he visited the House a few months
later. Ruth vividly remembers the weddings Shlomo performed in the
Jerusalem Forest just below the HLP for Ze'ev and Chaya Schwab, and
for Chanan and Channah Leah. It was typical of Shlomo that the *huppah*
alone lasted three hours.[58]

On June 22, 1970, at 2:30 AM, a fire broke out in the Kiryat Yovel
wooden House of Love and Prayer. The house was destroyed and all their
possessions lost in the flames. The police officer wrote a report indicating
arson. The rumor was that ultra-Orthodox fanatics had started the fire.
Bella Gerstner, a cousin of Shlomo recounted what happened next:

> We called Reb Shlomo and told him about the crime squad's
> findings. He was extremely agitated, fearing that the police would
> make trouble for those zealots and worrying even more about the
> disgrace that Orthodox Jewry might incur as a result of this *hillul
> ha-Shem*. He decided to ring the police investigator and had a
> lengthy conversation with him on the phone . . . On the following
> day, reports of the fire appeared in Israeli newspapers – together
> with the conclusion . . . that arson was *not* suspected.[59]

---

58. Interview with Ruth Fogelman, Oct. 2, 2011.
59. Brandwein, *Reb Shlomele*, 257–258, and Brand, *Reb Shlomele*, 176–178. See

After the House burnt down, Shlomo would lead Friday night Shabbat programs on the roof of King David's Tomb. He also led programs at Moadon Tikvateinu on Shivtei Yisrael St., the Torah Outreach Program's Center on Chabad St. in the Jewish Quarter (Rabbi Yaakov Fogelman's Center), Emuna and Yehoshua Witt's home when they lived on Ovadiah St., and at the home of Gavriel and Monique Goldberg[60] on Ramban St. in Rehavia.[61]

In May 1970, Rabbi Shlomo Carlebach visited Israel for two weeks, and the newspapers reported in advance the anticipated arrival of "the Dancing Rabbi."[62]

In 1971, Elyah and Miriam Succot, together with two other couples, Gedalia and Zahava Druin, and Ze'ev and Chaya Schwab, settled in Migdal, a town 8 km north of Tiberias on the slopes of Mount Tabor. Gedalia and Zahava became beekeepers. They planted trees mentioned in the Bible. Gedalia would bring visitors and dramatize the historical biblical events.[63] Nechama Yasskin (Silver) was one of the visitors sent by Shlomo to visit the Migdal families. She came in the summer of 1972 and described her impressons:

> It was a real opportunity for me to see "spirituality" in action. They were the holiest of families, living a simple, happy life, receiving guests with the utmost of joy and spreading the light of G-d's Torah in the most loving way.[64]

The families stayed in Migdal for a few years and as their children grew older, they moved back to Jerusalem.

When Shlomo was in Israel at the end of September 1970, he was interviewed in Tel Aviv in mid day by a *Maariv* reporter named Nili at the Bohemian meeting place Café Rowal on Dizengoff St. After describing his success in San Francisco, Shlomo shared his vision with Nili – he would turn Dizengoff Square into a giant synagogue and sit with the youth all

---

there for a reprint of the article about the fire by Yehiel Limor in *Maariv*, June 23, 1970.

60. Shlomo had made the *shidduch* of Monique and Gavriel, and performed their marriage.

61. Personal interview with Ruth Fogelman, Oct. 2, 2011. For the tune of "*Shochein 'Ad*" and the *niggun* "*M'loch al Kol*," composed by Reb Shlomo in the home of Monique and Gavriel in 1978, see Solomon, *Shlomo Shabbos*, 39.

62. *Maariv*, May 17, 1970 [Hebrew].

63. Yehiel Yisrael, personal communication, Sept. 14, 2011.

64. Nechama Yasskin (Silver), personal interview, Oct. 6, 2012.

Friday night singing "*Lecha Dodi*." This was Shlomo's picturesque way of explaining his unusual outreach vision.[65]

But there were very few outreach rabbis with whom Shlomo could share his vision. One exception was Rabbi Mordechai Goldstein. After studying at the Chofetz Chaim Yeshiva in Queens, Mordechai moved to Israel in 1964. After the Six-Day War, he founded Yeshiva "Toras Yisrael," later known as the Diaspora Yeshiva, on Mount Zion in the Old City of Jerusalem. This was the first *baal teshuva* yeshiva in Israel.[66]

Shlomo encouraged many of his followers to learn in Jerusalem, thus helping create the first class of Rabbi Goldstein's Yeshiva. One of these students was Joe Schonwald. When the Six-Day War broke out, 19-year old Joe was at the City College of Santa Monica.

> I flew to Israel to volunteer with the war efforts. My friend and fellow activist, David Zeller, was also there, and one evening he brought Reb Shlomo to meet us in Herzliya. Shlomo encouraged us to go study Torah, and thus eight of us became the first class at the Diaspora Yeshiva! I stayed there for seven years and received rabbinical ordination.[67]

After returning from Jerusalem to Los Angeles, Joe joined other activists in forming an urban kibbutz, *Ohr Hadash*, and ran workshops and outreach on college campuses. Rabbi Joe worked closely with Shlomo as a friend and confidant, and when he served as rabbi for 25 years at Temple Beth Abraham in Oakland, California, he often organized visits and performances of Shlomo in California (see below, Chapter 11).

Meir Zvi Spitzer, who met Shlomo in Jerusalem[68] helped Rabbis Goldstein and Carlebach in setting up this yeshiva – on his business card

---

65. Nili in *Maariv*, Sept. 30, 1970. See Brand, *Reb Shlomele*, 160, for a photocopy of this article.

66. Like Shlomo, R. Goldstein had studied with Rabbi Aharon Kotler at Lakewood Yeshiva. See Diaspora.org.il, http://diaspora.org.il/staff. When visitors began to come to the Western Wall, R. Goldstein's yeshiva was at the forefront of welcoming the secular and unaffiliated Jewish youth and offering them opportunities for religious practice and learning.

67. Personal interview with Rabbi Joe Schonwald, Feb. 5, 2012.

68. Meir Zvi Spitzer was 13 years old and studying in the Klozenberger Rebbe's Yeshiva in Kiryat Sanz in Jerusalem when he first met Shlomo. Spitzer described to his interviewer how Shlomo was dressed with a jacket and tie and charcoal hat. The two of them went together to the tish of the Satmar Rebbe in Jerusalem and the Rebbe gave Shlomo five books from his grandfather on "how to *mekarev* people with broken hearts and *neshamas*" and then blessed Shlomo. See Avigayil Witt's interview with Zvi Spitzer in "The Rebbe and the Rebbe," *Kol Chevra*, vol. 7, 2000, 101.

he identifies himself as "Director-Manager" of Yeshiva "Toras Yisrael."[69] Spitzer also participated with Shlomo in various happenings at the HLP[70] and he helped Shlomo's organizing in Israel from around 1969–1971. Aryae Coopersmith recalls:

> I remember Rabbi Zvi Spitzer coming with Shlomo several times to the House on Arguello Blvd. Sometimes he would stay for a while. Zvi was short, spoke English with a thick Israeli accent, often dressed similarly to Shlomo, or else would wear a suit without a tie. He was very energetic, always seemed to be doing something, would bustle about importantly and tell us about the arrangements he was making for Shlomo in Israel as his manager there. When I asked Shlomo if this was true, Shlomo put his arm around Zvi, flashed a big smile and a "v" with his fingers. "Greatest manager in the world!" he said.[71]

Reb Shlomo was back in Israel sometime after Pesach 1971. Simcha Holtzberg, who was known in Israel as the "Father of the Wounded Soldiers,"[72] arranged for Shlomo to perform at a special evening in Moadon Tzavta in Tel Aviv in honor of the paratrooper Yair Dori who had been returned to Israel after almost a year in Egyptian captivity. Shlomo sang "*Motzi Asirim Ufodeh Aanavim*."[73]

On July 25, 1971, Spitzer was involved in organizing "A Religious Woodstock," a weeklong learning program featuring Reb Shlomo and Rabbi Goldstein at the Diaspora Yeshiva and near Nahum Arbel's gallery close to the Kotel. Because it took place during the week before

---

69. In the upper left corner is the address of the House of Love and Prayer on Arguello Blvd. in San Francisco, and in the lower right corner is Spitzer's Jerusalem address, 6 Nechemiah St. (in the Bucharim neighborhood). http://www.bhol.co.il/forum/topic.asp?cat_id=19&topic_id=2956273&forum_id=18615.

70. For example, he appears in the photos from the wedding of George Gorner and Pamela Klein on March 24, 1969 in Golden Gate Park. See below, Chapter 5.

71. Aryae Coopersmith, personal correspondence, Jan. 4, 2013.

72. Simcha Holtzberg (1924–1994), a Holocaust survivor, received the Israel Prize in 1976 in recognition of his lifelong dedication to helping wounded soldiers and terrorist victims.

73. On May 30, 1970, Yair was driving a convoy of armored vehicles in the north area of the Suez Canal when his paratrooper unit was attacked, and his companions murdered in a cruel battle. Yair, seriously wounded, was taken captive. His life was saved by amputating his right arm at the elbow. Blinded in one eye and with wounds all over his body, he was returned to Israel on March 29, 1971. See http://www.encuentro-jdcla.org/11vo/concurso/ingles/jurado.asp. A recording of this evening with Reb Shlomo telling a story and singing can be heard at a program of Yedidya Meir at http://www.bhol.co.il/Article.aspx?id=33342.

Tisha BeAv the singing was without a guitar. Rabbi Spitzer, as the festival's spokesman, explained that the main purpose was to reach out to American youth visiting Israel. A few hundred youth came, not only from the Diaspora Yeshiva, but even from Meah Shearim.[74]

The impact of Shlomo via the Diaspora Yeshiva is illustrated in the colorful story of Chaim Dovid Saracik. Born as David Saracik in South Africa on December 3, 1952, he was talented musically and began playing guitar at age 11. At age 21, David met Shlomo in Amsterdam. At the time, David was living a Sufi type existence at a 3HO ashram[75] when he heard that a "singing, dancing Rabbi" would be visiting De Kosmos, a New Age meditation center in Amsterdam.[76] When Shlomo arrived he embraced everyone individually. David, who was dressed in white robes and a Sufi turban, greeted him with "Shalom Rabbi": "Shlomo gave a real *krechtz* and I was really embarrassed because everybody was looking at me. Shlomo sensed that I was a Jew."[77]

After another year in Sufi settings in Amsterdam and Paris, David arrived in London. When Shlomo visited in June 1975, David went to see him and Shlomo invited him to the Diaspora Yeshiva for his two-week teach-in. David arrived in Jerusalem on July 5, 1975, studied at the Diaspora Yeshiva for seven years and was married there on March 2, 1982. Known today as Chaim Dovid,[78] he has become one of the leading Carlebach musicians in Israel. Chaim Dovid accompanied Shlomo in hundreds of concerts in Israel and has produced a dozen albums. Chaim Dovid sums up his mission: "Reb Shlomo's smile and love of Am Yisrael changed my life and I'm trying to pass that on."[79]

While in 1969 Shlomo's business card had listed the Dan Hotel in Tel Aviv for his contact information in Israel,[80] in the 1970s, he had a

74. Tzvi Lavi, "A Religious Woodstock in the Capital – by the Dancing Rabbi," *Maariv*, July 23, 1971 [Hebrew]. Gil Sadan, "The Dancing Rabbi in Music and Song," *Yediot Ahronot*, July 28, 1971 [Hebrew]. Both articles are reproduced in Brand, *Reb Shlomele*, 153.

75. For details on Yogi Bhajan's 3HO Foundation, see Chapter 7.

76. De Kosmos was the most important New Age center in the Netherlands. It hosted visiting New Age celebrities such as Timothy Leary and Swami Satchidanada. See DeKosmos.net, http://www.dekosmos.net.

77. Interview with Chaim Dovid Saracik, Sept. 3, 2012.

78. The first name of Chaim was given to him by the Diaspora Rosh Yeshiva, Rabbi Mordechai Goldstein.

79. Personal interview, Sept. 3, 2012. See Chaim Dovid Saracik, "Far East, Middle East . . . and Home," *Kol Chevra*, vol. 16, 2011, 116.

80. On his card, Shlomo listed the Dan Hotel phone number as 03–241111. A copy of this card is preserved in the AJA Jacob Radar Marcus file on Carlebach. The Dan Hotel was Tel Aviv's first luxury hotel, and Shlomo's selection of this hotel was at

residential Jerusalem address, 16 Lincoln Street. His disciples, such as Michael Golomb, Yankala Shemesh, and Zipporah, organized classes there and sometimes Shlomo stayed there.[81] A House of Love and Prayer was established in the Shaarei Hesed neighborhood of Jerusalem on Teveriah St.

Sometime around 1971, Israeli TV filmed R. Shlomo with his song *"Am Yisrael Chai"* in its studio with an accompaniment of five of his disciples, Elyah Succot (Alex Scott), Yankala Shemesh, Natan Schafer, Baruch Goldberg, and Eliezer Garner.[82]

Israeli television filmed Shlomo on September 28, 1971, right before Yom Kippur, in front of the arch of the Hurva Synagogue in the Jewish Quarter of the Old City in Jerusalem, accompanied by Avshalom Katz on the accordion and two guitar players.[83] Shlomo began with a cantorial rendition of *"Uvechen,"* from the High Holiday liturgy for *Musaf.* Then he addressed the audience in Hebrew: "It is already time that there should be peace in the world, it is time for all of Am Yisrael to unite together with joy in a 'complete building' and we should sing together." Then he sang *"Samchem."* The participants, mostly religious youth, provided harmony in a responsive chorus. Finally, Shlomo concluded: "We are a holy people waiting all year long for Sukkot, for the day to leave our houses and enter the house of the Lord." Then he sang the verse from *Hallel* (Psalms 118:24) *"Zeh Hayom,"* "Today is the day that God has created, let us rejoice."

From February 14–24, 1972, Shlomo was in Europe on a concert tour which ended on Thursday night. He decided that he was so close to Jerusalem that he should "jump over" for Shabbat. A last minute concert was organized for Motzei Shabbat, *Parshat Zachor,* February 26, 1972, at the Hebrew University of Jerusalem Givat Ram campus.[84] Rabbi Kerry M. Olitzky, currently the Executive Director of the Jewish Outreach Institute, was 16 years old when he attended this concert. He became "a big fan of Carlebach music and liturgy that is *davened* (prayed) in the Carlebach style."[85] Larry and Evelyn Yellin, who were also present, reported:

---

least partially because of the phone service, which in the late 1960s was not a readily accessible commodity in Israel.

81. For example, Yankala Shamas told me that he recalls that in the summer of 1975, Shlomo stayed there with his wife and baby girl Neshama.

82. http://www.youtube.com/watch?v=rmWUyOBmwdU&playnext=1&list=PL5 48CE39DABB6BD87. Although the YouTube caption states 1972/3, Eliezer Garner told me that the original recording was made in 1971, as later than that he was living in the United States.

83. http://www.youtube.com/watch?v=TxPZ56tUbaw. My thanks to Nachman Futterman for identifying the accordionist.

84. My thanks to Rabbi Moshe Pesach Geller for providing these dates.

85. Personal communication, Rabbi Kerry Olitzky, Sept. 15, 2012.

Our daughter Linda was studying at Hebrew University, and we joined her for one of Shlomo's most memorable concerts. At first, the students, mostly secular, were cool to his music and message. But as the concert progressed, Shlomo's spirit captivated the audience and soon the entire auditorium was echoing Shlomo's song, "The Whole World is Waiting to Sing a Song of Shabbos" and the students were dancing up and down the aisles.[86]

The concert ended at midnight and then Reb Shlomo led a *Sheva Berachot* celebration on Mount Zion for Yosele Rosenblum which lasted until 3:00 A M.[87] Rabbi Moshe Pesach Geller who accompanied Reb Shlomo reconstructs what happened next early that Sunday morning, February 27, 1972:

At 4:00 A M, after stopping at the Kotel, our taxi driver drove us to the airport. Suddenly, we had a flat tire. Shlomo was distraught. If he were to miss the flight, then he wouldn't be back in Manhattan in time to lead the Purim program. Finally, we arrive at the airport half an hour after departure time. The El Al check-in clerk spots him and announces: "Shlomo, we are holding the plane for you." He goes straight to the departure gate and finds Rabbi Shneur Kotler, the son of Rabbi Aharon Kotler,[88] standing there, holding up the plane until he is aboard.[89]

This connection to rabbis of stature in the *haredi* community was of considerable importance to Reb Shlomo whose maverick type of outreach to the hippies in the early 1970s was criticized by some Orthodox rabbis. However, several Orthodox rabbis in Israel who were personal friends of Shlomo included Rabbi Gedalia Koenig,[90] Rabbi Yitzchak Ginsburgh,[91]

---

86. Personal communication, Larry and Evelyn Yellin, Sept. 15, 2012. Interview, Oct. 10, 2012.

87. Yosele was the brother of Avraham Rosenblum from the Diaspora Yeshiva Band

88. Rabbi Shneur Kotler (1918–1982) succeeded his father as the Rosh Yeshiva of the Lakewood Yeshiva.

89. Interview with Rabbi Moshe Pesach Geller, Jan. 14, 2013. Compare Geller, "I Remember," 106.

90. For a photo of Shlomo with Rabbi Gedalia Koenig, see Brand, *Reb Shlomele*, 37, Brandwein, *Reb Shlomele*, 45, and Ritchie, *A Friend to Our Generation*, 122. See below for his teaching Breslov Chasidut at the program that Shlomo led in mid-July 1975 at the Diaspora Yeshiva. He also came to teach at Moshav Me'or Modi'im.

91. For a brief clip of the two singing together at a rally in the Shomron in Israel, see http://www.youtube.com/watch?v=GAnSEPd_8JI&feature=player_embedded. For a photo of this rally with Shlomo, Rabbi Yitzchak Ginsburgh, and Benny Katzover, see

and Rabbi Uzi Schwietze of Kfar Yona.[92] The latter was a Modzitz Hasid. He tells the story of how Shlomo visited the Shabbat *tish* of the Rebbe of Modzitz, Shmuel Eliyahu Taub, on Dizengoff Street.[93] The Rebbe seated Shlomo next to him and recited the blessing of *shehakol barah l'chvodo* belonging to the *Sheva Berachot* recited at weddings. Then he whispered to Shlomo:

> That was no mere slip of the tongue, you know, for a heavenly voice just called out: Shlomo ben Naftali! You have been single long enough and very soon you will get married.[94]

Indeed, the prophecy of the Modzitz rebbe came true and Shlomo's marriage took place soon after, on December 26, 1972.

Shlomo was very friendly with the Chief Rabbi of Israel, Rabbi Yisrael Meir Lau, whom he visited several times over the course of thirty years. They first met in the 1960s when Shlomo performed in the courtyard of the Beit Zionei America cultural center in Tel Aviv.[95] Their paths came together several times,[96] as for example in the annual bar mitzvah celebration of the children of Israel Aircraft Industry workers when Rabbi Lau was invited to give the blessings and Reb Shlomo came to sing. On Motzei Shabbat, July 21, 1973, Shlomo came to the celebration in Tel Aviv of the birth of Rabbi Lau's daughter Shira. This was a special festivity after several years of worried anticipation, and was held in a hall on Hamasger Street. Shlomo arrived at 1:00 AM, sang songs, told stories, and stayed until 3:00 AM leaving a memorable impression on many participants.[97]

On August 16, 1973, Shlomo held a concert at the Sephardic Educational Center in the Old City of Jerusalem. Afterwards at 1:00 AM, Shlomo

---

Brandwein, *Reb Shlomele*, 269. Compare Brandwein, *Reb Shlomele*, 135 and Ritchie, *A Friend to Our Generation*, 80.

92. See two photos of Shlomo teaching in Rabbi Uzi Schwietze's home in Brand, *Reb Shlomele*, 41, 71. Compare Brandwein, *Reb Shlomele*, 55. For the eulogy delivered by Rabbi Schwietze at Shlomo's funeral, see Brandwein, *Reb Shlomele*, 302–304. On YouTube there are several videos of R. Schwietze speaking in memory of Reb Shlomo at the 16th and 17th *yahrzeit*s of Shlomo at Jerusalem synagogues. See, for example, in Ohel Rivka: http://www.youtube.com/watch?v=cbr1oumUp5E.

93. Shlomo, in the late 1940s when he was in the Lakewood Yeshiva, had been close to the previous Modzitz Rebbe in New York (see above, Chapter 1).

94. Brandwein, *Reb Shlomele*, 97–98; Brand, *Reb Shlomele*, 71.

95. Personal interview with Rabbi Lau, on Jan. 1, 2013.

96. See below for the wedding they performed together in Sept. 1974 and about their trip to Sebastia in Nov. 1975.

97. Shira Lau (now Schweitzer), who was born on July 11, 1973, explains how this event left a lasting impression on all present with memorable stories such as that of "Yossele the Holy Miser." Personal interview with Shira on Jan. 8, 2013.

invited everyone to join the wedding he was about to perform for Dina
and Ben Zion Solomon. Actually they were already married but not in
a halachic ceremony and they had recently come on aliyah. The *huppah*
was three hours and the wedding lasted until sunrise. The Solomons were
the first settlers of Moshav Me'or Modi'im (see below).

In 1973, Reb Shlomo was filmed in the Herzliya Television studio accompanied by two tambourines, four guitars, and about sixty people,
including many children.[98] The program was entitled *Pe'er Vechavod*
and was produced by Paul Selinger and Yisrael Goldwicht. It included
the following songs: "*Pe'er Vechavod*,"[99] "*Lemaan Achai*,"[100] "*Uvnei
Yerusholayim*,"[101] "*Lecha Dodi*," "*Yisrael Betach BaShem*,"[102] "*Esa
Einai*,"[103] "*Barchenu Avinu*,"[104] "*Ki Hem Hayenu*,"[105] "*Ki Mitziyon*,"[106] "*Boi
Beshalom*,"[107] "*Mizmor Shir*,"[108] and *El Adon*.[109] Reb Shlomo inserted
stories emphasizing expectations for Peace and a future Messianic Day
of Shabbos.[110]

5.   AFTERMATH OF THE YOM KIPPUR WAR (1973–1975)

The Yom Kippur War broke out with a fury on October 6, 1973. On Hol
HaMoed Sukkot, October 16, 1973, Reb Shlomo led a passionate heart-

---

98. http://www.box.com/shared/jba33jj3sx/1/34341330/652181323/1#/s/jba33jj3sx/
1/34341330/1061148106/1; http://www.youtube.com/watch?v=QxvfcodXWMQ. The
entire program is reproduced in two parts – 28:42 minutes at http://www.box.net/
shared/86ztu36k69tba7josa7u, and 16:58 minutes at http://www.box.net/shared/trg
psok16ct6etmxeb5l; http://www.box.net/shared/86ztu36k69tba7josa7u.

99. http://www.youtube.com/watch?v=nXlPqSzrCYQ.

100. http://www.youtube.com/watch?v=kYO7fTcYb6M.

101. http://www.youtube.com/watch?v=EAarYUhkuPs.

102. http://www.youtube.com/watch?v=e2sioksLAug. Shlomo introduces this
tune with an expectation of Messianic redemption.

103. http://www.youtube.com/watch?v=fMeBDgLol5M.

104. http://www.youtube.com/watch?v=b_cFSjS1J8Q.

105. http://www.youtube.com/watch?v=VdehlV1VyFI.

106. http://www.youtube.com/watch?v=1of6UYzvyxI;

107. http://www.youtube.com/watch?v=QxvfcodXWMQ. http://www.youtube
.com/watch?v=1KaPasvN1Ao

108. http://www.youtube.com/watch?v=V5K85uKZ3wE. The song begins at segment 3:05.

109. http://www.youtube.com/watch?v=Uys5nksowwM. The song begins at segment 3:04.

110. The two stories are in the second part of 16:58 minutes – http://www.box.net/
shared/trgpsok16ct6etmxeb5l. See also http://www.youtube.com/watch?v=V5K85u
KZ3wE Holy Beggar.

rending concert in San Francisco.[111] The United Nations ceasefire was adopted on October 22, 1973. Shlomo and a few followers boarded the first available flight to Israel. However, the ceasefire was broken and the passengers were sequestered at the departure gate in Rome. Shlomo played his guitar and taught in the airport.[112] To an interviewer in 1975, Shlomo recalled:

> It was impossible to get onto El Al, so I went with Pan Am to Rome. At the airport in Rome, my wife and I were sitting for nineteen hours . . . our plane came and the director of El Al there said it's impossible to get on the plane. There were about 2,000 people waiting at the airport, you know, besides us. So how many can get on the flight? Let's say 200–300. That's it. So I told him, you know, I got to go because I'm playing for the soldiers. So he went up and spoke to the captain. And you know, the crew has a little room where they can sleep or they can do their thing. So, my wife and I, the crew gave us their seat. So I went to Israel.[113]

The war officially ended on October 25. Shlomo arrived in Israel, singing at numerous army units, and visiting the wounded in the hospitals. He composed a new song meant to provide courage and fortitude, *"Gam Ki Elech"* (Psalms 23:4): "Even as I walk in the valley of the shadow of death, I fear no evil for You are with me."[114] Simcha Holtzberg arranged for Shlomo to visit Hadassah Hospital in Ein Kerem to sing with soldiers wounded in action. Shlomo's famous song *"Am Yisrael Chai"* now acquired a new connotative meaning of survival.[115]

Atara Beruchim accompanied Shlomo to the hospital and took a photo of him shaking the hand of a soldier named Tzion Segev whose armored truck had sustained a direct hit on the Syrian side of the Hermon Mountains. Tzion had been seriously wounded in the spinal cord and

---

111. Preserved in the Ami Weisz collection of 44 audio recordings archived by the Shlomo Carlebach Foundation. My thanks to Alon Teeger for this recording, #34.

112. Personal interview with Fay Bluime, Sept. 13, 2012 who was on this flight.

113. Radio interview on KQED (88.5 FM) in San Francisco, 1975.

114. The song can be heard in the album with a live recording from Feb. 24, 1974 at Brooklyn College.

115. Reb Shlomo plays *"Od Avinu Chai"* at 11:35–13:20 in the 26-minute video prepared in the wake of the Yom Kippur War by Hadassah Women's Zionist Organization on behalf of Hadassah Hospital http://www.youtube.com/watch?v=VFWljkjnlB4&feature=player_embedded#at=774; http://www.nrg.co.il/online/1/ART2/171/324.html.

For just the segment of Shlomo's visit to wounded soldiers in Hadassah Hospital, see http://www.youtube.com/watch?NR=1&v=obvVMe57vFc and http://il.utabby.com/v?i=obvVMe57vFc.

Reb Shlomo's Hasidim in Jerusalem are on the album cover "VeHaer Eynenu,"
1970. Seated are Eliyahu and Miriam Scott with their children. Behind Shlomo
with guitar is Eliezer Garner. Next to him is Yankala Shemesh. The women
include Anna from England and next to her is Tzipora.

leg. Five years later, Atara again met this soldier. The couple fell in love.
Shlomo flew especially from America to perform the wedding.

Atara had first met Shlomo on the street in the summer of 1973 near
the Kings Hotel in Jerusalem when he invited her to join the singing
service at the Kotel that Friday evening: "That was the beginning of a very
special relationship with Shlomo and Neila. We became very close friends
and they adopted me as if I were their daughter."[116] The Segev wedding
took place in the Central Hotel in Jerusalem on December 19, 1979 and
the *huppah* ceremony was a musical event that lasted 2.5 hours. Later,
when the boys of the Segev couple were born, Shlomo came especially

---

116. Personal interview with Atara (Beruchim) Segev, Aug. 27, 2012.

from abroad for the *brit milah* celebrations, on February 10, 1982 and June 17, 1987 respectively.[117]

The impact of the Yom Kippur War on Shlomos songs is illustrated in the album *Rabbi Shlomo Carlebach Live in Concert* recorded on February 24, 1974 at the Walt Whitman Auditorium at Brooklyn College.[118] Shlomo took his tune from "*Shema Yisrael*" and superimposed the words of "Israel Trust in God," "*Yisrael B'tach BaShem*," to raise the morale and encourage the soldiers. The words were chosen as the name of the album and Shlomo wrote a dedication to the fallen and wounded soldiers and "to those who are desperately waiting for Peace and for the arrival of the Moshiach to melt away the loneliness of the world." The cover design became a very popular and symbolic poster. It pictured an Israeli soldier wearing a *tallit* and waving a *lulav* on his tank.[119] Nine songs from the concert were put onto the record and they included "*Od Yishoma*" and "*Adir Hu*" from the 1972 and 1973 Hasidic song festivals respectively. "*Gam Ki Elech*" (Psalms 23:4) became a most significant song to reflect on the Yom Kippur War. The song "*Hashem Oz L'Amo Yiteyn*" (Psalms 29:11) was given an interpretation on the record jacket:

> God gives strength from the highest place unto His people to hold out. God will bless His people with peace. Now more than ever, we know that Peace will start in Jerusalem. Only from there can it expand to the whole world.

Shlomo's concert on September 7, 1974,[120] at the Tzavta Theater, Tel Aviv[121] was recorded live and entitled *Together with Rabbi Shlomo Carlebach*. It was produced with Hed Arzi by Nachum Beitle, Shlomo's manager, and contained nine popular Carlebach tunes.

On July 4, 1975 at 10:00 AM, a huge explosion ripped through Jerusalem's Zion Square as Palestinian terrorist Ahmed Jabara detonated a bomb hidden in a refrigerator that killed 13 and injured 72. The next evening,

117. Personal interviews with Atara Segev on Aug. 27 and Sept. 11, 2012.

118. The record was arranged by Yisroel Lamm whose Neginah Orchestra accompanied Shlomo. Yisroel Lamm and Yitzchok Gross (Y and Y Production) produced the record in cooperation with Reb Shlomo's company, Zimrani Records. The backup choir was Jerry Pollack and Meir Sherman.

119. Alan Alperin designed the poster based on a concept proposed by David Greenblatt.

120. I am calculating the date of Motzei Shabbat, Sept. 7, based on the evidence of Eleonora Shifrin that she attended this concert two days before her wedding which Shlomo performed on Sept. 9, 1974.

121. For a series of three pictures from Shlomo's performances at the Tzavta Theater in Tel Aviv see the State of Israel's National Photo Collection, picture code D596-004, D596-005, and D596-006.

Visit of Shlomo to Hadassah Hospital in Ein Kerem, Jerusalem after the Yom Kippur War. He is shaking hands with Tzion Segev whose armored truck had sustained a direct hit on the Hermon.

Motzei Shabbat, July 5, Shlomo gave one of his most memorable concerts. It took place at the Diaspora Yeshiva on Mount Zion and Shlomo led the crowd in singing, dancing, and praying "on Mount Zion for the dead of Zion Square."[122]

One of those injured in the blast was a 21-year old named Chanan Avital who had just completed his army duty. Chanan needed to be hospitalized in Shaarei Zedek Hospital for more than a year. Shlomo visited him many times, specially arriving on Fridays towards Shabbat. Chanan describes how the entire hospital would be filled with song and joy when Shlomo arrived. The two became close personal friends and when Chanan recovered he decided to invest the monetary compensations from his injury in designing a Hasidic Song Festival for children in Binyanei Hauma. Soon thereafter he founded Pirchei Yerushalayim, the

---

122. See the account by Perle Epstein (Besserman), *Pilgrimage: Adventures of a Wandering Jew* (Boston: 1979), 34–35. In this autobiographical novel, Epstein uses a pseudonym for Carlebach. In a book on Kabbalah and meditative paths, Besserman devotes a chapter to describing the Hasidic "Path of Song and Dance" and notes that "In the twentieth century no Hasidic teacher better embodied this ecstatic way to God than Rabbi Shlomo Carlebach," Perle Besserman, *A New Kabbalah for Women* (New York: 2005), Chapter 7.

Wedding of Atara Beruchim and Tzion Segev, Central Hotel in Jerusalem, December 19, 1979.   *Courtesy of Atara Segev*

Jerusalem Boys Choir, for ages 9–14.[123] The Choir recorded close to 50 record albums and Avital established 22 boys' choirs around the world, contributing greatly to the expansion of Carlebach-type Hasidic music. Chanan acted as Shlomo's manager, arranging many concerts for him with the Jerusalem Boys Choir opening the program.

In mid-July 1975, Reb Shlomo led a two-week Teach-In for the Tisha BeAv period based at the Diaspora Yeshiva in the Old City of Jeruslaem. Nechama Silver reports:

> Moshe Shur, a student at the Diaspora Yeshiva was in the band. Rabbi Gedalia Koenig, a Breslov Rebbe from Meah Shearim came to teach. The program concluded with a grand finale concert at King David's tomb for Tu BeAv on July 23, 1975.[124]

---

123. See Dudu Cohen, *"Perachim BaTzameret,"* *BeSheva*, 480, 10–14, Feb. 9, 2012, http://www.inn.co.il/Besheva/Article.aspx/11422. In English, see "Pirchei Yerushalayim Celebrates 40 Years with a Song for Pollard," May 15, 2012, SOS-Israel, http://www.sos-israel.com/64168.html. Chanan modeled Pirchei Yerushalayim on the precedent of Yigal Calek's Pirchei London which had been established four years earlier in 1972.

124. Personal correspondence, Nechama Silver, Jan. 8, 2013.

Shlomo performs at the Tzavta Theater in Tel Aviv.
Photo taken by Chanania Herman
Courtesy of the Israel Government Press Office, National Photo Collection

On November 30, 1975, Gush Emunim demonstrated at the old rail-road station near Sebastia.[125] Shlomo joined Rabbi Yisrael Meir Lau on a mission to encourage the settlers. This is the story as told by Rabbi Lau:

> It was a very rainy evening, the third night of Hanukkah and we were on our way to encourage the Gush Emunim activists. We had three young boys in the back seat, one of them my 11-year old son David Lau. At the first army roadblock, they let us through. At the second roadblock, one of the soldiers identified me as "the rabbi from the TV" and they waved us on. At the third roadblock, they wouldn't let us pass. I opened my car trunk and showed them the wedding canopy and four poles decorated in blue and white. I explained that I am a rabbi and next to me is a cantor, Shlomo Carlebach. They let us through. Arriving at Sebastia, I announced:

---

125. From late 1974 until November 1975, a Gush Emunim group led by Menachem Felix, Hanan Porat, Moshe Levinger, and Benny Katzover attempted several times to establish a settlement at the old railroad station near Sebastia. Each effort lasted a few days before the army evacuated them until finally on Dec. 8, 1975, the government allowed 25 families to settle in the army camp near Nablus (Shechem). The Sebastia agreement was a turning point that opened up the southern West Bank to Jewish settlement.

This album cover design from 1974, following the Yom Kippur War, shows an Israeli soldier wearing a tallit and waving a lulav on his tank. Alan Alperin designed the poster based on a concept proposed by David Greenblatt.

"Now is the time to renew our engagement between the Land of Israel as the bride and the people of Israel as the groom" and Shlomo sang his wedding tune "*Od Yishoma.*" It was truly a memorable event.[126]

6.   MOSHAV ME'OR MODI'IM (1976–1979)

In the mid-1970s, Shlomo's *chevra* began looking for a rural settlement where they could create their own communal life and raise their children. Furthermore, they wanted "to build a center for the Rebbe," to create a New Age type yeshiva where all could "turn on to the beauty of Yiddishkeit."[127] Early in 1975, Pinhas Sapir, then chairman of the Board of Directors of the Jewish Agency, was impressed by Reb Shlomo and his *chevra* and offered to help.[128] Yankala Shemesh began a search across Israel. In March 1976, he was asked to take a look at Moshav Mevo Modi'im (literally, entry to Modi'im), the first pioneering foothold in the strategic area connected to the Maccabean heritage. The Moshav seemed attractive with its beautiful feeling of nature, being situated in the middle of the Ben Shemen Forest, the largest planted forest in Israel. The first planning meeting took place at the home of Yankala Shemesh

---

126. Personal interview with Rabbi Lau on Jan. 1, 2013. Compare the story as told by Shaul Maizlish and recorded in Brandwein, *Reb Shlomele*, 270–275.

127. Zusha Frumin, personal communication.

128. Pinhas Sapir died on Aug. 12, 1975. The story of Sapir's role in encouraging the establishment of the Moshav is brought by Brand, *Reb Shlomele*, 106–107 in the name of "Reb Betsalel Bokshin, a member of the original nucleus of Mevo Modi'in." A somewhat different version is related in the English translation (Brandwein, *Reb Shlomele*, 145–147).

*Reb Shlomo and Reb Gedalia Koenig (1921–1980) at the Diaspora Yeshiva
on Mt. Zion in Jerusalem 1973.   Courtesy of Rabbi Sarah Leah Grafstein*

in Sanhedria, Jerusalem in the beginning of April 1976.[129] Zusha summed
up the rationale:

> We were tired of *davening* in other people's *shuls*. It was uncom-
> fortable and inhibited. Even at the Kotel, we felt like freaks in a
> circus. Wasn't anyone else singing and dancing there? We wanted
> to create a new House of Love and Prayer – where all the world
> could come for Shabbat – but this time, it would be centered
> around our families and children.[130]

But there was a reason that this Moshav was up for grabs. For over a
decade, several groups failed consecutively in settling this area. The only
road to the Moshav reached a dead end at the site of an ancient cemetery
labeled the Graves of the Maccabees.

Nechama Silver recalls:

> You had to be a real pioneer; there was nothing there but scor-
> pions, rocks, weeds, and one bus a day on the main road. The
> electricity would go off whenever there was a rainstorm. There
> was only one telephone line. The water system would fail and the

---

129. See Zusha Frumin, "Jerusalem!," *Kol Chevra*, vol. 16, 2010, 45–48.
130. Zusha Frumin, personal communication.

army bailed us out with a water tank to distribute in jerry cans. In the summer the heat was stifling, and in the winter we were freezing.[131]

Mevo Modi'im was a result of persistent prodding beginning already in March 1949 by Yosef Weitz, director of the Land and Forestation Department of the Jewish National Fund. It was only in 1963 that he convinced the army generals to establish a settlement. In July 1964, the first buildings were built as part of a grand plan called Metzudot Sefar, "Fortresses of the Periphery." Poalei Agudat Yisrael, PAI, the *haredi* political party and settlement movement, asked to be put in charge as it was near their settlement of Kibbutz Sha'alvim. PAI organized Nahal soldiers from their youth movement Ezra and from a group called then Nahal Haredi. A big celebration was set for the day before Hanukkah, December 29, 1964, and a Torah scroll was brought into the synagogue in a procession led by the two Chief Rabbis of Israel, Rabbi Isser Yehuda Unterman and Rabbi Yitzhak Nissim. It was a major event that Sunday in the presence of the President of Israel, Zalman Shazar, the Chief of Staff, Yitzhak Rabin, and the Deputy Defense Minister, Shimon Peres.[132]

Serious problems began at the end of 1965 with the onset of the Shemittah year because PAI policy followed the Hazon Ish and not Rav Kook, thus limiting agricultural work for an entire year. Army Chief Rabbi, Shlomo Goren, set up a yeshiva, the first in the history of the Nahal, and the soldiers devoted time to study instead of agriculture. Then, after the Six-Day War, it was decided rather hastily to turn the army outpost into a civilian settlement. The ceremonial transition took place on August 28, 1967, 22 Av. However, the hastiness resulted in the failure of PAI to organize a homogenous group of settlers.[133] For almost a decade, several groups came and went, and PAI had not yet created a successful settlement.

Rabbi Dr. Joshua Ritchie, a key figure in the HLP core group, was a close confidant and personal driver of the Amshinover Rebbe, R. Yerahmiel Yehuda Meir Kalish. The Amshinover Rebbe spoke to Rabbi

131. Personal communication from Nechama Silver, Sept. 23, 2012 supplementing an interview with Yankala Shemesh, Aug. 17, 2011.

132. Yair Douer, *Our Sickle Is Our Sword: Nahal Settlements until 1967*, vol. 1 (Tel Aviv: 1992 [Hebrew]), 135–141. The entire book can be found at Bterezin.Brinkster. net, http://bterezin.brinkster.net/nahal/Nahal-hechzut-part-1_output/web/flipview-erxpress.html.

133. Ibid., 138–140.

David Halahmi, a PAI leader who was born into an Amshinov Hasidic family. Soon PAI accepted the HLP *chevra*.[134]

Uzi Narkis, head of the Aliyah Department of the Jewish Agency, was skeptical how the hippie Hasidim could earn a living. The *chevra* themselves had little idea what to do, but at the time, Avraham Leader, Michael Golomb, and Avraham Sand had started a granola business in Jerusalem named Amud HaShachar.[135] So when Yankala Shemesh and Avraham Leader met with Narkis, they told him they would develop a granola industry:

> They had never heard of granola before. We all passed individual and group psychological testing and moved to the Moshav and began producing granola.[136]

The Amshinover Rebbe died on May 27, 1976. The *chevra* then asked to change the name of the settlement from Mevo Modi'im to Me'or Modi'im, thus memorializing the Amshinover Rebbe's middle name Meir and at the same time emphasizing a connection to the light of the Maccabees.[137] The "foundation scroll" of the Moshav was signed in June 1976. It proclaims that anyone whom Reb Shlomo meets in his travels around the world and whom he judges to be downcast and in need, and anyone who is lost on an alien path and wishes to come to Israel, will be welcomed whether for a short period or a long time no matter what the financial situation of the Moshav will be.[138]

The first pioneers settled in bringing with them a hippie dream of growing their own food and getting back to nature.[139] But they were living in poverty. Avraham Sand recalls:

---

134. Brand, *Reb Shlomele*, 267. Personal interview with Dr. Ritchie, Oct. 6, 2012.

135. Avraham Sand, personal interviews Sept. 9–10, 2012.

136. Yankala Shemesh, personal interview, Aug. 19, 2011.

137. About the choice of the name see Ben Zion Solomon, "A History of Me'or Modi'im," "What's in a Name? – Me'or Modi'im," in *The Moshav Me'or Modi'im, 25th Anniversary Journal*, 1976–2001, 1–5: "We used the word Meir but altered it to Me'or" to connect to the Maccabees who had lived in the Modi'im area.

138. Brand, *Reb Shlomele*, 106–107. I translated from the Hebrew. For a different translation see Brandwein, *Reb Shlomele*, 146–147.

139. Nechama Silver reported (Sept. 23, 2012): The first two families moved in during mid-June, 1976 – Ben Zion and Dina Solomon, Avraham and Rachel Trugman. They were followed on July 1 by Reuven and Zahava Gilmore, Avraham and Chaya Leader, Liliane and Josh Ritchie, Yankala and Shoshana Shemesh, Emuna and Yehoshua Witt. The singles included Michael Golomb, Nechama Yasskin, and Mickey Moshe Shur. Soon after, David and Feigi Pam, and Zusha Frumin joined them.

We didn't have much food. So Ben Zion Solomon and I began producing about 15 or 20 kilogram of tofu a week and delivering it to each family. We curdled our tofu with Dead Sea water, a nice innovation, and it was thick like goat's cheese and very delicious. We also began producing tempeh and miso. The Jewish Agency found out about our tofu production, and arranged a meeting to discuss setting up a commercial soy food industry. The Moshav women made fantastic tofu dips and other soy delicacies for the meeting. The Jewish Agency people flipped! They declared that they would gladly fund the equipment from Japan and set up a tofu and soy foods dairy on the Moshav. It was decided that I would go to America to visit tofu shops and learn everything.[140]

Avraham spent a year in the U.S. visiting over twenty major tofu shops. But when he returned to the Moshav, he was dismayed to learn that the Jewish Agency had decided not to fund the project. This is merely one example of the trials and tribulations in settling the Moshav. Somehow, the Moshav succeeded.

The story of Avraham Sand illustrates the influence of Reb Shlomo. Born October 17, 1951 as Roger Wayne Sand in Stamford, Connecticut, he grew up with just a taste of Hebrew school and concluded that "Judaism was an ancient dying ritual, and spirituality needs to be sought elsewhere." Sand attended Northeastern University in Boston when his math-physics professor advised him to learn about life by traveling. In 1971, Roger began an odyssey around the world and eventually passed through Jerusalem. There he met Michael Golomb who introduced him to the Carlebach *chevra*, taught him basic Judaism, and guided him to the Diaspora Yeshiva. While in the yeshiva, Sand learned how to play the dumbec, the popular Middle East hand-drum. With his dumbec, he accompanied Shlomo in about fifty performances around the world. In 1986, Avraham met Leah Rivka Soetendorp, who had come to Israel in 1979 from Amsterdam. She was a devoted follower of Reb Shlomo. Their first date was a Carlebach concert in Jerusalem at the Pargod Theater. A month later, Shlomo officiated at their engagement ceremony on the Moshav. Then, Shlomo flew specially to Israel to perform their wedding on June 9, 1986 at Kehillat Yedidya in the Baka neighborhood of Jerusalem.[141]

Today, the Sands live on the Moshav. Leah is on the *vaad*, the governing committee of the Moshav. She organizes the Moshav Country Fairs twice

---

140. Avraham Sand, interview, Sept. 10, 2012.
141. Avraham Sand, interview, Sept. 9, 2012.

a year, on Hol HaMoed Pesach and Sukkot. For the past fifteen years, Leah Sand has been organizing the monthly Rosh Chodesh women's gatherings for an average of fifty women each month. Avraham works as a professional Aromatherapist, importing oils to Israel, and providing Organic Essentials Oils worldwide.[142] Avraham sums up the influence of Reb Shlomo by stating emphatically: "I wouldn't be practicing Judaism in any way if it weren't for Shlomo." This is but one illustration of the people who raised their families on the Moshav and became the core group of an extended Carlebach *chevra* community around the world.[143]

To help strengthen the Moshav, Reb Shlomo came to lead the Rosh Hashana program on September 12–14, 1977. The unusually dramatic service was described by Betsalel Bokshin:

> "My friends," he said, "let us go out to welcome the New Year in a manner fit for a king. We all gathered outside and then walked in procession to the entrance of the Moshav, singing and dancing along the way . . . Between one *niggun* and the other, Shlomo stood like a general facing his troops, pointed to the sun going down on the horizion, and sang three times: Let the old year with its maledictions end; let the new year with its blessings begin! "[144]

Musical talent was encouraged at the Moshav. This is illustrated by Ben Zion Solomon, a co-founder in 1973 of the Diaspora Yeshiva Band. His band is Ben Zion Solomon and Sons, and his sons formed other bands: Soul Farm, HaMakor, and the Moshav Band.[145] Every so often, Shlomo would invent a tune. At *seudah shlishit* on Shabbat in the summer of 1981, he composed a tune for *"Ledor Vodor Nagid Godlecho"* from the *Kedushah* of Shabbat *Musaf*.[146] At *seudah shlishit* on July 27, 1985, the Ninth of Av, Reb Shlomo composed a tune for *"Shuva HaShem"* (Psalms 126:4–6), "Lord, bring back our exiles as streams in the Negev. They that sow in tears will reap in songs of joy."[147]

Eventually a Hasidic rock band called Modiim L'Simcha was established at the Moshav and included Reuven Gilmore (bass), Mordechai Levy

---

142. See Avraham Sand, *Mystical Aromatherapy: The Divine Gift of Fragrance* (Twin Lakes, Wisconsin: Lotus Press, 2012). Their website is AvAroma.com, http://www.AvAroma.com.

143. Interestingly enough, their daughter, Chanita Sand, married Elnatan, the son of Michael Golomb. The couple set up their house on the Moshav.

144. Brandwein, Reb Shlomele, 91–92.

145. The eight Solomon children are: Noach, Yemima, Yehuda, Meir, Yosef, Hanan, Nahman, and Sruli.

146. Ben Zion Solomon, *Shlomo Shabbos*, 53.

147. Ibid., 59.

(trumpet), Moshe Duskis (guitar), Yankala Shemesh (percussionist, drummer and guitar), Nechama Yasskin (autoharp), and Avraham Sand (dumbec).[148] Yankala Shemesh served as Reb Shlomo's personal assistant (*shamash*) for twenty-six years and played with him in "over a thousand concerts."[149] Other musicians such as Aryeh Naftaly who moved to the Moshav in 1987 were also recruited by Shlomo. Aryeh accompanied Shlomo in about 100 concerts all over Israel, playing bass, guitar, and sometimes saxophone and flute.[150]

Shabbatot at the Moshav became major events when Shlomo came. Hundreds of guests would join. The impact of these Shabbatot is exemplified in the story of Baruch Melman. Baruch had taken a year off from Brandeis University and was studying at Pardes Institute in Jerusalem in 1978 when he "ran into Shlomo in the parking lot near the Kotel" and was invited to the Moshav for Shabbat, November 3–4, 1978:

> Kabbalat Shabbat lasted for hours. The meal lasted for hours. The singing lasted for hours. The joy lasted a lifetime.[151]

Baruch became one of the devoted disciples of Reb Shlomo and during the last decade of Shlomo's life, Baruch joined Reb Shlomo in the Shabbat programs of the Carlebach Shul in Manhattan:

> Only when I started to reconnect with Shlomo was I able to live an integrated Jewish observant life, fully tasting the sweetness of Yiddishkeit. I had been observant on my own terms all through high school, but to fully feel my *neshama* express itself on all levels at once in a real organic way required me to connect with Reb Shlomo. It all came together and finally made sense to me and it allowed me to fully blossom spiritually in a way I never could before.[152]

Engagements and weddings at the Moshav were special events. One wedding that Shlomo performed on the Moshav was for Yankele Shemesh, one of the founding members. His wedding to Bracha took place on Tuesday, September 18, 1979. Hundreds of people attended.

Finally, the Moshav was a site for a variety of educational activities.

---

148. My thanks to Nechama Yasskin (Silver), and Yankala Shemesh for this information.

149. See Yankala's website, RebYankalaShemesh.weebly.com, http://rebyankalashemesh.weebly.com/about-reb-yankala.html.

150. Personal interview with Aryeh Naftaly, Oct. 17, 2011. See also segment 3:07–3:45, http://www.youtube.com/watch?v=BYbVXvKLhDs&feature=relmfu.

151. Personal communications with Rabbi Baruch Melman, Oct.–Nov. 2012.

152. Ibid.

One unusual example is a peace initiative organized from August 18 to August 30, 1977. Entitled The 2nd Annual Jerusalem Camp, the idea was spearheaded by Benefsha Gest,[153] the coordinator in Israel of Sufi Sam's Hallelujah! The Three Rings.[154] Reb Shlomo and Reb Zalman were the featured teachers at this Moshav event. The Sufi part was led by Benefsha and Mansur Johnson.[155] The program was organized by Murray Jacob Kabb[156] and Bruce (Hashir) Ginsberg.[157]

Shlomo was back on the Moshav in the summer of 1979. A major event with Reb Shlomo was held on August 1, 1979, the eve of Tisha BeAv. One of the organizers, Chaim Cohen, recalls:

> Reb Shlomo conducted the evening Tisha BeAv Ceremony that was broadcast live on Israel Radio. On Thursday, August 2, there were Tisha BeAv teachings in the late afternoon, and many of us remember the day, as Elana Schachter helped deliver Niflaah, the baby of Mordechai and Morasha Levy.[158]

For ten days, August 12–23, 1979, Murray Jacob Kabb and Bruce Ginsberg organized another "Festival of Peace." A publicity flyer announced a "Spiritual Gathering in Israel" whose purpose was "to kindle a fire of love and peace until the world becomes one." About sixty people arrived

---

153. Born July 1, 1944, 23-year old Benefsha was a volunteer in Jerusalem during the Six-Day War and had a life changing vision of how peace could be achieved. Upon returning to California, she befriended Aryae and Ruth Coopersmith and began going regularly to the Friday night program at the HLP where she became a close admirer of Reb Shlomo. Yet her main inspiration was found in Sufi Sam who asked her to return to Israel. There, Benefsha organized a peace center on the Mt. of Olives, established the Jerusalem Sufi Center and initiated the first peace camp near Latrun in the summer of 1976. Personal interview with Benefsha Gest, Dec. 19, 2012.

154. The idea of three rings refers to Sufi Sam's program to get Jews and Arabs and Christians, representing the three rings, to eat, dance, and pray together. Sufi Sam asked Benefsha to bring peace to Israel and Palestine as coordinator of Hallelujah! The Three Rings.

155. The original publicity flyer listed several Sufi teachers, but they couldn't attend, and Benefsha asked Mansur Johnson to replace them (interviews in Dec. 2012 with Benefsha and Mansur). Mansur Johnson, who accompanied Reb Shlomo on the drums referred me to his version of the story as recorded in his book *Shamcher: A Memoir of Bryn Beorse and His Struggle to Introduce Ocean Energy to the United States*, 1991, Shamcher.org, www.shamcher.org/6.html. Mansur quotes from the publicity flyer: "The 1977 Jerusalem Camp, to be held in the Judean Hills west of Jerusalem, will host a multi-national, multi-cultural convocation of students, seekers, and lovers of God, who wish to come together in the attitude of brotherhood."

156. Jacob Kabb was influenced by Sufi Sam and had become involved with the Sufi Order of the West under Pir Vilayat Khan (see above, Chapter 7).

157. Personal communication from Bruce Ginsberg, Nov. 28, 2012.

158. Chaim Cohen, personal correspondence, Jan. 6, 2013.

from the U.S. and Europe.[159] Participants camped out in the forest adjacent to the Moshav.[160] Reb Shlomo gave a talk entitled "Vessels to Keep Secrets and to Make Secrets," and Reb Zalman spoke about the "Variety of Kabbalistic and Other Meditations through the Ages." Sufi Sheik Murshid Hassan came with his young American wife, Maryam and their baby daughter, from the Balata refugee camp southeast of Nablus.[161] Another presenter was Reb Meir Fund. Chaim Cohen reports:

> Reb Shlomo quoted Genesis 1:27–28, emphasizing that the angels said to God that we should make mankind in our images as our likenesses in a *plural* form. This implies that the variety of types of people all reflect diverse Images of the Creator.[162]

Sometimes, Reb Shlomo's egalitarian-type approach to men and women singing together led to a clash with Orthodox authorities. *The Jerusalem Post*, August 19–25, 1979, reported that the Rabbi of the Western Wall ordered a mixed group of people singing with Rabbi Shlomo Carlebach to leave the area.

On Tuesday, September 18, 1979, Reb Shlomo performed the wedding for Yankele and Bracha Shemesh (Shames) at the Moshav. The Shabbat before the wedding, Shlomo led a program at the Moshav with a few hundred people and celebrated Yankele's *aufruf.* Bruce (Buzzy) Ginsberg tells the story of how Shlomo gave him a very special and unusual Hebrew name at the Torah reading on this Shabbat:

> I had come to Israel in late January 1977 and studied with Reb Shlomo and played concerts with him around the country. I had told him that my name is Bruce, people call me Buzzy, and my Hebrew name is Dov but I don't feel bearlike. On Shabbat,

---

159. Americans were encouraged to join for only $975 including airfare, touring, and all expenses. To keep expenses down, participants were advised to bring their own sleeping bags. *Aquarian Minyan Berkeley Newsletter*, May–June 1979, 9. My thanks to Reuven and Yehudit Goldfarb for showing me the original announcement of this event. The Goldfarbs together with Yitz and Shonna Husbands-Hankin organized the American contingent to the Peace Festival.

160. Bruce (Hashir) Ginsberg who organized the program told me that several Moshav people who helped in organizing the program included Reuven Gilmore, Yitzhak ben Yehuda, Yankele Shames, Emuna Witt, Jacob and Reva Rautenberg.

161. In the early 1970s, Benefsha met Hassan in the Balata refugee camp adjacent to the city of Nablus, and arranged for him to visit the U.S. in 1975 as a Sufi peace promoter. Among the more unusual interfaith programs, he led a joint Yom Kippur service with Reb Zalman.

162. This was related by Chaim Cohen (Jan. 6, 2013) who made an audio recording of the event.

September 15, 1979, at the *aufruf* for Yankele Shemesh, Shlomo calls out at the Torah reading and asks where is Buzzy. I come up and he takes me under his *tallit* and says, "I have been thinking about it and I have two possible names for you, either Tzur Yisrael or Hashir v'Hashevach." I chose Hashir. Shlomo announced that from this day forth Buzzy will be known as Hashir v'Hashevach.[163]

On December 18, 1979, the third night of Hanukkah, Reb Shlomo appeared in concert at the Hebrew University Givat Ram campus in the Wise Auditorium.[164] The next day, December 19, he led the wedding of Atara and Tzion Segev at the Central Hotel in Jerusalem (see above).

7.   ISRAEL AS A SECOND HOME (1980–1994)

In August 1980, Shlomo was again in Israel. One of those who attended Shlomo's teachings and concerts that summer was Barbara Holdrege, who at that time was a graduate student specializing in Jewish and Hindu traditions at Harvard University and is now a Professor of Religious Studies at the University of California, Santa Barbara. Holdrege had been awarded a Dorot Foundation Grant by Professor Frank Moore Cross in the Department of Near Eastern Languages and Civilizations at Harvard to support her summer of study in Jerusalem. She recalls how Reb Shlomo played an important role in this early stage of her career:

> I told Shlomo about my research on Torah as well as about my broader project comparing Torah with Veda, the ancient scriptures of India. He listened carefully and expressed genuine interest not only in my studies of Torah but also in my comparative project. I was moved that an Orthodox rabbi whom I deeply respected did not dismiss my comparative venture, but instead encouraged me to continue my unusual quest. I subsequently completed my Ph.D. and, after joining the faculty at the University of California, Santa Barbara, published a book entitled *Veda and Torah: Transcending the Textuality of Scripture.*[165]

---

163. Personal communication with Hashir Ginsberg, Nov. 28–29, 2012. The Hebrew expression הַשִּׁיר וְהַשֶּׁבַח is found in the *piyut "Ha'aderet VeHaemunah"* הָאַדֶּרֶת וְהָאֱמוּנָה which is recited in the Hasidic *nusach* of the Shabbat and Festival morning service.

164. The date and place of this concert with a list of 18 songs that Shlomo sang was posted by a user named חוקי on the Carlebach Forum in *Behadrey Haredim,* on Dec. 7, 2012, http://www.bhol.co.il/forum/topic.asp?cat_id=19&topic_id=2988740&forum_id=18615.

165. Personal interview with Barbara Holdrege, Feb. 9, 2013.

"Festival of Peace" August 12–23, 1979. In the first picture (left to right): Chaim Cohen, Reb Shlomo and his daughter Neshama, Reb Zalman, Sheik Murshid Hassan and his wife Maryam and their two children, Jacob Kabb, and Reb Meir Fund and his wife.   *Photo courtesy of Elana Schachter*

During the summer of 1980, Shlomo was invited to visit Sharm El Sheikh to raise the morale of the soldiers preparing to transfer the Sinai to Egypt.[166] He took along a dozen *chevra* from the Moshav. Morasha Levy, who came with her baby daughter Niflaah,[167] reminisced about the trip:

> Shlomo and all the *chevra* took a glass-bottom boat ride out to the coral reef and then we all jumped into the water and were snorkeling around the reef seeing the amazing colored corals and the amazing fish. We slept in the air force barracks. The concert was out of this world and took place on the beach. The *chevra* were playing and dancing with the soldiers all around the beach.[168]

166. Although the peace treaty with Egypt was signed on March 26, 1979, Israel withdrew gradually from Sinai, completing the evacuation on April 25, 1982.

167. See above that Niflaah Levy was born on Tisha BeAv, Aug. 2, 1979 at the Moshav.

168. My thanks to Morasha Levy and Nechama Silver for this information, Oct. 21, 2012.

Shlomo was invited for all kinds of *mitzvot*. On September 2, 1980, he performed for residents of an old age home in Yad Eliyahu, Tel Aviv.[169] In December 1980, Shlomo led a sheva berachot at Moshav Me'or Modi'im for Ari and Chana Wolff.[170]

Sometime around the end of 1980, Shlomo was invited to the Neve Tirza Women's Prison in Ramleh. He was accompanied by his *chevra*, mostly from the Moshav. Upon arriving, Shlomo realized that only Jewish prisoners were in the audience, and insisted on inviting the Arab prisoners, fifteen of whom then arrived. Shlomo asked a woman who was jailed for having placed a bomb in a Jerusalem supermarket to translate his stories about the Ishbitzer Rebbe into Arabic. By the end of the concert, Arabs and Jews, prisoners and guards, were all dancing together.[171] Nechama Yasskin (Silver) who was part of the entourage recalls:

> The Arab women didn't want to come. So Shlomo went to visit them in their cells. Somehow he convinced the head terrorist, and the others followed. Thereafter, in prison, whenever she would see Shlomo performing on TV, she would exclaim to her fellow inmates that Shlomo was her rebbe.[172]

On May 7, 1981, Shlomo was one of the performers at the Likud rally, "We Are on the Map," on Israel Independence Day in the settlement of Ariel. Prime Minister Menachem Begin delivered one of his memorable speeches in which he swears that he will not relinquish any part of Judea, Samaria, Gaza, and the Golan. Shlomo sang his popular theme song *"Am Yisrael Chai."* Then to the astonishment of his bodyguards, Begin grabbed Reb Shlomo's guitar and gave it to Shlomo's assistant, Yehoshua Witt, and began dancing ecstatically with Shlomo on the stage. This scene was recorded by Haim Yavin, the Israeli TV anchorman who had been commissioned to do a documentary on the political campaign. After Begin was reelected in June, it was shown on Israel State television.[173]

---

169. For a picture of this event, see the State of Israel's National Photo Collection, picture D525-081.

170. A photo from this event was published in the *L'Koved Reb Shlomo Remembrance Journal*, Nov. 1995.

171. I reconstructed the story from the various versions that are extant. The earliest recorded version was told by Reb Zalman and can be heard in a recording from March 19, 1994 in Berkeley. The first appearance of this story in print is in 1997 by Mandelbaum, *Holy Brother*, 33–34 and by Brandwine, *Reb Shlomele*, 71–72.

172. Nechama Silver (Yasskin) personal communication, Oct. 22, 2012.

173. My thanks to Rami Shtivi, archivist of the Menachem Begin Heritage Center, for identifying the TV clip and helping me date it. For a picture of Shlomo and Begin at this rally, see Brandwein, *Reb Shlomele*, 264. A series of pictures from this rally can

On Thursday night, November 19, 1981, Reb Shlomo performed the wedding of Zusha Frumin and Rachel Bryna. It took place in Moshav Me'or Modi'im. Zusha recalls:

> As was Reb Shlomo's custom for his closest friends, he would always try to bring down a new *nigun* for the wedding. We merited that night that the tune he invented was eventually used for "*Yah Ribon*" and later became the standard melody for "Lecha Dodi." It came down to the world on that night. We got married like the orphans of the Moshav. No money. No family came. The Moshav was our only family. The band was the Moshav band consisting of Moshe Duskis, Mordecai Levi, Yankala Shamesh, and Ben Zion Solomon. We had no invitations but hundreds of people came because Shlomo invited folks at every concert he played.[174]

In the early 1980s, a professional photographer, Israel Korenbrot, was invited to the Moshav. His pictures were later published in a special book about the Moshav and presented to donors (see below, Chapter 11). The sixty-seven photos provide a rare glimpse into the daily life on the Moshav from 1980–1982.[175] Yael (Susan) Mesinai wrote the introduction and portrayed the vision and challenges of the settlers:

> They called themselves "Holy Beggars" and took great pride in their openness and joy, a life style that turned its back on material values to emphasize the wisdom of the heart. . . . A community of mystics, its members have had to learn how to ground their cosmic consciousness without losing the essential spirit, heartfelt commitment, and freedom necessary for their personal quest. . . . A group of highly individualized members, each of whom has been guided by guru [sic] or his/her own inner voice, must learn to function as a community, to address the business of life which in its particulars often seems contrary to visions of Messiah.[176]

Mesinai concluded with a description of "the true miracle" on the Moshav when Shabbat arrives and tensions of the week vanish:

---

be seen at the State of Israel's National Photography Collection, http://147.237.72.31/topsrch/abcole.htm.

174. Reb Zusha Frumin, personal correspondence, March 28, 2013. I have a recording of 1:09 minutes containing much of the *huppah* ceremony.

175. Israel Korenbrot, *Return to Modi'im* (Jerusalem: 1985).

176. Susan Yael Mesinai, "Moshav Meor Modi'im," *Return to Modi'im* (Jerusalem: 1985).

At a Likud Party rally in Ariel in honor of Israel's Independence Day, 1981.
Prime Minister Menachem Begin, front row, right, applauds during a perfor-
mance of Reb Shlomo. He then joined him on the stage, dancing ecstatically.
Photo taken by Yaakov Saar
  Courtesy of the Israel Government Press Office, National Photo Collection

A chord, vibrant with life, rich in its depth and Oneness is heard.
There's a unity, a joy to this congregation which makes those of
troubled heart sob, those of open spirit shine.[177]

In March 1982, Shlomo participated in another political statement, this
time towards the final stages of the Sinai evacuation. Meisha Mishkan,
a leading activist fighting to stop the evacuation, undertook a lengthy
hunger strike. Meisha proposed marriage to Nechama Yasskin of Moshav
Me'or Modi'im and the date was set for a wedding in Yamit on the 7th
of Adar, March 2, 1982. Shlomo and the Carlebach *chevra* who had been
invited by Nechama, managed to get past the army roadblocks. The wedding was performed in Moshav Sadot by Rabbi Yisrael Ariel, Chief Rabbi
of Yamit. Shlomo did the *bedeken* ceremony.[178]

On March 4, 1982 (9 Adar), Reb Shlomo performed the wedding on
the Moshav of Shalom Schwarz to Tova Sherman. Shalom had moved to

---

177. Ibid.

178. The marriage only lasted a short time and Nechama remarried shortly after
(see above). Personal communication with Nechama Yasskin Silver, Oct. 3, 2012.

the Moshav at age 23 on Hol HaMoed Pesach 1980 and became one of the central figures in the Moshav activities.[179]

On April 21, 1982, Shlomo somehow was able to enter the city of Yamit and lead a farewell concert for the last residents and remaining protestors just two days before the city was evacuated and given to Egypt.[180]

On June 6, 1982, war broke out in Lebanon. By the third week of the war, Shlomo was brought to Sidon to raise the morale of the IDF soldiers. Gil Bashe's reserve paratrooper unit had just been mobilized and sent into battle:

> On June 12, 1982, our forces were ambushed in heavy fighting at the Syrian-held town of Sultan Yacoub near the Beqaa Valley. Eighteen IDF soldiers were killed, thirty wounded and three captured. We were surrounded by enemy fire, but managed to fight our way out and make our way to the coast. There, on the outskirts of Sidon, we were involved in the heavy fighting at Ain al-Hilweh, the largest Palestinian refugee camp in Lebanon with over 70,000 refugees. Somehow, Shlomo arrived smack in the middle of the third week of the war.[181]

The IDF was fighting for Damur and the Beirut airport, pushing toward Beirut via the Suf Mountain range. There was constant danger and snipers were all over:

> This was no place for civilians to visit . . . and yet . . . Shlomo came to Sidon to be with us! I was so struck at everyone's reaction – I knew Shlomo as a kid and always thought of him as uniquely part of the New York Jewish scene – not here! It was incredible how all the non-religious soldiers ran to see Shlomo – he was theirs too! He played, and everyone sang and danced! Shlomo was just being his lovable self – engaging people and speaking in a reassuring way – concerned for our well-being, physically and spiritually. It was a great omen. I will always think of Shlomo as going where he was needed. Wherever Jews needed his love and strength, he was willing to travel. And for me, as a new immigrant, at a very

---

179. I have a recording of this wedding in two parts. My thanks to Shalom Schwarz for dating the wedding. After their divorce, Shalom married Bracha in 1992.

180. Don Canaan, who in 1974 had come on aliyah and settled in Yamit together with a group of Americans, mentions the concert in his obituary of Reb Shlomo: Don Canaan, "Shlomo Carlebach Dies in New York," Israel Faxx, Oct. 24, 1994, http://israelfaxx.com/webarchive/1994/10/4fax1024.html#shlomo_carlebach_dies_in _new_york.

181. Interview with Gil Bashe, Nov. 16, 2012.

Baking granola on the Moshav. In the center is Mordechai Gess, son-in-law of Reb Zalman Schachter-Shalomi. Next to him are Mordechai Morgenstern and Daphna. My thanks to Jonathan Daniel who was chief granola baker at the time (1980–1982) for identifying the people in this series of photos from the book by Israel Korenbrot.

Shlomo with Michael Golomb (right) and Reuven Gilmore (center)

Purim Feast, March 9, 1982, at the house of Alon and Rena Teeger. Avraham Arieh Trugman has his arm raised. To his left, wearing glasses, is Rachel Trugman. To his right is Michael Golomb. Across from Rachel is (Chana) Rachel Bryna Frumin. In the foreground is David Drexler.
Photos from Korenbrot, Return to Modi'im.

scary moment in life, it was a powerful reminder of our special connection to Klal Yisrael.[182]

On July 11, 1983, Rosh Hodesh Av, Shlomo officiated at the engagement of Josh Lauffer and Orly Dekel at the Kabbalah Center on Ben Yehuda St. in Jerusalem. Then on December 1, 1983, the first day of Hanukkah, Shlomo performed their marriage in Moshav Ora.[183]

Later on Hanukkah, December 1983, Reb Shlomo performed a concert at the Orthodox Union (OU) Israel Center in Jerusalem on Strauss Street. In the middle of the concert, a group of young German tourists walked in. Raphael Harris who was present was astonished to see how graciously Shlomo greeted them:

---

182. Email exchanges with Gil Bashe, Nov. 16–19, 2012.

183. My thanks to Armond Lauffer, the father of Josh, for the above information. Josh is a performing guitarist, singer, and songwriter. Born May 27, 1963 and raised in Ann Arbor Michigan, Josh came to Israel in 1981, studied with Reb Shlomo and accompanied him on stage from 1982–1986. Josh lived for a while at the Moshav and also ran a center for prayer, study, music, and meditation with Rabbi David Herzberg (on Herzberg, see above, Chapter 5).

I had recently been to the Holocaust Museum and I was angered by these intruders. Yet Shlomo who had fled right before the Holocaust welcomed the Germans as if they were long lost dear friends. He put out a vibe of loving forgiveness. I watched with awe and absorbed a lifelong lesson.[184]

In 1984, Shlomo was back in Israel shortly before Pesach. On April 8, 1984, Shlomo performed a "triple header" with two weddings and one engagement ceremony sandwiched in between. The engagement was for Nechama Yasskin and Shmuel Silver. Two months later, on June 26, he performed their wedding at the Moshav.[185] Nechama was one of the mainstays from the HLP who moved to Israel and settled on the Moshav.[186] She played a key role in the Moshav administration and steering committee.[187]

On March 4, 1985, Shlomo performed the wedding of Jonathan (Yonatan) Daniel and Susan Meyers on the Moshav. This was very much a Carlebach *chevra* wedding: Reuven Gilmore read the *ketubbah*, Menachem Kallus and Itzchak Marmorstein were the witnesses, and the band included Ben Zion Solomon, Mordechai Levy, and Yankala Shames.[188]

In the settlement of Efrat, Elana (Elaine), the wife of David Zeller, was struggling valiantly with cancer and Reb Shlomo came there to spend Shabbat and encourage the family.[189] On Sunday, July 27, 1986, Elana died at the young age of 41. Shlomo returned to lead the funeral service. He had performed the marriage of David and Elana a decade earlier and was to officiate at David's second marriage three years later.[190]

In the summer of 1986 on Moshav Me'or Modi'im, Shlomo and Neila celebrated the bat mitzvah of their daughter, Neshama.

At the end of August, Reb Shlomo performed the wedding of Tzvi

---

184. Raphael Harris, personal communications Dec. 3–5, 2012.

185. Nechama and Shmuel had two children, Noam and Leah. Shmuel passed away March 3, 2010. In the early hours of the morning, after this wedding, Shlomo performed an engagement ceremony for Shaul Glick.

186. Nechama first met Shlomo on June 4, 1966 at a concert at Temple University in Philadelphia. She moved into the HLP in 1973 (see above, Chapter 5). In 1974, with Shlomo's encouragement, she went to study in Jerusalem at Shapell's College of the Itri Yeshiva.

187. Personal interviews and communications with Nechama (Yasskin) Silver, Sept. and Oct. 2012.

188. Personal communication with Jonathan Daniel.

189. Zeller, *The Soul of the Story*, 219.

190. Ibid., 221.

Moshe Cooper to Ruti Hafsadi at a school in Emek Refaim, Jerusalem.[191]

On Thursday, September 4, 1986 (Rosh Hodesh Elul), Reb Shlomo performed the wedding of Benzion Lehrer on Moshav Me'or Modi'im. Shlomo began the wedding with praise for Benzion's mother. He had met her in 1958 when she was a teacher at the Epstein Hebrew Academy in St. Louis when Shlomo spent a year teaching there. Recently, Benzion recounted the background for their first acquaintance:

> One day my mother was asked to pick up a new rabbi who was coming to teach in St. Louis, but because she didn't drive much, she was apprehensive. In the midst of heavy traffic, she began panicking and instead of turning left, just froze. At that moment, Shlomo took out his guitar and began to sing, calming her. During his year long stint in St. Louis, Shlomo became a frequent visitor in our home.[192]

At weddings, Shlomo was sometimes inspired to invent new songs. For example, on December 1, 1987, Shlomo invented his second version for the popular wedding song, "*Siman Tov uMazal Tov*" at the Moshav Me'or Modi'im wedding of Avraham Simcha and Yael Malka Rothbard.[193] This tune is so famous that few people realize it is from Reb Shlomo.

On January 27, 1988, Shlomo performed the marriage of Rabbi Micha Odenheimer to Naama Cifroni in Habayit Haadom in Motza. He also attended the naming celebrations of the Odenheimer girls, the circumcision ceremony of their son Chaim Natan on July 19, 1988 and his *upsherin* (haircutting) in 1991.

Sometime around March 1988, NBC TV filmed a model Passover Seder with Rabbi Shlomo Carlebach in Moshav Me'or Modi'im at the home of Alon and Rena Teeger. The reporter, Ed Rabel, an Emmy Award-winning broadcast journalist, narrated a description of the Seder celebration. This video provides a rare glimpse of the Moshav residents.[194]

---

191. My thanks to Tzvi Cooper for providing a recording of this event. Shlomo's brother, Eli Chaim, can be heard reading the *ketubbah*. Tzvi had first met Reb Shlomo in 1968. His family was living in the San Francisco Bay area and his father took Tzvi who was 9 years old at the time to the House of Love and Prayer. In 1984–1985, Tzvi became part of the Carlebach *chevra*. He asked Shlomo to perform his marriage.

192. Benzion Lehrer, personal interviews, Sept. 26, 2012, March 29, 2013.

193. For the two versions of *Siman Tov* see Ben Zion Solomon, *Shlomo Shabbos*, 76–77. My thanks to Benzion for adding identifying information about this wedding.

194. See http://www.youtube.com/watch?v=EKiK1oLAHuc. Rabbi Yehoshua Witt can be seen dancing with his children Yahad and Tiki. Rabbi Avraham Trugman is at segment 0:12, Dov Landesman sings the "*Mah Nishtana*" at segment 0:23, Zusha Frumin dances with his daughter Chemla Tamari at segment 0:39, Tzedek Gilmore, Eliasaf Galor, and Yahad Witt are at segment 0:41, Alon and Rena Teeger and family

On July 25, 1988, Shlomo suffered a heart attack in Jerusalem and was rushed to the hospital.[195] He was fitted with a heart pacemaker and warned to take it easy. It is reported that even though ordered to stay in his hospital bed, he went from room to room visiting patients and offering encouragement. In response to a nurse who tried to have him rest, he is said to have replied:

> Now I have an ideal opportunity to console other patients, because they are able to see how cheerful and optimistic I am while undergoing treatment here.[196]

In 1989, Israeli TV celebrated the thirtieth year of Shlomo's musical career with a special filming of Shlomo together with Israel Gottesdiener and Binyamin (Benny) Rosenbaum of Tzemed Reim, the duo who in the Second Hasidic Festival in 1970 had sung Shlomo's "*Shema Yisrael*" (see above).[197]

In the summer of 1989, Michelle Barr became Shlomo's business agent in Israel. She set up performances at non-religious clubs in Jerusalem such as Rasputin next to the Mount Zion Hotel, and Carlos and Charley's in Talpiot. A reporter from *The Jerusalem Post* described the variety of Shlomo's appearances:

> He sang for a collection of top military brass at a retirement party for OC Central Command Aluf Amram Mitzna, played for a group of Gentile Swedish teenagers visiting the capital, and was dragged by an admiring street band into giving a brief impromptu performance before the crowds ambling on the Ben Yehuda pedestrian mall. Perhaps most surprising was his invitation to appear before the Orthodox Rabbinical Council of America convention at the Ramada Renaissance Hotel Saturday night. Though himself an

---

are at segment 1:02. Reb Shlomo sums up with pathos at segment 0:46 how God took us out of Egypt just to bring us to the Holy Land. My thanks to Zusha Frumin, Asher Landesman, and Tzedek Gilmore for identifying the people (March 22, 2013).

195. Shlomo was taken to Shaare Zedek and then transferred to Hadassah Ein Kerem for treatment by Prof. Marvin Gottesman, an expert on pacemakers. Aryeh Bender, "The Dancing Rabbi had a heart attack and was rushed to the hospital," *Maariv*, July 26, 1988 [Hebrew] – reproduced in Brand, *Reb Shlomele*, 191.

196. Brandwein, *Reb Shlomele*, 159–161, quoting Dov Mendelson, an Amshinover Hasid.

197. See http://video.yahadoot.com/5521; http://www.youtube.com/watch?feature=player_embedded&v=XbQxsGlnpIM#.

On stage with Shlomo were Benzion Lehrer (guitar), Reuven Gilmore (bass), Yankele Shames (hand cymbals), Michael Golomb (tambourine), C. (Shimon) Lanzbom (guitar), and Natan Rothstein (keyboards). My thanks to Aryae Naftali and Benzion Lehrer for identifying the band members.

ordained Orthodox rabbi and graduate of New Jersey's respected Lakewood Yeshiva, Carlebach has long been ostracized by many in the rabbinical establishment . . . . "Ten years ago they wouldn't have invited me there," Carlebach says, "Who knows, maybe they're beginning to realize now that my approach works better?"[198]

Shlomo also appeared that summer in Gush Katif at the Palm Beach Hotel overlooking the sea. Baruch Ben Yosef was present and reports:

> There was a nice crowd, but his band didn't show up. So he had to play with people from the audience. He kept calling for his daughter Neshama to join him and help, but she wasn't around. He asked for people whom he recognized to come up and sing along.[199]

In mid-November, 1989, Shlomo was again in Israel. Pini Dunner, at the time a 20-year old studying at the Mercaz HaTorah Yeshiva in Jerusalem, a *haredi* yeshiva for English-speaking students, struck a deal with the owner of the Off the Square Restaurant and arranged for Shlomo to appear late at night. More than 100 young people came. The event as described by Dunner typifies both the spontaneity and the emotional relevance of Reb Shlomo's performances:

> Suddenly this flamboyant looking Negro walks in and Shlomo greeted him with a hug and a kiss – "Holy Brother Jimmy!!" It turned out to be a philo-Semitic Zionist Caribbean singer called Jimmy Lloyd.[200] Shlomo handed the mike to Jimmy who sang ca-lypso in Hebrew, Carlebach songs, and *"Mein Yiddishe Mamme,"* to the delight of everyone there. It was a few days after the fall of the Berlin Wall and Shlomo spoke about this historic event, and sang *"Av Horachamim"* with the hauntingly responsive *"Tivneh Chomos Yerushalayim."* Now that the walls of hate in Berlin had been torn down, he said, God could rebuild the Walls of Love in Jerusalem. It was very moving. One of the most memorable evenings I ever spent with Shlomo.

---

198. Calev Ben-David, "Sway of the Singing Rabbi," *The Jerusalem Post*, Aug. 4, 1989, 13.

199. Baruch Ben Yosef, personal interview, March 31, 2013.

200. My thanks to Rabbi Pini Dunner for this story. Jimmy (James) Lloyd was born in Trinidad in the southern Caribbean and as a teenager migrated to London where he attended the Ivor Mirants school of music. He first came to Israel in April 1963. In the Ninth Hasidic festival in 1977, he entered with Carlebach's song *"Ki B'simcha Tetze'un."*

By linking the fall of the Berlin Wall to the rebuilding of Jerusalem, Reb Shlomo was creating a direct connection between the historic events of the twentieth century to the utopian Messianic vision of the future. By honoring Jimmy Lloyd and inviting him to sing, Reb Shlomo was transmitting an ecumenical message to a primarily *haredi* audience.

By January 1990, Reb Shlomo was in Israel again. An informative anecdote about an impromptu concert at the Kotel is told by Pini Dunner:

> It was raining that Thursday night. We came to the Kotel from a wedding that took place on the roof of the house of R. Yehoshua Witt in Mahane Yehuda. Hundreds of American boys studying in Jerusalem at the *haredi yeshivot* of Mir and Brisk were waiting. Reb Shlomo sang and told stories about his time in yeshiva, including his reminiscences about R. Aharon Kotler. It was an informal post-midnight concert at the Kotel.[201]

Word of the concert was reported to a leading *haredi* Rosh Yeshiva. He announced that if the fellow who organized the concert is discovered, he should be excommunicated. After all, yeshiva boys should stay up late Thursday night, Erev Shabbat, to learn Torah and not for a Carlebach concert.

In Zionist religious educational institutions, however, Shlomo was well received. On January 9, 1990, he performed in Petach Tikvah for the high school girls of Ulpanat Yeshurun. In a video interview with a Yeshurun student, Shlomo explained how he began to play guitar, and how at a very young age he and his brother dreamt of becoming rabbis.[202]

In the summer of 1990, Reb Shlomo performed the wedding of Yankala and Amira Shemesh on August 2, 11th of Av at Moshav Me'or Modi'im. There he composed a new tune for "*Ein KeEloheinu.*"[203]

In September 1990, Shlomo took part in the weeklong SecondFestiNegev that began on Motzei Shabbat, September 8. He was the featured performer on September 11 at Beersheba's Desert Inn Hotel.[204]

On Sunday, November 11, 1990, Shlomo led an impromptu concert

---

201. Personal communication from R. Pini Dunner.

202. The concert was organized by Shmuel Zeltzer, manager of the Tarbut Toranit in the youth department of the Petach Tikvah municipality. It was posted in Oct. 2012 on http://www.youtube.com/user/tartporanipt; http://www.youtube.com/watch?feature=player_embedded&v=-yOKCHoaLBs.

203. Ben Zion Solomon, *Shlomo Shabbos*, 55.

204. Tirzah Agassi, "Rocking and Bopping in the Negev," *The Jerusalem Post*, Sept. 7, 1990, 16.

at the Kotel and Pini Dunner brought his guitar. This time it was for an American tour group.[205]

Reb Shlomo spent the summer of 1991 in Israel. On July 24, he performed the wedding for Moshe and Shira Stepansky at Moshav Me'or Modi'im. On Motzei Shabbat, July 27, 1991, he led a concert at the Ramada Renaissance Hotel in Jerusalem and then at 1:00 AM organized an impromptu *Sheva Berachot* for the Stepansky couple that lasted until early in the morning.

On August 17, 1991, Shlomo performed the engagement ceremony for Simcha Hochbaum and Leah Brodt at the Torah Outreach Program's Center on Chabad St. in the Old City. The couple had met on May 2, 1991 in the Carlebach Shul in Manhattan, and Shlomo had a part in this match. Three days after the engagement ceremony, August 20, 1991, Shlomo led their wedding ceremony on the rooftop at King David's tomb on Mount Zion.[206]

The tenth annual Arad Hebrew Music Festival began on Sunday July 12, 1992. It was billed as "Woodstock of the Negev," included leading Israeli song artists,[207] and attracted some 200,000 participants. Shlomo was a featured performer. The indoor concert was recorded in excellent quality and was released as *Shlomo Chai – Live at Festival Arad*.[208]

In July 1992, Reb Shlomo appeared at the OU Israel Center in Jerusalem together with his disciples as back up musicians: David Zeller, Benzion Lehrer, Natan Rothstein (keyboard), and Shoshana Shoshana (drum).[209]

---

205. A photo appeared the following day in the *Yediot Aharonot* newspaper with the 3 guitar players, Shlomo, Benzion Lehrer, and Pini Dunner. My thanks to Pini Dunner for sending me a copy of this photo.

206. See below, Chapter 11, about the rabbinical ordination given by Reb Shlomo to Simcha Hochbaum and to Leah's father Sholom Brodt as well as Shlomo's special connection to Judy Brodt (Leah's mother).

207. These included Shlomo Artzi, Meir Banai, Yitzhak Klepter, and Margalit Tzanani.

208. The record was produced by Aryeh Naftaly of Third Age Productions and then sold to Gal Star. It included a dozen of Shlomo's most famous songs. The only new song was *Teshuatam*. The musicians accompanying Shlomo included Michael Golomb (tambourine), Aryeh Naftaly (guitar, harmony, vocals), Don Slovin (percussion), Ben Zion Solomon (mandolin, harmony, vocals) and Dovid Swirsky (bass).

209. Photo courtesy of Joy Krauthammer, posted on http://rebshlomocarlebach-ztl.blogspot.co.il. Reb Shlomo performed at the OU Israel Center about 10 times in the last decade of his life. My thanks for this information to Shai Solomon who was the director of the OU Israel Center during those years.

On November 11, 1990, Yediot Aharonot reported an impromptu concert of Reb Shlomo at the Kotel.   *Courtesy of Rabbi Pini Dunner*

On August 23, 1992, Reb Shlomo performed the wedding of Sarah Leah Grafstein to Steve Klemow at Moshav Me'or Modi'im. Among the interesting guests was Ram Dass.[210]

On November 15, 1992, there was an Evening with Reb Shlomo Carlebach accompanied by Aryeh Naftaly's Ayn Safeq band in the Pargod Theater, Nachlaot, Jerusalem.[211] As Reb Shlomo was walking off the stage, everybody crowded around trying to speak to him. Rachel Yona-Shalev approached and asked to consult with him about her marital difficulties:

> Shlomo pulled out a crumpled piece of paper and added my name
> and number. He had never met me before and I really didn't think
> he would phone. But very late that night, I received a phone call.
> I was amazed. I told him how my marriage was falling apart, and
> described my husband as an Israeli secular hippie using a Hindu
> name totally uninterested in Yiddishkeit. Reb Shlomo promised

---

210. For this information, I thank Shalom Schwarz, longtime resident of Me'or Modi'im, who catered this event. My thanks to Sarah Leah Grafstein for informing of the wedding date.

211. The band was Danny Roth on drums, Dovid Swirsky on bass, and Aryeh Naftaly on acoustic guitar. Shlomo played a nylon string guitar.

to help. Sure enough, he actually met with my husband and tried to help solve our problems.[212]

Reb Shlomo was in Efrat for the Shabbat bar mitzvah of Mordechai Zeller on July 30–31, 1993.[213] Then, on Motzei Shabbat Nahamu, July 31, 1993, Shlomo was filmed in a live performance at The Great Synagogue in Jerusalem with songs of consolation as befitting a post-Tisha BeAv concert. He recounted his popular "Blind Chazan" story which reflects on consolation after the terrors of the Holocaust.[214]

On August 2, 1993, Tu BeAv, Reb Shlomo performed the wedding for Mordechai and Yonah at Moshav Aminadav.

For three summers in Jerusalem, from 1992–1994, Shlomo led an intensive learning program at the newly opened Beit Midrash of Yakar in Katamon, Jerusalem during the days prior to Tisha BeAv. Between 50–100 people participated. Mimi Feigelson and Yonatan Gordis were in charge of directing preparatory study sessions and then Reb Shlomo would follow with innovative expositions.[215] Sometimes, guest speakers who appeared with him, such as Prof. Moshe Idel, provided a contrast.[216]

While visiting Israel in December 1993, Reb Shlomo celebrated Hanukkah on Moshav Me'or Modi'im.[217] Then, a couple of weeks later, on December 24–25, he spent Shabbat in the settlement of Efrat. Shlomo had made a tradition of coming to Efrat for Shabbat at least once a year after his first Shabbat there in 1986 when Elana (Elaine) Zeller was dying of cancer. In the past, he had been hosted at various synagogues in Efrat, but this Friday night was the conclusion of a fast day, the Tenth of Tevet, and no congregation wanted to host a Carlebach service with prolonged

212. Rachel Yona-Shalev, personal interview, Dec. 29, 2012.

213. For Reb Shlomo's singing *Ani Ma'amin* accompanied by David Zeller and Yehudah Katz at the bar mitzvah of Mordechai Zeller, see http://vimeo.com/1148092?pg=embed&sec=1148092 and http://davidzeller.org/videos, segment 35:00–42:30. My thanks to Mordechai Zeller for providing the date of the bar mitzvah.

214. Breslev.co.il, http://www.breslev.co.il. The record was produced and released in 2005 by David Holstein's Noam Productions.

215. Yoni Gordis, personal communication, Aug. 3, 2011. For a transcription of Reb Shlomo's talk on July 29, 1992, two days before Rosh Hodesh Av, about eager waiting for the Messiah, see the transcription of Emuna Witt, "Achishena: Before the Appointed Time," *Kol Chevra*, 10, Oct. 2004, 32–38. For a videotape from mid-July 1993 of Reb Shlomo in conversation with Rabbi Meir (Micky) Rosen at Yakar, see http://www.box.net/shared/h9zpz4hxk2 (part I) and https://www.box.com/s/4029hmg3tsfs3g8kdiw2 (part II, 29:49).

216. My thanks to Prof. Moshe Idel for this information.

217. See "In Modi'in, Reb Shlomo Carlebach speaking at the house of R. Yankele & Amira (Lilien) Shamas, Chanukah 1993," *Kol Chevra*, 10, Oct. 2004, 27.

Reb Shlomo performing at the OU Israel
Center, July 1992, with Benzion Lehrer,
David Zeller, Natan Rothstein, and
Shoshanna Shoshana.
    Photo courtesy of ©Joy Krauthammer

singing. So David Zeller and friends set up their own services in the local
library and invited everyone to come. It was packed. Many people came
regardless of the fast.[218] The enthusiastic success led to the establishment
of the first independent Carlebach-type *minyan* in Israel (besides Me'or
Modi'im).[219] Back in Jerusalem on December 28–29, 1993, Shlomo taught
at Yakar.[220]

In mid-July, 1994, Shlomo's last summer on Moshav Me'or Modi'im,
he celebrated a surprise birthday party for his daughter Nedara (Dari):

> My father created "birthday seasons." He would emphasize that
> birthdays are a time when the heavenly gates are opened. All my
> very good friends from the Moshav crowded into our small home
> and we sang and exchanged blessings. This was a very special
> custom that he had invented, that everyone give and receive a
> special *beracha*.[221]

The last album in Shlomo's liftetime was recorded live in a concert in
Bnei Brak on Motzei Shabbat Nahamu, 15 Av, July 23, 1994, with the
accompaniment of Aryeh Naftaly's band, Ayn Safeq, including Dovid
Swirsky and Betzalel Edwards. This concert in the *haredi* city of Bnei
Brak was meaningful for Shlomo as part of a long-awaited reconciliation
with the *haredi* world.[222]

On 18 Av, Tuesday, July 26, 1994, Reb Shlomo led his last kumzitz in
Jerusalem. It took place at the home of Rabbi Yehoshua Hartman in Har
Nof.[223] Then Shlomo went to Safed to perform at the Klezmer Festival. In
Safed, he also entertained at a geriatric institution where most residents

---

218. Mordechai Zeller, personal communication, Jan. 21, 2013.

219. See the blog by Yitz written May 28, 2007 in HeichalHaneginah.blogspot.com,
http://heichalhanegina.blogspot.com/2007_05_01_archive.html.

220. Tamara (Edell) Gottstein, "Teaching on Anger," *Kol Chevra*, 2008, 18–28.

221. Nedara Carlebach, personal interview, Dec. 6, 2012.

222. Personal interview with Aryeh Naftaly, Oct. 17, 2011.

223. My thanks to Rabbi Yisroel Roll for sending me details about this event.
Yehoshua's father, Rabbi Yecheskel Hartman, had brought Reb Shlomo to St. Louis in

were confined to wheelchairs. Journalist Yedidya Meir described how the old people came alive and "a few even danced for joy."[224]

One unusual concert of Reb Shlomo took place in the Tel Mond prison in the summer of 1994. Several followers of Rabbi Meir Kahane had been held in administrative detention in the aftermath of the tragic massacre in Hebron by Baruch Goldstein. One of those detained was Baruch Ben Yosef. He recounts:

> Shlomo had a gig in Haifa the night before and someone arranged for him to visit on the way back to Jerusalem. Shivi Keller was his driver, but they wouldn't let him in to the prison. Shmali Witt was playing the darbuka and they let him in. When we came into the room where Shlomo was, he was playing the guitar with his eyes closed. We danced to the music until the guards told us that it was over. Since then, I have participated in the creation of two Carlebach *minyanim*, one in Mizpe Nevo, Maaleh Adumim and one in Tekoa.[225]

Selections from Reb Shlomo's last summer in Israel can be seen in a documentary film produced by Aryeh Naftaly and Shlomo Kabakov (Third Age Productions) entitled *Gevalt! On the Road with Shlomo Carlebach*.[226] The film contains video excerpts from an interview in July 1994 on Israel Army Radio with Muli Shapira.[227] It features clips of Shlomo at events from the end of July through August, 1994: the Klezmer

---

1957, thus setting in motion the dynamics that led to the production of Reb Shlomo's first record in June 1959 (see above).

224. Brandwein, *Reb Shlomele*, 282–283.

225. Personal interview with Baruch Ben Yosef, March 26, 2013.

226. My thanks to Aryeh Naftaly for supplying the identifying information for his documentary film which was posted in six parts on YouTube as Givalt 1/6, 2/6 etc. http://www.youtube.com/watch?v=WhFHekXNAVU&feature=related; http://www.youtube.com/watch?v=BYbVXvKLhDs&feature=related; http://www.youtube.com/watch?v=8OJwFVw9Wuc&feature=related; http://www.youtube.com/watch?v=zWOgPYAs9uI&feature=related; http://www.youtube.com/watch?v=8eRSoMCH1Ho&feature=related; http://www.youtube.com/watch?v=KVKtDHEVmfo&feature=related. The film credits are posted on this last part in segments 3:23-4:01.

227. The interview was conducted by Muli Shapira who headed the Israel Army Radio's culture department and presented the popular Friday morning *Bilui Naim* covering cultural happenings. In the radio studio, Shlomo was accompanied by two of his followers living on the Moshav, Aryeh Naftaly on the flute and Dovid Swirsky on acoustic guitar. See http://www.zingmit.com/2011/08/interview-with-shlomo-carlebach.html; http://www.youtube.com/watch?v=WhFHekXNAVU&feature=related 0:05–0:51, 3:00–3:20, 5:22–6:14; http://www.youtube.com/watch?v=BYbVXvKLhDs&feature=related 1:28–3:06.

Festival in Safed,[228] the wedding of Tiki Witt and Shahar Bashan in the Old City of Jerusalem on August 21, 1994, an engagement ceremony at 2:00 AM of Emmanuel Krassenstein to Menorah Tehora,[229] and concerts in Hebron,[230] Rehovot, the Tzavta Club in Haifa, and Beit Bamberger, a community center in Bnei Brak.[231] It also includes a number of clips from a discussion with actor Shmuel Vilozny and his manager Shumi Berkowitz in the latter's Ramat Gan apartment.

On the last day of Reb Shlomo's stay in Israel, some 10,000 people attended his last concert.[232] Entitled Nigun Atik, it was free entry in the open air at Gan Sacher in Jerusalem.[233]

Peforming for free was typically characteristic of Shlomo. This was dramatized in another one of his last concerts in Jerusalem in August 1994. It was a concert on behalf of Israeli MIAs[234] and Shlomo received an award from Jerusalem Mayor Ehud Olmert for his life's work in the realm of reinvigorating Jewish music and for being the father of Hasidic music.[235] The concert took place at the newly built Safra Square next to the Jerusalem Municipality, and hundreds of youth were loitering at the entrance, unable to enter. Chaya Kaplan was one of them. Later she was to exclaim how this concert changed her life:

> Suddenly, the music stops. We heard the mysterious singer call
> out to the powers-that-be – "Hey, you guys at the gate. Forget

---

228. The 7th Annual Klezmer Festival in Safed took place at the end of July 1994. Shlomo was accompanied by Aryeh Naftaly (acoustic guitar, sax, flute, and background vocals), Dovid Swirsky (electric guitar), Bezalel Edwards (bass), Yankele Shames (hand cymbals and background vocals) and Michael Rosen (tambourine).

229. This was one of Shlomo's last and most original name innovations. Emmanuel Krassenstein informed me that the name Menorah Tehora was given in connection with the reading in *Parshat Emor* (Lev. 24:4).

230. My thanks to Chaim David Saracik, who played on stage with Shlomo in Hebron, for supplying details of this concert.

231. For Beit Bamburger, see http://www.youtube.com/watch?v=BYbVXvKLhDs& feature=related 4:34–5:27.

232. This estimate of the numbers was posted in 2008 by Betzalel Edwards as a comment to the video footage on http://www.youtube.com/watch?v=WhFHekXN AVU&feature=related.

233. http://www.youtube.com/watch?v=8eRSoMCH1Ho&feature=relmfu 1:50– 4:24, and much of http://www.youtube.com/watch?v=KVKtDHEVmfo&feature=re lmfu.

234. See the comment by Nachum (May 18, 2012) at http://torahmusings.com/ 2012/05/new-periodical-hakirah-13. Nachum was one of the participants at this concert.

235. Personal interview with Ruth Fogelman, Oct. 3, 2011. See also Ruth Fogelman, "Within the Walls of Jerusalem – A Personal Perspective," *Kol Chevra*, vol. 7, 2000, 126.

about the money. Just let everybody in!" Was it a joke?! Was he talking about us?! Sure enough, they opened up the gates and we all started gleefully streaming in. It was the first and only time I have ever been suddenly let in to a concert for free! . . . We flooded in to find a world of hundreds of circle-dancing, Hebrew singing, funky and FRUM members of the tribe. . . . It was so pure, yet wild. It was fresh and new and yet old-world, old-style. I looked around and knew I had found my home in the homeland. I had no idea who Shlomo was. Little did I know that he was about to change my life, even from a distance.[236]

In conclusion, in many ways, Israel was Shlomo's second home where he had an extended family of both natural relatives and close personal friendships. This gradual process is reflected on his business card which at first showed the Tel Aviv Dan Hotel, then a rented apartment on 16 Lincoln Street in Jerusalem, and finally, in the last decade, his home in Moshav Me'or Modi'im.[237] Shlomo's impact on Israel was a result of the growing number of devoted followers who sang his songs and disseminated his teachings.

---

236. Chaya Kaplan-Lester "In Honor of Reb Shlomo Carlebach," Spoken Word Torah, *The Jerusalem Post* Blog, Nov. 1, 2012, http://blogs.jpost.com/content/honor-reb-shlomo-carlebach.

237. For a photo of Reb Shlomo's calling card with Moshav Me'or Modi'im and Congregation Kehilat Jacob, see Brandwein, *Reb Shlomele*, 147.

CHAPTER 9

Lifting the Iron Curtain

1.   AM YISRAEL CHAI, SSSJ, AND "WHITE FIRE" JEWS (1965–1988)

Shlomo Carlebach's catchy melodies played a vital role in two major phenomenon of the 1960s and 1970s – the *baal teshuva* movement and the struggle for Soviet Jewry. Rabbi Shlomo Riskin, founding Rabbi of Lincoln Square Synagogue (LSS) at West 69th in Manhattan, just ten blocks from the Carlebach Shul, was a prominent activist in both movements. In his memoirs, he remarks about the significance of Reb Shlomo's music:

> Rav Shlomo Carlebach provided the much needed musical expression for our rallies, as he did for the newly burgeoning *ba'al teshuva* movement; indeed it is difficult to imagine these two major activities . . . without Shlomo Carlebach's music, which gave our words and goals soulful expression.[1]

The Student Struggle for Soviet Jewry (SSSJ) was founded by Jacob Birnbaum in April 1964.[2] Popular folk songs had proven their importance

---

1. Rabbi Shlomo Riskin, *Listening to God: Inspirational Stories for My Grandchildren* (New Milford, Connecticut: 2010), 222–223.

2. For a comprehensive survey of SSSJ and Birnbaum, see "A Brief History of the Student Struggle for Soviet Jewry (SSSJ)" posted Oct. 19, 2011 on the website of the Russian-Speaking Community Council of Manhattan & the Bronx, www.RCCMB.org, http://rccmb.org/sssj-brief-history.pdf. See also Yossi Klein Halevi, "Jacob Birnbaum and the Struggle for Soviet Jewry," *Azure*, vol. 17, Spring 2004, 27–57. The files of the SSSJ were transferred by Jacob Birnbaum to Yeshiva University in 1993, and can be found in the Yeshiva University SSSJ Archives, http://www.yu.edu; A collection of 416 boxes of manuscripts, records and other artifacts is available at http://libfindaids.yu.edu:8082/xtf/view?docId=ead/SSSJ/SSSJ.xml;query=;brand=default. My thanks to Shulamith Z. Berger for sending me selected PDF copies from these files.

In mid-April 1964, Birnbaum issued a manifesto calling on students to join him in the American protest movements, and similarly, Birnbaum sought to create SSSJ songs. For that purpose, he recruited Sherwood Goffin[3] and Shlomo Carlebach.[4] Birnbaum asked Shlomo to compose a tune using the words *"Am Yisroel Chai"*:

> I vaguely recalled that the song *"Am Yisroel Chai"* had been an expression of defiance and hope in Nazi Germany, and after the war it had been sung in Displaced Persons camps.[5] As the Soviet Jewish resistance movement developed, the distinguished Yiddish poet Yosef Kerler composed his own version. However, when I enlisted Shlomo's aid in 1964, none of these versions were current.[6]

It was on Rosh Hashana, October 4, 1948, that Golda Meyerson (later Golda Meir), arrived at the Moscow Synagogue as the head of the first diplomatic delegation of the fledgling State of Israel. Reportedly, she was greeted with cries of *"Am Yisrael Chai"* and an astonishingly large crowd of some ten thousand people.[7] This was a jubilant milestone in the history of Soviet Jewry. Birnbaum's felicitous choice of these simple yet

---

at Columbia University on April 27 to create a national grassroots movement for Soviet Jewry. Some 250 students came. This was the first national meeting of the SSSJ. Four days later, on the Soviet holiday of May Day, May 1, 1964, Birnbaum pulled off the first grassroots confrontation of the Kremlin at the Soviet UN Mission in Manhattan with some 1,000 students. Personal communications with Birnbaum, March 2013. Compare Adam S. Ferziger, "'Outside the Shul': The American Soviet Jewry Movement and the Rise of Solidarity Orthodoxy, 1964–1986," *Religion and American Culture*, vol. 22, no. 1, 2012, 83–130.

   3. Sherwood Goffin began singing publicly in 1961. He became the cantor of the Lincoln Square Synagogue in 1965 shortly after its formation in 1964 and became known as the troubadour of Soviet Jewry thanks to his many years of singing at Soviet Jewry events.

   4. Jacob Birnbaum told me that he knew Shlomo well as their paths had crossed frequently. They had a nostalgic connection going back to their grandparents. Jacob's grandfather, Nathan Birnbaum, was elected secretary-general at the first Zionist Congress in 1897 in Basel, Switzerland where Shlomo's grandfather, Rabbi Asher Cohn, served as Chief Rabbi. Personal communication, Oct. 4, 2012.

   5. Birnbaum spent much time in the years 1946–1951 working with young survivors of Nazi and Soviet totalitarianism who had come to the U.K.

   6. My thanks to Jacob and Freda Birnbaum for the detailed explanations and clarifications, Sept.–Oct. 2012 and March 2013. See also Jacob Birnbaum, "Am Yisroel Chai – Shlomo Carlebach's Version and Earlier Versions," Chazzanut.com, http://www.chazzanut.com/articles/on-am-yisraeil.html, May 2003 (updated April 30, 2006). This article was reprinted with some omissions as "Am Yisrael Chai" in *Kol Chevra*, vol. 16, 2010, 30–31.

   7. Mordechai Altshuler, *Religion and Jewish Identity in the Soviet Union 1941–1964* [transl. from Hebrew by Saadya Sternberg] (Waltham, Mass.: 2012), 239–241.

evocative three words was monumentous. After being set to dramatic music by Shlomo the song became the SSSJ anthem.

At first, Birnbaum sent his requests to Shlomo but to no avail. Then, in mid-March 1965, Shlomo sang in Frankfurt, Germany and decided to try and enter Communist-controlled Czechoslovakia to celebrate Purim in the hometown of the 16th century Maharal of Prague, to whom the Carlebach family traced their ancestry. On Purim evening, March 18, 1965, Shlomo found a few young Czechs and together they went to a small concert hall. At first, the youth were hesitant and reluctant to sing and dance, but Shlomo persisted and finally won these reluctant and fearful kids over. Inspired by the transformation that he had witnessed, Shlomo began working on the task that Birnbaum had assigned him.[8]

Late on Friday afternoon, April 2, 1965, Birnbaum's phone rang, "and Shlomo's exhausted voice said, Yankele, I've got it for you!"[9] On Sunday, April 4, two weeks before Passover, some 3,000 protestors led by seven men wearing prayer shawls encircled the Soviet Mission to "topple the walls of hate" in Jericho style. They blew on seven *shofarot* seven times. For the first time, Shlomo sang *"Am Yisrael Chai."*[10]

Shlomo's inspirational invention was to add three additional words, *"Od Avinu Chai"* (Our Father is Still Alive), thus providing an exegetical link to both biblical and rabbinic tradition. The biblical verse, "Our father is still alive" (Genesis 43:28), is the brothers' consoling rejoinder to Joseph's query about his father (43:7). The rabbinic thematic expansion commentary is that Jacob = Israel still lives on even after his body is interred.[11] By inserting these words, Shlomo created both alliteration and a metaphoric homily. The expression, "Our father is alive," is a double entendre, i.e., the phrase is understood in its simple straightforward

---

8. Personal correspondence with Jacob Birnbaum, March 31, 2013. See also Gal Beckerman, *When They Come for Us, We'll Be Gone: The Epic Struggle to Save Soviet Jewry* (Boston, New York: 2010), 125–128.

9. Birnbaum, "Am Yisroel Chai."

10. For photos of Reb Shlomo at the Jericho March, see the YU SSSJ Archives, box 1, folder 10. For a video clip with R. Shlomo at the SSSJ demonstration at the UN, see http://www.youtube.com/watch?v=64DjIvG2Dbo&feature=player_embedded. The original recording of Shlomo singing "Am Yisroel Chai" on April 4, 1965 is preserved in the Yeshiva University SSSJ Archives Jacob Birnbaum collection, LibFindAids.Yu.Edu, http://libfindaids.yu.edu:8082/xtf/view?docId=ead/SSSJ/SSSJ .xml;query=;brand=default.

11. R. Yochanan in Talmud *Taanit* 5b explicating Jer. 30:10 that Israel need not fear as there is hope of Salvation and Return to the land. Similarly, Shlomo composed a tune for the rabbinic exclamatory conclusion in blessing the New Moon (Talmud *Rosh Hashana* 25a) where the words are similar – *Hai VeKayam*, "David King of Israel is alive and existing."

meaning that Jacob/Israel is alive, and also in its theological sense that God, the father of Israel, exists and protects His people. The musical notes reflect the juxtaposition of the two themes.

The simple words, easy to pronounce and repeat, attracted a wide following even of those who didn't know any Hebrew. The message was an expression of pride, existence, continuity, and solidarity and it became the signature song of the Soviet Jewry freedom movement.[12] It also turned into a quintessential exclamation of hope in the face of adversity and ultimately became a grand liberation song of the Jewish people.

Shlomo was featured at SSSJ rallies such as at the Riverside Plaza Hotel on the first day of Hanukkah, December 19, 1965, in conjunction with the Freedom Lights Menorah March through Central Park.[13] Similar to the anti-war and civil rights protests where folk singers such as Bob Dylan, Joan Baez and Pete Seeger excited the crowds, so also, the performances of Carlebach and Goffin energized the SSSJ rallies, created solidarity, and enthused the crowd to dance and sing. Jacob Birnbaum recalls:

> Shlomo felt deeply connected to the SSSJ passionate sense of redemptive mission, and the SSSJniks in turn loved Shlomo for his joyful exuberance and greatly respected his devotion to *Klal Yisrael*. Shlomo enjoyed interacting with these dedicated young people, many of whom later made aliyah. Among them were Yossi Klein (Halevi), who joined me in 1965 at the age of twelve; David Stahl, my deeply dedicated longtime Assistant National Coordinator; Yisrael Winkelman (Medad), now with the Menachem Begin Heritage Center, and the enthusiastic Bernie Marinbach, leader of SSSJ's "We Who Care" band.[14]

Bernie Marinbach was a student in Brooklyn College when he created the SSSJ band of young college students. His band appeared regularly at dozens of SSSJ demonstrations, often playing the theme song of "*Am Yisrael Chai*," thus popularizing it as the SSSJ anthem of freedom and hope.[15]

Israel's victory in the 1967 Six-Day War evoked a Jewish pride and a willingness to challenge the Kremlin. On Saturday evening October 28,

12. See Birnbaum, "Am Yisroel Chai." Compare Avi Weiss, "Student Struggle for Soviet Jewry (SSSJ)," *Encyclopaedia Judaica*, 2nd ed., vol. 19 (Detroit: 2007), 269. Rabbi Avi Weiss became SSSJ's chairman in 1983 succeeding Rabbi Riskin.

13. YU Archives, SSSJ collection, box 1, folder 14.

14. Jacob Birnbaum, personal communication, March 10, 2013.

15. Personal interview with Bernie Marinbach, March 21, 2013.

1967, just after Simchat Torah, Shlomo helped lead a demonstration in front of the Soviet Union delegation in New York.[16]

Shlomo appeared on March 20, 1969, at the Hillel Foundation of the University of Wisconsin.[17] On October 2, 1969, the sixth day of Hol HaMoed Sukkot, Reb Shlomo sang at the pre-Simchat Torah demonstration at Dag Hammarskjold Plaza near the United Nations where New York's Jewish community expressed its solidarity with Soviet Jews. The event was meant to be a counterpart to the Simchat Torah celebration of Soviet Jews who were dancing outside the Central Synagogue in Moscow.[18]

The Exodus March took place on Sunday, April 26, 1970, the sixth day of Hol HaMoed Pesach, and drew some 20,000 participants who marched down 5th Avenue to the UN building.[19] At Birnbaum's request, Shlomo composed a new tune for this rally using the words "*Lo Amut Ki Echyeh*" (Psalms 118:17), "I shall not die, but live to recount the works of the Lord."[20] Shlomo urged the crowd to sing "*Am Yisrael Chai*" in a way that "our souls should go straight up and tear apart Heaven until God opens the gates of Russia for our brothers and sisters."[21] By 1970, Birnbaum had compiled a booklet of songs and a record entitled *Songs of Hope for Russian Jews*. He dedicated it to "Cantor Sherwood Goffin, beloved troubadour of the Soviet Jewry Movement."[22]

In August 1970, Shlomo was in Haifa, Israel giving a concert when he was greeted by Avraham Shifrin who had immigrated to Israel two weeks earlier. Shifrin had been convicted as an espionage agent for the U.S. and Israel. While in the Lubyanka and Lefortovo prisons in Moscow,

---

16. This demonstration was organized under the auspices of the American Jewish Conference on Soviet Jewry (AJCSJ). An Israeli reporter stationed in New York wrote that 5,000 youth came from 24 Jewish organizations. See Shlomo Shafir, "Demonstration for Soviet Jewry," *Davar Newspaper*, Oct. 30, 1967, 2. However, Jacob Birnbaum told me (March 31, 2013) that the number 5,000 was greatly exaggerated.

17. *Wisconsin State Journal*, March 16, 1969, 32.

18. "Mayor Lindsay Calls on Russia to Let Jews Emigrate to New York or Israel," *Jewish Telegraphic Agency*, Oct. 3, 1969. See the Yeshiva University Archives, SSSJ collection, box 5, folder 11.

19. YU Archives, SSSJ collection, box 6, folder 6.

20. This is the original translation used in 1970. Personal communication from Birnbaum, Oct. 25, 2012. For Shlomo singing "*Lo Amut*" in the winter of 1970 at Ohio University, B'nai B'rith Hillel Foundation, see the Yeshiva University Archives, SSSJ collection, recordings item 441. My thanks to Shulamith Z. Berger, Yeshiva University's Curator of Special Collections file.

21. Yossi Klein Halevi, *Memoirs of a Jewish Extremist: An American Story* (New York-Boston: 1995).

22. The original title was *Songs of Protest for Russian Jews*.

he was made to stand in freezing waters and eventually had to have his war-wounded leg amputated. After ten years of imprisonment and four in exile, he was released, moving to Israel in August 1970.[23] Avraham convinced Shlomo that it would be possible for him to visit Moscow for Simchat Torah and have a powerful effect on Soviet Jewry. Shifrin forewarned his friends in Moscow to prepare a guitar and tape-recorders for a surprise clandestine visitor.

On Hol HaMoed Sukkot, October 19, 1970, Reb Shlomo sang at an assembly of 2,300 people at Hunter College.[24] Later that evening, Shlomo flew to Moscow hiding his Jewish identity under "the most ordinary hat."[25] He arrived just in time for the Simchat Torah celebrations at the Moscow Synagogue on October 23, 1970. Shlomo sang for a few hours near the synagogue on Archipov St. Later, Shlomo described with awe how the Jews in Moscow stood with him "under pouring rain and sang the only song they knew," "*Am Yisrael Chai,*" which he had just taught them.[26] The next day, he was officially escorted out of the USSR. It was not until almost two decades later, September 1989, that he was able to visit again.

Tapes of the improvised concert were copied and sent out throughout the USSR. Glenn Richter, the SSSJ national coordinator, described how Shlomo's records inspired and "sustained" the Jewish activists.[27] Eleonora Poltinnikiova[28] lived at the time in Novosibirsk, Siberia and was actively distributing underground anti-Soviet literature (the samizdat).

---

23. Avraham was born in 1923 in Minsk, Belorussia. His father Isaak was arrested when Avraham was 14 "which overnight turned a light-hearted lad into an enemy of the hypocritical and ruthless Soviet system. He swore to avenge his father." During World War II, he fought at the front lines in the Red Army, was twice badly wounded, many times decorated and finished the war as an army major. He then served as chief legal advisor to the Soviet Ministry of Weapons and became a secret espionage agent for the U.S. and Israel. When his spying was discovered, he was sentenced to be shot. Just before his execution, the chief prosecutor and KGB head, Lavrenti Beria, was executed himself in the upheaval that followed Stalin's disappearance, and Avraham's sentence was commuted to 25 years of strict prison camps plus 5 years of exile in Siberia and another 5 of civil rights curtailment. I thank Eleonora Shifrin for helping reconstruct this story (personal discussions, Sept. 2012). See also Eleonora Shifrin, "Avraham Shifrin *zt"l,*" *Kol Chevra*, vol. 5, 1998, 11–14. Cf. Conservapedia.com, http://www.conservapedia.com/Essay:_Avraham_Shifrin:_KAL_007_Researcher.

24. "Call Issued for Nationwide 'committees for the Release of the 32' Soviet Jews," *Jewish Telegraphic Agency*, Oct. 20, 1970.

25. *Kol Chevra*, vol. 5, Nov. 1998, 12, 15–17.

26. *Kol Chevra*, vol. 5, 1998, 18.

27. Larry Yudelson and Susan Birnbaum. "Shlomo Carlebach, Beloved Rabbi and Songwriter, Dies at Age 69," *Jewish Telegraphic Agency*, Oct. 24, 1994.

28. See below in this section about Eleonora's wedding to Avraham Shifrin.

She received a tape-reel with an inscription on the cover that said "The Dancing Rabbi." Eleonora recalled:

> Our life was suddenly burst into by a real life, by light and joy . . . a joy that was squeezing out the fear and hopelessness of our dreadful existence, a joy that was stirring in us pride of our Jewishness . . . Our hearts responded to the Jewish prayer whose single word we did not know. Now we could fly to the land of our dream on the wings of that music and this journey made us stronger for our struggle.[29]

In 1970, a group of sixteen refuseniks, organized by longtime dissidents Eduard Kuznetsov and Mark Dymshitz, prepared to hijack an aircraft and fly it via Finland to Sweden. Under the guise of a trip to a wedding, they bought all the tickets for the flight Leningrad to Priozersk on a twelve-seater aircraft. On June 15, 1970, after arriving at Smolny Airport near Leningrad, the "wedding guests" were arrested by the Russian Ministry of Internal Affairs and charged with high treason. Birnbaum reports:

> There were persistent reports that a major Soviet trial was planned for October. I organized a major event of song, drama, and speeches at Hunter College on Hol HaMoed Sukkot, October 19, 1970. Some 2,300 people paid to participate. Reb Shlomo made his usual dramatic and heartfelt appearance.[30]

The actual trial began in Leningrad on December 15, and harsh sentences were announced on December 24. Reb Shlomo was at the Kotel on Shabbat, December 26, 1970, the fifth night of Hanukkah when he heard the news that Kuznetsov and Dymshitz had been sentenced to death. Shlomo read the liturgy of the morning service after *Keriyat Shema* and was inspired to compose a song "to open prisons" to the words of *"Motzi asirim ufodeh anavim."* The song later appeared in his 1972 album *Uvnei Yerushalayim.*[31]

On Sunday, April 4, 1971, Shlomo participated in a pre-Passover Exodus Freedom Rally. Then on Sunday, April 18, 1971, the day after Passover, Shlomo was invited to a rally together with Rabbi Abraham

---

29. Eleonora Shifrin, "We All Miss You," *Kol Chevra*, vol. 4, 1997, 28–30.

30. Jacob Birnbaum, personal communication, March 31, 2013.

31. On the jacket cover, Shlomo wrote an expanded social commentary to the liturgical words: "Release all prisoners" – the whole world is still a prison. "Redeem the humble" – redeem the world from false humility. "Help the poor" – help the rich to know how poor they are and help the poor to know how rich they are. "Please God answer Israel's prayer" – God's answer to the world is "Have you ever heard my people cry."

Joshua Heschel. It was entitled the "Ninth Day of Passover for Soviet Jews" and it took place in Glen Cove, Nassau County on Long Island, New York opposite the Killenworth Mansion, site of the Soviet delegation to the UN:

> More than 500 people gathered today on a sloping hillside directly opposite Killenworth, the Soviet Compound . . . the hillside was transformed into one swaying mass of people who were led in dancing and singing by Rabbi Shlomo Carlebach.[32]

On Sunday, October 10, 1971, Shlomo was the featured singer at the solidarity rally in New York before 2,800 youths. He had hurt his back in an accident in Israel and was walking on crutches. Accompanying him were Sherwood Goffin, Jo Amar, and the Clei Zemer Band. Shlomo dramatically described his secretive visit to Moscow for Simchat Torah the year before:[33]

> I am not the same person any more. I can't forget all of those beautiful kids. You know, if I had a chance to dance with the Baal Shem Tov on Simchat Torah or to be in Moscow, I would have still chosen Moscow.

One of Shlomo's favorite stories about his visit to Moscow as "a real underground" relates how a 15-year old girl summoned him into an alleyway the morning after the Simchat Torah dancing and whispered the first five letters of the Hebrew alphabet, the only Jewish sounds she knew. Shlomo dramatized this story to introduce his tune for "*El Adon,*" the Shabbat morning *piyut* which is structured according to the *alef bet*.[34]

Shlomo used the term "white fire"[35] to illustrate the inner light of knowing of the Russian Jews who came on Simchat Torah.

---

32. "Rally for Soviet Jews Opposite Soviet Compound Draws 500 Persons," *Jewish Telegraphic Agency*, April 19, 1971 – Archive.JTA.org, http://archive.jta.org. The rally was sponsored by the SSSJ and the Long Island Committee for Soviet Jewry. See also Myron Fenster, *Up From the Straits: A Memoir* (2011), 188–189, where Rabbi Fenster describes the "sing along" and "clap along" led by Shlomo Carlebach whom he had invited together with Abraham Heschel to appear at this rally.

33. Philip Ben, New York correspondent for *Maariv*, Oct. 13, 1971. The article is reproduced in Brand, *Reb Shlomele*, 84.

34. This story has many versions. For one of them see http://www.youtube.com/watch?v=yKF14_4Sgho&NR=1.

35. This expression is based on a *Midrashic* notion quoted originally in the name of Resh Lakish that the letters of the Torah were engraved in black light but the parchment was white light. This idea is developed in over a dozen rabbinic sources, e.g., Talmud Yerushalmi *Shekalim*, 6:1 and *Sotah* 8, *Devarim Rabbah*, 3:12. In the Zohar, the term "white fire" indicates the empty spaces between the black ink letters. These

> Out of the 20,000 kids, there must have been 19,500 who did not
> know even what the word Simchat Torah means. But do you know
> what kind of Jews they are? They are "white fire" Jews. They have
> the message from God, the white fire which we forgot. . . . we are
> waiting for them to teach us the white fire, the real message, the
> real thing.[36]

Shlomo concluded with a mystical description of how these Jews are
instructed *directly* by God:

> I'm not so sure when the High Priest walked into the Holy of
> Holies and he really knew that God is One and he pronounced
> God's ineffable name. Maybe those kids knew even more. Because
> the High Priest had a father and mother who taught him. But
> these people had no one to teach them. It is the first time since
> Mt. Sinai that the whole generation is really God's pupils. And if
> you have such a Teacher, such a Teacher, they are the best pupils
> God ever had.[37]

Shlomo's exclamatory drama as he encounters "white fire" Jews in
Moscow sounds strikingly similar to how he related to hippies in 1966.
He discerns an intuitive devotion implicit in an "innocent" spiritual
quest. In both cases, he exaggerates with a natural naivety. Many Soviet
Jews did not become religious nor did they choose to go on aliyah.
However, Shlomo's utopian vision is based on a kabbalistic insight, that
underlying superficial expressions are spiritual yearnings inspired by the
Providential Hand of God. It blended well with the redemptive passion
that Jacob Birnbaum had injected into the Soviet Jewry Movement.

Shlomo's dramatic involvement with Russian Jewry came to a remarkable climax in a wedding that he performed on September 9, 1974 for
Avraham Shifrin and Eleonora Poltinnikiova on the Tel Aviv beach at
midnight. Eleonora Poltinnikiova had arrived in Israel from Novosibirsk
in 1972, and after she met Avraham at an anti-Soviet demonstration in
Tel Aviv, they decided to get married. However, rabbinic bureaucratic
difficulties prevented their receiving approval for their wedding. When
Shlomo arrived in Israel, the couple went to his concert on Motzei
Shabbat, September 7, 1974 in the Tel Aviv Tzavta Theater and shared

---

are considered to be the deepest Torah teachings because they are inexpressible. Cf.
Serkez, *The Holy Beggars' Banquet*, 94–95, where Reb Shlomo states: "The Torah was
written with black fire on white fire. White fire is when everything is clear. Black fire
is when everything is dark."

36. BooMP3.com, http://boomp3.com/mp3/rz5gz4j30g-12-russian-jews-1.
37. Ibid.

their problem with Shlomo. Somehow, he managed to obtain the necessary permissions.[38] Because he was scheduled to leave for Amsterdam and he had concerts scheduled in Eilat and Givataim, the wedding was held two days later next to the hotel where Shlomo was staying in Tel Aviv. Rabbi Yisrael Meir Lau performed the wedding:[39]

> I was delighted to agree to my friend Shlomo's request to perform this wedding. At the Plaza Hotel they gave us a box of oranges and some cake and we went outside to the beach adjoining the hotel and erected the *huppah* on the sand. Reb Shlomo led the singing and explained each blessing.

A few dozen of Shlomo's *chevra* added the joy, and the celebration lasted three hours. Hotel workers directed floodlights from the roof to the "free concert on the beach."[40] There Shlomo was inspired on the spot to compose one of his most inspirational songs, *"Shomerim Hafked."*[41]

Shlomo's tapes and records, clandestinely distributed in the Soviet Union, had an inspirational, educational, and nationalistic impact. Here, for example, is how Avital Sharansky, the wife of Natan (Anatoli) Sharansky, described the impact of Shlomo's record in the early 1970s:

> Someone sent us a record as a gift . . . When we heard the songs, we immediately fell in love with them. We heard the Judaism of 2000 years. We heard *Yerushalayim, Am Yisrael*. We heard so much love . . . Natan and I listened to the record constantly. These were our first encounters with Jewish songs.[42]

---

38. In order to acquire an exit permit separately from her "refusenik" family, Eleanora had arranged a "marriage" in Russia and after arriving in Israel arranged for a divorce. However, the Rabbinate did not grant permission for the new marriage because Avraham was unable to convince them that he was not a *kohen* and thus forbidden to a divorcee. When Shlomo arrived, he contacted Rabbi Simcha HaCohen Kook and Rabbi Yisrael Meir Lau and they expedited the wedding.

39. At the time, Rabbi Lau was serving as a rabbi in Northern Tel Aviv and had considerable influence in the Tel Aviv rabbinate. R. Lau is the son-in-law of Rabbi Yitzhak Yedidya Frankel who was the Chief Rabbi of Tel Aviv from 1973–1986.

40. Reconstructed from Eleonora Shifrin's various accounts – Groups.google.com, http://groups.google.com/group/shlomo-carlebach/browse_thread/thread/3cf5362a oe33dd2e#; Eleonora Shifrin, "We All Miss You," *Kol Chevra*, vol. 4, 1997, 28–30; "Rav Shlomo Carlebach, the Dancing Rabbi, Interview in *Vesti*, Oct. 1997," *Kol Chevra*, vol. 5, 1998, 18–20 and "Rav Shlomo Carlebach, the Dancing Rabbi," *Kol Chevra*, vol. 16, 2010, 17–21.

41. Shlomo on the album *Ani Maamin* produced by Emes Records in 1975 brings the words from the piyut at the end of the Pesach Haggadah which mean "place guards around Your city all day and all night." They hint at the futuristic vision of Jerusalem (Isaiah 62:11).

42. Avital and Natan Sharansky, "The Jumping Rabbi," *Kol Chevra*, vol. 16, 2010,

Avital and Natan were married on Thursday, July 4, 1974. The next day Avital left for Israel, certain that Natan would soon follow. However, he was imprisoned and served three years in jail and five years of forced labor camps in East Siberia. The Soviet regime made dozens of arrests among the refuseniks and by 1979 halted emigration.

Shlomo sang at several Soviet Jewry rallies in the mid-1970s: June 24, 1974; September 23, 1975; October 8, 1975, and January 4, 1976.[43] On Hol HaMoed Sukkot, September 23, 1975, he and Sherwood Goffin led the singing for some 1,000 New Yorkers at the "Simchat Torah Festival of Freedom" in Manhattan near the UN. It was there that Sylva Zalmanson announced her famous hunger strike on behalf of her husband, Eduard Kuznetsov (see above) and the other Prisoners of Conscience.[44] On January 4, 1976, Shlomo appeared in a Benefit Concert for Soviet Jewry in the prestigious Carnegie Hall in Manhattan.[45]

However, it took almost a decade before a significant breakthrough was achieved. In February 1986, Mikhail Gorbachev exchanged Natan Sharansky for a few Soviet spies who had been caught in the West. After making aliyah, Sharansky invited Shlomo to the Renaissance Hotel in Jerusalem to a party celebrating his aliyah, and together they sang "*Pitchu Li*" (Psalms 118:9), Open the Gates.[46]

On December 6, 1987, at the National Mall in Washington, on the eve of the decisive summit between Ronald Reagan and Mikhail Gorbachev, more than 250,000 protesters shouted "Let My People Go." Soviet policy began changing. On January 19, 1988, Iosif Ziselovich (Yosef) Begun, a prominent refusenik, was allowed to leave Moscow, ending a 17-year emigration battle that included prison and Siberian exile.[47] His crime was teaching Hebrew and protesting for free emigration to Israel.[48] In 1977, when he had been arrested for teaching private Hebrew lessons, he was

12–13. Compare Brandwein, *Reb Shlomele*, 258–259 where Natan Sharansky is quoted as singing in his jail cell two of Shlomo's songs, "*Am Yisrael Chai*" and "*Lemaan Achai*."

43. See the YU SSSJ archives, box 12, folders 2–3, box 14, folder 7, box 15, folder 10.

44. The program was sponsored by the GNYCSJ – Greater New York Conference on Soviet Jewry. For details, see the American Jewish Committee Archives, National Interreligious Task Force, 1975/6, http://www.ajcarchives.org/ajcarchive/DigitalArchive.aspx.

45. See the YU SSSJ archives, box 12, folders 2–3, box 14, folder 7, box 15, folder 10.

46. Sharansky, "The Jumping Rabbi," 13.

47. "Begun Leaves Soviet, Ending 17-Year Emigration Struggle," *New York Times*, Jan. 19, 1988, NYTimes.com, http://www.nytimes.com/1988/01/19/world/begun-leaves-soviet-ending-17-year-emigration-struggle.htmlAP.

48. "Iosif Begun, A Defiant Man," *New York Times*, Feb. 13, 1987, NYTimes.com, http://www.nytimes.com/1987/02/13/world/iosif-begun-a-defiant-man.html.

"depressed, frightened, and beyond hope." In those "terrible moments" he was comforted by singing Shlomo's melody, *"Gam Ki Elech"*: "Even though I walk through the valley of the shadow of death, I will have no fear." Begun wrote: "The lyrics inspired me and the melody comforted me."[49] Then in 1983, when he was sentenced to twelve years of prison and Siberian exile, he responded by yelling *"Am Yisrael Chai"* at the judge. He and his fellow prisoners sang Shlomo Carlebach melodies. After Begun's release, one of his most exciting visits was with Carlebach himself.[50]

In 1988, 18,919 Jews left the Soviet Union, more than double the previous year. In 1989, the numbers jumped to 71,196.[51] The doors of the Soviet Union were beginning to open. The "Solidarity Ethos" that Shlomo had been promoting now jumped to a new phase when he and his entourage of musicians and followers were invited to tour the Soviet Union.[52] Jacob Birnbaum sums up the significance of this phase transition:

> This is an incredible saga in Jewish history. All told, since we initiated the Soviet Jewry Movement, some two million Jews have left the USSR, completely revitalizing the face of world Jewry. Our mission was now transformed from "Let My People Go" to "Let My People Know" (their heritage).[53]

2.   FIRST JEWISH MUSIC TOUR IN RUSSIA (SEPTEMBER 1989)

On August 22, 1989, the *Los Angeles Times* announced "an unprecedented culture exchange" with the Soviet Union which would feature a folk rock Jewish Soul Music tour led by Shlomo Carlebach.[54] For three weeks, from September 7–27, 1989, Shlomo Carlebach toured the Soviet Union accompanied by the ten-man Los Angeles band, Promised Land with Jerry (Yehudah) Katz,[55] the band director and leader,[56] and Chanan

---

49. Yosef Begun, "The American Rabbi vs. the KGB," *Kol Chevra*, vol. 16, 2010, 22–24.

50. Steven Plaut, "The Man the Gulag Couldn't Break," *The Jewish Press*, Oct. 21, 2009.

51. Beckerman, *When They Come*, 528.

52. For a discussion of how "Solidarity Orthodoxy" developed as an outgrowth of the Soviet Jewry Movement see Ferziger, "American Soviet Jewry Movement."

53. Jacob Birnbaum, personal communication, March 31, 2013.

54. Claudia Puig, "Pop/Rock," Entertainment Calendar, *Los Angeles Times*, Aug. 22, 1989.

55. He started using his Hebrew name Yehudah after being inspired in his tour with Reb Shlomo in Russia. Personal communication, Aug. 31, 2011.

56. For pictures from the end of the concert with Shlomo signing autographs of his picture for Russian children, see http://www.youtube.com/watch?v=L9wh8EeVUVY.

(Michael Ian) Elias, lead singer.[57] Shlomo appeared in Leningrad,[58] Kiev, Vilna, and then returned to Leningrad. He completed his whirlwind tour in Moscow.[59] Twenty shows were held in halls holding thousands of seats, and all sold out.

This was "the first Jewish Music Tour of the Soviet Union,"[60] the first time a Jewish singer with Hebrew stories performed in Soviet concert halls. Stuart Wax and David Jonathan Waksberg from Los Angeles were the driving forces organizing the trip.

Stuart Wax was born May 15, 1957. His father Lazer, a cantorial prodigy who had lost his entire family in the Holocaust, served as the cantor in Congregation Sons of Israel, Woodmere, Long Island. Lazer was involved in inviting Reb Shlomo to perform in his synagogue several times during the years 1968–1972. Wax also would attend Shlomo's summer concerts at Riverhaven in the Catskills bungalow colony. Wax, who was himself musically inclined, became a devoted admirer of Shlomo. In 1988, he set up a company in Los Angeles to promote concerts named Midnight Music Management.[61]

Wax was also a Soviet Jewry activist, and in 1987, he heard about a refusenik named Julia, an orphan connected to one of the long-standing refusenik families. Stuart decided to go to Russia, arrange for a civil marriage and thus enable Julia to leave under the law of "family reunification." It was not simple to obtain a visa. Wax heard that rock and roll singer Billy Joel was planning a tour of the USSR and Wax presented himself as a journalist who would join Joel's entourage.

August 1987 was just after the dawn of glasnost. For the first time, the Soviet Union was allowing its citizens to really sample Western pop

---

For five sections of this concert, see http://www.youtube.com/watch?v=X9gM3T uzBBE&feature=related – "*Vehavienu*"; http://www.youtube.com/watch?v=TlWrA 3Uy75w&feature=related – "*Shalom Aleicheim Malachei Hashalom*"; http://www .youtube.com/watch?v=dU162ZvRfCU&feature=related – "*Siman Tov uMazal Tov*" with spirited dancing; http://www.youtube.com/watch?v=Enw4SlnobEE&feature= related – "*Romemu*"; http://www.youtube.com/watch?v=LqtxoR5444w&feature=re lated – "*Hashiveinu*."

57. Elias later added the background vocals for the record of Neshama and Reb Shlomo, *HaNeshama Shel Shlomo*. See JewishJukeBox.com, http://www.jewishjuke box.com/products/jewish_contemporary_music/434.asp.

58. For video clips from Motzei Shabbat, Sept. 9, 1989 in Leningrad and on Sept. 10, see http://www.youtube.com/watch?v=upeYoKC6TY8&feature=em-subs_digest -newavtr-vrecs; http://www.youtube.com/watch?v=IF1U9IFauyA&feature=youtube.

59. My thanks to Stuart Wax and Yehudah Katz for providing this information.

60. This was the title of the publicity according to Stuart Wax. Much of the information below is from interviews with Stuart Wax during July 2011.

61. Stuart Wax, personal interview.

culture. Joel's concerts were hyped as "the first time an American pop music star had brought a fully staged rock show to the Soviet Union." Actually, other American singers had been to Moscow earlier, however, Joel's concerts were unique. He gave three rock and roll concerts in Moscow and three in Leningrad, and the fans went wild in receiving him.[62]

Wax traveled to Russia with Joel's entourage. "Whenever we met refuseniks they would say 'Billy Joel is nice, but can't you bring us Shlomo Carlebach?'"[63] The refuseniks were suggesting that Carlebach, whose songs and records had been distributed clandestinely in the USSR for close to a decade, would have a direct effect on Soviet Jewry.

David Waksberg was an activist with hundreds of connections with refuseniks. Waksberg was born December 14, 1956 in New York City and as a young student became involved in the SSSJ. In 1981, he moved to California and began working for the Bay Area Council for Soviet Jews (BACSJ), soon becoming the Executive Director. In 1985, he became National Vice-President of UCSJ, the Union of Councils for Soviet Jews. Shlomo's tour in 1989 was a major achievement for Waksberg.[64]

From the Soviet side, it was refusenik Boris Kelman who met with Waksberg. Kelman was the inspirational force behind the Jewish Cultural Society of Leningrad, the first Jewish cultural group to receive official recognition in the USSR. Waksberg had deliberately decided to work in partnership with Soviet Jewish groups rather than on an official basis with the Soviet government. The tour was presented as part of glasnost and perestroika. Stuart Wax raised close to $100,000 and arranged for Reb Shlomo to be paid $15,000.[65] Shlomo, true to his generous and benevolent nature, distributed the money to enable others to join the trip and about 30–40 people joined his entourage. Wax describes his surprise at discovering how the trip eventually unfolded:

> At first we thought that we were simply going to be playing in refuseniks' private homes or for small groups. Instead, we found

---

62. Michael Sauter, "Billy Joel: To Russia With Love," Ew.com Entertainment, Aug. 9, 1996, http://www.ew.com/ew/article/0,,293632,00.html.

63. Wax, personal communication, July 13, 2011.

64. David Waksberg Papers, American Jewish Historical Society, New York, FindingAids.cjh.org, http://findingaids.cjh.org/?pID=973769.

65. Wax told me: "At the time, I represented Denise Rich as a songwriter, and I asked her if the Rich Foundation would fund the tour. She introduced me to Abraham Kalikow of the Rich Foundation, and $50,000 was pledged. Then the Wiesenthal Center gave $10,000, the LA Jewish Federation $5,000, and with David Waxberg's help, I raised another $25,000 from individuals in San Francisco, New York, and Los Angeles."

large concert halls each having 1,500–2,500 seats. In Vilna we even played in a giant stadium.[66]

In personal encounters with Russian Jews, Shlomo explained his outlook on life and justified an optimistic joy in affirming Jewishness.[67] In an interview in Leningrad, Shlomo explained the rationale of his warm welcoming attitude to every person he met and justified his vision as part of a Divine Plan for the chosen people to spread a universal message of love to all:

> I told the steel workers we always pray to God that our dreams should be fulfilled . . . But, I never dreamt I would play for the steelworkers in Leningrad. Imagine I would have prayed to God, please fulfill my dreams, I would never have played in Leningrad for the steelworkers. The truth is that God has even better dreams for us . . . God's dreams are so much more beautiful. We have to pray that God should fulfill history . . . the dream that God has for the world . . . If we Jewish people want to make it in the world . . . my heart has to be filled with tomorrow . . . I have to assume that every person I meet is my brother, my best brother . . . we are the chosen people, because God gave us the strength to do it, it takes heavenly strength to do it.[68]

In the mornings, Shlomo would visit local schools to sing and meet with the children. In Leningrad, on a Thursday morning, Shlomo arranged for people to be called up to the Torah. People came up with their Russian names, and on the spot, Shlomo would suggest a Jewish name. As the women's section in the upstairs balcony was crowded, Shlomo asked for the women to come downstairs and sit behind a makeshift *mechitza* of chairs. For some, this was the first time in their lives that they ever heard a Torah reading, and tears rolled down from their eyes. Joel Segal, a San Francisco attorney who joined the tour, exclaimed: "It was amazing . . . I've never seen such joy and enthusiasm in my entire life."[69]

One of the reasons for the unprecedented success was that surprisingly

---

66. Wax, personal communication, July 13, 2011.

67. See the discussion in the Leningrad Synagogue where a Russian Jew asked "just one question," why are you so happy and joyous, why not be in mourning? Video footage posted courtesy of Stuart Wax at http://www.bestjewishvideos.com/?best -video=russian-to-shlomo-carlebach-why-are-you-so-happy.

68. Slightly edited from a 2-minute excerpt of an interview with Reb Shlomo in Leningrad (preserved by Stuart Wax) – http://www.youtube.com/watch?v=re-uZL 11dvY&sns=fb.

69. Winston Pickett, "A Rockin' Rabbi Rocks the USSR," *Jewish Exponent*, Oct. 20,

enough, the Soviet government promoted the concerts, rented the halls, and sold the tickets. The interest in a cultural exchange was part of the thawing of relations after the Cold War, and the Soviets utilized this opportunity to garner revenues to benefit the victims of the earthquake in Armenia.[70] The earthquake had hit the Leninakan-Spitak-Kirovakan area of northern Armenia on December 7, 1988. At least 25,000 people were killed, 19,000 injured, and 500,000 left homeless. More than 20 towns and 342 villages were affected, and 58 of them were completely destroyed. Damage totaled 16.2 billion U.S. dollars.[71] Despite the Cold War, Mikhail Gorbachev had turned to the West for humanitarian help. The cultural exchange which brought Shlomo to Russia was a natural for fundraising. From the perspective of the Jewish organizers, it was a momentous opportunity to reach Soviet Jewry.

In a report written on February 22, 1990 to Abraham Kalikow of the Rich Foundation, David Waksberg summed up the incredible success of Carlebach's Jewish Music Tour of the USSR:

> This tour was historic by all accounts. We reached approximately *60,000 Jews* in the Soviet Union. We produced a major Jewish cultural event in each city visited by our tour. In Leningrad and in Kiev, Shlomo led services at the synagogue . . . In Moscow, Shlomo led a group in public song on the Arbat,[72] surely a first. Most importantly, those who were touched by this tour were able to reclaim pride and dignity in their Jewish identities. . . . The tour succeeded not only in content, in bringing Yiddishkeit to Soviet Jews, but in . . . promoting self-help cultural renewal efforts by Soviet Jewry groups.[73]

1989, 3, 44. The article was originally published as "First-ever Cultural Tour Inspires Thousands of Jews . . ." in *The Northern California Jewish Bulletin*, Oct. 6, 1989.

70. Reb Shlomo mentions this as an aside in his interview with Zachary Goldman, *His Life,* third part of the interview, segment 2:50–4:30, http://www.youtube.com/watch?v=cMZzuvLdGBY&annotation_id=annotation_793120&feature=iv.

71. "Historic Earthquakes – Spitak, Armenia," U.S. Geological Survey. See earthquake.usgs.gov, http://earthquake.usgs.gov/earthquakes/world/events/1988_12_07.php.

72. The Arbat is a kilometer long pedestrian street in the historical center of Moscow. During perestroika, the restructuring of the Soviet political and economic system in the late 1980s, the street was a gathering place for informal youth movements and street musicians and artists.

73. David Waksberg correspondence to Abraham Kalikow, Rich Foundation, 4 Rue De Lota, Paris, France. My thanks to the American Jewish Historical Society, New York, for sending me this letter found in the Waksberg Papers, box 6, folder 6, Carlebach, Shlomo, 1989.

In a video interview with Zachary Goldman, Shlomo exclaimed: The concerts were "fire, fire," there was so much holiness.[74] Stuart Wax recalls Shlomo exhorting his entourage before embarking on the trip, "many of our Russian brothers have never smiled before; so few of them have known real joy. It is our mission to make them smile; it is our mission to bring them joy!"[75]

At the concert in Leningrad, Reb Shlomo asked the crowd, whom do you think is on this stage? It is not only the band you see here, but all our ancestors, Abraham, Isaac, and Jacob. He exhorted his listeners to go out and proudly say hello to everyone on the street. Let all know that we are Jewish.[76] On Motzei Shabbat, September 23, 1989, Shlomo and the band organized an after-midnight *Selichot* program at the Leningrad Railroad Station.[77]

For Friday evening services in Kiev, after five sold-out concerts, more than 1,000 people lined up outside the Central Synagogue. The next morning, on Shabbat, R. Shlomo organized bar mitzvah *aliyot* for six Jewish boys from Kiev.[78]

Shlomo is quoted as proclaiming: "You can't imagine the depth, the emotion, the closeness. Imagine 2,800 people in the audience in Moscow for our last concert of the tour. For the last song, everyone got up from their seats and came close to the stage and held each other." All told, an estimated 50,000 Soviet Jews, most with little or no Jewish background, "came away with their first dose of Yiddishkeit."[79]

Darlene Rose who participated in the tour described Reb Shlomo's "loving, strengthening, and stirring spiritual leadership as he reached out to over 50,000 Soviet Jews in three weeks."[80] Darlene quoted Shlomo's message to the Russian audiences: "The job of a Jew is to warm up the world and make it beautiful again."[81]

Indeed, Shlomo's message was to awaken the warmth, the mission, and the love for Jerusalem. He told a Hasidic parable about Rebbe Elimelech

---

74. Zachary Goldman, *His Life*, third part of the video interview, segment 4:16, posted at http://www.youtube.com/watch?v=cMZzuvLdGBY&annotation_id=annotation_793120&feature=iv

75. Mandelbaum, *Holy Brother*, xxxiv.

76. This and the entire concert can be heard in a downloadable audio recording, 613.org, http://www.613.org/music/niggun.html.

77. Yehudah Katz told me that Shlomo was scheduled to leave Leningard that evening in order to arrive on time to play in Kiev, therefore they used the venue of the Railroad Station for the musical *Selichot*.

78. Pickett, "A Rockin' Rabbi."

79. Ibid., 3.

80. Darlene Rose, "Holy Sister," *Kol Chevra*, vol. 10, 2004, 53–55.

81. Darlene Rose, "Watch Me!," *Kol Chevra*, vol. 7, 2000, 192–193.

of Lizensk who was sick and couldn't eat. So he asked his son (R. Lazer) to bring him the soup of the wife of the impoverished water carrier. His son went and asked for the soup. She explained that once when R. Elimelech visited her, she didn't have anything to offer except warm water. So she took a spoon and stirred the warm water and prayed to God, "I have nothing, but You have so much, can You please put a little bit of paradise in this warm water." The parable, Shlomo explained, is that each person has a drop of warmth in his heart, a bit of paradise, and can give it to warm the world:[82]

> Some of us don't even know the alphabet, but everyone has a little warmth in their heart, so I bless you and me that God should put a little bit of paradise in this warm drop of water. When you love someone very much, this one drop can give water to the whole world. The world is so thirsty for that warm water . . . and sometimes I have the feeling that the world is angry at us that we don't give enough warm water. But you know where the headquarters of the warm water is? Where the kitchen is where the Jews warm the holy water is? It is Jerusalem. The dream of every Jew that one day the whole world is coming to Jerusalem, the holy city for just one prayer and I can swear to you that on that day there will be peace in the world, so much goodness.[83]

In November 1989, the Berlin Wall began to be taken down. By 1990, as the Gorbachev-era reforms took hold, the Soviet Union opened its gates, and close to two million Jews eventually emigrated.[84]

When Shlomo returned to California, he appeared in concert on February 18, 1990 at Temple Beth Shalom in Santa Ana, Orange County[85] and recounted with pathos his impressions from visiting Russia. He dramatically portrayed the yearning of Russian Jews to discover their heritage as "one of the holiest experiences" in my life:

---

82. This story is transcribed in Midlo, *Lamed Vav*, 181–183. The version there is that R. Lazer discovers the secret of the "holy soup" of Malka which has a taste of paradise inside because of the genuine heartfelt tears, and understands that it "can *mamash* bring people back to life."

83. 613.org, http://www.613.org/music/niggun.html. See the section "Reb Shlomo Carlebach Concert in Russia 1989."

84. In 1990, 181,802 Jews emigrated; 178,566 in 1991; 108,292 in 1992; 101,134 in 1993. By the end of the 1990s, over one million Soviet Jews had immigrated to Israel. Another half a million had gone to the United States, and about 200,000 to other countries in the West, such as Germany. See Beckerman, *When They Come*, 528.

85. *Los Angeles Times*, Feb. 17, 1990, 19.

How can I tell you what we felt, Richard[86] and I, Darlene and all the people who were with us in Russia, what we felt when we had the privilege of uplifting the spirits of our brothers and sisters. It was not from this world. . . . Their inside is *so* pure, *so* holy. . . . They want something *so* deep, and *so* holy and *so* exalted.[87]

Was this optimistic naïveté? After all, the vast majority of Soviet Jews were not refuseniks and many were not even Zionists.[88] But it is through the prism of a Hasidic-Kabbalistic Messianic vision that Reb Shlomo observed sparks of holiness revealing themselves in the simple Jews who came to his concerts seeking to find a connection to their Jewish roots. In his vision, these were "the white fire" Jews. They had a hidden, unperceivable fire inside, connecting them to the long lost traditions.

Shlomo's passionate plea to empathize with Soviet Jews stirred a chord of Jewish solidarity in his audiences while simultaneously inspiring them to enliven their own spiritual lives as Jews. But his humanitarian passion was also fired up by a drive to reach out with a message of love and hope to non-Jews behind the Iron Curtain. This was dramatically demonstrated in his concert tour of Poland in January 1989.

3.   LOVE AND HOPE IN POLAND (JANUARY 1989)

From January 1–10, 1989, Reb Shlomo visited Warsaw, Cracow, Majdaneck, Biala, and Lodz, giving eight concerts in ten days. He was the first openly religious Jew to perform in Poland since the 1967–1968 wave of anti-Semitism in Communist Poland.[89]

In agreeing to visit Poland, Shlomo faced three challenges. First, Poland was still under Communist domination. Could he travel and perform freely and easily? Second, this was the land that had come to symbolize

---

86. Shlomo referred here to Richard Hardy, a classically trained saxophone, horns, flute, and woodwinds player who performed with the Denver Symphony Orchestra. Darlene Rose notes that Richard "had a special place in Shlomo's heart, as he was the only non-Jewish musician on the tour to Russia and he surprised Shlomo by coming to this concert in Orange County." Darlene Rose, personal communication, April 16, 2013.

87. See http://www.youtube.com/watch?v=upeYoKC6TY8&feature=related; http://www.youtube.com/watch?v=upeYoKC6TY8&feature=em-subs_digest-new avtr-vrecs. The video clips here were taken in Leningrad on Sept. 9 at midnight (this was Saturday night) and Sunday noon on Sept. 10, 1989.

88. Beckerman, *When They Come*, 529.

89. Menachem Daum, "Opening the Gates – A Film in Progress," *Kol Chevra*, vol. 15, 2009, 9–10.

the extermination camps filled with the most horrifying traumatic atrocities. Would his performance be seen as an act of forgiveness for the past? Finally, this would be the first time a rabbi from the Western world would sing religious songs and tell Hasidic stories in Polish concert halls. How would the predominantly Catholic population receive him?

The significance of this visit is illustrated in the story of Miroslawa (Mira) and Andrzej Boryna, two underground anti-Communist activists.[90] For a decade, Mira and Andrzej had been persecuted by Communist authorities.[91] In Stargard Szczeciński, northwestern Poland, Mira and Andrzej established The Association of Spiritual Unity for Love, Light and Life and organized a festival-conference in Cracow, Poland entitled a Week of Wholeness and Healing, April 25–May 1, 1988. There they met Reb Zalman who suggested contacting Reb Shlomo. In January 1989, when Mira and Andrezej heard that Reb Shlomo was visiting Poland, they phoned and were immediately invited to his hotel. They flew to Cracow and joined Shlomo on the full day bus trip around the city and then in his walk towards the Slowacki Theatre. Along the way, Shlomo encountered people on the streets and invited them. Before long, about 100 people were following, all personally invited to the concert. When the entourage arrived at the hall, it was packed and there were no more tickets. Mira Boryna:

> Rabbi Carlebach went in through the back door. Like small puppies, we grabbed the sides of his long black coat and followed him. There were no empty seats so we sat on the edge of the stage by the curtain.[92]

When Shlomo asked the audience to get on stage, Mira and Andrej were closest and quickly joined to dance.[93] Mira recalls: "My memory of the concert is so vivid and I just sense the atmosphere and Blessing and Peace that came from his singing."

Subsequent to Shlomo's 1989 visit, Mira and Andrzej set up a program

---

90. The description here is based on email correspondence with Mira during July 2011.

91. Andrzej was interrogated and beaten by the SB (*Sluzba Bezpieczenstwa*, Communist Security Services) for his role in Solidarity strikes in Toruń and Stargard Szczeciński.

92. Personal correspondence of Miroslawa Boryna, July 11, 2011.

93. Mira can be seen (with long brown hair) in segment 5:20–5:28 of the film clip from this concert See below for more details of Menachem Daum's film, PBS.org, http://www.pbs.org/wnet/religionandethics/episodes/may-2-2008/shlomo-carle bach/77/.

to spread music for peace in Poland called Ananda Music[94] with Reb Shlomo as a "spiritual patron."[95]

Reb Shlomo's trip to Poland was conceived by Chana Fisher, a New Yorker, and her friend Greizyna Powle, a sociologist from Warsaw.[96] The Polish host was Andrew Souchichinski from the Art Studio Center who coordinated the technical planning and the concerts. Reb Shlomo brought along a large group of his followers.[97]

The actual planning was engineered by Rabbi Yechezkel (Chaskel) Besser, director of Central European Programs for the Ronald S. Lauder Foundation. His brother-in-law, Nachman Elbaum,[98] organized the travel details.[99] Besser was astounded to see "what a colossal impact" Shlomo had on the *non-Jews* who listened to his songs and speeches. "I was stupefied. The people just went wild about him," said Besser.[100]

Chaskel Besser (1923–2010) was born in Katowice, Poland. In 1939, with the ominous Nazi dangers, his parents immigrated to Palestine. Chaskel was a boy of 16 studying in the Radomsker Yeshiva in Lodz, and he planned to join his parents when the yeshiva vacation was to begin in July 1939. As it turned out, his safe passage out of Poland was nothing short of miraculous.[101] The dual Nazi and Soviet invasions of Poland began September 1, 1939 and with it the devastation of Jewish life in Poland.

In 1949, after his father died in Israel, R. Besser moved with his wife Liba and their two small children to New York where he had been doing

---

94. In 2005, it evolved into the BORYNA Foundation Centre of Sound and Music Therapy. On the BORYNA Foundation, see BorynaFoundation.com, http://www.borynafoundation.com/index.php?option=com_content&view=article&id=120&Itemid=120.

95. BorynaFoundation.com, http://www.borynafoundation.com/index.php?option=com_content&view=article&id=177&Itemid=75.

96. Greizna first saw Reb Shlomo during a visit to New York and brought some of his tape cassettes back to Poland where she organized tape recorded concerts of his music in Warsaw. See Rabbi Sammy H. Intrator, "On the Road with Reb Shlomo," special issue on Poland, *Hakrev Ushma* (*Connections*), vol. 4, issue 2, 1989, 19–30.

97. See Intrator, "On the Road," especially pp. 21, 28–29.

98. Rabbi Nachman Elbaum, the founder of Ideal Tours, is the son of Rabbi Yitzchok Isaac Elbaum (1900–1986), a Holocaust survivor from Warsaw. He organized many tours to Russia and Ukraine.

99. This is what Reb Shlomo says in an interview to Zachary Goldman, *His Life*, third part of the interview, segment 2:30–2:45. In the interview, Shlomo mentions the trip to Russia, but the details are confused with his trip to Poland, http://www.youtube.com/watch?v=cMZzuvLdGBY&annotation_id=annotation_793120&feature=iv.

100. Yudelson and Birnbaum, "Shlomo Carlebach."

101. My thanks to Rabbi Shlomo Besser, son of Chaskel, for this information, Nov. 4, 2012.

business. Initially, they lived in Crown Heights. In 1952, they moved to 84th St. in Manhattan and eventually Chaskel became the spiritual leader of Bnei Yisroel Chaim on 353 West 84th Street, just five blocks from the Carlebach Shul.[102]

It was the Lubavitcher Rebbe who introduced the two men sometime around 1952.[103] In the early 1980s, Rabbi Besser began devoting his life to reviving Jewish life in Poland[104] and restoring hundreds of Jewish cemeteries.[105] When he felt that the time was ripe to bring Jewish music to Poland, he approached Shlomo telling him how a concert tour could bring thousands of Polish Jews to reclaim their Jewish identity.

The trip to Poland was documented with video coverage thanks to Menachem Daum who was invited by R. Sammy Intrator to join the entourage.[106] The live footage captures the unique experience of the Polish people and shows how this was not merely a cultural concert tour. It became a breakthrough in altering stereotypes and breaking down animosity. Daum reported:

> When we got off the plane, the television crews and reporters gathered around right by Carlebach. They had heard a singing rabbi was coming to Poland, and they asked him what he would like to accomplish . . . Shlomo told the reporters, "I'd like to shake the hand of every man, woman, and child in Poland." That was an answer I hadn't anticipated; nor had the Polish media. They played this clip over and over throughout Poland, so the entire ten days we were there, wherever we went, people had already seen this clip . . . They couldn't get enough of his stories and songs. To me it was quite amazing.[107]

---

102. See Warren Kozak, *The Rabbi of 84th Street: The Extraordinary Life of Haskel Besser* (New York: 2005). Vosizneias.com, http://www.vosizneias.com/49003/2010/02/09/new-york-noted-asken-reb-chaskel-besser-passes-away.

103. See above for the story of the Rebbe's request and how Chaskel set up employment for Marilyn who was studying in Shlomo's TSGG group in 1951–1952. Personal communications from Rabbi Shlomo Besser, Nov. 4, 2012.

104. In a eulogy for Chaskel Besser, the Chief Rabbi of Poland, Rabbi Michael Schudrich, commended Besser as the person who "started the Jewish revival in Poland" and as "the spiritual father of everything that was rekindled and re-emerged here in Poland." JTA – *The Jewish Daily Forward*, Feb. 10, 2010, Forward.com, http://www.forward.com/articles/125374/#ixzz1OtYhQWJZ.

105. "Orthodox Jews, Polish Government in Accord on Jewish Cemeteries," *Jewish Telegraphic Agency*, Sept. 2, 1983.

106. Daum's particular interest in filming Shlomo's trip is because Daum was born on Oct. 5, 1946 in a displaced persons camp in Germany to Polish parents who survived the Holocaust and came to America in May 1951.

107. Interview with Menachem Daum, *Religion & Ethics Newsweekly*, April 29,

Daum explained how Reb Shlomo responded to the Holocaust by stressing how every individual can become God's partner in fixing the world and replace anger with love and joy:

> After the Holocaust it's so easy to be angry at the world, and it's so easy to condemn the world. But we have to continue to love the world. The most important thing today every person has to do is to cleanse their hearts from anger, and fill the heart with a lot of joy.[108]

In Majdaneck, Reb Shlomo said: "On the one hand, I cannot forget what happened in Europe. On the other, I know that I have to help rebuild a new world." He explained that he was bringing a unique message of religious Jewish Orthodoxy. Precisely because Poland is the site of extermination camps, "that's the very reason that it makes Poland a prime choice for change." Shlomo explained that honoring the six million entails returning to their burial grounds and swearing to them "that we shall dedicate ourselves to spreading their values and their dreams to the entire world." He cited a biblical precedent to connect the locus of tragedy to the beginning of redemptive healing:

> In the Bible we find that Shechem is the city where Dina was raped. Years later it was the city where the brothers sold Joseph and the split of the twelve tribes began. But it's also the headquarters for the tribe of Joseph who symbolizes the start of the redemption.[109]

In the concert hall in Bielsko Biala, Reb Shlomo asked how can we "repair the hate of the past?" His answer: "Only by filling ourselves with absolute and complete love and joy."[110] He taught a song:

> Let the whole world get together again. Let the whole world be filled with joy again. Let the salvation of the world grow every second.[111]

In Cracow, Reb Shlomo performed at The Jewish Culture Festival (*Festiwal Kultury Żydowskiej w Krakowie*) in the former Jewish district

---

2005, Episode # 835, PBS.org, http://www.pbs.org/wnet/religionandethics/week835/interview.html.

108. Adapted/edited from PBS.org, http://www.pbs.org/wnet/religionandethics/week1135/profile.html; http://www.youtube.com/watch?v=5KxhJFeLr_w&feature=related; http://wn.com/Yeshiva_Rabbi_Chaim_Berlin.

109. Transcribed by Rabbi Sam Intrator and printed in *Hakrev Ushma* (*Connections*), April 29, 1989.

110. Intrator, "On the Road," 21.

111. Transcribed by Emuna Witt and printed in *Kol Chevra*, vol. 6, 1999, 16–17.

of Kazimierz. This festival was launched in 1988 by Janusz Makuch and Krzysztof Gierat.[112] Makuch was amazed to see Carlebach moving from row to row, literally shaking hands with all 600 members of the audience:

> It was amazing, because for most of them, this was the first time they were seeing a rabbi face to face . . . The only previous contact they'd had with rabbis had been visiting their graves.[113]

There were merely 300 Jews in Cracow, compared with a pre-war population of about 70,000. Reb Shlomo visited the synagogues in Kazimierz, including the synagogue named after R. Moshe Isserles (1520–1572).[114] There he composed his famous "Cracow Niggun." Later, as a promo to this tune, Shlomo would describe his dream where he saw Jews boarding the trains, arriving at an extermination camp, and walking towards the doors. Suddenly, in the dream, all the Jews are leaving, dressed in white with big smiles on their faces.[115]

From Cracow, Reb Shlomo and his entourage traveled five hours by bus to spend the Shabbat in Warsaw. Reb Shlomo led a spirited Friday evening service at the Nozyk Shul, the only synagogue in Warsaw to survive the ghetto's destruction. The Shabbat morning highlight was a bar mitzvah celebration for Yahad Witt, oldest son of Shlomo's "right-hand man" from Israel, Rabbi Yehoshua Witt.[116]

On Motzei Shabbat, January 7, 1989, Reb Shlomo appeared in concert at the Warsaw Yiddish Theater. Afterwards he attended a reception in his honor at the home of Alice Le Maistre, the U.S. cultural attaché in Poland. Reb Shlomo returned to his hotel after midnight where several hundred people awaited him to celebrate the engagement ceremony

---

112. Craig S. Smith, "In Poland, a Jewish Revival Thrives – Minus Jews," *New York Times,* July 12, 2007, NYTimes.com, http://www.nytimes.com/2007/07/12/world/europe/12krakow.html?pagewanted=1&ei=5124&en=ceb7c359b7a7976a&ex=1341979200&partner=permalink&exprod=permalink.

113. Makuch as quoted by Schaechter, "Monday Music," *The Jewish Daily Forward.*

114. Sacred-Destinations.com, http://www.sacred-destinations.com/poland/krakow-remuh-synagogue-and-cemetery.htm; http://www.krakow-info.com/synagogs.htm.

115. Versions of this story and tune can be heard: on http://www.youtube.com/watch?v=sbKgrRoo7kA; http://www.youtube.com/watch?v=6sS736syJUA&feature=related; http://www.youtube.com/watch?v=uPbNv4g-kRM&feature=related; It is recorded on several albums such as *A Melava Malka in Notting Hill* (1994) and *Shabbos Songs.* See Last.FM, http://www.last.fm/music/Shlomo+Carlebach/_/Cracow+Nigun. For the musical notes, see JewishGuitarChords.com, http://jewishguitarchords.com/Carlebach_Krakow.txt.

116. Intrator, "On the Road," 23–24. Personal interview with Yahad Witt, Sept. 11, 2012.

of Nathan Moheban, a Jewish Iranian living in Brooklyn, to Karen Shulman.[117] The couple had met at Shlomo's concert on Hanukkah in December 1988. Reb Shlomo related the story of how he had discovered Karen as a spiritual seeker when he came for Shabbat to the Omega Institute. Then in December 1988 Karen had met Nathan at Shlomo's Hanukkah concert in New York. Also joining in the engagement party were members of the Israeli basketball team, Maccabi Tel Aviv, who had earlier in the night defeated their Polish rivals and entered the European championship finals.[118]

Gebert Constanty, Shlomo's interpreter, described the excitement in Warsaw – "Carlebach's concert was the first public Jewish event since the fall of the government, and everyone was absolutely enthusiastic." Stan Krajewski, a Jewish philosophy professor at the University of Warsaw, recalls that by the end of the Warsaw concert, many in the audience had joined Carlebach on the stage singing "*Lemaan Achai*" Early Sunday morning, Stan and Monika, his wife, invited Reb Shlomo to their apartment.[119] The Krajewski home contained a Jewish library and was a meeting place for Polish dissidents, part of a growing movement of intellectual groups dedicated to renewing the glory of Polish Jewry. Many had only recently discovered their Jewish roots. Reb Shlomo's visit gave the group a new momentum.[120] Menachem Daum explains:

> The great accomplishment of Shlomo's visit was that he started the process which emboldened hidden Jews to come out of the closet. For many years, long before Shlomo arrived, many Poles saw the Jew as the "anti-Pole," as only caring about their own and exploiting Poles. The Jews were also blamed by many Poles as having imposed Communism on occupied Poland against Polish national interests. So thousands with Jewish ancestors felt they had to hide their Jewish background from their Polish neighbors. Shlomo's embrace of Poland and Poles showed that one could be a real Jew and care about every single Pole. Shlomo's behavior and warmth started a gradual process, accelerated by Pope John Paul's

---

117. Also joining in the engagement party were members of the Israeli basketball team, Maccabi Tel Aviv, who had earlier in the night defeated their Polish rivals and entered the European championship finals.

118. Intrator, "On the Road," 27.

119. Rukhl Schaechter, "Monday Music: Shlomo Carlebach in Poland," *The Jewish Daily Forward*, April 9, 2012, Blogs.Forward.com, http://blogs.forward.com/the-arty-semite/153814/monday-music-shlomo-carlebach-in-poland. The original Yiddish version was published on March 23, 2012.

120. Intrator, "On the Road," 28.

teachings about Jews, to the point where today it is actually exotic and chic in Poland to admit having Jewish ancestors.[121]

Due to the tremendous demand for tickets, two more concerts were added on Sunday in Warsaw in the afternoon and evening. The final concert was held on January 9 in Lodz. Every seat in this magnificent grand opera theater was taken and soon the gigantic stage filled with hundreds dancing ecstatically.[122]

Throughout the trip, Menachem Daum recorded Reb Shlomo's explanations. One is an optimistic message recited in a sing-song:

> When I walked the gas chambers it was clear to me – dawn is breaking. I want you to know, my beautiful friends, don't ever give up on the world. Don't ever give up on any human being, because we all are God's image.

Daum's film concluded with a universal exhortation by Shlomo: "My message is that there's one God. We are one world. We are all brothers and sisters."[123]

In sum, Shlomo developed a boldly conciliatory approach of love towards the Polish people. When challenged how he could shake hands and even hug children of the perpetrators, he replied: "If we had two hearts like we have two arms and two legs, then one heart could be used for love and the other one for hate. Since I have but one heart, then I don't have the luxury of hating anyone."[124]

In 1990, the first free and democratic elections in Poland since World War II brought an end to Communist dominance and a victory for the Solidarity party. Lech Walesa won the presidency in December 1990 heralding the collapse of Communism across Eastern Europe. Viewed in this context, Shlomo's message of love and hope to Poland was part of both the spiritual-cultural revolution and the religious revival of Polish Jewry.

---

121. Email correspondence with Menachem Daum, June 3, 2012.

122. Intrator, "On the Road," 29.

123. Menachem Daum and Oren Rudavsky, "Hiding and Seeking: Faith and Tolerance after the Holocaust," *Religion & Ethics Newsweekly*, May 2, 2008, PBS.org, http://www.pbs.org/wnet/religionandethics/week1135/profile.html; http://www.youtube.com/user/fullofcontradictions#p/u/4/5KxhJFeLr_w; http://www.youtube.com/user/fullofcontradictions#p/u/3/y5j-vbvDoeo.

124. Interview of Menachem Daum with Mimi Feigelson, Aug. 1995 where she attributes this quote to Reb Shlomo.

CHAPTER 10

Jewish Renewal in the U.S.

1. WORLD SYMPOSIUM FOR HUMANITY, DECEMBER 1976

There were Swamis, Yogis, Indian medicine men, and psychological experts, but Reb Shlomo was the only overt Jewish presenter at the World Symposium for Humanity at the Hyatt Regency Hotel in Vancouver, British Columbia, Canada, November 27–December 4, 1976.[1] Stephen Gaskin, the Master of Ceremonies, invited Shlomo to the closing night, Saturday evening, December 4. The Grand Ballroom was dimmed and Shlomo led a *Havdala* candle ceremony. This is one of the most moving performances of Reb Shlomo. His message was a radical interpretation of the first fratricide. True, that the Bible tells how Cain murdered Abel. True, that throughout history, and especially in the Holocaust, the Cains of the world murdered their brothers Abel. But in the future, there will be a resurrection and the brothers will be reconciled. The audience swayed together in a trance-like state of ecstasy and fraternity:[2]

> And our holy rabbis tell us that for three days,
> Cain was lying next to Abel, begging him.
> And our holy rabbis teach us that all of nature,
>   the whole world, was crying with him.
> Now my most darling friends, on the great day,

---

1. The event was sponsored by the 3HO Foundation (Healthy, Happy, Holy Organization) led by Yogi Bhajan.

2. GreenStar.org, http://www.greenstar.org/remember/shlomo-video.htm; http://www.youtube.com/watch?v=qvWWBK91lSg; Video.Yehudim.net, http://video.yehudim.net/play.php?vid=313. See also IsaacWalters.com, http://www.isaacwalters.com/play/qvWWBK91lSg/Reb_shlomo_carlebach-The_Tragedy_of_Cain_and_Abel.html.

on that great day we are waiting for, the most unbelievable thing
will happen. All the Cains of the world will lie next to the Abels
they killed,

and they will begin to cry. . . .

And they will say, my precious brother, forgive me Forgive me . . .
I am begging you, forgive me for being angry at you. I am begging
you, come back. I am begging you, come back.

So on that great day, the miracle will happen: Abel will open his
eyes. And he and Cain, what a moment . . . The world has not been
privileged to feel the love Between brother and brother, Between
one human being and the other, That will be on that day. Then
Cain and Abel will begin to dance, And the whole world will join
them. And all the creatures of the world will begin to dance. Let
it be soon . . . let it be soon . . .

Let it be soon, let it be soon, let it be soon.

The style, structure, and hyperbole of this "half story, half song" resonate
as if taken from a *midrash*. All of nature, the whole world, is crying with
Cain, begging for forgiveness. Then the miracle occurs and Abel opens
his eyes. Brotherly love is restored. Cain and Abel dance together. The
entire creation joins. Shlomo has invented a *midrash* suited specially for
a universalistic approach to interfaith outreach.

At the Symposium, Reb Shlomo's *midrash* made an indelible impression on Yitzhak (Yitz) Hankin, who at the time was 29 years old.
Many years later, in a sermon as the senior rabbi at Temple Beth Israel
in Oregon, Yitz retold the Carlebach *midrash* of Cain and Abel as an
illustration of how to eliminate prejudices and religious animosity and
transform the world into a trusting and compassionate place.[3]

Shlomo himself would reuse this Cain and Abel *midrash* for rebuking
Jewish audiences for not going out to the world and teaching the joy of
loving God. According to this alternative version, the sin of Abel was that
he did not teach Cain the secret of joy in serving God. When Messiah
arrives, God will turn the clock back. It will be as if there never was
persecution or destruction of the Holy Temple. Cain will beg Abel, please
do not remain dead. Open your eyes. The nations will plead for the revival
of the Jewish people and demand that they openly teach the secrets to
serving God. They will challenge the Jews to fulfill their task and truly be
a light to the nations.[4]

---

3. The sermon was given on Rosh Hashana, September 29, 2008, TBIEugene.org,
http://www.tbieugene.org/RYHH_ErevRH_5769.html.

4. This is the version of the story brought in Yahad Witt, *Open Gates of the Heart,*

About 3,000 people attended this week-long symposium in 1976. Young Jewish people were everywhere, yet hidden, wearing turbans and following Yogis.[5] For some of them this became a life-changing experience.

Avraham Moskowitz was in his last year of Naturopathic School in Seattle and nominally Jewish. He had come to the symposium out of curiosity to see this "smorgasbord of spirituality." He was attracted by the "gathering of all the top holy men" at the Hyatt. Avraham was particularly impressed when a little 14-year old boy came to Shlomo before Shabbat and told him that he never had a bar mitzvah. Not only did Shlomo take the boy the next day to a local Orthodox synagogue and arrange for his *aliyah*, but at the closing event of the conference, Shlomo invited the bar mitzvah boy to be his guest on stage and accompany him by drumming:

> He absolutely shone from happiness underneath this huge, opulent chandelier, surrounded by circle after circle of swaying spiritual seekers in turbans, feathers, barefoot . . . Instead of the usual Om we were singing Shalom. The heights were reached.

The next morning, Avraham approached Shlomo and asked: "Brother, are you for real?" Shlomo responded by inviting Avraham to Moshav Me'or Modi'im. After much deliberation, Avraham decided, "I had to find out if there was something to this Jewish business or if it was all nonsense." So Avraham went to Israel and spent six years in yeshiva study.[6]

Yitz Hankin had met Reb Shlomo in 1974 at the University of Oregon and had been in touch with him several times. Yitz was an accomplished cellist and a member of the Eugene Symphony Orchestra. He began taking an interest in Shlomo's Jewish music. At the momentous closing evening in the Grand Ballroom, Reb Shlomo invited several musicians to join him on stage including Yitz with his cello and Stephen Gaskin with his drums. Together they led a musical finale of the Symposium.

Shonna Husbands also attended the World Symposium. Later she was to recount what a powerful impact that evening made:

> The teachings and songs of Reb Shlomo brought the whole group energy together, singing as one vibrant illuminated pod of humanity, colorfully diverse, yet united fully in spirit. With tears in my eyes, he became my Rebbe that night.[7]

---

vol. 3, 398–399 [Hebrew].

5. Shonna Husbands-Hankin, "Bridging Worlds," *Kol Chevra*, vol. 8, 2001, 127.

6. Avraham Moskowitz, "The First and Last Time I Met Shlomo," *Kol Chevra*, vol. 6, Nov. 1999, 35–36.

7. Shonna Husbands-Hankin, "Radiant Souls," *Kol Chevra*, vol. 17, 2011, 78–79.

As the World Symposium was closing, several Jewish seekers gathered to plan their own Jewish Spiritual Gathering. The result was the *first* Northwest Jewish Spiritual Gathering.

2.   JEWISH RENEWAL IN THE PACIFIC NORTHWEST

Just as the 1966 Berkeley Festival paved the way for Reb Shlomo to inspire a hippie generation in San Francisco, now the 1976 Symposium in Vancouver served as a catalyst for spiritual renewal in the Pacific Northwest. Three couples who met at the Symposium decided to organize a weekend with Reb Shlomo. They found a place midway between Vancouver and Portland, Camp Solomon Schechter, near Olympia, the capital city of Washington. The Shabbat weekend took place on March 18–20, 1977. A contingent from the AMB (Aquarian Minyan of Berkeley) drove some seventeen hours from San Francisco to join them.[8]

The organizers described themselves as "a group of young Jewish people searching for a spiritual lifestyle appropriate for a New Age consciousness of caring for each other and the earth."[9] They billed Reb Shlomo as a "Chassidic troubadour," "a joyful musician and storyteller," who will "share the ecstasy, mysticism and timeless truths of the Hebraic tradition."[10] This 1977 event was a harbinger of Jewish Renewal in the Pacific Northwest, an area distant from the major urban centers of vibrant Jewish life. Shonna Husbands-Hankin describes how Shlomo's agreement to bring his spirituality and religious enthusiasm from afar was so significant:

> We "found" each other at this retreat, Jewish seekers who were alone, now felt part of a community. This retreat became a catalyst for a regional relationship of Jewish spiritual communities up and down the West Coast. What Reb Shlomo really did was to affirm our quest for Judaism and for living a Jewish life. He was gathering the holy sparks that were scattered. By agreeing to come to a *fairly remote location*, one of the fringes of the Jewish world, he brought his authenticity and big heart and made a rightful place for all of us. He welcomed us home to a spiritual place in Judaism.[11]

---

8. The group included Sarah Leah (Ayla) Grafstein, Eshyah Tony Sargent, Avraham Sand, and Marty Hauser.

9. The organizers listed in the AMB bulletin were Shonna and Yitz Husbands-Hankin from Oregon; Mordechai and Hana Wosk from Vancouver, British Columbia; Nathan and Sharna Cheifetz from Portland, Oregon, and Riva Zeff from Seattle, Washington.

10. The quotes are from the *Aquarian Minyan Newsletter*, March 1977, 4.

11. Shonna Husbands-Hankin, personal communication, May 29, 2012.

The personal biographies of Yitz and Shonna Husbands-Hankin provide an illustration of how key figures in the Jewish Renewal Movement integrated Shlomo's teachings and music into their own innovative programming.

Yitz was born on January 27, 1947 in Pittsburgh, Pennsylvania.[12] His maternal grandmother had emigrated from Poland as a 14-year old. His father was born in Russia and immigrated to the U.S. when he was 12 years old. His earliest Jewish education was with his grandfather, Reb Shmuel Hankin, and his musical grandmother, Rivka Etkin Hankin. Yitz was the soprano boy soloist in the Orthodox Shaare Torah choir under Cantor Jacob Lefkowitz.

On November 8, 1977 Shonna and Yitz were married in Eugene, Oregon. They invited Reb Shlomo and Reb Meir Fund to officiate. The wedding ceremony was attended not only by members of the local Eugene congregation, but also by members of the newly emerging Jewish Renewal community from throughout the Northwest:

> The ceremony went beyond time and space. It traversed different territories of spirit, as Reb Shlomo read in the *ketubbah* the white spaces between the black letters, and also made reference to the six million – the following night, November 9, being Kristallnacht.[13]

Over the years, Yitz remained in touch with Reb Shlomo, accompanying him in about fifteen concerts, often in a duo with Aryeh Hirschfield.[14] When Yitz and Shonna founded a Moshav in Dorena, Oregon named Shivtei Shalom,[15] Reb Shlomo came to visit on July 10, 1984. There he presented Yitz with a certificate, ordaining him as a *baal tefillah*, a prayer leader.[16]

Yitz served as cantor at Temple Beth Israel, and after receiving his rabbinic ordination from Reb Zalman in July of 1987, also served as one of

---

12. His parents named him Edward Hankin, but as an adult he selected the Hebrew name of his great-grandfather, Yitzhak, and after marriage added his wife's name Husbands.

13. Shonna Husbands-Hankin, personal communication, May 29, 2012.

14. Aryeh was a talented musician who recorded his own music and produced a number of albums. He had been raised in an Orthodox home in the Bronx but had rejected Orthodoxy and followed other spiritual paths until after the Yom Kippur War in 1973, subsequent to which he found his way to Reb Shlomo's House of Love and Prayer. In 1985, he received ordination from Reb Zalman. He died, tragically drowning, on Jan. 6, 2009. For more about Reb Aryeh, see RebAryeh.com, http://www.rebaryeh.com.

15. The settlement existed until 1993. Personal correspondence with Shonna, May 28, 2012.

16. See Chapter 11 for a detailed description of this document.

Reb Shlomo in Eugene, Oregon, 1989 at the home of Avraham and Leah Sand. Courtesy of Avraham Sand (sitting at Shlomo's left)

the congregation's rabbis.[17] As a cantor/singer/composer, Yitz integrated Carlebach music in the Temple Beth Israel liturgy.[18] His wife, Shonna Husbands-Hankin, is a leader in the Jewish Renewal Movement.[19]

In the last years of his life, Reb Shlomo came three times to Eugene, Oregon to help their pre-Pesach program. The following two stories illustrate the inspiration he created.

The first story is a classic Baal Shem Tov type Shlomo story – recognizing a simple child with a rich spirit who loves God and wants to be close to the Torah with joy. It took place on March 19–21, 1991 at Temple Beth Israel. Lotus Blossom Cahn, a 19-year old with developmental disabilities, had been continuously asking, "When is my bat mitzvah?" Shonna tells her story:

> With her inquisitive brown eyes, her searching, stuttering, and demanding presence, she was insistent that she needed a bat mitzva.... In the after concert hubbub, I approached Reb Shlomo, described Lotus and asked if it would be ok for Lotus to celebrate at the next morning's service. "It would be my greatest honor!"

Thus, on Thursday morning, March 21, 1991, Lotus celebrated her bat mitzvah:

---

17. Randi Bennet, "Cantor Strives To Become A Rabbi," *The Eugene Register-Guard*, Oct. 31, 1987, 18.

18. Yitz recorded a CD of his original compositions, *Treasure Each Day* and *Dancing Through Eden*, music for Erev Shabbat sung at Temple Beth Israel. Reb Shlomo's music along with compositions by Reb Yitzhak and Reb Aryeh serve as the foundation for the music at Temple Beth Israel in Eugene where he serves as senior rabbi.

19. She is renowned as a Judaic artist, writer, spiritual director and community organizer who has taught at the Aleph Kallah and Elat Chayyim.

In the most incredible, awesome, profound warbling primal voice, she uttered the memorized Hebrew, as though she was the first human ever uttering sounds that were shaped to become words. . . . The room full of adults was all in tears, hearing, for the first time, a calling out of the most profound blessings one could imagine. Lotus proceeded to give a spontaneous *devar Torah* of her own making, and then went around the room giving deep blessings, straight to the core essence, for each participant in the room. Reb Shlomo held the space for this remarkable event and guided it back into "Jewish standard time."[20]

Libby Bottero adds: "The story of Lotus especially touches the heart – she wanted her four favorite rabbis (Shlomo, Myron, Yitz, and Aryae) to be at her bat mitzvah and amazingly it happened – it meant so very much to Lotus and was one of the peak moments in her life."[21]

The second story illustrates Reb Shlomo as a versatile Rebbe who facilitates the creation of a social-spiritual community with unique pre-Pesach preparations. It began with Shlomo's concert at Temple Beth Israel in Eugene, Oregon on Sunday, April 12, 1992. The next morning some seventy-five women, men and children gathered in the backyard of Yitz and Shonna to bake *shmura* matzot.[22] Fresh spring water was collected and kneaded with the *shmura* flour that Shlomo brought from New York. Shlomo led *Hallel* singing on the guitar together with Yitz and Aryeh Hirschfield, then rabbi at Havurah Shir Hadash in Ashland. Shonna summed up the significance of this unique event:

> We wrapped the *matzot* in new foil, and each participant took one home for their Seder. Reminder: We are out in Oregon where there were no kosher facilities for 250 miles . . . trying to be Jewish in our fashion![23]

---

20. My thanks to Shonna for sharing this story, May 30, 2012. Lotus, the daughter of Shanti and Alan Cahn, was born on Jan. 20, 1972. At age 30, she developed cancer and died on Feb. 27, 2005.

21. Personal communications from Libby Bottero, June 2012. For more about the story of Lotus Cahn and the overall context and meaning of this celebration see Shonna Husbands-Hankin with Reb Yitzhak Husbands-Hankin, "My Greatest Honor," *Kol Chevra*, vol. 18, 2012, 11–15. The write-up includes 7 photos by Libby Bottero.

22. *Shmura* matzah entails special supervision from the time the wheat was harvested to ensure no fermentation.

23. Shonna Husbands-Hankin, May 30, 2012.

In the evening, Shlomo taught at the home of Avraham and Leah Sand.[24] The next day, the group set out to the Cougar Hot Springs geothermal pools in the Willamette National Forest where Reb Shlomo told Hasidic stories about *mikveh* and expounded upon the teachings of Reb Nachman of Breslov how *mikveh* waters remove anger and brokenness and envelop us with God's love.[25] Finally, in the evening, the group went to the restaurant of Nazir Zahra on 5th St. in Eugene where Reb Shlomo led a dinner concert.

Shonna Husbands-Hankin sums up how Shlomo had a lasting effect on Jewish Renewal in the Pacific Northwest by his travels to communities scattered all over: Victoria, Vancouver, Seattle, Eugene, Portland, Ashland, and Phoenix: "We are eternally grateful for his and Reb Zalman's unique weaving of the web of Jewish Renewal in our area and beyond."[26]

3. INFLUENCE ON JEWISH RENEWAL RABBIS

A thorough analysis of Reb Shlomo's influence on the Jewish Renewal Movement deserves a separate study. Here are sample stories from five Jewish Renewal rabbis in different areas of the United States: San Francisco Bay area, the East Coast, and the Pacific Northwest. I interviewed them about the influence of Reb Shlomo on their lifework.

#

Reuven (Robert) Goldfarb was born on April 30, 1945 in Brooklyn and grew up in a Conservative household. In 1965, he graduated from Lafayette College in Easton, Pennsylvania, with a BA in English, and in the fall entered a Master's Program in Creative Writing at Syracuse University. In January 1967, Robert dropped out of graduate school, and in June traveled to California in search of love and adventure. After experiencing diverse spiritual settings and teachers,[27] Reuven began attending the HLP regularly during 1970–71 and experiencing Shabbat

---

24. See Chapter 8 for a description of Avraham and Leah Sand in Me'or Modi'im.

25. Libby Rivka Bottero, creator of the Eugene *mikveh* and a former HLP member had written to Reb Shlomo, asking him to devote a teaching to the significance of *mikveh*. The talk was recorded and printed in *Kol Chevra*, vol. 10, 2004, 39–42. See also HomeMikveh.org, http://www.homemikveh.org/shlomo/shlomik.html. My thanks to Libby for sending me 13 CDs containing the recordings of Reb Shlomo's teachings during his visit to Eugene, Oregon, April 12–14, 1992.

26. Skype conversation May 31, 2012.

27. These included the San Francisco Zen Center, Ram Dass, Chogyam Trungpa Rinpoche, Sufi Sam, Krishna Das, and Stephen Gaskin.

with its exuberant dancing and silent devotion. In 1973, he found an apartment from which he would walk to the HLP on Shabbat. In the summer of 1974, David Drexler, a friend from the House, recommended the new Aquarian Minyan. Soon Reuven became involved in co-creating the innovative Friday evening services at the Minyan. Reuven recalls:

> I began to be more focused. The spiritual learning that I had absorbed from Reb Zalman, Reb Shlomo, and Steve Gaskin, my main teachers, were now things that I could put into practice in my life in general and, of course, in the Aquarian Minyan community.[28]

At the AMB, Reuven met Yehudit (Judith Wallach). They were married on Lag B'Omer, May 5, 1977, in Lakeview Picnic Area, Tilden Park, Berkeley. As a co-founder of the AMB, Yehudit was involved from the onset in formulating the vision of a spiritual community where the spirit and "alive Judaism" could be tapped to form a living, relevant, and inspiring Jewish community in the Bay Area:[29] "We viewed ourselves as establishing a major revival, a New Age Judaism."[30]

When Shlomo came to events co-sponsored by The Aquarian Minyan and the Berkeley Hillel, Reuven would record and edit his talks, as for example on June 30, 1981.[31]

After eighteen years of co-leading and facilitating AMB programming, Reuven was honored on Simchat Torah 1993 and received *semicha* from Reb Zalman as Moreinu, Maggid, and Rabbinic Deputy, empowering him to serve as a teacher, counselor, and facilitator of life cycle events.[32] The Goldfarbs moved to Israel in 1999 and made aliyah on November 5, 2003. They now live in Safed where they direct the Bayt Maor HaLev Center for Movement, Healing and Language Arts and host a weekly *Chug TaNaKH*, a Bible class.[33]

❉

---

28. The story told here is based on conversations with Reuven Goldfarb from Aug. – Sept. 2011.

29. Yehudit Goldfarb, "The Weaning of the Minyan, An Historical Overview of the Minyan's First Three Years" in Gross, Goldfarb, Goldfarb, Gross and Stampfer (eds.), *Ancient Roots*, 3–5 (originally published in the *Aquarian Minyan Newsletter*, June 1977).

30. Personal interviews with Reuven and Yehudit Goldfarb, Aug. and Sept. 2011.

31. "The Taz and the Bach, " recorded and edited by Reuven Goldfarb, *Hakrev Ushma (Connections)*, vol. 1, issue 5, 25–28.

32. The other signers of the document were Rabbis David Wolfe-Blank, Gershon Winkler, Leah Novick, and Pamela Frydman Baugh.

33. Reuven continues to write poetry, fiction, and essays. He hosts a monthly salon for writers and conducts bi-weekly sessions called Short Story Intensive.

The Bat Mitzvah of Lotus Blossom Cahn at Temple Beth Israel in Eugene,
Oregon, March 1991. To her left is Rabbi Aryeh Hirschfield, and to her right
is Rabbi Myron Kinberg, the rabbi then of Temple Beth Israel.

Courtesy of Libby Bottero

Rabbi Stan Levy received ordination from the Jewish Renewal ALEPH
Rabbinical program.[34] He is the co-founder of the Academy for Jewish
Religion, California a transdenominational Rabbinical, Cantorial and
Jewish Chaplaincy Seminary in Los Angeles. He is also very musical and
produced albums and concerts. In 1968, he founded Congregation B'nai
Horin in West Los Angeles. When asked what he found so inspirational
about Reb Shlomo, Stan responded:

> I loved Shlomo's passion, integrity, and authenticity, and how
> he made each person feel important and special. He brought
> relevancy, meaning, and spirituality to a living Judaism and in-
> spired me to try to do the same. My congregants would go to hear
> Shlomo whenever he came to LA. I myself will often sing Reb
> Shlomo's "*Esa Einai*" when I officiate at funeral services.[35]

⊞

Rabbi/Cantor David Shneyer received rabbinic ordination from Jewish
Renewal's ALEPH Seminary. From 2006–2008, he served as president
of OHALAH, The Association of Rabbis for Jewish Renewal. Today, he

---

34. Stan Levy is also a practicing lawyer who founded Bet Tzedek which provides
free legal services to about 15,000 poor and elderly people in Los Angeles annually.
See BnaiHorin.com, www.bnaihorin.com.

35. Personal correspondence, June 1, 2012.

sees himself as a "holy Hasid of Reb Shlomo," adding that "90% of what I do can be credited to Reb Shlomo."

David was born in Brooklyn on November 22, 1948 and raised in Lakewood, New Jersey. He was active in a Conservative Synagogue named Congregation Ahavat Shalom that his parents helped found in Lakewood. The synagogue cantor, a former Chabadnik, gave him Shlomo's album, *At the Village Gate*:

> Here I was, a 14-year old guitar player in a rock and roll band performing in the Lakewood hotels. I was enchanted by Shlomo's Hasidic music. I found the connection with guitar and Jewish music amazing. I had a curiosity for liturgy and hearing his *niggunim* set to *tehilim* really excited me.

In March 1966, David attended Shlomo's concert at Woodbridge High School sponsored by Adas Israel of Woodbridge, New Jersey:

> Several hundred people attended. After the concert I went up to meet Shlomo. His look embraced me. His persona, his heartfelt teachings and *niggunim* touched me. We promised to stay in touch.

David studied at Rutgers State University from 1966–1970. When Reb Shlomo was brought by the Hillel campus organization to the University student center, David backed him up on guitar. In 1970, David moved to Washington, D.C. to work at B'nai Israel, a Conservative congregation. Shlomo asked David to organize a concert for him at B'nai Israel. That was the beginning of David's calling.

At this concert, David met Alan Oresky and together with Frank Sparber they formed a klezmer band. In 1971, they founded the Fabrangen Fiddlers, "the first *simcha* band in the D.C. area." They performed at more than 1,000 concerts and celebrations over the years. The band accompanied Reb Shlomo whenever he came to D.C. in the 1970s–1980s.

The Fabrangen Fiddlers were a part of the Fabrangen, "a Jewish Free Culture Center" in Washington D.C., founded by Rob Agus and David Shneyer with a vision of creating a center where young Jews could celebrate Jewish life, gather for learning, spiritual nourishment, and receive counseling (draft and drug).[36] With the aid of a $15,000 grant from the UJA Federation of Washington, they began programming in January 1971. David brought Reb Shlomo for several Shabbatonim in D.C.

---

36. Ellen Garshick and Fran Goldman (eds.), *Fabrangen: Celebrating 36 Years*, Washington DC, 2007, 49. See Fabrangen.org, http://www.fabrangen.org/activity/36th/Memory_Book_Final.pdf.

Reb Shlomo had a "major impact" on the early Fabrangen: "He gave us a neo-Hasidic egalitarian Judaism that fueled the community spirit."[37] Similarly, Chava Weissler, the first president of Fabrangen, describes how the group of young people in their twenties felt that "we were creating a new and revolutionary form of Judaism, one that included equality for women, renewed spirituality, and taking charge of our own Jewish lives."[38] Eventually Fabrangen evolved into a *havurah* type community.

David organized hundreds of Jewish music concerts and helped create several alternative and independent communities. In 1978, he co-founded *Kehila Chadasha*, an independent *havurah*, devoted to education, celebration, and community service based in Bethesda, Maryland. Shlomo's music became an integral part of the High Holiday Services that catered regularly to as many as 1,200 participants. In 1990, David founded *Am Kolel*, a Jewish Renewal community centered in Montgomery County, Maryland and dedicated to outreach.

David recounts: "*Am Kolel* would not exist if it were not for Reb Shlomo." He sums up the influence of Shlomo on his own lifework:

> Reb Shlomo taught me how to play a *niggun*, the lift off, the rise to higher orbits and the soft landing. I learned what *kavvanah* means as a *shaliach tzibbur* whose primary task is to inspire his congregants to join in. Reb Shlomo also encouraged me to compose my own *niggunim*. He bequeathed to me a gift of how music brings us closer to God and to each other. I was impressed by his commitment to inclusiveness, and his spontaneous way of seeing the preciousness of each individual soul. Just by witnessing his acts of kindness and understanding, I discovered what *hesed* can really be. In brief, Reb Shlomo inspired me on my life path. To this day, I feel that his presence is very much still alive.[39]

❊

Rabbi Alvin (Avraham) Wainhaus has served thirty years as rabbi of Congregation Or Shalom in suburban Connecticut. He states emphatically: "Shlomo made me who I am – no exaggeration." Alvin leads his congregation with his guitar in joyful "sing-along" services:

> It was Shlomo Carlebach who innovated this new style of prayer worship. It was a complete revolution in his time. As a rabbi who

---

37. Personal interviews and emails with Rabbi David Shneyer, June 5–10, 2012.
38. Garshick and Goldman, *Fabrangen: Celebrating 36 Years*, 51–52.
39. Personal interviews and emails with Rabbi David Shneyer, June 5–10, 2012.

also serves as cantor, this combination has determined my rabbinic style.[40]

Alvin was born on September 30, 1948 to Holocaust survivors.[41] Alvin
grew up in the Yiddish-speaking world of Borough Park, Brooklyn and
studied in *haredi* yeshivas. When he was about 15 years old, he went to
hear Shlomo in concert at a local *shul* in Flatbush: "I realized that music
really attracted me as a primary vehicle to feel close to Hashem." While
at yeshiva, he attended Brooklyn College at night and Queens College in
the summer. As a philosophy major, Alvin was exposed to other religions
and philosophies. He completed his BA in 1971 and his rabbinic ordination at a *haredi* yeshiva in Bnei Brak in 1972. But although he found a
Rabbinic position in Yarmouth, Nova Scotia and flew there once a month
to conduct Shabbat services, Alvin felt bewildered:

> I began a three year period in the wilderness, not knowing who I
> was, but knowing who I was not. I was estranged from my *haredi*
> family. During those years that I felt lost and depressed it was
> Shlomo's music that kept me Jewish. His songs spoke to my heart.
> When I rediscovered Judaism, I found a spiritual Judaism in Jewish
> Renewal.

At age 25, Alvin joined a group led by Jeff Oboler in New York's East
Village, the East Coast equivalent to Haight-Ashbury in San Francisco.
Oboler, known later as Reb Yosef Ben Shlomo Hakohen, was offering an
innovative form of Orthodox outreach to the non-Orthodox world:

> We were all in our twenties and searching spiritually. Jeff was our
> guru. Every two weeks we would meet at Bet Café for lectures
> and discussions. Oboler would often lead the singing of Carlebach
> tunes. What was unique about the Carlebach message and mys-
> tique is that there was a sense of authentic spiritual Yiddishkeit
> outside the Orthodox establishment and that was very attractive
> for us.

In 1975, Alvin was hired as an associate rabbi and cantor at the
Brotherhood Synagogue at Gramercy Park, Manhattan, and he brought
Shlomo to perform there. Alvin completed his MA in education at NYU.

---

40. This quote and those following are based on personal interviews, Sept. 6–7,
2012.

41. His father, Anshel Wainhaus, was rescued by the Japanese diplomat Chiune
Sugihara who risked his life and career to save Polish Jews by signing thousands of
transit visas through Japan. Anshel met his future wife in Shanghai.

He also began developing his musical career as guitarist and soloist, and recorded half a dozen original songs. Together with Shlomo, he entered the First Hasidic Song Festival at Brooklyn College – Shlomo Carlebach won first place. In 1981, he was hired as rabbi of Congregation Or Shalom of Orange, Connecticut where he has been to this day.

⁂

Hanna Tiferet Siegel was born as Anne Sacks on May 1, 1948. She first encountered Reb Shlomo in January 1967 at a Shabbaton at the Hillel Foundation at Western Reserve in Cleveland. Hanna was deeply moved: "Reb Shlomo opened the gates of music and prayer for me." Hanna attended Shlomo's concerts whenever she could.[42]

On October 12, 1969, Hanna married Daniel Siegel. Together they embarked upon a career of Jewish communal service and became leading figures in what was soon to be known as the Jewish Renewal Movement.[43] Hanna and Daniel were instrumental in bringing Reb Shlomo to Canada three times.[44] On January 15, 1976, Hanna brought Reb Shlomo to Congregation Emanuel in Victoria, British Columbia. This was the oldest functioning synagogue in Canada. During the concert, Reb Shlomo was asked whether the antiquated synagogue building should be restored or torn down. He responded: "These walls are filled with prayers." The congregants took his message to heart and the building was refurbished. Today it stands as a vibrant monument to 150 years of Jewish history.[45] After the Siegels moved to Vancouver, they began to create a spiritual community where "the music of Shlomo, and the Hasidim he inspired to compose new melodies, brought the ancient liturgy to life." This eventually became Congregation Or Shalom. Twice, Hanna brought Reb Shlomo to perform and teach in Vancouver – November 10, 1977 at the JCC and January 9, 1980 at International House.

On Shavuot in 1982, Hanna became the first woman to receive the title

---

42. Skype interview with Hanna, June 1, 2012.

43. Rabbi Daniel Siegel was raised in New York where he attended Yeshiva of Central Queens and Ramaz High School. He was in the first class at the Reconstructionist Rabbinical College in Philadelphia but completed his rabbinical studies with Reb Zalman in Winnipeg. On March 24, 1974, he became the first person to receive rabbinical ordination from Reb Zalman. Today he is the Director of Spiritual Resources for ALEPH: Alliance for Jewish Renewal and Associate Dean of the ALEPH Ordination Programs.

44. My thanks to Hanna Tiferet Siegel for the stories here related to me June 4, 2012.

45. CongregationEmanu-el.ca, www.congregationemanu-el.ca.

of *Eshet Hazon* (Woman of Vision) and *M'yaledet N'shama* (Midwife of the Soul). In January 2003, Hanna received rabbinical ordination from Reb Zalman and a group of rabbis at the OHALAH conference in Denver, Colorado. Currently, she serves as a spiritual guide on the Hashpa'ah faculty of the ALEPH Ordination Programs. Hanna is a singer-songwriter and liturgical artist, recently releasing her eighth album, *TIFERET * Heart of Compassion*.[46]

The stories above are just a few of the multitude of impressions left behind by Reb Shlomo. In the next chapters, we explore the last two decades of Shlomo's life and try to better understand the neo-Hasidic revival he was creating.

---

46. See HannaTiferet.com, www.hannatiferet.com.

CHAPTER 11

Global Rebbe

1.   MARRIAGE AND DAUGHTERS

On a Friday night in August 1972, Shlomo met Elaine Glick at the Kotel in Jerusalem. That Sunday he composed a new tune for "*Eishet Chayil*" ("A Woman of Valor Who Can Find," Proverbs 31),[1] and on Monday he proposed to her. She didn't agree. But Shlomo was sure that they were true soulmates and he kept on proposing.

The next Shabbat, Shlomo and his *chevra* were again at the Kotel. The following was described by Nechama Yasskin (Silver):

> We finished a beautiful *davening* at the Kotel by midnight, and at 1:00 AM we were back at 16 Lincoln St. for the Shabbat meal, crowded on the living room floor eating brown rice and vegetables. Shlomo rented a couple of rooms for the chevra in the President Hotel. I remember sharing the suite with Violette Witt and Elaine Glick and several other women. For the next six weeks, we traveled with Shlomo to concerts and teach-ins. He would rent a group of taxis and we all would ride from place to place. A feeling of love and unity pervaded every group activity. One night, Shlomo told us we were going to a birthday party for Elaine at her relative's home in Ramat Gan. It was very clear that Shlomo was interested in her.[2]

Shlomo and Elaine were married on December 26, 1972. He suggested calling Elaine "Neila,"[3] thus referring to the final prayer of Yom Kippur,

---

1. Ben Zion Solomon, *Shlomo Shabbos*, 22.

2. Nechama Yasskin (Silver), personal interview, Oct. 6, 2012.

3. Neila wrote to me (Sept. 28, 2012): "My original Hebrew name is Aliyah and I always include it when asked my whole name. Aliyah is from my parents and Neila is a gift from Shlomo."

a time of unique closeness with God just as the Gates are closing.[4] The wedding invitation emphasized the opening of the Heavenly Gates:

> Open the gates even if we closed the gates
> For we will never leave the gates.
> Please be with us when G-d in His mercy
> opens all the gates of love and oneness.[5]

Before the wedding, Shlomo went with a few disciples to the Bobover Rebbe to receive a blessing.[6] The wedding took place in the giant banquet hall of Terrace on the Park, Flushing Meadows in Queens, New York where the World's Fair had taken place in 1964–1965.[7] The hall could hold 1,100 people, but about 1,800 arrived, all having been invited by Shlomo, and the management wouldn't let them all in. But, when Shlomo came with his entourage from the HLP in San Francisco, he arranged for everyone to be seated next to each other on the floor!

This World's Fair Pavillion contained four ballrooms mounted twenty flights up in the air atop of a central pillar of elevators. The *bedeken* was in the first room, the *huppah* in the second, the reception in the third, and the meal in the fourth room. Reb Shlomo's twin brother Eli Chaim officiated. The Fabrangen Fiddlers led by David Shneyer played before the wedding.[8] Another two bands played during the wedding: Clei Zemer under the direction of Noach Dear, and Howie Kahn's band – Ruach Revival.[9] During the week of *Sheva Berachot*, Itzik Aiesenstadt drove the *chevra* around in his van to join Shlomo in celebrating. Shlomo was inspired at one of his *Sheva Berachot* to compose a special tune to the words "*LeShana HaBa'a BeYerushalayim.*"[10]

---

4. In a San Francisco radio interview in 1975, Shlomo explained that he chose the name Neila because "she was like my last big stop in this world, my last prayer. And, she's like a little holy master on her own also."

5. This optimistic theme, based on Psalms 118:9 was first highlighted by Reb Shlomo in his third LP, *At the Village Gate*.

6. See Coopersmith, *Holy Beggars*, 308–309. Compare Ne'eman Rosen, comment April 6, 2009 on HolyBeggars.ning.com, http://holybeggars.ning.com/forum/topics/ shlomos-wedding.

7. Sarah Ariella Kauffman posted nine pictures from the wedding on HolyBeggars .ning.com, http://holybeggars.ning.com/photo/shlomo-and-neilas-wedding-1?con text=featured.

8. Personal communication from Rabbi David Shneyer on June 5, 2012.

9. Howie recalls how he was chosen by Shlomo's mother Pessia, to play "*Boi Veshalom*" on the accordion to accompany Shlomo and his mother to the *huppah*. Personal interview with Howie Kahn, Aug. 2, 2011.

10. Although never actually recorded in Reb Shlomo's lifetime, this tune was redis-covered by Shlomo Katz who released it in Nov. 2012 as a single. The tune was placed

Neila's parents, Chaya and David Glick, had emigrated in 1924 from Kishinev, Russian Bessarabia to Toronto, Canada. David (1898–1991) served as a cantor in several Toronto synagogues. Of Neila's four brothers, Earl (Ezriel Aaron), Norman (Nachum), Danny (Daniel), and Srul Irving (Israel), three were involved with Shlomo's music. Earl and Norman worked as executive producers of Hal Roach Studios which produced Shlomo's record *Days Are Coming* in 1978 (see below, this chapter, section 2). Srul, one of Canada's most prolific composers, arranged many of Shlomo's melodies, and incorporated some of them into the musical legacy of the synagogue choir he conducted in Toronto.[11]

Neila worked in Toronto as a school teacher, teaching French and theater. She also served as a corporate executive in Toronto in the family company Hal Roach Studios. So now Shlomo had another home base – Canada. This partially explains the heightening of Shlomo's impact in the late 1970s in Canada and the Pacific Northwest.[12]

A new phase of Shlomo's life began. On Simchat Torah, October 9, 1974, their first child was born and named Neshama Tehorah Shlucha Ester. Neila was inspired to name her Neshama Tehorah. Shlomo added Shlucha as a reference to the biblical blessing in Genesis 49:21, hinting at the name of Naphtali, Shlomo's father. Ester was added for Neila's sister-in-law Essie Glick, who died just before Neshama was born. Esther was also the namesake of Esther Adler, Shlomo's grandmother.

The evening after his first daughter was born, Shlomo went to Montreal and in his indomitable way invited the crowd to his daughter's wedding "to be held in Jerusalem in twenty years time."[13]

---

on numerous sites as for example: http://www.chasidinews.com; http://www.inn.co .il/News/News.aspx/246113; http://www.babakama.co.il/?q=showArticle&id=463; http://www.youtube.com/watch?v=GaQpwo1NMzo; http://www.kipa.co.il/tarbut/ 186/49847.html.

11. Srul Glick (1934–2002) became conductor in 1969 of the choir at Beth Tikvah Synagogue, a Conservative Synagogue in Toronto, and in 1978, became the choir's composer-in-residence. He wrote liturgical music and Yiddish folk song arrangements for the choir. See "Srul Irving Glick," *The Encyclopedia of Music in Canada*, CanadianEncyclopedia.com, http://www.thecanadianencyclopedia.com/articles/ emc/srul-irving-glick.

12. See, for example, in this chapter, sect. 2 about the World Symposium for Humanity in Toronto in April 1979. Compare Chapter 10 about Shlomo's participation in the Vancouver World Symposium in 1976 and the resulting influence on Jewish Renewal in the Pacific Northwest.

13. This was told to me by Rabbi Yisroel Roll who was 16 years old at the time. Twenty years later, when he was rabbi of The New West End Synagogue in London, invited Reb Shlomo to perform at his synagogue in what turned out to be Reb Shlomo's last public concert.

The birth of his daughter influenced Shlomo's music as is reflected in his album *Shlomo Carlebach and The Children of Jewish Song Sing Ani Maamin*, released in 1975 by Emes.[14] The song *"Ani Maamin,"* "I Believe," serves as both the title and theme for this album. Shlomo introduces the record by emphasizing the purity and innocence of a child's belief and teachings:

> I believe so much in children. The Torah is only given to children as it says "Speak to the children of Israel" and the Land of Israel was given only to the children of Israel. God also blessed children with true belief, so their vision is pure . . . I have been blessed with many holy teachers but none has reached as deeply or as clearly as my own baby.

Shlomo concludes by thanking the children's chorus who accompanied him and adding the wish that "the Land of Israel once again become the land of the Children of Israel."

When she was 9 years old, Neshama accompanied her father to Zurich, Munich, and Israel.[15] At age fifteen, she began singing with her father on stage, and in December 1993, when she was twenty, she left acting school and accompanied her father on his concert tours around the world. After Shlomo's untimely death in 1994, Neshama was asked to fill in for her father at the many concerts that had been booked in advance, and soon she began her own musical career. Her first record, released in 1996, was entitled *Neshama – Soul*. Her second record in 1997, *HaNeshama Shel Shlomo* featured Neshama as a 19–year old singing in a duet with her father, blending his "baritone voice with her sultry tenor harmonies."[16]

Neshama found innovative ways of continuing her father's legacy. One of her eight CDs,[17] *Higher and Higher*, features the New York-based Green Pastures Baptist Church Choir.[18] Neshama is a divorcee with two

---

14. This is the record company of Baruch Chait, composer and founder of The Rabbis' Sons. There are 11 songs, most from the liturgy. The orchestra arranger was Martin Lewinter who also played bass and classical guitar. The vocal arranger was Abie Rotenberg (D'veykus was his first commercial music venture). Also participating was the Dave Nulman Orchestra. The children's chorus included Michael Chaneles, Eli Klein, Ezra Kramer, and Mordechai Respler.

15. Neshama Carlebach, "My Merna," in *L'Koved Reb Shlomo Remembrance Journal* produced by the Carlebach Shul.

16. Steven A. Rosenberg, "Carlebach gives new life to American Jewish music," *Boston Globe*, March 11, 2011.

17. Facebook.com, http://www.facebook.com/neshama.carlebach?sk=info; http://www.neshamacarlebach.com/home.htm. The 8th recording is *Every Little Soul Must Shine*.

18. Neshama's CDs are produced by Sojourn Records founded by Mark Ambrosino

Wedding of Shlomo and Neila, in Queens, New York, December 26, 1972
Courtesy of Menachem Daum

sons, Rafael Lev Shlomo,[19] born October 27, 2006, and Micha (Micah) Or Shalem, born August 22, 2010.

Shlomo's second daughter was born in New York on July 13, 1977 (28 Tammuz). Shlomo named her Chana Nedara[20] Amra Nafshi,[21] or in short, Nedara (Dari). Dari married Ari Leichtberg in 2003, and they came on

---

and Tom Laverack. Mark is both Neshama's business manager and drummer, SojournRecords.com, http://www.sojournrecords.com/prod/artist/neshama_carlebach.

19. The play on words on the name is illustrative – following the paradigm of the healing angel, Rafael, Shlomo is to heal the heart. At the *brit* ceremony, Neshama's blessing to her son was that he should "heal all the things that my father left behind, all the brokenness." Recorded by Menachem Daum, segment 28:50.

20. The name Chana was chosen as the namesake of two great grandmothers of both Shlomo and Neila. Dari explained to me that the name Nedara was selected to connect to the Torah reading of the Shabbat after her birth which was from *Parshat Matot* and begins with vows. The idea is connected to I Samuel, 1:11, where Chana takes a vow to dedicate her son to God and then Samuel is born. In his 1981 record *L'Kovid Shabbas* [*sic*] with his two little daughters on the cover, Shlomo writes about Neshama as "little soul" and Nedara as "little promise."

21. The original expression of *Amra Nafshi* (my soul has declared) is found in Lamentations 3:24 where it is used in the context of a deep yearning for God.

Shlomo and Neila   Courtesy of Menachem Daum

aliyah in 2008. Dari's daughter is Ra'eya Ayalah Tair, born January 3, 2007. Her son was named Shlomo Li'av Marom and was born on July 29, 2009.

Although Neshama and Dari grew up with their mother in Toronto, Canada, they spent the summers with their father on Moshav Me'or Modi'im and joined him in New York for all the major holidays. These were most memorable times. Today Nedara looks back and comments:

My father was his own Living Torah. He was so present in the moment. When he hugged someone as his best friend it was being fully present with that individual. So also each mitzvah on the holidays was celebrated with such devotion as if nothing else existed. For example, on Sukkot he could be so engrossed in the mitzvah of eating that he didn't notice that it was actually raining. When he shook the *lulav*, it was as if he was shaking heaven and earth, and when he brought the *lulav* to his heart, there was an overwhelming sense of emotion. On Pesach, when he ate the matzah, he would close his eyes and shuckle back and forth with the taste of paradise as if he were on another plane of existence. I remember once on Shavuot at 4:00 AM as he was walking with us from the Carlebach Shul to our hotel after the all night learning, he noticed a homeless person on a 79th St. stoop. He ran back to the Shul to bring him food. And then gave him his winter coat.

2. BLOSSOMING CAREER (1974–1980)

One way that Reb Shlomo's message began spreading to broader audiences was via the counterculture radio station WBAI in New York City.[22] Shlomo was interviewed several times by Lex Hixon.[23] On Thursday evening, January 10, 1974, Hixon hosted Reb Shlomo for "a chassidic rock jam session" backed up by Mickey Lane, Zal Schrieber, David Nulman, and Joey Fishof.[24] At other sessions on the radio program, Shlomo was asked to address "controversial issues." Once he was joined by Ram Dass.[25]

In Philadelphia, at the beginning of 1974, Kenny Ellis arranged a performance for Reb Shlomo at Temple University and interviewed him on

---

22. With a transmitter in the Empire State Building and a studio location at 359 East 62nd St. in Manhattan, radio WBAI played a major role in the counterculture movement of the late 1960s and early 1970s. With its signal reaching nearly 70 miles beyond New York City, its reach and influence were significant.

23. From 1974–1987, Lex Hixon (1941–1995) hosted a program on WBAI called *In the Spirit*, and interviewed a broad spectrum of cultural and spiritual figures including several rabbis mentioned in our story – Gedaliah Fleer, Zalman Schachter Shalomi, Meir Fund, and Dovid Din.

24. Archive.org, http://archive.org/stream/wbaifoliojan74wbairich#page/n9/mode/2up.

My thanks to Menachem Daum who told me about the recordings of WBAI radio.

25. Srv.org, http://www.srv.org/index.php?option=com_content&view=article&id=72&Itemid=267. See #158: "Lex Hixon and Shlomo Carebach celebrate the Shabbat with song and teachings and Ram Das makes a guest appearance."

WRTI 90.1 FM, the classical and jazz radio station of Temple University where Shlomo described his musical career and his experiences during the Yom Kippur War.[26]

On 9 Nisan, 5734, April 1, 1974, shortly before Pesach, Reb Shlomo performed the marriage of Reuven Gilmore and Zahava Alexander in Hillside, New Jersey. The couple had first met in 1972 in Jerusalem at the House of Love and Prayer in Shaarei Hesed. One of Shlomo's original innovations was to explain the visitations of Elijah the Prophet in Jewish life rituals – at the Pesach Seder and at the circumcision *brit* of newborn boys. Shlomo asked when Elijah comes for girls. He answered that Elijah appears at her wedding bringing with him the souls of the children who are destined to be born. Later, Reuven and Zahava were among the founding families of Moshav Me'or Modi'im.

On October 22, 1974, Reb Shlomo recorded a single at Mickey Lane's Sound Cube in Manhattan. Produced by Mickey Lane with Stanley Miller it included *"Uvau Haovdim"* (Isaiah 27:13) and *"Mimkomcho."* This was the final release by Zimrani Records, Shlomo's recording company.

The album *Tanchumim*, recorded shortly thereafter, was released in 1975 by Tanchum Portnoy, a cousin of Shlomo, who had prepared ten original compositions for liturgical verses and Shlomo was to be his guest soloist in the recording studio at Mickey Lane's Sound Hut. However, Shlomo arrived very late, so Portnoy asked Rabbi Alvin (Avraham) Wainhaus to fill in as vocalist.[27] Wainhaus sang six tunes including *"Etz Hayim"* (Proverbs 3:18), the most famous of Portnoy's compositions.[28] When Shlomo finally did arrive, he sang *"Shema Koleinu"* (from the *Amidah* daily prayers) and *"Yimloch Hashem Leolam"* (Psalms 146:10).[29] This album is a rare example where Shlomo sang liturgical songs that were not his own composition.[30]

On October 26, 1974 at Randallstown Senior High School in Baltimore, Reb Shlomo had hundreds of young people dancing on stage. The *Baltimore Jewish Times* reporter described the "mass outpouring of joy"

---

26. My thanks to Kenny Ellis for this information and for sending me the audio recording of the radio interview. One of the interesting comments that Shlomo makes is that the first tune that he composed was for the verse beginning *"Od Yeshoma"* (Jer. 33:10–11), and he then sang it at a friend's wedding.

27. On the record credits, the name Avraham Yanon is listed. This was the pseudonym used by Rabbi Avraham Weinhaus.

28. Portnoy's tune is sung in synagogues around the world to accompany the returning of the Torah to the Ark. See http://www.youtube.com/watch?v=4LRKx-5 ENJM&feature=related.

29. The other two songs were sung by Bency Schachter and Avigdor Bernstein respectively.

30. My thanks to Howie Kahn for providing much of the above information.

on Saturday night at the concert, sponsored by the Pickwick Jewish Center. A clinical psychologist, Dr. Morris Lasson, commented: Psychologically, this is fantastically healthy. It is definitely fulfilling a need . . . he's using a skill to bring out the spontaneity in people."[31]

On Purim, February 25, 1975, Shlomo was invited after the *megillah* reading by Rabbi William Berkowitz, the rabbi of Congregation B'nai Jeshurun (BJ) on West 88th St. in Manhattan, just ten blocks from the Carlebach Shul. The concert and dialogue hosted by the two rabbis created a tradition that continued for almost a decade as an annual BJ Purim concert that drew thousands.[32] David Stahl, at the time a student at Brooklyn College, remembers how students would travel from all over New York to join this standing-room only event.[33] When Rabbi William Berkowitz died in 2008, his son, Rabbi Perry Berkowitz, exclaimed in his eulogy about the extraordinary annual Purim celebration with Reb Shlomo where all types of Jews celebrated together:

> Only at Dad's B'nai Jeshurun on Purim night would 3,000–5,000 people come to be with him and Reb Shlomo Carlebach, and you could see on the pulpit a Squarer chasid and the head of the Reconstructionist movement dancing together while secular Jews clapped and Buddhist Jews kvelled . . . That was Dad's vision of Klal Yisrael, the totality of the Jewish people – unity but not uniformity, and the blessing of inclusive diversity.[34]

Shlomo was sometimes invited to perform and speak at The New York Open Center on 22 East 30th Street in Manhattan, "New York's Leading Center of Holistic Learning and World Culture." Thus, on March 25, 1975,

---

31. Eileen R. Pollock, "Carlebach Instructs and Inspires With His Songs," *Baltimore Jewish Times*, Nov. 1, 1974.

32. See the obituary by E.B. Solomont, Rabbi William Berkowitz, 83, "Bridge Builder," *New York Sun*, Feb. 12, 2008, NYSun.com; www.nysun.com/obituaries/rabbi -william-berkowitz-83-bridge-builder/71126: "Berkowitz was ordained at the Jewish Theological Seminary in 1952, and he immediately took a position at Congregation B'nai Jeshurun, where he served as a rabbi until 1984 . . . Each year, Berkowitz and Rabbi Shlomo Carlebach hosted a Purim concert that drew thousands of worshippers." This was confirmed in a response that I received from Frederic S. Goldstein of BJ who informed me that Reb Shlomo performed at BJ after Purim services for a number of years until 1984 (email Nov. 21, 2012).

33. David Stahl, personal interview, Nov. 18, 2012. See below for a description of Shlomo at BJ for Purim in 1979 and 1984.

34. Steve Lipman, "A Great Communicator," *The New York Jewish Week*, Feb. 13, 2008. TheJewishWeek.com; http://www.thejewishweek.com/features/%E2%80%98 _great_communicator%E2%80%99.

Neila with her two daughters Neshama and Nedara.
Courtesy of Menachem Daum

Reb Shlomo with his two
daughters, Moshav Me'or
Modi'im, summer 1980

he arranged to lead *Sheva Berachot* at The Open Center for Michele and Eliezer Garner, two of his close disciples.[35]

On May 11, 1975 (Rosh Chodesh Sivan), Reb Shlomo officiated at the wedding of Reb Zalman to Elana Rappaport in the outdoor amphitheater of John Hinkel Park in north Berkeley.

On Motzei Shabbat, November 1, 1975, Shlomo appeared at the Jewish

35. Personal interview with Michele and Eliezer Garner Dec. 24, 2012.

Community Center sponsored by the Beth Shalom Synagogue in Ottawa, Ontario.[36]

On April 23–24, 1976, *Parshat Aharei Mot*, Reb Shlomo joined Rabbi Eugene and Annette Labovitz in Miami Beach, Florida for the Shabbat bar mitzvah of their son. Eugene Labovitz would regularly bring Shlomo to Miami arranging for him to stay in a hotel and spend a few days teaching.[37] One of those who met Shlomo at the Labovitz apartment was Channah (soon to be Schafer), who was living then on a houseboat in Miami. Soon Channah became a devoted Carlebach follower and was known for her special hospitality in hosting the *chevra* on her boat. In 1976, Channah was invited for Shabbat to the home of Neila and Shlomo in Manhattan. They invited three eligible bachelors for the three meals, including Natan Schafer for *seudah shlishit*. The couple became engaged, and the wedding was performed by Shlomo in his Manhattan apartment on September 16, 1976. The Schafers lived in Boston where they hosted Shlomo about thirty times over the years. Shlomo attended all their family celebrations. Thus, for example, he was the *sandak* at the *brit milah* ceremony for their son Uriel Benyamin Eli Segal Dodi (or Ben for short) who was born April 25, 1977 in Boston. The Schafers would come often to be with Shlomo for Shabbat in Manhattan, even after they already had four children.[38]

On Thursday, the first night of Hanukkah, December 15, 1976, Reb Shlomo performed the wedding of Yoel and Nomi Glick in Toronto, Canada. This was a real family *simcha* because Yoel is the son of Earl Glick, Neila Carlebach's brother.[39] Shlomo began the wedding by turning off the electric lights and having a dozen candles. He interspersed original explanations with musical interludes such as how the bride is to give a *tallit* to the groom as a message to learn how to stand before God and talk to Him in prayer.[40]

On May 18, 1977, Reb Shlomo together with Reb Zalman performed the wedding of David and Elaine (Elana) Zeller at Menlo Park near Palo Alto in the San Francisco Bay area.[41]

---

36. *The Citizen*, Ottawa, Oct. 24, 1975, 75.

37. Personal interview with Dr. Annette Labovitz, May 2012.

38. Personal interview with Channah and Natan Schafer, Oct. 6, 2012. See below, Chapter 11, on Natan as the first person to receive ordination from Reb Shlomo.

39. Shlomo distributed the *Sheva Berachot* under the *huppah* to Earl Glick's brothers: Nahum received the second blessing, Danny the fourth, and Srul the fifth. The grandfather, David Glick, a cantor, sang the last blessing.

40. The entire wedding with Reb Shlomo's music and explanations is preserved in a 12-part recording that I was given.

41. See Zeller, *The Soul of the Story*, 166. My thanks to Mordechai Zeller for the details.

From June 1977 through 1978, Shlomo performed more than thirty times late on Motzei Shabbat, 10:00 PM, at the fancy kosher French cuisine restaurant La Difference in Midtown Manhattan.[42] He was backed up by the Kenny Ellis trio."[43]

In September 1977, Susan Yael Mesinai had a life-changing encounter in the Carlebach Shul. She was living on the Upper West Side of Manhattan, and pursuing a Tibetan Buddhist path "meditating six hours a day under a very ancient noble lama":

> I kept running into Shlomo on Broadway and of course for the *hagim* I went to his *shul*. Shlomo gave a *devar Torah* that ended on this note: "You can climb the highest mountain, go to the bottom of the sea, you can meditate on the Buddha, do your Native American dances, whirl like a dervish – but I'll tell you now, sweetest friends, none of this matters if you are not a good Jew. And do you know what else, my friends; do you know what is the hardest thing of all? It is to really know there's Only One God." Shlomo's dark eyes burned through me and I felt not only that he was addressing that to me but that he was utterly right. That Oneness was and is the Key. This set off a whole chain reaction within me because I was deeply committed to the Enlightenment Path of the Buddha. I felt that my soul was like a flickering candle – that the Buddhist teachings which extinguish the ego were snuffing out that part of me which corresponded to my reasons for being in this world. So I went to my Rinpoche and asked permission to leave, and told him that I had things to do involving my ancestors – things to fix in this world. I was thinking then of my Jewish grandmother, who had a very difficult and lonely life, whose relatives almost all died in the Holocaust – and the Holocaust was very important to me. That is how I began to become a follower of Shlomo. Two years later, I began editing his stories towards publication.[44]

---

42. La Difference, owned by Murray Wilson, was located at the Roosevelt Hotel on Madison Avenue at 45th Street.

43. Kenny Ellis played the tambourine and sang in harmony with Shlomo. Gil Dor played guitar and Menachem Wiesenberg piano. Kenny had known Shlomo from 1969 and suggested inviting him as the star performer. I thank Kenny Ellis for sending me the poster and explanations about this event (Dec. 19, 2012). A special thanks to Yitta Halberstam Mandelbaum for referring me to Kenny. Yitta wrote about this event in her book *Holy Brother*, 105–107.

44. Personal correspondence with Susan Yael Mesinai, April 2, 2013. On the book's publication, see below in this chapter.

On May 11, 1975 (Rosh Chodesh Sivan), Reb Zalman married Elana Rappaport in Hinkel Park, Berkeley. Reb Shlomo officiated with his guitar. In the second photo, from left to right: Reb Zalman, Elana, and Reb Shlomo. In the back row are Menucha Gleich, Carol Rose, and Barry Barkan.

Courtesy of Libby Bottero

One Friday afternoon, Susan again ran into Shlomo on Broadway. This time he was carrying a fish and rushing home for Shabbat:

> I walked right over to him and said: "Rebbe! Are you going to save my soul or not?" He asked, "What's hurting you?" I told him that my mother was not Jewish and I would like to convert. So he sent me to Reb Meir Fund. In November 1978, Reb Shlomo and another two rabbis converted me, giving me a Hebrew name Yael. Reb Shlomo blessed me that I should always have access to Eretz Israel. That summer I went back to Israel and stayed on the Moshav where I met Tzlotana Barbara Midlo who eventually was to support me in writing the first collection of Shlomo's stories.

On Wednesday, September 28, 1977, Shlomo was invited by Rabbi Alvin Wainhaus to lead a Simchat Beit Hashoeva at the Brotherhood Synagogue at Gramercy Park, Manhattan.[45] One of the people in attendance was Judy Tibor (Brodt) who soon became a close disciple of Reb Shlomo.[46]

On Sunday afternoon, November 13, 1977, Rabbi Meyer Leifer hosted Reb Shlomo, together with two other famous singers, Jo Amar and

---

45. On Rabbi Alvin Wainhaus, see above, Chapter 10.

46. See below on Judy's role in the Carlebach Shul in 1979–1981, and how she and her husband, Rabbi Sholom Brodt, set up a Carlebach yeshiva in Jerusalem.

Havdala *service at the home of Rabbi Eugene and Annette Labovitz in Miami Beach, Florida. Shlomo came for their son's Bar Mitzvah, Parshat Aharei Mot, April 23–24, 1976. Courtesy of Annette Labovitz*

Shlomo Rabinovici, for a Pre-Hanukkah Festival of Song at Congregation Emunath Israel in Manhattan.[47]

David Sacks was 14 years old when he visited the Carlebach Shul a block away from his home.[48] David had grown up in a non-observant family, and at the time, he was a student at the Bronx High School of Science. David describes the seminal experience that transformed his outlook on spirituality and religion:

> I remember that first Simchas Torah in the Shul, holding the Torah and dancing with it, and feeling like this was my whole life and that this is all that I wanted. It took me many years to manifest these feelings on a level of practical observance.[49]

David went on to graduate Harvard University and become a successful Hollywood writer and producer of comedy television shows. The Carlebach experience remained and he co-founded the Carlebach Happy Minyan in Los Angeles, where "many people say that we celebrate Simchas Torah every week."[50]

Gradually, Reb Shlomo's followers set up their own centers. Ohr Chadash, an organization devoted to "spiritual upraising" in the Northwest Los Angeles area, was set up by David Montag, Jeff Mann, and

---

47. My thanks to Rabbi Leifer for this information and for sending me the publicity flyer.

48. His family lived on 79th and Broadway in a building called the Apthorp, a historic condominium apartment building named for Charles Ward Apthorp.

49. Personal communication, Oct. 26, 2012. See also the website of David Sacks, TorahOniTunes.com, http://torahonitunes.com, and especially Sacks's article "A Place for the Light," http://www.livingwithgod.org/articles/a-place-for-the-light.

50. See HappyMinyan.org, http://www.happyminyan.org/#About.

Joe Wasserman. Amongst other innovations, David Montag organized a group to learn farming techniques in preparation for making aliyah and called the group "Zippies" for "Zionist Hippies."[51] He set up various programs with Shlomo such as the Shabbat Retreat on Thanksgiving, November 24–26, 1977, at the Hillel Retreat House in Malibu,[52] an affluent, beachfront city in northwestern Los Angeles County, California. A year later, Shlomo was invited again to the Hillel Retreat House for the weekend of September 15–17, 1978.[53] In the publicity for this event advertised the "world-renoned singer . . . master of joy" who "has appeared on French, German, Austrian, Amercian, and Israeli television" and "has performed in Australia, New Zealand, the Fiji Islands, and the Soviet Union."[54]

In 1978, a live concert of Shlomo was recorded in England[55] and he gave a concert in Dubrovnik, Yugoslavia.[56] Effectively, he was assuming a role as the first musical rebbe to have a worldwide following, a "congregation without walls."

On February 15, 1978, Reb Shlomo spoke in a pre-Purim program at the Kol Emet Hebrew Day School. Then on February 17–18, 1978, Reb Shlomo led a Shabbat program in the San Francisco Bay Area. On Motzei Shabbat he gave a concert entitled Let There Be Peace at the Norse Auditorium in San Francisco. On Sunday, February 19, 1978, he appeared in a special children's concert at 2:00 PM at the Fort Mason Building.[57] In the evening, Reb Shlomo gave "an evening of Hasidic teaching and song" at the Community Congregational Church in Tiburon.

In 1978, Neil and Patricia Seidel produced in Los Angeles the album *Days Are Coming* at the request of Shlomo. The project was funded

---

51. See the website of Mark Hurwitz, Davka.org, http://www.davka.org/2011/04/26/close2torah/#ixzz26eI5woFZ.

52. Handwritten poster preserved in the files of the Jacob Rader Marcus Center – "Shlomo Carlebach," Nearprint Biography, American Jewish Archives, Cincinnati, Ohio.

53. The Shabbat program was at the Hillel House and the Sunday evening concert was held at Plummer Park at 1200 N. Vista, West Hollywood, California. See *B'nai B'rith Messenger*, Sept. 1, 1978. I thank Kevin Proffitt and Michelle Wirth of The Jacob Rader Marcus Center of the American Jewish Archives for sending me the documents from the "Shlomo Carlebach Nearprint File."

54. Ibid.

55. See the discography at Sojourn Records which was selected by The Estate of Rabbi Shlomo Carlebach "to release newly discovered recordings of performances previously not available to the public" – ShlomoCarlebachMusic.com, http://shlomocarlebachmusic.com/?page_id=64.

56. Mandelbaum, *Holy Brother*, 75.

57. My thanks to Yehudit Goldfarb for the poster.

and released on the Hal Roach Studios' label.[58] In reality, Shlomo had not produced a high quality musical album since his first records in the 1960s.[59] Neil reinterpreted Shlomo's music.[60] He brought musicians who did not have prior experience in Jewish music, yet "would respond to Shlomo in a creative manner."[61] Shlomo dedicated this record to his parents, wife, and daughters, as well as to "all the young people I have met who have carved their hunger of God into my soul." On the jacket cover, Reb Shlomo interpreted the prophecy of a spiritual hunger expressed by Amos 8:11 as the "wake up" message to "our generation" to tell them that our children are begging to hear the Word of God.

On May 12, 1978, Shlomo was the featured performer for the 30th anniversary celebration of Israel Independence Day performing in front of nearly 1,000 people at Central Park's Delacorte Theater in Manhattan.[62] He was accompanied by Kol b'Seder, a band led by Rabbi Daniel Freelander and Cantor Jeff Klepper.[63] In an article they published in January 1978, they described the influence of Reb Shlomo on the music of the American synagogue.[64] They represented a new trend in American Jewish music,[65]

---

58. The Hal Roach Studios executive producers were Neila Carlebach's brothers, Earl A. Glick and Norman Glick. They produced the movie "Starship Invasions" (1979).

59. Neil and Patricia Seidel also produced "Shlomo Stories" which features Neil's solo guitar playing and Shlomo's storytelling. Neil appears on "Open Your Heart," "Holy Brother" and several other CDs with Shlomo, CDUniverse.com, http://www .cduniverse.com/productinfo.asp?pid=7131392; http://www.cduniverse.com/product info.asp?pid=7925999&style=music.

60. Two albums of guitar instrumental renditions of Carlebach melodies were interpreted by Neil Seidel in *The Heavenly Melodies of Shlomo Carlebach*, vols. 1 & 2. Samples of the 13 tunes (without words) on vol. 2 can be heard at IndependentCreativeSources.com, http://independentcreativesources.com/shlomo cd2.htm.

61. On the record, arranged and conducted by Richard Hieronymus, were Neil Seidel on the guitar, Andrew Simpkins – bass, Jeff Castleman – electric bass, Ralph Humphrey – drums, Rod Rozzelle – percussion, Terry Harrington – flute and English horn. See Neil Seidel, "Musical Communication," *Kol Chevra*, vol. 8, Oct. 2001, 163–165.

62. David Friedman, "1000 People Celebrate Israel's Anniversary in Open Air Program," *Jewish Telegraphic Agency*, May 12, 1978.

63. KolBseder.com, http://www.kolbseder.com/main.html; JeffKlepper.com, http:// jeffklepper.com. Freelander was the assistant director of NFTY, North American Federation of Temple Youth, the Reform Movement's Youth Movement. Klepper was "one of the first cantors to champion congregational singing."

64. Daniel Freelander and Jeff Klepper, "Jewish Rock: Music for a New Generation," *Sh'ma: A Journal of Jewish Responsibility*, Jan. 20, 1978, 51–52, http://www.bjpa.org/ Publications/details.cfm?PublicationID=8979.

65. Jeffrey K. Salkin, "The New Trend in Synagogue Music," *Reform Judaism*,

an "American *nusach*,"[66] "a new Jewish song style using harmonies and rhythms borrowed from the folk-rock music of the late 1960s" that gained popularity especially in the Reform and Conservative summer camps.[67]

In May 1978, Shlomo was invited to Maharishi International University (MIU),[68] in Fairfield, Iowa to lead a full Shabbat program of prayers, meals, and music.[69] At MIU, Jews constituted about 25% to 30% of the 700 undergraduates, six of the seven founding faculty, and three of the four college's top four administrators.[70] Eliezer Ben Baruch (Berkeley), president of Chavurat Shlemut, the Jewish student club at MIU, described how they organized their own synagogue with a kosher kitchen and Shabbat programming:

> Maharishi was actively encouraging his followers to develop "cultural integrity," i.e., to enliven their own religious traditions. As a result, our student club was funded by the University. The problem was to find rabbis who would offer religious programming without alienating the students. The Chabad representative who came was not accepting of our meditative life style. He would put up a picture of the Rebbe on top of our picture of Maharishi. Contrastingly, Shlomo offered a dynamic model of Judaism in its full expression without criticizing our meditative understandings of life. He taught us what it meant to be a religious Jew with a direct connection to Hakadosh Barukh Hou. For that we were very grateful.[71]

Nov. 1980, 4.

66. American *nusach* is defined here as the late 20th century refashioning of liberal Jewish worship to reflect the attitudes and beliefs of life in North America.

67. Benjamin Dreyfus, "Hear the Echoes of Miriam's song: American nusach in concert." *Studies in Jewish Musical Traditions: Insights from the Harvard collection of Judaica Sound Recordings*, Kay Kaufman Shelemay (Cambridge, MA: Harvard College Library, 2001), 33–50.

68. MIU was founded in 1973 as the American campus of the Transcendental Meditation (TM) Movement led by Maharishi Mahesh Yogi. By the late 1970s, TM had been taught to over one million people.

69. My thanks to Hananya Goodman for telling me about this story (Nov. 2012). Hananya (Andy) Goodman became a devoted disciple of Reb Shlomo in the late 1970s. He helped organize the program at MIU as well as programs for Shlomo at the Hillel House at Yale University.

70. Lawrence Tabak, "Learning to Levitate in Fairfield Iowa," *Moment Magazine*, vol. 4, no. 3, 26–32.

71. My thanks to Eliezer Ben Baruch for sharing this story (Nov. 24, 2012). Eliezer graduated MIU in 1978 and moved to Israel in 1981.

On Motzei Shabbat, Shlomo's concert at MIU was attended by 200 TM meditators. Even the president of the University, Prof. Larry Domash, came.[72] Reb Shlomo initiated a direct contact with Maharishi and tried to help him in his plan to set up a community of meditators in Israel.[73]

On June 7, 1978, Reb Shlomo and Reb Zalman led a Fabrengen at the Hillel Foundation, 2736 Bancroft Way, Berkeley, similar to the Farbrengen they had led four years earlier on June 16, 1974. In fact, the flyer was the same, with merely a change of date.[74]

On October 23, 1978, Reb Shlomo led the Simchat Torah program at the Carlebach Shul. One of those present was Sharie Yasgur Sofair. When she told Shlomo that she was studying music therapy in graduate school at New York University, he suggested that they play music together, and indeed from then on, Sharie accompanied him to many concerts and learning sessions. Sharie was deeply inspired by Shlomo. As a professional music therapist, she composed her own songs in addition to singing those of Shlomo.[75] Sharie recalls how years later, married with children, "Shlomo asked me in my home, Are you still my right hand man?"[76]

On Hanukkah, December 24, 1978, Shlomo was the featured performer at the Brotherhood Synagogue, 28 Gramercy Park South, a progressive congregation (Conservative) in downtown New York.[77]

Reb Shlomo had "managers" the world over. For example, Alex Klein, Shlomo's personal manager in England, arranged for his performances:

> From 1978 onwards, I arranged many concerts with Reb Shlomo. The first was for the ZCC (Zionist Central Council) at Mamlock House in Manchester. Shlomo played in Liverpool, Manchester, Leeds, and Stanmore. He went to the Edgware King David Primary School in Manchester and to the Oxford student club with Rabbi Shmuley Boteach. He *davened* at the Holy Law Synagogue in Manchester when Rabbi Ivan Wachmann was minister, and at Gatley, a suburban area of Manchester. He also went to Sale, a

72. Years later, Domash left the TM movement and became affiliated with Chabad. See Natan Ophir, "The Lubavitcher Rebbe's Call for a Scientific Non-Hasidic Meditation." *B'Or Ha'Torah*, vol. 22, 2013, 109–123.

73. Shacham, "Enfant Terrible."

74. The flyer was reproduced in Victor Gross, et.al., *Ancient Roots*, 17.

75. For her record *Sharie - My Heart/Leebee*, and her acknowledgements of Shlomo's role in her music see www.cduniverse.com.

76. Sharie Yasgur Sofair, "The First Moment," *Kol Chevra*, vol. 7, 2000, 100.

77. Eleanor Blau, "City Rings in Holiday Music and Pageantry; The City Rings In Holiday Music and Pageantry Concerts Around the City Motets and Masses Christmas-Carol Suite," *New York Times*, Dec. 22, 1978, The Weekend Section, C1.

town in Manchester with Rabbi Reuben Livingstone, and to Childwall, a suburb of Liverpool, with Rabbi Lional Cofnas.[78]

On March 13, 1979, Reb Shlomo continued his annual tradition of appearing on Purim at Dr. William Berkowitz's Congregation B'nai Jeshurun in Manhattan (see above). However, 1979 was unique because the Shah had just been overthrown in Iran, and Purim was the natural time to bring up concern for the welfare of the 70,000 Jews in the land of Ancient Persia where Purim began. David Friedman reported:

> Rabbi Shlomo Carlebach . . . sang several songs directly aimed at the Iranian Jews. The audience, under Carlebach's leadership, sounded a loud and enthusiastic Good Purim to the Iranian Jews.[79]

In April 1979, Shlomo was in Toronto with his wife Neila and their two young daughters when the World Symposium on Humanity was held in Toronto from April 7–14, 1979. This New Age ecumenical event was similar to one held in Vancouver 1976 (discussed above), but this time the idea was to have simultaneous events in Toronto, Los Angeles, and London, connected by interactive video satellite to demonstrate a theme of Universal Unity. Shlomo performed on Tuesday night, April 10, the night before Pesach when it is customary to check the house for *hametz*. Reb Shlomo remembered later: "There were hundreds of kids. I told them about *bedikat hametz*, how holy it is."

Although the interactive satellite connection failed, copies of Shlomo's prayer for peace in the Middle East, were distributed to the Jewish/ Moslem interfaith service held at London's Wembley Conference Centre. This was done in live time via a computer – a technological feat for the time.[80] Vocalist/percussionist Susan Slack was volunteering as a stage manager at that concert and reported her impressions of Reb Shlomo:

> He strummed while sing-songing words of compassion and brotherhood with such conviction you knew he had to be right. For the last half hour he invited everyone to come and join him in a circle, Schlomo [sic] at the top of the gently rising steps that led to the stage and the other couple hundred dancing and swaying

---

78. Personal communication from Alex Klein, Aug. 15, 2011.

79. David Friedman. "Teheran's Chief Rabbi Says Iran's Jews Have Nothing to Fear," *Jewish Telegraphic Agency*, March 14, 1979.

80. *AJR Information*, vol. XXXIV, no. 6, 3 issued by the Association of Jewish Refugees in Great Britain, June 1979, AJR.org.uk, http://www.ajr.org.uk/journalpdf/1979_june.pdf.

as they sang. This was totally mystical and transformational for everyone.[81]

Although raised a Presbyterian, Susan was so impressed that she spent that summer in Toronto attending Shlomo's classes in people's homes. Shlomo, who knew about her musical talents, invited her to sing:

> Not knowing any better I broke into "Amazing Grace." When people complained that it was not a Jewish song, he said it was a holy song, good for all to hear. He was a person who inspired universal love through the lense [*sic*] of Judaism. It seemed easy and natural to become a better person while singing with him.[82]

In Toronto, Reb Shlomo realized that there were many Jews at the Conference, and although they were celebrating Easter celebrations there was nothing planned for Pesach:

> It was during Easter and they had special Easter prayers. Nothing for Pesach. The leader of the group was named Yossi Cohn. *Gevalt.* As it so happens, Yossi is a good friend of mine. I said, "Yossi, you respect every religion except your own. We have two Seder nights, there will be thousands of people, many Jews. Can't you do something for them?" He said, "Okay, you do something."

This was Canadian astrologer, Joseph Mark Cohen, who had begun leading Kabbalistic astrology retreats in 1975.[83] He spoke to Carol Sokoloff, one of the volunteer organizers asking to arrange for Shlomo to lead a "Cosmic Seder" for the first night of Pesach. Sokoloff recalls:

> I knew that Shlomo would be with his family in a northern district of Toronto for the Seder so I didn't really think it possible. But Shlomo invented a solution. After finishing his family Seder, he would walk the few miles downtown to the university and the program could begin at 11:00 PM. He suggested the Seder consist of only symbolic foods, e.g., greens for the growth of spring, eggs for rebirth and the cycle of life. I arranged candles and greens, and Manischewitz donated matzah for our cause.[84]

---

81. Susan Slack, March 2, 2011, http://susanslackblog.wordpress.com/tag/world-symposium-on-humanity.

82. Ibid.

83. http://www.linkedin.com/in/josephmarkcohen; http://www.treeoflifeschool.com/ast.html.

84. Personal communications from Carol Sokoloff, Sept. 27, 2012, March 21, 2013.

Carol had a friend, Bob Wise, hand draw a poster advertisement using attractive Hebrew calligraphy. The conference copied it and had volunteers distribute it, saturating the Toronto campus with the following personal message from Reb Shlomo:

> Dear Brothers and Sisters,
>
> Please come and celebrate with us the holiest night of the year. The night when God's light is shining so strong that the lowest slave becomes free and the most unholy becomes holy. The night when all gates of heaven are open, let us be together to open our hearts. The night when we and our children are so close that Elijah the Prophet has come to tell us Redemption is near.[85]

In a postscript to the poster, guests were asked to bring a bottle of kosher-for-Passover grape juice and a hard-boiled egg. The Seder was held on April 11, 1979 in the Great Hall of Hart House in the University of Toronto. Shlomo walked an hour and twenty minutes with his brother-in-law Srul Glick and a few friends, arriving at the Toronto University campus shortly before midnight. Carol Sokoloff reports:

> We expected only a few people, but hundreds came. There were Buddhist monks and First Nations chiefs, each in colourful traditional garb. Here indeed was a splendid array of humanity from different countries and cultures, all joined in an ancient celebration of spiritual liberty.[86]

Shlomo was astonished at the huge crowd patiently awaiting him. His recollections of the event were enthusiastic and hyperbolic:

> To my most unbelievable surprise, 1,500 people were sitting at the tables, 1,500 people of every race, every religion were there. As far as I was concerned, that was the highest Seder on the planet. The fire and the holiness, their readiness was unbelievable. . . . About 3:30 AM, we went out to greet Eliyahu HaNavi. I want you to know, there were 1,500 candles standing by the door until a quarter to five.[87] I was telling Eliyahu HaNavi stories and all kinds of other

---

85. My thanks to Carol Sokoloff for discovering the original poster and sending it to me (March 21, 2013).

86. Carol Sokoloff, "Reb Shlomo's Cosmic Seder," *Jewish Independent*, April 7, 2006, JewishIndependent.Ca, http://www.jewishindependent.ca/Archives/April06/ archives06Apr07-11.html, and clarifications via email.

87. Shlomo had a Seder custom of taking candles to the door to greet Eliyahu HaNavi. Shlomo explained this custom in a teaching in Los Angeles at the Ritchies' home on March 16, 1972. A transcription of this teaching can be found in the Pesach collection by Rabbi Moshe Pesach Geller entitled "A Reb Shlomo Carlebach Pesach

things. Until this very day, I travel all over the world, I meet people who tell me they were at that unforgettable Seder.[88]

Recently, Carol commented:

> The recollections of Reb Shlomo convey the spirit of an amazing event. Indeed, we had a huge surprise at the impressive attendance filled with "fire and holiness." My memory is that there were much less than 1,500 people and that by the time we opened the door for Elijah we were about 30 people. But we felt so high that we probably had the power of 1,500.[89]

In November 1979, Reb Shlomo came to Berkeley for a three-day teaching and concert program beginning Sunday, November 25, 1979 at the Berkeley Hillel House, followed on November 26 at the home of David and Elaine Zeller in Palo Alto, and on November 27 at Congregation Beth Ami in Santa Rosa.[90]

In the beginning of September 1979, Susan Yael Mesinai was invited to prepare a collection of Shlomo's stories:

> I came home one day to my home in Manhattan and pinned on my door were two airplane tickets for my son and I. Tzlotana Barbara Midlo, at the request of Nechama Silver, had invited me to Israel to prepare a book of Shlomo Stories. And so I began collecting every tape and written version of the different stories. It was quite a creative challenge. Shlomo's oral teachings are meant to be heard. They dissolve when you transfer them to a printed page. To allow the story in its essence to rise out of his exposition requires a lot of restraint and listening as well as courage.[91]

Susan came to Jerusalem to write the book:

> It had to be in Eretz Israel because the whole thing was part of the *shefa* of Shlomo's blessing when I converted to Judaism. Yoel and Nomi Glick were very important to the project. They gave me

---

Guide: Teachings and Stories Collected from Various Sources over the Years." My thanks to Rabbi Geller for graciously sending me his book, which hopefully will soon receive the necessary funding for publication.

88. This memory of Shlomo from the early 1980s is part of a Pesach teaching that was transcribed in Rabbi Moshe Geller's collection.

89. Personal communication from Carol Sokoloff, March 25, 2013.

90. *The AMB* (Aquarian Minyan Berkeley) Nov.–Dec. newsletter, 1979 under the title "Reb Shlomo Returns."

91. Personal correspondence with Susan Yael Mesinai, April 2, 2013.

a place to live next to their home on 2 Hakinor St. in the Jewish Quarter of the Old City of Jerusalem.[92]

Susan consulted with Shlomo over the years "at least twenty times." Her book *Shlomo's Stories: Selected Tales* was published a month before Shlomo died. Mesinai wrote in her preface: Like everyone's dreams, these stories are filled with angst – constant questions of survival . . . of trying to live in a hostile environment. . . . They are tales that belong to the universe, spoken with a Jewish tongue. In putting them into literary form, I have been true to the hearing of them, for herein lies their power and their soul.[93]

In 1980, Shlomo toured the Far East for the first time.[94] In June 1980, Shlomo was scheduled to perform at the Clearwater Festival.[95] This annual folk music festival, known officially as the Great Hudson River Revival, was designed to raise environmental awareness. The founder and inspiration of the festival was Shlomo's esteemed friend, the famed folk singer, Pete Seeger.[96]

In the summer of 1980, Reb Shlomo was invited to the Unification Church training center for priests. This was an institution of Rev. Sun Myung Moon whose followers are known as the Moonies and it was highly unusual for outsiders to be allowed in past the barking dogs and wired fenced gates protecting the Belvedere International Training Center.[97] Estimates of the number of Jews in the Unification Church in 1980 ranged from 6% to as high as an incredible 50%![98]

---

92. Personal correspondence with Susan Yael Mesinai, April 2, 2013.

93. Mesinai, *Shlomo's Stories*, pp. xiii–xix.

94. Sam Weiss, "Shlomo Carlebach" in *Nine Luminaries of Jewish Liturgical Song*, 2003, KlezmerShack.com, http://www.klezmershack.com/articles/weiss_s/luminaries/#carlebach.

95. My thanks to Robert L. Cohen who provided this information (Nov. 5, 2012). However, Cohen added: "I don't know if Shlomo (who was scheduled, of course, only for Sunday) actually played there."

96. In 1966, Seeger first announced his plan to "build a boat to save the Hudson River" which at the time was filling with raw sewage, toxic chemicals, and oil pollution. In 1969, Seeger launched the *Clearwater* as a replica of the sloops that had sailed the Hudson in the 18th and 19th centuries. The Festival takes place annually on a weekend in June. For the story of this festival and Pete Seeger's involvement, see Clearwater.org, http://www.clearwater.org/about/the-clearwater-story.

97. Founded by the Korean evangelist, Rev. Sun Myung Moon, the official title of the Church is The Holy Spirit Association for the Unification of World Christianity. It is considered an evangelical enterprise where devotees are taught a mix of Pentecostal Christianity, Eastern mysticism and pop-psychology.

98. John Gordon Melton and Robert L. Moore, *The Cult Experience: Responding to the New Religious Pluralism* (New York: 1982), 30. Compare Arnold James Rudin

Naomi Mark was one of the *chevra* accompanying Shlomo. She recalls that although they were greeted with initial distrust, soon Shlomo's word-less tunes felled the differences and by 4:00 AM, "the entire seminary was dancing with us in a circle," singing *"Yerushalayim,"* hugging and kissing us.[99]

What was the secret of Shlomo? How did he break down barriers of suspicion? Shlomo spoke that night about the difference between errors in the physical world that require retracing your steps as opposed to the spiritual world where "the moment that you realize you've been off, you're already on – and on your way to being closer to God than ever." This message was well-received. Naomi, herself a trained psychotherapist, concluded:

> Shlomo planted subliminal messages in their consciousness that they too can return. Undoubtedly, at least one of those ministers must have been influenced positively by the events of that night.[100]

In retrospect, there are three ingredients in this type of outreach (or "wide-reach"). First, a love and respect for others of a totally different mindset. Second, using song, even wordless tunes, to communicate and establish rapport. Finally, the astute way of conveying a message that could be interpreted as non-threatening yet meaningful.

Shlomo's working assumption for groups like the Moonies and Transcendental Meditation was that there was a genuine spiritual mo-tivation just waiting to be channeled towards Judaism. To a journalist interviewer, Shlomo explained:

> I am in contact with the Moonies. The leaders of the Moonies are Jewish. There are signs that the youth will be disillusioned and then come to me. I also have a direct contact with the Maharishi, leader of Transcendental Meditation (TM). He has many adherents, also in Israel. The Maharishi would like to issue an imperative to the Jews that they should return to their sources. He is willing to send hundreds of his Jewish followers to set up a yeshiva in Israel. I met with him for that purpose. However, the program was jettisoned because the Chief Rabbis of Israel ruled that TM was idolatrous.[101]

and Marcia R. Rudin, *Prison or Paradise? The New Religious Cults* (Norristown, Pennsylvania: 1980), 101.

99. Naomi Mark, "Reb Shlomo and Tshuva," *Kol Chevra*, vol. 2, Nov. 1995, 9. Naomi Mark, personal communications, June 20, Sept. 5, 2012.

100. Naomi Mark, personal communication, Sept. 5, 2012.

101. Shacham, "Enfant Terrible." The interview was in March 1985 and Shlomo's explanation reflects an attempt by several Jewish leaders in the TM Movement both

On March 16, 1980, Reb Shlomo performed for a packed auditorium at Centre Rachi (now Centre d'Art et de Culture) in Paris. Elaine Rotstain was 24 years old. She had come to France from South America and was so deeply moved by the concert that she began a process of *teshuva*:

> Like many French Jews, I was merely a "cultural" Jew. But Shlomo's concert instilled in me the painful realization that Hashem was absent in my life. I began to feel an irrepressible desire for true Yiddishkeit even though it would entail a revolution in my life. At the time, I liked all aspects of Yiddish folklore, Jewish history, literature, etc., but Shlomo's concert made me realize that I was looking for something much more, for a true living presence of Hashem. Eventually, I became a *baalat teshuva*.[102]

A broadcast on French television entitled "*La Fiancée Chabbat*" (Shabbat Bride) was shown on November 9, 1980, with Reb Shlomo singing Kabbalat Shabbat tunes such as "*Shabbat Shalom*," "*Mikdash Melekh*," and "*Mizmor Shir*." It was directed and produced by Rabbi Josy Eisenberg as part of his Sunday television program, "*La Source de Vie*" (The Source of Life).[103]

On Sunday, June 8, 1980, Shlomo and the Neginah Orchestra performed at two street festivals in Manhattan – at the Jewish Peoplehood Week celebrations on West End Avenue and at the fourth annual Jewish Spring Festival on East Broadway on the Lower East Side.[104]

Shlomo's deep caring for people is illustrated in the story of Reva Rautenberg. Reva was a midwife who had delivered many babies on Moshav Me'or Modi'im when she was a resident there. In 1980, Reva was living on a farm in Rensselaer County, Upstate New York, when she became ill with cervical cancer. On Sunday, July 13, 1980, Shlomo traveled 150 miles by train from New York City just to be with her, singing and comforting. Reva died on July 15, 1980 and Shlomo again traveled some

---

in the U.S. (e.g., Lawrence Domash) and in Israel (e.g., Gad Tick) to set up a meditating community in Israel. This venture had begun in an advanced TM-Sidhis course in Safed, Israel, Nov. 19, 1978 – Jan. 10, 1979 with 400 participants mostly from the U.S. See above for Shlomo's Shabbat visit to the TM University campus in May 1978.

102. Personal interview with Elaine Rotstain, July 1, 2012.

103. The four parts were posted on YouTube on March 10, 2013: http://www.youtube.com/watch?v=rFS5niCneDo; http://www.youtube.com/watch?v=rWmjbQ83NA8; http://www.youtube.com/watch?v=ASnYVRno8ZM; http://www.youtube.com/watch?v=EMpclJ6H7EQ.

104. Ari L. Goldman, "4 Festive Affairs for a June Weekend," *New York Times*, June 6, 1980, C13.

eight hours back and forth from Manhattan, just to be there during the mourning and lead a *minyan*.[105]

3.   LONELINESS AND INNOVATION (1980–1983)

Three events in 1980 caused Shlomo loneliness and sadness: his ill health, his divorce, and his mother's death. For a while, he came to concerts on crutches because of a spinal infection.[106] With the divorce, Neila moved with their two daughters back to her home town, Toronto. Shlomo's mother, Rebbetzin Pessia, died on Shabbat, June 21, 1980 (7th of Tammuz) and was buried on Har HaMenuhot in Jerusalem next to her husband, R. Naphtali.[107] At the funeral Shlomo, instead of speaking, began to sing Psalms 23 ("*Mizmor L'David Hashem Roi*"):

> Someone taped it and gave me a copy. Later I decided that this is a good melody for *Nishmas*. That whole year I was singing it to *Nishmas* in honor of my mother.[108]

Rebbetzin Pessia had played a dominant role in running the Manhattan Synagogue and organizing the meals on Shabbat and festivals. She had been very involved in her son's life and welfare. Now, Shlomo was alone in his Manhattan home.

In September 1980, Judy Tibor (Brodt) moved into the Carlebach Shul upstairs apartment and gradually assumed the role as "manager" of Shlomo's learning programs and Shabbatot.[109] Shlomo would come to Manhattan once a month or so. But when he came, word spread rapidly.

---

105. My thanks to Bruce Ginsberg for this story. Bruce together with Reva's husband Jacob Rautenberg, picked up Shlomo from the train station and drove him back. After Reva died, Jacob changed his name to Yaakov Rahmana. Later he married Morasha, the widow of Mordechai Levy, one of Shlomo's disciples on the Moshav who had received *semicha* from him. My thanks to Chaim Cohen for this information (Jan. 6, 2013).

106. See Jack Sandhaus, "A Varmer (Warm) Yid," *Kol Chevra*, 17, 2011, 86. Sandhaus attended a Shlomo concert at the Café Baba in Queens, New York in 1980 where Shlomo "hobbled on crutches."

107. The inscription on her tombstone reads: "Her love for Torah and *b'nai Torah* knew no boundaries. She pursued *tzedakah* and *hesed* until her last moments" (my translation).

108. See Ben Zion Solomon, *Shlomo Shabbos*, 35. See below that when Reb Shlomo died, that Psalms 23 was sung at his funeral.

109. Judy had first met Shlomo in Sept. 1977, and under his influence gradually became religious and made aliyah. In 1980, Judy needed a place to live with her 10-year old daughter in New York, and Yoel Glick (Neila Carlebach's nephew) arranged for her to stay in the Carlebach apartment. Personal interview with Judy Tibor (Brodt), Oct. 15, 2012.

Melinda (Mindy) Ribner remembers how she helped prepare Friday evening meals for dozens of people on the "Shlomo Shabbatot."[110] In the summer of 1981, Shlomo and Eli Chaim decided to organize a rotation system for Shabbatot. Judy moved to Philadelphia where she worked as the program coordinator for Reb Zalman. This was a time that many Modern Orthodox families were moving into Manhattan's Upper West Side and the local synagogues were flourishing.[111]

On November 30, 1980 (two days before Hanukkah), Shlomo traveled to teach at Temple Beth Ami in Santa Rosa, California.[112] The following year, he returned to Santa Rosa to teach on Hanukkah, December 25, 1981. Shlomo spoke about hope in times of darkness – on Hanukkah the nights are longest and darkest and it is then that light can reach. This is God's Light. "If there is light deep inside you," then "you are the one to open the doors for God's light to shine into the world."[113]

In December 1980, on Hanukkah, Shlomo was invited to an interfaith program organized by Rabbi Joseph H. Gelberman.[114] The event took place at the Methodist Episcopal Church in Manhattan. Nachman Futterman, who was president of Gelberman's interfaith organization, was so impressed that he subsequently arranged for Shlomo to lead a *Kiddush HaLevana* new moon celebration every month at Futterman's Manhattan home on East 35th Street. This program continued for half a dozen times during 1981. Nachman became a devoted follower of Shlomo, soon moving to an apartment in close proximity to the Carlebach Shul where he took an active role in the Synagogue's reorganization.[115]

In 1981, Shlomo's last LP record was published.[116] It was entitled *L'Kovid*

---

110. Mindy was one of the active organizers in the Carlebach Shul from 1977 until Shlomo's death in 1994. Personal interviews with Mindy Ribner on Nov. 3, 2010 and June 25, 2012.

111. The Modern Orthodox renaissance actually began in the early 1970s when apartments on West End Avenue and its side streets were at relatively low rents. The people who moved in contributed to the development of several synagogues on the Upper West Side such as Lincoln Square Synagogue.

112. These teachings were recorded and transcribed by Reuven Goldfarb.

113. This was in Los Angeles at the home of his disciples, the Ritchies. See "Chanukah 1981 LA: A Teaching at the Ritchie's," *Kol Chevra*, 10, Oct. 2004, 20–24.

114. For an obituary of Rabbi Gelberman who died at age 98 on Sept. 9, 2010, see http://blog.beliefnet.com/inspirationreport/2010/09/interfaith-pioneer-rabbi-joseph-gelberman-dies-at-98.html#ixzz2G2YYPM6U.

115. Personal interview with Nachman Futterman, March 11, 2013.

116. This was Reb Shlomo's 15th LD. The record was produced by Sound Part Records, Oakville, Ontario. Shlomo gives special thanks to Bill Drew and Batsheva Paul for producing the record. The music was arranged, orchestrated and conducted by Milton Barnes. Accompanying Shlomo were Milton Barnes (percussion and

Shabbas[117] and dedicated to his two little daughters whose picture adorns the cover. Shlomo explained on the cover:

> Stories are pure and holy like children. That is why my stories are meant for children – for the child in us – all that is still untouched by facts and theory.[118]

On April 8, 1981, Reb Shlomo and Reb Zalman led a group of about 300 people in Blessing the Sun atop the Empire State Building.[119] They said *Hallel* and released seventy balloons, evoking the seventy bulls sacrificed on Sukkot for the mythical seventy nations of the world.[120]

Another innovative performance took place in February 1982 when David Zeller, who was active in the International Transpersonal Association (ITA), arranged to have Reb Shlomo and Reb Zalman speak and perform as the Jewish representatives at the Seventh Conference of the ITA in Bombay, India.[121] Reb Shlomo later described how the conference was organized by a woman who "was a Jew hater who didn't want any Jews there but every other religion was invited":

> We were the only religious leaders who had to pay our own way there, and we even had to pay admission to get in. When I got on stage I said I'm so privileged to be here in India, and I told them I am a real Jew from all four sides, and I want you to know what Judaism is all about. And this woman saw me the next day and

---

piano), Joseph Macerolla (accordion), Paul Pulford (Cello), Alan Torok (classical guitar), and Larry Sereda (saxophone, clarinet, and flute).

117. This unusual transliteration might reflect a connection to the Yiddish.

118. The stories on this record include "The Holy Hunchback," "Beyond Paradise," and "The Creation." The Shabbat songs include *"Shalom Aleichem," "Lecha Dodi," "Mizmor Shir," "Yismechu," "Harachaman," "Kol M'kadesh," "Va'ani B'chasdecha," "Shabbat Shalom,"* and *"Gut Shabbas."*

119. The *Birkat HaChama* blessing, recited merely 3 times a century, marks the sun's return every 28 years "to its original point in the heavens."

120. The number of 300 participants is given by Julie Wiener, "Love the Earth, Bless the Sun," *The Wall Street Journal*, April 3, 2009, OnLine.WSJ.com, http://online.wsj.com/article/SB123872560930985495.html. Cf. Jonathan Mark, "When The Blessing Was Born," *The New York Jewish Week*, March 24, 2009, TheJewishWeek.com, http://www.thejewishweek.com/features/when_blessing_was_born.

121. Some 700 people participated and the proceedings were published in 22 chapters – Stanislav Grof (ed.), *Ancient Wisdom and Modern Science*, SUNY series in Transpersonal and Humanistic Psychology (Albany, New York: 1984), SunyPress.edu, http://www.sunypress.edu/p-23-ancient-wisdom-and-modern-scien.aspx; http://books.google.com/books?id=UMkzkPqyPYoC&printsec=frontcover&dq=Ancient+Wisdom+and+Modern+Science&hl=iw&ei=2wXzTePGB4z2sgbUip2tBg&sa=X&oi=book_result&ct=result&resnum=1&ved=0CCoQ6AEwAA#v=onepage&q&f=false.

hugged me and was crying. She said: "When you said that you were disgustingly Jewish, I said to myself, whom am I fooling? I'm not a Buddhist or a Hindu. I'm a Yid." She went to Israel and is now a *frum* woman.[122]

Reb Zalman appeared on stage replete in his *streimel* and *kapote* as befitting a Hasidic rebbe. He led a meditation based on the four Kabbalistic worlds.[123] At the musical program on Wednesday evening, Reb Zalman invited musician Paul Horn up to the stage and they had a musical exchange of flute and *shofar*.[124] Shlomo led the singing that for the first time at that conference brought everyone to hold hands and dance "for what seemed like hours," and the management feared that the stage would collapse.[125]

Mindy Ribner, who was invited by Reb Shlomo to join the trip, describes their visit to the synagogue of the Jewish community in Bombay:

> Reb Shlomo instructed me to get all the women dancing and we danced together with great joy. These Jews had met very few rabbis from the West before. You can imagine how overjoyed they were to meet rabbis like Reb Shlomo and Reb Zalman.[126]

In 1982, Shlomo invited Shoshannah, a composer pianist, to accompany him at the Lincoln Square Synagogue in Manhattan. Shoshannah soon became a regular with Reb Shlomo. She describes her experience:

> Reb Shlomo hired me to accompany him on both piano and on African Gjembe Drum in about forty concerts in New York and Israel. He even asked me to lead off several events with my own Jew/New Age renditions of his music. When I would play on stage with him, it was if Divine love was flowing through me with sublime melodies soothing the soul.[127]

---

122. Brenner, *Talkline*, segment 38:50. A similar story is told by Zeller, *The Soul of the Story*, 205.

123. For an explanation of Reb Zalman's 4-world meditation, see Kamenetz, *Stalking Elijah*, Chapter 4, 16–18. Reb Zalman told me in a Skype conversation on Aug. 7, 2011 that it was a "Transpersonal Mass" intended to resonate with the ideas of the Transpersonal Association.

124. Skype interview with Reb Zalman, Aug. 7, 2011.

125. Zeller, *The Soul of the Story*, 204–205.

126. Personal communication, June 25, 2012.

127. Personal interview with Shoshannah, Oct. 3, 2011. In 1989, Shoshannah performed at venues such as Lincoln Center, United Nations and Carnegie Hall, and played with famous recording artists such as David Darling, Giora Feidman, Laraaji and Glen Velez. Today, Shoshannah lives in Jerusalem and has developed Piano Therapy and Spiritual Piano Playing, as well as producing piano albums: *Sanctuary*,

Shoshannah was deeply impressed by Reb Shlomo:

> When I would hear his songs, tears would fall down uncontrol-
> lably. My *neshama* was opening up. From Shlomo I learned that
> music is channeling, just letting God's inspiration flow through
> you. I began a spiritual search, eventually entered "into the Torah
> world" and moved to Jerusalem.[128]

On June 28, 1982, Reb Shlomo officiated together with Reb Zalman
and Reb Meir Fund at the wedding of Sholom Brodt and Judy Tibor
in Pottstown, Pennsylvania. The couple worked in Jewish education in
Montreal. There Judy would arrange concerts and learning events for
Shlomo in Montreal five or six times a year.[129]

The three rabbis (Shlomo, Zalman, and Meir), together with Reb
Dovid Din, were invited by Gedalya and Naomi Persky to a retreat en-
titled "Ruach: Spirit of Judaism" from July 1 – July 5, 1982. It took place at
The Abode of The Message, a Sufi retreat center founded in 1975 by Pir
Vilayat Khan in New Lebanon, Upstate New York.[130] More than one-third
of the commune members had been born Jewish. Both Reb Zalman and
Reb Shlomo had visited there before.[131]

John (Gedalya) Persky had known very little about his Judaism when
he came to the Sufi center in 1975 "looking for spirituality." When Reb
Zalman visited there, John discovered that he "had a Jewish name," and
it was Gedalya. Over the next few years, he began seeking Judaism.[132]
Gedalya and Naomi[133] convinced The Abode members to allow them

---

Gifts from Heaven, and *Deepheart Awakening, Eternal Love* and *Rivers of Light*. See
www.aish.com/family/heart/Spiritual_Piano_Lessons.asp;   http://www.myspace
.com/shoshannahpiano.

128. Personal interview with Shoshannah, Oct. 3, 2011. See also Shoshannah Sarah,
"Spiritual Piano Lessons," *Mishpacha Magazine*, 2006, Aish.com, http://www.aish
.com/f/hotm/48936052.html.

129. Personal interview with Judy Tibor (Brodt), Oct. 15, 2012.

130. See above, Chapter 7, how both Zalman and Shlomo were friendly with Pir
Vilayat Khan.

131. Bruce (Hashir) Ginsberg who was living at the time in Upstate New York about
15 miles from The Abode of The Message, remembers how he brought Reb Shlomo
"to play concerts at The Abode in December 1979/January 1980 and again in early
1981." Personal communication, Nov. 28, 2012.

132. Gedalya Persky, "How I Met Shlomo," *Kol Chevra*, vol. 16, 2010, 110. After
graduating Boston University in 1974, John Persky lived a hippie life under the name
Otis East Wind in the East Wind Community in the Missouri Ozarks. After seeing
the *Sunseed* movie (see above, Chapter 7), he moved to Pir Vilyat Kahn's Abode of
The Message. My thanks to Gedalya Persky for this story (Jan. 9, 2013).

133. Gedalya and Naomi were married in a Sufi ceremony at The Abode, then with
a Justice of the Peace, and finally, in a Jewish religious Chabad ceremony.

to host a Jewish Retreat. After all, this was a liberal minded commune with all kinds of New Age events from Buddhist meditation to Native American Indians – so why not have a Jewish event.[134]

A commune member, Tzilia Sacharow, recalls what happened at the retreat:[135]

> We camped out on top of a mountain at the Abode,[136] the Sufi community where Naomi and I lived. There was a beautiful round tent where the sessions were held and a little kitchen without electricity. We made an *eruv* in the woods and stayed within it for the five days of Ruach. I think sixty people came.[137]

Before the retreat, Shlomo phoned Gedalya and asked if he could have a *Sheva Berachot* celebration for a newlywed couple. Gedalya agreed even though he was not yet even familiar with what a *Sheva Berachot* was.[138] So Shlomo brought Judy and Shalom Brodt, whose marriage he had performed a few days before, and led an ecstatic celebration on Motzei Shabbat, July 3. Wally Speigler, one of the participants, later described how Shlomo created great excitement with his singing and dancing:

> The gathering in the tent went wild. We were high on celebration. Some of the Sufi residents from the commune below heard the commotion and joined in the celebration with their twirling dances. We were ecstatic, intoxicated on life.[139]

Shlomo would continue to be a regular featured speaker/performer at fifteen Ruach Retreats organized by Gedalya and Naomi Persky. These events reflect an important part of Reb Shlomo's outreach programming in the last decade of his life.[140]

On Sunday, December 19, 1982 at 7:00 PM, Shlomo appeared at Town Hall in Manhattan.[141]

In January 1983, Shlomo sang in Germany at a "festival of hope" on the fiftieth anniversary of Hitler's rise to power. But when he returned

---

134. Naomi Persky, "Ruach Retreats – 25 Years New," *Kol Chevra*, vol. 14, 2008, 157–159.

135. Tzilia (Meyers) Sacharow met Shlomo in 1961 (see above, Chapter 3).

136. The Abode of The Message maintained a commune at the foot of a mountain and a retreat center on the top.

137. http://www.facebook.com/pages/Ruach-the-Spirit-of-Judaism/19671136837.

138. Gedalya Persky, personal interview, Jan. 9, 2013.

139. Wally Speigler, JewishHealing.com, http://www.jewishhealing.com/spirituality 12.html#top.

140. I thank Gedalya Persky for supplying the dates, places, and participants of these 15 retreats.

141. For the announcement, see *New York Magazine*, Dec. 20, 1982, 104.

home to Manhattan on Thursday, February 3, 1983, he faced an eviction order. The court had ruled in favor of his landlord who had been trying for a long time to raise the rent to $800 a month instead of $260. An eviction order was prepared for both Reb Shlomo and the Synagogue.[142] The congregants planned a protest for Sunday, February 6, 1983. Steve (Simcha) Goldstein, the president of the Carlebach Shul, announced: "If the marshals come, we'll demonstrate outside."[143]

Bruce (Hashir) Ginsberg recalls how the landlord, Sol Goldman, was a wealthy real estate developer who could have made a veritable fortune if he had ousted the synagogue and built a skyscraper with dozens of luxury co-op apartments:

> Goldman owned the "air rights" over the building and wanted to construct a high-rise on top of the two-story *shul*. However, he knew that the development plan would not be approved so long as a synagogue existed on the ground floor because he would need a lobby for his planned co-op. The controversy intensified when he tried to forcibly evict the *shul* and had City Marshals padlock the entrance. We had to break in through a side window from the courtyard and bring the Torah scrolls to the Carlebach apartment upstairs. We demonstrated to publicize our plight and Rabbi Avi Weiss was one of our speakers.[144]

Eventually Goldman was convinced to allow the Synagogue to continue, and $5,000 was paid for back rent and security. Later, when Goldman raised the rent to $1,500 a month, the Congregation launched a campaign to purchase the building, but it took until 1991 before they succeeded.[145]

4.   REORGANIZATION (1983–1988)

One of the practical results of the eviction threat was to galvanize the Carlebach regulars to fundraise and organize a budget. In 1983, Nachman

---

142. "The Appellate Division permitted the landlord, under city rent regulations, to empty both the downstairs synagogue and the rabbi's apartment upstairs" – Laurie Johnston and Robin Herman, "New York Day by Day," *New York Times*, Feb. 3, 1983.

143. Ibid.

144. Personal communications with Bruce (Hashir) Ginsberg, Nov. 28–Dec. 3, 2012. Hashir was one of Shlomo's concert musicians and a member of the Carlebach Shul. At Shlomo's personal request he served on the Synagogue's Board of Trustees from 1989 until 1994. See the photo with Hashir and Elli-Moshe Kline who helped save the Synagogue.

145. See below for the Eliyahu the Prophet incognito event in 1991 that enabled the eventual purchase. Based on communications from Rebbetzin Hadassa Carlebach, Sept. 24, 2012 and Nov. 1, 2012.

Futterman became president of the Carlebach Shul and for the first time an actual salary was budgeted for Reb Shlomo in the amount of $36,000 a year.[146] Reb Eli Chaim and his wife Rebbetzin Hadassa moved in the second floor and paid the rent. Hadassa was appointed executive director. She also prepared the Friday night communal meals and published a regular newsletter.[147] A board of directors was formed and many people assumed leadership roles.[148]

A key figure in the reorganization of the Carlebach Shul beginning was Rabbi Sammy (Shmuel Chaim) Intrator. Born in Baltimore, Maryland in 1955,[149] Sammy first met Shlomo at a Purim concert in February 1975 at the Congregation B'nai Jeshurun in Manhattan (see above, section 2). In 1983, Shlomo asked Sammy to organize his concert bookings. Sammy studied with Reb Shlomo for many years and received ordination from him. Together with Rivka Haut, he edited *Connections*, a bi-monthly newsletter/magazine put out by Hakrev Ushma, an organization that Shlomo set up to offer "a full schedule of classes, concerts and religious events." Beginning in 1985 some fifteen issues were published and they helped create a sense of community for followers of Reb Shlomo scattered the world over.

With Sammy's efficient management, Reb Shlomo pursued innovative programming. On June 29, 1983, Shlomo participated in a public meeting together with Grandfather Semu Huaute, an Indian healer, Chumash Medicine Man, at the Hillel Foundation, Berkeley, California.[150] Then, for Shabbat, Shlomo traveled back to New York to join the second annual Ruach Retreat which took place from June 30 – July 4, 1983 at The Abode of The Message.[151]

For Dr. Bonna Devora Haberman, this 1983 Ruach Retreat, changed her life when Reb Shlomo involved her in the liturgical readings:

---

146. Personal interview with Nachman Futterman, March 11, 2013.

147. Personal communication with Hadassa Carlebach, Nov. 2, 2012.

148. Some of the women activists at Kehilath Jacob in the 1980s included Chaya Adler, Chana Klemberg, Devorah Preiss-Blum, and Louise Temple (Barret). Barbara Meyer, who was a founding member of the board and served for 4 terms as vice president, was one of those who helped put together Reb Shlomo's visits in 1989 to Poland and Russia (see above, Chapter 9).

149. Sammy studied at Ner Yisroel Rabbinical College, Yeshivat Derech Chaim, and Yeshivat Kol Yaacov, where he received his rabbinic ordination. He also earned a degree in political science and worked for the New York City Council for 16 years. My thanks to Rabbi Sammy Intrator for interviews in July 2011 and Aug. 2012.

150. Reuven Goldfarb, "Joy," *Kol Chevra*, vol. 8, 2001, 87–88.

151. Also participating were Reb Dovid Din, Reb Meir Fund, Miriam Minkoff, and Lev Friedman.

> When Reb Shlomo invited me to chant *Shir HaShirim* – Song of Songs – one Erev Shabbat, and called me up to the Torah for an *aliyah* the next morning at a Ruach-Spirit retreat in 1983, he changed my life. I stood trembling by him at the *bimah*, encompassed by my *tallit*, engulfed by his tangible affirmation and love. Having grown in an Orthodox community, I had struggled to be permitted to learn Rambam, to study *gemara*-Talmud. This was the first time I had witnessed a formidable religious leader respect, include, and celebrate women at the core of Jewish practice, as full participants and as leaders. Shlomo welcomed me, affirmed my desire for public Jewish practice.[152]

Bonna eventually went on to become one of the primary movers of Women of the Wall (see below).

Reb Shlomo was a featured speaker/singer in San Francisco on a Sunday afternoon, September 25, 1983 (Hol HaMoed Sukkot). He was the only rabbi to appear in this three-day conference on Nuclear Disarmament: Moving Forward sponsored jointly by the Association of Humanistic Psychology, the Ecumenical Peace Institute, and Meeting of the Ways. This was the second annual gathering of peace activists, human potential leaders and spiritual teachers. It took place in a warehouse on Fort Mason's Pier Three. Dio Urmilla Neff reported about the event in a feature article in *Yoga Journal* and summarized how Rabbi Shlomo differentiated between two kinds of teaching, the transfer of information as opposed to the more essential and important holy transfer of light which is what is needed now.[153]

In November 1983, Shlomo gave a Sunday morning concert for 400 students and parents at the Ohav Sholom Hebrew School in Merrick, Long Island in Nassau County, New York.[154]

In March 1984, a pre-Purim concert was organized for Reb Shlomo at the Walt Whitman Auditorium located at the Brooklyn Center for the Performing Arts at Brooklyn College. Dov Shurin, who played guitar

---

152. Personal correspondence with Bonna Devora Haberman, June 9, 2013 and based on Bonna's blog http://bonnadevorahaberman.wordpress.com.

153. Dio Urmilla Neff, "Men and Peacemaking: A Meeting of the Ways," *Yoga Journal*, March–April, 1984, no. 55, 35–37, 64. For the program advertisement and list of participants, see *Yoga Journal*, Sept. 1983, no. 52, 58.

154. See Isaacs, "A Teacher." The principal, Mel Isaacs, picked up Shlomo and his daughters from his Manhattan hotel. Mel had met Shlomo earlier that year when Goldie, his future wife, had invited Shlomo to sing at her home in Brooklyn (see above for the story of Goldie Stern as a 17-year old fan of Shlomo in 1957). Personal interview with Mel Isaacs, Dec. 20, 2012.

Rally to save the Carlebach Shul after February 3, 1983 eviction order. In the photo with Shlomo are Bruce (Hashir) Ginsberg and Eli-Moshe Kline. Photo courtesy of Bruce (Hashir) Ginsberg

with Reb Shlomo, recalls how this was intended as a rapprochement with the *haredi* religious world. Seating was separate and Reb Shlomo wore a tie and suit and added Yiddish explanations. According to Shurin, Reb Shlomo said in Yiddish to his audience: "Maybe I went too far. At the time I had no one to talk to. But my intention was to bring lost souls back to Judaism." However, only a mere 700 tickets were sold for the 2,500-seat theater.[155]

On March 17, 1984, Purim after the *megillah* reading, Shlomo and the Neginah Orchestra played at Congregation B'nai Jeshurun on West 88th St. in Manhattan.[156]

On June 1–3, 1984, Shlomo and David Zeller led a Shabbat retreat at the Joy Lake Community near the Sierra Nevada Mountains, 30 minutes south of Reno, Nevada. This was scheduled to be followed by a Shavuot retreat from June 3–8. Susan Jacobs, a San Francisco freelance writer who specializes in health and healing, and serves as a contributing editor of *Yoga Journal*, was there for Shabbat together with about twenty people. Susan discovered her spiritual roots:

> Born a Jew, I never felt particularly Jewish . . . I just couldn't understand why anyone would choose to center their whole life around religion. On the outside I was Jewish, but Judaism failed to touch me deeply . . . Rabbis Shlomo Carlebach and David Zeller became

---

155. Dov Shurin, personal interview, July 21, 2011.

156. Ari L. Goldman, "Special Joys of Purim Marked Around City," *New York Times*, March 16, 1984, C20.

guides who helped me navigate the path back to my roots. . . . Since then I have travelled to various other locations including Israel to hear them speak, listen to them play, and basically learn from them about the richness and joyousness of Judaism.[157]

Reb Shlomo led the teaching at the third annual Ruach Retreat which took place over the weekend of June 29–July 3, 1984 at The Abode of The Message in New Lebanon, New York.[158]

Then for July 7, 1984, Shlomo was scheduled to appear at the Rainbow Family Peace Gathering in the Modoc National Forest in Northeastern California.[159] This was a major annual event of the counterculture peace movement and drew about 28,000 participants.[160] Shlomo was scheduled to perform on Motzei Shabbat after Richie Havens. As it was getting really late at night, people told him that he should forget it and go home as nobody would stay. Shlomo began at 11:00 PM and mesmerized the crowd until 3:00 AM. Even Richie stayed and then complimented him saying "You have the whole world at your feet." Shlomo, laughing, recalled that "it was *gevalt* to receive *semicha* from Richie Havens."[161]

On Sunday, September 9, 1984, Shlomo performed at the Jewish Peoplehood Festival on West End Ave. in Manhattan.[162]

On January 23, 1985, Rosh Hodesh Shevat, Shlomo was hosted for a

---

157. Susan Jacobs, "A New Age Jew Revisits Her Roots." *Yoga Journal* 61, March–April 1985, 32–34, 59.

158. Also teaching there were Reb Meir Fund, Reb Dovid Din, Reb Dovid Zeller, and Dr. Blema Feinstein (her name at the time was publicized as Dr. Bahira Feinstein).

159. For the reconstruction of this event, I am basing myself on Shlomo's response to Alon Teeger's interview question in Johannesburg in Sept. 1992. Teeger had asked Shlomo to tell about his greatest concerts and Shlomo recalled a "Rainbow Festival" in California "in 1982 or 1983." However, the only Rainbow Gathering then in California was during the week of July 4, 1984. For the listing of the annual sites of the Rainbow Gatherings in North America, see WelcomeHome.org, http://www .welcomehome.org/rainbow/sites/allsites.html.

160. The Rainbow Gathering was a free festival designed to celebrate the ideas of "equality and love." It was organized during the week of July 4, American Independence Day. For the 1984 festival, see Michael I. Niman, *People of the Rainbow: A Nomadic Utopia*, 2nd ed. (Knoxville, Tennessee: 1997), 175–176. Compare Richard Dannelley, *Sedona: Beyond the Vortex* (Flagstaff, Arizona: 1995), 7: "The silence was to be held until noon, at which time we were to say many unending OMs as we focused our thoughts on world peace and healing." Approximately 3,000 people were in that circle "convinced that the power of our prayers had changed planetary destiny."

161. Interview with Teeger 1992 (Rena Teeger's transcription, p. 17). An excerpt from this interview was printed in *Kol Chevra*, 13, 2007, 37.

162. Ari L. Goldman, "Ethnic Celebrations Bid Summer Farewell, *New York Times*, Sept. 7, 1984.

concert/teaching in Temple Beth Abraham, Oakland, California by his close friend Rabbi Joe Schonwald.[163] Towards the end of the concert, Reb Shlomo heard about a woman named Bella Tobias who was very ill. He heard that it would be most meaningful for Bella to receive *semicha*. Reb Shlomo called up Reuven Goldfarb, Barry Barkan, and Joe Schonwald, and presented a *"semicha"* type document to Bella. Unfortunately, she died a week later.[164]

For the Shabbat weekend of March 22–24, 1985, Reb Shlomo was featured at a Ruach Retreat that was held in Florida.[165]

On May 20, 1985, a special event was organized to honor Reb Shlomo and to raise funds for Moshav Me'or Modi'im. It was hosted by Bob and Clare Goldman at the elegant restaurant La Difference, on Manhattan's West Side. Speakers included Rabbis Eli Chaim Carlebach, Avi Weiss, Meir Fund, and Chaim Brovender.[166] The guests were presented with a book containing sixty-seven photographs of the Moshav Me'or Modi'im community.[167] This was one of the very few fundraising events organized for Shlomo's endeavors.[168]

In the summer of 1985, Shlomo led a July 4th program in the Catskills at the Fialikoff Bungalow Colony. Then for Shabbat, July 5–6, he joined the fourth annual Ruach Retreat which took place this time at Mt. Tremper, a Zen Mountain Monastery in the Catskills about ten miles west of Woodstock, New York.[169] After that, Shlomo traveled to Israel where he spent the rest of the summer from July 10 until August 26, 1985.[170]

Reb Shlomo's followers helped spread his songs and teachings around the world to far-flung Jewish communities. Pearl Atkin visited Romania

---

163. The concert was recorded and I received a copy in 37 digitalized files.

164. Personal interview with Rabbi Joe Schonwald, Feb. 5, 2012.

165. Other participants included Reb Dovid Din, Reb Meir Fund, and Dr. Blema Feinstein.

166. Rivka Haut, "Tribute to Shlomo," *Hakrev Ushma* (*Connections*), vol. 1, issue 3, June–July, 1985, 26–29. Musicians included Martin Davidson and Yoel Sharabi. For pictures from this event see pages 30–31.

167. Korenbrot, *Return to Modi'im*. See above, Chapter 8. On the book cover is a picture of a hand sifting sand with a concentration camp number. This was meant to symbolize the connection to the Holocaust. My thanks to Jonathan Daniel for this explanation.

168. Alon Teeger reports that Shlomo and Neila traveled to the New York airport to pick up the 3 Moshav Me'or Modi'im representatives: Alon Teeger, Michael Golomb, and Avraham Trugman. The 3 had arrived in sandals and informal dress so Shlomo took them to buy suits and shoes. About $150,000 was raised for the Moshav.

169. The Ruach Retreat was from July 4–7, 1985 and included Reb Dovid Din, Reb David Zeller, Dr. Blema Feinstein, and Miriam Minkoff.

170. *Hakrev Ushma* (*Connections*), vol. 1, issue 3, June/July 1985, 45.

in 1982 to locate the graves of her father's parents.[171] She became close to the Jewish communities there and brought them Shlomo's tapes. Then in 1985, Pearl arranged for Shlomo to give three concerts in Romania (one in Iași and two in Bucharest). "We were all touched by Shlomo's speaking to them in Yiddish and telling them how proud he was that they had come through Hitler, Fascism, and Communism."[172]

On Sunday, September 22, 1985, Shlomo participated in a Ruach Retreat event at the Midtown YMCA in New York City.

The schedule of events from October 1985 was detailed by Rabbi Sammy Intrator in the *Carlebach Synagogue Bulletin*:

On Friday, October 18, 1985, Shlomo flew to Seattle, Washington where he was hosted by Sara and Robert (Bob) Kupor for Shabbat *Parshat Noah*. They celebrated the birth of their daughter Daniella Miriam with a *kedushat bat*. The Kupors had a tradition – they celebrated with Shlomo the *kedushat bat* in 1974 in San Francisco[173] of their daughter Devra Rachelle, and in 1975 in Chattanooga of Elana Ruth.[174] The Kupors were members of the Beth Shalom Synagogue, an egalitarian synagogue affiliated with the United Synagogue for Conservative Judaism, and on Motzei Shabbat, Shlomo was the guest performer in the synagogue. During the week of October 20–23, Shlomo appeared before children at several schools and in the evenings taught at private homes. Sammy Intrator described what transpired in between Shlomo's public appearances:

> Swamis, Sufis, and Yogis knock on his door, most of whom are Jewish by birth but their only Jewish identification is through Shlomo. They talk theology, spirituality, and Bible.[175]

On October 23, Shlomo performed at the San Francisco Jewish Community Center. Then, on October 24, he taught at the home of Don Rothenberg, about "humility, holiness, and secrets of life." Finally, on Friday, October 25, 1985, Shlomo arrived in Los Angeles to spend Shabbat with Dr. Joshua and Liliane Ritchie and to perform at a *Melaveh Malkah*.[176]

---

171. Pearl Atkin, "In Memoriam to Haim Ghidale," *Hakrev Ushma* (*Connections*), vol. 3, 1987, 7–8.

172. Pearl Atkin, "At Shlomo's Shloshim," *Kol Chevra*, vol. 7, 2000, 55–56.

173. After receiving a Ph.D. from Harvard in microbiology, Bob did research at the University of California in San Francisco. See Diana Brement, "Examining Politics from the Inside," jtnews.net, The Voice of Jewish Washington, Sept. 7, 2007, JTNews .net, http://www.jtnews.net/index.php?/columnists/item/3332/C7.

174. *L'Koved Reb Shlomo Remembrance Journal*, Nov. 1995.

175. *Hakrev Ushma* (*Connections*), vol. 1, issue 5, Oct.–Dec., 1985, 3–12.

176. Ibid.

On November 16, 1985, Shlomo gave a benefit concert for the Merrimack Valley Hebrew Academy in Lowell, Massachusetts.[177]

※

Here is a busy list of Shlomo's touring in December 1985:[178]

Friday, December 6–7: Shabbaton at Congregation Shomrei Israel, Poughkeepsie, New York, including a Motzei Shabbat concert.

December 8: First Day Hanukkah Concert at Congregation Agudath Israel in Newburgh, New York.

December 9–10: Paris, France.

December 11–12: Me'or Modi'im, Israel.

Friday–Shabbat, December 13–14: Shabbaton at Congregation Havurat Israel,[179] Forest Hills, New York including a Motzei Shabbat Hanukkah concert with NCSY youth at Congregation Ezrath Israel at Ellenville, New York.[180]

December 15: Kehilath Jacob in Manhattan, and in the evening at 7:30 PM a concert at the Alternative Healing Center at Public School 192, Brooklyn.

Friday–Shabbat, December 20–21: Flatbush, Brooklyn Shabbaton at an old age home, the Scharome Manor,[181] including a Motzei Shabbat concert.

Sunday, December 22: Concert at Temple Emanuel, a Reform congregation in Great Neck, New York.[182]

December 23: Miami Jewish Community Center with a children's performance at 2:00 PM, and a concert for adults at 7:30 PM.

December 24–26: Concerts at various Miami Beach resort hotels.

Friday, December 27 until January 1: Five-day retreat at Monterey, California.[183]

---

177. I thank Rabbi Baruch Melman for this information (Nov. 7, 2012). He was a teacher at the Merrimack Hebrew Academy and attended this concert.

178. *Hakrev Ushma* (*Connections*), vol. 1, issue 5, 16.

179. The original in *Hakrev Ushma* (*Connections*) says "Havuth Israel" but I assume this is a spelling mistake and that the reference is to a synagogue named Havurat Yisrael Congregation which held Shabbat services at 113th St. in Forest Hills.

180. EzrathIsrael.org, http://www.ezrathisrael.org. The synagogue is located in the foothills of the Catskills, 90 miles from New York City.

181. This is an assisted living facility for adults located on 631 Foster Avenue, Brooklyn, New York off Ocean Parkway in Flatbush. See ScharomeManor.com, http://www.scharomemanor.com/index.html.

182. Emanuelgn.org, http://www.emanuelgn.org/index.htm.

183. Monterey is a waterfront community on the central coast of California where many musical festivals are hosted. See Monterey.org, http://www.monterey.org.

Finally, for January 1986, Reb Shlomo was scheduled to travel again to
France and Israel.

✳

For the weekend of January 31 – February 2, 1986, Shlomo was invited
by Rabbi Gerald Friedman, executive director of Hillel at the University
of Florida. During his tenure at Hillel, Rabbi Friedman invited Shlomo
many times to Florida, but this Shabbat was a response to a tragic
event – the crash of space shuttle *Challenger* on January 28, 1986. Rabbi
Friedman recalls:

> It was a very emotional time for the American people. For Jews
> there was an additional reason of mourning because one of the
> seven crew members killed was Judith Resnik, the first American
> Jewish astronaut to go into space. I knew we needed something
> very special so I invited Shlomo. He came to campus for Shabbat.
> People were crying in *shul*. Many faculty members and leading
> University officials attended, anxious to respond to the tragedy
> from a Jewish perspective. It was Shabbat *Parshat Yitro* and
> Shlomo spoke about "the Torah of standing, even when you feel
> like collapsing." He made it so pertinent.[184]

Reb Shlomo was again in Florida during the weekend of February 28 –
March 2, 1986, this time as a keynote celebrity at the Ruach Retreat.[185]

The diversity of innovative outreach work is also illustrated in Reb
Shlomo's tour of South Africa, July 9–23, 1986. Organized by Tzvi Matz,
under the auspices of JSUP (Jewish Students University Program), the
highlight of the tour included two major concerts at the Civic Theatre
in Johannesburg on July 22–23, 1986.[186] In addition, Alon Teeger, the
manager of Shlomo's programs in Israel and Europe in the 1980s, set up
a variety of events.[187] The visit began in Pretoria with a learn-in at the

---

184. Personal interview with Rabbi Gerald Friedman, Feb. 5, 2013.

185. Other participants included Reb Dovid Din, Reb Meir Fund, Dr. Blema
Feinstein, and Rabbi Chaim Richter.

186. Alon Teeger produced a double tape of the second concert which he called
Alive in South Africa, Vol. 1–2 (1986). This tape is listed in the discography, compiled
at Sojourn Records, ShlomoCarlebachMusic.com, http://shlomocarlebachmusic.
com/?page_id=64.

187. Alon and his wife, Rena, had first met Reb Shlomo in London in July 1977.
The Teegers moved to Moshav Me'or Modi'im in the summer of 1979, and Alon
served on the Moshav management committee until 1988 when they returned with
their 4 daughters to South Africa for a few years. The information here is based on a
personal interview with Alon in his home in the Moshav on April 10, 2012.

home of Rabbi Lewis Furman, and stories/songs at the Carmel Jewish Day School in Pretoria. Then, in Johannesburg, Reb Shlomo appeared in many different places including a restaurant with Cantor Ari Klein[188] and a major event on Sunday, July 13 at Congregation Imanu-Shalom, Temple Emanuel, 38 Oxford Road, Parktown. This event was hosted by a personal friend of Reb Shlomo, Rabbi Adi Assabi, a leading figure in the Progressive Judaism community, who had previously been an Orthodox rabbi.

Alon also arranged for Shlomo to be interviewed on a popular Sunday Christian radio program. It was so successful that he was then invited to address a large Christian community church, in Rosebank, Johannesburg. Alon recalls:

> Shlomo, with guitar in hand, sang a Midrash about how God had created the world and why He had chosen Jerusalem as His holy city. At the end of the story, one thousand people rose as one person and began clapping their hands in appreciation.

❉

Despite all the globe-trotting, a focal point of activities remained the Carlebach Synagogue in Manhattan with programming led by Shlomo's brother Rabbi Eli Chaim. Thus for example, the two brothers organized a "Hanukkah Feast" on December 29, 1986.[189]

One of the most unique aspects of Reb Shlomo's career was how he would set his priorities. Sometimes, a personal mitzvah to be with a close friend would override other considerations such as a concert. This is what happened when the parents of his close student/friend and guitarist, Bruce (Hashir) Ginsberg, were killed in a car crash in New Jersey.[190] Shlomo heard the tragic news and cancelled a sold-out concert scheduled for Thursday night in Miami and flew back to New York. Sammy Intrator then drove him to the Farmingdale Jewish Center for the funeral on Friday, February 20, 1987, where he co-officiated with Rabbi Paul Teicher. Bruce adds a sequel:

---

188. For a YouTube recording from this event, see http://www.youtube.com/watch?v=9nO1keWWgvA.

189. Ari L. Goldman, "Hanukkah, with Latkes and Light." *New York Times*, Dec 26, 1986.

190. Albert Ginsberg was 59 years old and his wife Edith was 57. They lived in Farmingdale, Long Island, New York.

A year later, he came to Farmingdale to play a Memorial Concert for my parents as a fundraiser for the Memorial Fund, and took not a penny for his time or travel.[191]

Another example of how Reb Shlomo was involved in the life cycle events of his followers is the story of Nachman and Miriam Futterman. Nachman had become a devoted follower in 1981 and served as president of the Carlebach Synagogue for nine years (see above). Miriam had met Shlomo in November 1981 in Los Angeles at the home of Joshua and Liliane Ritchie. The two were introduced to each other in Jerusalem on December 29, 1986, and several days later they went to see Shlomo perform at the Pargod Theater in Nachlaot, Jerusalem. Shlomo looked at them and realized they were a match. On March 11, 1987, Shlomo led their engagement (*tena'im*) ceremony,[192] and on April 6, 1987 offici-ated together with his brother Eli Chaim at their wedding at The Jewish Center on Manhattan's upper West Side.[193]

Shlomo would often build his program of activities around the Shabbat weekends. Here is an accounting by Sammy Intrator who accompanied Shlomo on four Shabbatot in mid-1987:[194]

May 29–30, 1987. Shlomo flew to Atlanta, Georgia and was picked up by Miriam and Jacob Kapp who hosted him in Cheeha State Park in Alabama for the Shabbat retreat. Then on Sunday evening, May 31, 1987, he led a concert in Atlanta, Georgia.

June 11–14, 1987. Reb Shlomo joined the annual Ruach summer retreat. This time it was held at the pastoral Berkshire Hills Emanuel Camps in Copake, Upstate New York.[195] The *Melaveh Malkah* together with Reb Shlomo and Reb Dovid Zeller began after midnight and lasted till about 4:00 AM.[196]

June 19–20, 1987. Shlomo vacationed at Fialikoff, a Catskills Bungalow

---

191. Personal correspondence with Bruce (Hashir) Ginsberg, Nov. 30, 2012.

192. The event is described by Nachman and Miriam Futterman in the *L'Koved Reb Shlomo Remembrance Journal*, Nov. 1995. See also Miriam Futterman, "Heilige Yid," *Kol Chevra*, vol. 7, 2000, 91–92.

193. Personal interview March 11, 2013. My thanks to the Futtermans for the series of wonderful photos from this wedding.

194. Rabbi Sammy Intrator, "On the Road with Reb Shlomo: Four Summer Weekends," *Hakrev Ushma (Connections,)* vol. 3, 2–3, 1987, 20–31.

195. The Emanuel Camps are located in the Berkshire Mountains with a private 60-acre natural spring fed lake, wooded terrain, trails and pine forests in Copake, a small township in Columbia County, Upstate New York.

196. Sammy Intrator, "On the Road with Reb Shlomo – Four Summer Weekends," *Hakrev Ushma (Connections)*, vol. 3, 23–25. Other participants included Reb Dovid Din, Dr. Blema Feinstein, and Reb Meir Fund.

Colony hosted by the owners, Naomi Adler and her son Shimon. For several summers, Reb Shlomo has vacationed there and led Motzei Shabbat concerts.[197]

July 10–11, 1987. Shlomo led a Shabbat retreat at the home of Dr. Felix and Margaret Rappaport in Great Neck, Long Island and celebrated *seudah shlishit* at the Young Israel of Great Neck. Sammy Intrator described the experience which was organized by two doctors (Dr. Felix Rappaport, a pioneer in heart transplant surgery, and his neighbor, Dr. Nathan Edelstein, a family doctor), with the purpose of exposing their professional friends "to the joy that can be experienced in Shabbos celebration." Intrator adds: "This is a straight Jewish, WASPY, professional crowd, but slowly, they loosen up," and there is lively dancing during the latter part of *Lecha Dodi* and the meal lasts until past midnight.[198]

Shlomo spent the rest of the summer in Israel but was back in Manhattan in mid-September 1987 to lead the *Selichot* service in the Carlebach Shul.[199]

An illustration from 1987 of how Reb Shlomo brought major changes to the lives of his followers is the story of Meron and Taharah Gil. Meron Meir Gil, born in 1955 in Poland was living in Amsterdam when Reb Shlomo came there to give a concert. In 1987, he introduced his future wife to Reb Shlomo and he gave her a Hebrew name, Taharah Elyona. The couple moved to Jerusalem. Reb Shlomo performed their marriage in 1988 in the Old City above the tomb of King David.[200]

In the last decade of his life, Reb Shlomo went through some trying times. Jeffrey Howard (Yossi) Chajes, who accompanied him musically in many of his last performances, recalls how sometimes very few people would show up.[201] Sometimes, the reason was that the Orthodox rabbinical leadership boycotted Shlomo resulting in disappointing turnouts. This is illustrated in the story of Rabbi Pini Dunner. In mid-October 1987, as a 17-year old student at the Gateshead Yeshiva, Dunner organized a Shlomo concert at the Walthamstow Town Hall in Northeast London on Hol HaMoed Sukkot. Dunner recollects:

---

197. Ibid., 25–27.

198. Ibid., 29–31.

199. The video which is part of a series filmed by Rabbi Eliezer and Michele Garner is posted at http://www.youtube.com/watch?v=waF8Fo6UyAI.

200. See Taharah Gil, "In Memory of Meron Meir Gil, *z"l*," *Kol Chevra*, vol. 7, 2000, 36 and Rabbi Yehoshua Witt, "My Dear Friend," *Kol Chevra*, vol. 7, 2000, 38. Meron Gil was tragically injured in a car accident on Erev Yom Kippur in 1998 and died a year later.

201. Dr. Yossi Chajes, interview, Sept. 15, 2011.

Shlomo officiated together with his brother Eli Chaim on April 6, 1987 at the wedding of Nachman and Miriam Futterman at The Jewish Center on Manhattan's Upper West Side. Besides Nachman and Miriam, the photos include Reb Shlomo and his brother Reb Eli Chaim who co-officiated, Rebbetzin Hadassa Carlebach greeting the bride; Itzik Aisenstadt and Moshe Shur with Reb Shlomo.

My association with the concert almost got me thrown out of the Yeshiva. Shlomo was *treif* and exposure to him was considered dangerous. As a result of the Yeshiva's opposition, I was not able to sell tickets and attendance was poor.[202] Shlomo suggested that we record the concert and that the record help defray the concert

202. Leiser Morawiecki: "Only 70 people showed up in a hall with 700–800 places because "the local rabbis forbid people to attend." Leiser, who was there with his

expenses, most of which had been paid for with borrowed money. The 2+ hour recording was made live at the concert and edited to fit onto a 60-minute cassette. The recording was bought by Jonathan Tischler of the now defunct House of Menorah record company of the Lower East Side and released as "Shlomo Carlebach Live in London."[203]

In the decade of the 1980s, Reb Shlomo remained closely connected to his followers. For example, Jerry and Leah Strauss would frequently invite Shlomo to their home to teach wherever they were living, whether in Topanga Canyon, Santa Rosa, or Poway or elsewhere in California.[204] Although they had been married for seventeen years, they never had a Jewish wedding and Reb Shlomo performed it for them at their home in Santa Rosa. There were nostalgic gatherings such as on Sunday, February 14, 1988, in downtown Berkeley, California at the Magnes Jewish Art and Life Museum where Shlomo's *chevra* met together to see an exhibition of photos from Shlomo's Moshav, Me'or Modi'im, reminisce about their days at the HLP, and sing songs.[205]

For the weekend of June 9–12, 1988, Reb Shlomo was at the annual Ruach Retreat which was again in the Berkshire Hills in Copake, New York.[206]

On June 28, 1988, Reb Shlomo together with his colleague Rabbi David Stavsky,[207] performed the wedding of Harvey Wasserman and Susan Saks. Their wedding video is unique in that it is posted in full on the web.[208] Shlomo intersperses explanations and songs for twenty minutes as he recites each of the seven blessings of the *Sheva Berachot*. He continues during the wedding reception with storytelling, hermeneutical explanations, and personal references, all the while transmitting empathy and

---

family: "Shlomo performed with all his heart, although he knew very well why the place was empty. He never spoke badly against people who wronged him. It was all love!!" Personal communication, Jan. 16, 2012.

203. Personal communication with Rabbi Dunner, April 19, 2012.

204. For a description of a meeting in May 1986 of the Shlomo Chevra and an excerpt from the teaching in the Strauss home see Kuki-Leah Yudelvitz-Strauss, "Who Are We?," *Kol Chevra*, vol. 3, 1996, 19–20.

205. Yehudit Goldfarb, personal communication, Sept. 2, 2011.

206. Other participants included Dr. Blema Feinstein, Yehudis Fishman, Reb Meir Fund, and Reb Dovid Zeller.

207. Rabbi Stavsky (1930–2004), a graduate of Yeshiva University and RIETS, served for 47 years as the Rabbi of the Beth Jacob Congregation in Columbus, Ohio. He was instrumental in bringing Shlomo to Ohio several times.

208. Blip.TV, http://blip.tv/days/wasserman-wedding-with-rav-shlomo-carlebach-and-rabbi-david-stavsky-5101899.

sincerity that enliven what otherwise would be considered moralistic preaching. A secret of Reb Shlomo's charisma is demonstrated in his versatility at creating different meanings and moods while pointing to practical life teachings and inspirations.

In July 1988, Reb Shlomo came to Pikesville, a northwestern suburb of Baltimore, to appear at a concert meant to inspire "disconnected Jewish boys and girls from Central and South America."[209] At the end of July, Reb Shlomo was in Israel, but on July 25, 1988, he suffered his first heart attack (see Chapter 8).

On November 20, 1988, Shlomo appeared in concert at the Beth Israel Synagogue in Borough Park.[210]

On December 11, 1988, the last day of Hanukkah, Shlomo performed the marriage of Wendy Borodkin and Ira Brandwein.[211]

5.   GLOBAL WIDE-REACH (1989–1992)

The two major highlights of 1989 were Shlomo's trips to Poland (January 1–10) and to Russia (September 7–27). These are discussed at length above in Chapter 9. The stories in between illustrate the global "wide-reach" that created an incredibly variegated career filled with remarkable vignettes that provide the backdrop to understanding Shlomo's public teachings.

On January 24, 1989, Reb Shlomo performed in Minnesota.[212] In February 1989, Shlomo performed at the Robbins Auditorium at the Albert Einstein College.[213]

---

209. The concert was organized by R. Pini Dunner who was studying at the time in Yeshivas Ner Yisroel in Baltimore and would often travel to the Carlebach Shul in Manhattan to be with Reb Shlomo for Shabbat. R. Dunner wrote to me in April 2012 that the concert took place at Chapps Chinese Restaurant in Pomona Square, Pikesville. It was part of an outreach program organized by Rabbi Moshe Fuller to bring Mexican kids to the Baltimore yeshiva for a "taste of Torah atmosphere." See R. Eliezer Bulka, "Reb Moshe Fuller, z"l, on His 3rd Yahrzeit," *Baltimore Jewish Life*, March 23, 2011, http://baltimorejewishlife.com/news/news-detail.php?SECTION_ID=1&ARTICLE_ID=4970.

210. Miriam Rubinoff, "Shabbos Gives Life," *Kol Chevra*, vol. 14, 2008, 61–63.

211. Wendy Borodkin and Ira Brandwein, "Love At First Sight," *Kol Chevra*, vol. 18, 2012, 80–81. The couple had met the year earlier, on June 12, 1987 at a Ruach Shabbaton (see above).

212. http://www.box.com/shared/jba33jj3sx/1/34341330/652181323/1#/s/jba33jj3sx/1/34341330/530460759/1; http://www.box.com/shared/jba33jj3sx/1/34341330/652181323/1#/s/jba33jj3sx/1/34341330/530499877/1.

213. http://www.youtube.com/watch?v=hZ-yOSr1l9Q – *"Lemaan Achai"*; http://www.youtube.com/watch?v=Ttz50O6oxN8&feature=related – *"Mimkomcha."*

On March 6, 1989, Shlomo participated with his disciple Diane Wolkstein, a well-known international storyteller, at the American Museum of Natural History in Manhattan. Their joint song/story event was entitled *Drunkards and Water Carriers*.[214]

Then Shlomo was in London for Shabbat. On Motzei Shabbat, March 11 and Sunday, March 12, 1989, Shlomo performed at two consecutive concerts at the Yakar Educational Center in London.[215]

In the early spring of 1989, R. Pini Dunner arranged for Reb Shlomo to be hosted for a Shabbat program at the Beth Shalom Congregation in Frederick, Maryland.[216]

In May 1989, Shlomo was in Los Angeles and taught for a week at the home of Rabbi Dr. Joshua and Liliane Ritchie. On Shabbat, May 20, 1989, Shlomo was hosted at the home of Louis Kemp in Pacific Palisades, Los Angeles, where more than one hundred people participated. On Lag B'Omer, Monday night, May 22, Shlomo led a concert at the Young Israel of Santa Monica in western Los Angeles, and taught about the significance of weddings and Jerusalem. There he composed "*Mehayra*" מְהֵרָה ה' which became one of his most popular wedding songs.[217]

On June 2–4, 1989, Shlomo again participated in the annual Ruach Retreat held at Copake together with Reb Dovid Zeller, Reb Meir Fund, Dr. Blema Feinstein, and Yehudis Fishman.

On June 11, 1989, Shlomo presided over a funeral in Passaic, New Jersey. Sydell Deitchman Power recounts how Shlomo came a few days before to New York Hospital to be with her mother as she was on her death bed. This is an aspect of Shlomo's career that is rarely mentioned,

---

214. About Diane's connection to Reb Shlomo and his influence on her career, see above, Chapter 6. They appeared on stage together a second time at the American Museum on Sept. 13, 1989 – see below, Chapter 12.

215. This event was recorded by video by Leiser Morawiecki who also hosted Shlomo in his home for dinner before the Sunday night concert. Four years later, Reb Shlomo performed at the bar mitzvah of Leiser's son – see below, Chapter 12. Leiser had first met Reb Shlomo in 1972 at a concert in Savigny-sur-Orge in the southern suburbs of Paris. Personal correspondence, Leiser Morawiecki, Jan. 8, 2013.

216. See BethSholomFrederick.org, http://www.bethsholomfrederick.org/index .php where the synagogue is identified variously as a Conservative-affiliated congregation and a post-denominational congregation. The spiritual leader from 1961–2010 was Rabbi Morris Kosman.

217. I thank Yehudah Katz for the information in this paragraph (March 19, 2013). Yehudah's marriage to Michelle took place on May 23, 1989, but Reb Shlomo did not perform their wedding because he had a prior commitment for a bat mitzvah in New York.

but illustrates his personal involvement as a global rebbe in the lives of countless people around the world.[218]

Another one of his disciples whose life was intricately connected to Reb Shlomo was Rabbi David Zeller. On June 19, 1989, Reb Shlomo officiated together with Reb Meir Fund at the wedding of David and Hannah Sara Zeller which took place at the Brooklyn Botanical Gardens in New York.[219] This was after David's first wife had died tragically of cancer three years earlier.

On November 3–4, 1989, Shlomo was hosted for Shabbat at the Ohav Shalom Synagogue in Cincinnati. On Shabbat, he delivered the sermon and led the *Musaf* service. On Friday evening, he was the guest of honor at the congregational dinner and during the day he led a Kiddush hosted by the Couples' Club. On Motzei Shabbat, he performed for a community audience accompanied by the David Lieberman Ensemble. Shlomo related to the problems of anti-Semitism facing the Cincinnati community, saying that it is "an absolute waste" of time to talk about anti-Semitism. Reb Shlomo announced his solution:

> We Jews can make the world our friends. It's up to us. Every Jew has to begin shining. If all of us Jews, would be the way that God wants us to be – so, so lofty and so full of love, full of joy – the world would look at us with different eyes.[220]

Reb Shlomo was an expert at "shining" this joy and love, always on the lookout to find ways of expressing empathy and celebrating life. Isabella Kaydanova and her parents (Abram and Asya) had emigrated from Kharkov, in the Ukraine, in the former Soviet Union in late 1981 and, after an extended stopover in Italy, arrived in America right before Passover in 1982 when she was almost 26. She originally lived on the Lower East Side and occasionally came to the Upper West Side for Shabbat, and moved into the neighborhood in 1988, for about a year. Occasionally, during this time, she visited the Carlebach Shul, where she discovered a scene unlike anything she had seen in her country of origin:

> At Carlebach's, it was shocking, exhilarating, and inspiring. For me, in the country of my birth, Jewishness was often associated with hatred and intimidation. I had never witnessed such an

---

218. Tribute written to Shlomo Carlebach by Sydell Deitchman Power in the Carlebach Shul Journal, *L'Koved Reb Shlomo*, Nov. 1995.

219. Zeller, *The Soul of the Story*, 228.

220. Don Canaan, "Shlomo Carlebach Spreads Message of Hope," *The American Israelite*, Nov. 23, 1989. My thanks to Kevin Proffitt of the Jacob Radar Marcus Archives for sending me this article from the AJA collection on Shlomo Carlebach.

atmosphere of unrestricted cheerfulness and joy in a Jewish setting.[221]

During occasional Shabbat meals, Isabella told Shlomo about how she
had risked her safety to study Torah and learn Hebrew, and described
the discrimination against her mother who was a doctor and her father
who was an engineer. She told Shlomo about her clandestine trips to
purchase Jewish books from a man in the St Petersburg synagogue – the
Torah, a prayer-book, a calendar, and two books of *Elef Meeleem* (1000
basic Hebrew words).[222] Shortly afterward, Isabella went to the Moscow
Institute of Defectology on an internship. At that time, she would go to
Moscow's main synagogue. One Rosh Hashana, the young people began
dancing in circles right in front of the synagogue and singing Jewish
Zionist songs, even though the knowledgeable ones in their midst told
them to wait for Simchat Torah. The thrill and excitement did not last
too long. Huge military trucks ominously approached, with headlights
glaring, and spotlights from above, creating a daytime effect, like in a
Hollywood horror movie:

> The trucks almost touched us, and some people screamed in
> fear and wanted to disperse. But others shouted defiantly, "Let's
> continue dancing and show we're not afraid." We held onto each
> other tightly to stay together.[223]

Shlomo listened attentively with wide open eyes. This was an affirmation
of his working assumptions about the spiritual questing in the Soviet
Union. This first-hand evidence explains some of the incredible exclama-
tions of Reb Shlomo during and after his trip to Russia in September
1989 (see above, Chapter 9) about the purity of the spiritual yearning in
Russia and how these Jews are the first generation since Sinai who are
direct disciples of God.

At first, life in the Golden Land for Isabella was not so welcoming. She
confided in Reb Shlomo about her problems as a lonely new immigrant:

> In Russia, we had been discriminated against because we were
> Jewish. In America, I was humiliated because of my accent and

---

221. Personal communications from Isabella Reichel, Oct. 25–28, 2012.

222. It was a miracle to get books like this at that time, especially for someone from
Kharkov. But, Isabella couldn't find anyone in Kharkov, a city of close to two million
people, who could teach her, until another miracle happened. Isabella's mother had a
colleague whose husband was a professor and a linguist in Kharkov University, who
had studied in a *heder* in Poland as a child, so he was able to teach Isabella Hebrew
and Torah. Isabella traveled two hours each way, twice a week, to get to him.

223. Personal communications from Isabella Reichel, Oct. 25–28, 2012.

mistreated because I was an immigrant. Rabbi Carlebach empa-
thetically understood as he himself was an immigrant and had an
accent! He was kind and uplifting. He raised my spirits.[224]

Isabella had been a speech pathologist in Russia specializing in stuttering,
but in America she had to begin studying anew for her master's degree
before she could recreate her career: "Rabbi Carlebach encouraged me
to believe I could make it in this country and he proved to be prophetic."
Isabella eventually became an associate professor at Touro College in
New York and a renowned world expert on stuttering.

On November 12, 1989, Isabella married Aaron Reichel whom she
had met at an Orthodox Union Torah Retreat at the Homowack Hotel.
On Friday night the couple celebrated their *Sheva Berachot* at Aaron's
parents' home on 79th Street (his father, Rabbi Dr. O. Asher Reichel,
was the rabbi of the neighboring West Side Institutional Synagogue) and
then walked over to the Carlebach Shul to share the good news with Reb
Shlomo. Isabella recalls:

> Reb Shlomo was overjoyed that we had found each other since
> he knew both of us. The *chevra* were still in the middle of their
> Shabbat meal. Shlomo declared, let's have a *Sheva Berachot*, even
> though we told him that we already had *Sheva Berachot* earlier
> in the evening. So it came about that we had two sets of *Sheva
> Berachot* on the same Friday night![225]

This story of Isabella illustrates not only how Reb Shlomo helped individuals overcome adversity, but also how he turned their private celebrations into a communal spiritual enthusiasm and a Jewish *joie de vivre*.
Furthermore, it demonstrates how Shlomo's seemingly hyperbolic stories could have a basis in real life events that he heard from individuals.

On November 14, 1989, Reb Shlomo led a *Sheva Berachot* for Aviva
and Barry Luden at the home of Barry's parents, Meyer and Helga Luden,
in New Rochelle.[226]

Another way that Reb Shlomo celebrated life in a unique way for an
Orthodox rabbi was to invite women as musical accompaniment.[227] In

---

224. Ibid.

225. Interviews with Isabella and Aaron Reichel, Oct. 16–27, 2012.

226. Barry Luden had married Aviva Grodner on Sunday, November 12, 1989.
Aviva's parents, Reuven and Goldie had first met when they were 17-year old coun-
selors at the Pioneer Hotel in the summer of 1957. See above for Reb Shlomo at
the Pioneer and his leading programs at Goldie's parents' apartment. My thanks to
Goldie Isaacs for this information (Dec. 20, 2012).

227. The women mentioned above as accompanying Shlomo on stage include:

this spirit of empowering women, when 150 women from Women of the Wall[228] were marching in Jerusalem on Shabbat, November 25, 1989, Shlomo reportedly addressed them as the "noble ladies whom all of Israel should be here to greet."[229] Bonna Devora Haberman, who helped initiate Women of the Wall, recently elaborated on this:

> Reb Shlomo was quick to support Women of the Wall during the tumultuous months in 1989. While so many threatened and violated, he strengthened us with music and teachings. He knew well the anger and cruelty as well as the sweetness and ecstasy of Jewish souls. Through years and tears, Reb Shlomo nurtured my spiritual unfolding.[230]

Reb Shlomo's motivating force throughout his life was to reach out to Jews in their spiritual quests, even if it meant going where other Orthodox rabbis did not enter. On December 25, 1989, the third night of Hanukkah, Reb Shlomo came to the Sivananda Ashram Yoga Camp founded in 1963 by Swami Vishnudevananda (1927–1993), located in the Laurentian Mountains, an hour's drive from Montreal, Canada. The director of the Ashram, Swami Mahadevananda (disciple of Swami Vishnu Devananda)[231] sat on stage in a lotus position and can be seen clapping his hands to Shlomo's music. Shlomo on guitar was accompanied by Eliezer Garner on the tambourine.[232] Eliezer recalls that many of the Swami's followers were of Jewish origin and Shlomo who surreptitiously handed them his business card with his address at the HLP and Manhattan and

---

Shoshannah (piano), Joy Krauthammer (percussion), Shirley Perluss (mandolin), Sara Shendelman (guitar), and Jocelyn Siegal (drums).

228. The mission of WOW (Women of the Wall) is "to achieve the social and legal recognition of our right, as women, to wear prayer shawls, pray, and read from the Torah collectively and out loud at the Western Wall." See WomenOfTheWall.org.il, http://womenofthewall.org.il.

229. Phyllis Chesler, "A Song So Brave – Photo Essay," *On the Issues Magazine*, Summer 1990, OnTheIssueMagazine.com, http://www.ontheissuesmagazine.com/1990summer/summer1990_CHESLER.php. Compare Rachel Jaskow, "Women of the Wall: A Personal Account," *Kol Chevra*, vol. 5, 1998, 59–60.

230. Bonna Devora Haberman, May 22, 2013, http://bonnadevorahaberman.word press.com/blog.

231. A decade before, David Zeller, Shlomo's disciple, had been invited as a guest speaker in 1978 at Swami Vishnu Devananda's yoga retreat center in the Bahamas. See Zeller, *The Soul of the Story*, Chapter 51.

232. http://www.youtube.com/watch?v=z-iVGFo9fME. Also in this video is Rabbi Sholom Brodt who had recently received ordination from Reb Shlomo in April 1989 (see below).

whispered to Eliezer that he didn't want the Swami to feel that he was taking away his business. Michele Garner walked into the kitchen:

> We had been traveling all day and were starving and we walked into the kitchen to see if anything might be kosher. I asked one of the Swami's disciples who was decked out in orange robes and a shaven head about the food, explaining that we were with a rabbi. He responded: My name is Moshe and I am from Brighton Beach, Brooklyn and I keep a kosher kitchen. On further inspection I found kosher symbols on most of the products.[233]

Eliezer contrasted the opposing messages of the Swami and Shlomo:

> The Swami spoke about the unity of all and how all religions say the same thing. Reb Shlomo began his presentation by humming the tune for the Motzei Shabbat blessing of "*Hamavdil ben kodesh lechol*" (He who separates from the sacred and profane). It was quite ironic how Shlomo's agenda was different than that of the Swami.[234]

Shlomo's visit in Montreal was not only to celebrate Hanukkah, it was also a time when Montreal was still reeling in shock from the massacre on December 6, 1989, in which fourteen students at École Polytechnique were killed and fourteen others wounded by Marc Lépine, a 25-year old Quebecker.[235]

Invitations to Reb Carlebach spanned the gamut of locations, affiliations, and synagogues. Shlomo performed on February 18, 1990 at Temple Beth Shalom in Santa Ana, Orange County.[236] On Purim, Sunday March 11, 1990, he performed with an orchestra at Martin Luther King Jr. High School in Manhattan.[237]

On March 23, 1990, Rabbi Eli Chaim died of a heart attack at age 65.[238] He was buried in the Har HaMenuhot cemetery in Jerusalem near his parents' grave and where his brother Shlomo would be interred four years later. After his passing, Sammy Intrator was appointed assistant rabbi.

On Sunday, April 1, 1990, Shlomo performed the marriage of Jeffrey

233. Personal interview with Michele Garner, Dec. 23, 2012.

234. Personal interview with Eliezer Garner, Dec. 23, 2012.

235. The article on Marc Lépine in Wikipedia is a good summary – http://en.wikipedia.org/wiki/Marc_L%C3%A9pine#cite_note-0.

236. *Los Angeles Times*, Feb. 17, 1990, 19.

237. "Celebrating Purim's Joy," *New York Times*, March 9, 1990, Arts Section.

238. *New York Times*, obituaries, March 27, 1990, NYTimes.com, http://www.nytimes.com/1990/03/27/obituaries/eli-c-carlebach-65-rabbi-of-synagogue-on-upper-west-side.html.

and Linda Fine. Actually, they had had a civil marriage several years before, but when they moved to Manhattan, they became religious under
the guidance of Shlomo and Eli Chaim Carlebach. Jeffrey even became
president of the Carlebach Shul. They were planning a "remarriage" with
the assumption that R. Eli Chaim would officiate. But when he died suddenly, Shlomo stepped in to perform the ceremony.[239]

On Sunday, April 29, 1990, Reb Shlomo was the featured singer at a
Yom HaAtzmaut concert to support Operation Exodus to enable "hun-
dreds of thousands of Soviet Jews" to emigrate to Israel. The concert took
place at Temple Beth Abraham, a Conservative synagogue in Oakland,
California. Shlomo was accompanied by Daniel Lev (guitar), Richard
Merman (clarinet), Steve Saxon (trumpet), Sara Shendelman (guitar),
Jocelyn Siegal (drums), Nathan Siegal (flute), and Aryeh Trupin (flute).

For the weekend of June 8–10, 1990, Shlomo was featured at the Ruach
Retreat which was held this time at Chalet Vim in Woodbourne, Sullivan
County, New York.[240]

On Motzei Shabbat Nahamu, August 4, 1990, Reb Shlomo appeared
in the bungalow colony at Woodlake, New York. He was invited by
Judith Graber, program director, to perform in the synagogue. Judith
had first heard Reb Shlomo when she went with her parents, Morris and
Gertrude Ross, to the Pioneer Hotel in the summer in the late 1950s.[241] In
a video recording, Shlomo can be heard singing and was featured singing
"*Mimkomcho*" with Meir Gross, Sammy, Harry, and Zvi Roth.[242]

On August 26, 1990, Reb Shlomo performed the marriage of Ilene
Paula Chugerman to Steven Jay Amiel at the James House in North
Tarrytown, N.Y.[243]

On September 3, 1990, Reb Shlomo performed at the wedding of the
youngest son of Rabbi Eugene and Annette Labovitz in Miami Beach,
Florida.[244] Reb Shlomo flew back to Israel to take part in the Second

---

239. Interview with Linda Fine, Oct. 16, 2012. My thanks to Raquel Z. Grunwald
for telling me about this event.

240. In addition to Shlomo, participants included Reb Meir Fund, Dr. Blema
Feinstein, and Yehudis Fishman.

241. My thanks to Azi Graber for this information, April 14, 2013. See above,
Chapter 3, for the video from the Pioneer Hotel in 1959.

242. http://www.youtube.com/watch?v=kfKHrxl8oQo&feature=related; http://
web.me.com/benkatz/Site_4/R_Shlomo_in_Woodlake.html.

243. *New York Times*, Aug. 27, 1990, B8.

244. A video of Shlomo singing "*Uvechen*" at the wedding with Jo Amar, father of
the bride, and famous singer himself, adding harmony, can be seen at http://www
.youtube.com/watch?v=m-f1GqFte-o&feature=player_embedded#!; http://www.you
tube.com/user/elabovitz. See also http://www.youtube.com/watch?v=Ke9lTpNzZjQ
&feature=plcp for Shlomo singing "*Yah Ribon Olam*" with Jo Amar.

FestiNegev, where he was the featured performer on September 11 at Beersheba's Desert Inn Hotel.

The albums produced in his last four years included *Shlomo Carlebach Sings with the Children of Israel* (1990); *The Best of Shlomo Carlebach,*[245] and *The Very Best of Shlomo Carlebach* (1991); *Sh'vochin Asader, Live at the Arad Music Festival, Shabbos with Shlomo* (1992); *Tora's Times* (1993).

The uniqueness of Reb Shlomo's work was not only a result of a resolute desire to reach out to all people, but also a natural expression of empathy for all. This was poignantly illustrated in June 1990 during his visit to Soweto, the most populous black urban residential area in South Africa. Rena Teeger recalls how Reb Shlomo accepted the invitation of Irene Mtintinlili to visit her craft center in Soweto,[246] and sang, offering words of hope and encouragement. He warned against being angry and embittered despite the apartheid discriminatory system:

> Your people were chosen by God to show the world what freedom is. But don't be angry. Anger will make you a slave again. The Germans killed six million of my people. I can walk around and be angry and bitter. But this is not what God wants me to do. He wants me to love the whole world . . . I want to bless you that you should see your children grow up in a better world.[247]

On December 10, 1990, Shlomo led a *Sheva Brachot* at his *shul* in Manhattan for Naomi Mark and Rabbi Tsvi Blanchard who had been married the day before.

On February 19, 1991, Shlomo led a concert at the Shir Ha-Ma'alot Temple in Newport Beach, in Orange County, California.

In March 29–31, 1991 Reb Shlomo lead the Pesach Seders at the Carlebach Shul in Manhattan. Then he took his daughter Dari to Hawaii, where he was the resident rabbi at a hotel in Kauai from April 1–7, 1991. Dari remembers the trip as a highlight of her life – "we had an unbelievable vacation in Hawaii, touring the towering cliffs, panoramic views, and exotic beaches."[248]

On May 20, 1991, Shlomo appeared in concert at the Brown's Hotel in the Catskills, New York.[249]

---

245. *The Best of Shlomo Carlebach 1960–1990* is a collection that includes 90 songs and 24 stories.

246. Mtintinlili provided the elderly Black Africans with a daily hot meal and enabled them to sell their handmade wares.

247. Personal communications from Rena Teeger. See also Rena Teeger, "South Africa Revisited – Soweto, June 1990," *Kol Chevra*, vol. 18, 2012, 54–55.

248. Dari Carlebach personal communication, Dec. 9, 2012.

249. My thanks to Sherwood Goffin for relating this event. Goffin was the second performer and Shlomo concluded this Motzei Shavuot concert.

Reb Shlomo was at the annual Ruach Retreat for the weekend of June 7–9, 1991 which was again held at Hotel Chalet Vim in the Catskills, New York.[250]

On September 10, 1991, Motzei Rosh Hashana, Shlomo performed a wedding. That month he also visited Everett, Massachusetts to be at the bat mitzvah of Sara Henna Polen, the daughter of Shlomo's good friend, Nechemia Polen.[251]

On October 17, 1991, Shlomo invented one of his new tunes without words at the *brit* of Yehuda Yosef Eliyahu Chaim Futterman.[252]

At the end of October, 1991, Reb Shlomo gave a concert sponsored by the Lechayim Society at the Oxford University Student Union under the leadership of Rabbi Shmuley Boteach.[253]

On November 24, 1991, Reb Shlomo was at an Orthodox synagogue in San Francisco, Congregation Chevra Thilim, and he spoke about how Hanukkah is a time for healing.[254]

Reb Shlomo adapted his messages for specific audiences. In Germany in 1991, when introducing his famous song *"Dovid Melech Yisrael, Hai VeKayam,"* Reb Shlomo explains to the Germans that in actuality everyone is royalty, a king and queen of God, designated as such by God Himself, The King of the Universe.

> God is the King of everybody. Do you know what a God King is like? A human being says: I am a king, and you are not. But God the King says: You are also a king. After all, are you not a child of God? And He is the King of the entire world. Therefore, you are also a king. We all are kings and queens. Therefore, let's sing together. Stand up on your feet, be strong, and go forward towards the Great Day of Redemption.[255]

---

250. Again, Reb Meir Fund, Reb Dovid Zeller, Yehudis Fishman, and Blema Feinstein were the additional presenters.

251. Photos of these events were published in the *L'Koved Reb Shlomo Remembrance Journal*, Nov. 1995.

252. See the video posted by Michele Garner with the permission of Nachman and Miriam Futterman, http://www.youtube.com/watch?v=YIxOO-VwVmY&feature=plcp. See above for Shlomo at the engagement of Miriam and Nachman Futterman on March 11, 1987.

253. My thanks to Mike Tabor for this information. Tabor played on the fiddle and this was his first of many times to accompany Reb Shlomo: http://www.youtube.com/watch?v=erfddHBDBMQ&NR=1; http://www.youtube.com/watch?v=QtwycV-4Yco&feature=related; http://www.youtube.com/watch?v=tCob7AlN8rY; RebShlomoCarlebach.blogspot.com, http://rebshlomocarlebach.blogspot.com.

254. Reuven Goldfarb, "On Scars and Healing," *Kol Chevra*, vol. 14, 2008, 64–65.

255. http://www.youtube.com/watch?v=IU-7ERkdvGs, segment 0:09–0:51. My free translation from the German.

On December 10, 1990, Shlomo led a Sheva Brachot at his Shul in Manhattan for Naomi Mark and Rabbi Tsvi Blanchard who had been married the day before. Naomi had been very active for a decade in the Carlebach Shul, organizing Shabbat programs and accompanying Reb Shlomo on excursions to different communities.   Courtesy of Naomi Mark

By providing a universal twist to a particularistic song, he is validating the German individual both spiritually and existentialistly, a most significant exclamation as it comes from a rabbi who escaped from Austria just before the Holocaust began. When he sings *"Adir Hu Yivneh Beitcha,"* he asks the audience to join in giving harmony and explains that the words *El Beneh* imply a universal message that God will build, and that all must scream out this hope. The audience, even the more staid participants,

Dr. Jacob Birnbaum, founder of the SSSJ, and Reb Shlomo on December 10, 1990, at the Sheva Brachot *for Naomi and Rabbi Tsvi. Courtesy of Naomi Mark*

join in enthusiastic response – with singing and lively clapping.[256]

In March 1992, Shlomo performed in concert in Chicago in the old Jewish neighborhood of West Rogers Park at the Mather High School Auditorium. Ruby Harris, who accompanied him on stage with mandolin, violin, vocals, and guitar, recalls how Shlomo sang the Yiddish folk song *"Oyfn Pripetshik,"* a major musical memory of pre-Holocaust Europe, about a rabbi teaching his young students the *alef bet*, because Shlomo wanted the elderly Yiddish people in the audience to feel comfortable.[257]

For Pesach in mid-April 1992, Reb Shlomo vacationed with his daughters at the Americana Resort Hotel in Aruba in the southern Caribbean Sea. Accompanying him was his disciple, Simcha Sheldon.[258]

On the eve of Holocaust Day, April 29, 1992, Reb Shlomo spoke and sang about the Last Will of the Six Million in a special program at the Carlebach Shul in New York.[259]

---

256. http://www.youtube.com/watch?v=X1CNJM9_rUA; http://www.israelvideo network.com/rabbi-shlomo-carlebach-in-germany-adir-hu. See segment 1:25 and 2:32–2:40.

257. Ruby Harris, email correspondence, Jan. 14, 2013. For a recording of Shlomo singing this song in a live performance, see ningmp3.com, ningmp3.com/ carlebach-mp3-download.html; http://ningmp3.com/onply.php?q=VXFISnc3ZVRO MHc=&tl=Shlomo%20Carlebach%20Singing%20Nice%20Old%20Yiddish%20songs.

258. My thanks to Simcha Sheldon for telling me about this event. I have reconstructed the date of Pesach 1992 based on information provided by Neshama Carlebach who was in her last year of high school at the time.

259. The event was filmed by Rabbi Eliezer and Michele Garner and posted on YouTube in five parts by the Carlebach Legacy: Part 1, Can't Stop Crying, http://www .youtube.com/watch?v=6hUhTteFElI&list=TL5cIHfbjoplE; Part 2, Jew by Choice, http://www.youtube.com/watch?v=qkW_-rfQka4&list=TL5cIHfbjoplE; Part 3, Holding Onto the Shoes, http://www.youtube.com/watch?v=7HMYBzTgjsU&list= TL5cIHfbjoplE; Part 4, Living Ashes, http://www.youtube.com/watch?v=8NjHLS6 koO8&list=TL5cIHfbjoplE; Part 5, The Six Million's Last Will, http://www.youtube .com/watch?v=OclK3oTEgA8&list=TL5cIHfbjoplE.

On June 1, 1992, Reb Shlomo appeared in London at the R.D. Laing Institute founded by Joseph Berkey.[260]

Shlomo led the annual weekend Ruach Retreat on June 19–21, 1992 at a luxurious resort, the Golden Acres Farm and Ranch in Gilboa, New York, in the northern Catskills.[261] The program included panel discussions, formal learning, storytelling, *niggunim*, and *davening.* In a video posted on several Internet sites, one can hear Shlomo's explanations at *Havdala* of how Shabbat empowers a person to bring holiness into a broken world and turn ugliness into beauty:

> We are living on two levels. One level is that everything is good, everything is holy. But on the second level, certain things are good, certain things are not so good, something is holy, something is not so holy. Only a person who has experienced the first level of pure Good and Holiness can come to the broken world and turn ugliness into beauty and create holiness. Shabbos is the time that everything is Good and Holy. When we make *Havdala* as Shabbos ends, we enter the daily week with its problems to fix the few things that are not good yet, but we do so as a "good doctor" empowered by the beauty and holiness of Shabbos.[262]

Shlomo continues with a synopsis of several major themes such as how to focus in the value of a specific moment and discover the unexpected joy to an explanation that the world is angry at us because we don't shine forth our Light. He emphasized the importance of bringing the Fragrance of the Tree of Life to compensate for the dryness of the Tree of Knowledge.[263]

On June 25, 1992, Shlomo officiated at the wedding of David Montag to Olga Volozova.[264] It took place in Los Angeles in the backyard of the home of Liliane and Dr. Joshua Ritchie. David and Olga had gone through a difficult time in their lives, and Shlomo spoke about the significance of brokenness:

---

260. This is mentioned by Hadassa Carlebach in *Kavod: Following in the Footsteps of Reb Shlomo*, a journal produced by the Carlebach Shul, Dec. 1996, 5. Reuven Goldfarb transcribed the recording.

261. The faculty also included Dr. Blema Feinstein, Yehudis Fishman, Reb Meir Fund, and Reb David Zeller.

262. This is my synopsis/explication of what Shlomo explains in segment 0:50–2:06 of http://www.youtube.com/watch?v=22zIYFrwrBI&feature=plcp.

263. http://www.youtube.com/watch?v=NvoNm4x8AtU&feature=plcp segment 0:35–3:54.

264. Previously, in May 1992, Shlomo officiated at their engagement ceremony.

We get married with a ring because it has a hole in it. Unless both a *chasan* and *kallah* have a little hole in their heart, a little place where they are broken, they will never make it. Because if my heart is already whole, what do I need you for? Why do I need anybody? Why do I even need to get married? So I bless you both, Olga and David, that you should always have a heart with a little hole . . . not too cracked, God forbid, but not too whole either.[265]

David, who was instrumental in organizing many events for Reb Shlomo in the Los Angeles area, had received a non-rabbinical *semicha* from Shlomo in Israel in August of 1989.[266]

On Shabbat, November 21, 1992, at the Carlebach Shul, Reb Shlomo performed the naming ceremony of the first daughter of Eliezer and Michele Garner – "a real miracle after eighteen years of marriage." She had been born in October 21, but her parents waited to to celebrate the naming with Shlomo on Shabbat in the Carlebach Shul. They called her Nechama Batya, and Shlomo added the name Temima.[267]

On Sunday, December 6, 1992, Reb Shlomo was featured together with Avraham Fried and the Diaspora Yeshiva Band (DYB) at Carnegie Hall in a sold-out concert. The new generation of stars in Jewish music was creating a novel phenomenon of expanding the scope of Hasidic music to include Chabad singers (Fried) and Jewish Rock Music (DYB). Many of these new directions were influenced by Reb Shlomo's pioneering efforts at setting Hebrew verses to popular music.

6.   EMPOWERMENT AND RABBINIC ORDINATIONS (1976– 1992)

In his later years, Shlomo signed documents empowering his followers for leadership roles as rabbis, storytellers (*maggidim*), outreach/inreach workers, cantors/singers, and even meditation teachers. Various lists have been compiled. One is entitled Rabbeinu's Ordained Disciples and contains titles and contact information of forty-eight recipients,[268]

---

265. Personal communications from Olga Volozova, Sept. 2012 based on the recollections of Michael Ozair. See also Ozair's comment in the David Montag Scrapbook following Montag's death at age 68 on March 20, 2008 – http://davidmontag. blogspot.co.il/2008/03/announcing-passing-of-professor-rabbi.html.

266. My thanks to Jeff Mann for this information (Oct. 25, 2012).

267. Nechama Garner, "Grandpa-Shlomo," *Kol Chevra*, vol. 13, 2007, 221–223. Personal communication with Eliezer and Michele Garner, Dec. 24, 2012.

268. The list was dated Nov. 9, 2004 and was posted on rebshlomo.dafyomi.org and on www.rebshlomo.org, sites that are currently not functional. The accuracy of

twenty-three of whom are listed with an asterisk to indicate *semicha* granting authority to determine *Halacha* (*Yoreh Yoreh, Yadin Yadin*). Twelve are said to have established a House of Love and Prayer in their communities.[269] Such lists illustrate the inspirational importance of Shlomo's ordinations and the practical ramifications in perpetuating the Carlebach legacy.

The "ordinations" bestowed by Reb Shlomo constitute a unique genre. Some of the compositions were adorned with biblical, Talmudic and halachic references, original hermeneutical insights, and subtle inspirational nuances.[270] Sometimes, a specific program of study was involved, but in many instances the ordination was a form of honor and guidance. The stories below illustrate a range of ordination types and purposes.

#

One of the first rabbinical ordinations that Reb Shlomo wrote was for Natan (Nossen, Norman) Schafer, one of Shlomo's most veteran disciples. Born in 1945, Norman first met Shlomo in 1957 in Winnipeg when Reb Shlomo had been invited there by Reb Zalman. From 1963 through 1966, Norman would hitchhike to New York in order to be with Shlomo and to accompany him to his various engagements. Later he went with him to the HLP, and then in 1968 moved to Israel (see above). Almost a decade later, in 1976, Natan was living in Boston and working as a hospital and prison chaplain. Neila and Shlomo had arranged the match, and Shlomo had performed Natan's marriage to Channah on September 16, 1976. That same year, Reb Shlomo gave *semicha* to Natan enhancing his role as a pastoral counselor.

---

the list has been disputed partially because it was not always clear what was *semicha* and what was Shlomo's way of empowering disciples with special recognition and titles.

269. The 12 rabbis listed as leading communities are: (1) Joseph Cooper, Boulder, Colorado; Safed, Israel (2) Joel Dinnerstein, Ohr Ki Tov Carlebach Chassidim of Flatbush (3) Eliezer Garner, Rocking Rabbi, Or Pnimi (4) Yisroel Finman, Nishmat Kol Chai and Rabbi of Long Island Chassidic Center, Rosedale, New York (5) Zusha Frumin, Moshav Me'or Modi'im (6) David Montag, Ohr Chadash Congregation in Los Angeles (7) Yehoshua Ritchie, Jerusalem (8) Nossen Schafer, Sharon, Mass. (9) Shlomo Schwartz, Chabad Shaliach to UCLA (10) Shmuel Stauber, Achdut Group (11) Elyah (Eliyahu) Succot, Safed, Israel (12) Dovid Zeller, Efrat, Israel

270. In the 2nd edition of his book, *Depths of the Heart*, 234–262, Yahad Witt printed the text of the ordinations and semi-ordinations that Shlomo gave to 13 people: Sholom Brodt, Reuven Gilmore, Mordechai Levi, Yitzhak Miller, Mindy Ribner, Joshua (Yehoshua) Ritchie, Yaakov Mordechai Ritchie, Yehezkel Sasson, Yankala Shemesh, Avraham Arieh Trugman, Yehoshua Witt, and Dovid Zeller.

Street festival concert in Bensonhurst, Brooklyn sponsored by the Bensonhurst Council of Jewish Organizations, around 1989. From left to right: Dr. Yisrael Levitz, Reb Shlomo, and Prof. Chaim Waxman.

Courtesy of Rabbi Ari Waxman

⌗

On November 7, 1977 (26 Heshvan), Reb Shlomo gave David Zeller a preparatory document encouraging him to prepare for *semicha*. Rabbi Zeller later explained the process that led to his ordination. Zeller was working at the Institute of Transpersonal Psychology at Johnston College in Northern California and people would ask him if he is a rabbi. He confided in Shlomo who then gave him a list of subjects to study – "whenever we got together, he would ask questions to check my progress." A couple of years later, Shlomo gathered the Carlebach *chevra* and created an official *semicha* ceremony.[271]

---

271. The text of the *semicha* is printed in Witt, *Depths of the Heart*, 245–248. Zeller recounts how he was questioned as to the legitimacy of his using the title "Rabbi." He explains that when Rabbi Yaakov Yitzchok Ruderman, the head of Ner Yisroel Yeshiva in Baltimore, was visiting in Santa Clara, he consulted with him. After quizzing him, R. Ruderman affirmed that Zeller could "go out into the world" and use his "title of rabbi." See Zeller, *The Soul of the Story*, Chapter 45, 173–176.

Shlomo and Yitzhak Buxbaum

⌗

In the end of 1977, Reb Shlomo instituted the same idea of an official preparatory *semicha* document for three of his followers who had founded Moshav Me'or Modi'im. He presented letters to Reuven Gilmore, Yankala Shemesh, and Yehoshua Witt encouraging them to prepare to receive ordination "in two years time."[272] In actuality, the ordination for Yankala Shemesh was given a decade later,[273] but for Yehoshua Witt it was granted less than a year later, on August 25, 1978, at Moshav Me'or Modi'im. Shlomo used a word play in Hebrew on the two classical terms of ordination to expand the meaning to include: "*Yoreh Yoreh* (Teach, Teach) the Way of Hashem and *Yadin Yadin* (Judge, Judge) all of Israel in a meritorious manner."[274]

⌗

In the late 1970s, Reb Shlomo gave a non-rabbinical ordination to Yitzhak Buxbaum as a *maggid*, an inspirational teacher, and a storyteller.[275] Yitzhak recalls:

> I was raised as a fairly typical Conservative Jew. Like many of my generation, my bar mitzvah was not the beginning of a living Jewish connection, but the end. When I returned to Judaism in my mid-twenties, it was through Shlomo Carlebach and Lubavitch. I first met Shlomo in 1967 in Boston at Brandeis University and

272. See Witt, *Depths of the Heart*, 241–242, 259. The letters for Gilmore and Witt are dated 18th Tevet, 5738 (= December 28, 1977).

273. The idiomatic Hebrew expression "at the end of two years" (in the document for Yankala Shemesh) is borrowed from the verse in Genesis 41:1, and therefore does need not mean an exact count of two years. The actual ordination for Yankala Shemesh (pp. 260–261) is dated 15th of Av (= Aug. 18, 1978).

274. The Hebrew text of this ordination is printed in Witt, *Depths of the Heart*, 243–244.

275. In traditional literature, the term "*maggid*" referred to one who preaches and admonishes to go in God's ways.

remained close to him for twenty-six years. I wanted to follow in his footsteps as a *maggid* who inspired Jews to greater devotion and fervor for God. Actually, I had been doing the work of a *maggid* for some years; I just didn't know that there was a traditional role and title for what I was doing and I wanted spiritual support from my Rebbe so I spoke to Shlomo about it. He gave me *semicha* as a *maggid* in a special ceremony in the Carlebach Shul in New York. A decade after his death, I founded the Jewish Spirit Maggid Training Program and began to pass on that *semicha* that I had received from Shlomo.[276]

Shlomo begins this ordination document with the verse: *Maggid devarav leYaakov* (Psalms 146:19).[277] He uses three terms "*Yaggid Yaggid,*" "*Yeorer Yeorer,*" and "*Yahzir Yahzir.*" "*Yaggid*" refers to the role of the *maggid* to tell stories; "*Yeorer*" to his function in arousing and awakening, and "*Yahzir*" to his task of bringing Jews back to God and religion. Shlomo empowers Reb Yitzhak: We support, strengthen, and uphold Reb Yitzhak on his life mission to open the hearts of Israel, to bring them back to God and religion. Shlomo uses several word plays on Talmudic and Midrashic concepts to dramatize Reb Yitzhak's role as a *maggid*.[278] He is to go out and knock on the doors, to open the gates of the heart, to bring Jews to discover knowledge they have lost, knowledge of the Most High. With *aggadot* (literally, tales) that attract the heart, the *maggid* is to effectually return Israel in complete *teshuva* (literally, penitence) through love.[279]

With the granting of a *maggid* ordination, Reb Shlomo established

---

276. Personal email exchange 2011 with corrections in Jan. 2013. See also http://www.jewishspirit.com/about_yitzhak.html.

277. In the Biblical context the verse means that God tells His words to Jacob. These three words were known as the title of the anthology of teachings from the famous Maggid of Mezreritch, Rabbi Dov Ber (1710–1772), foremost disciple of the Baal Shem Tov.

278. I thank Reb Yitzhak for sending me his explanations of the word plays and the range of meanings. For example, by using the phrase "*aveida midaat,*" Reb Shlomo alludes to a person who has lost an object. In the Talmudic context, the term means "lost to mind" and refers to a case where the owner has given up hope of retrieving his lost object, thereby making it *hefker*, ownerless. But Shlomo turns the phrase around: Jews alienated from Judaism are "lost" and God is the owner who has "lost them." They are lost because they have no *daat Elyon*, knowledge of God. The task of the *maggid* is to return the "lost" Jews to God, their Owner, by providing them with knowledge of God transmitted through stories.

279. This is a reference to the classical Talmudic distinction (e.g., *Yoma* 86b) of two types of *teshuva*: through love or through awe. Shlomo concludes the *semicha* document with a citation from Isaiah 60:1, "Arise, shine, for your light has come," heralding the awakening and redemption. Then he adds the verse from Numbers 6:23,

a precedent that implies a revival of the Eastern European itinerant preacher yet offers an adaptation for the modern *teshuva* movement. Here he empowers Reb Yitzhak as an inspirational teacher and storyteller with a mission that is now being transmitted to another generation of *maggidim*.

#

On July 10, 1984 in Dorena, Oregon, Reb Shlomo presented Yitzhak Husbands-Hankin with a certificate, ordaining him as a *baal tefillah*, a prayer leader whose mission is "to awaken the hearts of Israel to prayer, to pray for all of Israel with love, and to guide the scattered holy flock of Israel to return in *teshuva* to Mt. Sinai and to Jerusalem."[280] Yitz clarified what this document meant:

> Reb Shlomo was particularly aware of me as a musician, cellist, singer, and composer of *niggunim*. I believe that his desire was to particularly bless and strengthen me in the expression of holy prayerful music as this was the way we connected most deeply. Reb Shlomo taught a whole new generation of Jewish musicians how to listen for holy melodies. He demonstrated for us this miraculous human capacity and through listening to his music we gained a sense of how to attune to the world of music and welcome holy melodies to flow into our lives as well.[281]

#

On October 5, 1984, Reb Shlomo gave *semicha* to Yitzhak Miller emphasizing his mission as a cantor to enthuse hearts – the broken hearts of the people of Israel.[282] Yitzhak was born in Israel but educated in San Francisco where from 1965–1981 he studied music and developed his vocal skills with leading opera singers. Yitzhak was active in the HLP and performed on stage with Reb Shlomo. He served as a cantor in San Francisco until moving to Israel in 1992.

#

"So shall you bless [Israel]." Finally, he expresses anticipation to merit seeing the future elevation of the honor of Israel through joy.

280. My thanks to Yitz for sending me a copy of the Hebrew original.

281. Personal correspondence with Rabbi Yitz Husbands-Hankin, May 30, 2012.

282. Witt, *Depths of the Heart*, 253–254.

On August 10, 1987, Tu BeAv, Reb Shlomo presented semicha to Avraham Arieh Trugman.[283] The document was signed on official stationery of Yeshivat Me'or Modi'im – "The New House"[284] where Avraham had studied for ten years, and the ceremony was held at the Moshav. Noting the significance of the 15th of Av as the traditional time for celebrating love and courtship in the vineyards, Shlomo began by comparing the yearning of the soul for God:

> Today is a Holiday for Israel – The Day of the Fifteenth of Av.
>
> We have gone out to the vineyards, G-d's vineyard, to find the one who our soul loves. He is oneness inside and out. Essence of my Essence, my soul flies away when He speaks (Song of Songs 5:6).
>
> The one who loves G-d and his people Israel, the great and praiseworthy Rabbi Avraham Arieh ben Chayim Nachum and Yehudit.
>
> *Yoreh Yoreh.* He shall teach, he shall teach
> To draw out preciousness from the dregs.
> *Yadin Yadin.* He shall judge, he shall judge
> Among the nations – one nation on the earth (I Chronicles 17:21)
> *Hakem Hakem.* He shall be lifted up, and lift up with him the *Shechina* out of the dust.
> *Yizkeh V'Yizkeh.* He shall merit and give merit to everyone he meets to find a path in the midst of the sea – the pure path when G-d brings back the returners to Zion (Psalms 126:1). . . .

Rabbi Avraham and Rachel Trugman are a founding family of the Moshav in 1976. Avraham served as the director of the Center for Jewish Education at the Moshav. Currently, they direct Ohr Chadash: New Horizons in Jewish Experience which in many ways continues the Carlebach legacy of outreach and inreach around the world.[285]

※

---

283. The Hebrew text is printed in Witt, *Depths of the Heart*, 249–250.

284. The name "New House" is a translation for *Bayit Chadash* the magnum opus written by Rabbi Joel Sirkis (1561–1640) on the Shulhan Arukh. Reb Shlomo traced his rabbinic lineage back to R. Sirkis, and this is even inscribed on Shlomo's tombstone.

285. My thanks to the Trugmans for the interviews and communications in Sept. 2012. See also TheTrugmans.com, http://www.thetrugmans.com/trugman_bios .shtml.

This is a widely publicized photo of Reb Zalman and Reb Shlomo together taken around 1989. Courtesy of Natan and Rhia Jacobi. Thanks to Rabbi David Zaslow for the investigative clarifications.

On September 27, 1987, Shlomo came especially to the house of Eliezer Garner in Staten Island and celebrated with him the granting of his *semicha*. Written with the inspiration of the Ten Days of Penitence, Reb Shlomo began the certification by noting that the Books of Life are open, the gates of *teshuva* have never been closed, and the gates of Torah are open eternally. He devoted the ordination "to our friend who is ready and prepared to be a glory to his people and a true lover of Israel. The gates of his heart are open and his life is open to all things of holiness."[286]

The personal story of Eliezer and his wife Michele is a striking illustration of how Reb Shlomo changed lives. Eliezer (Sonny) was part of the founding group of the HLP in 1967–1969. When he asked Shlomo what should be his next steps to understand his Jewishness, Shlomo told him, "Go and learn in Diaspora Yeshiva in Jerusalem." Eliezer studied there for six months and then attended other yeshivas in Jerusalem such as Mercaz HaRav Kook before going back to the U.S. to study full-time with Shlomie Twersky from Denver at his Torah Research Institute (TRI), and then in the Sh'or Yoshuv Yeshiva in Far Rockaway from 1971–1975. His *havruta* learning partner there, Dovid Din, had been a leader in the HLP (see above) and suggested that Eliezer meet Michele.

Michele Back, born in Brooklyn in 1949, was raised as Conservative Jew in Brooklyn with no connection to religious observance. She studied in Hunter College from 1967–1971 and became very involved in Eastern religions, meditations, yoga, and Zen. One day in 1968, her yoga teacher played a record to meditate on. It was *The Whole World is Waiting to Sing a Song of Shabbos*. Michele recalls how this led her to Shlomo:

> I went to my yoga teacher and asked whose song is that? She told me that it is Rabbi Carlebach, and that next Wednesday night he will be at the Integral Yoga Institute with Swami Satchidananda. So I went. First, Satchidananda spoke, and then Shlomo led music and dancing. I went over to him and said that's amazing. He gave me his business card. I never ever had spoken to a rabbi before.

---

286. My thanks to Eliezer Garner for sending me a copy of his original *semicha* document which I have translated here into English.

But, I finally dared to phone and left a message with Ann, his secretary at 7th Ave. Sure enough, he called me back and invited me to his concert at Brooklyn College. I told him I didn't have money to pay. So he invited me to meet him before the concert and enter as his guitar carrier.[287]

In 1974, Shlomo arranged for Michele to join his Shabbaton in the Catskills. There she met Stanley (Simcha) and Michol Leah Miller who influenced her to become religious. Stanley showed her the Carlebach album cover *VeHaer Eynenu* published in 1970 with a photo of Eliezer Garner next to Shlomo, and soon the *shidduch* was made. They met in February 1975 and were married March 19, 1975. In 1987, the Garners were encouraged by Shlomo in their founding of the Or Pnimi Center for Spiritual Judaism "as a vehicle to reach out to all Jews and to share with the world the universal message of Judaism." One of their more unique programs is Eliezer's weekly radio show on WSIA in Staten Island *The Kabballah Airwaves Show*, and Michele, the Rockin' Rebbetzin's *Kol Isha*.[288]

#

On October 13, 1987, the evening of Hoshanna Rabba, Reb Shlomo presented *semicha* to Zusha Frumin, one of the founders of the Moshav, who recalls, "It was a beautiful ceremony in front of all the hundreds of guests who came to be with Shlomo."[289]

#

On June 26, 1988, a very special *semicha* was given in Los Angeles to Matthew J. Ritchie, the father of Dr. Joshua Ritchie. Matthew was a chaplain in the Arizona state prison system and Shlomo composed a *semicha* type document with several word plays on the theme of *Hakem Yakim* (Lift and Uplift) recognizing the devoted service of Rabbi Yaakov Mordechai Ritchie to "help those imprisoned and support those who fall."[290] The *semicha* was signed by Rabbis Shlomo Carlebach,

---

287. Personal interview with Michele Garner, Dec. 23, 2012.

288. Personal interviews with Michele and Eliezer Garner, Dec., 2012.

289. Personal communication with Reb Zusha, March 28, 2013. On Zusha and the founding of the Moshav see above, Chapter 8.

290. This is a play on words from the second blessing of the *Amidah*, the standing prayer.

Joshua Ritchie, and David Moshe Montag as a "Holy Court of three." Shortly after, Matthew passed away.[291]

#

Sholom Brodt received *semicha* on April 13, 1989. He was born on August 2, 1949 and studied in Ner Yisrael in Toronto and at the Chabad Yeshiva Tomchei Temimim in Montreal. He completed a BA in economics at Concordia University in Montreal and an MA in Jewish education at Yeshiva University in Manhattan. He first met Reb Shlomo at a concert in Montreal in 1963, and over the years became close to him especially when Shlomo and Neila were living in Toronto during the late 1970s. Sholom married Judy Tibor, a devoted follower of Reb Shlomo (see above) and the couple worked in Montreal in Jewish education. In 1988/1989, the Brodts spent a sabbatical year in Jerusalem and Sholom studied in Knesseth Beis Eliezer of Rabbi Yaakov Moshe Poupko. One Sunday morning on April 9, 1989, after the Brodts had spent Shabbat at Moshav Me'or Modi'im, Reb Shlomo encountered Sholom and announced: "Sholom, I'm giving you *semicha* this week, whether you'll be there or not." Thus, on April 13, 1989, an official ceremony was held in the Brodts' apartment in Mekor Baruch, Jerusalem with Shlomo presenting a hand written document with inspirational blessings and lofty aspirations.[292] Using a range of idiomatic themes and associative wordplays intertwined with biblical and rabbinic citations, Shlomo broadened the classical ordination formula of *Yoreh Yoreh, Yadin Yadin*. He included the discernment of varying shades of truth, judgment in matters pertaining to both physical and monetary holiness and a devotion to all that is good.[293]

The Brodts came to live in Israel in 1994. In 2003, they founded Yeshivat Simchat Shlomo in Nachlaot, Jerusalem – the first full-time Carlebach yeshiva in Israel offering text-based and experiential programs in Talmud, Prayer, Meditation, Kabbalah, Hasidut, and Jewish storytelling.[294]

#

On August 16, 1989, Tu BeAv, Shlomo wrote out a *semicha* document for Dr. Yehoshua (Joshua) Ritchie enhancing his career as a medical doctor

---

291. My thanks to Dr. Joshua Ritchie for showing me this ordination. The document is printed in Witt, *Depths of the Heart*, 257–258.

292. Personal communications with Rabbi Sholom Brodt in Sept. 2012.

293. My summation of the Hebrew text. The document was printed in Witt, *Depths of the Heart*, 238–240.

294. ShlomoYeshiva.org, http://www.shlomoyeshiva.org.

who integrates a spiritual approach. This *semicha* recognizes the work of a devoted follower who played a pivotal role in the success of the Carlebach Movement.[295] The *semicha* was presented by Reb Shlomo to Joshua in the Amshinov Yeshiva, Jerusalem. It contains about 120 words and has ten key phrases – replete with biblical and Talmudic connotations some of which are noted below:

> And command Joshua,[296]
>
> God should save you from being directed by the force of habit.[297]
>
> And the steps of His Hasidim He will guard[298] with the highest protection.
>
> He who wishes to be a Hasid should be careful to avoid injurious words.[299]
>
> Your Words are a Lamp to my feet and a Light to my path (Psalms 119:105) – all her paths are Peace (Proverbs 3:17).
>
> Shalom to those far and near (Isaiah 57:19).
>
> By this we hereby lay our hands, the long hands of a long exile[300] to a complete redemption upon the head and heart, upon Haim Joshua son of Rabbi Yaacov Mordechai.
>
> 1. Our teacher, Rabbi, he shall be called.
> 2. A light in darkness[301] he shall be called.
> 3. A light which is good – true good which is Torah[302] – he shall be called.

295. For example, Joshua served as one of the 3 rabbis on the Rabbinical Court that Reb Shlomo convened for special purposes such as conversions.

296. This is a reference to Deut. 3:28 where Moses is told by God to strengthen and encourage Joshua to assume a leadership role in entering the Land of Israel. The theme here is specifically for Joshua Ritchie.

297. This apparently is an original word play of Reb Shlomo on the exegetical comment of Rashi that Moses was praying for Joshua to be saved from the advice of the spies. Reb Shlomo uses the term *"hergelim"* rather than *"meraglim"* to indicate the dangers of ingrained habits that need to be changed.

298. This is based on the verse in I Sam. 2:9 that God watches over the steps of his pious ones (*hasidim*).

299. This is a quote from the Talmudic comment of Rav Yehudah in *Baba Kamma* 30a that he who wishes to be a *"hasid"* should be careful to avoid injuring others. The ethical expositions of this cryptic statement are explained by R. Moshe Hayyim Luzzato in *Mesillat Yesharim*, Chapter 19, as referring to damages in body, money, and congeniality.

300. This is a play on words based on the idea of "a long hand" as the halachic interpretation of how a messenger is considered to be an extension of one's will. The idea of an extended exile is found in the Talmudic concept in *Berakhot* 4b.

301. This concept is based on the verse in Isa. 9:1.

302. The rabbinic word play on Gen. 1:4 that the Light is Good = Torah, can be

4. *Yoreh Yoreh*, Counselor he shall surely counsel those who have strayed from the path.[303]

5. Healer, he shall surely Heal[304] the souls of the people of Israel lost in captivity in spiritual exile.[305]

6. Uplifter, he shall surely Uplift[306] the fortunes of His people Israel.

7. Ascend, he shall surely Ascend from level to level in the service of God and in learning Torah.

8. Drawing Close, he shall surely Draw Close the outcasts of Israel from the four corners of the earth.[307]

9. Builder, he shall surely Build his house in Jerusalem in the holy city.

10. Learning, he shall surely Teach the depths of Torah, the treasures of Torah, words sweeter than honey.[308]

This document was intended to empower and inspire Joshua in adding the spiritual rabbinical dimension to his medical career.[309] Born in 1938, Joshua had completed his MD in 1962 at the University of Southern California School of Medicine in Los Angeles. His encounter with Shlomo at a concert in Berkeley changed his life and he became a life-long follower. When the House of Love and Prayer opened in May 1968, Joshua was the one to pay the first month's rent of $400. When Shlomo would visit the HLP for Shabbat, the Ritchie family would come to stay with their three children and sleep upstairs.

When the Ritchies moved to Jerusalem and settled in Bayit VeGan,[310]

---

found in *Avot* 6:3.

303. The classical formula for giving rabbinic ordination is *"Yoreh Yoreh."* Here and in other ordination documents, Reb Shlomo extends the connotation to the verse in Psalms 25:8 as a reference to showing the way to sinners.

304. The double term of "Heal," he shall heal is taken from the verse in Exod. 21:19 and applied specifically to Dr. Ritchie.

305. The concept of "exile of the soul" is developed in the writings of Rabbi Nachman of Breslov.

306. The double word play of *Hakem Yakim* is based on the verse in Deut. 22:4 and understood in rabbinic commentary to mean helping uplift the burden onto the donkey as opposed to Exod. 23:5 where the double verb refers to helping unload the burden.

307. This quote is based on Isa. 11:12.

308. The last expressions hint at the rabbinic commentaries to Ps. 19:11.

309. Joshua had spent hundreds, or probably as much as a thousand hours, witnessing the counseling sessions of the Amshinover Rebbe and of Reb Shlomo. He incorporated these into his personal practice.

310. Joshua accepted a position teaching pediatrics at Hadassah Hospital – the

Joshua met the Amshinover Rebbe, Yerachmiel Yehuda Meir Kalish, and became a *ben bayit*, a part of the family, even serving as his personal physician and driver. He began wearing an Amshinov *spodik*, an honor usually reserved only for homebred Amshinov Hasidim. The Amshinov connection was a key link for Shlomo to the Hasidic *haredi* world, even during the difficult years when he was ostracized because of his unconventional modes of outreach. The Amshinover warmly welcomed Shlomo, inviting him to sing and play his guitar at Amshinov celebrations,[311] and praising his outreach efforts.[312]

In 1976, the Ritchies were part of the pioneering group of eight families who settled the Moshav.[313] It was the intervention of the Amshinover Rebbe that proved crucial in the establishment of Me'or Modi'im (see Chapter 8).

The Ritchies returned to Los Angeles in 1978.[314] Their house at 613 N. Las Palmas was Shlomo's home base whenever he visited the LA area. Joshua estimates that they hosted Shlomo a total of about forty times. In 1991, the Ritchies moved to the New York area (Monsey) to be near Shlomo's home base in Manhattan. After Shlomo's death, they moved to Bayit VeGan in Jerusalem to be near the Amshinover Rebbe. In 1995, the Ritchies founded the Refuah Institute, an organization offering training programs, counseling, and coaching from a Torah perspective.[315]

Hebrew University School of Medicine after completing his residency in pediatrics at the Albert Einstein Medical Center in New York.

311. For a photo of Reb Shlomo singing at the wedding of the daughter of the Rebbe of Amshinov, see Brand, *Reb Shlomele*, 74. For video footage filmed by Eliahu Gal-Or where Shlomo can be seen playing his guitar at an Amshinover Rebbe *Sheva Berachot* in a summer in the 1980s, see http://www.zingmit.com/2012/02/old -footage-of-shlomo-carlebach-with.html; http://rebshlomocarlebach.blogspot.co. il/2010/04/shlomo-with-rebbes.html; http://www.youtube.com/watch?v=0x8-wal9 whw&feature=related.

312. See Brand, *Reb Shlomele*, 100, and Brandwein, *Reb Shlomele*, 136, citing the Rebbe of Amshinov as responding to criticism of Reb Shlomo by saying that Shlomo's faults are only due to his excessive love for Jews. For a photo of Shlomo and R. Ya'akov Aryeh, the Rebbe of Amshinov, see Brandwein, *Reb Shlomele*, 77. Brandwein there quotes "a reliable witness" about the Rebbe of Amshinov saying that Reb Shlomo's reward in heaven "will not only be greater than the one in store for me, it will even exceed the reward *you* think I am destined to."

313. The Ritchies lived on the Moshav for a year. Josh served as the founding secretary-general while he traveled to Rehovot to work as a pediatrician.

314. Dr. Ritchie served as the medical director of the Edendale Family Medical Center and at the Queen of Angeles – Hollywood Presbyterian Medical Center from 1978–1991.

315. Personal interviews with Rabbi Dr. Joshua and Liliane Ritchie, Oct. 2012. See also Refuah.net, http://www.refuah.net/faculty.php.

#

On December 19, 1989, Reb Shlomo presented his Manhattan assistant, Mindy (Melinda) Ribner, with a non-rabbinical *semicha* document, witnessed and signed by two other Orthodox rabbis, Rabbi Yidel Stein and Rabbi Dr. Seymour Applebaum.[316] In this document, he empowered Miriam Shulamit to "teach and transmit the Torah of *hitbodedut* (meditation) and the pouring forth of the soul."[317] Mindy reconstructs the event:

> Reb Shlomo wanted to give the *semicha* publicly, and chose to do so at the *yahrzeit* commemoration for his father when many people attended. He was in his rebbe mode more than I had ever experienced him. He spoke about being a conduit for the blessings of the holy rebbes from all generations, a chain of tradition going back to the Baal Shem Tov and Moses, and that this would all flow through him to me. Some people walked out yelling and screaming, contesting that no form of *semicha* should be given to women. But for me it was a tremendously powerful moment of transformation. I believe that he saw that I was destined to be a Jewish spiritual teacher and wanted to empower me and pave the way for other women to be similarly empowered.[318]

#

Simcha (Edward) Sheldon first met Shlomo in the lobby of the Pine View Hotel, in Upstate New York around 1960. Over the years, Simcha developed a close relationship with Reb Shlomo, and performed with him in concert. From the 1970s, Simcha worked as an educator and spiritual leader in New York and California, and in 1981 also became a licensed psychotherapist. In 1990, Simcha consulted with Reb Shlomo about how to deal with the fact that people would address him as "Rabbi Sheldon." Shlomo's answer was to design a tailor-made *semicha* learning program. On July 1991, the *semicha* was written and announced at a community learning session in Jerusalem. Later, on Shushan Purim, March 14, 1992, the *semicha* was presented in an official ordination ceremony at the

---

316. Personal interview with Mindy Ribner, Nov. 3, 2010. See Rahel Musleah, "Shlomo Carlebach – The Music Man," *Hadassah Magazine*, Oct. 28, 2008, 51–56, HadassahMagazine.org, http://www.hadassahmagazine.org/site/c.twI6LmN7IzF/b.5 766903/k.C3FB/October_2008_Vol_90_No_2.htm.

317. Translation from the Hebrew document in Yahad Witt, *Depths of the Heart*, 1996, 234.

318. Recorded interviews with Mindy Ribner, Nov. 2010.

annual Carlebach Shul dinner in Manhattan. Here is an excerpt from the English version of the ordination: To Decide and to Judge.

> To show those estranged in Israel to find His Place and their place,
> As on Shabbat you cannot leave your place
> To Learn and To Teach,
> To Bring Close and even Closer,
> Show the Way and Show the Way,
> The True Way Leading Up to the House of God and
> To the ladder whose head reaches Heaven Lift Up and Be Uplifted
> With Holy Fire Who Burns All Night Until the Morning . . .

Shlomo invented the terms *"Lehorot veLadun"* (literally, To Teach and To Judge) and *"Yaaleh VeYaaleh"* (Lift Up and be Uplifted).[319] He adapted the imagery of reaching up towards Heaven (Genesis 28:12), and the metaphor of being uplifted with Holy Fire (Leviticus 6:2). Rabbi Dr. Sheldon told me that this *semicha* helped empower him to integrate Torah spirituality, psychology, and music in his work and his teachings, and to develop innovative educational experiences "following in the footsteps of Reb Shlomo, as a composer, singer, musician, and rabbi promoting unity and spiritual growth." Simcha developed multifaceted outreach programs in Los Angeles such as Project L.E.A.R.N, and The Loving Heart Fellowship "to spread love, unity, Torah, and music." His newest project is Jews Are Good for the World – to enhance Jewish pride and unity and to facilitate a positive relationship towards Jews worldwide.[320]

❀

The final example here of a Shlomo *semicha* document is from June 30, 1992 for Israeli-born Itzchak Marmorstein. He first met Shlomo in 1974 at the Kotel and after that "he was an important and joyful part of my life." During the years he lived in Israel, Itzchak would go to hear Shlomo whenever he could – such as at weddings and weekends at Moshav Me'or Modi'im. After receiving ordination from Rabbi Zalman Nechemia Goldberg in Jerusalem in 1990, Itzchak served as rabbi in Vancouver. There he would bring Shlomo each June from 1990–1992 to serve as the head of a special conversion court (Beit Din):

---

319. This is a word play on the classical formula of *Yoreh Yoreh, Yadin Yadin*.

320. Personal interviews Sept.–Oct. 2012. See also LovingHeart.org, http://www .lovingheart.org and DrSimcha.com, www.drsimcha.com. Today he lives with his family in Israel and works as a practicing clinical and medical psychologist.

Dr. Joshua Ritchie in Hasidic garb with Shlomo, David Zeller, and Yehoshua Witt.   Courtesy of Dr. Ritchie

Reb Shlomo and Dr. Ritchie

His visits were a yearly highlight for many of us there. The deep mornings in the *mikveh* would often continue into a joyous *chuppah* or two in the afternoon for those married, freshly covenanted, who never had a real Jewish wedding. In the evening, our best musicians would back him as he did a concert for the larger community. We danced and then fabrenged long into the night.[321]

Shlomo had assigned a course of study to Itzchak towards awarding him ordination. On June 30, 1992, just before Reb Shlomo departed from Vancouver, he composed the *semicha* document. It begins with the classic ordination formula of *Yoreh Yoreh* and *Yadin Yadin*, literally, he will teach and judge. But a new terminology is added:

> Teach to distinguish between the pure and impure, light and darkness, and varying shades of holiness. Teach sinners the path (Psalms 25:8) until there are no more sinners in the land (Psalms 104:35). Judge life saving issues as well as monetary dilemmas through the device of the "holy shekel," and bring redemption for the soul and body . . . Listen, Israel, and discover the innermost value of each person regardless of their state in life, whether wicked or ignorant and unable to even ask.[322]

What Shlomo has done is to associate *Yoreh Yoreh*, the standard ordination form, with an outreach/inreach task to discover the inner value of each person and to work towards eradicating evil and sin and hastening redemption. It was these kinds of inspired letters that empowered his disciples in their life missions.[323]

✳

As a postscript to the Carlebach ordinations, I conclude with the story of Mimi Feigelson, an Israeli student of Reb Shlomo who was the first woman for whom Shlomo wrote out a syllabus towards receiving official ordination. Mimi's family came on aliyah when she was 8 years old. At age 16, Mimi began studying with Reb Shlomo and became one of his most devoted disciples, traveling with him all over Israel and the U.S.

---

321. Itzchak Marmorstein, "Meeting the Rebbe and Saying Goodbye," *Kol Chevra*, vol. 14, 2008, 131–133.

322. My thanks to Rabbi Itzchak Marmorstein for providing me a copy of the original document in Hebrew and discussing it with me, June 6, 2011. The English is my translation.

323. The last *semicha* given by Reb Shlomo was on April 25, 1994 to Rabbi Simcha Hochbaum – see below, Chapter 12.

She accompanied him, tape recorder in hand, on his 1989 trips to Poland and Russia. In 1992, she was involved in founding Yakar Jerusalem – A Center for Tradition and Creativity, and as associate director, created the Women's Beit Midrash program. Mimi, along with Rabbi David Zeller, brought Shlomo to Yakar for three consecutive summers of teaching. In the summer of 1994, Shlomo wrote out a syllabus, primarily Talmud and *Halacha*, towards granting official ordination to Mimi and her *havruta* Yoni Gordis.[324]

Mimi is one of the few women scholars to have studied intensively with Shlomo.[325] Currently she is the *Mashpiah Ruchanit* (spiritual mentor) and lecturer of Rabbinic Studies at the Ziegler School of Rabbinic Studies at the American Jewish University. In 2010, Reb Mimi was recognized by *The Forward* as one of the fifty most influential female rabbis in the U.S., and was accepted to the Board of Rabbis of Southern California as an independent Orthodox rabbi.

These are merely a few examples of a diverse range of ordinations. A thorough study of the documents can reveal more about the impact of Shlomo and the continuity of the Carlebach legacy.

---

324. Shortly after Shlomo's death, the Carlebach *semicha* was recognized by a panel of 3 Orthodox rabbis. I thank Reb Mimi for her responses to my questions in July 2011. For more details, Mimi referred me to her article written in Hebrew in *Eretz Aheret*, 31, Dec. 29, 2005, Acheret.co.il, http://acheret.co.il/?cmd=articles.139 &act=read&id=487.

325. Mimi completed her B.A. in 1985 and her M.A. in 2000 at the Hebrew University of Jerusalem.

CHAPTER 12

Last Two Years

1. TRAVERSING THE CONTINENTS (1993–1994)

Reb Shlomo continued to travel around the world, performing in South America (Brazil, Argentina, and Chile), South Africa, and Austria.[1] Here are some highlights from 1993:

In January 1993, Shlomo and a few of the *chevra* visited for a Shabbat at the Beth Israel Synagogue in New Orleans, Louisiana. On Motzei Shabbat, Shlomo and his entourage went to see Cajun dancing at Tchoupitoulas Street and the Mississippi River.[2]

On Sunday, January 10, 1993, Shlomo participated at the Lincoln Center for the Performing Arts, Avery Fisher Hall in Manhattan, New York in a concert on behalf of HASC (Hebrew Academy for Special Children) and sang *"Borchi Nafshi"* (Psalms 103:1)[3] and *"Veasau Chol Leovdecha."*[4] The concert, with a full orchestra and 101 male singers, was produced by Dovid Golding of Suki and Ding productions, conducted by Mona Rosenblum, and arranged by Yisroel Lamm. The Master of Ceremonies was Zale Newman. Reb Shlomo appeared in tie and suit, men and women sat separately,[5] and the MC asked for "all the men" (and not the women) to sing along. In a sense, this signified a significant mutual reacceptance of the *haredi* world and Reb Shlomo. Towards the end, there was a memorable appearance of popular American Hasidic singer, Mordechai Ben David singing *"Ana Hashem"* (Psalms 116:16) where he

---

1. Sue Ann Wood, "The Singing Rabbi," *St. Louis Post*, Jan. 10, 1993.

2. A photo and description of this event was published in the *L'Koved Reb Shlomo Remembrance Journal*, Nov. 1995.

3. Shlomo sings: http://www.youtube.com/watch?v=U6uOlDwvijM; wn.com, http://wn.com/Barchi_Nafshi; http://www.youtube.com/watch?v=AJqtL8KA-Lk; http://www.youtube.com/watch?v=CjtBHQQ4H-8.

4. http://il.utabby.com/v?i=1_pTCt1R3KM.

5. See the pictures of the audience on http://il.utabby.com/v?i=1_pTCt1R3KM.

embraces Reb Shlomo and then dances with him, in a sense signifying their reconciliation.[6]

Another example of how Reb Shlomo was now accepted and honored in some *haredi* communities can be seen on a video from Motzei Shabbat, January 16, 1993. Leiser Morawiecki from the Sassover Beth Hamedrash in Golders Green, London, invited Shlomo to perform at the bar mitzvah of his son Moshe Dov Morawiecki. The celebration took place in a marquee tent in the garden of the Morawiecki home on Finchley Road. This video illustrates how a *haredi* Hasidic audience in London is enthused and inspired by Reb Shlomo.[7]

Later that same evening, January 16, 1993, Shlomo performed at the Notting Hill Synagogue in London. Rabbi Pini Dunner recorded the concert using a "surround sound BBC orchestra microphone" to enrich the sound reproduction and capture the atmosphere of the Motzei Shabbat program. The result was a high quality recording, *A Melave Malka at Notting Hill*, which became a favorite of Shlomo aficionados.[8]

On February 28, 1993, over 900 people came to hear Reb Shlomo perform in Silver Spring, Maryland at the Northwood High School.[9] The event was organized by Am Kolel led by Rabbi David Shneyer as a special tribute to Reb Shlomo.[10] This was one of the *very few such events to honor Reb Shlomo in his lifetime*, although after his death this would become commonplace. Several speakers offered words of praise and appreciation and then Reb Shlomo sang, backed up by David's band, The Fabrangen

---

6. There had been a tension between the two because Mordechai had recorded songs very similar to those of Shlomo such as *"Tov Lehodot"* and Shlomo felt that the words and tunes had been incorrectly altered. The appearance on stage signaled reconciliation. For the performance, see WeJew.com, http://www.wejew.com/media/4139/Shlomo_Carlebach_Sings_with_MBD; IsraelVideoOnNetwork.com, http://www.israelvideonetwork.com/carlebach-and-mordechai-ben-david-singing-ana-hashem; http://www.youtube.com/watch?v=wMUYP8sVbHk.

7. The 15-minute video of Reb Shlomo performing at the Morawiecki bar mitzvah was posted at https://www.box.com/rashban/1/34341330/5154160038/1. My thanks to Dovid Reich of Kesher Torah, Stories & Nigunim Songs by Rabeinu Shlomo Carlebach *zt"l* for sending me the contact details and to Leiser Morawiecki for explanations about this event.

8. Personal communication with Rabbi Dunner, April 19, 2012. For the recordings, see MostlyMusic.com, http://www.mostlymusic.com/a-melave-malka-in-notting-hill.html; MileChai.com, http://www.milechai.com/product/Jewish_Music_Melava_Malka.html; Eichlers.com, http://www.eichlers.com/Product/Music/All_Music/Solo_Artists/Shlomo-Carlebach-CD-Melava-Malka-In-Notting-Hill-_ADCD225.html.

9. See Eve Zibart, *Weekend* section of the *Washington Post*, Feb. 26, 1993.

10. See above for a description of the impact of Reb Shlomo on Am Kolel and Rabbi David Shneyer.

Fiddlers. The program also featured two of Reb Shlomo's important musical disciples, Hanna Tiferet Siegel and Rabbi David Zeller.[11]

On March 7, 1993, Reb Shlomo led the Purim program at the Carlebach Shul in Manhattan and this is one of the few Carlebach video recordings that have been posted in full on the Internet.[12] The musical accompaniment for Shlomo is provided by C. Lanzbom and Noach Solomon.

On May 16, 1993, Shlomo performed the wedding of Bruce (Hashir) and Jan Ginsberg at Beacon, New York, overlooking the Hudson River:

> When Reb Shlomo officiated at my wedding, he wore the pants of one suit, the vest of another and the jacket of a third, prompting me to thank him for wearing not just one but his best three suits. His *huppah* time was miraculously abbreviated at my request, maybe an hour and a half. Following that, Shlomo's friend, the famous singer Pete Seeger, who lived just a few miles away, played his song *My Rainbow Race*, a favorite of mine.[13]

On Sunday, May 30, 1993, Shlomo recruited Afro-American folk singer Richie Havens to appear alongside him in a free six-hour concert at the Medgar Evers College amphitheater in Crown Heights.[14] This was a time of growing racial tension in New York City.[15] The Bensonhurst Council of Jewish Organizations organized a Brooklyn Jewish street festival with Reb Shlomo as the featured performer. It was billed as "the first-ever League of Neighbors Unity Concert," and sponsored by a coalition of several groups including JCS (The Jewish Chautauqua Society), an interfaith organization dedicated to improving intergroup relations.[16] The concert was a response to the Crown Heights Riot of August 19–21, 1991,

---

11. My thanks to Rabbi David Shneyer for this information.

12. See http://www.youtube.com/watch?v=BXr3ZIXDH-A&playnext=1&list=PL4 48B598460665A23 for a half hour clip from this event. For the full video of one hour, see http://youtu.be/oZvyguI8NdQ.

The lead theme song here is "*Teshuatam Hayita LaNetzach*" from the *piyut* on Purim, "*Shoshanat Yaakov.*"

13. Hashir (Bruce) Ginsberg, personal communication, Nov. 28–30, 2012.

14. The concert was produced by Moshe Liebert, Levi Garbose, and Paula George. A brief clip of Shlomo performing alongside Richie Havens in Crown Heights and the crowd joining in dancing can be seen in the film produced by Menachem Daum (segment 2:11–2:50), PBS.org, http://www.pbs.org/wnet/religionandethics/week1135/ profile.html. It is described with a photo by Paula George in the *L'Koved Reb Shlomo Remembrance Journal*, Nov. 1995.

15. On Aug. 23, 1989, Yusef Hawkins, a 16-year old African-American, was murdered by a white gang. See John DeSantis, *For the Color of His Skin: The Murder of Yusuf Hawkins and the Trial of Bensonhurst* (New York: 1992).

16. *New York Amsterdam News*, May 22, 1993.

Leiser Morawiecki from the Sassover Beth Hamedrash in Golders Green, London, invited Shlomo to perform at the bar mitzvah of his son Moshe Dov Morawiecki, January 16, 1993.

which began when a car from the Lubavitcher Rebbe's motorcade killed Gavin Cato, a 7-year old black child. Crown Heights was home to many Lubavitcher Hasidim who were Holocaust survivors or their descendants and this was their first anti-Semitic riot in America.[17] Richie Havens recalls:

> Black young people were dancing to Jewish melodies, and vice versa. The distinction of who the music belonged to went away.[18]

---

17. Bands of blacks roamed through Crown Heights assaulting Jews and damaging property. A 29-year old Lubavitcher Hasid from Australia, Yankel Rosenbaum, was stabbed to death. See Edward S. Shapiro, *Crown Heights, Blacks, Jews, and the 1991 Brooklyn Riot* (Lebanon, New Hampshire: 2006), xi, 1.

18. Ron Grossman, "Rabbi's joyful noise is a family tradition," *Chicago Tribune*, June 15, 2007, Articles.ChicagoTribune.com, http://articles.chicagotribune.com/2007-06-15/news/0706140666_1_shlomo-carlebach-berkeley-folk-festival-music. Richie Havens met Carlebach when they were playing unpaid gigs at clubs like Cafe Noir in Greenwich Village. Ever since his appearance at Woodstock on Aug. 15, 1969, Richie Havens had become famous. He was Woodstock's first performer and he was the longest, holding the crowd for *nearly two hours*, from 5:07–6:55 PM because all the other musicians were stuck in the traffic jam as the highway turned into a massive parking lot. Eventually, the performers were flown in by helicopter.

By 1993, Reb Shlomo's music had become so widespread that often it was forgotten that there was actually a composer. Such was the case with Gary Sinyor, a movie director and script writer, who used Shlomo's tune for "*Asher Bara*" in the wedding scene in a British comedy movie, "Leon the Pig Farmer." This was discovered by Rabbi Pini Dunner who then hired a lawyer, Leon Ruskin and filed a complaint. The producers duly acknowledged their error and paid Shlomo £5,000. R. Dunner described the anecdotal sequel:

> After the money arrived, I got a phone call from the director Gary Sinyor. He was desperately upset at what had happened and wanted to meet Shlomo to apologize personally. I arranged for my mother to invite Gary and Leon to a dinner party the next time Shlomo came to London in 1993. Thereafter, Shlomo was credited on the video cover. Gary was forever grateful. Later he became a member of my *shul*, the Saatchi Synagogue.[19]

In June 1993, Reb Shlomo gave a concert at Congregation Beth Sholom, a Conservative synagogue in San Francisco led at the time by Rabbi Alan Lew, known as the Zen Rabbi. This event is described by Ida Lewis as a concert in honor of going on aliyah. Ida wrote: "I couldn't think of a way to explain to my friends why I would want to live in Israel. I called Shlomo . . . 'All I can think of is giving my friends an evening with you!'" Four hundred people came and danced and listened to Shlomo's stories. Lewis reminisced: "In Israel during the following year, I met at least ten people who decided to make aliyah shortly after attending that concert in San Francisco."[20]

On June 11–13, 1993, Shlomo led the annual Shabbat weekend Ruach Retreat which this time was held in Monroe, Orange County, New York.[21]

On Monday evening, June 21, 1993, Shlomo came to Los Angeles to the home of his close disciples, Yehudah (Jerry) and Michelle Katz, to bless them as they were preparing to move to Israel.[22] Yehudah is an outstanding example of a musician who continues in the way of Reb Shlomo, traveling around the world performing music, telling stories, and inspiring thousands of people. He founded Reva L'sheva, a Jewish

---

19. Personal communication from R. Dunner, April 23, 2012.

20. Ida Lewis, "You Never Know . . . You Never Know . . . ," *Kol Chevra*, vol. 13, 2007, 57–58.

21. The program, organized by Reb Meir Fund, included again Reb Dovid Zeller, Blema Feinstein, and Yehudis Fishman.

22. Yehudah Katz, "Weddings and Marriage," *Kol Chevra*, vol. 2, 1995, 11.

rock and soul band, and many of the band members have been strongly influenced by Reb Shlomo.[23]

Then on Tuesday, June 22, 1993, Shlomo performed at the home of Selwyn Gerber in Beverlywood, Los Angeles.

On August 26, 1993, Shlomo led a program entitled Learning with Music at Congregation Agudas Achim Anshei Sfard, Adams Street Synagogue in Newtonville, Massachusetts.[24]

From September 19–22, 1993, just after Rosh Hashana, Shlomo appeared in the Los Angeles area in a series entitled The Joy of Tshuvah. On Sunday, September 19, 1993, he was hosted at the home of Simcha Sheldon in Venice, a beachfront neighborhood on the Westside of Los Angeles, California.[25] On Monday, September 20, Shlomo performed a concert at Beth Jacob, a Modern Orthodox congregation in Beverly Hills. On Tuesday, September 21, he was hosted at the home of Adrienne Scheff

---

23. The original line-up was Yehudah Katz, David Abramson, Adam Wexler, Zvi Yechezkeli, and Avi Yishai. Later band members include Eliezer "Lazer Lloyd" Blumen, Chanan Elias, Danny Roth – all of whom were directly influenced by Reb Shlomo. See CelebrateIsrael.com; http://www.celebrateisrael.com/DisplayVendor .asp?VID=233.

24. Congregation Agudas Achim Anshei Sfard Newsletter, Sept.–Oct., 1993, vol. 2, no. 1, AdamsStreet.org, http://adamsstreet.org/newsletters/vo2no1.

25. Interview with Dr. Simcha Sheldon, Oct. 12, 2012.

At the Silver Spring concert, 1993. Rabbi David Zeller playing the guitar near the piano together with the Fabrangen Fiddlers (left to right): piano Sue Roemer, guitar David Shneyer, fiddler Alan Oresky, mandolin Larry Robinson, and far right, Theo Stone. Courtesy ©Lloyd Wolf / www.lloyd-wolf.com

in Tarzana. Finally, on Wednesday, September 22, he was at the home of Selwyn Gerber. There his musical accompaniment was Richard Hardy (winds) and Joy Krauthammer (percussion).[26]

On November 21, 1993, Shlomo came to Dartmouth College in Hanover, New Hampshire where he performed for about 200 people.[27]

In December, Shlomo's daughter 19-year old daughter Neshama stopped her studies in acting school and began accompanying her father in his travels for the last months of his life. Concerned about his fragile health and problematic heart condition, Neshama tried to shield her father from the incessant demands on his time and energy. But it was very difficult. A performance in Israel in December 1993 turned into a real commotion on stage with people shoving in excited dancing. Shlomo was pushed, and his shoulder was dislocated. He suffered in pain for the next few months. Nonetheless, he continued traveling.

On December 12, 1993, Shlomo came with his family to London for the wedding of Pini and Sabine Dunner. Pini relates:

---

26. See the publicity advertisement and the photos taken and posted by Joy Krauthammer on her blog: http://rebshlomocarlebach-ztl.blogspot.co.il.

27. Shlomo was brought to Dartmouth by Hanna Tiferet Siegel (see above). At the time, her husband Rabbi Daniel Siegel was the Hillel director at Dartmouth.

Reb Shlomo in Silver Spring, Maryland, February 1993.
Courtesy ©Lloyd Wolf / www.lloydwolf.com

I had not expected him to come, but he called me the week before to say he was coming with Neila and the girls. At the wedding dinner, he sat next to Rabbi Mordechai Elefant, Rosh Yeshiva of Itri Yeshiva, with whom he had studied together in Lakewood Yeshiva. After *benching*, Shlomo sang and told stories and *divrei Torah* for almost an hour.[28]

---

28. Personal email from R. Dunner, April 2012.

Reb Shlomo with children, February 1993.
Courtesy ©Lloyd Wolf / www.lloydwolf.com

In January 1994, Shlomo participated in a Jewish-Muslim conference in Morocco entitled The Lessons of Maimonides for the Modern Age. The conference, co-sponsored by the Maimonides Research Institute of New York and Sidi Mohamed Ben Abdellah University of Fez, was part of a conciliatory approach of King Hassan II.[29] *New York Times* reporter, Ari L. Goldman, who accompanied Shlomo on the trip, described how on Friday evening, January 7, 1994, the group attended Temple Beth El Synagogue in Casablanca where in typical Moroccan style each section is chanted by different individuals. Shlomo was honored with leading *"Lecha Dodi."* As he did so in Carlebach style, all joined the singing. Afterwards Shlomo commented: "You can never bring peace in the world unless you have peace among us Jews."[30] Shlomo was paid an honorarium of $1,000, but he spent $900 on his phone bill alone, and he also had with him an entourage of musicians and his daughter Neshama.

---

29. The King, who expressed pride in his country's tolerance for Jews, had played a role in the Israeli-Palestinian talks. A few months earlier, on Sept. 14, 1993, Yitzhak Rabin and Shimon Peres had met with King Hassan in his seaside palace in Skhirat near Rabat on their way home after signing a peace agreement with the PLO in Washington.

30. See Ari L. Goldman, "To Honor a Philosopher," Religion Notes, *The New York Times*, Jan. 15, 1994, NYTimes.com, http://www.nytimes.com/1994/01/15/us/religion-notes.html. Also, Ari L. Goldman, "Why Carlebach Matters," *The Jewish Week*, May 8, 2009, TheJewishWeek.com, http://www.thejewishweek.com/viewArticle/c228_a16465/Special_Sections/Text_Context.html.

In the Beverlywood home of Selwyn Gerber, June 22, 1993
Collage created by © Joy Krauthammer

He sang with some Moroccan musicians who were members of the royal orchestra.[31]

Aboard the plane, Goldman discussed with Shlomo's business manager, Rabbi Sammy Intrator, how a Carlebach Institute should be set up "in Florida perhaps, where the Rabbi could be set up comfortably and visitors

---

31. Personal communications from Ari L. Goldman, Sept. 2012.

would come to him rather than him running to seek them out."[32] Indeed, Shlomo began seriously planning a change of pace. He discussed with his family how to "settle down" in one place without relinquishing his vision of a worldwide *teshuva* enterprise. One idea was to set up Carlebachian type yeshivas in Florida, California, and Jerusalem which would be led by his followers and Shlomo would stay in each yeshiva a few months a year. Furthermore, he and Neila began planning to remarry. Shlomo even joked that he would purchase the wedding ring in the airport which is what he had done for their first marriage in 1972. Yet all knew that Shlomo was motivated by a driving urge to help wherever needed and only the realization of his fragile health might slow him down.

On January 17, 1994, residents of the greater Los Angeles area were rudely awakened by the Northridge earthquake. A benefit concert was quickly organized to raise relief funds, and Shlomo was invited. The concert, entitled Rekindling the Flame, took place on February 1, 1994 at the Tatou Nightclub in the affluent city of Beverly Hills near Los Angeles.[33]

Then, on February 5–6, 1994, Reb Shlomo appeared at Temple Chai, a Reform synagogue in Phoenix, Arizona. There he spoke forcefully about Jewish rights to the Land of Israel.[34] The concert was organized by Rabbi Sarah Leah (Ayla) Grafstein and over 800 people attended. Sarah Leah had met Shlomo at age 8 in Toronto at her Orthodox synagogue "and he changed my life at a young age." She produced many concerts and gatherings for Shlomo over the years.[35]

On Motzei Shabbat, February 12, 1994, Shlomo led a Farbengen in Brooklyn on Rosh Hodesh Adar devoted to the teachings of the

---

32. Videotaped interview of Menachem Daum with Ari Goldman, Feb. 26, 2007, segment 45:50.

33. The musicians accompanying Shlomo included Robby Nathan Halperin, Bruce Berger, Skye Michaels, Simcha (Ed) Sheldon, Sam Glaser, Chanan (Michael Ian) Elias, P.F. Sloan, and two women, Joy Krauthammer (percussionist), and Shirley Perluss (mandolin). Joy Krauthammer posted pics at Rebshlomocarlebach-ztl.blogspot.com.

34. "A Celebration of Life and Peace," Teaching in Phoenix, AZ, Feb. 5, 1994, *Kol Chevra*, vol. 8, 2001, 49–51. Shlomo's talk in Phoenix about Israel's right to the land is dated Feb. 6, 1994. See http://www.youtube.com/watch?v=z7Ta2wOj52A, video released by Ruach Hamidbar founded by Rabbi Sarah Leah (Ayla) Grafstein. See also http://www.youtube.com/watch?v=FlxoNRwjHB0&feature=related, http://wn.com/shlomo_carlebach__awesome_live_speech_about_israel. As one of the proofs for Jewish ownership and rights to the Land of Israel, Shlomo mentions a childhood memory during the Nazi regime where "on every Jewish house the Nazis put up a sign saying Jews Go To Palestine" (segment 6:25–6:32).

35. Email correspondence with Sarah Leah, Nov. 4, 2011. In a ceremony in 1985 at the Shivtei Shalom community in Oregon, Sarah Leah became the second woman to receive the title of *Eshet Hazon*. See above, Chapter 10 for explanation of this title.

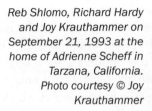

Reb Shlomo, Richard Hardy and Joy Krauthammer on September 21, 1993 at the home of Adrienne Scheff in Tarzana, California. Photo courtesy © Joy Krauthammer

Ishbitzer Rebbe. To illustrate the importance of Ishbitz, Shlomo mentions a discussion he had in Jerusalem with Rav Tzvi Yehudah HaCohen Kook[36] who asked Shlomo what he finds to be the best way to reach out to the youth in the House of Love and Prayer. When Shlomo answered Hasidut, Rav Tzvi Yehudah added that in accordance with his father's discourse likening Torah to food for the soul, the Hasidic writings of Breslov and Ishbitz are like drugs, powerful medicine. Indeed, Shlomo explained, these texts proved to be most effective "for all the heavily drugged up kids who came to the HLP."[37]

On February 13, 1994, Shlomo came to the home of Bruce (Hashir) Ginsberg in White Plains, New York, to participate in the naming of Hashir's first child, Alanna, who had been born ten days before.[38]

Towards the end of February 1994, Shlomo came to Vienna to play the star role in a movie for Austrian TV about the life of the Baal Shem Tov as the founder of Hasidism. The movie, entitled *"Der Meister des Guten Namens,"* was directed by Austrian film director, Georg Lhotsky. Shlomo told Hasidic Baal Shem Tov stories in German and his daughter Neshama was cast in the role of Hodol, the daughter of the Baal Shem Tov.[39] At the beginning of this documentary film, Shlomo dons his *tallit* and presents

---

36. Shlomo mentions here that Rabbi Tzvi Yehudah's father, Rav Avraham Yitzhak HaCohen Kook, had stayed in Shlomo's grandfather's house "for a year." See above, Chapter 1, that Rabbi Dr. Asher Michael (Arthur) Cohn hosted Rav Kook in 1915 in Basel, Switzerland. During World War I, Rav Kook lived in St. Galen, Switzerland for most of 1915 until he moved to London in the beginning of 1916.

37. The discussion with Rav Tzvi Yehudah took place sometime during the time period that Shlomo had the HLP in San Francisco. See the 3-minute video posted by Joel Goldberg, http://www.youtube.com/watch?v=3HEXmk7dXB0. The dating of this video is thanks to Rabbi Moshe Pesach Geller. It was reposted on http://koshertube.com/videos/index.php?option=com_seyret&Itemid=4&task=videodirectlink&id=11778

38. Hashir (Bruce) Ginsberg, personal communication, Nov. 28–30, 2012.

39. My thanks to Neshama Carlebach for this information. For a photo from the movie of Shlomo and Neshama, see www.lhotsky-film.at/meilensteine.html.

Shlomo and Neshama in Fez,
Morocco, January, 1994.
Courtesy of Rabbi Joe
Schonwald

a message of focusing joy and happiness even in times of adversity, with songs such as *"Ein KeEloheinu."*[40]

Shlomo was accompanied by two musicians, an accordionist and 22-year old Moscow-born violinist Alexei (Aliosha) Biz.[41] Biz also teamed up with Shlomo to perform together in Klagenfurt,[42] a three-hour drive from Vienna. On this last trip to Austria, Shlomo took his daughter Neshama to Baden and showed her the house where he had grown up and the remains of what had been his father's synagogue.[43]

On March 11–12, 1994, Shlomo led a Shabbaton program in the B'nai David-Judea (BDJ) Synagogue in the Pico-Robertson area in Los Angeles.[44] The program was so inspirational that afterwards Stuart Wax and Lewis Weinger opened a bank account and registered the name "Carlebach West" with the intent of establishing a Carlebach *minyan* in Los Angeles.[45]

---

40. A 2:44-minute clip from this film has been posted on YouTube by the http://www.youtube.com/watch?v=3Hx0YeHmUDM&feature=endscreen&NR=1. At segment 1:45, Shlomo says: "Friends, the holy Baal Shem Tov teaches us that the biggest sin in the world is to be in sadness. When you are sad, then you cannot be happy. Therefore, always be in joy, even in the times of trouble." (My synopsis/translation).

41. See aliosha.biz, http://www.aliosha.biz/bio_e.htm.

42. See Shulamit Mitchell, "Austrians flock to events promoting Jewish culture," *Jewish Telegraphic Agency*, July 10, 1997, JTA.org, www.jta.org/news/article/1997/07/10/1085/BAustriansflockt.

43. Neshama Carlebach, "My Merna," in *L'Koved Reb Shlomo Remembrance Journal* produced by the Carlebach Shul.

44. See Joy Krauthammer, "The Pied Piper – Dancing with Joy," *Kol Chevra*, vol. 15, 2009, 106–109. On p. 108, is a picture of Joy with Reb Shlomo at 2:30 A M when she completed duplicating tapes of this concert. See also Rebshlomocarlebach-ztl.blogspot.com.

45. The Happy Minyan of LA was actually founded in March 1995, the Shabbat after the wedding of Stuie and Enny Wax. The LA Happy Minyan "now draws 100 to 150 people to services at The Karate Academy of Pico-Robertson." My thanks to Stuie Wax for this information, June 28, 2012.

Reb Shlomo, Joy Krauthammer, and Shirley Perluss on February 1, 1994 in the Tatou Nightclub, Beverly Hills.   Photo courtesy of © Shira Solomon

On March 19, 1994, Reb Shlomo joined Reb Zalman in a *farbrengen* co-sponsored by the Aquarian Minyan and the Berkeley Hillel Foundation, marking the twentieth anniversary of the founding of AMB.

In New York at the Carlebach Shul, Shlomo led the last two Pesach Seders of his life on March 26–27, 1994. His daughter Dari was 17 at the time. She recollects her experience:

> The synagogue was completely packed through the night with a very elevating experience ending at 4:00 AM. Each part had uniqueness. For example, for *motzi matzah*, Shlomo gave a special blessing and a specific wish to each person with a piece of matzah. This took some forty-five minutes. For opening the door to receive Elijah the Prophet, we went outside on 79th Street and sang with the wind hitting us and my father shielding me with his coat. I felt as if Elijah was actually there.[46]

At the end of Pesach, Reb Shlomo was hosted at the LaCosta resort near San Diego.[47] Shlomo then flew to New York to be present on Friday morning, April 8, 1994 at the Lutowisker Shul on Delancey St. in the

---

46. Personal interview with Dari Carlebach, Dec. 6, 2012.

47. Joy Krauthammer who attended this event wrote to me on Nov. 3, 2011 that she

Lower East Side of New York for the *brit* of Simcha and Leah Hochbaum's son, Yedidyah Nisan.[48]

On Sunday, April 24, 1994, on the eve of the 14th of Iyar, Reb Shlomo gave a class in Newton, Massachusetts at the home of Michael and Brenda Edwards about the meaning of Pesach Sheni as the "holiday of the second chance" with the message "it's never too late . . . to fix even the scars."[49] Then, on April 25, 1994, at the Carlebach Shul in Manhattan, Shlomo elaborated on the idea of Pesach Sheni as a second chance for those who are on the "far path." He publicly announced the *semicha* of Simcha Hochbaum and with a play on words, Shlomo explained how Simcha's task is *somech lechol hanoflim* (Psalms 145:14), to give *semicha*, support, to all those who fall and provide a second chance – people should always know that they have someone upon whom they can rely (*somech*). This was the last ordination granted by Reb Shlomo.[50]

Rabbi Meyer Leifer, a lifelong friend of Shlomo,[51] hosted Shlomo for a Sunday evening concert in Emunath Israel for Yom Yerushalayim, 28th Iyar, May 8, 1994. For nearly two decades, from 1975 until 1994, Rabbi Leifer would invite Shlomo to Emunath Israel each year for either Yom Yerushalayim or Yom HaAtzmaut.[52]

On Sunday, May 22, 1994, Shlomo was one of the featured singers at New York's Salute to Israel celebration.[53]

On June 2–5, 1994, Shlomo led the Shabbat weekend of the annual Ruach Retreat that was held at Copake, New York.[54] On Sunday, June 5, 1994, Shlomo was back in New York for a Healing Concert and

---

was deeply saddened and offended that the rabbi in-charge refused to allow her and Neshama to come up on stage to sing and play with Reb Shlomo.

48. Personal interview Sept. 12, 2012 with Rabbi Simcha Hochbaum. This baby is the grandson of Rabbi Sholom and Judy Brodt – see above on their special connections to Reb Shlomo. For a photo of Reb Shlomo blessing the baby Yedidyah Hochbaum, see Ritchie, *A Friend to Our Generation*, 93.

49. "Rabbi Shlomo Carlebach Teaching on Pesach Sheni," transcribed by Reuven Goldfarb, *Kol Chevra*, vol. 17, 2011, 197–203. A precedent for this idea can be found in a talk in 1978 of the Lubavitcher Rebbe, *Likkute Sichos* XII 5738, *Parshat Emor*, 216–220: "The idea of Pesach Sheni is that nothing is irretrievable; we can always rectify our behavior."

50. My thanks to Rabbi Simcha Hochbaum for this information.

51. See above that Rabbi Meyer Leifer first met Shlomo in Yeshivas Chaim Berlin.

52. Personal interviews, Dec. 17 and 24, 2012. Rabbi Leifer served for 42 years (1958–2000) as the Rabbi of Congregation Emunath Israel of the Chelsea Jewish Center on West 23rd St. in Manhattan.

53. Larry Yudelson. "Clouds of Last Year Won't Rain on This Year's Parade for Israel." *Jewish Telegraphic Agency*, May 19, 1994.

54. Rabbi Hershel Yolles joined in addition to the regular presenters, Blema Feinstein, Yehudis Fishman, and Reb Meir Fund.

In the 1994 film "Der Meister des Guten Namens," Rabbi Carlebach portrayed the character of the Baal Shem Tov, and Neshama Carlebach was cast as Hodol, the Baal Shem Tov's daughter.

Symposium sponsored by the Carlebach Shul at the Symphony Space Theater in New York City. He was joined on stage by Dr. Bernie Siegel, who was famous for his work in healing cancer patients. The program was conceived of by Mike (Moshe Avraham) Weber, who had been helped by both Shlomo and Bernie while fighting a serious illness.[55]

Later in June 1994, Reb Shlomo performed in Manhattan at the Millinery Center Synagogue on 1025 Avenue of the Americas. Lazer Lloyd had been invited to accompany him on stage. Lazer was born in Madison, Connecticut on May 7, 1966 as Lloyd Blumen. He majored in music at Skidmore College and became a famous blues/rock singer/songwriter/guitar player. He had his own band, The Last Mavericks and a promising career with Atlantic Records. That evening at Millinery Synagogue changed Lazer's life:

> From the first note that Shlomo sang, I realized that this was not the same as the other gigs. For the first time in my life, I met someone whose goal in singing was to bring people to a high level of spiritual awareness, to bring joy and unity. The audience responded in kind, singing in harmony and dancing. I was mesmerized by Shlomo's personality and stories. In the middle of this concert, I decided that this is where I wanted to be, not the shallowness of my hippie friends who spoke about love and peace, but lived a life of pleasure seeking. I spoke to Shlomo and he convinced me to go to Israel. Soon I was playing with Carlebach bands in Israel like Reva L'sheva and Chaim Dovid Saracik.[56]

In July 1994, Shlomo was invited by his cousin (also named Shlomo Carlebach), to a program at Lincoln Square Synagogue in Manhattan to speak about the Lubavitcher Rebbe on the occasion of the *shloshim*,

---

55. My thanks to Emuna Witt-Halevi for providing me with a copy of the Carlebach Shul booklet for this event.

56. Personal communication with Lazer Lloyd March 21, 2013. Compare Ben Shalev, "American singer swears by blues and miracles," *Haaretz*, April 20, 2012, http://www.haaretz.com/weekend/week-s-end/american-singer-swears-by-blues-and-miracles-1.425545. See also www.lazerlloyd.com.

commemorating a month after his death. Shlomo reminisced about his special connection to the Rebbe who had sent him out on his mission.[57]

Shlomo was back in Israel for the rest of the summer of 1994. He led his last learning series in Jerusalem at Yakar in Katamon, and played his last concerts in Israel (described above in the section on Israel).

On September 5–7, Reb Shlomo led the Rosh Hashana *davening* at the Carlebach Shul in New York. A day before Erev Yom Kippur, on September 13, 1994, Shlomo appeared together with Diane Wolkstein in front of 800 people at New York City's American Museum of Natural History. They told stories of forgiveness, compassion, tolerance, and understanding. Diane had asked Shlomo for a title and he suggested "Celebrating Our Mistakes" as an appropriate pre-Yom Kippur mode of experience. Diane recalls:

> Shlomo said that instead of wallowing in sorrow over our errors, we should celebrate when mistakes can indicate how God is guiding us. By "celebrating" our mistakes, we optimistically acknowledge that we are transforming ourselves towards a greater good.[58]

Shlomo's parting exclamation as he left his audience that night was: "How good it is to be alive, I bless you that every minute of your life you should be alive."[59] These were to be his last words at his last concert in America.

Shlomo led his last Yom Kippur program on September 14–15, 1994. Moshe Pesach Geller who was with him describes how he watched with trepidation when Shlomo stood for forty-five minutes the night before Yom Kippur and looked at a bookshelf of 300 of his *sefarim*, and then exclaimed, "*Oy, oy, oy, al chet shechatanu b'yodim uvelo yodim,* for all the things that we have sinned knowingly, and for all the things that we wished we didn't know."[60]

On September 22, 1994, the third day of Hol HaMoed Sukkot, Shlomo was hosted by Nachman and Miriam Futterman in their home in Monsey,

---

57. The Rebbe died June 12, 1994 (3 Tammuz). See above, Chapter 2, for the citation from this event which was posted by the Carlebach Legacy Foundation, http://www.youtube.com/watch?v=E9_d1eVkwSE&feature=plcp. Shlomo sings a Chabad tune for *Eli Atah*.

58. In 2006, Wolkstein produced a 57-minute DVD based on this performance entitled *Celebrating Our Mistakes: Stories and Songs from the Jewish Tradition*. See MostlyMusic.com, http://www.mostlymusic.com/celebrating-our-mistakes.html; http://www.filmbaby.com/films/3168.

59. Diane Wolkstein, personal interview, Jan. 20, 2013.

60. Interview with Rabbi Moshe Pesach Geller, Jan. 14, 2013. Compare Geller, "I Remember," 106.

New York. It was pouring rain, and therefore a tarpaulin was placed on the top of the Sukkah as Shlomo led a special learning for the *yahrtzeit* of Rebbe Nachman of Breslov.[61]

On October 1, 1994, Shlomo led a *Melaveh Malka* on Motzei Shabbat *Parshat Bereshit*.

Shlomo's last Shabbat in New York was *Parshat Noah*, October 7–8, 1994. Then he flew to England where he gave the last concert tour of his life. Arriving on October 11, 1994 in London, Reb Shlomo performed the following day at the New West End Synagogue in St. Petersburgh Place, Bayswater, West London.[62] He was introduced by the synagogue rabbi, Rabbi Yisroel Roll, who explained that twenty years earlier, he had been inspired by Reb Shlomo in Montreal:

> In October 1974, I was 16 years old and attended Reb Shlomo's concert in Montreal on Motzei Simchat Torah. His daughter, Neshama, had just been born, and Shlomo invited the entire crowd to attend the wedding in Jerusalem "in twenty years time." Now we are here in London on Simchat Torah with Reb Shlomo, and I have brought my 7-year old daughter to see the man who ignited the fire of love for Hashem in so many people.[63]

From there, Reb Shlomo traveled to Leeds University to perform for the students and returned to London for Shabbat, October 15, 1994. There at the home of Rabbi Pini Dunner, he felt ill and had difficulty walking. What would normally be a five-minute walk to *shul* on Shabbat took twenty minutes with Shlomo stopping every ten or fifteen yards to catch his breath. Nonetheless, on Sunday, he performed at Ronnie Scott's jazz club in the West End of London. On Monday night, Shlomo sang in Hendon for a group of disabled Israeli army veterans who were in London on a special trip.[64] Then Shlomo visited the house of his first cousin Moshe Cohn in Golders Green, relaxed and shmoozed with family and friends, and played his guitar.[65] From there, he took his daughter Dari

61. Personal interview with Nachman Futterman, March 11, 2013.

62. My thanks to R. Pini Dunner for providing details of the venue. The video recording was posted on Box.net, http://www.box.net/shared/jba33jj3sx#/shared/jba33jj3sx/1/34341330/652181323/1. Reb Shlomo sang "*Od Yeshoma*," "*Simcha LeArtzecha*," and tunes from the High Holy Days liturgy and Simchat Torah. He told an inspirational story about how Avraham Shifrin observed Yom Kippur in Siberia and concluded with a comparison of Noah remaining "holy" and aloof as opposed to Abraham, the outreach worker.

63. Personal email from Rabbi Yisroel Roll, June 21, 2012.

64. Rabbi Pini Dunner, "Shlomo's Last *Shabbos*," *Kol Chevra*, vol. 8, 2001, 14–18. My thanks to Rabbi Dunner and Moshe Cohn for clarifying this information.

65. Moshe is the son of Rabbi Dr. Chaim (Heinrich or Heini) Cohn who was the

by taxi to the London airport for her flight back to Toronto and ended up missing his scheduled flight to Manchester. The organizers of the concert began panicking and sent Mike Tabor to pick Shlomo up from a later flight.[66] After arriving, Shlomo performed on Tuesday, October 18, 1994 at the Jewish Cultural Centre on Bury New Road.[67]

A humorous anecdote is recorded when Rabbi Yossi Chazan walked in late,[68] and Shlomo stopped to ask: "You have become so *frum* now that you don't speak to me anymore? You know, some people have become so *frum* that they don't speak to God any more." R. Chazan responded: "Yes, we have quite a lot of people like that in Manchester." The audience burst out laughing.[69] But this humorous exchange reveals a serious problem. Shlomo's affectionate greetings to all endeared him to a hippie generation but were anathema to the *haredi* world. Kids whom he had "turned on to Yiddishkeit" would become so "*frum*" that they disassociated themselves from him.[70] Unlike colleagues in Manchester, R. Chazan did not ostracize Reb Shlomo. After the concert, he invited Shlomo for dinner and this evolved into a *farbrengen* which was to be Shlomo's last activity.[71]

On Wednesday morning October 19, Shlomo flew back to New York.[72] On Thursday evening, October 20, 1994, Sammy Intrator drove Shlomo to the LaGuardia Airport to spend Shabbat with his family in Toronto. As the plane was taxiing for take off, he suffered a fatal heart attack.

It is said, that Shlomo was seated in business class next to the Skverer

---

eldest son of Rabbi Dr. Arthur Cohn (Shlomo's grandfather). Moshe and his wife Ruth lived at 7 Helenslea Ave., centrally located near the Golders Green Underground station. Therefore, when Shlomo came to London, he would invite all his many cousins living in London to join him there for an evening of song and stories. My thanks to Moshe and Ruth Cohn for this information (personal interview, Jan. 12, 2013).

66. Personal communication with Mike Tabor, Sept. 9, 2011. See also "Reflections of Michael Tabor," *Kol Chevra*, vol. 3, no. 1, 35.

67. Alex Klein, Reb Shlomo's manager for UK, filmed the concert and it is available on YouTube in four parts: http://www.youtube.com/watch?v=AZCVopHuhoc& feature=related; http://www.youtube.com/watch?v=ovYF-OgskQ8&feature=related; http://www.youtube.com/watch?v=dzyvueRXaDw&feature=email; http://www.you tube.com/watch?v=9OqsAykofo8. Shlomo tells a story about of the Modzitzer rebbe and the Cossacks with their conducter who was secretly a Jew – https://www.you tube.com/watch?v=E8iCXGitDNU&feature=player_embedded.

68. A New York born-Rabbi, who graduated both Torah VeDaas and Tomchei Temimim, Rabbi Chazan served as the Rabbi of Holy Law South Broughton Hebrew Congregation in Manchester.

69. This segment is reproduced with an incorrect caption on the YouTube video – http://www.youtube.com/watch?v=jOwZnDrBZwY&NR=1.

70. See Katz, *Torah Commentary, Part I*, 191–192.

71. My thanks to Mike Tabor for the details.

72. Dunner, "Shlomo's Last *Shabbos*," 18.

Rebbe of Borough Park and singing with him *"Hasdei Hashem ki lo tamnu"*: "God's Goodness has no end, and His Compassion is Infinite" (Lamentations 3:22). Shlomo had actually composed this tune after the Yom Kippur War as an optimistic way of faith in responding to tragedy and darkness. In fact, Shlomo once explained that these words were sung in the Nazi concentration camps to a tune composed by the Skulener Rebbe:[73]

> The words of this song, they were in a different melody, and were sung all over the concentration camps. The melody was written by the last of the holy people, the Skulener Rebbe, he's still alive, and his song was top, really like *the* song in the concentration camps. But then, I thought to myself, that after the Six-Day War and the Yom Kippur War, we have other stories to tell about God's goodness, so I composed a different melody.[74]

Shlomo was rushed to the Western Queens Community Hospital in New York where he was pronounced dead. It was the 16th of Heshvan, three months short of his 70th birthday.

2.   EULOGIES (OCTOBER 1994)

The eulogy in Manhattan was held on a rainy Sunday morning, October 23, 1994, right outside the Carlebach Shul.[75] Rarely, had anyone ever had such a diverse collection of mourners. In New York's *Jewish Week*, Jonathan Mark depicted the funeral:

> Satmar Chasidim standing shoulder to shoulder with bikers in studded leather jackets, Talmudists in hamburgs, artists, hippie women, Lubavitch, Belz, folkies, New Age, old age.[76]

---

73. Rabbi Eliezer Zusha Portugal was born in the town of Skulen in Bessarabia (which alternated between Romania and Russia). He is well-known for his heroic efforts of encouraging Jews during the Holocaust. The Skulener Rebbe arrived in the United States in 1960 and established his Beit Midrash in Williamsburg, New York. He died on Aug. 18, 1982.

74. These are the words of Shlomo in a radio interview with Kenny Ellis at the end of 1973 on WRTI, 90.1 FM, Temple University radio in Philadelphia. My thanks to Kenny for sending me the recording of this interview.

75. The MP3 eulogy of 1 hour 32 minutes can be heard at http://benkatz.com/music/carlebach_funeral.mp3. Parts can be heard in a YouTube video posted by go4joel in four parts "shlomo carlebach Historic Levaye": http://www.youtube.com/watch?v=CGXe6NTi19c; http://www.youtube.com/watch?v=G-7tyZLph1I&NR=1; http://www.youtube.com/watch?v=d7gCYNNYz7g&NR=1; http://www.youtube.com/watch?v=lFosp1XFsIs&NR=1.

76. Quoted by Cohen, "Jewish Soul Man," 83.

Rabbi Pini Dunner organized Rabbi Shlomo Carlebach's concert tour in London. The concert, at Ronnie Scott's Jazz Club in London's West End, October 16, 1994, turned out to be Reb Shlomo's last public performance. From left to right: Zev Dunner, Yankel Plitnick, Graham Morris (slightly obscured), Reb Shlomo, Raziel Davidoff, Nachmi Barsam, Aba Dunner, Pini Dunner.   *Courtesy of Rabbi Pini Dunner*

Here are a few highlights culled from over an hour of eleven eulogies. The speakers reflected not only on what Reb Shlomo meant to each person, but also on the mission to be carried forward.

Dr. Moshe Rothkopf described how R. Shlomo would warmly greet everyone who came to his *shul* because "he felt that after the Holocaust every Yid is a miracle. He wanted us to go out and hug and kiss every miracle."[77] Rothkopf exclaimed:

> I'm challenging all of the *Rabbeim* of the world, make your love sweeter, make your *davening* higher, reach out your arms, hold the people who need to be held. It is *mamash mesirus nefesh. Our generation is drowning. Shlomo was pulling them out of the water.* Please I'm begging you, I'm begging you.

---

77. Moshe and Zipporah Rothkopf had bought an apartment on 212 West 71st St. near the Carlebach Shul in order to be close to Reb Shlomo. See Tracie Rozhon, "Habitats/212 West 71st Street; Jimmy Walker Lived Here. . . . Well, Maybe He Did." See *New York Times*, April 16, 1995, http://www.nytimes.com/1995/04/16/realestate/habitats-212-west-71st-street-jimmy-walker-lived-here-well-maybe-he-did.html?src=pm. For the story of how Reb Shlomo helped Moshe Rothkopf in the conversion process of his wife-to-be Zipporah, see Brandwein, *Reb Shlomele*, 113–117, Brand, *Reb Shlomele*, 78–80. Today, Dr. Rothkopf lives in Lakewood, New Jersey, but he often visits Jerusalem and organizes a Carlebach *minyan* at the Kotel.

Rabbi Mordechai Tendler, at the time, rabbi of a congregation in New Hempstead, New York, described how his grandfather, R. Moshe Feinstein, the outstanding leader of twentieth century Orthodox Jewry, esteemed R. Shlomo and expressed "an extraordinary sense of appreciation." R. Tendler described Shlomo as "a *talmid chacham nisgav* (lofty scholar), a *maggid beYisrael* (storyteller in Israel) who chose a unique path to be *mekarev levavot l'Avinu she'baShamayim* (bring hearts closer to Our Father in Heaven)."

R. Zalman Schachter-Shalomi turned poignantly to his friend and declared: "Shlomele, holy beggar, you were also a banker. We gave you a deposit of our love, and you banked it in Torah, in God, in *davening*, and for this we are grateful."

Rabbi Avi Weiss, senior rabbi of The Hebrew Institute of Riverdale, asked: "Who was Reb Shlomo Carlebach?" His answer was a dramatic and piercing eulogy:

> Our friend, our Rebbe, Reb Shlomo, taught all Jews how to say to God, "*Haneshama Lach*" (the soul is Yours). Reb Shlomo, our friend and our Rebbe had faith in our souls. When we sometimes felt blocked in our pathway to God, when feeling blocked, Reb Shlomo gave us through the genius of his song, a personal channel to Hakadosh Baruch Hu . . . Reb Shlomo created a change that was so fundamental, so organic to Jewish music. It seemed like it was always there. This is the highest level of change. To create something so magical, so brilliant. You don't even know it occurs because it is so pervasive. When we *daven*, we *daven* with Reb Shlomo's tunes, and we don't realize it. We think that these tunes have been around for centuries, when in fact they've come from Reb Shlomo's soul. Who is Reb Shlomo, our friend, our Rebbe? A genius in creating melody that was natural, pure and profoundly simple. It was an extraordinary gift given by God to Reb Shlomo in a way that maybe comes to one person, once in many many generations . . . No one in this generation had more direct impact on teaching and touching Jewish souls than our friend, our Rebbe, Reb Shlomo.

Shlomo was buried the next day in Har HaMenuhot, Givat Shaul, Jerusalem, on Monday, October 24, 1994 in a gravesite near his parents and his twin brother. The burial was shortly after 11:00 AM, but the crowd stayed until late at night. During the eulogies, the Psalm, *Mizmor L'David Hashem Roi*, was sung to Shlomo's tune. This was the song Shlomo had chosen for his mother's funeral (see above).

The Chief Rabbi of Israel, Rabbi Yisrael Meir Lau, was asked by Neila

Collage created by © Joy Krauthammer

Carlebach to give the keynote eulogy.[78] Rabbi Lau described how he had often hosted R. Shlomo in Tel Aviv. Once Shlomo said to him: "Rav Yisrael, you are a child of the Holocaust. I want to sing a special tune for you," and then he composed a melody for "*Gam Ki Elech*" (Psalms 23:4).[79] Rabbi Lau exclaimed:

> We ask forgiveness and pardon in the name of those present here and in the name of many who should have been here but didn't come. They will come to value this great soul who moved among us, a soul from the world of *Atzilut* (Emanations) and purity, the world of awe, of melody, and *devekut*. . . . R. Shlomo was a great soul, a quintessential soul. Only once in a generation does such a soul appear. Who knows whence it was hewn? From the roots of the Supernal worlds.[80]

Additional eulogies in Jerusalem were given by the following four rabbis: Yosef Ba-Gad, Mordechai Kohen, Uzi Schwietze, and Yehoshua Witt.[81]

The inscription on the top of Shlomo's gravestone is his most famous

---

78. Personal interview with Rabbi Lau, Jan. 1, 2013.

79. Compare Brandwein, *Reb Shlomele*, 74.

80. This is my translation of Rabbi Yisrael Meir Lau's Hebrew eulogy at the funeral. Variant translations can be found in Brand, *Reb Shlomele*, 291–295, and Rachel Ebner on IsraelNationalNews.com, http://www.israelnationalnews.com/Articles/Article.aspx/9132.

Cf. also Greer Fay Cashman, "Pied Piper," *Jerusalem Post*, Oct. 30, 1994, 6.

81. Brand, *Reb Shlomele*, 297–306.

Reb Shlomo in summer 1994,
with Yehudah Katz and Daryl
Temkin   © Joy Krauthammer

After the concert, Pico-Robertson,
2:00 AM with tapes from the hundreds duplicated that very same
day by Joy Krauthammer.
Photo courtesy of © Shira Solomon

song – "*Am Yisrael Chai, Od Avinu Hai.*" "Our father is still alive." The
Hebrew inscription can be translated as follows:

> Here is buried our honorable, holy father, the teacher and rabbi,
> the *gaon*, the hasid, lover of Israel, unique in his generation, sweet
> singer of Israel, our holy Rabbi . . . descended from the Taz and
> Bach, and above them in holiness, tracing (his lineage) back to
> King David and Aharon the holy priest. Rabbi in the holy congre-
> gations Kehilath Jacob in New York, Me'or Modi'im, the House of
> Love and Prayer in San Francisco and Jerusalem. A trusted faithful
> of the Admor RaYaTZ of Lubavitch, an outstanding pupil of the
> great *gaonim* R. Aharon Kotler and R. Shlomo Hyman.

3.   GERMINATION OF A MOVEMENT

Until this point, we have documented the personal outreach career of
Reb Shlomo. Percolating behind the scenes was the nascent growth of a
Movement. Rabbis, musicians, storytellers and Carlebach Hasidim – all
were perpetuating the new message. By the late 1970s and early 1980s,
Carlebach followers were beginning to become prominent in many areas
of spiritual creativity. Some received rabbinical ordination from Shlomo

*Gravestone of Reb Shlomo in
the Har HaMenuhot Cemetery in
Jerusalem   Photos courtesy of
© Joy Krauthammer*

שיר ושבחה הלל וזמרה
קדושה ומלכות
שירים חדשים של ניגוני קודש
בעם ישראל פתח
לכבות רבבות אלפי ישראל הלהיב
וקירב לאבינו שבשמים
מעיין המתגבר בחידושי תורה
שירה זמרה ועבודת ה'
העמיד תלמידים רבים וניהל עדת
קדושים בכל רחבי תבל
קידש שם שמים בעמים פעמים אין ספור
ריץ ואז לכל אשר נברא בצלמו יתברך
לקדושה ילדים ולאהבתם הסיף
ישירו לעולם ועד אלפי ניגוניו הקדושים
בדרך הבעש"ט ותלמידיו הקדושים הלך
היה הגאון אדיר ונורא בנגלה ובנסתר
היה עמוד החסד כאברהם אבינו
היה מלא קדושה שבפניו הרגישו קדושת השכינה
במסירות נפשו העצומה הציל והקים
אלפים לאגדא רמה
סיפוריו מימים עברו מכיגים אותנו ליום שכולו
שבת, שמחתו ואהבתו קדושת גדיבתו ורוחב ליבו
כעין הדורות הקדמונים קודש קדשים
לירושלים עירך ברחמים תשוב.

עם ישראל חי
אבינו חי
פה נטמן
כבוד קדושת אבינו
מרנא ורבנא הגאון החסיד
אוהב ישראל יחיד בדור
נעים זמירות ישראל רבינו הקדוש
מוהר"ר שלמה בן הרה"ג ר'נפתלי זמרת פסיא
לבית קרליבך זצוקללה"ה
מצאצאי הט"ז והב"ח הקדוש ולמעלה בקודש עד
לדוד מלך ישראל חי וקים ואהרן כהנא קדישא
רב ורם בק"ק קהילת יעקב ניו-יורק ובקק מושב
מאור מודיעין ובקק בית אהבה ותפילה
סאן-פרנסיסקו ירושלים נאמן ביתו של
אדמו"ר הרד"ץ מליובאוויטש זיע"א
תלמידו המובהק של הגאונים האדירים
ר' אהרן קוטלר ור' שלמה היימן זצ"ל
נולד ח"י שבת התרפ"ה
ונתבקש לישיבה של מעלה
ששה עשר לירח רם-חשון
פרשת ותתברכו בזרעך כל גויי הארץ התשנ"ה
תהא נשמתו צרורה בצרור החיים
חסדי ה' כי לא תמנו

and served as educators or in congregations. Many used Carlebach music and storytelling as a tool for outreach activities. Others created *Happy Minyanim*, retreats, festivals and Carlebach events.

The fifteen annual Ruach Retreats in which Reb Shlomo participated are merely one illustration of how Reb Shlomo and his disciples/friends influenced the American *baal teshuva* movement. These weekend retreats from 1982 onwards brought together hundreds of people who were inspired to become more religious and more spiritual. The setting was halachic Orthodoxy including full Shabbat and *kashrut* observance, but the focus was on a Jewish New Age experiential alternative for spiritual seekers. Gedalya Persky summed up the significance of the Ruach Retreats and Reb Shlomo's role:

> The retreats always drew both unaffiliated and religious people who needed a spark/zetz in their Yiddishkeit. The teachers provided inspiration through various forms of presentation, always striving to be experiential rather than theoretical. Reb Shlomo was a keystone to the whole process, drawing people who had heard of him and humbly sharing the stage with the others through music, Torah, and his natural charisma.[82]

The three rabbinical figures besides Shlomo who came to almost all the Ruach Retreats were Dovid Zeller, Dovid Din, and Meir Fund. All three were Shlomo's disciples/colleagues. They transmitted to their own students a new revitalized form of religious Judaism and each in his own way provided a conduit for an individual transformation of the Carlebachian message. Reb Dovid Zeller (1946–2007) was mentioned above several times in the stories of his first meeting with Reb Shlomo in Berkeley and the rabbinic ordination he received. He founded the Network of Conscious Judaism in 1980, made aliyah in 1985, and co-founded Yakar in Jerusalem in 1992.[83] Reb Meir Fund studied at the Mir Yeshiva, and for six years with Rabbi Yosef Dov Soloveitchick from whom he received rabbinic ordination. He served as the Hillel rabbi at Brooklyn College. In the early 1980s, he founded Beis HaMedrash Sheves Achim, The Flatbush Minyan in Brooklyn.[84] Reb Dovid Din was born in Baltimore, Maryland in 1941 and died on July 9, 1988. He spent some time studying in John Hopkins University and in Yeshivas Ner Yisroel in

---

82. Gedalya Persky, personal correspondence, Jan. 10, 2013.

83. Zeller, *The Soul of the Story*. For an online photo of David Zeller with Reb Shlomo, see http://davidzeller.org/videos, http://www.youtube.com/watch?v=EVLVz09g7wg, segment 2:35.

84. FlatbushMinyan.org, http://www.flatbushminyan.org/about/about-rabbi-fund; http://www.flatbushminyan.com/about/flatbush-minyan.

Baltimore. He served as Reb Zalman's secretary in Winnipeg in the mid 1960s.[85] After much spiritual searching, including a stint at the HLP and with Rabbi Shlomo Freifeld in Far Rockaway, he settled in Borough Park and founded a center for *baalei teshuva*, Sha'arei Orah, in Manhattan.[86]

Two women were on the roster of the Ruach Retreat speakers. Dr. Blema Feinstein was Professor Emeritus in Renaissance and Comparative Mythology at C.W. Post College, Long Island University. Blema had studied at Neve Yerushalayim, Bais Rivka and with Reb Dovid Din. She came to almost all the Ruach Retreats. Yehudis Fishman came to five Ruach Retreats. She taught Hasidic philosophy at Clark University and lectured at Lubavitch women's conventions.

All told, these five teachers at the Ruach Retreats can be said to have furthered the Carlebachian development towards enhanced spirituality within a specifically religious Orthodox structure.

Similarly, Shlomo inspired a generation of professional musicians. A few dozen were mentioned above,[87] however, there are many more whose stories should be told.[88] Some of Shlomo's musically inclined students helped organize and produce new reproductions of his songs. Here is one example. Zale Newman was 10 years old in 1965 when he first heard Shlomo sing at the Shaarei Tefillah Shul in Toronto. He soon became an avid follower and carried Shlomo's guitar whenever Shlomo

---

85. My thanks for to Prof. Shaul Magid who studied with Dovid Din for several years for filling in some of the information.

86. Howard Jay Rubin, "Judaism's Mystical Heart – An Interview with Dovid Din," *The Sun*, 103, June 1984, SunMagazine.org, http://www.thesunmagazine.org/archives/2575?page=1. Rubin describes Dovid Din as a kabbalist who dresses like a *haredi* Hasid, draws his inspiration from Rebbe Nachman of Breslov but "claims no allegiance to any specific Chassidic branch."

87. Those mentioned above include Chanan Avital, Bruce Berger, Chanan (Michael Ian) Elias, Sam Glaser, Michael Golomb, Robby Nathan Halperin, Aryeh Hirschfield, Baruch Melman, Howie Kahn, Shlomo Katz, Yehudah Katz, Jeff Klepper, Josh Lauffer, Benzion Lehrer, Skye Michaels, Aryeh Naftaly, Menachem Ophir, Dov Shurin, Chaim Dovid Saracik, Neil and Patricia Seidel, Simcha (Ed) Sheldon, Yankale Shemesh, P.F. Sloan, Don Slovin, Hizki Sofer, Ben Zion Solomon, Dovid Swirsky, Mike Tabor, and Dovid Zeller. In addition, half a dozen women musicians were noted: Neshama Carlebach, Joy Krauthammer, Shirley Perluss, Sara Shendelman, Shoshanna Shoshanna, and Jocelyn Siegal.

88. Some of the famous singers influenced by Carlebach includes: Mordechai Ben David (Werdyger), Karni Eldad, Avraham Fried, Efraim Mendelsohn, Matisyahu Miller, Michael Streicher, and Yidel Werdyger. A partial list of Carlebach musicians, most of whom played with Shlomo in his lifetime includes: Naftali Abramson, Musa Berlin, Moshe Duskis, Yehuda Green, Raz Hartman, Ruby Harris, Shivi Keller, Shua Kessin, Roman Kunsman, C. (Shimon) Lanzbom, Lazer Lloyd, Aaron Razel, Yonatan Razel, Oneg Shemesh, and Sinai Tor.

came to Toronto. Newman graduated Yeshiva University in 1976,[89] and did graduate work in business administration at McGill University in Montreal, and marketing at York University in Toronto. He was also a talented musician and recorded *Uncle Moishy and the Mitzvah Men*. In 1987, Newman prepared a recording with Shlomo entitled *Shlomo Carlebach Live for the Jews of Russia* to distribute as cassettes for free to Russian Jews. After that, Newman and Dovid Woolf recorded Shlomo songs and stories in a ten-cassette series entitled *The Best of Shlomo Carlebach – 60s, 70s, 80s* and *Rest of the Best. Shabbos in Shomayim* was to have been a six-part series of his Shabbat davening, wherein Shlomo passed away after the first two parts were recorded, as well as a song and story set entitled *Shabbos with Shlomo* and *Shlomo Live*! The total came out to be a total of 115 songs and forty stories.[90]

Despite his globetrotting, Shlomo's home base was in Manhattan where he returned regularly to lead Shabbat and holiday services. He would alternate with his brother, Rabbi Eli Chaim, who also was an outgoing friendly personality with a knack for storytelling. Eli Chaim established a publishing house in memory of his father named Machon Zecher Naftali where he published some forty books on Hasidic masters. Several Carlebach Shul members studied with him on a personal basis.[91] Ongoing classes led to the founding of the Chassidic Institute at the Carlebach Shul, offering a range of courses from classical texts to New Age body/mind techniques and courses on relationships and transforming negative emotions.[92]

The New York *chevra* were a crucial factor in the ongoing operations of the Carlebach Shul. Micha Odenheimer is one such activist. A graduate of Yale University (1980), Micha moved to the upper West Side in Manhattan in 1982 to be close to Reb Shlomo. He received his rabbinic ordination in 1984 from Rabbi Moshe Feinstein and Rabbi Michel Birnbaum at Mesifta Tiferet Yerushalayim. When Shlomo and his brother Eli Chaim were not at the synagogue, Micha often led the program: "Shlomo put me in charge

---

89. Yeshiva University College Yearbook, *Masmid*, 97, Archive.org, http://www.archive.org/stream/masmid1976#page/96/mode/2up.

90. Zale Newman, "Holy Food," *Kol Chevra*, vol. 18, 2012, 97–99. See also Stewart Ain, "New NCSY Chief: Lanner 'Behind Us,'" *The New York Jewish Week*, July 11, 2003, TheJewishWeek.com, http://www.thejewishweek.com/features/new_ncsy_chief_lanner_%E2%80%98behind_us%E2%80%99.

91. For example, Michael Steinhardt reports that he had a regular weekly tutorial with R. Eli Chaim. Personal interview August 30, 2012.

92. This is described on pp. 8–9 of a publicity booklet published by the Carlebach Shul for An Inaugural Benefit Concert/Symposium on June 5, 1994 at the Symphony Space Theatre in New York.

of the *shul* when he was away in Israel for the summers of 1985–1986, and for a while, I even lived in his apartment above the *shul*." Micha describes how the inner circle of a dozen *chevra* discovered a different dimension to Shlomo's teachings:

> Shlomo was perhaps the greatest interpreter of the Hasidic tradition of the modern age. He held in his mind the Talmudic, Kabbalistic, and Hasidic traditions, and his genius was to marshal it all in touching people where they lived, in a post-religious age, to reveal a hidden dynamic to their inner life that could open up into a longing for God. I experienced him as a healer as did others I spoke to.[93]

With the looming threats of eviction that had begun in 1983, the Carlebach *shul* had been struggling to raise money to purchase the building. Sometime around 1991, in an Elijah the Prophet incognito type story, an anonymous person, perceived as a drifter by the community, became attached to Rebbetzin Hadassa Carlebach and in great secrecy donated a considerable sum to help reach the goal for the purchase.[94]

After the purchase of the building, Shlomo was in Manhattan more often and the Carlebach Shul began to become more popular. Rabbi Moshe Pesach Geller reminiscences:

> The Synagogue was thriving and a new management position was created – I was hired on October 1993, Hol HaMoed Sukkot, to be the manager of the Synagogue, a position that I retained until after Purim in February 1994. I organized the programs and was with Reb Shlomo constantly, accompanying him wherever he went.[95]

Shlomo began to implement his vision of a yeshiva with classes in Talmud and Hasidut that were organized late at night by Zwe Padeh (Zvi Padah).[96] After Shlomo's death, videos of his teachings were shown each Sunday by Zwe Padeh and it was as if Shlomo were still present. Many people who keenly felt Shlomo's absence began frequenting the Carlebach Shul, attempting to recapture the lost fervor and spirit. Regular Shabbat and holiday programs were supplemented with new initiatives, courses, and

---

93. Personal interview with Rabbi Micha Odenheimer, Sept. 1, 2012.

94. Personal communications from Shy Yellin and Rebbetzin Hadassa Carlebach, Sept.–Oct., 2012.

95. Interview with Rabbi Moshe Pesach Geller, Jan. 14, 2013.

96. Interview with Fay Bliume, Sept. 2012. Fay, who first met Shlomo in 1960, was a longtime follower of Shlomo. In 1992, she helped set up the Yeshiva program at the Carlebach Shul. In 1995, she went on aliyah and presently lives on Moshav Me'or Modi'im.

teachers.[97] In memory of Shlomo, a late *Maariv minyan* was established at 10:00 PM, the latest in all of Manhattan, and it continues to this day.[98]

In 1998, Shy Yellin became vice president. He recruited an outside executive director and together with the synagogue president Ted Cohen, began "a phased transition from a *shteibel* to an organization." In December 2000, Rabbi Sammy Intrator departed for Florida after nearly two decades at the synagogue (see above, Chapter 11, section 4). By then, membership had quadrupled in the six years following Shlomo's death.[99]

With the search for a new rabbi during 2001–2002, guest speakers were invited regularly, bringing a new vigor to the Shabbat programs. Shy Yellin became president in 2002 and introduced a donor, Sam Domb, to undertake a major renovation – the second floor was reconfigured so that events could be held there for dinners, programs, and lectures. The entire dynamics of Shlomo's shul was transformed.

In June 2003, Rabbi Naftali Citron, grandson of Rabbi Eli Chaim Carlebach, was hired. Named after his great-grandfather, Rabbi Naphtali Carlebach, Naftali had grown up in a rabbinic family in Los Angeles and was ordained at the Central Lubavitch Yeshiva in Brooklyn.[100] Following the path of his grand-uncle, Reb Shlomo, Naftali brought a wide perspective of Hasidic masters, teaching Rebbe Nachman, Ishbitz, and the Seer of Lublin.[101]

The Carlebach Shul in New York became a focal point for innovation. The annual *yahrzeit* for Reb Shlomo turned into a full weekend program and the annual dinner was upgraded to a 5-star hotel.[102] Under Rabbi Naftali's leadership, an annual international Carlebach conference was

---

97. In an ad placed in the Carlebach Shul Journal, *Kavod*, Dec. 1996, a total of 225 people are listed as students who had visited the Yeshiva at some time and a similar number of names are mentioned as having participated in The Carlebach Institute.

98. The late minyan was formed by Shy Yellin, Raanan Wolf and Hershy Broyde.

99. "Over the last six years, membership at the Shul, has grown to almost 400, from 75 in 1994." From Corey Kilgannon, "Resignation of Rabbi Known for Dancing Spurs Tumult," *New York Times*, Dec. 27, 2000, NYTimes.com, http://www.nytimes.com/2000/12/27/nyregion/resignation-of-rabbi-known-for-dancing-spurs-tumult.html?pagewanted=all&src=pm.

100. His father, Rabbi Chaim Zev Citron, teaches at Yeshiva Ohr Elhanan Chabad in Los Angeles. For an illustration of how Naftali views Shlomo Carlebach's legacy, see http://www.youtube.com/watch?v=KmP14groxw8&feature=related; http://www.youtube.com/watch?v=IaLKCKSrbjI&feature=related.

101. My thanks to Rabbi Naftali Citron for his comments, Oct. 29, 2012.

102. See http://www.flickr.com/photos/carlebach/collections for photos of 2 annual dinners at St. Regis, a 5-star Manhattan hotel (June 19, 2012, June 20, 2011), and of the annual Shlomo Carlebach Yahrzeit (Oct. 24, 2010) which was followed by a conference on Ishbitz Hasidut (Oct. 25, 2010).

Hadassa Carlebach and Shy Yellin at the Carlebach Shul Annual Dinner

inaugurated and new community learning programs were instituted. Yehuda Green, a preeminent Carlebach composer and singer, became the *baal tefillah*.[103] His leadership of the services created an excitement reminiscent of the days of his role model, Reb Shlomo.[104]

A full history of the Carlebach Shul would require interviewing board members, past presidents, *gabbaim*, and myriads of activists.[105] Here, in conclusion, is the description of the synagogue vision by the current President, Shy Yellin:

> The Carlebach Shul, as a gatekeeper of Reb Shlomo's legacy, sees its mission as promulgating his approach of serving God with joy through Torah learning and song infused prayer. Although firmly committed to Orthodox tradition, the Shul goes to great lengths to create a welcoming environment. Visitors will see jeans alongside black hats, women in long skirts alongside slacks, Jews of all complexions and people of all backgrounds. Today,

---

103. Yehuda Green is referred to as "the Carlebach of today's generation" by Yisroel Besser for *Mishpacha Magazine*, Dec. 3, 2009, Vosizneias.com, http://www.vosiz neias.com/113259/2012/09/09/new-york-singing-dancing-and-inspiration-abound -as-jews-gather-for-selichos-videos. Born in 1959 into a mixed Breslov and Lubavitch Chassidic family near Meah Shearim, Jerusalem, Green became a Carlebach fan at age 5 and over the years followed Shlomo to hear him at the Kotel and Mount Zion. He was first invited by Shlomo to join him on stage in 1980 at a concert in Golders Green, London.

104. Shy Yellin, personal interview, Oct. 11, 2012.

105. See Carlebach Shul.org, http://www.carlebachshul.org/About%20Us/Officers .htm (last accessed Sept. 27, 2012) where the following names are listed under Board of Trustees: Shy Yellin (President), Hadassa Carlebach (Vice President), Daniel J. Goldschmidt (Corresponding Secretary), Sherri Daniels (Recording Secretary), Leon Sutton (Treasurer), Barbara Chazan, Dr. Jeremy Chess, Steve Eisenberg, and Raphael Kellman. The list of past presidents goes back to the early days of the Synagogue and includes Morris Goldberg, Simcha Goldstein, Danny Mars, Bill Shernoff, Nachman Futterman, Dr. Yehoshua Leib Fine, Moshe Liebert, and Ted Cohen. Rabbi Moshe Stepansky, *gabbai* until 2005, was a key figure in leading the services. He was succeeded as *gabbai* by Rabbi Avraham Newman.

our Manhattan Shul has become the focal point of a worldwide
Carlebach community.[106]

Around the world, the unique style of Carlebach tunes and *nusach* is
growing in popularity. The distinguishing features of Carlebach *minyanim* are joy and friendliness, informality and hospitality, and *devekut*
and dancing. By 2004, a decade after Shlomo's death, 114 Carlebach
minyanim could be counted – forty-eight in Israel, sixty-four in North
America, and five in Europe. The greatest concentrations were in New
York with fifteen and Jerusalem with twelve[107]. It is estimated that the
number today is far greater.

But perhaps the most interesting part of the Carlebach phenomenon
is the continued growth of a worldwide *chevra*. This was phrased in 2000
by Miriam Futterman:

> One of the main gifts that Shlomo gave us is to know that we are
> a spiritual family and throughout the whole world we have our
> *chevra*, which is a strong spiritual family, and that we have *Am
> Yisrael*. All of *Am Yisrael* is our spiritual family.[108]

---

106. Personal communication, Sept. 27, 2012.

107. "Minyanim Around the World: The Worldwide Chevra Communities," *Kol
Chevra*, vol. 10, 2004, 173–179. Brief descriptions and contact information were
provided for each *minyan*.

108. Futterman, "Heilige Yid," 92.

CHAPTER 13

In Conclusion

1.   WHO WAS REB SHLOMO?

Who was Reb Shlomo Carlebach? This question was deliberated in the obituaries after his death. Elli Wohlgelernter of *The Jerusalem Post* tried to describe Shlomo's elusive uniqueness:

> The obituaries referred to Rabbi Shlomo Carlebach as the "Singing Rabbi," but that's like describing Yankee Stadium as just some ballpark in the Bronx. . . . To have spent any time with Shlomo – that's all he was called, never Rabbi Carlebach – was to understand this: he was his own kind of rabbi and they were his own songs, and they will be sung for as long as Jews gather to sing and dance. . . . He was part hippie, part yippie, part beatnik, and part New Age. He was Dylan, Elvis, Arlo and Seeger all rolled into one, with a touch of Sholem Aleichem and Mark Twain.[1]

Indeed, Shlomo just didn't seem to fit into any restrictive defining label. Menachem Daum, in a video report for *Religion News and Ethics*, labeled Rabbi Carlebach as the "most unorthodox Orthodox rabbi." Moshe Stern, the internationally renowned cantor, characterized Carlebach as a combination of "a prodigal *tzaddik*, a musical genius, perhaps a religious exegete, a hippie in religious-ultra-orthodox garb." Stern highlighted the all encompassing nature of Reb Shlomo's personality which defied catergorization:

> His greatest strength was and remains chiefly his ability to be all encompassing, a kind of prototype for felling the divides, for blurring the borders. This, it seems, is what the ears and souls of many in that younger generation latched onto, seeking as they did

---

1. Wohlgelernter, "Simply Shlomo."

an escape path from the rigid categorizing enforced on them by the split reality of Israeli life.[2]

Similarly, Robert L. Cohen asks: Was there ever such an "embodied paradox, a bundle of contradictions?"[3] Cohen enumerates some of the seemingly contradictory aspects of Shlomo's life. For example:

> A thoroughgoing traditionalist, with Orthodox yeshiva education and rabbinical ordination, he outraged the Orthodox; a man for whom "pluralism" was an alien, ill-fitting concept, he was an implicit pluralist – teaching and singing everywhere, honoring rabbis of every denomination and encouraging others' unorthodox paths.[4]

Shlomo was equally at home with the Admor of Amshinov, the homeless in Riverside Park, and Hadassah women. But there were subtle differences in how he presented himself. It was a different type of Shlomo comforting soldiers in hospitals during the Yom Kippur War, and another Shlomo singing for Christians in Poland and Germany.

A 1994 obituary by Yossi Klein Halevi in *The Jerusaelm Report* used the term "Pied Piper of Judaism" to describe how Shlomo "taught an orphaned generation numbed by the Holocaust and assimilation how to return to joy." Halevi captured the uniqueness of Shlomo's concerts:

> A Shlomo concert was part 60s-style happening, part hasidic revival. . . . Shlomo always appeared with an entourage – strung-out street people, rebellious yeshivah boys, spiritual seekers, groupies . . . The only constant was Shlomo himself: his beautiful melodies; his deep, sure voice; his at-once profound and hokey rap ranging from hasidic stories to exhortations for people to love each other, to mocking and very funny critiques of both ultra-Orthodoxy and Reform Judaism.[5]

The question of who was Reb Shlomo was often a reflection of how people related to him. Sometimes, it was Rabbi Shlomo Carlebach officiating in rabbinical functions such as weddings. Most disciples preferred the

---

2. Ronit Tzach in *Yediot Aharonot, Seven Day Magazine*, Feb. 4, 2005, 34. Cited in Shmuel Barzilai, *Chassidic Ecstasy in Music* (Frankfurt am Main: 2009), 152.

3. This witty aphorism is a quote from Charles Caleb Colton (1780–1832), *Lacon, or, Many things in a few words: addressed to those who think*, vol. 1, CCCCVII, p. 1980.

4. Cohen, "Jewish Soul Man," 59–60.

5. Yossi Klein Halevi, "The Pied Piper of Judaism," *The Jerusalem Report*, Nov. 17, 1994, 45.

appellation "Reb Shlomo" to indicate a Hasidic closeness and warmth.[6] But for many followers, it was simply "Shlomo," the best friend, informal confidant, eschewing titles or other artificial barriers. He was the rabbi poised at the entrance to his *shul* on West 79th St. to welcome all with a bear hug. In the setting of Manhattan's street corners, he was a "holy brother" to many a "holy beggar."

With a natural ease, Reb Shlomo also assumed the role of a charismatic prayer leader. For example, on Hoshana Rabbah services at West 79th St., wearing a white *kittel* and black *gartel*, he was like a choirmaster orchestrating the musical accompaniment of trumpet, violin and singing congregation. In the full hour-long video dated September 26, 1994 at the Carlebach Shul, one can see the epitome of the new religious structure invented by Reb Shlomo: integrating a selection of his songs for the *Hallel*, each setting a different mood and spiritual direction; the symbolic waving of the *lulav* and *arava* with joyful dancing, and interjections in English creating a thoughtful direction.[7] This is the Shlomo leading a new form of religious experience specifically adapted to the Orthodox community.

Shlomo was able to blend in to so many different types of communities because he reflected sundry images to diverse audiences. Prof. Shaul Magid uses the metaphor of a mirror:

> Most remember him as a mirror: They saw in him what they wanted him to be, or what they imagined themselves to be.... each of his followers heard what he or she wanted and constructed him in their image. The Orthodox offer one reading, the neo-Hasidim another, Diaspora Jews another, Israeli Jews another; leftists read him one way, Jewish militants another. The point is none of them really know . . . He bequeathed a "Judaism of uncertainty" ("what

---

6. Shlomo explained the advantages of using the designation Reb rather than Rabbi by playfully distinguishing the letters. "Rabbi" is a combination of *Ra* (Hebrew for "bad") and *Bi* ("he gets by"), whereas "Reb" is a shortened form of "Rebbe," and in Hebrew means "Rabbi" with the letter *yod*, signifying the Divine Presence – "God is so tremendous inside" – God's Light in you. Shlomo's explanation can be heard on segment 4:53–5:11 in part 4 of Rabbi Shlomo In Concert, YouTube, http://www.you tube.com/watch?v=5xWq93sR1Oo&feature=relmfu. This is from his concert in Feb. 1994 in Miami Beach.

7. For an hour long program of Reb Shlomo leading the singing for the Hoshana Rabbah service at the Carlebach Shul on 79th St., see Kikarhashabat.co.il; http://www.kikarhashabat.co.il/video.php?vid=49839-43433. Compare http://www.sharey ot.co.il/?p=3301; https://www.box.com/shared/od27gutop6. A record was produced entitled *R. Shlomo Carlebach – The Last Hoshana Raba*. http://he.israel-music.com/shlomo_carlebach/last_hoshana_raba/; http://he.israel-music.com/shlomo_carleb ach/hoshana_raba_part_1_for_pc; http://he.israel-music.com/shlomo_carlebach/hoshana_raba_part_2_for_pc.

do we know?" was his catchphrase) so that everything could be reviewed and revised, in the spirit of love and not separation, on compassion and not exclusion.[8]

Nonetheless, of all the images of Shlomo, the most well-known is that of the Singing Rabbi, the father of modern Hasidic music.

2.   THE FOREMOST SONGWRITER IN JUDAISM?

Ari Goldman, in *The New York Times* obituary in 1994, designated Shlomo Carlebach "the foremost songwriter in contemporary Judaism."[9] Recently, Goldman reiterated this statement, adding that it has never been disputed.[10] In 1997, music historian, Robert L. Cohen, referred to Shlomo as "the most prolific composer of liturgical folk melodies in this, perhaps any, century."[11] In a later article, Cohen explained that Carlebach "opened the gates for a new generation of *niggun* makers" by creating music with a Hasidic flavor that could be accessible to young Americans:

> Shlomo Carlebach had a phenomenal gift for melodies that conveyed yearning and joy, sweetness and exultation all at once . . . His example inspired an entire generation to set traditional, and some original, verses to their own new melodies . . . The result has been a garland of new Jewish music – of new wings for our prayers.[12]

This type of recognition recurs in various Jewish encyclopedias and year books. Mark K. Bauman in the 2011 *Jewish American Chronology*, recognized Shlomo as "the twentieth century's *most prolific and influential composer of Jewish music* and a key ambassador of spirituality, especially

---

8. Shaul Magid, "Carlebach's Broken Mirror," *Tablet Magazine*, Nov. 1, 2012, TabletMag.com, http://www.tabletmag.com; http://www.tabletmag.com/jewish-arts -and-culture/music/115376/carlebach-broken-mirror?utm_source=tabletmagazine list&utm_campaign=85f99372d7-11_1_2012&utm_medium=email.

9. Ari L. Goldman, "Rabbi Shlomo Carlebach," *New York Times*, Oct. 22, 1994.

10. Goldman, "Why Carlebach Matters."

11. Cohen, "Jewish Soul Man," 59.

12. Robert Cohen, "New Wings for Our Prayers: On American Jewish Music," *Open the Gates!*, vol. 1, 2005, excerpted in *Tikkun*, March 27, 2008, Tikkun.org, http://www.tikkun.org/article.php?story=20090327095511603.

Cohen's essay accompanies the CD *American-Jewish Music for Prayer* and describes Jewish religious folk music, its inspiration in the Hasidic movement and its cultural roots in American folk music. The CD includes 18 different composers and performers of prayerful melodies and #17 is *"Ein Keilokeinu"* of Shlomo Carlebach.

to Jewish youth."[13] Judah M. Cohen, in the *Encyclopaedia Judaica* entry, defined Carlebach's extraordinary influence:

> At the time of his death, Shlomo Carlebach had become a legend of sorts, having recorded over 25 albums, composed up to 5,000 songs, performed on five continents, released two official songbooks, amassed a broad following, granted *semikhah* to both male and female students, and given away nearly all his earnings. Several of his songs, moreover, had become "traditional" during Jewish events; revelers would sing such songs as *"Esa Einai," "David Melekh Yisrael," "Am Yisrael Chai,"* and *"Od Yeshoma."*[14]

Mark Kligman, professor of Jewish Musicology at Hebrew Union College in New York, in his survey of contemporary Jewish music in the *American Jewish Year Book* (2001) stated: "Jewish musical artists of today consider Shlomo Carlebach the *father of contemporary Jewish music*."[15] Kligman explains that the most innovative part of Shlomo's musical success was "the blending of Hassidic song with folk music":

> Combining the participatory ease of folk music, the energy of the newly created music from Israel, and the religious fervor of the Hassidic *niggun*, he succeeded in moving liturgical music out of the synagogue and into a wide range of other settings, including concert halls and night clubs, and used his music to educate and inspire Jews to renew their Jewish identity and discover the beauty of Jewish life.[16]

Nonetheless, not all Jewish musicologists have recognized Shlomo's importance. Cantor Macy Nulman in his 1975 comprehensive encyclopedia of Jewish music does not have an entry for Shlomo Carlebach.[17] Similarly, in his 1992 masterful survey of Jewish musical traditions, Hebrew University Professor of Musicology, Amnon Shiloah, does not mention Shlomo.[18] Presumably, part of the reason is that popular Hasidic folk songs are not on the same level as professional music. Indeed,

---

13. Mark K. Bauman, *Jewish American Chronology: Chronologies of the American Mosaic* (Santa Barbara, California: 2011), 119.

14. Judah M. Cohen, "Carlebach, Shlomo," *Encyclopaedia Judaica*, 2nd ed., vol. 4, 481–482.

15. Kligman, "Contemporary Jewish Music."

16. Kligman, "Contemporary Jewish Music."

17. Macy Nulman, *The Concise Encyclopedia of Jewish Music* (New Zealand: 1975).

18. Amnon Shiloah, *Jewish Musical Traditions* (Detroit: 1992). His book is based on a course in Hebrew that Shiloah prepared for the Open University in the years 1985–1987.

Shlomo's musical success is remarkable considering that he never really trained as a professional musician, and apart from a few voice lessons in Manhattan, was not an expert cantor. Or as Shlomo self-effacingly explained in an interview to Elli Wohlgelenter:

> I don't think I have a good voice. I think my voice is just good enough to inspire people to sing with me. If I would have a *gevalt* voice like, let's say, Moshe Koussevitzky, then nobody would want to sing with me, because then they'll think they don't want to miss my voice, but my voice is just good enough to make them sing.[19]

Shlomo's self-comparison to the renowned cantor Moshe Koussevitzky highlights a key ingredient of his musical success. Rather than impress an audience by a beautiful recital, Shlomo led a sing-along of catchy tunes. A typical Carlebach tune is easy to follow.[20] At Shlomo events, participants quickly learned his new songs thus furthering their popularity.

Musicologist Velvel Pasternak explained that if judged by objective musical standards, Shlomo was not the most outstanding composer, singer or guitarist, but his success was due to an uncanny ability to strike an immediate responsive chord in the ears of his listeners:

> Even a seemingly banal sounding melody became a hypnotic and mesmerizing chant. The simplicity of his melody line, the intensity of his performances, the charisma of his personality, served to create a worldwide musical following.[21]

Furthermore, by adapting the form and fervor of a Hasidic *farbrengen* (see above, Chapter 6), Shlomo constructed a new hybrid of folk singing and semi-prayer. To quote the insightful appraisal of Motti Regev and Edwin Seroussi:

> Armed with a guitar, dressed like an "orthodox hippie," and us-ing the most basic harmonies and short, repetitive melodies, Carlebach appeared at concerts that became a kind of unorthodox prayer that recalled the traditional Hassidic *tish*, an assembly of

---

19. Wohlgelernter, "Simply Shlomo."

20. A typical Carlebach tune has two contrasting sections of only eight bars each, with the second one in a higher register, melodic sequences, and constant syncopation (with the rhythm accenting a normally weak beat) – see Motti Regev and Edwin Seroussi, *Popular Music and National Culture in Israel* (Berkeley–Los Angeles–London: 2004), 129.

21. Velvel Pasternak, "A Musical Legacy," *Aquarian Minyan Newsletter*, Autumn–Winter, 1995, reprinted in David Wolfe-Blank (ed.), *The Aquarian Minyan KhaZak! Khazak!*, 388–389.

Hassidim around the table of the rebbe, held on special dates, and characterized by singing and dancing.[22]

In sum, the amalgamation of a Hasidic *tish*, inspirational storytelling, emotional insights, and ethical exhortations created the innovative Carlebachian musical experience. Samuel C. Heilman, professor of Sociology at Queens College CUNY, describes Shlomo Carlebach as a product of a synergy between Hasidic, Israeli, and American trends:

> He attached himself to Hasidic prayer styles from which he took the idea of expressive enthusiasms in prayer and devotional ecstasy as part of Jewish outreach. From American new folk idioms, he took the guitar, rhythms, the practice of sing-alongs, the "talking blues," concertizing, and the idea of making recordings. From Israeli culture, he borrowed the idea of *shirah b'tzibbur*, i.e., choral singing as a tool of social solidarity. All these he mixed syncretistically to develop his particular style.[23]

Indeed, this description sums up the secret of the appeal to Reb Shlomo's music. He was able to bring together the popular folk music of the 1960s and the fervor of Hasidic *niggunim* to create a new genre of music. But Heilman goes further and explains:

> Contemporary Carlebach *minyanim* have elevated him and his approach to a kind of mythic status. Reb Shlomo, as devotees refer to him these days, is the modern Jew's counterpart to the Hasidic rebbes and other immortals that the *Haredi* world has enshrined. Like these rebbes, he is frequently resurrected in stories, songs, aphorisms, and teachings that are meant to shape the attitudes and religious character of those who invoke his memory.[24]

Nonetheless, despite the accolades and adulation, there were also criticisms, some of them harsh and painful.

3.   APPRECIATING OR DEPRECATING?

David M. Weinberg wrote in *The Jerusalem Post* on the occasion of Shlomo's fourth *yahrzeit*:

---

22. Regev and Seroussi, *Popular Music*, 127–128.

23. Adapted from Samuel C. Heilman, *Sliding to the Right: The Contest for the Future of American Jewish Orthodoxy* (Berkeley and Los Angeles: 2006), 291.

24. Ibid.

So misunderstood and unappreciated in his lifetime, yet so celebrated and yearned-for after death – such was Rabbi Shlomo
Carlebach, the saintly singer and composer, storyteller, scholar
and saver of souls. . . . we all owe Reb Shlomo an apology. For not
appreciating him more. For not realizing just how deep he was,
and for not applauding him every step of the way.[25]

In truth, it is not a simple task to deal directly with the assorted criticisms against Reb Shlomo. The controversies began in the late 1960s,
when Shlomo asked the religious establishment to help with his outreach
work, but he was mocked.[26] Because of his work with the hippies in
Haight-Ashbury, some of his more strident antagonists went so far as to
label him a "drug user." Shlomo later recalled:

> I had the privilege, a little bit, in really un-drugging a lot of kids.
> I was *mamesh* showing them that there is something higher than
> drugs. So, what does the world do? The world says I'm a drug
> addict. . . . I was in Jerusalem and they asked me to *daven Musaf*
> in a certain shul. I'm just about to begin to *daven* and the President
> of the *shul* walks up to me and says, "We don't permit drug addicts
> to *daven Musaf.*" He *mamesh* said it out loud in front of the whole
> *shul*. Suddenly the whole *frum* community turned against me.[27]

In an interview in 1980, Reb Shlomo remarked: "I was an outcast, and I
still am a little bit of an outcast." He explained how he understood the
antagonism: "Whenever you want to do something great, suddenly everyone turns against you."[28]

One illustration of how some in the Orthodox establishment bitterly
disputed Shlomo's relatively liberal approach to a halachic issue is related
by his daughter Neshama who accompanied her father in almost all the
concerts during the last nine months of his life:

---

25. David M. Weinberg, "Missing Reb Shlomo," *Jerusalem Post*, Oct. 11, 1998,
DavidMWeinberg.com, http://davidmweinberg.com/1998/10/11/missing-reb-
shlomo.

26. In an undated recording archived in the Ami Weisz collection by the Shlomo
Carlebach Foundation, Shlomo can be heard plaintively describing how in 1969 he
told "one of the biggest Rosh Yeshivas" how "thousands of kids are coming back to
Yiddishkeit," and that "we need new yeshivas for *baalei teshuva.*" The Rosh Yeshiva
called somebody up to say "that he never saw a comedian like me."

27. Undated recording in the Ami Weisz collection.

28. Witt, "Reb Shlomo," 5. This petulant complaint is elaborated upon in the Ami
Weisz recording cited in the previous footnote.

Wherever we appeared, my father would invite me to sing with him. It was always just one short song, *BeShem Hashem*.[29] This prayer-song describes the protection of the angels. Our harmonizing together was extraordinarily moving. When we performed for religious audiences, my father would announce: "I am inviting my daughter to sing with me and for those of you who follow the halachic restriction of not listening to a female singer (*kol isha*), I won't be offended if you walk out for a few minutes." Sometimes, however, the organizers were so infuriated at his having me singing on stage that they actually reneged on their agreement to pay my father for the performance.[30]

Towards the end of Shlomo's life there was a growing appreciation in the *haredi* world of how his maverick approach was instrumental in creating the *baal teshuva* movement. This mutual rapprochement was illustrated for example in the 1993 HASC concert in Lincoln Center where a large crowd of men and women sitting separately, enthusiastically received Shlomo who appeared in a conventional tie and jacket (see above). However, some of the criticisms continued after his death.

In retrospect, it would seem that paradoxically, Shlomo's greatest strengths were also his weaknesses. His *hesed* and magnanimous behavior were legendary yet could be ruinous. He was known to respond generously to anyone in need even if he was left penniless. He operated in a realm beyond time to the chagrin of punctual people. His penchant for impromptu *mitzvot* could result in missing an appointment or even an airplane. Shlomo's non-judgmental welcoming enabled many an outcast to find an empathetic ear, but it also took a heavy toll on his time and organization. And finally, his hugging and affectionate gestures "saved" many lonely souls, but it also deterred, and sometimes offended, those who didn't appreciate his intentions.

It was during the 1967 Summer of Love in California that Shlomo had discovered the incredible power of hugs. With tens of thousands of

---

29. For a 30-second sample of this song from the record *HaNeshama Shel Shlomo*, see http://www.rhapsody.com/album/Alb.160513; http://www.mostlymusic.com/ haneshama-shel-shlomo.html; http://www.amazon.com/Ha-Neshama-Shel-Shlomo -Carlebach/dp/B0000U38WM/ref=cm_cr_pr_pb_t. The record was released Jan. 1, 1997.

To hear this song where Shlomo dedicates it to his second daughter Nedara, "my heart and my pride," see http://www.youtube.com/watch?v=_FhRjZeb_Zo. For Neshama's version of this song, see http://www.youtube.com/watch?v=UonWR28vNQA and http://www.youtube.com/watch?v=bR9UFbU5ilQ.

30. Personal interview with Neshama Carlebach, Dec. 27, 2012.

hippies converging on Haight-Ashbury, Shlomo was able to reach out to the alienated youth, some 30% of whom were Jewish. He walked up and down Haight Street and with his hugs discovered the key to their hearts. The very fact that an Orthodox rabbi offered an embrace provided a startling alternative to their estrangement from religious Judaism. Soon Shlomo established the House of Love and Prayer where the motto was "a place where, when you walk in, someone loves you, and when you walk out, someone misses you" (see above, Chapter 4).

This became Shlomo's trademark. When he entered a concert hall, he would first hug and greet every person, and only then ascend to the stage. He became known as the rabbi whose mission was self-defined as breaking down barriers. This expression of affectionate warmth was extended to all, even to non-Jews, as was illustrated in 1989 with his visit to Poland where he embraced thousands of non-Jews to the astonishment of the Polish press. As a result, some Holocaust survivors accused him of wrongly showering forgiveness onto the Polish people (see above, Chapter 9).

At the time that Shlomo was pronouncing his goal to hug and love every human being, the American counterculture was touting the slogan "Make Love Not War," and the Beatles were singing "All You Need Is Love." However, for an Orthodox rabbi to energetically assert that love, empathy, and hugs would solve the world's problems was considered going beyond the pale. With the exception of a handshake, public physical contact between men and women was not the norm in the Orthodox world; for a rabbi to hug intentionally and in such numbers was unprecedented. The public hugging and kissing was considered an anathema. It was a breach of normative halachic practice by a charismatic figure who had been trained in Lakewood Yeshiva and had publically represented Chabad. As a result, some Orthodox organizations refused to invite him and educational institutions even banned their students from attending his concerts.[31]

But there was a second issue percolating behind the social hugging that was to generate controversy even within non-Orthodox communities. During Shlomo's lifetime, accusations of sexual wrongdoings were publicized against some of Shlomo's Guru friends such as Yogi Bhajan, Satchidananda, and Ram Dass.[32] Gradually, there was a growing

---

31. I witnessed this personally in 1993 when I was working as the rabbi of Hebrew University. I arranged for Shlomo to perform for the students on Mt. Scopus. Someone contacted the sponsor of the event and convinced him that it was wrong to invite a rabbi who hugs women. The event was cancelled.

32. See Geoffrey D. Falk, *Stripping the Gurus: Sex, Violence, Abuse and Enlightenment* (Toronto: 2009). Falk discusses the wrongdoings of 26 gurus. The

awareness of how charismatic authority figures could abuse their power and take advantage of their devotees. At first, rumors that circulated about Shlomo sounded rather benign because they related mostly to his social hugging and his proclivity to phone at late hours. However, almost four years after Shlomo's death, an article was written by Sarah Blustain in the feminist magazine *Lilith*, and it opened a Pandora's box of accusations.[33] *Lilith* received dozens of emotional responses pro and con. Twelve were selected for a follow-up issue. These demonstrated the vociferous nature of the controversy.[34] The issue at stake was how to remember Shlomo.

In 2001, Vicki Polin established the Awareness Center with the avowed goal of exposing sexual offenders, and began publicizing allegations against dozens of religious leaders. Polin added Shlomo Carlebach to her list of people accused,[35] but unfortunately, obfuscated some of the issues.[36] In 2002, when the New York City municipality decided to name

---

book in PDF form can be downloaded at StrippingTheGurus.com, http://www.strip pingthegurus.com/ebook/download.asp.

33. Sarah Blustain, "A Paradoxical Legacy: Rabbi Shlomo Carlebach's Shadow Side," *Lilith Magazine*, vol. 23, 1, Spring 1998, 10–17.

34. Readers Respond, "Sex, Power and Our Rabbis," *Lilith Magazine*, Summer 1998, 14–16.

35. Besides general accusations and citing the *Lilith* article, Polin added one specifically new story, but did not vouch for its accuracy: "I am sharing Ariela's story with you. Please note there is no way to verify her words." Ariela (presumably a pseudonym) is identified as a Vancouver resident who wanted to convert to Christianity and who had an "unhappy marriage" with a non-Jew. See TheAwarenessCenter. blogspot.co.il/2012/06/case-of-rabbi-shlomo-carlebach.html. Polin did not provide enough information to enable contacting this woman.

36. For example, in a lead banner about the "Case of Rabbi Shlomo Carlebach," Polin states that "Rabbi Moshe Feinstein BANNED Music by Shlomo Carlebach back in 1959" [caps in the original]. She implies that this was because of "sexual predator behavior" – http://theawarenesscenter.blogspot.co.il/2012/06/case-of-rabbi-shlomo -carlebach.html (last accessed March 3, 2013). This is *simply incorrect.* On the contrary, in the Responsa written on May 30, 1959, Rabbi Feinstein allowed playing Carlebach tunes at weddings. His objection was to the singer's appearances in mixed audiences (*Even HaEzer*, 1, 96; see above, Chapter 3). Rabbi Feinstein labeled such behavior pejoratively as *peritzut* and *kalut rosh* (licentiousness and light-headedness). Previously, in May 1955, Rabbi Feinstein had praised Rabbi Carlebach (see above, Chapter 2 for the citation from *Iggerot Moshe, Even HaEzer*, 32, 69–75). But four years later, in 1959, he was angered by Shlomo's decision *to perform for mixed audiences.* Similarly, Rabbi Feinstein only grudgingly permitted fathers to be present at school performances where girls under the age of 11 sang (*Even HaEzer* 1, 26). Furthermore, he was unyielding in his opposition to co-ed classes. For an English synopsis of Rabbi Feinstein's rulings, see David Derovan, "Feinstein, Moses," *Encyclopaedia Judaica*, 2nd ed., vol. 6, 741–742.

the street of the Carlebach Shul on West 79th St. (from Broadway to Riverside Drive) as the Rabbi Shlomo Carlebach Way, Polin spearheaded a campaign successfully canceling this honor.[37]

What really happened during Shlomo's life? Did he misuse his charisma? Did he make mistakes in the ways that he hugged or related to women? And if so, should such stories be sought out and publicized?

Sarah Blustain's article in *Lilith* has been quoted so frequently that it has come to be thought of as an authoritative source. Indeed, Blustain is an accomplished writer and worked for many years as an editor at *Lilith*. However, in the case of Reb Shlomo, her stories are difficult to verify because her documentation is filed away in an archive labeled as "not available for 50 years."[38]

In trying to arrive at definitive conclusions, I conducted long hours of in-depth interviews.[39] Many people who had been close to Shlomo over extended periods of time stated emphatically that the allegations are incorrect, reflect tabloid journalism, and it is immoral to assail a person not alive to defend himself.[40] But others were harsh in their criticism. They cited stories to prove that Shlomo acted wrongly and that some women were hurt emotionally. After listening carefully and examining the stories in an attempt to determine their veracity, eventually I decided to leave room for other writers to undertake the challenging tasks of judge or jury.[41] What convinced me most was that the most prominent ethical message in Shlomo's legacy is to refrain from caustic judgments. His motto was "You Never Know." He illustrated time and again how external superficial actions can be misleading. Often Shlomo would

---

37. See Adam Dickter, "Facing a Mixed Legacy," *The New York Jewish Week*, Sept. 8, 2004, TheJewishWeek.com, http://www.thejewishweek.com/features/facing_mixed _legacy. The cancellation was announced on Sept. 14, 2004.

38. They are filed in the American Jewish Historical Society as part of the Rabbi Goldie Milgram Papers, series III, box 19 folder 3, http://digifindingaids.cjh.org/?p ID=552551.

39. I thank Karen Blake, Linda and Bill Elyad, Yehudit Goldfarb, Rabbi Lynn Gottlieb, Debbie Gross, Rabbi Goldie Milgram, Melinda Ribner, Sara Shendelman, Judy Tibor (Brodt), Diane Wolkstein, and numerous other people, for sharing their stories, answering my many questions, and helping me to try and understand the reasons for the accusations.

40. This position was well articulated by Rabbi Jack Riemer, "Due Respect," in Readers Respond, *Lilith Magazine*, Summer 1998, 14: "To tear down the name of someone who cannot defend himself if innocent, or do *teshuvah* if he is guilty, is contrary to Jewish ethics."

41. One problem is that most of the negative stories are told under pseudonyms making them difficult to verify. Secondly, events of a few decades ago are problematic to reconstruct accurately based merely on oral memories.

declare how vital it was to reveal the goodness of the other person and to abstain from critical verdicts.[42]

4. A MODERN DAY BAAL SHEM TOV?

It is symbolic that in the film made in the last year of his life, Rabbi Carlebach portrayed the character of the Baal Shem Tov, and Neshama Carlebach was cast as Hodol, the Baal Shem Tov's daughter. The announcer explains that the short stories of the Baal Shem Tov and of Reb Shlomo create a spark of joy in the world and a joy about God.[43] This comparison to the Baal Shem Tov was emphasized in 1965 on Shlomo's fourth record where his message was defined as a continuation of the visionary rejuvenation created by the Baal Shem Tov and Shlomo was described as "a link in our time to the heroic figure of the Baal Shem Tov."[44]

More recently, in 2010, Shaul Magid pointed out that Shlomo resembled the Baal Shem Tov "whom he emulated, consciously and unconsciously, in many ways."[45] This was phrased well by Hanna Tiferet Siegel when explaining Shlomo's influence in the Pacific Northwest:

> Reb Shlomo, like the Baal Shem Tov, was a healer who opened the hearts of ordinary people to the ecstatic and miraculous experience of God's Holy Presence. Through his profound *niggunim* and his transformative stories and teachings, he breathed new life into a broken and fragmented Jewish world.[46]

In a manner reminiscent of the Baal Shem Tov, Shlomo's charismatic personality and "Divine Fire" brought a spiritual healing to the weary soul, or as Sophia Adler phrased it: "In his presence one may experience that glow of warmth and courage, the Hassidic spark of divine fire that melt estrangement and soul weariness."[47]

Indeed, this historical precedent can help place the legacy of Reb

---

42. Because of this personality trait, Shlomo paid a price when people took advantage of his kindness or didn't pay for his music. Similarly, in the communities that he founded, borderline personalities whom he accepted might create disrepute for the entire group.

43. See above for the film produced at the end of February 1994 – www.lhotsky -film.at/meilensteine.html.

44. Liner notes by Sophia Adler on the jacket cover of the Shlomo's fourth record, *In the Palace of the King.*

45. Magid, "Rabbi Shlomo Carlebach," 18–21.

46. Skype interview with Hanna Tiferet Siegel, June 1, 2012.

47. Liner notes on the fourth record, *In the Palace of the King.*

Shlomo in perspective. In a sense, Reb Shlomo did for twentieth century Jewry what the Baal Shem Tov did in the eighteenth century. If the Baal Shem Tov created a Hasidic revival with joy, love, and simplicity, so Shlomo heralded a transformation based on reinserting emotion into prayer, feeling into ritual, and empathy into life. Just as the Baal Shem Tov had a popular appeal to the masses so too Shlomo's revivalist message in its easy to follow song and story had a widespread attraction. Shlomo can be said to be a "modern Baal Shem Tov" in that he presented a neo-Hasidic message based upon stories, traditions, and songs from Eastern European Hasidism adapted to a twentieth century American audience. He made Hasidut relevant by showing "that Hasidism is ultimately about the notion of relation – to God, to other humans, to oneself."[48]

Besides the parallels to storytelling and itinerant preaching/teaching, Reb Shlomo followed the path of the charismatic founder of Hasdism in the way he discovered the spark of good in each individual, and lifted up with respect the downtrodden and misfortunate. This was illustrated above in a number of stories such as the coat for the homeless person on a 79th St. stoop (related above by Nedara Carlebach) or the bat mitzvah of Lotus Blossom Cahn. It was this unique personal caring that led his followers to view him as a hidden *tzaddik*, one of the thirty-six righteous who ensure the existence of the world. Here for example is the testimony of one of his devoted followers, Liliane Ritchie:

> For so many people, Reb Shlomo was a most magnanimous, self-less, patient, devoted teacher, a giant Soul Master whose brilliant, profound knowledge revealed to us glimpses into the truth, the reality of the infinite kindness of the Almighty.[49]

Indeed, a good part of Shlomo's life was devoted to being a caring rabbi. This was noted by Rabbi Raphael Harris when he witnessed how Shlomo intervened to help Rachel Yona-Shalev at the Pargod Theater in November 1992 (see above, Chapter 8):

> The way Reb Shlomo counseled Rachel is astonishing. I was close to Shlomo for many years and witnessed how this occurred often. I personally heard people constantly asking Shlomo for advice and he never refused. One might have assumed that Shlomo was a trained social worker whose purpose in life was to bring consola-tion and hope to all.[50]

---

48. Magid, "Rabbi Shlomo Carlebach."

49. Ritchie, *Masters and Miracles*, 30–31. Liliane Ritchie, "A Blazing Trail of Heavenly Joy," *Kol Chevra*, vol. 16, 2010, 93.

50. Personal communication with Rabbi Raphael Harris, Dec. 30–31, 2012.

It was this unique caring that inspired Shlomo's followers and admirers. Rabbi Avraham Greenbaum first met Reb Shlomo in the mid-1980s and was deeply impressed by Shlomo's "incredible love and empathy":

> Reb Shlomo would do everything in his power to build the person up, make them feel good and positive so they would want to do real *teshuvah*. Merely to be in his presence made you want to emulate the goodness, kindness, and deep wisdom he always radiated.[51]

Reb Shlomo inspired his disciples to join him on a mission to change the world. In the words of Rabbi Yaakov Fogelman:

> He urges observant Jews to soar, to have no lesser goal than changing the whole world, rather than being content to just bring a few souls back to the faith. We're to bring the whole world to Jerusalem and teach them a Torah of loving God and other people, especially one's own children.[52]

These personal testimonies when viewed together depict a picture of Shlomo as a modern type Baal Shem Tov. To be exact, this was often at great personal expense in time, energy, and money. Shlomo did not develop the learning skills that he had exhibited during his yeshiva days in Lakewood. He did not write halachic responsa nor did he publish Talmudic commentaries. As Shlomo himself was fond of pointing out, he followed the exemplary biblical paradigm of Abraham who went out to the world to save others as opposed to Noah who was a private *tzaddik*.

In conclusion, it is interesting to read the quotation of how Reb Shlomo himself said that he would like to be remembered:

> Should your children and grandchildren ever ask who Shlomo Carlebach was, tell them that he was neither a saint nor a sinner, but merely a simple Jew who loved the Creator, the Torah, and his fellowman and whose only ambition was to draw them together.[53]

---

51. Rabbi Avraham Greenbaum, "Beware," *Kol Chevra*, vol. 16, 2010, 240.

52. Rabbi Yaakov Fogelman, *The Jerusalem Jewish Voice, The Weekly Torah Reading – A First Glance, Parshat Tzaveh*, http://www.israelvisit.co.il/top/tzaveh.shtml. Rabbi Fogelman is summing up the gist of the video interview of Reb Shlomo with Zachary Goldman, *His Life*.

53. Brandwein, Reb Shlomele, 13. See also Moshe Liebert, "President's Message, Carlebach Shul," *Kol Chevra*, vol. 5, 1998, 32. Moshe (Michael) Liebert, who first met Shlomo in 1982, was president of the Carlebach Shul from 1991–1998. He died on Aug. 4, 2000 at the age of 56. See "Moshe Liebert's Obituary," *Kol Chevra*, vol. 7, 2000, 23–24.

5.   REBBE OF LOVE, APPRECIATION, AND HOLINESS

Shlomo would often refer to himself as the "Rebbe of the street-corner." His potential constituency could be found in any forlorn corner that he encountered on the road. Like in the Baal Shem Tov tales and legends, so also Reb Shlomo discerned the goodness in the simpleton and uncovered holiness behind sordid exteriors. This approach to life is reflected in his stories about the hidden thirty-six righteous saints and Elijah the Prophet incognito.

To further clarify this designation of Reb Shlomo, below is a selection of ten quotes from people who experienced firsthand his message of love, appreciation, and holiness. These citations are subdivided into three categories: unconditional love for all, appreciation and close friendship, and discovering holiness in the other.

A.   *UNCONDITIONAL LOVE FOR ALL*

1.   Everyone Is Precious – Mimi Borowich
2.   Unconditional Love – Yitta Halberstam Mandelbaum
3.   How Everyone Can Be the Greatest – Menashe Bleiweiss

1.   *Everyone Is Precious – Mimi Borowich*

He was nicknamed the "Rabbi of Love" by many of his followers. Any time people were in need, whether monetary, emotional, or spiritual, they could always count on Reb Shlomo's help. When he walked into a room, he would hug everyone there. That was his first priority. He wanted to let people know that they were loved, that they were special. . . . He left me with the biggest and most important lesson of my life: if someone tells you that you are a nobody and that you will never amount to anything, don't listen. He is wrong. Everyone is precious.[54]

2.   *Unconditional Love – Yitta Halberstam Mandelbaum*

"Holy Sister Yitta," he would beam whenever we met. "You're the sweetest. The holiest." It didn't matter that I had just heard him utter the exact same greeting to 300 people before me. His luminous countenance radiated unmistakable sincerity, and I felt suffused with the warmth of his *unconditional love and acceptance*. This he had offered to me and to tens of thousands of Jews like me and unlike me.[55]

---

54. Mimi Borowich, "Reflections," *Kol Chevra*, vol. 8, 2001, 156.
55. Mandelbaum, *Holy Brother*, xix.

3.   *How Everyone Can Be the Greatest – Menashe Bleiweiss*

Reb Shlomo's allure came specifically through his modesty, his self-deflection.... "Rabbi," a skeptic once asked, "you tell everyone that they're the greatest. You can't mean it every time you say it!?" Reb Shlomo replied, "You know, when I tell Moishele that he's the greatest, at that moment, he is *mamash* the greatest in the whole world."... "If you know because of arrogance that you are special, then you cannot recognize that another person is special. But if you know because of holiness that you are special, then you can also recognize this is another."[56]

❋

B.   *APPRECIATION AND BEST FRIEND*

1.   Only Person in the World – Afro-American Riverside Park
2.   You Are *Mamash* the Best – Eleonora Shifrin
3.   Best Friend – Rabbi Naftali Citron

1.   *Only Person in the World – Afro-American in Riverside Park*

I had almost nothing and barely made it from one day to the next. One small light in my world of darkness was a man who would come down to the park almost every week. He would bring food to our small community and sit and talk with each of us, providing encouragement, advice and of course offering a big hug. That man was Shlomo Carlebach . . . He treated me like I was *the only other person in the world*. It mattered not that I lived on a bench rather than in a palace. He treated me like absolute royalty.[57]

---

56. Menashe Bleiweiss, "The Grateful Yid and the Grateful Dead: How Reb Shlomo Carlebach and Jerry Garcia Serenaded the Jewish Soul," *Jewish Spectator*, Winter, 1995–1996, MenasheBleiweiss.com, http://menashebleiweiss.com/articles/Grateful %20Yid%20and%20Grateful%20Dead.pdf.

57. This quote is reported by Rabbi Ezra Amichai as he heard it on the uptown Lexington Avenue train on a Sunday afternoon in 1997. Rabbi Ezra Amichai (Friedland-Wechsler), "A Subway Torah," *Kol Chevra*, vol. 13, 2007, 15–16. A similar story can be found in Ritchie, *A Friend to Our Generation*, 99 at Reb Shlomo's funeral where a "black beggar showed up crying bitter tears" and related that at 3:00 or 4:00 AM, Shlomo "would come down to the Hudson River, under the bridge where us homeless hang out. He would sing to us for hours on end."

2. *You Are* Mamash *the Best – Eleonora Shifrin*

[There were] those whose whole life was changed by Shlomo's blessings, or even by his one hug accompanied by those words he was never tired of saying: "You are the best, the cutest, the most beautiful, you are *mamash* the best!" Sometimes people who knew how far from being the best they were, who were used to being always cursed and rejected by everybody around, after hearing those words from Shlomo looked upon themselves anew and realized there was a spark of Hashem in them too and Shlomo had seen it.[58]

3. *Best Friend – Rabbi Naftali Citron*

I just want to say personally, that I don't know anyone who ever loved me the way that Reb Shlomo loved me. And I don't think that I am alone. Anyone who came close to Shlomo felt that love. . . . It's not that he was loving me because I was his nephew. There's no one that he met that he did not love like his son or his daughter.[59]

❋

C.   *DISCOVERING HOLINESS IN THE OTHER*

1. Finding the Holy Spark – Marvin (Moshe) Kussoy
2. Seeing People through God's Eyes – Estelle Frankel
3. Everyone is *Heilige* – Miriam Futterman
4. Holiness and Oneness in Everything – Rahel Sherman

1. *Finding the Holy Spark – Marvin (Moshe) Kussoy*

Every Jew has a holy spark in him/her, but only a few can find it on their own. Shlomo made it his mission to find, touch, and keep this spark alive and warm in each of us . . . I count myself blessed for all eternity to have known him in my own small way.[60]

2. *Seeing People through God's Eyes – Estelle Frankel*

Rabbi Shlomo Carlebach had an amazing gift for making people fall in love with God and with Judaism. He also had a way of making each of us feel beautiful, special, and loved . . . Reb Shlomo . . .

---

58. Eleonora Shifrin, "We All Miss You," *Kol Chevra*, vol. 4, Nov. 1997, 28–30.
59. Eulogy at Shlomo's funeral, BenKatz.com, http://benkatz.com/music/carlebach_funeral.mp3.
60. Marvin Kussoy in *What's Next?*, Winter/Spring 1995, 18.

had the gift of seeing people through God's eyes, mirroring back to each of us our highest potential.[61] Perhaps the greatest gift was that he modeled for me how to be a soul healer.[62]

3. *Everyone is Heilige – Miriam Futterman*

The bottom line is that everybody is a *heilige* Yid. Everyone's name is *"heilige."* Everyone is holy. That is how Reb Shlomo treated everyone. . . . It's all about acknowledging that *heilige* part in all of us. That's what Shlomo did. He acknowledged that *heilige* part in all of us, and that has changed my life. . . .[63]

4. *Holiness and Oneness in Everything – Rahel Sherman*

Shlomo taught me to see the *kedusha* and the oneness in everything and everyone – in Torah, in the Land of Israel, in Yehudim, in holy Goyalach. Only then can we have true Shalom and joy.[64]

6.   WHAT MESSAGE DID HIS FOLLOWERS RETAIN?

Indeed, the mutual admiration between Reb Shlomo and his followers created a most remarkable relationship. Shlomo was a Rebbe to Hasidim, but not in the classical sense of the standard Hasidic Rebbe. There was no separation and distance, but instead a first name basis. Reb Shlomo was often asked for his advice, but mostly he listened and somehow the questioner felt the answer. As noted in the vignettes above, lives changed dramatically for some of his followers simply by being around him, listening to a concert, or walking twenty miles in the rain on Shabbat in Los Angeles. Thus, one way of relating to the question of "Who Was Shlomo?" is by quoting the individuals who felt his charismatic influence. Here are nineteen statements subdivided into five categories:

A. Inspiration
B. Role Model
C. Virtuous Reality and Spellbinding Stories
D. Listening, Emotional Balance, and Joy
E. A Real Relationship to God

61. Frankel, *Sacred Therapy*, x.
62. Estelle Frankel, "Broken Hearts and Shattered Vessels," *Kol Chevra*, vol. 13, 2007, 191.
63. Futterman, "Heilige Yid," 92.
64. Rahel Sherman, "Memories," *Kol Chevra*, vol. 8, 2001, 155.

A.   *INSPIRATION*

1.   Magic of Shlomo's *Niggunim* – Dina Solomon
2.   His Music Set Me On Fire – Rabbi Prof. David Hartman
3.   Listening to All the Songs – Daniel Nakonechny
4.   Power of Shlomo's Blessings – Louise Barret

1.   *Magic of Shlomo's Niggunim – Dina Solomon*

Whenever Shlomo comes for Shabbos something magical happens in our village of Modi'im. Faces are shining, people are in high spirits, and a warmth is generated between friends. Something about Shlomo always makes you want to be better, to live up to the blessings he so freely bestows upon us. . . . Shlomo's *niggunim* transport us effortlessly to a place beyond our physical bodies . . . their power to uplift our souls and infuse us with joy is so strong.[65]

2.   *His Music Set Me on Fire – Rabbi Prof. David Hartman*

When I think of the foundational memories that shaped my life religiously, I cannot ignore the joyful influence of my beloved friend Shlomo Carlebach. His music set me on fire, and that fire has never been extinguished.[66]

3.   *Listening to All the Songs – Daniel Nakonechny*

Of all his teachings, what Reb Shlomo most bequeathed to us was to hear song . . . He taught us to listen to the song of the broken heart and the falling tears, the song of the setting sun and the rising moon, the song of the children and parents, the song of Jews and Jerusalem, the song of husband and wife, the song of Israel and the Holy Temple, the song of brothers and sisters, the song of love and God, the song of You and Me, the song of Shabbat and Yom Tov, the song of God and Torah, the song of Creator and Creation.[67]

4.   *Power of Shlomo's Blessings – Louise Barret*

He brought joy into my life and I am eternally grateful. The most significant thing he did for me, I truly believe, is that one Pesach

---

65. Dina Solomon, "Introduction to Solomon," *Shlomo Shabbos*, x.

66. David Hartman and Charlie Buckholtz, *The God Who Hates Lies: Confronting & Rethinking Jewish Tradition* (Woodstock, Vermont: 2011), 24.

67. Daniel Nakonechny, "Holy Messengers," *Kol Chevra*, vol. 8, 2001, 152–153. See also HeichalHanegina.blogspot.co.il, http://heichalhanegina.blogspot.co.il/2005_11_01_archive.html.

night, at five in the morning, he gave Dave and me a *bracha* to have children. . . . His *bracha* was so powerful that it led the way for Talya to come into this world.[68]

⁑

B.   *ROLE MODEL*

1.   How to Live Our Lives – Yossi Chajes
2.   Home Base of Tradition – David Barret
3.   A Synaptic Rebbe – Rabbi Yonatan Gordis

1.   *How to Live Our Lives – Yossi Chajes*

It was Reb Shlomo who kept, and continues to keep me Jewish. . . . Reb Shlomo gave over to me what I had known all along to be true: that we must serve God without holding anything back; that we never know about another person and his or her worth in God's eyes . . . All of us who were close to Reb Shlomo are living out our lives along a trajectory that is at once our own, and also an expression of our teacher. . . . inspired by his deep wisdom.[69]

2.   *Home Base of Tradition – David Barret*

For me, Shlomo was always home base, he represented centuries and centuries of Judaism, going back all the way to the desert . . . He was the Jew I had always had hidden deep within, and he represented the Jew that I could be and am aspiring to be. . . . He was a role model for me.[70]

3.   *A Synaptic Rebbe – Rabbi Yonatan Gordis*

Reb Shlomo was a synaptic rebbe and leader. He bridged time and teaching. He was a holy man who by personal example was able to model to us that we are all able to be. Mimi Feigelson and I were his teaching assistants at Yakar in Jerusalem for several years until 1994. Shlomo gave us a syllabus to study Talmud, *Halacha*, and Hasidut towards giving us official rabbinic ordination. He emphasized going beyond basic textual study and taught us to

---

68. David, Louise and Talya Barret, "He Did It with Love," *Kol Chevra*, vol. 7, 2000, 79–81.

69. Yossi Chajes, "Keeping Me Jewish," *Kol Chevra*, vol. 5, 1998, 81.

70. David, Louise and Talya Barret, "He Did It with Love," *Kol Chevra*, vol. 7, 2000, 79. Barret was a member of "the Carlebach *chevra*" in New York in the 1980s.

lead divinely inspired lives, to surpass our mortality and to sense our endless potential to help others. By being a paradigm shaker, he connected us to the whole.[71]

⁑

C.   *VIRTUOUS REALITY AND SPELLBINDING STORIES*

1. Creating Virtuous Reality – Reb Zalman
2. Creating Spellbinding Worlds – Elie Wiesel
3. Tree of Life Torahs of Love, Devotion, and Godliness – David Sacks
4. Revealing Hidden Lights – Maggid Gil Bashe

1. *Creating Virtuous Reality – Reb Zalman*

I call him the genius of virtuous reality because when he told you stories he would want you to get into a virtuous feeling or a virtuous behavior and then it was also important that that person would then start to thinking, "*Oy*, if only I could live that way. That would be so wonderful." And that yearning remained.[72]

2. *Creating Spellbinding Worlds – Elie Wiesel*

He attracted young people most of all, and they adored him. He made them laugh, dance, dream. He would help them overcome the bleak intoxications of daily life by modeling for them the spellbinding and mysterious worlds that every human being carries within himself. He would tell the Hasidic tales, giving wings to their imagination.[73]

3. *Tree of Life Torahs of Love, Devotion, and Godliness – David Sacks*

Reb Shlomo's stories were "Tree of Life Torahs."[74] They communicated a longing for Godliness and an understanding of holiness.

---

71. Personal correspondence from Yoni Gordis, Aug. 4–8, 2011.

72. Rabbi Zalman Schachter-Shalomi, "Afterword," in Dana Evan Kaplan, *Contemporary American Judaism: Transformation and Renewal* (New York, 2009), 392.

73. Elie Wiesel, "Foreword" (translated from the French by Joseph Lowin), in Mandelbaum, *Holy Brother*, xvii–xviii.

74. Reb Shlomo contrasted Tree of Life Torahs to "Tree of Knowledge Torahs." The latter has information which enters the head but not the heart and soul. "Tree of Life Torahs" transform a person's life.

By hearing the stories you were actually experiencing the highest levels of love and devotion that *tzaddikim* were capable of attaining. He made you them, if only for a moment. You could actually taste why Torah mattered and how essential it was to fixing of the world.[75]

4. *Revealing Hidden Lights – Maggid Gil Bashe*

We miss you Holy Rebbe. Your stories draw the heart like wine. Your teachings turn the hearts of parents to their children and the hearts of children to their parents. Even as time progresses, your lasting legacy continues to reveal Hidden Lights.

#

D. LISTENING, EMOTIONAL BALANCE, AND JOY

1. A Listening Psychotherapist – Pearl Atkin
2. Adding the Spiritual-Emotional – Rabbi Baruch Melman
3. Joy – Rabbi Sammy Intrator

1. *A Listening Psychotherapist – Pearl Atkin*

Shlomo was the deepest psychotherapist I know – it is no wonder that he has a large following of mental health professionals around the world that come to him to replenish their own sanity. He just listened with total unconditional love, never giving unasked-for advice. . . . He brought you to the essence of yourself, and gave you a taste of paradise.[76]

2. *Adding the Spiritual-Emotional – Rabbi Baruch Melman*

There was this whole spiritual, emotional side of Judaism that I was able to tap into on account of Shlomo. It was a world that had always existed, but because my connection to Judaism and the world was so very cerebral and intellectual, I barely knew it existed. Thanks to Shlomo I have been able to unite my right and left brains. Balance was restored![77]

---

75. Personal communication from David Sacks, Oct. 26–29, 2012. Sacks is an American television writer and producer. A graduate of Harvard University (1984), he is a co-founder of The Carlebach Happy Minyan in Los Angeles.

76. Pearl Atkin, "At Shlomo's *Shloshim*," *Kol Chevra*, vol. 7, 2000, 55–56.

77. Personal communication with Rabbi Baruch Melman, Oct. 26, 2012.

3.   *Joy – Rabbi Sammy Intrator*

What was so special about Reb Shlomo was that *simcha*, joy, permeated everything. . . . I saw that he really worked on being happy. He had a great sense of humor.[78]

✳

E.   *A REAL RELATIONSHIP TO GOD*

1.   *Davening* to Music – Rabbi Alvin Wainhaus
2.   Making God a Personal Reality – Daniel Nakonechny
3.   Godliness – Darlene Rose
4.   Spiritual Ecstasy in *Davening* – Asher Blachman
5.   The Amazing Kiruv Work – Jeff Mann

1.   *Davening to Music – Rabbi Alvin Wainhaus*

The popular modern practice of *davening* to folk music comes from Shlomo. His neo-Hasidic style of clapping, dancing, and participatory singing revamped the prayer experience. His catchy tunes for individual verses and entire sections revised the notion of what a synagogue service can or should be.[79]

2.   *Making God a Personal Reality – Daniel Nakonechny*

He literally opened up our hearts and souls to that special dwelling place where God's holiness resides. He showed each of us how we are uniquely connected to God, and he welcomed each of us into God's divine and magnificent Kingdom. For some of us he opened up the holy scholar that is inside, for others he opened up the holy musician, for others the holy teacher, and for others the holy listener and friend.[80]

3.   *Godliness – Darlene Rose*

Shlomo thrived on Godliness and holiness and it shined through for all to see. "There is nothing more charismatic than God!" he taught. "If we represent God in the most beautiful way, people will come." To Shlomo, warm smiles, singing, and dancing were part of being God's image. . . . He was trying to teach us that we

---

78. Devorah Preiss-Bloom, "The Real 'I and Thou', An Interview with Rabbi Sammy Intrator," *Kol Chevra*, vol. 7, 2000, 77–78.

79. Rabbi Alvin Wainhaus, personal conversation, Sept. 7, 2012.

80. Daniel Nakonechny, "Holy Messengers," *Kol Chevra*, vol. 8, 2001 (152–153).

can still soar and we can still dream of a world of peace where we are all brothers and sisters dancing in the streets of Jerusalem.[81]

4. *Spiritual Ecstasy in Davening – Asher Blachman*

I had never before experienced such an amazing feeling of spiritual ecstasy and true holiness. It felt as if heaven and earth were merging, and there was a wonderful outpouring of love among all of us in the *shul*. For Reb Shlomo, prayer was a meditation. His soul connected itself to Hashem through the words and song of the prayer, and his *davening* became a natural expression of his soul.[82]

5. *The Amazing Kiruv Work – Jeff Mann*

We owe a huge debt of gratitude to Reb Shlomo for all the amazing *kiruv* work he did, inspiring an entire generation of hippies and spiritual seekers. With dedication and perseverance he encouraged and enthused Jewish *neshamot* everywhere even where all other rabbis had given up.[83]

To sum up: True, there were and still are critics of Shlomo. But for many followers, Shlomo was a visionary who provided guidance and direction. Some perceived Reb Shlomo as a role model. Many emulated his way of discovering holiness in the other person, and his ability to radiate empathy. Other used his ideas to develop a new relationship to God. Finally, Shlomo's overall approach to life was a source of inspiration interpreted very differently by many kinds of people. In that way his influence was "wide-reach," going beyond congregational affiliations and denominational differences.

7.   THE LEGACY OF REB SHLOMO

The multifaceted story and, in particular, the micro-histories related in this book lead to one conclusion – the Carlebach legacy spells a different message to diverse communities.[84] For some people, Shlomo is a

---

81. Darlene Rose, "Watch Me!," *Kol Chevra*, vol. 7, 2000, 192–193.

82. Asher Blachman, "A Tribute to Reb Shlomo," *Kol Chevra*, vol. 8, 2001, 146–147. Asher Blachman who started a Carlebach *minyan* in Beersheba first met Shlomo in a concert in Brooklyn in May 1985. Asher describes an ecstatic experience of *davening* with Reb Shlomo on the Moshav in the summer of 1985.

83. Jeff Mann, Happy Minyan Los Angeles, personal communication, Dec. 10, 2012.

84. This was phrased succintly by Chaya Leader who lived at the first HLP and

founding father of the Jewish New Age,[85] while for his most devoted followers he is the saintly Rashban, an honorific acronym implying a reverence reserved for leading Talmudic scholars and Roshei Yeshiva.[86] A third group emphasizes the universalistic message. This aspect of Shlomo's life is emphasized in the "narrative" portrayed by the Broadway Musical *Soul Doctor*. Similarly, Sojourn Records advertises Reb Shlomo's music as an inspiration to broken-hearted and lonely souls:

> He sought to remind people that they are never alone, that there is one G-d who loves them, and that every person has a unique and important mission to discover for themselves. He was able to uplift the spirits and lives of the most broken, distraught people worldwide; people of all faiths and cultures. . . . Shlomo frequently stated that if we could see the best in each other and appreciate our own innate beauty, there would be no heartache in the world.[87]

If we highlight the most salient point of Reb Shlomo's innovative legacy, it would probably be that he was a pioneer. He did outreach to the unaffiliated before the term *baal teshuva* was even used. He retold legends in a way that made Hasidic teachings such as Breslov, Ishbitz, and Piaceszno sound existentially relevant to the twentieth century. He was the first rabbi to perform with a guitar. But often, he was just too far ahead of his time. For example, to be labeled a "Dancing Rabbi" in the 1960s was far from normative for an Orthodox Chabad rabbi, yet today, one can find unabashedly proud expressions of such activity.[88]

---

was one of the original founders of Moshav Me'or Modi'im before moving to Safed: "Everyone sees Shlomo in their own image." See Coopersmith, *Holy Beggars*, 152.

85. An example of this is the *New Age Encyclopedia* first published in 1990 which gives special entries to Reb Shlomo and Reb Zalman, emphasizing their major role in creating New Age Judaism. See J. Gordon Melton, Jerome Clark and Aidan A. Kelly (eds.), *New Age Encyclopedia* (Detroit: 1990), Sect. 70 (87–88), Sect. 171 (242–245), and Sect. 272 (404–406).

86. The acronym **R**abbenu **S**hlomo **B**en **N**aphtali is used by devoted Carlebach Hasidim. See for example, the facebook page of *Kesher Rashban*. One of the photos here describes Rashban in Yiddish as the continuation of the Besht (Baal Shem Tov) and an exponent of the Hasidut of Ishbitz and Breslov. Created in Dec. 2007, *Kesher* defines itself as the LARGEST online ARCHIVE for Reb Shlomo's Torah and Songs – see https://www.box.com/rashban.

87. SojournRecords.com, http://www.sojournrecords.com/prod/artist/shlomo _carlebach.

88. An illustration can be seen with Chabad rabbis dancing with the Houston NBA basketball team in the background at http://www.youtube.com/watch?v=URPSSxi8 G-U&feature=em-subs_digest-vrecs.

Another salient part of the Carlebach legacy was the poignant message of love and peace delivered with pathos to a post-Holocaust generation. In a TV feature story documenting Carlebach's 1989 visit to Poland, Bob Abernethy, *Religion & Ethics* anchorman, introduced him as "a Jewish troubadour in the 1960s and '70s who preached love and peace" and as "a Holocaust survivor who refused to lose his faith in God and in humankind."[89]

Shlomo's disciple, Rabbi Avraham Trugman, also emphasizes the significance of this universalistic message:

> In scores of interfaith gatherings, he was the "token" Jew. He represented Judaism without apologetics, portraying it as a spiritual path that had something to say to every human being. He used to say that perhaps the whole world is angry with us because we have something very special and yet are so reluctant to share it.[90]

Prof. Jonathan Sarna in his masterful survey of American Judaism sums up the tenets of spirituality and ethics that Shlomo's lifework embodied:

> Carlebach's work reflected, embodied, and advanced many of the central tenets of Jewish spirituality: a stress on the inner life and experiential religion; love for all human beings, particularly the oppressed and the downtrodden; gender egalitarianism; and the embrace of Hasidic and mystical forms of wisdom and worship, with a heavy emphasis on singing and dancing.[91]

An insightful appraisal of Shlomo's impact on Jewish life was offered by Prof. Shaul Magid:

> Shlomo changed the way Jews relate to their tradition and the world, something that only an itinerant can accomplish . . . . His accent, charming manner, rebellious persona, ungrammatical turn of phrase, and broad knowledge of the Talmudic tradition and the yeshiva world made him distinctly situated to be the consummate Jewish cultural translator in the late twentieth century.[92]

---

89. PBS.org, http://www.pbs.org/wnet/religionandethics/episodes/may-2-2008/shlomo-carlebach/77/.

90. Avraham Trugman, "Probing the Carlebach Phenomenon," *Jewish Action*, Winter 2002, OU.org, http://www.ou.org/publications/ja/5763/5763winter/CARL BACH.PDF.

91. Sarna, *American Judaism*, 348–349.

92. Magid, "Rabbi Shlomo Carlebach."

Benjamin Chaidell arrived at a similar conclusion:

> Carlebach provided young Jews what the new religious move-
> ments, Berkeley communes, drug culture, and folk revival could
> not: a return to an "authentic" past one could proudly call one's
> own. With his Austrian accent, Yiddishisms, and melodic voice,
> he recreated a pre-war Europe for his listeners of their (and his)
> imaginations, a simpler time of piety and goodness. Yet this "vir-
> tuous reality" was not a quaint, outmoded world, but rather a
> personal relatable model for the present. It provided lessons for
> real-world action aligned with the values of the counterculture.
> For Jewish youth, Carlebach offered a seamless synthesis of their
> own ethnic and religious tradition with contemporary norms and
> forms, so smooth that some considered his Judaism to be its most
> authentic form.[93]

But while Carlebach is considered the pioneer of religious outreach
in the twentieth century, the question remains to what extent will his
influence shape religious forms of Judaism in the twenty-first century. If
dating websites are an indication of sociological trends, then indeed, a
new definition is being created when "Carlebachian" is selected as an alternative to standard categories of religious identity.[94] Part of the reason
that some people choose to search for "Carlebachian" marital partners
is because the Carlebach name has become synonymous with a Judaism
imbued with spirit, joy, and love interspersed with individualism.

To conclude, I asked Shlomo's daughter, Nedara (Dari), what she
would like to say today to her father:

> What an unbelievable privilege it is to be your daughter. You gave
> me more love and strength in seventeen years than some daugh-
> ters find in a lifetime. You never told me what to do or how to be,
> you just believed in me and loved me infinitely. You were so in

---

93. Chaidell, "A Countercultural Tradition," 54.

94. For example, see Frumster.com and SYAS, SawYouAtSinai.com. SYAS offers
a wide spectrum of choices for self-identification from Conservative to a variety
of Orthodox affiliations. But Carlebach is the only category named after a specific
person. Frumster presents categories from Modern Orthodox Liberal to Yeshivish-
Modern, and Hassidish. Here too, Carlebachian is the only definition that is named
for a specific rabbi. A sociological study analyzing the categories of Frumster website
was presented by Sarah Bunin Benor, "Frumster.com and the Modern Orthodox to
Yeshivish Continuum," Association for Jewish Studies, San Diego, 2006. See now
Sarah Bunin Benor, *Becoming Frum: How Newcomers Learn the Language and
Culture of Orthodox Judaism* (New Brunswick, New Jersey: 2012). My thanks to
Sarah for sharing with me her sociological-linguistic insights.

tune with your inner light and your great mission to bring peace and holiness that you dared to explode the system and stand on your own, alone, to follow your heart and fix the world, one note at a time, one hug at a time.[95]

When asked about her father's message for today, Nedara responded:

He set out a beautiful clear map on finding the blueprint of one's own inner soul, in which each person would be able to gather his/her own personal strength and find a uniquely true way.[96]

What is this "map"? Can it be pieced together as a systematic blueprint replete with methodological assertions, philosophical underpinnings and psychological insights? To these types of questions, I devote a future volume two of this study as I collate and analyze the teachings, expositions, and homilies of Reb Shlomo.

A future challenge for students of Carlebachian thought is to determine if and how Shlomo's teachings can be systematized into coherent statements of exegetical insights or theological innovations. One might compare this to what is happening in the legacy of two other leading charismatic rabbinical figures of the twentieth century, Rav Avraham Yitzhak HaCohen Kook and Rav Yosef Dov Soloveitchik. Most of their teachings were spontaneous, inspired, and not systematically organized until their students began collating and organizing the teachings into distinct theological categories and philosophical statements. Reb Shlomo's teachings are currently scattered in thousands of recordings. When they are organized, annotated, and dated then it will become possible to evaluate his legacy more accurately.

---

95. Nedara Carlebach, personal communication, Dec. 4, 2012.
96. Ibid.

Timeline

The chronological framing of Reb Shlomo's lifework can provide a way of examining changes and developments in his lifework. However, as there were several thousand events, concerts, and happenings in Shlomo's life, it is only possible in the list below to offer scattered highlights.

A. *FORMATIVE PERIOD*

1917   Naphtali son of Rabbi Dr. Shlomo (Salomon) Carlebach, rabbi of Lübeck, marries Pessia, daughter of Rabbi Asher Cohn, Chief Rabbi of Basel.
Naphtali becomes rabbi of the Pestalozzistraße Synagogue in Berlin.

1925   January 14, Shlomo and Eli Chaim twins are born in Berlin.

1931   August 9, inauguration of Rabbi Naphtali as Chief Rabbi of Baden.

1937   The twins have private tutors from Ponevezh and Telshe.
Baden – waltz tunes in the courtyard.
Hasidic singing from Bobover and Tschortkover Hasidim.
Visit in Lithuania with Kahaneman family.
Shlomo learns in Ponevezh.
December 25, Shabbat celebration of the twins' bar mitzvah, Great Synagogue in Baden.

1938   July, travel to Lithuania.
Study in Telshe Yeshiva.

1939   Gradual escape from Europe via Denmark and England.
Williamsburg, Brooklyn.
Naphtali becomes rabbi of the Young Israel of Crown Heights.
Torah Vodaas. Influence of Rabbi Shlomo Hyman.
Musical influence of Modzitz.

1943   Lakewood Yeshiva. Influence of Rabbi Aharon Kotler.

1945   Carlebach family moves to 79th St., Manhattan.
Rabbi Naphtali becomes the rabbi of Cong. Kehilath Jacob.

	Influence of Bobov.
1949	Heart condition of R. Naphtali worsens.

1949 Heart condition of R. Naphtali worsens.
Shlomo leaves Lakewood and draws closer to Chabad.
Rosh Hashana, September 24–25, turning point in Shlomo's life.
Influence of the sixth Chabad Rebbe, the RaYaTZ.
December 10, *farbrengen*, Shlomo and Zalman receive mission
from RaYaTZ.
Outreach at Boston University, Brandeis, and Brown. Zalman
and Shlomo first outreach messengers to "lost souls" outside of
the committed Hasidic camp, *first "kiruv* workers."

1950 January 28, RaYaTZ dies.
R. Menachem Mendel sends Shlomo to Chicago, Cleveland, and
Detroit to gain new recruits for Lubavitch.
Shlomo studies Hebrew in *ulpan* at JTS.

1951 Shlomo learns English in a Columbia University program.
Shlomo, "right-hand man" of the Chabad Rebbe.
Teaches religious youth in Brooklyn basements.
Works in a small synagogue in Harlem, New York and tries
teaching in various yeshivas.

1954 Receives rabbinic ordination from R. Yitzhak Hutner.

1955 Shlomo leaves Chabad when the Rebbe forbids mixed singing.

B.   *1955–1959: INVENTING AN INDEPENDENT PATH*

Studies philosophy and abnormal psychology at the University
of Columbia and the New School for Social Research in
Greenwich Village. Becomes aware of Bohemian Beat culture.
Advisor for *The Dybbuk* in Greenwich Village.
Learns guitar with Anita Sheer who discovers his talent and
transcribes his songs.
Begins to perform at coffee houses and clubs in the Village.
Connects to folk singers and learns performing skills, audience
interaction, and storytelling.

1956– Weekend Rabbi in Dorothy, Atlantic County, New Jersey.

1957 Summers at the Pioneer Hotel in the Catskills.
Performs in schools, synagogues, homes of friends. The very fact
that an Orthodox rabbi plays guitar is revolutionary.

1957 Begins recording his songs towards producing a record.

1958 Youth director, Congregation Tpheris Israel, St. Louis, Missouri.

C.   *1959–1967: FIVE LPS, SIX EUROPEAN TRIPS*

1959   June, first LP, *Songs of My Soul*, produced by Zimra, Shlomo's
record company.
August, first trip to Israel.

1960   First performance in Jerusalem.
Second LP, *Sing My Heart*.

1961   Visits Belgium, Holland, England, France, and Israel.
October 22, Town Hall.

1963   Third LP, *At the Village Gate* by Vanguard Records, first time
a religious Jewish artist produces an album with a major
American record company.

1964   Eighth visit to Israel.

1965   Fourth LP, *In the Palace of the King*.
Fifth LP, *Wake Up World*.
By 1965, total of six European odysseys from Rotterdam to
Buenos Aires, Sydney to Rome.
SSSJ – Student Struggle to Save Soviet Jewry. His song, "*Am
Yisrael Chai*," created in April 1965, becomes its anthem.

1966   June 30 – July 4, 9th Berkeley Folk Music Festival.

1967   Haight-Ashbury, San Francisco.

⚓

D.   *1968–1972: KEHILATH JACOB, JERUSALEM, HLP*

1967   December 23, Rabbi Naphtali Carlebach dies and Shlomo
becomes rabbi of Congregation Kehilath Jacob.
Six-Day War, encourages disciples to go to Israel.
Soviet Jewry solidarity rallies

1968   May, first House of Love and Prayer (HLP) on 347 Arguello Blvd.
New York and Simchat Torah dancing rallies, Oct. 1967 and 1969.
Visits Moscow for Simchat Torah, October 1970 and 1972.
July 7, 11th Annual Folk Music Festival.
October, Los Angeles Shabbos Walk.
Visits Israel regularly. Base in Jerusalem.
Influence grows with the annual Hasidic song festival. In almost
every festival from 1969–1978, there is a Carlebach tune.
July 1970, Holy Man Jam.
June 1971, A Yoga of Joy.

1971   First HLP closes. *Chevra* meet at homes of older patrons.

1971   September 19, 1971, second HLP on 9th Ave. opens for High
Holidays.

1972 February, Meeting of the Ways.
Holy Beggars' Gazette, 12 issues, 1972–1977.

#

E.   *1973–1979: WORLDWIDE FOLLOWING*

1972 December 26, marriage to Neila.
HLP is established in Jerusalem.

1973 Yom Kippur War.

1974 Album Rabbi Shlomo Carlebach Live in Concert, February 24.
June 16, *farbrengen* at Hillel, Berkeley, launching of Aquarian Minyan Berkeley.
October 9, 1974, Neshama born.

1976 Founding of Moshav Me'or Modi'im in Israel.
July 13, 1977, Nedara (Dari) born.
November 27 – December 4, World Symposium for Humanity in Vancouver.

1977 March 18–20, Camp Solomon Schechter near Olympia (Jewish Renewal).
August, First Peace Festival at the Moshav.

1978 July, closure of the second HLP.

1979 August, Second Festival of Peace at the Moshav.

#

F.   *1980–1988*

1980 Death of Rebbetzin Pessia, Shlomo's mother.

1981 May 7, Independence Day Rally with Menachem Begin at Ariel.
Production of the fifteenth and last LP, *L'Kovid Shabbas*.

1982 April 21, farewell concert before evacuation of Yamit.
June 6, Sidon concert, Lebanon War.
December 19, Town Hall in Manhattan.

1983 January, Festival of Hope in Germany.

1984 March, Walt Whitman Auditorium at Brooklyn College (rapprochement with the *haredi* religious world).
July, Rainbow Family Peace Gathering with Richie Havens.

1985 May 20. Fund raising honoring Shlomo at La Différence.
Founding of Hakrev Ushma/*Connections*.

1988 July 25. Heart attack, rushed to the hospital in Jerusalem.

#

G.   *1989: HISTORIC TOURS OF POLAND, AND RUSSIA*

January 1–10, Warsaw, Cracow, Majdaneck, Biala, and Lodz, offering conciliatory approach of love and joy.

August, Israel, Orthodox Rabbinical Council of America.

September 7–27 Leningrad, Kiev, Vilnius, and Moscow with 21 performances.

December 25, Sivananda Ashram Yoga Camp.

Global Rebbe traveling around the world with personal attention, encouragement, and empowerment to an ever-growing constituency. Growth of Carlebach centers.

#

H.   *1994*

July, Last album recorded live, Bnei Brak.

August, Last concerts in Jerusalem.

September, Last recorded performance in America: Celebrating Our Mistakes.

Last album recorded – *In Concert with Ain Safek.*

October 11–18, Last concert tour, England.

October 20, Fatal heart attack in LaGuardia Airport.

October 23, Eulogies in Manhattan outside Carlebach Shul.

October 24, Burial in Har HaMenuhot, Givat Shaul, Jerusalem.

Bibliography

Agassi, Tirzah. "Rocking and Bopping in the Negev." *The Jerusalem Post*, September 7, 1990, 16.

Alpert, Zalman. "Carlebach, Shlomo (1925–1994)." In Jack R. Fischel, Zalman Alpert, Donald Altschiller, Alan Amanik, Susan M. Ortmann, *Encyclopedia of Jewish American Popular Culture*. Santa Barbara, California: 2009.

American Jewish Year Book. Obituaries, "Carlebach, Naphtali," vol. 69. New York: 1968, 605.

American Jewish Yearbook. Obituaries, "Carlebach, Shlomo," vol. 96. New York: 1996, 550.

Amichai, Ezra (Friedland-Wechsler). "A Subway Torah." *Kol Chevra*, vol. 13, 2007, 15–16.

Anders, Jentri. *Beyond Counterculture: The Community of Mateel*. Pullman, Washington: 1990.

Anderson, Terry H. *The Movement and the Sixties: Protest in America from Greensboro to Wounded Knee*. New York: 1996.

Ariel, Yaakov. "Can Adam and Eve Reconcile? Gender and Sexuality in a New Jewish Religious Movement." *Nova Religio*, May 2006, vol. 9, no. 4, 53–78.

Ariel, Yaakov. "Crisis and Renewal: From Crushed Hasidism to Neo-Hasidic Revival and Outreach." In Armin Lange, K.F. Diethard Romheld and Mattias Weigold (eds*.*) *Judaism and Crisis: Crisis as a Catalyst in Jewish Cultural History*, Göttingen: 2011, 317–335.

Ariel, Yaakov. "From Neo-Hasidism to Outreach Yeshivot: The Origins of the Movements of Renewal and Return to Tradition." In Boaz Huss (ed.), *Kabbalah and Contemporary Spiritual Revival*, Beersheba, 2011, 17–37.

Ariel, Yaakov. "Hasidism in the Age of Aquarius: The House of Love and Prayer in San Francisco, 1967–1977." *Religion and American Culture*, Summer 2003, vol. 13, no. 2, 139–165.

Ariel, Yaakov. "Paradigm Shift: New Religious Movements and Quests for Meaning and Community in Contemporary Israel." *Nova Religio*, May 2010, 13, 4–22.

Ariel, Yaakov. "Shlomo Carlebach." In Marc C. Carnes (ed.), *American National Biography – Supplement 2*. Oxford University Press: 2005, 77–78.

Atkin, Pearl. "At Shlomo's *Shloshim*." *Kol Chevra*, vol. 7, 2000, 55–56.

Atkin, Pearl, "In Memoriam to Haim Ghidale." *Hakrev Ushma* (*Connections*), vol. 3, 1987, 7–8.

Baker, Paul. *Contemporary Christian Music: Where It Came From, What It Is, Where It's Going.* Westchester, Illinois: 1985.

Balmer, Randall Herbert. "Ted Wise," *Encyclopedia of Evangelicalism.* Louisville, Kentucky: 2002.

Barkan, Barry. Ben Habeebe (a.k.a. Barry Barkan), "You Are Building It, and They Are Coming: The Aquarian Minyan and the Field of Rebbetude." In Victor Gross, Reuven Goldfarb, Yehudit Goldfarb, Nadya Gross and Miriam Stampfer (eds.), *Ancient Roots, Radical Practices, and Contemporary Visions: The Aquarian Minyan 25th Anniversary Festschrift.* Berkeley, California: Aquarian Minyan, 1999, 73–80.

Barkan, Barry. "Honoring David and Neila." *Kol Chevra,* vol. 17, 2011, 111–112.

Barret, David, Louise and Talya. "He Did It with Love." *Kol Chevra,* vol. 7, 2000, 79–81.

Barringer, Felicity. "Soviet Announces a Jewish Dissident Has Been Released." *The New York Times,* February 16, 1987.

Barzilai, Shmuel. *Chassidic Ecstasy in Music.* Frankfurt am Main: 2009.

Bauman, Mark K. *Jewish American Chronology: Chronologies of the American Mosaic.* Santa Barbara, California: 2011.

Beckerman, Gal. *When They Come for Us, We'll Be Gone: The Epic Struggle to Save Soviet Jewry.* Boston: 2010.

Begun, Yosef. "The American Rabbi vs. the KGB." *Kol Chevra,* vol. 16, 2010, 22–24.

Ben-David, Calev. "Sway of the Singing Rabbi." *The Jerusalem Post,* August 4, 1989, 13.

Bender, Aryeh. "'The Dancing Rabbi' Had a Heart Attack and Was Rushed to the Hospital." *Maariv,* July 26, 1988 [Hebrew].

Benhamou, Lea and Nethanel Shor. "A Shlomo Discography." *Kol Chevra,* vol. 15, 2009, 80.

Benor, Sarah Bunin. *Becoming Frum: How Newcomers Learn the Language and Culture of Orthodox Judaism.* New Brunswick, New Jersey: 2012.

Berry, Daniel. "The Performance Art of Reb Shlomo Carlebach." Undergraduate Thesis, Princeton University, 2009.

Birnbaum, Jacob. "Am Yisroel Chai – Shlomo Carlebach's Version and Earlier Versions." http://www.chazzanut.com/articles/on-am-yisraeil.html, May 2003 (updated April 30, 2006). Birnbaum's article was reprinted with a few changes as "Am Yisrael Chai" in *Kol Chevra,* vol. 16, 2010, 30–31.

Blachman, Asher. "A Tribute to Reb Shlomo." *Kol Chevra,* vol. 8, 2001, 146–147.

Blau, Eleanor. "City Rings In Holiday Music and Pageantry; The City Rings In Holiday Music and Pageantry Concerts Around the City Motets and Masses Christmas-Carol Suite." *The New York Times,* December 22, 1978.

Bleiweiss, Menashe. "The Grateful Yid and the Grateful Dead: How Reb Shlomo Carlebach and Jerry Garcia Serenaded the Jewish Soul." *Jewish Spectator,* Winter, 1995–1996.

Bliume, Fay (Faye bat Bluma). "He Brought Me Home." *Kol Chevra,* vol. 7, 2000, 66–68.

Blustain, Sarah. "A Paradoxical Legacy: Rabbi Shlomo Carlebach's Shadow Side." *Lilith Magazine,* vol. 23, 1, Spring 1998, 10–17.

Bokosky, Sidney M. *Harmony and Dissonance: Voices of Jewish Identity in Detroit, 1914–1967.* Detroit: 1991.

Borodkin, Wendy and Brandwein, Ira. "Love At First Sight." *Kol Chevra*, vol. 18, 2012, 80–81.

Borowich, Mimi. "Reflections." *Kol Chevra*, vol. 8, 2001, 156 –157.

Brand. The Brand Family, "Nachalat Yehuda." *Kol Chevra*, vol. 6, 1999, 9–10.

Brand, Meshulam H. *Reb Shlomele: The Life and World of Shlomo Carlebach*. Efrat, Israel: 1997 [Hebrew].

Brandwein, Meshulam H. *Reb Shlomele: The Life and World of Shlomo Carlebach*. Trans. Gabriel A. Sivan. Efrat, Israel: 1997.

Braunstein, Peter and Michael William Doyle (eds.). *Imagine Nation: The American Counterculture of the 1960s and '70s*. New York: 2002.

Bulka, Eliezer. "Reb Moshe Fuller, *z"l*, On His 3rd Yahrzeit." *Baltimore Jewish Life*, March 23, 2011.

Canaan, Don. "Shlomo Carlebach Dies in New York." *Israel Faxx*, October 24, 1994, israelfaxx.com/webarchive.

Canaan, Don. "Shlomo Carlebach Spreads Message of Hope." *The American Israelite*, November 23, 1989.

Carlebach, Naphtali. *The Carlebach Tradition: The History of My Family*. New York: The Joseph Carlebach Memorial Foundation, 1973.

Carlebach, Naphtali. *Joseph Carlebach and His Generation*. New York: 1959.

Carlebach, Neila. "Remembering Shlomo." *The Canadian Jewish News – Perspectives*, November 9, 1995.

Carlebach, Shlomo. *Ish Yehudi: The Life and the Legacy of a Torah Great, Rav Joseph Tzvi Carlebach*. New York: 2008.

Carlebach, Shlomo. "The Heart of Tomorrow." *Midstream*, vol. 16, no. 5, May 1970, 66–67.

Carlebach, Shlomo. "The Ingredients of Peace." In Elana Rappaport and Steven L. Maimes (eds.), *The Holy Beggars' Gazette*. Oakland, California, 1977, 3–4.

Carlebach, Shlomo. "The Soul of *Shabbos*." *Kol Chevra*, vol. 8, 2001, 10–11.

Carlebach, Solomon. *Geschichte der Juden in Lübeck und Moisling*. Lübeck: 1898.

Carter, Michael. "Memories of Reb Shlomo." *Kol Chevra*, vol. 16, 2010, 101.

Cashman, Greer Fay. "Pied Piper." *The Jerusalem Post*, October 30, 1994, 6.

Chaidell, Benjamin. "A Countercultural Tradition: Shlomo Carlebach and His Holy Hippielach." Yale University, Senior Essay in the Department of Religious Studies, April 11, 2011.

Chajes, Yossi. "Keeping Me Jewish." *Kol Chevra*, vol. 5, 1998, 81.

Chesler, Phyllis. "A Song So Brave – Photo Essay," *On The Issues Magazine*, Summer 1990.

Chipman, Jonathan. *Lekh Lekha* (Supplement) – "On Shlomo Carlebach – Rebbe and Minstrel." Posted http://hitzeiyehonatan.blogspot.com/2006_11_01_archive.html.

Chipman, Jonathan. "Thoughts on Shlomo (archives) An Abrahamic Soul (2001)." Posted October 30, 2004 on http://hitzeiyehonatan.blogspot.com/2004_10_01_archive.html.

Chipman, Yehonatan. "Memories of Shlomo." *Kol Chevra*, vol. 14, 2008, 137–140.

Cohen, Judah M. "Carlebach, Shlomo." *Encyclopaedia Judaica*. Michael Berenbaum and Fred Skolnik (eds.), 2nd ed. Detroit: 2007, vol. 4, 481–482.

Cohen, Robert L. "Jewish Soul Man." *Moment*, August 1997, 59–64, 83.

Cohen, Robert L. "New Wings for Our Prayers: On American Jewish Music." Open the Gates!, 2005.

Cohen, Robert L. "Shlomo Carlebach, Sweet Singer of American Jewry." *The Jewish Advocate*, December 16–22, 1994.

Cohn, Hermann (Tzvi Ahron). "The Basler Rav." In Marcus Cohn, *The Basler Rav: Rabbi Dr. Arthur Cohn: A Collection of His Writings*. Jerusalem: 2012.

Coopersmith, Aryae. "Communications." *Midstream*, vol. 16, no. 5, May 1970, 67–68.

Coopersmith, Aryae. "From House to Aquarian Minyan." In V. Gross, R. Goldfarb, Y. Goldfarb, N. Gross and M. Stampfer, *Ancient Roots, Radical Practices, and Contemporary Visions – The Aquarian Minyan 25th Anniversary Festschrift*. Berkeley, California: 1999, 30–34.

Coopersmith, Aryae. *Holy Beggars: A Journey from Haight Street to Jerusalem*. El Granada, California: 2011.

Coopersmith, Aryae. "House of Love and Prayer – Mechitzah." *Kol Chevra*, vol. 6, November 1999, 39–40.

Dannelley, Richard. *Sedona: Beyond the Vortex*. Flagstaff, Arizona, 1995.

Danzger, M. Herbert. *Returning to Tradition: The Contemporary Revival of Orthodox Judaism*. New Haven, Connecticut: 1989.

Daum, Menachem. "Opening the Gates – A Film in Progress." *Kol Chevra*, vol. 15, 2009, 9–10.

Daum, Menachem and Oren Rudavsky. "Hiding and Seeking: Faith and Tolerance after the Holocaust." *Religion & Ethics Newsweekly*, May 2, 2008.

Dershowitz, Yitzchok. *The Legacy of Maran Rav Aharon Kotler: A Vivid Portrait of the Teachings*. Lakewood, New Jersey: 2004.

Dickter, Adam. "Facing a Mixed Legacy." *The New York Jewish Week*, September 8, 2004.

Douer, Yair. *Our Sickle Is Our Sword: Nahal Settlements until 1967*, vol. 1. Tel Aviv: 1992, 135–141 [Hebrew].

Dreyfus, Benjamin. "Hear the Echoes of Miriam's song: American nusach in concert." In Kay Kaufman Shelemay, *Studies in Jewish Musical Traditions: Insights from the Harvard collection of Judaica Sound Recordings*. Cambridge, MA: Harvard College Library, 2001, 33–50.

Dunner, Pini. "Shlomo's Last *Shabbos*." *Kol Chevra*, vol. 8, 2001, 14–18.

Edelman, Marsha Bryan. *Discovering Jewish Music*. Philadelphia: 2003.

Edelstein, Yaakov. "The Dancing Rabbi, R. Shlomo Carlebach." *HaTzofeh*, August 18, 1961 [Hebrew].

Ehrlich, M. Avrum. *The Messiah of Brooklyn: Understanding Lubavitch Hasidism Past and Present*. Jersey City, New Jersey: 2004.

Elkins, Rabbi Dov Peretz. Communication in *What's Next* magazine, Winter/Spring, 1995, 24.

Elyad, Linda. "How the Minyan Has Affected Me and My Efforts to Create a Jewish Renewal in Israel, March 14, 1999." In V. Gross, R. Goldfarb, Y. Goldfarb, N. Gross and M. Stampfer, *Ancient Roots, Radical Practices, and Contemporary Visions – The Aquarian Minyan 25th Anniversary Festschrift*. Berkeley, California: 1999, 55–62.

Engel, Gerald. "The Singing Rabbi." *Congress Bi-Weekly*, July 25, 1960, 9–11.

Epstein (Besserman), Perle. *Pilgrimage: Adventures of a Wandering Jew*. Boston: 1979.

Falk, Geoffrey D. *Stripping the Gurus: Sex, Violence, Abuse and Enlightenment.* Toronto, 2009.

Falk, Ze'ev. "Carlebach, Joseph." *Encyclopaedia Judaica.* Michael Berenbaum and Fred Skolnik (eds.) 2nd ed. Detroit: 2007, vol. 4, 481.

Fenster, Myron. *Up From the Straits: A Memoir.* Xlibris, Corp.: 2011.

Ferziger, Adam S. "'Outside the Shul': The American Soviet Jewry Movement and the Rise of Solidarity Orthodoxy, 1964–1986." *Religion and American Culture*, vol. 22, no. 1, 2012, 83–130.

Finman, Yisroel. "Shlomo, My Bubie and the Soul of Judaism." *Kol Chevra*, vol. 7, 2000, 72–74.

Fleer, Gedaliah. *Rabbi Nachman's Fire: An Introduction to Breslover Chassidus.* New York: 1972.

Fogelman, Ruth. "Waking Up In Jerusalem." *Kol Chevra*, vol. 3, November 1996, 21–22.

Frankel, Estelle. "Broken Hearts and Shattered Vessels." *Kol Chevra*, vol. 13, 2007, 191–194.

Frankel, Estelle. *Sacred Therapy: Jewish Spiritual Teachings on Emotional Healing and Inner Wholeness.* Boston: 2003.

Freedlander, Daniel and Klepper, Jeff. "Jewish Rock: Music for a New Generation." *Sh'ma: A Journal of Jewish Responsibility*, January 20, 1978, 51–52.

Freedman, Shalom. *In the Service of God – Conversations with Teachers of Torah in Jerusalem.* Northvale, New Jersey: 1995.

Friedland, Ben-Arza, Sarah. "The Tune in Modzitz Hasidut." [Hebrew] http://www.piyut.org.il/cgi-bin/print_mode.pl?what=article&Id=761 (undated).

Friedman, David. "1000 People Celebrate Israel's Anniversary in Open Air Program." *Jewish Telegraphic Agency*, May 12, 1978.

Friedman, David. "Teheran's Chief Rabbi Says Iran's Jews Have Nothing to Fear." *Jewish Telegraphic Agency*, March 14, 1979.

Frumin, Zusha. "Jerusalem!" *Kol Chevra*, vol. 16, 2010, 45–48.

Futterman, Miriam. "Heilige Yid." *Kol Chevra*, vol. 7, 2000, 91–92.

Garb, Jonathan. *Shamanic Trance in Modern Kabbalah.* Chicago: 2011.

Garner, Eliezer. "Close Encounters of the Best Kind." *Kol Chevra*, vol. 7, 2000, 50–51.

Garner, Nechama. "Grandpa-Shlomo." *Kol Chevra*, vol. 13, 2007, 221–223.

Garshick, Ellen and Fran Goldman (eds.). *Fabrangen: Celebrating 36 Years.* Washington DC: 2007.

Gaskin, Stephen. *Monday Night Class.* Santa Rosa, CA: Book Farm, 1970.

Geller, Moshe Pesach. "I Remember." *Kol Chevra*, vol. 7, 2000, 102–106.

Gitlin, Todd. *The Sixties: Years of Hope, Days of Rage.* New York: 1993.

Goldberg, Hillel. *Between Berlin and Slobodka: Jewish Transition Figures from Eastern Europe.* Hoboken, New Jersey: 1989.

Goldberg, Jonathan Jeremy. "Radio Schmooze." *The Jerusalem Report*, January 27, 1994, 34.

Goldfarb, Reuven. "Joy." *Kol Chevra*, vol. 8, 2001, 87–88.

Goldfarb, Reuven. "On Scars and Healing." *Kol Chevra*, vol. 14, 2008, 64–65.

Goldfarb, Yehudit. "The Weaning of the Minyan: An Historical Overview of the Minyan's First Three Years." In V. Gross, R. Goldfarb, Y. Goldfarb, N. Gross and M. Stampfer (eds.), *Ancient Roots, Radical Practices, and*

Contemporary Visions: The Aquarian Minyan 25th Anniversary Festschrift. Berkeley, California: Aquarian Minyan, 1999, 3–5.

Goldman, Ari L. "Ethnic Celebrations Bid Summer Farewell." *The New York Times*, September 7, 1984.

Goldman, Ari L. "4 Festive Affairs for a June Weekend." *The New York Times*, June 6, 1980, C13.

Goldman, Ari L. "Rabbi Shlomo Carlebach." *The New York Times*. October 22, 1994.

Goldman, Ari L. "Special Joys of Purim Marked Around City." *The New York Times*, March 16, 1984, C20.

Goldman, Ari L. "To Honor a Philosopher," Religion Notes. *The New York Times*, January 15, 1994.

Goldman, Ari L. "Why Carlebach Matters." *The Jewish Week*, May 8, 2009.

Gottstein (Edell), Tamara. "Teaching on Anger." *Kol Chevra*, vol. 14, 2008, 18–28.

Green, Arthur. "Neo-Hasidism." In Adele Berlin and Maxine Grossman (eds.), *The Oxford Dictionary of the Jewish Religion*, 2nd edition, 2011, 532.

Green, Arthur and Schachter-Shalomi, Zalman. "A Dialogue on the Beginnings of Neo-Hasidism in America." *Spectrum: A Journal of Renewal Spirituality*, vol. 3, no. 1, Winter–Spring, 2007, 10–18.

Greenbaum, Avraham. "Beware." *Kol Chevra*, vol. 16, 2010, 240.

Grossman, Ron. "Rabbi's joyful noise is a family tradition." *Chicago Tribune*, June 15, 2007.

Gutwirth, Jacques. *La Renaissance du Hassidisme: De 1945 à Nos Jours, Paris.* 2004. (Translated into English by Sophie Leighton, *The Rebirth of Hasidism: 1945 to the Present Day.* London: 2005.)

Hacohen, Mordechai. "Kotler, Aaron." *Encyclopaedia Judaica*. Michael Berenbaum and Fred Skolnik (eds.), 2nd edition, Detroit: 2007, vol. 12, 323.

Hacohen, Moshe David. *For My Brothers and Friends: Teachings and Stories.* Jerusalem: 2003, 2nd edition [Hebrew].

Halberstam Mandelbaum, Yitta. *Holy Brother: Inspiring Stories and Enchanted Tales about Rabbi Shlomo Carlebach.* Lanham, Maryland: 1997.

Heilman, Samuel C. *Sliding to the Right: The Contest for the Future of American Jewish Orthodoxy.* Berkeley and Los Angeles: 2006.

Heilman, Samuel C. and Menachem M. Friedman. *The Rebbe: The Life and Afterlife of Menachem Mendel Schneerson.* Princeton and Oxford: Princeton University Press, 2010.

Husbands-Hankin, Shonna. "Bridging Worlds." *Kol Chevra*, vol. 8, 2001, 127.

Husbands-Hankin, Shonna. "Radiant Souls." *Kol Chevra*, vol. 17, 2011, 78–79.

Husbands-Hankin, Shonna and Yitzhak. "My Greatest Honor." *Kol Chevra*, vol. 18, 2012, 11–15.

Intrator, Rabbi Sammy. "On the Road with Reb Shlomo: Four Summer Weekends." *Hakrev Ushma (Connections)*, vol. 3, 2–3, 1987, 20–31.

Intrator, Rabbi Sammy. "On the Road with Reb Shlomo." Special issue on Poland, *Hakrev Ushma (Connections)*, vol. 4, issue 2, 1989, 19–30.

Intrator, Shmuel. "Sharing Memories." *Kol Chevra*, vol. 3, no. 1, November 1996, 7–8.

Jacobs, Susan. "A New Age Jew Revisits Her Roots." *Yoga Journal* 61, March–April 1985, 32–34, 59.

Jaskow, Rachel. "Women of the Wall: A Personal Account." *Kol Chevra*, vol. 5, 1998, 59–60.

Joffe, Lawrence. "Obituary: Rabbi Shlomo Halberstam: After escaping from the Nazis he revived an entire Jewish sect." *The Guardian*, London, September 2, 2000.

Johnson, Mansur. *Murshid, A Personal Memoir of Life With American Sufi Samuel L. Lewis*, Peaceworks, 2006.

Johnson, Mansur. *Shamcher: A Memoir of Bryn Beorse & His Struggle to Introduce Ocean Energy to the United States*. 1991, 2006, Shamcher.org, www.shamcher.org/6.html

Kamenetz, Rodger. *The Jew in the Lotus: A Poet's Rediscovery of Jewish Identity in Buddhist India*. San Francisco: 1994.

Kamenetz, Rodger. *Stalking Elijah: Adventures with Today's Jewish Mystical Masters*. San Francisco: 1997.

Kasimow, Harold, John P. Keenan, Linda Klepinger Keenan (eds.). *Beside Still Waters: Jews, Christians, and the Way of the Buddha*. Sommervile, MA: 2003.

Kaplan, Aryeh. *Meditation and Kabbalah*. York Beach, Maine: 1982.

Kaplan, Dana Evan. *Contemporary American Judaism: Transformation and Renewal*. New York: 2009.

Katz, Shlomo (ed.). *The Torah Commentary of Rabbi Shlomo Carlebach, Genesis, Part I*. Jerusalem: The Shlomo Carlebach Legacy Trust and Urim Publications, 2012; *The Torah Commentary of Rabbi Shlomo Carlebach Genesis, Part II*, Jerusalem: The Shlomo Carlebach Legacy Trust and Urim Publications, 2013.

Katz, Yehudah. "Weddings and Marriage." *Kol Chevra*, vol. 2, 1995, 11.

Kilgannon, Corey. "Resignation of Rabbi Known for Dancing Spurs Tumult." *New York Times*, December 27, 2000.

Klein Halevi, Yossi. "Jacob Birnbaum and the Struggle for Soviet Jewry." *Azure*, vol. 17, Spring 2004, 27–57.

Klein Halevi, Yossi. *Memoirs of a Jewish Extremist: An American Story*. New York-Boston: 1995.

Klein Halevi, Yossi. "The Pied Piper of Judaism." *The Jerusalem Report*, November 17, 1994, 45.

Kligman, Mark. "Contemporary Jewish Music in America." In David Singer and Lawrence Grossman (eds.), *American Jewish Year Book*. New York: 2001, vol. 101, 88–140.

Kligman, Mark. "New Jewish Music in the Orthodox Community." In Ilana Abramovitch and Seán Galvin (eds.), *Jews of Brooklyn*. Hanover, New Hampshire: 2002, 190–194.

Kligman, Mark. "Shlomo Carlebach." In Stephen Harlan Norwood and Eunice G. Pollack (eds.), *Encyclopedia of American Jewish History*. 2007, vol. 2, 669–683.

Korenbrot, Israel. *Return to Modi'im*. Jerusalem: 1985.

Kozak, Warren. *The Rabbi of 84th Street: The Extraordinary Life of Haskel Besser*. New York: 2005.

Krauthammer, Joy. "The Pied Piper – Dancing with Joy." *Kol Chevra*, vol. 15, 2009, 106–109.

Landau, David. *Piety and Power: The World of Jewish Fundamentalism*. New York: 1993.

Lavi, Tzvi. "A Religious Woodstock in the Capital – by the Dancing Rabbi." *Maariv*, July 23, 1971 [Hebrew].

Leary, Timothy. *Flashbacks, An Autobiography: A Personal and Cultural History of an Era*. Los Angeles: 1990.

Leiman, Shnayer Z. "Rabbi Joseph Carlebach – Wuerzburg and Jerusalem: A Conversation between Rabbi Seligmann Baer Bamberger and Rabbi Shmuel Salant." *Tradition* 28:2, 1994, 58–63.

Lerner, Michael. "Practical Wisdom from Shlomo Carlebach." *Tikkun Magazine*, September–October 1997, vol. 12, no. 5, 53–56.

Lerner, Michael. "Recent Losses: Jerry Rubin and Shlomo Carlebach." *Tikkun Magazine*, January 1995, vol. 10, no. 1, 7.

Levine, Yael. "Rabbi Shlomo Carlebach." *The Jerusalem Report*, 2000.

Levitt, Ellen. *The Lost Synagogues of Brooklyn*. Bergenfield, New Jersey: 2009.

Lewis, Ida. "You Never Know . . . You Never Know. . . ." *Kol Chevra*, vol. 13, 2007, 57–58.

Liebert, Moshe. "President's Message, Carlebach Shul." *Kol Chevra*, vol. 5, 1998, 32.

Magid, Shaul. "Carlebach's Broken Mirror." *Tablet Magazine*, November 1, 2012, TabletMag.com.

Magid, Shaul. "Jewish Renewal Movement." *The Encyclopedia of Religion* 2nd edition. Farmington Hills, Missouri: 2005, 7, cols. 4868–4874.

Magid, Shaul. "Rabbi Shlomo Carlebach and His Interpreters: A Review Essay of Two New Musical Releases." *Musica Judaica Online Reviews*, September 6, 2010.

Magid, Shaul. Shaul Magid on Rabbi Shlomo Carlebach, in "Jewish Spirituality in America – A Symposium." *Havruta: A Journal of Jewish Conversation*, vol. 2. no. 1, Spring 2009, 18–21.

Magid, Shaul. "The Triumph and Tragedy of Counter-Cultural Judaism: An inside Perspective on the Carlebach Revolution." *The Jewish Daily Forward*, July 22, 2011.

Maibaum, Matthew. *The New Student and Youth Movements, 1965–1972: A Perspective View on Some Social and Political Developments in American Jews as a Religio-National Group*. Ph.D. Thesis, Claremont Graduate School, 1980.

Mark, Jonathan. "When The Blessing Was Born." *The New York Jewish Week*, March 24, 2009.

Mark, Naomi. "Reb Shlomo and Tshuva." *Kol Chevra*, vol. 2, November 1995, 9.

Marmorstein, Itzchak. "Meeting the Rebbe and Saying Goodbye." *Kol Chevra*, vol. 14, 2008, 131–133.

McWilliams, John C. *The 1960s Cultural Revolution*. Westport, Connecticut: 2000.

Meir, Golda. *My Life: The Autobiography of Golda Meir*. London: 1984.

Meisl, Joseph, et al. "Berlin." *Encyclopaedia Judaica*. Michael Berenbaum and Fred Skolnik (eds.), 2nd edition, Detroit: 2007, vol. 3, 444–453.

Melton, John Gordon, Jerome Clark, Aiden A. Kelly (eds.). *New Age Encyclopedia*. Detroit: 1990.

Melton, John Gordon and Robert L. Moore. *The Cult Experience: Responding to the New Religious Pluralism*. New York: 1982.

Mesinai, Susan Yael and Shlomo Carlebach (1994). *Shlomo's Stories: Selected Tales*. Northvale, New Jersey: Jason Aronson, 1994.

Midlo, Tzlotana Barbara. *Lamed Vav: A Collection of the Favorite Stories of Rabbi Shlomo Carlebach*. Lakewood, New Jersey: 2005.

Miller, David Yisroel. "How It All Began: An Interview with Aryae Coopersmith." *Kol Chevra*, vol. 7, 2000, 60–65.

Miller, Timothy. Timothy Miller, *The 60s Communes: Hippies and Beyond*. Syracuse, New York: 1999.

Mintz, Jerome. *Hasidic People: A Place in the New World*. London: 1992.

Moskowitz, Avraham. "The First and Last Time I Met Shlomo." *Kol Chevra*, vol. 6, November 1999, 35–36.

Musleah, Rahel. "Shlomo Carlebach – The Music Man." *Hadassah Magazine*, October 28, 2008, 51–56.

Nakonechny, Daniel. "Holy Messengers." *Kol Chevra*, vol. 8, 2001, 152–153.

Neff, Dio Urmilla. "Men and Peacemaking: A Meeting of the Ways." *Yoga Journal*, March-April, 1984, no. 55, 35–37, 64.

Newman, Zale. "Holy Food," *Kol Chevra*, vol. 18, 2012, 97–99.

Nichols, Stephen J. *Jesus Made in America: A Cultural History from the Puritans to the Passion of the Christ*. Downers Grove, Illinois: 2008.

Niman, Michael I. *People of the Rainbow: A Nomadic Utopia*, 2nd edition, Knoxville, Tennessee: 1997.

Oberstein, Elchonon. "Early Days in Montgomery." *Where What When – Baltimore's Jewish Family Magazine*, March 2008.

Odenheimer, Micha. "On Orthodoxy: An Interview with Rabbi Shlomo Carlebach." *Gnosis* 16, 1990, 46–49.

Ofer, Tehila. "Prayer Accompanied by Guitar." *Haaretz*, December 1, 1964 [Hebrew].

Offenbacher, Elmer (2004). "The Association of Orthodox Jewish Scientists (AOJS) The First Two Decades (1947–1967)." *BDD, Bekhol Derakhekha Daehu: Journal of Torah and Scholarship*, Bar Ilan University Press, 15, September 2004, 5–36.

Offenbacher, Eric. "Interview with a Jewish Minstrel." *Jewish Life*, August 1959, 53–57.

Okun, Milton. *Along the Cherry Lane: My Life in Music*. Beverly Hills, California: 2011.

Olatunji, Babatunde. *The Beat of My Drum: An Autobiography*. Philadelphia: 2005.

Ophir, Natan. "How Sara (Edell) Schafler-Kelman Arranged Reb Shlomo's First Piano Performance for College Students (Manhattan, 1950)." *Kol Chevra*, vol. 18, 2012, 109–110.

Ophir, Natan. "The Lubavitcher Rebbe's Call for a Scientific Non-Hasidic Meditation." *B'Or Ha'Torah*, vol. 22, 2013, 109–123.

Ophir, Natan. "The Origins of Reb Shlomo's First LP Record: The Account of Rikki (Gordon) Lewin." *Kol Chevra*, vol. 18, 2012, 107–108.

Ophir, Natan. "The Story behind the Photos." *Kol Chevra*, vol. 17, 2011, 211.

Paley, Michael. "His Gift Will Last Long after Others Have Faded." *The Jewish*

Press, November 11, 2009 (an interview in 1993, originally submitted in 1996 to *The New Standard*).

Paley, Michael. "Shlomo Carlebach and the Synagogue of the Future." *Contact, The Journal of Jewish Life Network*, vol. 7, no. 1, Autumn 2004, 13–14.

Parles, Jon. "Robert Shelton, 69, Music Critic Who Chronicled 60's Folk Boom." *The New York Times*, December 15, 1995.

Pasternak, Velvel. "Hasidic Music and Modzitz: A Short Overview." *Journal of Synagogue Music*, vol. XVIII, no. 2, December 1988, 9–15.

Pasternak, Vevel. "A Musical Legacy." *Aquarian Minyan Newsletter*, Autumn–Winter, 1995.

Pasternak, Velvel. *The Shlomo Carlebach Songbook I–II*. Annotated, edited and arranged by Velvel Pasternak. Cedarhurst, New York: 1980.

Peli, Pinchas Hacohen. *"Barkhi Nafshi et Hashem."* *Panim El Panim*, March 28, 1964 [Hebrew].

Persky, Gedalya. "How I Met Shlomo." *Kol Chevra*, vol. 16, 2010, 110.

Persky, Naomi. "Ruach Retreats – 25 Years New." *Kol Chevra*, vol. 14, 2008, 157–159.

Persoff, Meir. "Bible with a Beat." *The London Jewish Chronicle*, July 7, 1961.

Pickett, Winston. "A Rockin' Rabbi Rocks the USSR." *Jewish Exponent*, October 20, 1989, 3, 44.

Plaut, Steven. "The Man the Gulag Couldn't Break." *The Jewish Press*, October 21, 2009.

Poll, Solomon. *The Hasidic Community of Williamsburg: A Study in the Sociology of Religion*. New Brunswick, New Jersey: 2006.

Pollock, Eileen R. "Carlebach Instructs and Inspires with His Songs." *Baltimore Jewish Times*, November 1, 1974.

Preiss-Bloom, Devorah. "The Real 'I and Thou,' An Interview with Rabbi Sammy Intrator." *Kol Chevra*, vol. 7, 2000, 77–78.

Puig, Claudia. "Pop/Rock." Entertainment Calendar, *Los Angeles Times*, August 22, 1989.

Regev, Motti and Edwin Seroussi. *Popular Music and National Culture in Israel*. Berkeley–Los Angeles–London, 2004.

Reichel, Aaron I. *The Maverick Rabbi: Rabbi Herbert S. Goldstein and the Institutional Synagogue – "A New Organizational Form."* 2nd edition, Norfolk, Virginia: 1986.

Reichman, Lynn. "A Story about a Niggun." *Kol Chevra*, vol. 17, 2011, 26.

Riemer, Rabbi Jack. "Due Respect." Readers Respond, *Lilith Magazine*, Summer 1998, 14.

Rigg, Bryan Mark. *Rescued from the Reich: How One of Hitler's Soldiers Saved the Lubavitcher Rebbe*. Yale University: 2004.

Riskin, Rabbi Shlomo. *Listening to God: Inspirational Stories for My Grandchildren*. New Milford, Connecticut: 2010.

Ritchie, Liliane. "A Blazing Trail of Heavenly Joy." *Kol Chevra*, vol. 16, 2010, 93.

Ritchie, Liliane. *Masters and Miracles: Divine Interventions – Messages of Love, Healing and Heart Wisdom*. Jerusalem: 2010.

Ritchie, Liliane. "The Wandering Messenger." *Kol Chevra*, 13, 2007, 40–47.

Ritchie, Zivi. *Shlomo Carlebach: A Friend to Our Generation*. The Rabbi Shlomo Carlebach Center, 1997.

Robinson, Ira. *Translating a Tradition: Studies in American Jewish History.* Brighton, MA: 2008.

Rose, Carol. "Introduction to Kavvanot for the Mikveh." In Shohama Harris Wiener and Jonathan Omer-Man (eds.), *Worlds of Jewish Prayer: A Festschrift in Honor of Rabbi Zalman M. Schachter-Shalomi.* London: 1993, 226–230.

Rose, Carol. "Memories that Continue to Hold Magic." *Kol Chevra*, vol. 7, 2000, 57–59.

Rose, Darlene. "Holy Sister." *Kol Chevra*, vol. 10, 2004, 53–55.

Rose, Darlene. "Watch Me!" *Kol Chevra*, vol. 7, 2000, 192–193.

Rosenberg, Steven A. "Carlebach gives new life to American Jewish music." *Boston Globe*, March 11, 2011.

Rotem, Avraham. "The Dancing Rabbi is Exciting Thousands." *Maariv*, September 4, 1961 [Hebrew].

Rotem, Avraham. "With the Inspiration of a Visit to Romania." *Maariv*, May 17, 1970 [Hebrew].

Roth, Chazkel. "Vintage Reb Zalman Schachter-Shalomi." *Kol Chevra*, vol. 15, 2009, 190–191.

Ruben, Michael (ed.). *The Teachings of Rabbi Shlomo Carlebach.* Northvale, New Jersey: 1997.

Rubin, Howard Jay. "Fixing the World – An Interview with Schlomo [*sic*] Carlebach." *The Sun*, issue 84, November, 1982.

Rubin, Howard Jay. "Judaism's Mystical Heart – An Interview with Dovid Din." *The Sun*, issue 103, June 1984.

Rubinoff, Miriam. "Shabbos Gives Life." *Kol Chevra*, vol. 14, 2008, 61–63.

Rudin, Arnold James and Marcia R. Rudin. *Prison or Paradise? The New Religious Cults.* Norristown, Pennsylvania, 1980.

Sadan, Gil. "The Dancing Rabbi in Music and Song." *Yediot Ahronot*, July 28, 1971 [Hebrew].

Salkin, Jeffrey K. "The New Trend in Synagogue Music." *Reform Judaism*, November 1980, 4.

Sandhaus, Jack. "A Varmer (Warm) Yid." *Kol Chevra*, 17, 2011, 86.

Saracik, Chaim David. "Far East, Middle East . . . and Home." *Kol Chevra*, vol. 16, 2011, 116.

Sarna, Jonathan D. *American Judaism: A History.* New Haven and London: 2004.

Schaechter, Rukhl. "Monday Music: Shlomo Carlebach in Poland." *The Jewish Daily Forward*, April 9, 2012.

Schachter, Zalman M. *The Condition of Jewish Belief: A Symposium Compiled by the Editors of Commentary Magazine.* New York: 1966, 207–216.

Schachter, Zalman. "How to Become a Modern Hasid." *Jewish Heritage*, 2, 1960, 33–40.

Schachter-Shalomi, Rabbi Zalman. "A Conversation: Rabbi Zalman Schachter-Shalomi & Rabbi Arthur Green." *Spectrum*, vol. 3, no. 1, Winter–Spring, 2007, 11–18.

Schachter- Shalomi, Rabbi Zalman and Joel Segel. *Davening: A Guide to Meaningful Jewish Prayer.* Woodstock, Vermont: 2012.

Schachter-Shalomi, Rabbi Zalman. *Spiritual Intimacy: A Study of Counseling in Hasidism.* Northvale, New Jersey: 1991.

Schachter-Shalomi, Rabbi Zalman. *Wrapped in a Holy Flame: Teachings and Tales of the Hasidic Masters*. San Francisco: 2003, 287–296.

Schärf, Thomas E. *Jüdisches Leben in Baden: Von den Anfängen bis zur Gegenwart*. Vienna: 2005.

Schlossberg, Eli W. "The Awesome Power of Music," *Where What When – Baltimore's Jewish Family Magazine*, September 1, 2011.

Schlossberg, Eli W. "The Sixties and Seventies: Turbulent Yet Wonderful Years – The Way We Were." *Where What When – Baltimore's Jewish Family Magazine*, March 2009.

Schlossberg, Eli W. "TA the Way It Was." *Where What When – Baltimore's Jewish Family Magazine*, February 2011.

Seidel, Neil. "Musical Communication." *Kol Chevra*, vol. 8, October 2001, 163–165.

Selvin, Joel. "Summer of Love: 40 Years Later / 1967: The stuff that myths are made of." *San Francisco Chronicle*, May 20, 2007.

Serkez, Kalman (ed.) *Holy Beggars Banquet – Traditional Jewish Tales and Teachings of the Late, Great Reb Shlomo Carlebach and Others, in the Spirit of the 1960s, the 1970s, and the New Age*. Northvale, New Jersey: 1998.

Shacham, Dan. "Rabbi Shlomo Carlebach: 'The Enfant Terrible' of Orthodox Jewry in the United States." *Israel Shelanu*, March 8, 1985, 29 [Hebrew].

Shaw, Steven and George E. Johnson. "Jews on an Eastern Religious Quest and the Jewish Response." *Analysis* 41, Institute for Jewish Policy Planning & Research of the Synagogue Council of America, November 1, 1973.

Shelton, Robert. "Rabbi Carlebach Sings Spirituals." *The New York Times*, October 24, 1961.

Sherman, Rahel. "Memories." *Kol Chevra*, vol. 8, 2001, 155.

Shifrin, Eleonora. "Avraham Shifrin *zt"l*." *Kol Chevra*, vol. 5, 1998, 11–14.

Shifrin, Eleonora. "Rav Shlomo Carlebach, the Dancing Rabbi: A Self-Interview of Avraham and Eleonora Shifrin for the Russian Newspaper *Vesti*, October 1997." *Kol Chevra*, vol. 5, 1998, 15–19.

Shifrin, Eleonora. "Rav Shlomo Carlebach: The Dancing Rabbi," *Kol Chevra*, vol. 16, 2010, 17–21.

Shifrin, Eleonora. "We All Miss You." *Kol Chevra*, vol. 4, 1997, 28–30.

Shoshannah Sarah. "Spiritual Piano Lessons." *Mishpacha Magazine*, 2006.

Siegel, Richard, Michael and Sharon Strassfeld. *The Jewish Catalog: A Do-It-Yourself Kit*. Philadelphia: 1973.

Siegel, Shefa. "Shlomo Carlebach – Rabbi of Love or Undercover Agent of Orthodox Judaism?" *Haaretz*, September 4, 2011.

Singer, Ellen (ed.). *Paradigm Shift: From the Jewish Renewal Teachings of Reb Zalman Schachter-Shalomi*. Northvale, New Jersey: 1993.

Skir, Leo. "Communications." *Midstream*, vol. 16, no. 5, May 1970, 68–69.

Skir, Leo. "Shlomo Carlebach and the House of Love and Prayer." *Midstream: A Quarterly Jewish Review*, February 1970.

Slevogt, Esther. *Die Synagoge Pestalozzistraße*. Berlin: 2012.

Smith, Craig S. "In Poland, a Jewish Revival Thrives – Minus Jews." *The New York Times*, July 12, 2007.

Snyder, Tova. "Blessings and Love." *Kol Chevra*, vol. 10, 2004, 118–119.

Sofair, Sharie Yasgur. "The First Moment." *Kol Chevra*, vol. 7, 2000, 100.

Sokoloff, Carol. "Reb Shlomo's Cosmic Seder." *Jewish Independent*, April 7, 2006.

Solomon, Aryeh. *The Educational Teachings of Rabbi Menachem M. Schneerson*. Northvale, New Jersey: 2000.

Solomon, Ben Zion (ed.). *Shlomo Shabbos: The Shlomo Carlebach Shabbos Songbook*. New York: 1993.

Solomon, Ben Zion. "What's in a Name? – Me'or Modi'im." *The Moshav Me'or Modi'im, 25th Anniversary Journal*, 1976–2001, 4–5.

Solomon, Heather. "Michael Ruben Celebrates Life." *The Canadian Jewish News*, March 1, 2001.

Stein, Regina. *The Boundaries of Gender: The Role of Gender Issues in Forming American Jewish Denominational Identity, 1913–1963*. Ph.D. dissertation, Jewish Theological Seminary, 1998.

Steinhardt, Michael H. *No Bull: My Life In and Out of the Markets*. New York: 2001.

Stern, Moshe (ed.). *To Shlomo, Jubilee Volume, Collection of Expositions and Scholarly Articles in Wissenchaft and Jewish History from His Relatives and Friends*. Berlin: 1910 [Hebrew and German].

Stevens, Jay. *Storming Heaven: LSD and the American Dream*. New York: 1987.

Sutton, Robert. *Modern American Communes: A Dictionary*. Westport, Connecticut: 2005.

Tabak, Lawrence. 1979. "Learning to Levitate in Fairfield Iowa." *Moment Magazine*, vol. 4, no. 3, 26–32.

Teeger, Rena. "South Africa Revisted – Soweto, June 1990." *Kol Chevra*, vol. 18, 2012, 54–55.

Tompkins, Vincent (ed.). "Hippies." *American Decades*, vol. 7, 1960–1969, Detroit: 2001.

Tourkin-Komet, Sue. "An Inter-Faith Date." *Kol Chevra*, vol. 7, 2000, 164–166.

Trugman, Avraham. "Probing the Carlebach Phenomenon." *Jewish Action*, Winter, 2002.

Trugman, Rachel. "Modzhitz Flash Mob." *Kol Chevra*, vol. 17, 2011, 31.

Wasserman, Chaim. "The First and Last Time We Met." *Kol Chevra*, vol. 13, 2007, 64–65.

Waxman, Chaim I. "From Institutional Decay to Primary Day: American Orthodox Jewry Since World War II." *American Jewish History*, vol. 91, no. 3–4, September–December 2003, 405–422.

Waxman, Chaim I. *Jewish Baby Boomers*. Albany, New York: 2001.

Weber, Bruce. "David Gahr, Photographer of Musicians, Dies at 85." *The New York Times*, May 29, 2008.

Weidenfeld, Sarah. *Rabbi Shlomo Carlebach's Musical Tradition in its Cultural Context: 1950-2005*. Ph.D. Thesis Submitted to the Senate of Bar Ilan University, January 2008.

Weidenfeld (Lerer), Sarah. *The musical tradition of R. Shlomo Carlebach: A definitive analysis of his works and musical style*, MA Thesis, Bar Ilan University, 2003 [Hebrew].

Weinberg, David M. "Missing Reb Shlomo." *The Jerusalem Post*, October 11, 1998.

Weinberg, Steve. *What's Next?* magazine, Ojai, California, Winter/Spring 1995, 18.

Weinreb, Tzvi Hersh. "Dr. Gershon Kranzler: Tiferet Personified." *Jewish Action*, Winter 5761/2000.

Weiss, Avi. "Student Struggle for Soviet Jewry (SSSJ)." *Encyclopaedia Judaica*. Michael Berenbaum and Fred Skolnik (eds.), 2nd edition, Detroit: 2007, vol. 19, 269.

Weiss, Sam. "Ben Zion Shenker." In *Nine Luminaries of Jewish Liturgical Song*, 2003, http://www.klezmershack.com/articles/weiss_s/luminaries/#shenker.

Weiss, Sam. "Carlebach, Neo-Hasidic Music, and Current Liturgical Practice." *Journal of Synagogue Music*, vol. 34, Fall 2009.

Weiss, Sam. "Shlomo Carlebach." In *Nine Luminaries of Jewish Liturgical Song*, 2003, http://www.klezmershack.com/articles/weiss_s/luminaries/#carlebach.

Weissler, Chava. "Performing Kabbalah in the Jewish Renewal Movement." In Boaz Huss (ed.), *Kabbalah and Contemporary Spiritual Revival*. Beersheba: 2011, 39–95.

Wertheimer, Jack. "The Turbulent Sixties." In Jonathan Sarna, *The American Jewish Experience*. New York and London: 1986, 2nd edition, 330–347.

Wilde, James. "Religion: Yogi Bhajan's Synthetic Sikhism." *TIME Magazine*, September 5, 1977.

Winkler, Allan M. *To Everything There Is a Season: Pete Seeger and the Power of Song*. New York: 2009.

Winkler, Gershon. "Shlomo." In *Pumbedissa: An Open Forum for Uninhibited Discussion of Judaic Issues*, printed in *What's Next*, Winter/Spring 1995, 18.

Witt, Emuna. "Achishena: Before the Appointed Time." *Kol Chevra*, 10, October 2004, 32–38.

Witt, Emuna. "Reb Shlomo 1980." *Kol Chevra*, vol. 13, 2007, 1–6.

Witt, Yahad (ed.). *Open Gates of the Heart*, 2010 [Hebrew].

Witt, Yahad (ed.). *Sparks of David: Rabbi David Herzberg zt"l Teaches Orot Shlomo – Commentary of Rabbi Shlomo Carlebach zt"l on Orot HaTeshuva of Rabbi Abraham Isaac HaKohen Kook zt"l*, Israel: 2006.

Wohlgelernter, Elli. "Simply Shlomo." *The Jerusalem Post*, April 20, 1995.

Wood, Sue Ann. "The Singing Rabbi." *St. Louis Post*, January 10, 1993.

Yudelson, Larry and Birnbaum, Susan. "Shlomo Carlebach, Beloved Rabbi and Songwriter, Dies at Age 69." *Jewish Telegraphic Agency*, October 24, 1994.

Yudelvitz-Strauss, Kuki-Leah. "Who Are We?" *Kol Chevra*, vol. 3, 1996, 19–20.

Zablocki, Avi. "Memories." *Kol Chevra*, vol. 17, 2011, 118.

Zablocki, Avi. "My Very First Concert with Shlomo." *Kol Chevra*, vol. 18, 2012, 68–69.

Zablocki, Rivka. "Little Did I Dream." *Kol Chevra*, vol. 7, 2000, 82.

Zeller, David. *The Soul of the Story: Meetings with Remarkable People*. Woodstock, Vermont: 2006.

Zivan, Shmuel. *Lev HaShamayim (Heart of Heaven): High Holidays and Sukkot, Passover, Hanukkah*. 2004–2006 [Hebrew].

Zivan, Shmuel. *Sippurei Neshama (Soul Stories)*. 2009, 2011 [Hebrew].

Sites Accessed

Note: The sites below were accessible as of September 2012.

613.org
Acheret.co.il
AdamsStreet.org
Aish.com
AjcArchives.org
Aleph.Nli.org.il
Aleph.org
AquarianMinyan.org
Archive.JTA.org
Archive.org
Articles.ChicagoTribune.com
AvAroma.com
Azure.org.il
BnaiHorin.com
BenKatz.com
BerkeleyFolk.blogspot.com
BethSholomFrederick.org
Beyondbt.com
Blip.TV
Blogger.com
Blogs.Forward.com
BooMP3.com
BorynaFoundation.com
Breslev.co.il
Bros-and-Sis.com
Bterezin.Brinkster.net
CanadianEncyclopedia.com
CarlebachLegacy.com
CarlebachShul.org
CdUniverse.com
CelebrateIsrael.com
Chabad.co.il
Chazzanut.com
Clearwater.org
CongregationEmanu-el.ca
Conservapedia.com
DavidAndLilatResemer.com

DavidMWeinberg.com
DeKosmos.net
DetroitYeshiva.org
Diaspora.org.il
DrSimcha.com
earthquake.usgs.gov
Eichlers.com
EmanuelGN.org
En.Wikipedia.org
Ew.com
EzrathIsrael.org
Fabrangen.org
Facebook.com
Fandango.com
FindingAids.cjh.org
FlatbushMinyan.org
Flickr.com
Forward.com
Frumster.com
GreenStar.org
Groups.google.com
HaAretz.com
HadassahMagazine.org
HannaTiferet.com
HareKsna.com
HavurahShiraHadash.org
HebrewAcademy.com
HeichalHanegina.blogspot.com
HitzeiYehonatan.blogspot.com
HolyBeggars.Ning.com
HomeMikveh.org
IndependentCreativeSources.com
IsaacWalters.com
Israelfaxx.com
IsraelNationalNews.com
IsraelVideoOnNetwork.com
Iyiny.org

JCNCF.org
JeffKlepper.com
JewishEntertainment.net
JewishGuitarChords.com
JewishHealing.com
JewishIndependent.Ca
JewishJukeBox.com
JewishMusicArchive.blogspot.com
JewishPressAds.com
JoshuaHammerman.blogspot.com
JStandard.com
JTNews.net
Juedischegemeinde.at
KlezmerShack.com
KolBseder.com
Koshertube.com
Last.FM
Lhotsky-film.at
LibFindAids.Yu
Lohud.com
LovingHeart.org
MenasheBleiweiss.com
MickeyHart.net
MileChai.com
MillionMonkeysPress.com
Modzitz.co.il
Monterey.org
MostlyMusic.com
MurshidSam.org
MyJewishLearning.com
NeshamaCarlebach.com
Nevey.org
NewsPaperArchive.com
NewVoices.org
NYSun.com
NYTimes.com
OnLine.WSJ.com
OnTheIssueMagazine.com
Ortav.com
OU.Org
PBS.org
Pekko.Naropa.Edu
Piyut.org.il
RabbiShlomo.co.uk
RCCMB.org
RebAryeh.com
RebShlomoCarlebach.blogspot.com
RebYankalaShemesh.weebly.com

Refuah.net
RLCWordsAndMusic.net
Ruhaniat.org
Rzlp.org
Sacred-Destinations.com
SacredTherapy.com
SalamResearch.com
Savethemusic.com
SawYouAtSinai.com
ScharomeManor.com
SeferChabibi.blogspot.com
Shamcher.org
Shii.org
Shituf.Piyut.org.il
ShlomoCarlebachMusic.com
ShlomoMusical.com
ShlomoYeshiva.org
ShorYoshuv.org
SikhiWiki.org
SimpleToReMember.com
SoferOfTzfat.com
SojournRecords.com
Srv.org
StephenGaskin.com
StrippingTheGurus.com
SunMagazine.org
SunyPress.edu
TabletMag.com
TBIEugene.org
TheFlamencoSociety.org
TheJewishRevolution.com
TheJewishWeek.com
TheTrugmans.com
Tikkun.org
Time.com
Toker.fm
USAToday.com
Ushmm.org
VanguardRecords.com
Video.Yehudim.net
Vosizneias.com
WeJew.com
WelcomeHome.org
WhereWhatWhen.com
WN.com
WomenOfTheWall.org.il
Zingmit.com

Discography

There have been several attempts at compiling a discography of Carlebach tunes.[1] The first official collection of Reb Shlomo's tunes with musical notes was produced in 1970 by Milt Okun and Zimrani Records. Entitled *The Shlomo Carlebach Songbook* it contained sixty-two songs from the first six official records put out by Reb Shlomo from 1959 until 1968. Then in 1980, the musical notes for Shlomo's most popular songs were published in *The Shlomo Carlebach Songbook* by Tara Publications, the publishing house founded by ethnomusicologist, Velvel Pasternak.[2] In 1992, these two songbooks were combined by Pasternak into one volume arranged according to the liturgy, thus effectively creating the first handbook of Carlebach tunes for prayer services.[3] Finally, in 1993, Tara Publications put out *Shlomo Shabbos: The Shlomo Carlebach Shabbos Songbook* edited by Ben Zion Solomon.[4]

Reb Shlomo performed in thousands of concerts,[5] recordings of some

---

1. For example, see Lea Benhamou and Nethanel Shor, "A Shlomo Discography," *Kol Chevra*, vol. 15, 2009, 80 where they list 26 albums produced during Shlomo's lifetime (these include several live recordings) and 25 albums after his death (including his song-stories, some of which had several volumes). Continuous updating attempts can be found at the "Shlomo Carlebach" entry in Wikipedia.

2. *The Shlomo Carlebach Songbook I–II*, annotated, edited and arranged by Velvel Pasternak (Cedarhurst, New York: 1980).

3. The 133 songs were divided as follows: 60 songs for the weekday, 18 for Friday night, 25 for Shabbat, 17 for the major festivals, 8 for High Holidays and 5 for weddings.

4. This Shabbos songbook was reproduced by Ben Zion Solomon and Kehilat Jacob Publications (i.e., the Carlebach Shul on 79th St.) as a spiral-bound book of 94 pages and 46 songs. Ben Zion estimates that after all of Reb Shlomo's songs are gathered together, there will be somewhere between 700–800 songs.

5. An estimate of 2,000 concerts is given by Cohen, "Sweet Singer". However, my calculations are that Reb Shlomo averaged 110 concerts a year from 1958–1994 and that the number is closer to 4,000. This does not include impromptu concerts, informal events, and sing alongs which often occurred, especially in the early years. Thus, for example, on a boat to Ness in 1963, Shlomo with his guitar in hand began

of which are now being made available.[6] Devoted Hasidim of Reb Shlomo, such as Yisroel Travis,[7] recorded hundreds of tapes thus preserving many songs that would otherwise have been lost. In 1999, Travis together with Zale Newman and Dovid Woolf, produced a record entitled *The Hidden Songs of Shlomo Carlebach*.[8] Other collectors, such as Hizki Sofer and Nethanel Shor, have amassed many recordings.[9] Several YouTube channels are dedicated to Shlomo's songs,[10] and Internet stations offer 24-hour playing of his songs and stories.[11] The Internet has created previously unimagined possibilities of playing Carlebach tunes. Thus for example, chords for 80 of the most famous Carlebach tunes can be accessed on line at Rabbi Joshua Yuter's site of The Jewish Guitar Chords Archive (www. JewishGuitarChords.com).

Although Reb Shlomo composed about 600 or 700 songs, the 52 original songs in the first five albums which appeared from 1959 until

---

spontaneously singing and "people in the first class section crossed over to hear him." See Intrator, "On The Road," 27.

6. For example, two performances that were recorded live in 1973 were published by Sojourn Records in 2009.

7. Yisroel Travis's father, Tzvi Dov Travis, was a year younger than Reb Shlomo and studied with him in both Mesifta Torah Vodaas and Lakewood Yeshiva. Yisroel first met Shlomo in the fall of 1965, when Shlomo came to perform at the Chelsea Hebrew Academy, near Boston, Massachusetts. My thanks to Yisroel Travis for this information, April 8, 2013.

8. Toronto, Ontario, *Jerusalem Star*, 1999. This record contains a total of 11 songs and stories of Reb Shlomo. The songs are sung by Yisroel Travis and The Har Nof Chevra choir. The record is not too well known but it can be found in the Jerusalem National Library, Aleph.Nli.org.il, http://aleph.nli.org.il:80/F/?func=direct&doc _number=003241273&local_base=NNL01. My thanks to Yael Levine for telling me about this record.

9. See for example the interview of Yedidya Meir on Arutz Sheva for Reb Shlomo's 17th *yahrzeit*, where video footage collected by Nethanel Shor is shown 091111-car-libach-yedidya-heb.wmv.

10. One outstanding collection of close to 400 videos is by Joel Goldberg from New York – http://www.youtube.com/user/go4joel. Another important source is "RabiShlomo" – "The official channel of Rabbi Shlomo Carlebach on YouTube," http://www.youtube.com/user/RabiShlomo, where since Nov. 20, 2010 they have been uploading Reb Shlomo's songs on YouTube "with a new song every Friday" with the anticipation that "all of Reb Shlomo's recordings" will be "available for everyone to listen to." In March 2013, they had reached 302 videos. A third valuable archival source is "CarlebachLegacyChannel" which joined YouTube on Feb. 22, 2011, http:// www.youtube.com/user/CarlebachLegacy/videos. Other collectors have taken from these sites and posted the videos, e.g., http://koshertube.com.

11. Toker.fm; TuneIn.com, http://tunein.com/radio/Reb-Shlomo-Carlebach-s95 906. Radio Carlebach 24 hours a day – Carlebach.net, http://carlebach.net; Chaim Rubin set up Carlebach Radio, http://radio.carlebach.net; RabbiShlomo.co.uk, http:// rabbishlomo.co.uk.

1966[12] form the basic core of the early Carlebachian legacy.[13] Below is the list in Hebrew followed by an annotated description in English from the first five jacket covers.

הנשמה לך 1959

1. אֶשָּׂא עֵינַי אֶל הֶהָרִים מֵאַיִן יָבֹא עֶזְרִי (תהילים קכ"א, א)
2. הנשמה לך והגוף פעלך (מהסליחות)
3. מִמְּקוֹמְךָ מַלְכֵּנוּ תוֹפִיעַ (קדושה בשחרית בשבת)
4. וּבְנֵה אוֹתָהּ בקרוב בימינו (ברכה 14 בתפילת העמידה)
5. שׁוֹמֵר יִשְׂרָאֵל (תחנון, אחרי נפילת אפיים)
6. אַל תִּירָא מִפַּחַד פִּתְאֹם (משלי ג, כה)
7. אָב הָרַחֲמִים הֵיטִיבָה בִרְצוֹנְךָ אֶת צִיּוֹן (תפילה קודם פתיחת הארון)
8. לוּלֵי תוֹרָתְךָ (תהילים קי"ט, צב)
9. אֶתְהַלֵּךְ לִפְנֵי ה' בְּאַרְצוֹת הַחַיִּים (תהילים קט"ז, ט)
10. כִּי לִישׁוּעָתְךָ קִוִּינוּ כָל הַיּוֹם (ברכה 15 בתפילת העמידה)
11. לֹא בְחַיִל וְלֹא בְכֹחַ כִּי אִם בְּרוּחִי (זכריה ד, ו)
12. עוֹד יִשָּׁמַע (ירמיה ל"ג, י–יא)

בָּרְכִי נַפְשִׁי 1960

13. בָּרְכִי נַפְשִׁי אֶת ה' (תהילים ק"ד, א)
14. הַשְׁמִיעִינִי אֶת קוֹלֵךְ (שיר השירים ב, יד)
15. כְּבַקָּרַת רוֹעֶה עֶדְרוֹ (קדושה במוסף של ימים נוראים)
16. קְחוּ עִמָּכֶם דְּבָרִים וְשׁוּבוּ אֶל ה' (הושע י"ד, ג)
17. מרן די בשמיא (יקום פורקן בתפילת שבת בבוקר)
18. קוֹל פְּנֵה אֵלַי וְהוֹשִׁיעוּ (תפילת הושענה רבה ע"פ ישעיה מ"ה, כב)
19. בְּךָ בָּטְחוּ אֲבֹתֵינוּ בָּטְחוּ וַתְּפַלְּטֵמוֹ אֵלֶיךָ זָעֲקוּ וְנִמְלָטוּ בְּךָ בָטְחוּ וְלֹא בוֹשׁוּ (תהילים כ"ב, ה–ו)
20. שִׂמְחָה לְאַרְצֶךָ וְשָׂשׂוֹן לְעִירֶךָ (תפילת ימים נוראים)
21. אִם אָמַרְתִּי מָטָה רַגְלִי חַסְדְּךָ ה' יִסְעָדֵנִי (תהילים צ"ד, יח)
22. וְכֻלָּם מְקַבְּלִים עֲלֵיהֶם (ברכת יוצר הַמְאוֹרוֹת לפני קריאת שמע בשחרית)
23. לְעוֹלָם לֹא אֶשְׁכַּח פִּקּוּדֶיךָ כִּי בָם חִיִּיתָנִי (תהילים קי"ט, צג)
24. רְאֵה נָא בְעָנְיֵנוּ (ברכה 7 בתפילת העמידה)

---

12. Although there are only 5 official Carlebach records produced from 1959 until 1966, some of the discography became confused because of the bootlegging. For example, the concert that took place in New York on Dec. 22, 1962 was bootlegged, i.e., recorded privately and then distributed without permission (see above, Chapter 3).

13. Actually, there are a total of 55 recorded songs in the first 5 albums, however one song is a Yiddish tune that Reb Shlomo did not compose, and 2 songs are repeats that were recorded in the live performance at The Village Gate.

פְּתְחוּ לִי 1963

25. פִּתְחוּ לִי שַׁעֲרֵי צֶדֶק (תהילים קי״ח, ט)
26. הִתְנַעֲרִי מֵעָפָר קוּמִי (מהפיוט לְכָה דוֹדִי)
27. רַחֵם בְּחַסְדְּךָ עַל עַמְּךָ צוּרֵנוּ (ברכת המזון)
28. וְכֹל הַחַיִּים יוֹדוּךָ סֶּלָה וִיהַלְלוּ וִיבָרְכוּ אֶת שִׁמְךָ הַגָּדוֹל בֶּאֱמֶת (ברכה 18 בתפילת העמידה)
29. הַשְׁמִיעִינִי אֶת קוֹלֵךְ (שיר השירים ב, יד)
30. יָמִין וּשְׂמֹאל תִּפְרוֹצִי (מהפיוט לְכָה דוֹדִי)
31. אֶשָּׂא עֵינַי אֶל הֶהָרִים מֵאַיִן יָבֹא עֶזְרִי (תהילים קכ״א, א)
32. וְזוֹכֵר חַסְדֵי אָבוֹת (ברכה 1 בתפילת העמידה)
33. וַאֲנִי תְפִלָּתִי (הוצאת ספר תורה)
34. יִתְבָּרַךְ שִׁמְךָ בְּפִי כָל חַי תָּמִיד לְעוֹלָם וָעֶד (ברכת המזון)

מִקְדַּשׁ מֶלֶךְ 1965

35. הָרַחֲמָן הוּא יָקִים לָנוּ אֶת סֻכַּת דָּוִד הַנּוֹפֶלֶת (תוספת לברכת המזון בסוכות)
36. אָנָּא ה׳ הוֹשִׁיעָה נָּא (תהילים קט״ז, כה, ותפילת הלל)
37. וְיִשְׂמְחוּ בְךָ כָּל יִשְׂרָאֵל מְקַדְּשֵׁי שְׁמֶךָ (מתוך ברכת וְהַשִּׂיאֵנוּ בעמידה לשבת ומועד)
38. קוֹל בְּרָמָה נִשְׁמָע נְהִי בְּכִי תַמְרוּרִים רָחֵל מְבַכָּה עַל בָּנֶיהָ (ירמיה ל״א, יד)
39. רַחֲמָנָא פְּרוֹק (פיוט ארמי מהסליחות)
40. חָנֵּנוּ ה׳ חָנֵּנוּ כִּי רַב שָׂבַעְנוּ בוּז (תהילים קכ״ג, ג)
41. לֹא תֵבוֹשִׁי וְלֹא תִכָּלְמִי (מהפיוט לְכָה דוֹדִי)
42. שְׁמַע קוֹלֵנוּ ה׳ אֱ-לֹהֵינוּ (ברכה 16 בתפילת העמידה)
43. מִקְדַּשׁ מֶלֶךְ (מהפיוט לְכָה דוֹדִי)
44. ה׳ מֶלֶךְ ה׳ מָלָךְ ה׳ יִמְלֹךְ לְעֹלָם וָעֶד (פסוקי דזמרה בשחרית)

שִׁפְכִי כַמַּיִם 1965

45. שִׁפְכִי כַמַּיִם לִבֵּךְ נֹכַח פְּנֵי ה׳ (איכה ב, יט)
46. מִמְּקוֹמוֹ הוּא יִפֶן בְּרַחֲמָיו לְעַמּוֹ וְיָחוֹן עַם הַמְיַחֲדִים שְׁמוֹ עֶרֶב וָבוֹקֶר בְּכָל יוֹם תָּמִיד פַּעֲמַיִם בְּאַהֲבָה שְׁמַע אוֹמְרִים (קדושה במוסף של שבת)
47. גְּוַואלְט בְּרִיידֶער (שיר עממי ביידיש)
48. אוֹדֶה ה׳ בְּכָל לֵבָב (תהילים קי״א, א)
49. לְךָ אֶזְבַּח זֶבַח תּוֹדָה וּבְשֵׁם ה׳ אֶקְרָא. נְדָרַי לַה׳ אֲשַׁלֵּם נֶגְדָה נָּא לְכָל עַמּוֹ בְּחַצְרוֹת בֵּית ה׳ בְּתוֹכֵכִי יְרוּשָׁלָיִם הַלְלוּ יָהּ (תהילים קט״ז, יז–יט)
50. כִּי בְשִׂמְחָה תֵצֵאוּ וּבְשָׁלוֹם תּוּבָלוּן הֶהָרִים וְהַגְּבָעוֹת יִפְצְחוּ לִפְנֵיכֶם רִנָּה וְכָל עֲצֵי הַשָּׂדֶה יִמְחֲאוּ כָף (ישעיה נ״ה, יב)
51. וְשִׂים חֶלְקֵנוּ עִמָּהֶם לְעוֹלָם וְלֹא נֵבוֹשׁ כִּי בְךָ בָּטָחְנוּ (ברכת על הצדיקים בתפילת שמונה עשרה)
52. הִנֵּה לֹא יָנוּם וְלֹא יִישָׁן שׁוֹמֵר יִשְׂרָאֵל (תהילים קכ״א, ד)

53. אֱ־לָהָא דִּי לֵיהּ יְקָר וּרְבוּתָא פְּרוֹק יַת עָנָךְ מִפֻּם אַרְיָוָתָא וְאַפֵּיק יַת עַמָּךְ מִגּוֹ גָּלוּתָא עַמָּךְ דִּי בְחַרְתְּ מִכָּל אֻמַּיָּא (מתוך יָהּ רִבּוֹן עָלַם וְעָלְמַיָּא פיוט בזמירות ליל שבת)

54. שֶׁבְּשִׁפְלֵנוּ זָכַר לָנוּ כִּי לְעוֹלָם חַסְדּוֹ (תהילים קל"ו, כג)

55. לשנה הבאה בירושלים (הגדה של פסח)

SONGS OF REB SHLOMO AS DESCRIBED ON THE JACKET COVERS OF THE FIRST FIVE RECORDS

1. *Hanshomo Loch*, or in English, *Songs of My Soul* was Reb Shlomo's first record. It appeared in June 1959. Two songs show the influence of the waltz: "*Shomer Yisroel*" and "*Av HoRachamim*." Two songs from the prayers have cantorial renditions: "*Hanshomo Loch*" and "*Mimkomcho*." The English translations on the jacket cover reflect subtle nuances, filling in gaps for ambiguous Hebrew expressions.

The first song "*Esa Einai*," אֶשָּׂא עֵינַי from Psalms 121:1 was a statement of faith and a plea for help: "I lift up my eyes towards the mountains, from whence will my help come? My help comes from the Lord who created heaven and earth."

The second song, "*Hanshomo Loch*," הַנְּשָׁמָה לָךְ, which is also the Hebrew title of the record, is a yearning of the soul towards God. It was reworked in translation: "The Soul is thine and the body is thy creation. Have compassion upon thy handiwork."

The third song, "*Mimkomcho*," מִמְּקוֹמְךָ is from the Shabbat morning *Kedushah* and is the only tune on this record in a major key and with a "*chazonish*" introduction. It is rephrased in translation:

> From Thy Place shine forth, O our King. And reign over us for we wait for Thee. Speedily, even in our days, do Thou dwell there and for ever. In the midst of Jerusalem thy city and to all eternity. O let our eyes behold the Kingdom according to the word that was spoken in the songs of the Might by David, Thy righteous anointed.

The fourth song, "*Uvneh Osoh*," וּבְנֵה אוֹתָהּ is taken from the conclusion of the fourteenth blessing in the *Amidah* prayer. It epitomizes the plea for rebuilding Jerusalem: "Rebuild it soon in our days as an everlasting building and speedily set up therein the throne of David Thy servant."

The fifth song, "*Shomer Yisroel*," שׁוֹמֵר יִשְׂרָאֵל from *Tahanun* is a prayer for preservation of Israel:

> Guardian of Israel, Preserve the remnant of Israel. And suffer not Israel to be destroyed, who say hear O Israel.

Similarly, the sixth song, "*Al Tiroh*," אַל תִּירָא from Proverbs 3:25 talks of not being afraid:

> Be not afraid of sudden fear, neither of the desolation of the wicked when it cometh. Take counsel together and it shall come to naught. Speak the word, and it shall not stand. For God is with us.

The seventh song, "*Av Horachamim*," אָב הָרַחֲמִים the prayer before opening the ark, also asks for the building of Jerusalem – "Father of Mercies, do good. In Thy favour unto Zion. Build Thou the walls of Jerusalem."

The eighth song, "*Luley torascho*," לוּלֵי תוֹרָתֶךְ is from Psalms 119:92. It is translated as "Unless Thy law had been my delight, I should have perished in mine affliction."

The ninth song, "*Eshalech*," אֶתְהַלֵּךְ is from Psalms 116:9: "I shall walk before the Lord in the land of the living."

The tenth song, "*Ki Lishuoscho*," כִּי לִישׁוּעָתְךָ, is from the fifteenth blessing of the *Amidah* prayer: "Because we wait for Thy Salvation all the day and hope for deliverance."

The eleventh song, "*Ruach*," רוּחַ ה׳, is based on Zechariah 4:6 which was translated on the record as: "Divine Spirit, not by might nor by power, but by my Spirit saith the Lord of Hosts."

Finally, the last song, popular for weddings, is "*Od Yeshoma*," עוֹד יִשָּׁמַע from Jeremiah 33:10–11:

> Soon may there be heard in the cities of Judah and in the streets of Jerusalem, the voice of joy and the voice of gladness. The voice of the bridegroom and the voice of the bride.

✣

2. The second album, entitled *Sing My Heart*, בָּרְכִי נַפְשִׁי appeared in 1960 with twelve original compositions of Reb Shlomo. The English translations printed on the record album transform the traditional Hebrew words into modern inspirational themes and emotionally evocative exhortations.

The first song, "*Borchi Nafshi*" from Psalms 104:1, is translated "Bless the Lord, o my soul." It contains just four words בָּרְכִי נַפְשִׁי אֶת ה׳ to be repeated again and again, creating a trance-like meditative effect of a yearning for God.

The second song is from Song of Songs 2:14 and expresses yearning of the soul for God, "*Hashmi'ni es Koleych*," "Let me hear Thy voice, for sweet is Thy voice and fair Thy countenance" (הַשְׁמִיעִנִי אֶת קוֹלֵךְ כִּי קוֹלֵךְ עָרֵב וּמַרְאֵיךְ נָאוֶה).

In the third song "*KeVakoras*," Reb Shlomo sings a noteworthy selection from the *Kedushah* of *U'netaneh Tokef* of the High Holidays:

> Even as a shepherd seeks out his flock and causes it to pass beneath his staff, so Thou causest to pass and numberest every living soul. Appointing the measure of every creature's life and decreeing his destiny.
>
> כְּבַקָּרַת רוֹעֶה עֶדְרוֹ מַעֲבִיר צֹאנוֹ תַּחַת שִׁבְטוֹ כֵּן תַּעֲבִיר וְתִסְפֹּר וְתִפְקֹד נֶפֶשׁ כָּל חַי וְתַחְתֹּךְ קִצְבָה לְכָל בְּרִיָּה וְתִכְתֹּב אֶת גְּזַר דִּינָם.

The fourth song is a verse from Hosea 14:3: "*K'chu Imochem*." It is translated as a plea for *teshuva*, return: "Take with you words (of Torah and prayer) and return unto the Lord" (קְחוּ עִמָּכֶם דְּבָרִים וְשׁוּבוּ אֶל ה').

"*Moron di Vish'mayoh*" is the fifth song. Taken from the Shabbat prayer after the Torah reading, it is translated as "May the Lord of Heaven be their help at all times and seasons" (מָרָן דִּי בִשְׁמַיָּא יְהֵא בְסַעֲדְּהוֹן כָּל זְמַן וְעִדָּן).

For the sixth song, R. Shlomo selected a verse from Isaiah 45:22 which is used in the Sukkot and Hoshana Rabbah prayers: "*Kol P'nuh*," and explained it as "The voice of the Lord calls. Turn to Me and be saved" (קוֹל פְּנוּ אֵלַי וְהִוָּשְׁעוּ).

Side Two of the record begins with a message of trust in God interwoven with a cantorial rendition to Psalms 22:5–6: "*B'cho Botchu*," translated here as "Unto Thee they cried and they were saved. In Thee they trusted and they were not shamed" (בְּךָ בָּטְחוּ אֲבֹתֵינוּ בָּטְחוּ וַתְּפַלְּטֵמוֹ, אֵלֶיךָ זָעֲקוּ וְנִמְלָטוּ בְּךָ בָטְחוּ וְלֹא בוֹשׁוּ).

The eighth song is "*Simchoh L'artzecho*," a prayer from the High Holidays, explained as a Messianic plea for joy: "O, grant joy to Thy land, gladness to Thy city, growing strength to David Thy servant and radiant light to the son of Yishai Thy Anointed" (שִׂמְחָה לְאַרְצֶךָ וְשָׂשׂוֹן לְעִירֶךָ וּצְמִיחַת קֶרֶן לְדָוִד עַבְדֶּךָ וַעֲרִיכַת נֵר לְבֶן יִשַׁי מְשִׁיחֶךָ).

The ninth song is a verse from Psalms 94:18, "*Im Omarti*," translated as "Whenever I thought my foot would stumble, Thy Mercy, O Lord upheld me" (אִם אָמַרְתִּי מָטָה רַגְלִי, חַסְדְּךָ ה' יִסְעָדֵנִי).

The tenth song, "*V'chulom M'kablim*," is a prayer from before *Keriyat Shema* in *Shaharit*, the emphasis is on accepting the Kingdom of heaven, "And they all take upon themselves the yoke of the Kingdom of Heaven one from the other" (וְכֻלָּם מְקַבְּלִים עֲלֵיהֶם עוֹל מַלְכוּת שָׁמַיִם זֶה מִזֶּה).

The eleventh song is from Psalms 119:93: "*L'olom Lo Eshkach*," and rendered as "I will never forget Thy precepts for they are my life" (לְעוֹלָם לֹא אֶשְׁכַּח פִּקּוּדֶיךָ כִּי בָם חִיִּיתָנִי).

The final song, "*Re'eh Naw*," is a selection from the *Amidah* prayer: "Behold our affliction and plead our cause and redeem us speedily with a full redemption for Thy Name's sake" (רְאֵה נָא בְעָנְיֵנוּ וְרִיבָה רִיבֵנוּ וּגְאָלֵנוּ גְאֻלָּה שְׁלֵמָה מְהֵרָה לְמַעַן שְׁמֶךָ).

#

3. Reb Shlomo's third LP, *At the Village Gate*, was released in March 1963 by Vanguard,[14] The song "*Pitchu Li*," פִּתְחוּ לִי chosen as the Hebrew title of the album was from Psalms 118:9 and one of his most famous. In this performance, Shlomo sang tunes from the prayer book such as "*Rachem*" and "*Yitbarach*," from *Birkat Hamazon*, from the *Shemoneh Esreh*, and from "*Lecha Dodi*." Here is the list of tunes in their order of appearance:

1. פִּתְחוּ לִי שַׁעֲרֵי צֶדֶק
2. הִתְנַעֲרִי מֵעָפָר קוּמִי
3. רַחֵם בְּחַסְדֶּךָ עַל עַמְּךָ צוּרֵנוּ
4. וְכל הַחַיִּים יוֹדוּךָ סֶלָה וִיהַלְלוּ וִיבָרְכוּ אֶת שִׁמְךָ הַגָּדוֹל בֶּאֱמֶת
5. הַשְׁמִיעִינִי אֶת קוֹלֵךְ
6. יָמִין וּשְׂמֹאל תִּפְרוֹצִי
7. אֶשָּׂא עֵינַי אֶל הֶהָרִים מֵאַיִן יָבֹא עֶזְרִי
8. וְזוֹכֵר חַסְדֵי אָבוֹת
9. וַאֲנִי תְפִלָּתִי
10. יִתְבָּרַךְ שִׁמְךָ בְּפִי כָּל חַי תָּמִיד לְעוֹלָם וָעֶד

#

4. Reb Shlomo's fourth record, *In the Palace of the King, Mikdash Melekh*, was released in 1965 again by Vanguard Records. This record jacket is unique in that the English explanations added to the Hebrew songs reinterpret the biblical passages as universal themes of hope, joy, and salvation. The translations reapply the verses to modern concerns and worries. The subtle yet innovative exegesis of the Hebrew terms creates a new ethical directive, an inspirational psychology and a theological statement.

The song "*Mikdash Melekh*," translated as "My King's Palace," provides the inspiration for the record title. It is based upon a stanza in the poem of "*Lecha Dodi*." The exegetical translation on the record jacket is: "Lead me back to my place, the city of holiness, the palace of my King, away from my ruins and despair. I dwelt too long in the valley of tears. Now let your loving tenderness show me the way."

The song "*Hannenu*," entitled "Give Me Light," is a modern reworking

---

14. CDUniverse.com, http://www.cduniverse.com/productinfo.asp?pid=1017091.

of Psalms 123:3. The translation reads: "My world is dark with disappointment. Give me your light, Lord."

"*Ana Hashem*" (Psalms 116:16) is given the title "Help Me to Start." Instead of the simple meaning of "Please God Save me," the commentary here is "I beseech You Lord, help me to start anew. I beseech You Lord, let me succeed to try again if I fail."

"*Rachmana Perok*," an Aramaic selection from the *Selichot* prayers, is entitled "Take Off My Heavy Burden" – "Merciful, unburden me, deliver me. Please don't wait any longer."

"*VeYismichu*, Rejoice" is the title for the prayer from Shabbat and festivals. The translation reads: "Give true joy to those who live to hallow your name."

"*Lo Tevoshi*" from a stanza of "*Lecha Dodi*" is entitled "Don't Wait": "Don't be ashamed. Don't wait. Trust Him and He will trust you and help to rebuild the whole world."

"*Shema Kolenu*," entitled "*Our Prayer*" is a reworking of the selection from the *Amidah*. The explanation is: "Hear our prayer, Merciful God. Let our life not be so empty, but let us feel that we are in Your Presence."

"*HaRachaman Hu Yakim*, Lift Me Up" is a prayer from the addition to *Birkat Hamazon* for Sukkot, but it is reworked: "All merciful, raise up the fallen tabernacle of David. Some people need only to be shown the way. Others need to be lifted up."

"*Kol BeRama*, Return Children" is the title for the song from Jeremiah 31:14. The English expansive rendition reads as follows: "A voice is shaking heaven and earth. A voice of lamentation and bitter weeping. Rachel is crying for her children because they are in exile. They are strangers in the world – without roots – without wings. Thus says the Lord: Please stop crying Rachel. You true Jewish mother. Your children will return to their homes."

"*Hashem Melekh*," a selection from *Pesukei d'Zimrah* of the morning prayers, is the only verse translated literally without embellishment: "The Lord is my King. The Lord was my King. The Lord shall be my King forever and ever."

In sum, the songs with their English exegesis on the record jacket take on a manner of succinct teachings emphasizing salvation, meaning, consolation, hope, and joy. The effect is to create a selection of pithy inspirational sayings, reminiscent of an American ethical tradition first set by Benjamin Franklin's *Poor Richard's Almanac*. But with Reb Shlomo, the aphorisms are reworkings of biblical verses.

The fifth album, in 1965 was entitled *Wake up World* and in Hebrew *Shifchi KaMayim* (Lamentations 2:19). That is also the lead song and is translated as "In His presence, My soul cascades with prayer."[15] Reb Shlomo describes how he was inspired to "discover" the tune in Paris at a gathering of French students at the home of his friend, Gutwirth "and we sang it as we marched through the streets of Paris." Reb Shlomo offers hope, consolation, and rejuvenation. Some of the titles in this record hint at this message: "*Mimkomo*, Lord Where Are You?" (from *Musaf Kedushah*); "*Ki Vesimcha*, Let Joy Lead You" (Isaiah 55:12); "*Hiney Lo Yonum*, The Lord Awakens You" (Psalms 121:4); and "*LeShana HaBa'a BeYerushalayim*, Next Year in Jerusalem."

❅

Below are the 52 original songs produced in Reb Shlomo's first five records organized here according to their source in the liturgy and Bible: The 29 from the liturgy include 12 from the daily prayer service, 11 from Shabbat songs and prayers, and 6 from the holidays; The 23 from the Bible include 14 from Psalms, and 9 from the other books of the Bible.

TWELVE SONGS FROM THE DAILY SERVICE

1. ה' מֶלֶךְ ה' מָלַךְ ה' יִמְלֹךְ לְעֹלָם וָעֶד (מתוך שחרית פסוקי דזמרה)
2. וְזוֹכֵר חַסְדֵי אָבוֹת (ברכה 1 בתפילה העמידה)
3. רְאֵה נָא בְעָנְיֵנוּ (ברכה 7 בתפילת העמידה)
4. וְשִׂים חֶלְקֵנוּ עִמָּהֶם לְעוֹלָם וְלֹא נֵבוֹשׁ כִּי בְךָ בָטָחְנוּ (ברכה 13 בתפילת הע־ מידה)
5. וּבְנֵה אוֹתָהּ בְּקָרוֹב בְּיָמֵינוּ בִּנְיָן עוֹלָם (ברכה 14 בתפילת העמידה)
6. כִּי לִישׁוּעָתְךָ קִוִּינוּ כָּל הַיּוֹם (ברכה 15 בתפילת העמידה)
7. שְׁמַע קוֹלֵנוּ ה' אֱ־לֹהֵינוּ (ברכה 16 בתפילת העמידה)
8. וְכֹל הַחַיִּים יוֹדוּךָ סֶּלָה וִיהַלְלוּ וִיבָרְכוּ אֶת שִׁמְךָ הַגָּדוֹל בֶּאֱמֶת (ברכה 18 בתפילת העמידה)
9. וְכֻלָּם מְקַבְּלִים עֲלֵיהֶם (ברכת יוצר הַמְּאוֹרוֹת לפני קריאת שמע בשחרית)
10. יִתְבָּרַךְ שִׁמְךָ בְּפִי כָּל חַי תָּמִיד לְעוֹלָם וָעֶד (ברכת המזון)
11. שׁוֹמֵר יִשְׂרָאֵל (תחנון, אחרי נפילת אפיים)
12. רַחֵם בְּחַסְדֶּךָ עַל עַמְּךָ צוּרֵנוּ (ברכת המזון)

---

15. To hear Reb Shlomo sing this song on YouTube, see http://www.youtube .com/watch?v=KfgNEr1LaWE; http://www.youtube.com/watch?v=FIRUPZeWPG8. Together with a dubbing of his daughter Neshama: http://www.youtube.com/watch ?v=o_3UYmn_Xa4. For additional versions, see Shituf.Piyut.org.il, http://shituf.piyut .org.il/piyut/2140; http://www.youtube.com/watch?v=siDb9_5Q6C4.

ELEVEN SONGS FROM THE SHABBAT LITURGY

1. מְקַדֵּשׁ מֶלֶךְ עִיר מְלוּכָה (מהפיוט לְכָה דוֹדִי)
2. לֹא תֵבֹשִׁי וְלֹא תִכָּלְמִי (מהפיוט לְכָה דוֹדִי)
3. הִתְנַעֲרִי מֵעָפָר קוּמִי (מהפיוט לְכָה דוֹדִי)
4. יָמִין וּשְׂמֹאל תִּפְרֹצִי (מהפיוט לְכָה דוֹדִי)
5. אֲ־לָהָא דִי לֵיהּ יְקָר וּרְבוּתָא פְּרֹק יַת עָנָךְ מִפֻּם אַרְיָוָתָא (יָהּ רִבּוֹן עָלַם וְעָלְמַיָּא פיוט בזמירות ליל שבת)
6. אָב הָרַחֲמִים הֵיטִיבָה בִרְצוֹנְךָ אֶת צִיּוֹן (תפילה קודם פתיחת הארון)
7. וַאֲנִי תְפִלָּתִי לְךָ ה' עֵת רָצוֹן (מתוך שחרית שבת)
8. מִמְּקוֹמְךָ מַלְכֵּנוּ תוֹפִיעַ (קדושה בשחרית בשבת)
9. מָרָן דִּי בִשְׁמַיָּא (יקום פורקן בתפילת שבת בבוקר)
10. וְיִשְׂמְחוּ בְךָ כָּל יִשְׂרָאֵל מְקַדְּשֵׁי שְׁמֶךָ (מתוך ברכת וְהַשִּׂיאֵנוּ בעמידה לשבת ומועד)
11. מִמְּקוֹמוֹ הוּא יִפֶן בְּרַחֲמָיו לְעַמּוֹ וְיָחֹן עַם הַמְיַחֲדִים שְׁמוֹ (קדושה במוסף של שבת)

SIX SONGS FROM THE FESTIVAL LITURGY

1. הַנְּשָׁמָה לָךְ וְהַגּוּף פָּעֳלָךְ (מהסליחות)
2. רַחֲמָנָא פְּרֹק (פיוט ארמי מהסליחות)
3. הָרַחֲמָן הוּא יָקִים לָנוּ אֶת סֻכַּת דָּוִד הַנּוֹפֶלֶת (תוספת לברכת המזון בסוכות)
4. כְּבַקָּרַת רוֹעֶה עֶדְרוֹ (קדושה במוסף של ימים נוראים)
5. שִׂמְחָה לְאַרְצֶךָ וְשָׂשׂוֹן לְעִירֶךָ (תפילת ימים נוראים)
6. לשנה הבאה בירושלים (סוף ההגדה של פסח)

FOURTEEN SONGS FROM PSALMS

1. תהילים כ"ב, ה–ו: בְּךָ בָּטְחוּ אֲבֹתֵינוּ בָּטְחוּ וַתְּפַלְּטֵמוֹ אֵלֶיךָ זָעֲקוּ וְנִמְלָטוּ בְּךָ בָטְחוּ וְלֹא בוֹשׁוּ
2. תהילים צ"ד, יח: אִם אָמַרְתִּי מָטָה רַגְלִי חַסְדְּךָ ה' יִסְעָדֵנִי
3. תהילים ק"ד, א: בָּרְכִי נַפְשִׁי אֶת ה'
4. תהילים קי"א, א: אוֹדֶה ה' בְּכָל לֵבָב
5. תהילים קט"ז, ט: אֶתְהַלֵּךְ לִפְנֵי ה' בְּאַרְצוֹת הַחַיִּים
6. תהילים קט"ז, יז–יט: לְךָ אֶזְבַּח זֶבַח תּוֹדָה וּבְשֵׁם ה' אֶקְרָא
7. תהילים קי"ז, כה: אָנָּא ה' הוֹשִׁיעָה נָּא
8. תהילים קי"ח, ט: פִּתְחוּ לִי שַׁעֲרֵי צֶדֶק
9. תהילים קי"ט, צב: לוּלֵי תוֹרָתְךָ
10. תהילים קי"ט, צג: לְעוֹלָם לֹא אֶשְׁכַּח פִּקּוּדֶיךָ כִּי בָם חִיִּיתָנִי
11. תהילים קכ"א, א–ב: אֶשָּׂא עֵינַי אֶל הֶהָרִים מֵאַיִן יָבֹא עֶזְרִי. עֶזְרִי מֵעִם ה' עֹשֵׂה שָׁמַיִם וָאָרֶץ
12. תהילים קכ"א, ד: הִנֵּה לֹא יָנוּם וְלֹא יִישָׁן שׁוֹמֵר יִשְׂרָאֵל
13. תהילים קכ"ג, ג: חָנֵּנוּ ה' חָנֵּנוּ כִּי רַב שָׂבַעְנוּ בוּז
14. תהילים קל"ו, כג: שֶׁבְּשִׁפְלֵנוּ זָכַר לָנוּ כִּי לְעוֹלָם חַסְדּוֹ

NINE SONGS FROM OTHER BIBLICAL BOOKS (ISAIAH,
JEREMIAH, ZECHARIAH, HOSEA, LAMENTATIONS,
PROVERBS, AND SONG OF SONGS)

1. ישעיה מ״ה, כב (תפילת הושענה רבה): קול פְּנוּ אֵלַי וְהִוָּשְׁעוּ
2. ישעיה נ״ה, יב: כִּי בְשִׂמְחָה תֵצֵאוּ וּבְשָׁלוֹם תּוּבָלוּן
3. ירמיה ל״א, יד: קוֹל בְּרָמָה נִשְׁמָע נְהִי בְּכִי תַמְרוּרִים רָחֵל מְבַכָּה עַל בָּנֶיהָ
4. ירמיה ל״ג, י–יא: עוֹד יִשָּׁמַע
5. הושע י״ד, ג: קְחוּ עִמָּכֶם דְּבָרִים וְשׁוּבוּ אֶל ה׳
6. זכריה ד, ו: לֹא בְחַיִל וְלֹא בְכֹחַ כִּי אִם בְּרוּחִי
7. משלי ג, כה: אַל תִּירָא מִפַּחַד פִּתְאֹם
8. שיר השירים ב, יד: הַשְׁמִיעִינִי אֶת קוֹלֵךְ
9. איכה ב, יט: שִׁפְכִי כַמַּיִם לִבֵּךְ נֹכַח פְּנֵי ה׳

Abbreviations

AMB	Aquarian Minyan Berkeley
HLP	The House of Love and Prayer in San Francisco
JTS	The Jewish Theological Seminary
SSSJ	Student Struggle for Soviet Jewry
TSGG (TASGIG)	"Taste and See God is Good" – the program set up by Shlomo at his father's synagogue
YU	Yeshiva University

Index of Carlebach Songs

Below is an index of about 100 Carlebach songs mentioned in this book. It does not include the songs in his repertoire which were not his own compositions.[1]

Some of the transliterations below follow the spelling on the early Carlebach record albums and reflect Shlomo's original Ashkenazic pronunciation, as for example, *Uvnai Yerusholayim, Uvneh Osoh* and *Hanshomo Loch*. Transliterations of the later songs follow the Israeli Sephardi inflection which became more common and acceptable for most singers of Carlebach music.

SONGS IN ENGLISH[2]

Because of My Brothers and Sisters (see *Lemaan Achai*)
Lord Get Me High (lyrics composed with George Gorner)   118,
     160–161, 219
My Lord Is Coming Back To the City of David   214
Return Again (lyrics composed with Ronnie Kahn)   162
The Whole World is Waiting to Sing a Song of Shabbos   144, 226

SONGS IN HEBREW (AND ARAMAIC)

Adir Hu (*piyut* from the Pesach Haggadah) אַדִּיר הוּא   216, 216n39, 231,
     360
Al Tiroh (Proverbs 3:25) אַל תִּירָא מִפַּחַד פִּתְאֹם   474, 468, 465

---

1. The Yiddish folk songs were *"Oyfn Pripetshik,"* and *"Gevaldishe Bruder."* The songs composed by Rabbi Eliyahu Hartman and sung by Reb Shlomo were *"B'nai Vescho," "Tiveeanu," "Zul Shoin Zein," "Gal Einai,"* and *"Hodu LaShem."*

2. The popular English songs that Shlomo sang which were not his own composition include "Don't You Weep Over Me," "Kumbaya," "We Shall Overcome," and "When Irish Eyes Are Smiling."

Index of Names

An asterisk indicates people who provided information directly via email and/or were interviewed in person or by Skype.

The family relationships presented in parentheses indicate how the person is related to Rabbi Shlomo Carlebach.

References to photos are in italics.

Index of Places

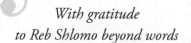

With gratitude
to Reb Shlomo beyond words

From the members of
AM KOLLEL
and KEHILA CHADASHA
Spiritual Leader, Rabbi David Shneyer

"Come join us for Shabbos"

KEHILA CHADASHA

www.am-kolel.org

www.e-kehila.org

How can I thank you, Reb Shlomo?
For enriching my world.
For being my mentor and Rebbe.
For teaching me esoteric and exoteric truths.

Here in this dedication I express just a bit of my gratitude
for your gifts:
Your affirmation of my Weltanschauung.
Your music that both penetrated and revived my soul.
Your introducing me to the wisest and kindest people I've
ever met.

Raquel bat Pinchas Elimelech Grunwald
And my children & children-in-law
& sweetest granddaughter Zoe Sara'le.

Raquel Z. Grunwald, Ph.D.
New York, La Jolla, and Israel

LEGACY TRUST

The Shlomo Carlebach Foundation
is preparing a digital archive to preserve
Reb Shlomo's legacy as a Jewish National Treasure.

The Shlomo Carlebach Heritage Center will be
built in Moshav Mevo Modiim to serve as an educational
institution, performing arts center, and guest house.

This will be a Living Memorial where visitors will be inspired
by the teachings, stories, music and legacy of Reb Shlomo.

See www.ShlomoCarlebachFoundation.org

Twelve Testimonials

(1) Reb Zalman Schachter-Shalomi; (2) Prof. Chaim I. Waxman; (3) Prof. Shaul Magid; (4) Menachem Daum; (5) Rabbi Reuven Goldfarb; (6) Prof. Yaakov Ariel; (7) Rabbi Sammy Intrator; (8) Shonna Husbands-Hankin; (9) Prof. Jonathan D. Sarna; (10) Rabbi Aaron Reichel; (11) Aryae Coopersmith; (12) Shy Yellin

1. Dr. Natan Ophir (Offenbacher) is to be thanked and congratulated for his exhaustive and detailed work on the life and the creative legacy of Rabbi Shlomo Carlebach, *a"h*. Avoiding both the adulation of hagiography and the dry description of the "facts" of Shlomo's life, he is able to make visible to us the impact Shlomo had in Judaism the world over. He also is able to bring out the distinctive features that have to do with the spiritual as well as the musical creations of that religious genius. As much as I knew of Reb Shlomo, I learned much that I did not know about him from Reb Natan Ophir.

> Reb Zalman Schachter-Shalomi, author of *Davening, Jewish Lights*, and *The Hidden Light*. First Chabad emissary to the college campuses together with Reb Shlomo, Prof. Emeritus of Jewish Mysticism and Psychology of Religion at Temple University, holder of World Wisdom Chair at Naropa University and founder of the Jewish Renewal Movement

2. Dr. Natan Ophir (Offenbacher) has written a poignant in-depth biography of Shlomo Carlebach in which we get to see him as a unique individual who was both a product of and a producer of his times. Ophir analyzes the man, his music and his message within the context of the social and cultural patterns of the worlds within which he lived, which enables us to understand his continuing, if not growing, influence.

> Prof. Chaim I. Waxman, Professor Emeritus of Sociology and Jewish Studies at Rutgers University and Senior Fellow at the Van Leer Jerusalem Institute

3. Dr. Natan Ophir Offenbacher's *Rabbi Shlomo Carlebach: Life, Mission and Legacy* is a lucid, engaging, and highly informative documentary

history of arguably one of the most significant and influential Jews in the postwar era. I have always thought such a study would be impossible to write given the unorganized way material about his life has been collected, the way many people whose life he touched and changed were sometimes less-than-willing to share their stories with a scholar who may distort their "rebbe's" image, and the extent to which much of his life remained the product of oral transmission. Ophir worked tirelessly not only collecting and organizing data on three continents but gained the trust of hundreds of people who told him their experiences with Reb Shlomo. The result is a documentary history that promises to be the definitive biographical study of Reb Shlomo's life and career. Ophir captures the itinerant nature of his subject as well as the way he lived in, and through, tumultuous periods in European, American, and Israeli history from the 1930s until the 1990s. It seems that Reb Shlomo was a part of every significant event in Jewish history during those years and Ophir gives his reader the requisite social and historical context to understand the role Reb Shlomo played in those events. While the book is the product of a loving disciple, it is largely not plagued by hagiography and courageously confronts some of the more challenging aspects of his subject's complicated life. This book will be a joy to read by fellow travelers as well as those who did not know Reb Shlomo during his life or follow his path after his passing.

Prof. Shaul Magid, Jay and Jeannie Schottenstein Professor of Modern Judaism at Indiana University Bloomington

4. I had the pleasure of being hosted by the author for a while and witnessed him working tirelessly day and night on his manuscript. I have rarely witnessed such love and devotion by a Hasid for his Rebbe. The engrossing book that has emerged from Dr. Ophir's meticulous research covers not only the famous episodes in the incredible odyssey of Reb Shlomo, but also scrupulously explores the seemingly minute details of his life. There is a famous story about a Hasid who was about to make a long pilgrimage to spend time with his Rebbe. "What are you going to learn from your Rebbe?" asked one of the Hasid's friends. "Kabbalah? Cleaving to God? The secrets of the Torah?" "No," answered the Hasid. "Mostly I want to learn how the Rebbe ties his shoes." Reading this book will inspire readers not only to appreciate Shlomo's unique revelation of the mysteries of Judaism but also how he discovered a Divine pulsating Love, Empathy and Joy in each and every action and encounter.

Menachem Daum, documentary filmmaker, co-producer of *A Life Apart: Hasidism in America*, and *Hiding and Seeking: Faith and Tolerance after the Holocaust*

5. Natan has accomplished what many thought couldn't be done. Through painstaking and conscientious research, he has reconstructed Shlomo's life and career and has managed to offer readers a glimpse of this *illui*'s many sides. As someone who was interviewed for the book, I can testify that Natan wanted this portrayal to be as accurate as possible, and to that end he was willing to accept multiple corrections and make multiple revisions until he and his informants were all satisfied with the result.

We are now in an era when many of Shlomo's most ardent adherents did not actually know him or had very limited contact with him. Without accurate information readily available, legends about an already legendary figure can easily proliferate, and people can, without realizing what they are doing, recreate a hero according to their own preferred image, and ascribe views to him that they hold but that he did not. Natan's book brings clarity to the often asked questions, "Who was Reb Shlomo?" and "What was he like?" Those of us who knew him can still tell our stories, sing and play his music, and give over his teachings, but now there will be a factual version to serve as a check upon many of the exaggerations and distortions that have frequently been circulated.

> Rabbi Reuven Goldfarb, part of the *chevra* at the San Francisco House of Love and Prayer and later a spiritual leader of the Aquarian Minyan of Berkeley. He received *semicha* as Moreinu, Maggid, and Rabbinic Deputy from Reb Zalman Schachter-Shalomi. Today, Reuven and his wife Yehudit reside in Safed where they co-direct the Bayt Maor HaLev Center for Movement, Healing, and Language Arts.

6. Scholars and lay persons interested in Jewish culture will welcome Dr. Natan Ophir's biography of Shlomo Carlebach. There is growing awareness in the last years in the centrality of Carlebach's work to the rise of neo-Hasidism and the movement of return to tradition. Ophir's is to date the most detailed biography of "the Singing Rabbi," and the author should be commended for his extensive research, which both illuminates many unfamiliar corners in the life and career of the neo-Hasidic rabbi and also provides a comprehensive picture of a unique religious leader.

> Prof. Yaakov Ariel, Department of Religious Studies at the University of North Carolina. He has published extensively on Jewish renewal and Jewish new religious movements.

7. Kudos to Rabbi Dr. Natan Ophir for undertaking the long overdue and Herculean task of offering the first in-depth study of Rabbi Shlomo Carlebach's multi-talented spiritual expressions that have left a legacy that supersedes even his colorful and luminous career. Reb Shlomo's life does not lend itself to an easy analysis as he defied simplistic categorization and conventional limitations of intellectual study. Through his profound soul, he revolutionized Jewish music, inspired tens of thousands

to deeper spiritual experience and was a highly creative teacher with a unique style of Torah learning; all the while being a caring and loving friend to the many who called upon him. If such a multifarious life was lived it must have a binding thread that wove it all together. Dr. Ophir takes us through the adventures and travails of Reb Shlomo's experiences to discover the hidden DNA that powered and propelled his remarkable achievements.

> Rabbi Sammy Intrator received ordination from Rabbi Carlebach and served as Assistant Rabbi of the Carlebach Synagogue, and after Shlomo's death, as the Synagogue Rabbi. Currently, he is the Rabbi of the Carlebach Shul in Miami Beach, Florida.

8. There are physical biographies and there are spiritual biographies. This book is both. In it we can see how we were part of Reb Shlomo's broad, expansive life, and how he was a significant part of our personal spiritual journeys. Together, we shared a renewing of Jewish life, filled with learning and music, love and joy. Thanks to Rabbi Dr. Natan Ophir for his unique effort to research, document and sequence Reb Shlomo's life path, and in doing so, illustrate his inspirational impact on many holy times and holy places. We are honored to be part of the story.

> Shonna Husbands-Hankin, a leading figure in the Jewish Renewal Movement, is a Judaic artist, writer, spiritual director and community organizer living in Eugene, Oregon.

9. At last! A carefully researched and meticulously annotated biography of Shlomo Carlebach. A must-read for anyone interested in Reb Shlomo and his legacy.

> Prof. Jonathan D. Sarna, Joseph H. & Belle R. Braun Professor of American Jewish History, Brandeis University, and author of *American Judaism: A History*

10. This *magnum opus* is sweeping in scope and destined to become the definitive biography of a unique personality whose influence on Jewish prayer as expressed musically may be more far-reaching than that of anyone since King David. Reb Shlomo inspired a "Nusach Carlebach," forming the basis of *minyanim* perpetuating his unique approach to prayer in virtually every meridian of the globe where Jews gather to share their common destinies. Many wonderful books have been written about Rabbi Carlebach, but this book goes beyond them in terms of comprehensiveness and the placement of each individual event and anecdote in historical and cultural context, with intriguing lists, such as the names of each song Reb Shlomo composed, its English and Hebrew title, its source, and where it can be downloaded and heard on the Internet. Imagine how many novel insights the average reader can absorb and savor about such an exciting, spontaneous, and holy personality!

Rabbi Aaron I. Reichel, Esq., author of *The Maverick Rabbi, Rabbi Herbert S. Goldstein and the Institutional Synagogue, "A New Organizational Form"*; formerly attorney editor at Prentice-Hall and national president of Yavneh

11. I've swapped stories with many people who knew Rabbi Shlomo Carlebach at different periods of his life. What we all had in common, including those of us who wrote about him, is that we each had experienced only a small piece of the much larger story of this great and complex soul.

Dr. Natan Ophir has given us all a huge gift by bringing so much of this story together: a richly detailed picture built on years of meticulous research that encompasses and reflects on *all* periods of Reb Shlomo's life. This book is sure to make a major contribution to how the world understands Reb Shlomo and his legacy.

Aryae Coopersmith was co-founder of Rabbi Shlomo Carlebach's House of Love and Prayer in San Francisco in 1968. He is author of *Holy Beggars: A Journey from Haight Street to Jerusalem*, a memoir which chronicles the story of Reb Shlomo, the "holy beggars," and the "House" in 1960s and '70s San Francisco. He received *semicha* from Reb Zalman as a Jewish Spiritual Teacher.

12. It is with great honor that I write a tribute to Reb Shlomo, one of the greatest men of faith that I have ever met. Reb Shlomo saw the world of his youth destroyed and his people decimated. Then, as a young and brilliant yeshiva student on safe shores in the United States, he perceived the looming dangers of destruction from assimilation. With a resolute determination, he set out to save Jewish souls.

Rabbi Dr. Natan Ophir first visited the Carlebach Shul in 1969. Now, in this new biography, he documents the career of Reb Shlomo, and illustrates how Shlomo bestowed compassion and boundless love onto his fellow man, and bequeathed to us melodies that allow our souls to soar. Reb Shlomo traveled around the globe, sharing with all his love of Torah study and guiding thousands in deepening their connection to the Divine. Some construed his methods to be outside the bounds of the "straight and narrow," but it was so sought after by the flower children of the '60s, the Jewish kids in the ashrams, and those in search of their heritage. Reb Shlomo's *neshama* undoubtedly came from a place very close to the Heavenly throne and hence, when he spoke of G-d or taught Torah he did so with the utmost conviction. May his meritorious deeds defend his people on high from all evil forces and may his teachings continue to be a source of great inspiration.

Shy Yellin, President of the Carlebach Shul in Manhattan

About the Author

Dr. Natan Ophir (Offenbacher) grew up in Philadelphia and graduated from the Talmudical Yeshiva of Philadelphia. He first met Reb Shlomo in 1969 when his family moved to 81st Street in Manhattan, two blocks from the Carlebach Shul. Natan graduated Yeshiva University in New York in 1974 and then moved to Israel. He studied for seven years at Yeshivat Mercaz HaRav Kook where he received ordination from the Chief Rabbinate of Israel. Then he completed his M.A. and Ph.D. in Jewish Philosophy at the Hebrew University of Jerusalem where he served as rabbi of the campus from 1982–1998. Currently, he directs JMIJ, the Jewish Meditation Institute Jerusalem, whose goal it is to teach practical Jewish Meditation in the light of research in neuropsychology. He also teaches at the Jerusalem College of Technology and at the Ono Academic College where his expertise is developing Computer Aided Instruction and Blended Learning.